Gender and Modernization in the Spanish Realist Novel

JO LABANYI

OXFORD
UNIVERSITY PRESS

OXFORD
UNIVERSITY PRESS

Great Clarendon Street, Oxford OX2 6DP
Oxford University Press is a department of the University of Oxford.
It furthers the University's objective of excellence in research, scholarship,
and education by publishing worldwide in
Oxford New York

Athens Auckland Bangkok Bogotá Buenos Aires Calcutta
Cape Town Chennai Dar es Salaam Delhi Florence Hong Kong Istanbul
Karachi Kuala Lumpur Madrid Melbourne Mexico City Mumbai
Nairobi Paris São Paulo Singapore Taipei Tokyo Toronto Warsaw
and associated companies in Berlin Ibadan

Oxford is a registered trade mark of Oxford University Press
in the UK and certain other countries

Published in the United States
by Oxford University Press Inc. New York

© Jo Labanyi 2000

The moral rights of the author have been asserted
Database right Oxford University Press (maker)

First published 2000

All rights reserved. No part of this publication may be reproduced,
stored in a retrieval system, or transmitted, in any form or by any means,
without the prior permission in writing of Oxford University Press,
or as expressly permitted by law, or under terms agreed with the appropriate
reprographics rights organizations. Enquiries concerning reproduction
outside the scope of the above should be sent to the Rights Department,
Oxford University Press, at the address above

You must not circulate this book in any other binding or cover
and you must impose the same condition on any acquirer

British Library Cataloguing in Publication Data
Data available

Library of Congress Cataloging in Publication Data
Data available

ISBN 0-19-815178-0
ISBN 0-19-816009-7 (Pbk.)

1 3 5 7 9 10 8 6 4 2

Typeset by Graphicraft Limited, Hong Kong
Printed in Great Britain
on acid-free paper by
Biddles Ltd,
Guildford and King's Lynn

Oxford Hispanic Studies

General Editor: Paul Julian Smith

THE last twenty years have seen a revolution in the humanities. On the one hand, there has been a massive influence on literary studies of other disciplines: philosophy, psychoanalysis, and anthropology. On the other, there has been a displacement of the boundaries of literary studies, an opening out on to other forms of expression: cinema, popular culture, and historical documentation.

The *Oxford Hispanic Studies* series reflects the fact that Hispanic studies are particularly well placed to take advantage of this revolution. Unlike those working in French or English studies, Hispanists have little reason to genuflect to a canon of European culture which has tended to exclude them. Historically, moreover, Hispanic societies tend to exhibit plurality and difference: thus Medieval Spain was the product of the three cultures of Jew, Moslem, and Christian; modern Spain is a federation of discrete autonomous regions; and Spanish America is a continent in which cultural identity must always be brought into question, can never be taken for granted.

The incursion of new models of critical theory into Spanish-speaking countries has been uneven. And while cultural studies in other language areas have moved through post-structuralism (Lacan, Derrida, Foucault) to create new disciplines focusing on gender, ethnicity, and homosexuality, it is only recently that Hispanists have contributed to the latest fields of enquiry. Now, however, there is an upsurge of exciting new work in both Europe and the Americas. *Oxford Hispanic Studies* provides a medium for writing engaged in and taking account of these developments. It serves both as a vehicle and a stimulus for innovative and challenging work in an important and rapidly changing field. The series aims to facilitate both the development of new approaches in Hispanic studies and the awareness of Hispanic studies in other subject areas. It embraces discussions of literary and non-literary cultural forms, and focuses on the publication of illuminating original research and theory.

Preface

THIS book has grown out of three articles (Labanyi 1986, 1988, 1990) written in response to Tony Tanner's *Adultery and the Novel: Contract and Transgression*, which proposes that the fascination in the European realist novel with adultery (and its frequent alternative, incest) should be read as the expression of worries over the breakdown of the nature/culture opposition. Tanner's brilliant study, written in 1979, did not take into account the now substantial body of feminist theory. Nor did it provide answers to other questions posed by the late nineteenth-century Spanish novel. Why—apart from the obvious fact that sex outside the family is easier in large communities—did so many urban novels focus on adultery and wives, and rural novels on incest and husbands? Why did novels of adultery pay so much attention to rubbish, and to money (Galdós) and health (*La Regenta, Los Pazos de Ulloa*)? Why were all these novels obsessed with masculine women and feminine men? And why did all of them, to varying extents, insist on State employees and electoral vote-rigging? As I attempted to rethink Tanner's perceptions in the light of these issues, it became clear that concern with the breakdown of the nature/culture opposition was part of a wider anxiety over the redefinition of the public and private spheres in a period of rapid and (in Spain) uneven development. The position of the family as cornerstone of privacy yet source of civic values, at a time of growing State and social interference in individual life, made it the key to locating the shifting boundary between public and private, and the basis for alternative remappings. What interests me in this study is the way the family is used to talk about wider social, political, and economic issues. The increasing overlap between public and private spheres is shown by the impossibility of separating the two questions jointly taxing the late nineteenth-century European imagination: the 'woman question' and the 'social question'. They are linked by a common fund of imagery whose function is to articulate anxieties that cannot be directly acknowledged or resolved.

It is this textual unconscious that I want to explore. To do so I have immersed myself in works in, and on, late nineteenth-century political, economic, and social theory, medicine, and town planning, to form a sense of the period's underlying worries and the recurrent patterns linking them. I have been particularly interested in the ways that different discourses—economic and medical in particular—invade each other, on the supposition that such spillages betray anxieties that cannot be contained. Indeed, the dominant recurrent patterns convey anxieties about flow, leakage, and blockage. I have been consistently surprised —and gratified—to find that the insights of historians writing about Britain and France, where excellent work has been done in the field of gender, apply equally, if not more, to late nineteenth-century Spain where rapid and uneven development made the issues especially visible and urgent. All the ideas in this book are indebted to the work of others. I hope that, in making connections between a wide range of disparate material, I have been able to offer a new reading of the Spanish realist novel that allows the modern reader to appreciate its contribution to the contemporary project of nation formation.

In particular, I am grateful to Catherine Jagoe, Alison Sinclair, Lou Charnon-Deutsch, Akiko Tsuchiya, Noël Valis, Maryellen Bieder, Alda Blanco, and Elena Delgado for keeping me up to date with their own excellent work on the representation of gender in late nineteenth-century Spain, and to my former research student Teresa Fuentes for her acute insights into the construction of 'the social' in the Restoration period. My thanks also to my colleague John Kraniauskas for being a walking bibliography in political theory, and to Jesusa Vega for her bibliographical help on the role of historical painting and landscape painting in nation formation in Spain. I should also like to thank Sophie Goldsworthy of Oxford University Press for her efficiency and patience, and Jackie Pritchard for her meticulous copy-editing. The preliminary preparation of this book was assisted by a research grant from Birkbeck College, University of London, in 1993. The later stages of research were funded by a British Academy/Leverhulme Trust Senior Research Fellowship for 1993–5, without which this book would have been very different and, for me at least, much less interesting.

J. L.

Contents

Introduction: Writing the Nation 1

PART I. REDEFINING THE PUBLIC AND PRIVATE SPHERES

1. Liberal Political Theory: Freedom and the Market 31

2. The Construction of 'the Social': Reform and Regulation 52

PART II. THE URBAN NOVEL: FEMALE ADULTERY AND THE EXCHANGE ECONOMY

3. Mapping the City: Galdós's *La familia de León Roch* (1879), *La desheredada* (1881), *Lo prohibido* (1884–1885) 91

4. Excess and the Problem of Limits: Galdós's *Tormento* (1884) and *La de Bringas* (1884) 139

5. The Consumption of Natural Resources: Galdós's *Fortunata y Jacinta* (1886–1887) 165

6. Pathologizing the Bodily Economy: Alas's *La Regenta* (1884–1885) 209

PART III. THE RURAL NOVEL: HUSBANDRY OR KEEPING IT IN THE FAMILY

7. Making *Caciquismo* Respectable: Valera's *Pepita Jiménez* (1874) 265

8. Patriarchy without the State: Pereda's
   Peñas arriba (1895)   299

9. Problematizing the Natural: Pardo Bazán's
   Los Pazos de Ulloa (1886) and *La madre
   naturaleza* (1887)   337

Conclusion: Modernity and Representation   385

References   417
Index   453

Introduction
Writing the Nation

HISTORIANS have in recent years started to study the process whereby, from the eighteenth through to the late nineteenth century, Spain was constituted as a modern nation-State (Gortázar 1994; Bahamonde Magro and Martínez 1994; Mar-Molinero and Smith 1996). The construction of a Spanish national literary canon from around 1870 has also started to be critically examined, particularly in the United States where resistance to attempts to revise the canon has highlighted the political issues at stake (Blanco 1993a; Jagoe 1993a, 1993b). In 1980s Britain too the 'return to Victorian values'—meaning 'family values' but also the ethos of the market—saw the imposition of a 'national' curriculum. This was indeed a return to 'Victorian values' for, as historians have shown, it was in the last three decades of the nineteenth century that nationalism developed throughout Europe as nation-States (and regions claiming statehood) fabricated a national tradition, building on (or, in the case of local nationalisms, resisting) the earlier but continuing extension of central State control through which the nation's inhabitants were turned into citizens (Anderson 1983; Hobsbawm and Ranger 1984; Hobsbawm 1990; Corrigan and Sayer 1991). Then, as now, the construction of privacy through a series of discourses centring on the family was accompanied by the privileging of an economic discourse based on the 'free' market: twin forms of individualism that complement yet contradict each other. My first chapter will look at the implications for the public/private divide of liberal market theory. The second will trace the ways in which this divide was reinforced and eroded by the discourses of social control. As we shall see, both sets of discourses construct women as the main objects of anxiety.

In this book I want to bring together recent historians' concern with nation formation and recent literary interest in

2   *Introduction*

canon formation, by examining the ways in which the canonical texts of those writers considered by Restoration critics to be the major exponents of the 'national novel' contribute to contemporary debates on the nation's transition to modernity.[1] Although it is obvious that nation formation and canon formation go together, they have not in the case of Spain been studied in tandem.[2] Hobsbawm insists that 'Nations do not make states and nationalisms but the other way round' (1990: 10). In a key essay, Fusi observes that the notion of a national language, art, and history started to develop in the late eighteenth century under the absolutist State, at a time when the process of unifying the country was only just beginning (Gortázar 1994: 80–1). In their recent history of nineteenth-century Spain, Bahamonde and Martínez note that Spanish nationalism as a cultural process is still 'huérfano de estudios' (1994: 496). Their own brief outline (1994: 496–500) shows how, from the 1850s to the 1890s, historians and painters 'nationalized the past' by constructing a version of Spanish history based since origins on a teleological progression towards national unity. Critics of Galdós's massive attempt to give fictional form to Spain's historical progression towards modernity, the *Episodios nacionales*, could usefully draw on their insights. Indeed, there is urgent need for study of the contribution to nation formation of the Spanish historical novel in general, from the Romantic period through to the turn of the century. It is however the period after the 1868 Revolution, particularly after the Restoration of 1875, that is decisive, for

---

[1] The inclusion here of Alas's *La Regenta* should perhaps be justified since, despite its obviously canonical status today, it is commonly said that it was ignored in its time, and it was re-edited in Spain only in 1901, 1908, 1947, and 1963 (with editions in Argentina in 1946 and Mexico in 1960) before its 1966 publication in paperback by Alianza established it as a national classic. However, Tintoré (1987: 32) establishes that Alas was initially satisfied with the novel's sales and critical reception (Galdós praised it warmly and wrote the prologue to its 1901 2nd edition), and Alas's status as Restoration Spain's major literary critic necessarily accorded his novel national significance, regardless of professional jealousies on the part of fellow critics.

[2] Interesting work here has been done in relation to Latin America by Sommer (1991) and Masiello (1992). The latter notes that the fictional treatment of prostitutes in the 1880s Argentine novel reflects anxieties about the breakdown of the boundary between home and market, and that adultery became a frequent subject at the same time (6, 114, 116): these themes will be discussed here in relation to Spanish novels of the 1880s. Sommer notes the frequency of gender-crossing in Latin American 'foundational romances' (80): something we shall also examine in the Spanish case.

it was then that a series of legal codes standardizing all areas of national life were drawn up (some remaining in force for nearly a century), and that a serious attempt was made to create a 'national novel'. The attempt to write the nation into existence through the law is paralleled by the attempt to construct it in fiction. Both Castelar and Cánovas del Castillo—Republican President and Conservative Prime Minister respectively—were historical novelists as well as historians; Castelar was also Professor of Spanish History at Madrid University. It is symptomatic that Cánovas spent the September 1868 revolutionary period working in the national historical archives at Simancas.[3] As Álvarez-Junco observes (Mar-Molinero and Smith 1996: 96), Modesto Lafuente's thirty-volume history of Spain, published 1850–66, was the first of a dozen such works produced in the second half of the century.[4] In many cases, these historical reconstructions do not simply glorify national unity but explore the conflicting issues arising from it. Most nineteenth-century Spanish historians were progressive liberals rather than conservatives (Bahamonde Magro and Martínez 1994: 498). Historical painting was promoted through the Exposiciones Nacionales de Bellas Artes instituted in 1856—reviewed by Valera and Galdós—and the national parliament's commissioning of work for its walls, but also by local government bodies who offered painters bursaries and commissioned work for public buildings (Reyero 1989; Valera 1942: 2248–9; Pena López 1993–4: 225–6). The top prizes awarded to entries to the Exposiciones Nacionales were for paintings in the historical genre; these prizes were offered by the Ministerio de Fomento, making it clear that the genre was seen as an instrument of nation formation. Reyero (1989: 100) notes that 1887 was the year when the number of historical paintings entered for the National Art Exhibition peaked. Painters chose as their topics not only historical episodes illustrating national unification and expansion, but also the Comuneros and local heroes who resisted the imposition of central State control. As in the novel, female subjects—notably Juana la Loca —tend to disturb the sense of destined progression towards a

---

[3] For Cánovas's concept of nationhood, central to his political thought and practice, see Dardé's essay 'Cánovas y el nacionalismo liberal español' (Gortázar 1994: 209–38).
[4] On mid-19th-century Spanish historiography and nation-building, see Cirujano Marín, Elorriaga Planes, and Pérez Garzón (1985).

rationally coordinated nation-State (Reyero 1989; Díez 1992). Bahamonde Magro and Martínez (1994: 500) note that late nineteenth-century historical painting is narrative painting for, like historiography and the novel, its function is to 'narrate the nation'. The realist novel is not constructing a past national tradition but depicting contemporary society. Galdós called his non-historical novels 'novelas contemporáneas' for the realist novel is by definition about modernity. Spain's realist novel—beginning in the 1870s and peaking in the 1880s—occurs later than that in France or Britain because the modernization process did not affect the whole of the national territory, constructing it (theoretically) as a unified nation, until the Restoration period. A large number of novels are set in the *sexenio revolucionario* of 1868–74 for it was the political hesitations following the 1868 liberal revolution—moving through the interim revolutionary government of 1868–71, Amadeo of Savoy's liberal monarchy of 1871–3, the First Spanish Republic of 1873–4 with its federal and unitarian phases, to the 1875 restoration of the Bourbon monarchy with strengthened constitutional guarantees—that defined Spain's transition to modernity. By showing the political prevarications of this period, the novel of the Restoration period is able to present the current regime as the 'inevitable' outcome, if only *faute de mieux*, while also showing the tensions involved in the construction of the modern nation-State. For these novels of modernity are highly critical of political, economic, and social modernization. This does not mean that they reject the modern world, for modernity as a cultural project has always been constituted by anxieties about modernization. What matters is that their authors, whatever their response to modernity, all agree that it is an established 'fact'; even Pereda's autarkic rural dream depends on the bringing of modernization from the city. This, rather than any supposed accuracy in copying the real world, is what constitutes them as realists.

In examining the ways in which the realist novel contributes to the process of nation formation, I do not wish to propose a simplistic scenario in which writers function as undercover agents of the State in its attempt to construct model citizens. The realist novel is not crudely prescriptive, but neither is it descriptive. Rather than copy reality, it functions as a forum for critical debate, airing issues of contemporary concern. Like the contemporaneous legal codifications of national life, it deals with what happens when things go wrong. In this sense, the novel forms part of the public sphere of critical debate that Habermas (1989) has seen as the centrepiece of modern civil society, alongside the press and intellectual clubs, academies, and debating societies, including the coffee houses (Galdós's cafés). The Restoration censorship laws, introduced in 1879 by Cánovas and rescinded by Sagasta's Liberal government in 1883, were aimed more at controlling the dissemination of socialist and anarchist ideas than at curtailing bourgeois freedom of expression. The novel is better placed than other public-sphere institutions to air collective anxieties for it can invent its stories, tailoring them to highlight specific concerns. Characters also acquire unprecedented density in the realist novel, allowing positive and negative identifications through which readers construct their own sense of what is proper and improper. This density results from the characters' enmeshing in the social fabric in such a way that their behaviour raises social issues; their problems are the nation's problems. As Stuart Hall has said, 'nationalism constructs identities by giving us images to identify with'. As he also notes, the function of nationalism is 'to represent difference as identity' for the modern nation-State, constructing its citizens as members of a common 'imagined community' (to borrow Benedict Anderson's term), is a homogenizing agent.[5] But such identity formations are complex, for they may enact anxieties without resolving them, and the multiplicity of characters allows plural if not contrary identifications. What we find in most Spanish realist novels is precisely a critique of this homogenizing process, encapsulated in Ana's dilemma in *La Regenta* as to whether or not to be 'como todas'. The issue of the maintenance and erosion of difference—between town and country, middle and lower classes, public and private, masculine and feminine—is central to these texts, as it was to contemporary public debate. The urban novels express anxiety at the standardization and imitation which come with democracy; the rural novels show the often negative effects of the central State's attempt to incorporate the regions. Only two of the novels studied—Valera's *Pepita Jiménez* and Pereda's

[5] Plenary lecture 'Ethnicity, Race and Nation: Narrating Cultural Identities' to the conference on 'Empire, Nation, Language' (Institutes of Advanced Study, University of London, Dec. 1993).

Peñas arriba—use the romance format ending in marriage as a way of resolving oppositions, and Pereda's novel does so in order to resist the central State. The other novels start with marriage and show its progressive breakdown—or, in Pardo Bazán's *La madre naturaleza*, end with possible alliances rejected—for they are not providing blueprints for a model society but illustrating dilemmas which have no resolution or whose resolution is tragic, as for example in the working-class Fortunata's incorporation into bourgeois society: the incorporation of a 'savage' into the nation, for which she pays the price of death.

But although these novels mostly illustrate the problems arising from modernity's homogenizing project, they nevertheless serve this same project by constructing the reading public as an 'imagined community' united by common anxieties. Such an 'imagined community' based on shared anxieties can cut across belief systems, incorporating different sectors of the population into a shared cultural system: a useful way of 'representing difference as identity' that allows difference to stand. Apart from which, the emotive nature of anxieties makes them a more effective bonding agent than rationally held beliefs. Of course, any cultural form appealing to a nationwide mass public can be said to contribute to nation formation; nationalism is dependent on the existence of modern forms of mechanical mass reproduction. But the realist novel contributes to nation formation in a specific way. As Anderson has argued, the creation of a mass reading public through the capitalist commercialization of print and a standardized education system creates a sense of the nation as an 'imagined community' sharing common cultural values. The members of civil society are 'the reading classes' (Anderson 1983: 73). In particular, Anderson notes the importance of the national press which developed in the mid-century with the construction of a nationwide railway network, for not only do readers throughout the nation read the same news, but they are aware of each other's existence as simultaneous consumers of the same information (1983: 39). Practically all Spanish realist novels of the Restoration period show, or at least mention, characters reading the national press. As Anderson demonstrates (1983: 30–7), this sense of belonging to a nationwide community is reproduced in, and reinforced by, the realist novel's construction of a complex social network whose members take each other's existence for granted though most of them never meet. Part II of *Fortunata y Jacinta* traces the Rubín family history back over the same period covered by the Santa Cruz family history narrated in part I, constructing the sense of a continuous 'imagined community' precisely because the two families have so far coexisted without converging. This illusion of social continuity across space makes us wonder with Maxi what Fortunata is doing while she is separated from him in the convent reformatory, for we are convinced—as we are meant to be—that the characters go on existing when they are absent from the printed page: an illusion confirmed by the narrator 'filling in' the missing information about Fortunata's parallel but separate existence during this time. If we call a novel 'realist' it is not because we believe it narrates events that really happened, but because it constructs an 'imagined community' that corresponds to the illusion of a homogeneous society that is the modern nation. In both cases, we are dealing with a fictional construct. In the course of this book I shall develop the argument that realism is based on an awareness that modernity is in various ways constituted by representation.

As Anderson shows, this concept of society as an all-embracing web of parallel but largely independent lives makes simultaneity as important as chronology to the realist novel's construction of society as an organism continuous in both space and time. Anderson's insight helps explain the apparent anomaly whereby the narrator of *Fortunata y Jacinta* can claim that modern Spanish society is one big melting-pot while his plot demonstrates the difficulties of class integration.[6] For this novel, more than any other ever written in Spain, constructs society as a vast network of individuals who, despite their differences, take it for granted that they are all members—or must become members—of the same 'imagined community'. For Fortunata membership of this community is defined as being 'like' Jacinta, even though the two women hardly meet. In his 1870 essay 'Observaciones sobre la novela contemporánea en España', Galdós proposed the 'clases medias' (the 'intermediate' classes) as the subject matter of a modern Spanish novel because he saw them as a melting-pot 'unifying' the different strata of the population (Pérez Galdos 1972: 122–4). His other

[6] Bahamonde Magro and Martínez (1994: 455) note that the term 'clases medias' was abused by mid-century intellectuals, for social mobility and homogenization were a project more than a reality.

major literary statement, his 1897 speech on admission to the Spanish Royal Academy, lamented the current standardization but argued that it had allowed the creation of a national novel, for the latter requires the sense of homogeneous community (1972: 177–82). Alas ended his 1882 article 'Del naturalismo' by insisting that the modern novel should express 'la solidaridad en que existen en la realidad los acontecimientos', with characters integrated into 'una acción compleja, en que hay muchos más agentes, el resultado de todos los cuales es la vida' permitting a 'conocimiento y conciencia total del mundo'. He observed that this required the novelist to be not so much an accurate observer as a skilful constructor, for the 'slice of life' constructs society as a totalizing whole (Alas 1972: 142–3). Alas, Galdós, and Pardo Bazán all argued repeatedly that the novel is the serious study of modern society. This is an important statement for what is meant by 'society' is something radically new. If we now take it for granted that the nation is 'a society', allowing us to talk of 'Spanish society' in the singular despite obvious social differences, this is partly due to the realist novel's success in propagating the concept. As Anderson (1983), Hobsbawm (1990), and Giddens (1985) have shown, before the extension of the central State's powers to the whole of the national territory in the course of the eighteenth and nineteenth centuries, creating the modern nation-State by making the State coterminous with the nation for the first time, the various inhabitants of the national territory had little or no awareness of each other's existence, and did not expect to have anything—language, race, or culture—in common. The sense that the State and the nation are not yet coterminous but should be is illustrated by the tendency of all the novels studied to call the urban and rural masses 'savages'; this term is used precisely when describing the attempt to turn them into citizens (which means converting them from 'masses' into individuals). We should not forget how radical Galdós's decision, in *Fortunata y Jacinta*, to narrate this process from the viewpoint of his 'savage' must have seemed to contemporary readers who, as such, were 'citizens'.

Blanco (1993a; Charnon-Deutsch and Labanyi 1995) and Jagoe (1993a, 1993b) have denounced the Restoration critics who 'masculinized' the Spanish literary canon by ignoring or vilifying the substantial body of mid-century novels by women. Jagoe has argued that these women writers were excluded because they were seen as sentimental and idealist; that is, not concerned with the objective portrayal of reality. As she puts it, 'only realist novels could represent "lo español"' (1993*a*: 230–3, 1993*b*: 432). In a suggestive essay (Charnon-Deutsch and Labanyi 1995), Blanco has shown how the gender stereotyping whereby men were seen as active originators, and women as passive consumers or imitators of fashion, was used to devalue women's writing on the grounds that it was based on the imitation of foreign models, thus making it possible to argue that 'masculine' realism was by contrast authentically Spanish. (In practice, of course, realism was also based on the imitation of foreign—largely French—models.) Thus, as Blanco notes, Galdós can start his 1870 essay 'Observaciones sobre la novela contemporánea en España', which proposes realism as the basis of a national novel, with the statement:

> El gran defecto de la mayor parte de nuestros novelistas, es el haber utilizado elementos extraños, convencionales, impuestos por la moda prescindiendo por completo de los que la sociedad nacional y coetánea les ofrece con extraordinaria abundancia. Por eso no tenemos novela. (Charnon-Deutsch and Labanyi 1995: 129)

Galdós is here attacking the popular serialized novel which, despite being written by male as well as female authors, was seen as a 'feminine' genre because of its supposed consumption by a female reading public. Although female literacy was rising, particularly in Madrid where in 1877 64.27 per cent of women could read, the 1877 national average of 19 per cent female literacy (Martínez Cuadrado 1973: 124) makes it unlikely that women did constitute the mass of the reading public when *folletines* sold up to 13,000 copies (Jagoe 1993*a*: 226, 229).[7] The reason that the reading public for this 'domestic literature' was constructed as feminine is, I would argue, precisely because it was 'domestic'; that is, concerned exclusively with the private sphere.[8] Regardless of whether it was idealist and sentimental,

---

[7] Bahamonde Magro and Martínez (1994: 486) give national illiteracy rates as 75% in 1860, 72% in 1877, 68% in 1887, and 64% in 1900. See Vilanova Ribas and Moreno Julià (1992). For detailed information on female literacy and on women's education, see Jagoe, Blanco, and Enriquez de Salamanca (1998: 105–217).

[8] Much mid-century melodrama was the vehicle for social criticism, attacking a corrupt aristocracy in the name of bourgeois virtues, but this moral message is articulated through private relationships, not through the construction of a cohesive social canvas. See Elsaesser (1987).

and of whether it was read by men or women, fiction that did not deal with the public sphere of social relations—the new 'society' that constituted the modern nation-State—could not provide a basis for the creation of a new 'national' novel. The debate over the respective merits of idealism and realism was a debate not so much over literary procedure or fidelity to reality as over content; that is, over what constituted the modern nation and was thus appropriate subject matter for a modern national novel. Women were members of the nation but they did not have civic rights and were thus excluded from civil society. It is, I suggest, because of their uneasy relationship to nationhood that the realist novel is so interested in women, but the stress is precisely on their problematic relationship to the public sphere.

In an interesting article, Enríquez de Salamanca (1993) has argued that the criterion for literary quality was related to the contemporary criterion for the full exercise of political rights known as 'capacidad'. This suggests that what was at issue in both cases was membership of the public sphere. The 1845 and 1876 Constitutions gave suffrage to property-holders paying tax above a specified amount and to 'las capacidades' comprising the new liberal professions; that is, the educated or 'possessors' of culture. The Suffrage Law of 1846 required 'capacidades' also to fulfil the minimum tax requirements, but that of 1878 stipulated no such requirement for culture was seen as a capital possession in its own right. One is reminded of Matthew Arnold's *Culture and Anarchy* (1867) which views culture as the prerequisite for citizenship. As Enríquez notes, the 'owners' of culture—a definition which automatically excluded women and the lower classes—were those variously entrusted with 'writing' the modern nation:

Los literatos redactaron las Constituciones y las Leyes electorales, compusieron los Códigos y construyeron el sistema de educación. Desde la prensa los literatos formularon y difundieron el lenguaje político del nuevo Estado y con ellos construyeron la opinión pública. Pero también, los literatos idearon la literatura española. (1993: 456)

This last sentence refers to the histories of Spanish literature written in the Restoration period, which proposed the realist novel as the national literary form both because it depicted modern Spanish society and because realism was supposedly an indigenous Spanish product. Blanco (Charnon-Deutsch and Labanyi 1995: 120–36) has shown how the development of literary criticism as a specialist discipline in the Restoration period was tied to a nationalist project.[9] Here Spanish intellectuals were echoing the invention of national traditions which took place throughout Europe in this period: the creation of the autochtonous was itself a foreign imitation. This process was orchestrated through the various institutions whose role was to form national public opinion: the universities (dominated by Madrid's Universidad Central), the academies and learned societies (in particular, the Academia de Ciencias Morales y Políticas, founded 1857, and the Sociedad Española de Higiene, founded 1882), the Ateneo (Madrid's major debating society, founded 1835), the press, and book publishing (both overwhelmingly centred in Madrid).[10] Practically all post-1868 Spanish public figures spoke at the Ateneo; the Restoration Prime Minister Cánovas was its president twice while in political opposition; Valera and Galdós served on its literary committee (Ruiz Salvador 1971).

It must be stressed that the role of such cultural institutions—like that of the novel—was not to produce a single, monolithic version of national culture but to provide a debating forum, within the evident limits of what could be thought by their members. Its protagonists covered the whole of the bourgeois political spectrum for this was a debate about what constituted the nation.[11] Many of them were affiliated to Krausism, with

[9] The first history of 'Spanish Literature' was published in 1861–5 by José Amador de los Ríos, appropriately dedicated to Queen Isabel II.

[10] Bahamonde Magro and Martínez (1994: 489) describe this cultural centralization as the conversion of the capital into a 'museum city' storing the nation's cultural heritage. Madrid's major museums, beginning with the Museo del Prado in 1819, were mainly founded in the course of the 19th century. For an important study of museums and collecting in Galdós's novels, see Gold (1988).

[11] Gold (1993: 174) notes the political nature of the critical debate on the national literary canon, but tends to assume that this was a debate between 'the two Spains'. This Manichaean simplification of public opinion into two diametrically opposed camps is itself a construct of the early Franco regime's nationalist project, concerned to label all who were not 'with us' as the enemy. Gold rightly notes (178) the Franco regime's expurgation of Alas and, apart from the *Episodios nacionales* with their explicitly nationalist project, Galdós from textbooks and the curriculum. Indeed, their novels raise issues about the relationship of public and private spheres, and particularly about the State's invasion of private life, that were totally inimical to the early Franco regime's attempt to construct an all-invasive, monolithic State apparatus. If Pereda's novels had been read carefully they would also have been banned, for their patriarchal rural autarky is based on a visceral hatred of the State.

its belief in culture as an instrument for creating a sense of citizenship.[12] All the novelists studied in this book took part in this national debate as journalists or as speakers at the Ateneo or Spanish Royal Academy (Alas and Pardo Bazán never achieved admission to the latter), though Pereda's contribution was small. It was Pardo Bazán's insistence in forcing herself on the public sphere as a journalist publishing in the national press, and by 1887 as a public speaker at the previously all-male Ateneo,[13] that made her so unpopular but also earned her a place in the national literary canon: the only woman writer of the Restoration period to be admitted. As Blanco notes, her novels were included in the canon because, unlike those of her fellow women writers, they were realist (Charnon-Deutsch and Labanyi 1995: 133). I would argue that what is at stake here is not her supposed use of 'masculine' analysis and objectivity, but the fact that her novels are concerned with the feminine space of the home only inasmuch as it relates to the public sphere. Ironically, the same focus on women's difficult relationship to a public sphere monopolized by men allows her to make some extraordinarily radical feminist proposals while at the same time earning her novels the 'national' status that could not be accorded to less radical women novelists who restricted themselves to the private sphere.

The fuss over Pardo Bazán's articles defending French naturalism, *La cuestión palpitante* (1882–3), was at least partly due to the way they highlighted the uncomfortable fact that the Spanish realist novel was dependent on foreign models. Both Pardo Bazán and her critics bent over backwards to argue that Spanish realism was 'different' because it derived from an indigenous realist tradition going back to the sixteenth century if not earlier. On this there was no disagreement; the argument was over what would happen if Spanish novelists wrote like the French. As Hobsbawm has shown (Hobsbawm and Ranger 1984: 1–14, 263–307), all nationalisms try to mask the fact that they are

[12] In his foundational Krausist text, *Ideal de la humanidad* (1860: 70), Sanz del Río had insisted that art should be an 'idea fundamentalmente social y con efectiva influencia sobre el pueblo'; in effect, a plea for a national literature.
[13] In *La cuestión palpitante* (1966: 32), published in the conservative paper *La Época* in 1882, Pardo Bazán points out that she was not able to attend the Ateneo lectures because women were not admitted. Jagoe (Jagoe, Blanco, and Enríquez de Salamanca 1998: 130) notes that the first women to attend a course at the Ateneo in 1882 were a group of students from the Krausist-backed Escuela de Institutrices.

the product of a recently created nation-State by positing a national tradition stretching back to mythical origins: a hazy concept whose identity shifts depending on the kind of tradition being invented. It was during the Restoration, particularly the 1880s and early 1890s, that the myth of the 'quintessential realism' of Spanish literature and art was born. Its function was twofold: to legitimize contemporary realism as the expression of the nation and, since realism supposes the existence of a 'national society', to suggest that the modern concept of a distinctive, homogeneous Spanish national identity was not a modern invention at all. Thus Pardo Bazán included in *La cuestión palpitante* an essay titled 'Genealogía' which traced a supposed national realist tradition back through Cervantes, Velázquez, and Murillo to *La Celestina*.[14] The existence of a traditionalist realist writer like Pereda was, she argued, living proof that realism was not 'smuggled' into Spain from France but the continuation of an indigenous tradition. Echoing the preface to her 1881 novel *Un viaje de novios*, she concluded that Spanish realism would be 'different' from the French variety because it was a native product and because Spanish society was different from that of France (1966: 68–70, 171, 181–2). The nationalist project underlying Spanish realism is here explicit. What is also clear is that Spanishness is constructed as that which is not French: a perennial problem since the creation of the liberal nation-State had, from its beginnings under the Enlightenment-inspired Bourbon Carlos III, been based on French models, but one that was inevitable given that, as Carr notes (1966: 105), modern Spanish nationalism originated in the resistance to Napoleonic invasion.

Pardo Bazán was criticized for opportunism in taking up the naturalist cause but, as Alas noted in his prologue to the book version of *La cuestión palpitante*, naturalism, being the expression of modernity, was necessarily 'un oportunismo literario' (Alas 1972: 152). In claiming that naturalism, as a form of realism, was the expression of modern Spanish society and the basis of a centuries-old national literary tradition, Pardo Bazán was succumbing to the inevitable contradictions involved in inventing a tradition to legitimize the modern. Galdós had made the

[14] Pena López (1994: 45) notes that art criticism of the 1870s and 1880s (by the Krausists Giner and Cossío) 'nationalized' Golden Age art by insisting on painters' 'Spanishness'.

same contradictory claim in his 1870 essay (Pérez Galdós 1972: 116–17).[15] What is being constructed here is a teleological version of national literary history whereby origins are invented in the image of the present in order to present the latter as the realization of a manifest destiny. The same teleological structure underlies Padre Blanco García's rabidly nationalist *La literatura española en el siglo XIX* (3 vols., 1891–4) which claims Spanish American literature as 'Spanish'; and most notably Menéndez Pelayo's massive construction of a national intellectual tradition in his *Historia de los heterodoxos españoles* (5 vols., 1880–2), *Historia de las ideas estéticas en España* (5 vols., 1883–91), and *La ciencia española* (3 vols., 1887–9)—coinciding with the dates of publication of most of the novels studied here —in which, in a manœuvre typical of late nineteenth-century discourses of social control, the 'normal' is affirmed through discussion of the 'deviant'.[16] In his 1882 essay 'De la filosofía española', Valera constructed a very different national intellectual tradition including Spanish Jewish and Arab thinkers and culminating in Krausism, using heterodox roots to justify the contemporary secularization of Spanish culture (1882: 55–103).[17] Again, we see how the debate over what constitutes a national culture is a debate about what should be included and what excluded. If contemporary discussion on the relative merits of idealism and realism centred on subject matter, this was not due to literary naivety but because, if the function of the novel was to 'write the nation', what was included and what was excluded was crucial. Valera's own insistence that he was an idealist writer has rightly been seen as an alibi (Tierno Galván 1977: 108–13, 117–18) allowing him to deal with sexuality while claiming that his novels had nothing to do with reality and thus did not threaten the constitution of the 'imagined community'. I have

---

[15] Galdós's 1901 prologue to the 2nd edition of *La Regenta* also argued at length that realism was a native product subsequently exported to England and France, and now reimported back into its homeland (Alas 1981: i. 79–92). He is of course right to point out that the English novel in particular continued the Cervantine and picaresque traditions. But 19th-century realism, as the expression of the modern nation-State, is a very different animal in both its structures and function.
[16] Appropriately, Menéndez Pelayo was appointed head of the Biblioteca Nacional when its present building, first mooted in 1866, was completed in 1892.
[17] In an 1861 parliamentary speech, Valera had insisted that the study of Spanish national culture should be compulsory at university; again, he included Spanish Jewish and Arab thinkers (Valera 1929: 41–4).

included him in this study of the realist novel since *Pepita Jiménez* is precisely about the construction of an 'imagined community' through the marriage of town and country.

Although Valera and Pereda are predominantly rural novelists, both depict the effects of modernization and both—like Galdós, Alas, and Pardo Bazán—argue passionately for the need to create a national novel to counter the 'flood' of foreign imitations. The work of both has been related to *costumbrismo*, seen as a nostalgic resistance to modernity. I would argue that the relationship of *costumbrismo* to modernity is more complex for its principal writers, Mesonero Romanos and Estébanez Calderón, were both active participants in liberalism's modernizing project. Estébanez Calderón went into exile with other liberals in 1824; was Provincial Governor of Logroño in 1835, of Cádiz in 1837, and of Seville in 1837–8 (provincial governors being the agents of central State control under the 1833 territorial division of Spain into forty-nine provinces on the French centralized model); was parliamentary deputy from 1846, in 1847 becoming War Minister, in 1849 Councillor of State, and in 1853 Life Senator. The political patron of the future Restoration premier Cánovas, he also worked as a lawyer and journalist, and was editor of the official State *Boletín* and *Diario de la Administración*, literally 'writing the nation'. Cánovas wrote his biography in 1883. He was, in other words, involved at a high level in the mid-century moderate liberal administrations responsible for extending centralized control.

Mesonero Romanos's biography is particularly telling, for he was personally responsible for initiating the rebuilding of Madrid which would make the popular 'types' described in his *Escenas matritenses* (1842) redundant: if he is protesting against modernity, he is protesting against his own political efforts. In 1831 he published his *Manual histórico-estadístico de Madrid* (updated 1833, 1844, 1854), mapping the city. The appendix to the 1833 edition, 'Rápida ojeada sobre el estado de la capital y los medios de mejorarla', sets out proposals for the following: modern sanitation, water supply, and public baths; covered markets; the building of new residential districts ('ensanches') and of long, wide avenues and squares with central parks; hackney cabs; paving and street-lighting; regular numbering of houses; street names and public monuments; new cemeteries; the elimination of begging and the creation of asylums, hospices, hospitals, and prisons; public safety; savings banks and reformed Montes de Piedad (pawnbrokers); the encouragement of commerce through the building of shopping arcades and modern shops with window displays ('bazares') plus restaurants and inns; improved educational facilities, including bringing to Madrid the old University at Alcalá de Henares, and creating an Ateneo and new academies and museums, with popular libraries to be built on the site of disentailed monasteries and scholarships for artisans; improved public entertainment; town planning and public health regulations, and revised municipal ordinances; regular population censuses and city maps—in short, a modern town planner's dream of total rationalization in the best Benthamite panoptical tradition. Anderson has noted the function of the census, the map, and the museum in contructing the nation (1983: 163). Mesonero Romanos's street names and public monuments were to commemorate national heroes.[18] The streets of the new *ensanches*, when built in the 1860s to 1880s, would also be named after the Restoration's statesmen (this was the time when politicians started to be referred to as 'hombres de Estado').[19] As Galdós mentions in *Fortunata y Jacinta* (Pérez Galdós 1992: i. 138), many of Mesonero Romanos's proposals were implemented by the Marqués de Pontejos in the mid-century.[20] In 1833 and 1840 Mesonero Romanos toured the major European cities to study modern town planning and, on election to the Ayuntamiento de Madrid in 1846, put forward his *Proyecto de mejoras generales de Madrid*, followed in 1849 by a further *Memoria*. His 1861 *El antiguo Madrid* is a guide to the city he himself was instrumental in demolishing.[21]

[18] An 1844 Royal Order required all provinces of Spain to 'protect their cultural monuments' (Reuben Holo 1997: 304).

[19] Álvarez Junco (Mar-Molinero and Smith 1996: 100), who argues that the Spanish State failed to instil in the populace the sense of belonging to a common national community, states that national glories were not exalted in street names (as Mesonero Romanos had proposed). While this is not entirely true, it must be conceded that the predilection for naming streets after statesmen gave the populace little opportunity for emotional identification.

[20] For the modernizing measures of the Marqués de Pontejos, see Martín Muñoz in Otero Carvajal and Bahamonde (1986: i. 193–209). These included proposals for bringing running water to Madrid, not realized till work started in 1848 on the Canal de Lozoya, whose consequences are charted in Galdós's *Fortunata y Jacinta*.

[21] Biographical information on Estébanez Calderón and Mesonero Romanos is from the *Enciclopedia universal ilustrada europeo-americana* (Madrid: Espasa Calpa, 1987–91). Fernández (1992: 107) notes that Mesonero Romanos 'writes Madrid' through his activities as town planner as well as his *costumbrista* writings.

I would argue that in practice Estébanez Calderón's and Mesonero Romanos's *costumbrista* writings reinforce their political activities, contributing to the liberal project of mapping the nation by making educated Spaniards aware of the urban and rural popular masses, and in the process incorporating the latter into the nation as fellow members of the 'imagined community'. Bahamonde and Martínez (1994: 499) have argued that the *costumbrista* insistence on the picturesque, and particularly on the Andalusian, should be seen, not so much as an archaizing project, but rather as an attempt to construct a national identity out of those features that most clearly distinguished Spaniards from Europeans. It can also be argued that this emphasis on 'exotic', frequently racially alien (gypsy or Arab) 'others' was an attempt to construct the nation on colonial lines, through the incorporation into the centralized nation-State of what were seen as indigenous ethnic groups: a colonial concept of the nation which anticipates the realist novel's habit of referring to the lower classes as 'savages'. The popularity of *costumbrista* publications titled *Los españoles pintados por sí mismos* (or *Las españolas pintadas por los españoles*) makes it clear that the function of such works was to turn the people into 'Spaniards'; that is, members of a single national community. Indeed, the *costumbrista* cataloguing of popular 'types' perfectly incarnates the contradictory liberal project of constructing a unified nation based on individual freedom or difference.[22] That men were largely responsible for the creation of these stereotyped images of national identity suggests that the project was seen as one pertaining to the public sphere. The one pre-1868 female writer admitted by Restoration critics to the national literary canon was Fernán Caballero (male pseudonym for Cecilia Böhl de Faber). This was not on account of her domestic novels, rarely mentioned, but because her *costumbrista* writings made her a precursor of the modern national novel by contributing to the formation of a Spanish national identity.

---

[22] Comparison could usefully be made with Mayhew's cataloguing of popular London types in his *London Labour and the London Poor* (1851, expanded edition 1861). Eugen Weber's classic *Peasants into Frenchmen: The Modernization of Rural France, 1870–1914* charts the incorporation of the French rural populace into the nation. Hobsbawm (1990: 44) quotes the Italian statesman d'Azeglio's words at the first meeting of parliament of a newly unified Italy: 'We have made Italy; now we have to make Italians.'

That she was here continuing her German father's Romantic interest in the 'primitive' *Volk* is another ironic manifestation of the debt to foreign models of constructions of national culture. Gellner (Hutchinson and Smith 1994: 65) notes that nationalism involves 'the imposition of a high culture on society, where previously low cultures had taken up the lives of the majority'. Costumbrismo, in which the educated speak for the 'folk', marks the first stage in this shift to 'specialist-transmitted' culture (Hutchinson and Smith 1994: 66), completed with the creation and canonization of the realist novel.

Hobsbawm (1990: 60–1) notes the role print culture has played in unifying the nation through the imposition of a single national language. In 1789, only 12–13 per cent of Frenchmen spoke standard 'French' and only 50 per cent spoke it at all; at the time of Italy's unification in 1860, only 2.5 per cent of the population spoke 'Italian' for everyday purposes. But literacy gave them access to a common written language. Valera repeatedly urged the Spanish parliament to recognize the new Italian nation on the grounds that the existence of a common Italian literary language made Italian nationhood a *de facto* reality.[23] Both Valera and Menéndez Pelayo acknowledged Castilian, Catalan, and Portuguese (subsuming Galician) as Spanish national languages, but were hostile to other minority languages' claims to such status on the grounds that they did not have a literary tradition (Valera 1958: 1395–6; Gortázar 1994: 118 n. 14, 164).[24] As Anderson (1983: 69) and Hobsbawm (1990: 61) insist, national languages do not evolve naturally but are constructed through the standardizing efforts of grammarians, lexicographers, philologists, teachers, and the State administration. What this meant in Spain's case was that Castilian acquired a monopoly of all non-literary written usage. The dictionaries of the Spanish language

---

[23] See Valera's parliamentary speeches of 1861 and 1863 (1929: 5–25, 98–143). In his 1861 speech, Valera showed a clear understanding of the difference between 'nation' and 'state', arguing that Spain had been a nation 'desde que España es España' but had been a State only since the Catholic Kings. He further noted that Italy's case showed that it is possible to have a sense of national unity without the existence of a central State (1929: 9). In his 1896 essay 'El regionalismo filológico en Galicia' (1942: 900), Valera acknowledged that that before the Catholic Kings there was not even such a thing as a Spanish nation or 'Spaniards'.

[24] The inclusion of Galician under Portuguese was a tactical move legitimizing both men's support for Iberian unity. Not surprisingly, the Portuguese were less enthusiastic about the claim that Portuguese was a 'Spanish' national language.

produced by the Spanish Royal Academy, founded in 1713, were dictionaries of Castilian, and members had to be resident in Madrid—Menéndez Pelayo had to secure an exemption for Pereda in 1897 (Madariaga de la Campa 1991: 397). Quintana's 1813 education plan imposed Castilian as the sole language of State education, ratified by Moyano's 1857 Education Act. Castilian was also the sole language of the State administration from its eighteenth-century beginnings; the *oposiciones* system ensured that all State officers spoke and wrote 'proper Spanish'. Hobsbawm notes (1990: 82) that throughout nineteenth-century Europe the State administration was 'the largest single body of employment requiring literacy'.

The story of State formation in Spain is the story of the imposition of Castilian culture, not only through language but also through the progressive abolition of local customary law. Valencia, Aragon, and Catalonia were brought under Castilian jurisdiction in 1707, 1711, and 1716; Navarre in 1841. The Basque and Navarrese *fueros* were revised in 1839 and 1841, and largely abolished on Carlist defeat in 1876. This meant incorporation into a national legal and fiscal system, whose operations were conducted in Castilian, and incorporation into a national market through the abolition of internal customs controls. As we shall see, in the 1880s unease about excessive centralization led to demands for the revival of local customary law; indeed, the 1889 Civil Code included concessions to foral rights (Clavero 1982: 9, 21, 26). The rise of peripheral nationalisms in the 1890s will be discussed in Chapter 8. As Fusi (Gortázar 1994: 81–2) and Ucelay da Cal (Graham and Labanyi 1995: 32) note, from the start local and State nationalisms fed off each other. The intensification of the latter in the Restoration period was a response to the threat to national unity posed during the *sexenio revolucionario* by the third Carlist War of 1873–6, the Cuban War of 1868–77 (the Cuban independence struggle directly affected national integrity since Spain's American colonies had since 1812 been constitutionally defined as provinces), and federal republicanism which additionally represented the spectre of popular insurrection. The 1873 cantonalist uprisings in Andalusia and the Levante were perceived as 'proof' that federal republicanism meant the break up of the nation-State. In fact, as Jover Zamora has shown (Gortázar 1994: 105–67), the federalist politicians of the First Spanish Republic unanimously saw federalism as a way of preserving national unity by countering grassroots disaffection. The short-lived federalist experiment of 1873 led to an intense debate about the relative merits of State centralization versus decentralization continuing throughout the Restoration period. The debate was based on differing interpretations of national history. The former Federal Republican President Pi y Margall's *Las nacionalidades* (1879) argued that Spain's historic nationalities stretching back to the Middle Ages proved that federalism was the 'natural' form of national government (Gortázar 1994: 107). The Conservative Prime Minister Cánovas argued in his 1882 Ateneo lecture 'El concepto de la nación', attacking Renan's controversial lecture 'Qu'est-ce qu'une nation?' of the same year, that Spain's progression toward national unity obeyed an ineluctable historical law (Ruiz Salvador 1971: 155; Gortázar 1994: 211–13; Díez del Corral 1943: 573–5).[25] As Hobsbawm (1990: 19) and Giddens (1985: 179–221) stress, the nation-State is based on the concept of national sovereignty for it presupposes that all the nation's inhabitants are citizens. The 1869 Constitution introduced universal manhood suffrage and placed sovereignty in the nation, but the Restoration Constitution of 1876 reneged on universal suffrage (formally abolished by the 1878 Electoral Law) and placed sovereignty, as before the 1868 Revolution, in the Crown and parliament. As we shall see in Chapter 3, this prompted discussion as to who exactly constituted the nation if only some of its inhabitants were citizens.

The extension of State control in post-1868 Spain has to be seen in the context of such debates—essential to nineteenth-century Spanish political life, as Fusi notes (Gortázar 1994: 77) —over the nature of the nation-State. Even the brief federalist interlude was an attempt to decentralize the State but not to reduce its powers; hence popular disenchantment.[26] Galdós's obsession with *empleomanía* (wanting a job with the State administration) reflects contemporary concern not just with the 'brain drain' that took the best minds out of productive labour, but also with the State's increasing invasion of public and private

[25] Renan's lecture (printed in Bhabha 1990: 8–22) had claimed that the nation is an act of collective will ('a daily plebiscite') that depends on forgetting much of national history; see Gellner (1987: 6–10).

[26] See Giddens (1985) and Corrigan and Sayer (1991) for an analysis of nation formation as the extension of State control over all areas of public and private life.

life. In his 1897 Royal Academy speech, Galdós criticized the bourgeois ruling classes for subjecting the whole of national life to 'un sin fin de reglamentos, legislando desaforadamente sobre todas las cosas' (Pérez Galdós 1972: 178). But he, as a parliamentary deputy 1886–90 (admittedly pretty inactive), was part of this legislative process. His practical positioning, whatever his sympathies, is made clear in his 1913 preface to the French edition of *Misericordia* where he relates how, in his research for *Fortunata y Jacinta*, he toured lodging houses with a police escort and brothels disguised as a municipal medical inspector (1972: 223). Valera was also a deputy in successive parliaments as well as holding appointments in various ministries; Pereda was a parliamentary deputy 1871–2; and Pardo Bazán's father had had a brief parliamentary career. All the writers studied here (Pereda in his youth, Pardo Bazán in later life) were political as well as cultural journalists; Alas's political journalism, predominantly concerned with excessive government centralization, is particularly impressive (Lissorgues 1980–1).

The legal codification of the public sphere began with the 1812 liberal Constitution (never fully implemented), culminating in what has been called the 'fiebre codificadora' (Jutglar 1971: 83) of the Restoration. As we shall see in Chapter 8, the standardization and centralization of local government initiated by the 1833 division of the national territory into forty-nine provinces, modelled on French lines and ignoring the boundaries of Spain's historic communities, was increased by successive legislation through to the 1880s, during which decade the issue of centralization versus decentralization dominated political debate. Most standardizing and centralizing legislation was aimed at creating a national economy. The Madrid Stock Exchange was set up in 1831. The Bank of Spain was formally constituted in 1856; in 1874 it was granted a monopoly over the issue of paper money. A single national currency, based on the peseta, was imposed in 1868 with the stipulation that coins should bear the national insignia, rather than the monarch's head as previously (Bahamonde Magro and Martínez 1994: 544). Sardá (1948: 99) and Vicens Vives (1969: 713) estimate that in 1842 half the currency circulating in Spain was foreign, apart from the mass of regional variants. The standardization of the multiple regional systems of weights and measures was begun in 1858 with the introduction of the metric system (Vicens Vives 1969: 692).

Decisive in the formation of a national market were the creation of a telegraph system in the 1840s, electrified in the 1850s (Bahamonde Magro and Martínez 1994: 413–20), the completion 1840–68 of the national road network begun in the eighteenth century, and, crucially, the construction from 1848 to the mid 1880s, peaking in the period 1855–65, of a national railway network. All of these communications systems furthered centralization through their radial structure converging on Madrid.

As Hobsbawm notes (1990: 25), it was not fortuitous that nation-making coincided with the classic era of free-trade liberalism for, perhaps more than anything else, it was the incorporation of the whole of the nation's inhabitants into a single market that turned them into citizens. The power of the guilds, first curtailed in 1813, had been ended in 1836. The Company Acts of 1848 and 1856 allowed Spain's entry into the international credit and banking system. The years 1868–9, following the 1868 Revolution, saw a flood of free-trade legislation, abolishing import restrictions and reducing customs tariffs; allowing anyone (in theory) to set up a company, act as a business agent, or exploit mineral resources; and affirming freedom of contract. Contradictorily, free trade not only constructed a national market but threatened the nation's integrity by opening the door to foreign trade and investment. These free-trade measures were formalized in the Commercial Code of 1885 (García Delgado 1985: 401–12). Free trade remained the buzzword of both progressive and conservative liberals until Cánovas reintroduced protectionist tariffs in 1891. This free-trade legislation highlights the paradox at the heart of the liberal nation-making project, for the object of central State control—as liberal politicians of all shades never tired of saying—was to create and guarantee individual freedom. Thus the 1869 Constitution—the parliamentary debate on which was witnessed by Galdós as a political journalist (Elorza 1973: 157)—in addition to confirming the above economic reforms proclaimed freedom of expression, religion, association, education, place of residence, and inviolability of the home and correspondence: these last two inviolabilities being a key affirmation of individual privacy. For the modern concept of the individual has to be enforced through legislation: that is, written into existence. As Giddens notes (1985: 200–1), the slogan 'liberty, equality, fraternity' means being equal before the law but also equally subject to the law. This is made explicit by Cánovas's statement: 'He creído siempre que únicamente cabe la libertad donde hay un Estado muy fuerte' (Díez del Corral 1943: 590). What was meant by individual freedom was, essentially, the right to private property. The central plank of the liberal nation-making project was disentailment, proposed in the 1812 Constitution and implemented by the mid-century legislation of Mendizábal (1835–7) and Madoz (1855). This abolished the old ecclesiastical and seigneurial jurisdictions, all forms of entail (including the *mayorazgo* system of sole, unalienable inheritance by the eldest son), and, in 1855, the village common lands, declaring all such land 'bienes nacionales' and placing it on the 'free' market. The goals were multiple. First, to alleviate the national debt since the sales of land were payable in government bonds. Second, to extend State control to those parts of the national territory—an estimated two-thirds (Shubert 1990: 57)—previously under noble and Church jurisdiction. As Carr notes (1966: 171), the desire to bring the Church under State control was exacerbated by its support for the Carlist attack on national unity. With this integration of noble and Church lands into the State, the distinction in the 1812 Constitution between 'Spaniards' and 'citizens' disappeared from the 1837 and later Constitutions (Artola 1973: 129). The third goal was to break up the large estates, creating more property-holders and thus citizens since suffrage, giving one a personal 'investment' in the nation, was tied to a property qualification. Mendizábal's 1836 disentailment decree explicitly stated that the aim was to 'crear nuevos vínculos que aten al hombre con la Patria y con sus instituciones' (Rueda 1986: 138). This division and privatization of the big estates additionally brought more of the nation's surface under cultivation, stimulating agricultural output but also—as Carr notes (1966: 425)—destroying perhaps half the nation's forests. Rueda (1986: 176) emphasizes that such privatizing measures were never intended to alleviate the lot of the rural masses, who lost their previous rights of use to noble, Church, and common lands and were forced to migrate to the cities, creating a useful pool of cheap surplus labour but also a swarm of vagrants provoking a succession of Anti-Vagrancy Laws rounding them up and returning them to their place of origin (Bahamonde Magro and Toro Mérida 1978: 47–50, 57).

Raymond Williams (1975: 121–34) has written eloquently about the impact on the English realist novel of the Enclosure Acts of the eighteenth and early nineteenth centuries. The impact of Spain's mid-century disentailments—combined with separate legislation in 1770, 1788, 1813, 1833, and 1836 giving landowners right of enclosure—was infinitely more devastating. Shubert (1990: 60) calculates that from 1836 to 1895 between a quarter and a third of the nation's surface changed hands.

Mooers (1991) has argued convincingly that the nineteenth-century European liberal revolutions were 'bourgeois' not because they were carried out by a dominant bourgeoisie, for in most European countries the middle classes were still relatively small, but because they imposed bourgeois forms of organization. He notes that the existence of a large State administration, such as developed in Spain in the course of the nineteenth century, was useful in helping backward countries 'catch up' by implementing rapid capitalist transformation from above (1991: 95–6, 105). Shubert (1990: 1–6, 90) accordingly insists that, despite the late development of its middle class, nineteenth-century Spain did experience a bourgeois revolution for the mid-century disentailment laws, plus the free-trade legislation passed after 1868, subjected the nation to the law of the market. Indeed, in Spain—unlike France—the nobility largely supported the liberal revolution. In this book I shall use the term 'modernity' to refer to post-1868 Spain, despite the country's evident economic backwardness, for contemporary legislation and public debate were as 'modern' as anywhere else in Europe; indeed, the introduction of universal manhood suffrage in 1869 (rescinded by Cánovas in 1878, reinstated by Sagasta in 1890) antedated many other European nations (it was introduced in Britain in 1918). I shall examine in my conclusion the consequences of contemporary awareness that Spain's modernity existed largely on paper.

These economic reforms, designed to bring the whole of the national territory under State jurisdiction and into a single market economy, clearly had massive effects on private as well as public life. Further legislation was specifically aimed at constituting the nation's amorphous inhabitants as individualized but standardized citizens. The abolition of local *fueros* extended military conscription to the whole of the national territory (a constant source of local grievance), subjecting all young males unable to buy themselves out to a common disciplinary system and inculcation of patriotic values (a national anthem and flag were first introduced in 1770 and 1785 (García de Cortázar and González Vesga 1994: 375)). Even more important, it allowed nationwide fiscal control, facilitated by Mon's 1845 creation of a uniform tax system; in Galdós's *Miau*, Villaamil, obsessed with further standardizing the tax system, had originally worked under Mon.[27] As Bahamonde and Martínez note (1994: 67), to pay taxes (*contribuciones*) is literally to contribute to the nation. The gathering of statistics—particularly for tax purposes—by the State administration, initiated in 1768, was systematized through the introduction of regular national censuses in 1857 and the establishment in 1870 of a Civil Registry, with which all births, marriages, and deaths had to be recorded. The compilation of statistics was part of civil governors' centralizing brief. The word 'statistics', of course, means pertaining to the State; in becoming statistics, the nation's inhabitants were 'nationalized' in every sense.[28] The year 1870 also saw the interim revolutionary government's introduction of civil marriage; Cánovas abolished this in February 1875 immediately on coming to power, ceding to pressure from the extreme-right Moderate Party in exchange for their agreement to continued freedom of worship (Varela Ortega 1977: 101). For many rural inhabitants the most tangible sign of the State's presence was the Guardia Civil, created in 1844 as a centrally controlled nationwide police force, deployed in a radial network corresponding to the national road and rail systems which they were additionally charged with defending (López Garrido 1982: 125, 149–50). The penal system was standardized through the introduction of a State-wide Penal Code in 1822 (modelled on centralized Napoleonic legislation), strengthened by the Penal Code of 1848, influenced by Bentham and greatly increasing penalties for offences against private property (Bahamonde Magro and Martínez 1994: 270–1), the

---

[27] Mon was also responsible in 1838 for centralizing the credit operations of the Banco de San Fernando (renamed the Banco de España in 1856) and in 1849 for putting it under State control by making its governor and deputy governors State appointments (Vicens Viyes 1969: 725).

[28] Giddens (1985: 41–6, 178–9) argues that the rise of the nation-State was dependent on literacy inasmuch as writing originated as a way of recording and classifying information for purposes of administrative control. As he notes, writing led to the replacement of local customary law by standardized legal codes that could be read, and enforced, anywhere in the nation.

1855 Civil Justice Act, 1870 Penal Code and Judiciary Reform Act, 1872 Criminal Justice Act, 1881 Civil Justice Act, and 1882 Criminal Justice Act. The culmination of this 'fiebre codificadora' was the 1889 Civil Code, debated in parliament and the press throughout the 1880s, which laid down norms governing private property, marriage, and the family, and the relative roles of the State and civil society (García Delgado 1985: 369–99). The centralizing obsession of Spanish liberal governments, especially those of the right, not only provoked an eloquent Krausist critique of State control but also ensured that the Spanish lower classes opted predominantly for anarchism rather than socialism.

The State's assumption of responsibility for the nation's education, enshrined in the 1812 Constitution, made it the Church's direct rival in the battle for ideological control. Given this, and the dissolution of the monasteries under the disentailment laws, it is not surprising that nineteenth-century catechisms declared liberalism to be a sin. The 1845 Moderate Constitution's attempt to compensate by committing the State to paying priests' salaries, confirmed by the 1851 Concordat with the Vatican, also gave the State leverage in controlling appointments; in practice, the State budget covered only around one-third of the clergy (Jutglar 1971: 50; Shubert 1990: 151–2). Education was standardized and centralized by the 1845 Plan Pidal, introducing a national curriculum and centralized appointments system, and giving the State exclusive control of higher education, with Madrid University—renamed the Universidad Central in 1850 after its transfer from Alcalá in 1836 (Hernández Sandoica in Otero Carvajal and Bahamonde 1986: ii. 379)—having a monopoly of higher degrees. Moyano's 1857 Education Act ensured that all the nation's youth would (in theory) have a training in citizenship by instituting compulsory, free primary school education to the age of 9, with curriculum and textbooks subject to central approval.[29] It was this tight State control that allowed the sacking of Krausist professors at Madrid University in 1867 and prompted their mass resignation on its reimposition in 1875. From 1855 to 1900, education was controlled by the Ministerio de Fomento, responsible

---

[29] For a Foucauldian discussion of the beginnings of State education in Spain and its role in enforcing State control, see Varela and Álvarez-Uría (1991).

for public works, for it was in every sense a branch of national development.[30] In 1870 Echegaray as Ministro de Fomento made it obligatory for all State primary schools and teachers' training colleges (Escuelas Normales) to teach the national Constitution (Fernández Valencia and Anadón Benedicto in Otero Carvajal and Bahamonde 1986: ii. 399).

Both the State education system and the Institución Libre de Enseñanza, created by the Krausist Giner de los Ríos in 1876 as an independent, secular educational establishment encouraging critical debate, attached great importance to geography as a way of giving the young a sense of citizenship. The same Madoz who was responsible for the second wave of mid-century disentailments compiled his sixteen-volume *Diccionario geográfico-histórico-estadístico de España* in 1845–50, complemented by Coello's contemporaneous *Atlas de España*. All local government bodies were instructed to buy these texts (Castro 1987: 28–9); the map of Spain joined the crucifix on the walls of Spanish classrooms. Giner's close contacts with geologists led him in 1885 to create his Sociedad para Estudios del Guadarrama (Pena López 1990: 142; Litvak 1991: 24). His country excursions with his students (which inspired Antonio Machado's Guadarrama poems) were part of a nationalist project—his famous 1885 essay 'Paisaje' noted that there was no need to go abroad to find beautiful scenery (1915: 369–70)—but effectively made Castile the basis of a 'national' landscape. Rodríguez Esteban (1994) and Casado (1994) have described the patriotic activities of the Sociedad Geográfica de Madrid (founded 1876) and the Sociedad Española de Historia Natural and Sociedad Linneana Matritense (founded 1871 and 1878), all with strong Krausist connections, which encouraged the publication of maps and surveys of the nation's geology, flora, and fauna, in the former case undertaking explorations in Africa to further Spanish colonial expansion. As Litvak (1991) and others (Vega in *Carlos de Haes* 1996; Pena López 1982, 1993–4) have shown, the creation in 1844 of a Cátedra de Paisaje at the Academia de Bellas Artes de San Fernando, first held by Carlos de Haes who instituted the practice of *plein air* painting, led to the development of a

---

[30] Prior to 1855, education was successively under the Ministries of the Interior, Trade, Education and Public Works, and Justice. Proposals to set up a separate Ministry of Education, finally instituted in 1900, were put to parliament by Krausist politicians in 1883, 1885, and 1886 (Salaün and Serrano 1991: 69–70).

school of Spanish landscape artists (initially realist, in the 1880s moving towards impressionism) who took advantage of the new railway network to chart Spain's varied geography, in an attempt to construct both local and national identities. For the railways not only created a national market but allowed Spaniards—like the honeymoon couple Jacinta and Juanito in *Fortunata y Jacinta*—to 'discover' 'their' country; this was also the time—as Galdós's, Pereda's, and Alas's novels testify—when seaside and country holidays were invented.

The realist novel can be seen as a parallel attempt to map the nation. We shall see how, in charting the modernization process which incorporated Spain's inhabitants into a centralized State apparatus, a single market economy, and a common print culture, the realist novel in many ways anticipated turn-of-the-century regenerationism. Indeed the complementary terms 'degeneration' and 'regeneration' started to be used in the 1860s and were common currency by 1880. Particularly striking is novelists' almost ecological concern from around 1880 with the ways in which a modernity conceived in terms of the city was exhausting natural resources; it was in the 1880s that the regenerationist Joaquín Costa started his campaign for irrigation and reforestation projects. As at the turn of the century, it is concern with the nation as a problem that engenders a sense of nationalism. For, in a curious way, the failure of the modernization process that constructs the nation-State produces an even more acute sense of national awareness than success. I have devoted separate sections to the urban and rural novel, but both share in the realist project of mapping a national life seen as problematic. As in contemporary degeneracy theory, with which there are important overlaps, the issue is where modernity has gone wrong. In my readings of the novels, I shall pay particular attention to textual details which would have functioned for contemporary readers as indicators of a shared fund of anxieties so commonly articulated in journalistic, political, and medical writing that they did not need to be spelled out. Such textual details should not be dismissed as 'background' for it was precisely their taken-for-grantedness that allowed them to construct contemporary readers as members of a common 'imagined community'.

PART I

Redefining the Public and Private Spheres

1
Liberal Political Theory: Freedom and the Market

IN this and the next chapter, I shall outline the theoretical framework to my analysis of the novels, indicating its application to late nineteenth-century Spain. Much has been written about the capitalist creation of separate public and private spheres, and the ways in which this division affected women, but most of it makes little or no reference to Spain. In her article 'Rethinking the Public Sphere' (1990), Fraser usefully reminds feminist historians that the public/private split is not a straightforward divide between what goes on inside the home and all the other things that comprise the 'outside' world.[1] The issue of defining the boundary between the public and private spheres was central to the European realist novel in general, as it was to public debate, because the two spheres overlap in a way which makes precise distinctions impossible. In Spain's case the problem of definition was particularly acute, since the uneven nature of the modernization process produced a superimposition of the old and the new, while its rapidity meant that the new divisions started to be eroded by further developments before they had had a chance to become consolidated—a problem illustrated, as we shall see, in *Fortunata y Jacinta*.

The establishment of the public/private division is complicated by the fact that the passage from the *ancien régime* to modernity took the form of two parallel splitting processes. On the one hand, the State separated off from the Crown through the creation of government ministers, backed by ministries of specialist administrators, and through the transfer of authority to parliament. This signified the change from a system based on personal (private) authority—that of the monarch and of

[1] See also Walby (1990) and Pateman (1989: 118–40).

those endowed with privileges by him—to one in which authority lay in public institutions 'representing' the citizenry, with even the monarch representing (under absolutism) divine authority and (under constitutional monarchy) the nation. As Habermas (1989: 5–26) notes, this produced a corresponding shift in the meaning of the term 'public'. In the pre-modern period, those in authority represented their personal power publicly; that is, before a public constituted as an audience. There was no private/public divide; the royal bedroom was a place of court ceremonial. With the passage to modernity, those in authority came to exercise a public power as representatives of the public. This constituted the latter as what came to be called 'civil society', for the first time creating the concept of 'society' as a homogeneous body of public opinion (homogeneous not because everyone was in agreement but because it was united by common concerns). Initially, of course, as Habermas observes (1989: 31–43), this new 'society' comprised only that small sector of the population which constituted the 'reading public', since public opinion was formed not only by debate in the coffee houses but above all through the press. Carr (1966: 207) notes that the new 'society' which emerged in Spain after the fall of absolute monarchy in 1833 was above all a 'discussing society'. Debating societies and the press flourished after the 1869 Constitution's granting of freedom of the press, and again after its restoration in 1883 (Martínez Cuadrado 1973: 66). As journalists Galdós, Alas, Valera, and Pardo Bazán all repeatedly stressed the need to create a healthy civil society through the encouragement of public debate.

It is this 'discussing society' that was, in Europe generally from the late eighteenth century, called the 'public sphere'. As Habermas emphasizes (1989: 52–6), it was separate from the State (which he refers to as 'public authority') and functioned as a critical monitor of its activities. In other words, the public sphere was constituted by the public opinion of private citizens. 'Private' here has the meaning it had under the *ancien régime* of those excluded from public (State) office. If before 'the public' consisted in private citizens constituted as an audience, now it was formed by private citizens playing an active, participatory role in public life. In Habermas's phrase (1989: 26), the public sphere was 'the sphere of private people come together as a public'. As a 'reading public', its members formed public opinion by getting together to discuss their private reading. Habermas divides the public sphere into the literary and the political. Both reading publics were influential in forming public opinion; however, he notes that the former included women whereas the latter, centred on the coffee houses and debating societies, was an all-male preserve (1989: 33). It is in this sense of forming public opinion that the novel contributed to nation formation.

Civil society, as the public sphere made up of private citizens, is however further subdivided. For private citizens come together to play a public role not only through public opinion, in its literary and political versions, but also through the market. This is where the second splitting process comes in. As Habermas notes (1989: 3–4), the Greek *oikos*, from which the term 'economy' derives, referred to the household as a production unit, including slaves as well as kin. The separation between the *polis* and the *oikos* was not one between public and private in the modern sense, for citizens enjoyed political status inasmuch as they were masters of a household. It has been noted that the rediscovery of Roman Law in medieval Europe facilitated the development of a legal and ultimately political system based on private property, but the Roman distinction between the *res publica* (State) and the patrician household was modelled on the Greek scheme, and Roman Law had to be substantially reinterpreted to fit changing European definitions of public and private (Giddens 1989: 99–100). Casey (1989) has studied the evolution of the family as a unit of economic production in the pre-modern period, with abundant examples from Spain. The Greek *agora* and the Roman *forum* were markets not in the modern economic sense, for economics was a household matter, but in that of a public opinion which coincided with the State or Republic. When, as we shall see, Alas (Professor of Roman Law at Oviedo University 1883–8) lamented the loss of the tangible public participation in political life that had characterized the Roman *res publica*, based on the *forum*, he was in practice arguing for a strengthening of public opinion as a check on the State. Restoration Spanish intellectuals, the Krausists in particular, constantly lamented the public sphere's increasing subjection to the State, illustrating Habermas's description of how, in the mid- to late nineteenth century, the expansion of the State administration and the incorporation of civil society's leading spokesmen into parliament blurred the division between a supposedly independent public sphere of private citizens and public authority (1989: 141–51). This is viewed as a problem in most of the novels studied.

The passage from the Greek *agora* and the Roman *forum* to the modern market required the separation of economic production from the household unit which took place with capitalist industrialization. For under capitalism what is understood by economic production is production for a profit ('capital' meaning money whose purpose is to make more money). It is this split which inaugurates the 'private sphere' in the commonest sense of the term: that of the domestic home based on privacy and love. Habermas calls this the 'intimate sphere', to avoid confusion with civil society (in its double form of public opinion and the market). Civil society thus constitutes a public sphere by contrast with the home but a private sphere by contrast with the State. The overlap of 'public' and 'private' inherent in the new concept of 'society' that emerges in the course of the nineteenth century is what makes it a source of novelistic concern. As Habermas notes (1989: 43–51), the concept of 'privacy' in the new sense of the intimate (as opposed to its original meaning of that which is excluded from the State) could develop only once economic activity had ceased to take place in the home. Ariès (1973), Hall (1992; Davidoff and Hall 1987), and others have shown how the growth of the capitalist economy was accompanied by the invention of childhood and of the nuclear family held together by sentimental bonds, as economic production and the home became separate public and private spheres respectively.[2] Habermas (1989: 44–5) observes that this process was paralleled by the increasing separation of private from public rooms in domestic architecture—a separation shown in *Fortunata y Jacinta* when Jacinta keeps slipping from the Santa Cruz dining room (public) to report the political conversation to the sick Juanito in the bedroom

---

[2] The derivation of the term 'family' from the Latin *famulus* (servant) indicates the word's pre-modern meaning of 'household' as an economic unit, rather than a unit based on blood ties (Nicholson 1986: 80). Casey (1989: 103) notes that prior to Adam Smith's *Wealth of Nations* (1776), the term 'economics' referred to the household enterprise, not to a 'market' conceived as a separate sphere. For a statistical analysis of family structures in Spain from the 17th century to the present, see Reher (1997).

(private).³ As Hall in particular has demonstrated (Davidoff and Hall 1987), this splitting off of economic activity from the home had devastating consequences for women, excluding them from production (except as hired labour) and reducing them to those domestic tasks connected with reproduction. As modern society came to be constituted in terms of exchange relations (the exchange of information as well as goods), the home became increasingly peripheral to the extent that it was not clear whether it formed part of society or not. It certainly did not form part of civil society. But if, with the rise of the nation-State, all the nation's inhabitants were to be turned into citizens, the home had somehow to be incorporated without losing its private status. Habermas (1989: 43) calls the bourgeois family 'a privateness oriented to an audience' for it became the subject of literature and of public opinion; indeed, the latter were responsible for constructing it as a private zone. The contradictory process whereby the State (through institutional regulation and the new codification of private life through civil law) and the public sphere (in the guise of social reformers) invaded domestic privacy in the name of manufacturing it will be discussed in Chapter 2.

Liberalism, as the political doctrine of the bourgeoisie, had a vested interest in keeping the home—and women—private, for women's admission to civil society logically required that of the lower classes. In his classic study *The Political Theory of Possessive Individualism* (1990), Macpherson explains how liberal political theory was able to sustain belief in universal freedom while excluding all but property-holders from franchise. As he notes, from its seventeenth-century origins liberal political theory defined freedom as the ability to dispose of one's property as one pleased. Liberalism is market theory because freedom was (and in contemporary neo-liberalism still is) seen as the ability to enter the market. If one did not have property, one was necessarily unfree in the sense that, having no access to the market, one was financially dependent on another. Franchise was seen not as a way of conferring freedom, but as something that could be exercised only by a free citizen, whose independent opinion would allow 'him' to contribute to public critical debate. The

---

³ For a detailed study of changes in domestic architecture in 19th-century Madrid, across the social spectrum, see Díez de Baldeón (1986).

opinion of servants (and of women, whom Macpherson barely mentions) was subsumed in that of the male head of household on whom they were financially dependent. This point was made by many Restoration opponents of women's suffrage, the Krausists included, who argued that granting the vote to wives and daughters as well as to male heads of household would be to give more than one vote to one body (Giner de los Ríos 1969: 202–8). But servants and women were still 'free citizens' because, although they mostly did not own property in the form of wealth, they did own 'property in their persons': that is, personal properties or skills. This notion is reflected in the word 'property' itself, whose original meaning of 'that which is proper to one' (*propio* in Spanish) implies that property is not just what one has but what one is. As Locke puts it (Macpherson 1990: 198), 'By *Property* I must be understood [. . .] to mean that Property which Men have in their Persons as well as Goods.' 'Men' here means what it says, as Kant's formulation makes clear:

> The only qualification required by a citizen (apart, of course, from being an adult male), is that he must be his *own master* (*sui iuris*), and must have some *property* (which can include any skill, trade, fine art, or science) to support himself. In cases where he must earn his living from others, he must earn it only by *selling* that which is his, and not by allowing others to make use of him; for he must in the true sense of the word *serve* no one but the commonwealth. (Habermas 1989: 110)

The second part of Kant's statement makes a crucial distinction between the trader or industrialist, who sells his property, and the wage-earner, who sells his labour and thus 'allows' another to exploit him. The definition of freedom as the ability to alienate one's property, including property in one's person, permitted the selling of one's labour to be seen as a voluntary alienation of freedom: workers were thus free but had 'chosen' to be unfree. Consequently it could be argued that wage-earners had 'chosen' to disqualify themselves from citizenship. As Macpherson shows, beggars were included here since they had 'voluntarily' made themselves dependent on alms.[4] The apparently crazy logic of the liberal definition of freedom as the ability to alienate

---

[4] Bahamonde Magro and Toro Mérida (1978: 57) note that 1868 Vagrancy Law defined vagrants as (i) those who possessed no property, income, trade, or skill, and (ii) those who possessed no property or income but did have a trade or skill which they did not employ. This careful wording places workers in a double-bind:

one's freedom is, as Macpherson notes, a brilliant sleight of hand which makes it possible for the bourgeoisie to maintain that, although all men are free, only those with property in the form of wealth (as opposed to property in their persons) can be members of civil society. Civil society is constituted by the market, but those who put their persons on the market 'exclude themselves'.[5]

Liberal market theory is contract theory because the exchange relations that constitute the market take the form of a contract between buyer and seller which, in legal terms, both enter into 'freely'. Macpherson nicely sums up Locke's argument: 'Since the individual is human only in so far as free, and free only in so far as a proprietor of himself, human society can only be a series of relations between sole proprietors, i.e. a series of market relations' (1990: 164). Giddens (1985: 68–70) notes that, although the concept of private property existed in the pre-modern period, it was only with capitalism that it came to be understood as meaning 'property that is freely alienable and, thus, can change hands in a manner governed wholly by its exchange-value'. With capitalism, land came to be seen as capital like any other form of property; that is, subject to contract law. As Shubert (1990: 57–60) and Rueda (1986: 12, 163) comment, the mid-century Spanish disentailments, putting noble and Church land on the market, signified the replacement of a property system governed by status with one governed by contract. Given the liberal definition of freedom as the ability to alienate one's property (and, if all one has is property in the person, one's freedom) on the market, the liberal politicians responsible for these measures were quite sincere in claiming

---

if they do employ their trade or skill, they are seen as having voluntarily alienated their property in their persons and thus their civil rights; but if they do not employ their property in their persons, they are seen as vagrants and thus again as having voluntarily forfeited their rights.

[5] The Lockean definition of freedom as the ability to dispose of one's labour and the property resulting from it is summarized as follows by the Spanish economist Álvaro Flórez Estrada, who introduced the principles of English classical economics into Spain, in his *Examen imparcial* of 1811: 'La prerrogativa más preciosa de que puede disfrutar el hombre [. . .] es la seguridad de su propiedad, derecho que no existe a menos que el ciudadano tenga absoluta libertad de disponer del fruto de su trabajo' (cited by Álvarez-Uría in Seminario de historia 1988: 128). The 1872 Spanish parliamentary debate on the abolition of slavery (not granted for Cuba till 1888) focused public attention on the freedom to dispose of one's 'property in one's person' (Bahamonde Magro and Toro Mérida 1978: 182).

that, by creating more private property-holders and forcing the peasants into wage-labour or vagrancy, they had instituted a free society.

Liberal theory is contract theory, not only because it defines freedom as the ability to 'contract away' one's property, but also because it supposes that society is created through a social contract whereby men agree, for their mutual convenience, to abandon the state of nature and abide by commonly agreed laws. In the late seventeenth century, Locke elaborated the notion of the social contract in opposition to Filmer's patriarchal theory which maintained that, just as sons were 'naturally' subject to the authority of fathers, so the nation's members were 'naturally' subject to the authority of the king (a theory which, of course, produced problems if the monarch was a woman). Locke's innovation was to argue that society was not subject to natural law like families, and that political authority was conventional; that is, agreed by the members of the body politic. This argument not only transformed 'subjects' into 'citizens' (those whose ownership of property in the form of wealth made them 'free'), but instituted a political division between public and private—parallel to the emerging economic division between market and home—by subordinating the family to different laws from the *polis*. The members of the body politic were 'free citizens', but the members of the family were still 'subjects'; that is, subject 'by nature' to the father. In her brilliant book *The Sexual Contract* (1989), Pateman notes that another sleight of hand is concealed here for the story of the social contract, while talking only about fathers and sons, is in effect a story which legitimizes men's authority over women (fathers over daughters, husbands over wives). She argues that Freud's social contract narrative—his Primal Horde theory—is not usually included in political discussion because it makes explicit the fact that the overthrow of the father by the sons is a dispute over the control of women (1989: 12). Pateman's treatment of social contract theories as 'stories' or 'fictions' is suggestive. The liberal slogan 'liberty, fraternity, equality' is, she notes (1989: 77–8), literally about the brothers' ownership rights to both property and women (which means the rights to women's property, and to women as property). Unlike Victorian Britain where, until the Married Women's Property Act of 1882, wives could not own property, those European countries like Spain whose civil legislation was based on the 1804 Napoleonic Code did allow women to own property, but on marriage the right to administer it, and all income from its use, passed to the husband, as did any wage income earned by the wife. The husband's signature was required if the woman wanted to sell her property, because married women were not legally entitled to make contracts except for wills (Scanlon 1986: 124, 128–30).[6]

However, as Pateman notes (1989: 54), there was one contract which women, although deemed minors (subject to the father if unmarried, to the husband if married), were all expected to make: the marriage contract. Indeed, as she comments, there is something very peculiar about the marriage contract for, unlike any other contract, it takes place not between two 'free individuals' but between one 'free individual' and one 'natural subordinate'; is non-negotiable (the two parties have no say in its terms); cannot be terminated except on death; and contains a clause whereby one party promises to obey the other unconditionally (Pateman 1989: 55, 58, 181; Corrigan and Sayer 1991: 23). As John Stuart Mill, author of *The Subjection of Women* (1869), nicely put it (Mill 1988: p. xiii), no right-minded businessman would sign such a contract explicitly relinquishing his rights for life (nor, for that matter, would any worker). Mill —whose book Pardo Bazán translated in 1892—opposed the legal subordination of married women's property to the husband, as he opposed slavery, on the grounds that 'It is not freedom to be allowed to alienate [one's] freedom' (Pateman 1989: 75). Why, Pateman asks, did liberalism constitute marriage as a contract (rather than a sacrament, which it continued to be in the eyes of the Catholic Church) when women were anyway deemed 'naturally' subject to male authority (1989: 54)? Her answer is that, first, the marriage contract was necessary to place wives within the social contract, giving them social obligations, while at the same time denying them social rights since they thereby signed away their status as citizens. And secondly, the fact that they had 'freely' signed their rights away made it possible to justify their subordination, like that of workers and beggars, while still maintaining that all human beings were free. For the

---

[6] The 1889 Civil Code, which made married women legally subordinate to husbands in the ways stipulated here, made no significant changes to previous legislation on women's rights and duties. As Scanlon notes (1986: 136), they had many of the latter but few of the former.

subordination of 'equals' can be justified only if it is entered into freely (Pateman 1989: 40, 112). The marriage contract and the wage contract placed wives and workers respectively in and not in civil society (1989: 11). The realist novel is so interested in married women because it was not clear where they stood, particularly if they were members of the property-owning classes which by definition constituted 'society'. Several novels—again *Fortunata y Jacinta* is paradigmatic—show awareness that the issue of women's membership of civil society (the 'woman question') was tied to that of the lower classes (the 'social question'), for both were part of, and yet outside, 'society'. Tony Tanner (1979: 12–13) has pointed out that adultery is more problematic than premarital promiscuity or even divorce, because it supposes that the adulterer is inside and outside marriage at once. For if it is possible to be simultaneously inside and outside, the boundary between the two positions disappears. In fact, the nineteenth-century wife could not help but be simultaneously inside and outside the private sphere of the family, since the marriage contract placed her inside society while excluding her from it. She was thus in a potentially adulterous position whether or not she was unfaithful. Male adultery was not seen as a social threat, and was thus less interesting to novelists, because the marriage contract did not require men to sign away their civil rights; there was thus no problem about their moving freely between the public and private spheres.[7]

Rousseau's theory of the social contract complicated the matter since he argued that families did not exist in nature but, like society, were constituted by contract.[8] This made the marriage contract seem both desperately urgent and precarious.

---

[7] The 1870 Penal Code, subsumed in the 1889 Civil Code, made female adultery punishable with two to six years' imprisonment (Scanlon 1986: 131), while male adultery was a crime only if committed with 'public scandal' or on the matrimonial premises. The punishment for a husband or father killing a wife or daughter who 'stained the family honour' was internal exile; causing bodily injury was not a punishable offence.

[8] Carr (1966: 74, 96) notes that the 1812 liberal Constitution of Cadiz, at the time the most radical in Europe, was based on contract theory largely derived from Rousseau, who was widely translated in Spain (Montesinos 1966: 235 lists Spanish translations of Rousseau's fictional works, including *Émile*, for the period 1814–50). For discussion of Rousseau's views on women and marriage, see Lange in Shanley and Pateman (1991: 95–111); Pateman (1989: *passim*); Canovan in Kennedy and Mendus (1987: 78–105); and Schwartz (1984) (who defends him). See also Tanner's brilliant discussion of *La Nouvelle Héloïse* (1979: 113–78).

In proposing nature as an ideal to be 'improved on' by the social and marriage contracts, rather than a state of barbarism to be repressed, he additionally made it unclear what the boundary between the social and the natural was. Most importantly, in arguing that families were conventional arrangements, he opened the way for recognition that the family had a history and did not have to be the way it was. Indeed, in his hypothetical state of nature, mothers had rights over children and were free from male control. However, as Canovan notes (Kennedy and Mendus 1987: 87–8), Rousseau contradicted himself by arguing that, although the patriarchal family did not exist in nature, it was still 'natural' and therefore necessary, since it was based on 'natural' sexual differences between the female and the male which suited the latter to citizenship and the former to dependence: a blatant contradiction since in Rousseau's hypothetical state of nature women fended for themselves and their offspring unaided. It is this ambivalent view of women as 'naturally' weak and yet 'naturally' not needing men except for reproduction that makes their subjugation through marriage so important to Rousseau. His evident fear of women's power makes him posit adultery as the ultimate evil: 'The unfaithful woman [...] dissolves the family and breaks all the bonds of nature [...] I have difficulty seeing what disorders and what crimes do not flow from this one' (Shanley and Pateman 1991: 105). Schwartz (1984: 96) notes that Émile's Sophie would, in the unfinished sequel to *Émile* titled *Émile et Sophie*, go on to commit adultery despite her education to be a perfect wife. As Laqueur has argued (1990: 94–7), it was not coincidence that the notion of 'natural sexual difference' came into existence in the late eighteenth century at the same time as the liberal declaration of universal rights. For, if all human beings were 'naturally' free, the old argument that women were inferior to men (essentially the same but unequal) no longer held. The notion that they were equal but 'naturally different' was yet another sleight of hand that allowed belief in universal freedom to coexist with women's continued subordination.

The 1804 Napoleonic Code, on which nineteenth-century Spanish civil legislation was largely based, for the first time defined marriage legally as a contract rather than a sacrament (Armstrong 1976: 14). Contract theory in general, and Rousseau in particular, were consistently attacked by the Krausist thinkers who in other respects were the most progressive elements in late nineteenth-century Spanish liberalism. Krausist hostility to contract theory will be discussed further in Chapters 2 and 6; it is worth noting here that a key reason why Rousseau was singled out for criticism was his suggestion that marriage was a contract. By contrast with Rousseau, the Krausists insisted on the concept of 'natural law', according to which the ethical (the basis of justice) was not the product of contract but inherent in nature; this meant that the family, as the embodiment of the ethical, was 'natural' and had always existed. In their view of the family as the embodiment of the ethical, the Krausists were clearly largely indebted to Hegel. Although, as Díaz has shown (1973: 21–6, 31, 48, 61), the initial elaborator of Krausist theory Sánz del Río chose Krause as his model because he was unhappy about the overwhelming supremacy of the State in Hegel's writings, there were in effect considerable overlaps between Krause's and Hegel's thought in other areas. Marriage was one of them.[9] Hegel argued that, although marriage was contractual in origin, its goal was to 'transcend contract' through the subordination of private interests ('particularism') to the common good ('the ethical', constituting the higher realm of 'the universal'). Marriage was seen by Hegel as the ethical foundation of society because, being based on love, it necessarily involved the subordination of particular to group interests; whereas society, being based on the market, attained the higher domain of 'the universal' only if its members sacrificed their egoistic interests in the name of justice. The family was thus a school in ethical citizenship. Hegel's critique of Adam Smith's model of free competition based on self-interest was highly attractive to the Krausists, who were worried about the moral consequences of basing society on market forces but —like Hegel—regarded private property as the foundation of individual freedom.[10] Hegel recognized, however, that 'Love is

---

[9] For Hegel's views on women and marriage, see Landes in Elshtain (1982: 125–44); Stillman in Cornell, Rosenfeld, and Gray (1991: 205–27); Pateman (1989: 173–81); Benhabib in Shanley and Pateman (1991: 129–45); Lloyd (1984: 80–93); Hodge in Kennedy and Mendus (1987: 127–58).

[10] Stillman defines Hegel's view of property as 'the embodiment of the free will in the world' (Cornell, Rosenfeld, and Gray 1991: 207). For the Krausists, property-ownership, being the mark of citizenship, brought social responsibilities. The two key Krausist legal theorists, Giner and Azcárate, both wrote extensively about property rights: see Giner de los Ríos (1875) and Azcárate (1879).

[...] the most tremendous contradiction' (Elshtain 1982: 136) for, in allowing the family's individual members to attain the supreme state of selflessness, it meant the destruction of the individual self. The conflict between self-interest and the good of the family group, dramatized in the realist novel by marital infidelity, figures a wider social problem raised by capitalist market relations. As the Krausists commented, if the family unit could not sacrifice self-interest to the comon good, there was little hope of schooling the nation's youth in responsible citizenship. And women were a special problem here since for Hegel (as for most of his contemporaries, including Rousseau) women were incapable of transcending subjective emotion. Their 'natural' capacity for love disposed them to sacrifice their own interests for another individual, but they were incapable of the kind of impersonal self-sacrifice, in the name of objective principles, required to implement social justice.[11] For this reason it was essential to confine them to the private sphere. Senhabib notes that Hegel's insistence that women cannot get beyond the particular means that they cannot enter history, which in turn means that 'women have no history, and are condemned to repeat the cycles of life' (Shanley and Pateman 1991: 135). For Hegel, the same capacity for love that made women examples of the ethical also made them an obstacle to its realization. This makes female adultery a special threat, both because the loss of a woman's love for her family means the loss of an ethical basis for society, and because women's lack of objective judgement makes them likely to lavish their love on the wrong object. As Hegel put it, woman is 'the everlasting irony in the life of the community' (Lloyd 1984: 82).

This issue of whether or not marriage was contractual was made urgent in Spain by the *sexenio revolucionario*'s introduction of civil marriage in 1870. Although the 1870 Civil Marriage Law allowed 'divorcio' only in the form of legal separation (this remained on the books till the Second Republic's 1932 Divorce Law), the demotion of marriage from religious sacrament to civil contract raised the spectre of its possible dissolution. In his 1869 contribution to the Krausist-organized 'Conferencias dominicales sobre la educación de la mujer', Rafael María de

---

[11] See Pateman's essay 'The Disorder of Women: Women, Love and the Sense of Justice' (1989: 17–32) on this topos in Hegel and Rousseau, notoriously repeated by Freud (1991*a*: 168).

Labra—exceptionally for a Krausist—supported the introduction of civil marriage since it separated 'el contrato del sacramento y hace posible la aplicación al primero de la libertad de contratación', noting correctly that, for marriage to function as a genuine contract, women should first be granted full civil rights, including the vote and *patria potestas* held jointly with the husband (di Febo 1976: 61). Even after the abolition of civil marriage at the start of the Restoration, it remained obligatory to register all Church weddings with the Civil Registry, implying that in the State's eyes it was a contract.[12] It should be remembered that the legal right to divorce was re-established in France in 1884, around the time several of the novels studied in this book were written (Showalter 1991: 7) As we shall see, the general Krausist rejection of contract theory for a belief in man's natural sense of justice and sociability showed their increasing disquiet, despite their defence of free trade, about a society governed by the laws of the market. Conservative liberals were also torn by contradictions: they passionately defended employers' rights to freedom of contract and a market economy based on private property rights (Bahamonde Magro and Toro Mérida 1978: 157), but their Catholic traditionalism clashed with the idea that society was contractual and therefore renegotiable. Thus Cánovas would argue that 'The *patria* is an association of and for the mutual aid of consumers and producers in order to create a life of its own as an individual family is created' (Carr 1980: 28), while maintaining that the nation was indissoluble (Gortázar 1994: 213). Cánovas's two formulations encapsulate the Restoration's contradictory view of the family as indissoluble and yet legally based on contract (the marriage contract ratified by the State through the Civil Registry). Indeed, Martínez Cuadrado (1973: 326) notes that the Restoration's culminating piece of legislation, the 1889 Civil Code, treated marriage as a contract about the ownership of property, to the extent that peasant and working-class families, lacking property, were not explicitly covered by its provisions.

---

[12] The narrator of *María . . . (Memorias de una huérfana)* (2 vols., Madrid: Miguel Guijarro, 1868), by the writer of popular serialized fiction Manuel Fernández y González, notes the Church's opposition to the introduction of a Civil Registry since 'el registro civil lleva encerrado en sí mismo el principio del contrato civil, y esto horroriza á Roma' (i. 269). I am grateful to my former research student Christine Spier for this reference.

Pateman (1989: 20) notes that patriarchy has been an urgent matter of discussion at three historical moments: the seventeenth century, with Locke's dispute with Filmer; the second half of the nineteenth century; and the later twentieth century, when it has been challenged by feminists. The issue was given added urgency in the mid- to late nineteenth century by the 'discovery' that 'primitive' societies were matriarchal. Rosalind Coward (1983) has traced the body of anthropological writing on primitive matriarchy: Bachofen's *Das Mutter-recht* (1861), McLennan's *Primitive Marriage* (1865), Tylor's *Primitive Culture* (1871), Lubbock's *Prehistoric Times* (1874), Post's *The Evolution of Human Marriage* (1875), and Morgan's *Ancient Society* (1877). The last was the source for Engels's discussion of the subject in *The Origins of the Family, Private Property and the State* (1884). As Coward observes (1983: 57), these works provoked a series of counter-publications which insisted that patriarchy was 'natural'. The suggestion that patriarchy was a contractual form of organization superseding an original 'natural' matriarchy had two-edged effects. Its main thrust was to contribute to degeneracy theory by arguing that matriarchy was, precisely, primitive and that patriarchy marked the evolutionary passage to civilization (a view upheld by Freud's later Primal Horde theory). It could thus be argued that women's emancipation was a regression to a lower stage of human evolution: an argument we shall encounter in later chapters. Like Rousseau, these anthropological texts based their arguments on a supposed 'natural' sexual difference that suited women for reproduction and men for intellectual tasks. But they also lent scientific weight to Rousseau's potentially revolutionary suggestion that the patriarchal family was conventional and matriarchy natural. Engels would thus argue that monogamy, by which men claimed women as their private property, 'was the first form of the family to be based not on natural but on economic conditions' (1988: 128)—a view which *Fortunata y Jacinta* and *Los Pazos de Ulloa* largely endorse, though of course neither Galdós nor Pardo Bazán approved Engels's consequent support for 'primitive' common ownership. (Perhaps not coincidentally, shortly after writing these two novels exposing the conventional status of marriage Galdós and Pardo Bazán had an affair.) The concern with the family in the late nineteenth-century novel has to be seen in the context of such debates which, in showing the modern patriarchal family to be the result of an evolutionary process, demonstrated that it was 'unnatural' and subject to change; that is, contractual and open to negotiation. It is logical that the emphasis on the father–daughter relationship in the mid-century *folletín*—and still in Galdós's *Gloria* (1876–7)—should shift in the realist novel to the husband–wife relationship. Concern with the father's abuse of his 'natural' male authority, based on inheritance, figures anxieties appropriate to the old absolutist order. The marriage relationship, based on a male authority that is contractual, figures the modern capitalist era. The Spanish realist novel, with its focus on marriage, coincided with intense public discussion, particularly after the 1871 Paris Commune but continuing through the Restoration, on the need to defend private property. For once property rights and marriage had come to be seen as contractual, neither could be seen as 'natural'.

The notion that marriage was contractual inevitably invited comparisons with the wage contract. As Macpherson notes (1990: 272), the contradictions in the liberal definition of freedom as the right to alienate one's property on the market surfaced when, in the mid-nineteenth century, workers started to claim that, if they could make wage contracts, they were entitled to citizenship like any other seller of property. Pateman (1989: 131) notes that, although legally not entitled to make contracts, many lower-class women did in fact work. Walter Benjamin (1989: 56–7, 171) took as his emblem of modernity the prostitute, for she is the woman who enters the market; in Chapter 2 we shall discuss the simultaneous legal and medical concern with prostitution. Prostitutes did not start to be seen as a threat until the rise of workers' movements (which took place in Spain after the 1869 foundation of the Spanish branch of the First Workers' International) because previously they, like workers, were deemed to have voluntarily alienated their property in their persons. But if it could be argued that workers were entitled to civil rights, then women who put their property in their persons on the market were similarly entitled. Indeed, given that property in the person was the only property most women had and the only property they could dispose of without a male signature, the logic of liberal market theory led to the conclusion that prostitutes were the only free women.[13]

---

[13] Pateman (1989: 189–218) discusses the problems posed by prostitution given contract theory's equation of freedom with access to the market, noting that the chief anxiety is over the fact that prostitution is a contract with a woman.

This helps explain why prostitutes, and not their male clients, were seen as being to blame for prostitution. Prostitutes were, of course, called 'mujeres libres'; they were also called 'mujeres públicas' for they inhabited the public sphere of the street. Late nineteenth-century urban growth necessarily increased the threat of access to the public sphere by women and workers, since the city street is a public domain open to all.

By the mid-century another kind of woman was starting to take to the streets: the female shopper. The fictional interest in the prostitute coincided with an even greater interest in the adulteress, for the two raised similar issues about women's relationship to the public sphere. That the late nineteenth-century European realist novel's fascination with female adultery was linked to the rise of consumerism is made clear by the genre's prototype, *Madame Bovary* (1857). Consumerism was seen as a largely female activity because the private sphere of the home, having ceased to be a unit of production, increasingly became a unit of consumption (Davidoff and Hall 1987; Hall 1992). The separation of home and market instituted by capitalist development became eroded by that same process as, in the mid-nineteenth century, it moved from its early industrial to its later consumerist phase, reinscribing the family in the market (Nicholson 1986: 124). The lateness of industrialization in Spain meant that the second phase took place contemporaneously with, if not before, the first, placing the family in a particularly complex position. Aldaraca has described mid-nineteenth-century Spanish conduct manuals' warnings to wives who fill their leisure, created by their removal from production, by going shopping. But, as she notes, all wives were expected to oversee domestic consumption. It is no doubt because women were associated with consumption that they were regarded as the chief 'consumers' of mass-marketed fiction. The adulteress is like the prostitute in that she is venturing out of the private sphere of the home by freely disposing of her property in her person; but she is more disturbing because, unlike the prostitute who is assumed not to have a family, she tries to live in private and public spheres at once, blurring the boundary between the two. In fact few nineteenth-century fictional wives commit adultery for financial gain; Rosalía de Bringas is a notable exception. Most of them commit adultery out of an avid desire to 'consume' love; their egoism in consuming rather than giving is frequently stressed. The shopper is thus a more appropriate model for the adulteress than the prostitute, particularly since shoppers, unlike prostitutes, move to and fro between street and home. The logic of this ironically makes the prostitute Fortunata a rare example of a selfless adulteress for she offers love rather than consuming it. As an avid consumer of money rather than love, Rosalía de Bringas also has to be both adulteress and prostitute in one person.

The history of shopping in late nineteenth-century Spain will be traced in Chapters 3, 4, and 5. The creation of a national market in the course of the nineteenth century meant the creation of an exchange economy where goods—and people—went into circulation. As Marx put it: 'The circulation of commodities is the starting-point of capital' (Marx 1990: 455). In the period 1850–80 the population of Madrid doubled; by 1898 over half its inhabitants were first-generation immigrants (Bahamonde Magro and Toro Mérida 1978: 97, 104). The 1856 Company Act led to a proliferation of credit companies, most financed by French capital: notably the Spanish branch of the Crédit Mobilier, the Sociedad General de Crédito Mobiliario, whose name made clear the aim of putting wealth into circulation. This aim was, of course, furthered by the concurrent disentailments converting *propiedad inmobiliaria* or *inmueble* into *propiedad mobiliaria* or *mueble*. The 1856 Banking Act additionally authorized the creation of private banks licensed alongside the Bank of Spain, created that year, to issue currency up to three times the value of their metal holdings; this generated a big increase in paper money, speeding up the circulation of wealth. The railway construction boom of the late 1850s and 1860s not only allowed goods and people to circulate, but led to a large-scale mobilization of private and State capital. The 1869 post-revolutionary economic reforms totally freed the banking system from State control (Artola 1973: 88). The 1874 concession to the Bank of Spain of a monopoly over currency issue, although restricting this freedom, revived the market by restoring confidence in paper money after the 1866 financial crash (which saw the liquidation of 5 of Madrid's 10 credit companies, 14 of the 28 provincial credit companies, and 6 of the country's 21 banks) and after the political turmoil of the *sexenio revolucionario*. The same 1874 banking law further increased the amount of money in circulation by authorizing the issue of paper money up to five

Liberal Political Theory 49

times the Bank of Spain's metal holdings (Bahamonde Magro and Martínez 1994: 322, 361, 371–2, 530, 544, 605). As Vicens Vives notes (1969: 743), it was in 1874 that consumer expenditure took off. The years 1876–86 saw a consumer expansion that Vicens Vives (1969: 743) has described as a 'gold fever', borrowing the title of Narcís Oller's 1890–2 novel in Catalan *La febre d'or*.[14] In fact, the term should properly—as in Oller's novel—be restricted to the Barcelona Stock Exchange boom of the early Restoration years (a boom specifically in banking shares) which peaked in 1881, crashing spectacularly that winter with severe repercussions on the financial sector as a whole, which never got back to its 1881 level. The ensuing period—when all but one of the novels discussed in this book were written—was marked by continued financial crisis, details of which will be given in the following chapters. The important point to note is that this financial crisis takes place precisely at the time when capitalist development has become accepted as the norm by all the major political parties. As Varela Ortega notes (1977: 244–5, 265–6, 279), the many critics of the Restoration's political and economic system all took it for granted that modernization was a good thing and, despite increasing protests from agricultural and industrial producers, all political parties remained committed to the principle of free trade till 1888, when Cánovas's Conservatives adopted a timid protectionist platform, implemented by the reintroduction of tariffs in 1891. The sense that capitalist development was desirable but was producing problems created a gap between theory and practice that made discussion of the new economic mobility especially urgent.

The urban rebuilding of the old city centres and the construction of the new *ensanches* which accompanied this capitalist development were also intended to facilitate the circulation of goods and people, as well as the circulation of water and fresh air—the sanitary aspects of this will be discussed in the next chapter. Giddens (1985: 4, 22, 146–7) notes that capitalist development created the nation-State by breaking down the boundary separating city and country; the demolition of the old city walls represented the creation of a unified market in which goods and people circulated freely. One of the first

---

[14] See Resina (1994–5: 259–75) for an excellent analysis of Oller's novel as a response to the Barcelona World Fair of 1888.

acts of the new revolutionary government of 1868 was to order the demolition of Madrid's city walls, first mooted by Castro's 1860 plan for modernizing the city.[15] As we shall see, worries about women going into circulation are in several realist novels associated with the blurring of the city/country divide. Ildefonso Cerdá's *Teoría general de urbanización* (1867), which first coined the term 'urbanization' to name the new science of town planning, attempted to create a taxonomy classifying cities according to their form of circulation (Choay n.d.: 7, 26). Cerdá's grid system, promoted by him since 1856, was adopted as the basis of Barcelona's *ensanche* in the 1860s (Bahamonde Magro and Martínez 1994: 443). One of the most progressive town planners in Europe was Arturo Soria, who from 1882 to 1890 propagated in the press his plan for an infinitely extendable Ciudad Lineal on the outskirts of Madrid. His design proposed a series of parallel ground-level and underground 'arteries' along which trains, trams, water, sewage, gas, electricity, steam heating, telephone and telegraph cables, and an automated mail delivery service would flow rapidly and efficiently, while blending city and country in a harmonious whole (Choay n.d.: 99; Artola 1973: 122).[16] As Soria stated in 1882, his planning theories were based entirely on the principle of 'locomoción'. In the 1870s he had built one of Madrid's first tram lines; he unsuccessfully tried to get permission to build a Madrid 'metro', and spent the whole of his life trying to improve the city's transport system (Collins and Flores 1967: 17, 20, 36, 193). A republican, he was also a supporter of women's emancipation, making a point of employing women in the Compañía Madrileña de Urbanización which he set up in 1894 to build his Ciudad Lineal (never completed). In an 1882 article for *El Progreso*, he proclaimed his enthusiasm for women's entry into the public sphere with the unfortunate slogan: '¡Viva la revolución femenina! ¡Arriba las faldas!' (Collins and Flores 1967: 105).

---

[15] See Hauser (1979: 83); also Fernández García (1993: 422, 428) who notes that, contrary to Castro's 1860 proposals, certain military and fiscal city boundaries were retained. Burgos demolished its walls as early as 1831, Almería in 1854, San Sebastián in 1864, Valencia in 1865, and Madrid and Barcelona both in 1868 (Bahamonde Magro and Martínez 1994: 443).

[16] Choay (n.d.: 101, 107) notes that Le Corbusier effectively 'stole' Soria's notion of the 'linear city', and that Soria saw Ebenezer Howard's 'Garden City' (started at Letchworth in 1903) as an extension of his own ideas, though Howard rejected Soria's rational stress on standardization.

In supporting the circulation of women as well as that of goods and men, Soria was more consistent than the majority of his contemporaries who tried to exclude women from the new capitalist mobility. But all of them realized that the threat of women emerging from their confinement to the private sphere was linked to an exchange economy which put everything into circulation. Bahamonde Magro and Martínez (1994: 456) note that the 'discurso de la movilidad' which became a late nineteenth-century Spanish topos exaggerated the actual extent of social mobility in order to mask the continued existence of inequality. The urban novels studied here use female adultery as a similar rhetorical strategy which exaggerates the threat posed by women's mobility in an age when the only professions open to women (apart from the convent, which represented confinement rather than mobility) were that of prostitute, servant, wet-nurse, factory worker, or shop assistant (the last two, largely male preserves), or, if they were lucky enough to attend one of the new women's training colleges set up by the Krausists in the 1870s–1890s, teacher or telegraphist (Scanlon 1986: 34–41). Even in such cases, it was assumed that women would stop working on marriage (many working-class women, of course, did not). I suggest that this exaggerated fear of women's mobility should be read, not as a sign of moral panic at the prospect of women dishonouring their promise to obey, but rather as a way of working out wider anxieties about a society dominated by the market. This chapter has tried to show what issues are at stake when women leave the private for the public sphere. The next chapter will set out the theoretical model for a converse figuration in which the social regulators invade the privacy of the home. The novels we shall study are concerned with both of these contrary violations of the public/private divide.

2
The Construction of 'the Social': Reform and Regulation

As we have seen, the statement that the novel is about society —the definition par excellence of the realist novel—could not have been made before the nineteenth-century process of nation formation, which created the concept of 'society' (meaning a particular 'national society') as a homogeneous whole. But the term took on a more specific meaning and a particular urgency in the last three decades of the century, as it became increasingly clear that, despite growing standardization, the effects of modernization were not in practice creating a homogeneous society but intensifying class conflict. The Paris Commune of 1871, which precipitated a parliamentary debate in Spain banning the First Workers' International by near unanimity, was crucial in forcing even the most enthusiastic advocates of *laissez-faire* to recognize that society was not a self-regulating and self-repairing organism, and that a measure of intervention was needed. In Spain's case, this meant that the triumph of *laissez-faire* liberalism with the 1868 Revolution was almost immediately overtaken by awareness of the need for some form of social control; the debate from 1871 onwards, intensifying as the social disturbances under the Federal Republic threatened national disintegration, was no longer about whether intervention was needed, but about what kind and (above all) who should implement it. The birth of the 'social question' gives rise to the new concept of 'the social'. Carr (1966: 247) finds the term 'cuestión social' used already in 1855; the creation of the Academia de Ciencias Morales y Políticas in 1857 stimulated discussion of the issue (Álvarez Junco in Seminario de historia 1988: 139). 'The social' was different from 'society', since the latter had either the general meaning of the whole nation or the more restricted meaning of 'civil society' (a politically useful, but problematic, terminological slippage); whereas 'the social', meaning an area of concern rather than a specific social entity, referred to those sectors of the population in need of intervention. 'The social' thus referred to those sectors which were not integrated into civil society but which were nevertheless within society in its wider sense. The problems of definition here are precisely what made 'the social' a matter of contemporary concern. In practice, 'the social' referred to the working classes. However women, also excluded from civil society but within society in its wider sense, occupied the same ambiguous status. Hence the 'woman question' and the 'social question' are inseparable, to the point that they end up blurring in the case of the bourgeois as well as the working-class woman. The problem was: how could these excluded-but-included elements of the population be integrated ideologically without granting them full citizenship?

The peasantry were not on the whole included in 'the social' since they were outside the network of social relations of the modern city which constituted 'society' par excellence: a third meaning of the term, creating further confusion as to what exactly 'society'—and the criterion for membership of it—was. Peasant revolt in the south under the Federal Republic and in the early 1880s (the latter reported on at first hand by Alas[1]) was met with straightforward military repression; it was only when the rural poor invaded the cities in search of work or other pickings, as they did in large numbers, that they became the object of social reform. Indeed, from the 1860s onwards, unemployed migrants were systematically rounded up as 'vagrants' and expelled from the city, in an attempt to relegate them to the status of 'outsiders' who could simply be repressed (by the Civil Guard whose function this was) rather than needing to be reformed (Bahamonde Magro and Toro Mérida 1978: 47–50, 57). In effect, social reform—by which was meant the integration of the 'alien' elements of the population into a homogeneous social 'body'—was always envisaged, not as the reform of political and economic structures, but as a moral campaign

---

[1] In 1882–3, at the time of the so-called Mano Negro peasant unrest in the south, particularly in the Jerez region, Alas spent over a month touring the area to document his twenty-one articles written for *El Día* under the title 'El hambre en Andalucía': see Lissorgues (1980–1: i. p. xlii), who reprints article 15 (157–60).

to 're-form' the urban masses via the inculcation of standardizing bourgeois 'norms'. In other words, the urban masses were to be 'helped' to 'choose freely' to reform themselves, thus maintaining the liberal fiction of the social contract whereby citizens volunteered for subjection: 'subjects' in the double sense of being free agents and objects of control.

The Krausists, who were responsible for keeping the issue of social reform on the political agenda throughout the Restoration, rejected liberal contract theory, as we have seen. But they did so to reinforce the liberal belief in 'universal' freedom by diminishing the role of the State: if 'men' were by nature social animals and if an ethical sense therefore existed in nature (the basis of the Krausist theory of 'natural law'), then it was not necessary for them to underwrite a social contract agreeing to be 'subject' to the State. Indeed, such a contract, handing power wholesale to the State, would be an irresponsible avoidance of individual civic responsibility. Hence the Krausists' passionate belief in education as a means of instilling civic virtues into the populace; their defence of 'natural law' made it essential for them to regard social reform as the conversion of the 'masses' into responsible individuals. There is however a contradiction here, for if 'man' has a 'natural' ethical sense (the Krausists' views on women will be discussed later), why should some sectors of the population need to have this instilled into them? The Krausists' answer to this was consistent with their attitude to the role of the State: namely, that intervention—whether by private or State initiatives—be limited to removing the obstacles to the realization of individual freedom. How this could be done without a measure of coercion was not clear. Indeed, the whole concept of creating individuals (seen as helping all members of the nation to realize their innate potential) involved a huge amount of social engineering. As Foucault has shown (1971, 1973, 1987, 1991), the creation of the modern individual central to the liberal political project was the other side of the invention of the 'delinquent' (Rabinow 1984: 219): a term whose newness is indicated by the dwarf Ujo's misrendering of it (as 'relincuente') in Galdós's *Nazarín* (Pérez Galdós 1895: 234). Thus, to cite Foucault, the new concept of reform 'compares, differentiates, hierarchizes, homogenizes, excludes. In short, it normalizes' (Rabinow 1984: 194). Foucault's insights into the contradictory nineteenth-century project of 'normalizing' 'deviant' behaviour (which labels such behaviour as deviant in the first place), through the construction of individualized subjects who 'freely' consent to their subjection, are crucial to an understanding of the Krausist reform programme, which sincerely proclaimed that its moralizing discourses were aimed at furthering individual freedom.[2] The Krausists were active in the anti-slavery lobby which succeeded in getting the issue debated in parliament in 1872, securing the abolition of slavery in Puerto Rico, though the war of independence in Cuba postponed abolition there till 1888 (Bahamonde Magro and Toro Mérida 1978: 82–3). The abolitionist debate—less overtly tied to women's emancipation in Spain than in the United States and Britain, but nevertheless raising similar issues—was a debate not so much on social equality as on the right of individuals freely to alienate their freedom by selling their labour on the market, rather than being born into slavery. As we shall see, the Krausists' rejection of contract theory meant that, where women were concerned, they opted for an attenuated version of the 'natural servitude' line.

As Foucault notes, modern liberalism, from the second half of the eighteenth century, was characterized by a new kind of power that did not emanate solely from the State:

the juridical system [. . .] is utterly incongruous with the new methods of power whose operation is not ensured by right but by technique, not by law but by normalization, not by punishment but by control, methods that are employed on all levels and in forms that go beyond the state and its apparatus. We have been engaged for centuries in a type of society in which the juridical is increasingly incapable of coding power, of serving as its system of representation. (1987: 89)

Giddens notes (1985: 172) that 'The nation-state [. . .] is the sociologist's "society"', since the 'social question' created the new concept of 'the social' as a problem area requiring intervention by a variety of private social agencies. But at the same time, as Giddens stresses, the nation-State set up its own normalizing agencies (prisons, asylums, workhouses, schools,

---

[2] See in particular Varela and Álvarez-Uría (1979, 1991), and Álvarez-Uría (1983 and in Seminario de historia 1988: 117–46), which apply Foucault's perceptions to 19th-century Spain with immensely productive results. Their insights are applied perceptively to Galdós's fiction by Fuentes Peris (1996, 1996–7, 1997a, 1997b).

the collection of fiscal and other statistics) which replaced pre-modern forms of local community sanction intended to punish rather than reform (1985: 100). Giddens insists that the modern nation-State is defined by a process of 'internal pacification' made possible by the extension of the central State administrative apparatus, for the first time turning the nation into a 'bounded and unitary whole': 'Unlike traditional states, the nation-state is a power-container whose administrative purview corresponds exactly to its territorial delimitation' (1985: 173). Giddens notes that this administrative exercise of power through techniques of control and surveillance allowed nineteenth-century capitalism to present itself as 'essentially pacific' since it made possible 'the withdrawal of the military from direct participation in the internal affairs of state' (1985: 192). Cánovas's main political objective as architect of the Restoration was to create a parliamentary democracy run by professional politicians, confining the military to their barracks. As Carr comments (1966: 356), he was hugely successful in this respect. His success depended on the acceptance by all legalized parties of the concept, central to Restoration politics, of the 'Estado tutelar': a concept which makes clear the objective of implementing social control through 'supervisory techniques' rather than the use of force (though recourse to the Civil Guard, as a paramilitary body separate from the army, allowed the central State to resort to violence while maintaining the fiction of civilian rule). As Álvarez-Uría puts it: the 'Estado tutelar' represented 'una política de individualización de masas que institucionaliza la "autonomía sometida"' (Seminario de historia 1988: 145). The 'Estado tutelar' is not the same thing as the 'welfare state', because technically it limits the State's role to that of 'overseeing' social control measures, without specifying whether these should be implemented by the State or by civil society. In practice, there was major disagreement between Cánovas's Conservatives and Sagasta's Liberals over whether the State's tutelary role involved direct responsibility for social control or was limited to the supervision of private initiatives. Despite his outright hostility to socialism, Cánovas advocated what he called a 'socialismo de Estado'—an ideal Galdós attributes to his State functionaries Onésimo Redondo in *La familia de León Roch* and Manuel Pez in *La de Bringas*, as we shall see—meaning that the State should take responsibility for social matters in order

The Construction of 'the Social' 57

to palliate social conflict (Seco Serrano in Gortázar 1994: 197). The difference between Cánovas's 'doctrinaire' brand of liberalism, putting social control in the hands of the State, and socialism proper was, of course, that the former was defined as the maintenance of individual freedom via the defence of private property. In effect, the few State welfare measures passed in Spain before 1900 were introduced by Cánovas's Conservatives (Seco Serrano in Gortázar 1994: 197–8).

The majority of Krausists supported Sagasta's Liberal Party because of its defence of individual and local freedoms, and its criticism of the extent of State control imposed by the Conservatives; indeed, many Krausists were founder members of the Liberal Party in 1880 (Varela Ortega 1977: 106). Other Krausists, like Alas, supported the Republicans because they felt the Liberals' critique of central State power did not go far enough. The Republicans' main quarrel with the Liberals was over Sagasta's 1883 concession to Cánovas in dropping the principle of national sovereignty and agreeing to the 1876 Constitution's placing of sovereignty in the Crown and parliament, for the principle of national sovereignty gave legal primacy to civil society. (In practice, Cánovas gave the State clear primacy over the Crown, keeping the young Alfonso XII under his 'tutelage' by placing his mistresses and confessors under strict surveillance (Varela Ortega 1977: 99; Carr 1966: 349).) Alas's political writings, like those of other Krausist political thinkers, insist on the difference between the State and society.[3] He needed to keep repeating this, both to combat Cánovas's 'socialismo de Estado', and because of the dispersal of power which, with the growth of new private social control agencies alongside those of the State, made it unclear who was in control of what. As Giddens notes (1985: 4), 'Nation-states are inherently polyarchic.' The fact that control was not only dispersed but

---

[3] Gil Cremades (1975: 41) notes that in his early works Giner talks only about the State, but from the mid-1870s makes a clear distinction between the State and society. His 1875 essay 'Estado presente de la ciencia política' contains a section 'Relación del Estado con la sociedad humana' whose aim is to establish 'una distinción esencial entre ellas' (1875: 250). Galdós's library contained a copy of Miguel Moya's *Conflictos entre los poderes del Estado* (1879), with a prologue by the leading Krausist political philosopher and reformer, Gumersindo de Azcárate. An attack on Conservative 'doctrinarismo', the book's central argument is the need to distinguish between the State and society, the role of the former being limited to that of 'arbiter' between the multiple 'powers' constituting the latter.

disguised as the 'removal of obstacles to the exercise of freedom' obfuscated matters further. Many Krausist political philosophers, including Alas, were professors of law, both because of the ethical importance they attached to the concept of 'natural law', and because they wanted to be precise about what the State as a legislative body should and should not do. The shocking conditions in Spain's State penitentiaries and 'charitable' institutions (asylums, hospitals, workhouses), repeatedly attacked by social reformers, provided additional grounds for arguing that the reform process should be controlled by 'society' rather than the State.[4]

The Krausists' main contribution to national life was their insistence on the importance of 'society' (meaning 'civil society') as a mediator between the competing claims of the State and the individual. The Krausists introduced the complementary disciplines of sociology and psychology into Spain, for the construction of an active public sphere required the construction of individualized citizens. In keeping with the Krausist belief in man's 'natural' sociability and sense of justice, Giner de los Ríos defined individual freedom, not as the right to do what one liked, but as the independent exercise of moral judgement (Díaz 1973: 136). This differed significantly from the Catholic notion of free will in its stress on critical thinking and respect for the opinions of other free individuals. The Krausist defence of a society of free individuals, each working in their separate autonomous sphere for the good of the whole through a process of collaboration and mutual respect for the autonomy of the others, was above all a defence of democratic pluralism. The Krausist idea of 'armonía' needs to be viewed in this context. Scholars have done Krausism a disservice by presenting it as an attempt to 'marry' idealism and materialism via a kind of mystical 'panentheism' (López Morillas 1956, 1977). Díaz (1973), sadly long out of print, is right to stress that Krausism was above all a school of political philosophy, concerned with creating an active civil society based not on competition but on cooperation. There is nothing mystical about this political

---

[4] For conditions in State institutions of social regulation, see Huertas and Campos (1992), Hauser (1979), and Pla et al. (1987). Moretti (1987: 53) notes that the 19th-century *Bildungsroman* is based on the supposition that private forms of control (that is, self-regulation) are preferable to State control.

conception of 'armonía', though Krausist political philosophy can be accused of naivety—or wilful blindness—in failing to recognize the reality of class conflict.[5]

Despite the Krausists' rejection of the social Darwinist competitive model of a 'free' society, measured by norms of health rather than justice, their 'harmonic' view of society (here meaning 'the nation') was, like that of Spencer, based on a biological analogy with the body, whose various organs contribute through their separate specialized functions to the functioning of the whole. The Krausists' defence of individual and local freedoms in some ways echoed Spencer's complaints, from the 1850s on, about liberalism's move towards a new tyranny of the State. Indeed, as Carr notes (1966: 301–2), Krausism signified an attempt to move away from the highly centralized French political model, on which nineteenth-century Spanish centralizing legislation, including the 1889 Civil Code, was largely based, towards a British model based on the primacy of civil society and the Protestant ethos of self-improvement. However, Spencer's later works recognized that society did not 'naturally' tend towards equilibrium, as he had hoped. Spencer, first known in Spain from around 1870, was widely translated into Spanish from 1879 on and much cited by Krausist political thinkers (Villacorta Baños 1980: 82; Gil Cremades in Costa 1984: 34), for his worries about increasing social disequilibrium echoed contemporary Spanish concerns about the need for social 'armonía'. Spencer felt that it was preferable to pay the price of human suffering rather than intervene in the 'natural' workings of the social organism. The Krausists' belief in 'natural law' —meaning not (as in Spencer's case) that society was determined

---

[5] An excellent political definition of Krausist 'racionalismo armónico' is given in Canalejas's essay 'La escuela krausista en España', in *Estudios críticos de filosofía, política y literatura* (1872), reproduced in Villacorta Baños (1980: 261–4). To cite the key passage: 'La organización social no es el comunismo, que suprime la libertad individual, ni es el individualismo que desconoce toda dirección superior; admite y concierta ambos elementos extremos; consiste en la distribución de todas las formas sociales en esferas distintas, independientes unas de otras, y cada una con propia actividad, con una misión especial que cumplir, aunque ligadas entre sí y concurrentes a un mismo fin general, como funciones de un mismo organismo. Así como el hombre está organizado en el espíritu, y en el cuerpo, y en la relación de ambos; y así como las funciones de la vida humana se reparten entre órganos distintos, sin que ninguno quede aislado ni separado de los otros, así también, la sociedad es orgánica cuando el trabajo de todos está repartido entre asociaciones diversas, cada una propia en sí y todos en concertada relación' (263).

by biological laws, but that men 'naturally' possessed a sense of social responsibility (Díaz 1973: 78–121)—allowed them to reconcile their demand for a more just society with a belief in 'natural organicism'.

The autonomous organs comprising the Krausist social 'body' were hierarchically arranged according to a double principle of complementarity and subsidiarity, in the following ascending order: individual, family, society (comprising the market, the liberal professions, and the Church), and State (itself a hierarchical structure of municipality, province, central government). The individual and the State were clearly private and public entities respectively, except that the principle of complementarity required each to defend the interests of the other. But the family and society posed problems of definition. According to Sanz del Río's *Ideal de la humanidad* (1860), society was a public sphere made up of private individuals, who came together in the form of different social groupings or 'families' to defend both the collective and the individual good; while conversely the family was a 'private society' (or 'personal society') whose function was to procure the welfare both of its individual members and of the collective, by providing a training in responsible citizenship. The same terminology is used by Giner de los Ríos and Azcárate (the latter a major political philosopher), writing in the 1870s and 1880s. Effectively, this social model meant that the mother was responsible for teaching future citizens to put group interests before their own, with the family seen as a blueprint for the social organism as a whole: the mother's private role is thus not so private after all. Indeed, the very notion, central to the Krausist concept of 'natural law', that men (and women) are 'by nature' social animals breaks down the private/public division. In his essay 'Concepto de la persona social' (1969: 202–8), Giner stated that the intrinsic human urge to enter into social relations is what turns a 'ser' into a 'persona' in the legal sense of the word: that is, someone with legal responsibilities (204). This definition of personhood was consonant with the Krausists' encouragement of women's entry into the public sphere as moral 'improvers'. Krausist organicism provided a handy way of still denying women civil rights, since it made it possible to argue that the family was an organic 'body' or single legal 'person' (hence the term 'personal society'), with wife and children legally subsumed under the 'headship' of the husband. The wife's role as 'heart' rather than 'head' of the household made her subsidiary and complementary, but in fact the most vital 'organ'.

The purpose of Krausist organicism, as Sanz del Río makes clear, was to delimit the sphere of action of each of the nation's constituent parts. But in practice, the principle of complementarity, while a defence of democratic pluralism designed to counterbalance the hierarchical principle of subsidiarity, meant that everything was everybody's business, opening the door to intrusions on an unlimited scale (a problem explored, as we shall see, in Galdós's *La familia de León Roch*). The Krausist organic scheme was intended as a model of representative government (also referred to by the English term 'self-government'), a subject on which all Krausist political philosophers wrote extensively, citing British sources (while rejecting Locke's contract theory).[6] What was meant by representative government was that each individual, instead of acting in his (or her; the Krausists included women here) own interests, 'represented' the particular sphere or spheres in which he or she operated. The problem, given the principle of complementarity, was to define which spheres were the responsibility of whom. The Krausists could state that women's responsibilities were confined to the family and at the same time provide education to enable women to undertake certain kinds of 'social' work, because social bodies were 'families' and families were 'societies' (albeit 'personal' ones). The Krausist model of the national 'body', in its attempt to delimit political, social, and individual responsibilities, did provide a basis for safeguarding individual and local autonomy against the intrusions of the State. But it made the boundary between 'family' and 'society' hard to pin down.[7] Indeed, as Sanz del Río kept insisting (1860), the whole nation was—or should be—'one big family'. Thus the Krausist reformers would promote private reform initiatives based on a 'política familiarista': that is—as Álvarez-Uría observes (Seminario de historia 1988: 124–5, 133)—a series of surveillance techniques, including 'los socorros a domicilio', designed to reinforce (or create) 'lazos de familia'.

[6] See Giner (1875), Azcárate (1877a, 1883, 1885); also Segismundo Moret, *La representación nacional, teoría del sufragio* (Madrid, 1884) cited by Elorza (1973: 186–7).
[7] Díaz (1973: 60) notes that the Krausists were totally opposed to State intervention but nevertheless supported intervention by 'los grupos sociales intermedios'.

The Krausists got their chance to put their political philosophy into practice in Sagasta's Liberal government of 1881–3, as they would again, on a larger scale, under the Second Republic of 1931–6. Ironically given the Krausist hostility to State intervention, the Comisión de Reformas Sociales—set up by parliamentary decree in 1883 on the initiative of the Krausist Ministro de Gobernación, Segismundo Moret, from 1879 to 1913 president of the Institución Libre de Enseñanza—marked the beginnings of the welfare State in Spain. On completion of its task in 1889, it evolved into a consultative body drafting labour legislation, in 1903 becoming the Instituto de Reformas Sociales, which in 1920 became the Ministerio de Trabajo (de la Calle 1989: 10–11). The bill proposing this parliamentary Commission of Inquiry, penned by Azcárate who in 1881 had published a book-length summary of the 1877–8 Ateneo debate on the 'social problem', envisaged it as a government-sponsored initiative undertaken by private members of civil society.[8] The Commission's seventeen members included seven Krausist university professors, the largest professional group represented being lawyers, followed by doctors, with two economists plus the editor of the pro-Liberal newspaper *El Imparcial* (de la Calle 1989: 45): civil society is represented exclusively by the liberal professions, with industrialists surprisingly excluded (workers were by definition excluded since they were not members of civil society). Its president was Cánovas, representing the State (Álvarez Junco in Seminario de historia 1988: 151). The Commission's mixed State–private status proved a major problem: on the Liberals' fall from power in December 1883, funding ceased and the Commission's findings were published piecemeal through till 1889, with many gaps remaining; conversely, workers were suspicious of a State initiative which they rightly saw as an attempt to pre-empt organized protest. In Oviedo, where the Krausist Professor of Political Economics, Adolfo Buylla, held two sessions with workers, the latter afterwards issued a statement retracting all they had said (de la Calle 1989: 15, 82). By contrast, bourgeois institutions such as the Ateneo and the Krausist Institución Libre de Enseñanza collaborated fully, for the 'social question' was a bourgeois problem. The most heated replies related to the issue of State

---

[8] For discussion of Azcárate, see Elorza (Lida and Zavala 1970: 239–53).

intervention (de la Calle 1989: 208). As Pérez Ledesma notes (Seminario de historia 1988: 156), the Commission's chief importance was that it made 'the social' a matter of nationwide public discussion.

Moret (half-Scottish and familiar with the work of Spencer, Darwin, and J. S. Mill) had earlier defended *laissez-faire* liberalism on the grounds that society was 'naturally' cooperative and self-regulating. His 1861 doctoral thesis 'El capital y el trabajo, ¿son armónicos o antagónicos?' had defended Bastiat's *laissez-faire* treatise *Harmonies économiques* (translated into Spanish in the 1840s and made a textbook at Madrid's Universidad Central in 1858) against Proudhon's 1844 *Contradictions économiques* which argued that capital and labour were antagonistic (Elorza 1973: 134, 155–201). In 1872, the Real Academia de Ciencias Morales y Políticas held a competition for the best essay on the same topic (Elorza 1973: 133–4); in the wake of the Paris Commune of the previous year, it was no longer so clear that capital and labour were 'armónicos'. By 1883 Moret, like most other Spaniards regardless of whether they supported State or private social control, had changed his mind about the possibility of the harmonious coexistence of capital and labour. But the Commission's full title—*Comisión para el estudio de las cuestiones que interesan a la mejora o bienestar de las clases obreras como industriales y que afectan a las relaciones entre el capital y el trabajo*—shows that the question remained the same. It is, of course, a question that Galdós's *Fortunata y Jacinta* sets out to answer, with inconclusive results. In practice, the Commission was a massive surveillance exercise, setting out to document every aspect of working-class life across the nation, including health, morals, education, and culture, at work and in family life.[9] One of the Krausist professors on the Commission was González Serrano, responsible for developing the discipline of psychology in Spain, for this sociological survey was also an attempt to turn the masses into 'individuals' by intensively describing their most intimate behaviour; that is, by constructing their privacy in the act of massively invading it. The questionnaire, drafted by Azcárate,

---

[9] Corrigan and Sayer (1991: 124) note that commissions of inquiry proliferated in Britain after 1800 as part of the new reform movement, with over 100 royal commissions set up between 1832 and 1846 alone. Corrigan and Sayer insist (169) that the interventionism of the modern State, usually seen as dating from the 1870s and 1880s in the British case too, can be traced back much earlier.

which was to be put to workers and social bodies throughout the land, consisted in 223 questions classified in 32 sections, in each case requesting statistics as well as opinions. Female and child labour was a particular concern, as were delinquency, prostitution, and women's influence on domestic life. In addition to gathering information about 'social' problems (meaning problems pertaining to the working classes, whether public or private), the questionnaire also asked for data about the effectiveness of existing solutions: specifically, charitable bodies and institutions (private and State) and education.

The reply of the Institución Libre de Enseñanza argued that women's education was more urgent than that for men, because of 'la influencia que [la mujer] ejerce en la familia y en las costumbres nacionales' (de la Calle 1979: 215), though they also argued that women needed to be able to earn a living to avoid the moral risks of destitution. One exceptional response from Alejandro San Martín, Professor of Therapeutics, replying on behalf of the Fomento de las Artes, argued for women's right to work on the grounds that they were as physiologically suited to it as men. Ramiro Pérez Liquiñano, replying for the same organization, claimed that work would rob women of their 'misterioso encanto' and 'velo de virtud y recato', jeopardizing the 'cariñoso éxtasis' of their husbands and making them spend more money on clothes and food for lack of time to shop around: even this respondent takes it for granted that women spend their time out of the home shopping (de la Calle 1979: 215, 219–21). Question 56 of section 9 ('Condición de la familia obrera') requests information on the following: 'Edad a que suelen contraer matrimonio los obreros; suavidad o dureza de las relaciones entres los cónyuges; frecuencia en la separación de hecho y de adulterio' (de la Calle 1979: 337). This prying into workers' private lives—seen as the key to public morals—was satirized in *La Voz Pública: Revista de Ayuntamientos* (17 August 1884), which suggested that the Commission add to its list of questions the following:

II. Familias.
1. Si son legítimas o adulteradas.
2. Si la adulteración hace degenerar la raza.
3. Si el marido da palos a la mujer o viceversa. (de la Calle 1979: 57)

The Construction of 'the Social'

In fact, these questions were effectively already included in the above-quoted section 9. As we shall see, the same three questions (the last figuratively) were central to the realist novel of the 1880s which, while critically exploring the contradictions inherent in the new forms of social control, was a parallel attempt—albeit fictional—at the surveillance of private life and its interface with the public sphere. The very fact that contemporary novelists and critics insisted that the novel documented, rather than invented, reality demonstrates that it was conceived as a surveillance exercise. As Foucault notes (Rabinow 1984: 202), the new obsession with documenting and classifying every troubling aspect of society (as in the Comisión de Reformas Sociales' 223 questions organized into 32 sections) was above all an attempt to make society 'describable'; that is, to control it by turning it into an ordered narrative. It is also worth noting that what was described was not the 'normal' but that which was construed as 'abnormal': the incidence of adultery, prostitution, or crime in the realist novel is an index not of its occurrence but of the anxiety it caused. As in the realist novel, the compilation of information about private life was central to the Comisión de Reformas Sociales' information-gathering exercise, for the construction of self-regulating individuals through the family unit was seen as the way to 'solve' (in practice, pre-empt) social conflict. As Le Play noted in his 1877 study *Ouvriers européens*, concerned with the same issues: 'Private life stamps public life with its character. The family is the foundation of the state' (Perrot 1990: 106–7). Like Le Play, the Krausists were attracted to this model of moralization via the family because it offered an alternative to State intervention.

De la Calle (1979: 186–90) notes that the medical members of the Commission argued that, because of their professional experience, they knew better than anyone else what the problems of the working classes were; but that in fact they mostly blamed bad living conditions on moral weaknesses such as sloth, gambling, drink, and a lack of thrift. The role of the newly professionalized discipline of medicine was central to attempts to regulate those elements of the population regarded as a problem—the working classes and women—in late nineteenth-century Spain. In fact, this process dates back to the mid-century: Carr (1966: 50) notes that doctors gained prestige in

Spain only after 1850, a development evidenced in *La Regenta* by Ana Ozores's change of doctors from the blundering old Somoza to the highly professional young Benítez. Unlike the Krausist reformers, the new medical experts had a largely positivist formation. 'Hygiene'—as the old 'art' of medicine was renamed—was above all an experimental science, concerned with material symptoms, causes, and effects, the detection of which allowed medical experts to play an interventionist role in preventing and controlling 'sickness'. The new discipline of 'hygiene' was also referred to as 'medicina social', which effectively constructs society as sick. Indeed, the new concept of preventive medicine implied that society needs 'treating' even before it has become sick. Social problems, traditionally referred to by the Church as 'social vices', from the mid-century started to be reclassified as 'enfermedades sociales', taking some of the blame off the poor (though in practice doctors continued to use the moralizing discourse of religion), but principally serving to legitimize medical experts' intervention. As Santero puts it in the concluding paragraph to his 1885 treatise on private and public medicine: 'El potente desarrollo de la industria y la llamada cuestión social llevará al higienista al consejo de los gobernantes' (1885: ii. 832). The notorious use of medical analogies by turn-of-the-century *regeneracionista* intellectuals has a prehistory of several decades.

Late nineteenth-century medicine was an 'experimental science'—as Claude Bernard's famous 1865 *Introduction à l'étude de la médecine expérimentale* stressed—not only because it was based on controlled laboratory experiments, but in the more important sense that it turned the whole of 'society' into a giant controlled laboratory experiment, in which the 'ill' (even before they became ill) would be subjected to clinical observation and regulation so as to restore the social 'body' to health. This concentration on society's problem areas constructed a proliferation of categories of the 'abnormal' or 'deviant' which spilled over from the working classes into other sectors of the population, with the result that 'society' (in its widest sense of 'the nation') and 'the social' (in the sense of that which is in need of reform) started to blur. The Krausist conception of the nation as 'body' was a humanist one stressing the exercise of individual moral responsibility; the medical notion of the 'cuerpo social' saw the body as a material organism that needed the medical expert's intervention. The use of the 'body' metaphor by Krausists and doctors alike produced a combined discourse of social control fraught with contradiction and confusion. This was compounded by the fact that even the medical experts needed to pay lip-service to the notion of free will to argue that their regulation of bodies had as its goal the production of healthy citizens, which in liberal terminology meant autonomous individuals able to exercise their freedom. This, in turn, provided an alibi justifying medical experts' intervention in mental as well as physical health. If the Krausists were responsible for developing the study of psychology in Spain, the hygienists were responsible for founding the discipline of psychiatry. They were also responsible for inventing the separate medical specialism of gynaecology which constituted women as a special medical 'problem', consolidating the notion of sexual difference and additionally putting women's bodies under the new male experts' control; indeed, the invention of gynaecology as a separate discipline is attributed to a Spaniard, Baltasar de Viguera, in his 1828 book on 'female pathology'. The Sociedad Ginecológica was founded in 1874; we shall be hearing more about its secretary Ángel Pulido. The notion that women were a special medical 'problem' is shown by the fact that the 1857 Moyano Law instituting compulsory universal free State primary education prescribed hygiene as an obligatory subject for girls only (Jagoe, Blanco, and Enríquez de Salamanca 1998: 116).

The new medical experts' conversion of society into a giant controlled laboratory experiment is what permitted Zola to make Claude Bernard's book the basis of literary naturalism. The latter cannot be understood without reference to the new concept of 'social medicine'; hence Zola's insistence on the novelist as social reformer.[10] Catholic objections to Zola's reduction of human behaviour to material bodily functions have misled critics ever since into regarding the controversy over naturalism—which flared up in Spain 1882–4—as a debate between supporters of idealism and supporters of materialism. The real battle between naturalism and the Church was over the new medical experts' threat to the latter's previous monopoly

---

[10] Valis (1992a: 209) notes that naturalist discourse is present in *La Regenta* through its medical projection of social fears onto the female body.

control over the population. The two sectors of the population over which the Church had traditionally held influence were the same sectors targeted by medical experts: namely, women and the working classes. The Church controlled the former through the confessional, the latter through its extensive involvement in charity. As we shall see in later chapters, the Church extended both of these activities during the nineteenth century, particularly in the second half, in direct response to competition from the new hygienists.[11] Indeed, one of the major social features of the Restoration was the religious revival produced by the influx of French orders—dissolved and expelled in the wake of Jules Ferry's anticlerical legislation of 1879, banning them from teaching—which quickly restored the Spanish Church to the prominence it had lost with the mid-century disentailments (the point of which had been to transfer the Church's monopoly of social control to the State). Numbers of the religious in Spain rose dramatically under the Restoration: the 1,500 monks remaining in 1867 had by 1910 swollen to 22,000, with 34 new male orders created after 1875; members of the female orders rose from 11,600 in 1854 to over 42,000 by 1900 (Shubert 1990: 150). The creation of a new religious order by the protagonist of Galdós's 1890-1 novel *Ángel Guerra*—unorthodox among other things in its refusal of sexual segregation—has to be set in this context. The majority of these religious orders were involved in forms of social control through education and charity, particularly hospitals, asylums, and reformatories. Indeed, the majority of private reform initiatives took the form of aristocratic endowments to religious orders to found a charitable institution. A classic case, though dating from the mid-century, is the 1845 foundation by the Vizcondesa de Jorbalán, Micaela Desmaisières, of the Comunidad de Adoratrices Esclavas del Santísimo Sacramento, originally the Colegio de María Santísima de las Desamparadas (the model for Las Micaelas in *Fortunata y Jacinta*, discussed in Chapter 5), which devoted itself to the regeneration of fallen women; the reformatory's title makes it clear that its nuns had 'freely' opted for female servitude (Rivière Gómez 1994). Further convent

---

[11] Carr (1966, 45, 54-5) observes that late 18th-century moves to set up State institutions for the relief of poverty were aimed explicitly at curbing the power of the Church; and that throughout the 19th century the Spanish State retained this hostility to religious charity, but without introducing State initiatives to replace it.

reformatories were founded in Madrid in 1864 (the Oblatas del Santísimo Redentor) and 1876 (the Hijas de María Inmaculada). In 1885, the year before Galdós started writing *Fortunata y Jacinta*, another reformatory for fallen women, that of La Santísima Trinidad known as 'las Trinitarias', was founded by Francisco de Asís Méndez and Mariana Allsop (Rivière Gómez 1994: 108). Scanlon (1986: 112) notes that this last new order aimed to set up workshops and factories for girls over 14, and created further reformatories in Santander, Barcelona, and Seville. Education gave the Church control over the offspring of the bourgeoisie, particularly girls; hospitals, asylums, and reformatories, placing them in direct rivalry with the hygienists, ensured their control over large sections of the poor. As we shall see, this rivalry led to a mutual poaching of each other's discourses by the religious and medical 'improvers', causing further ideological confusion. The hygienists' insistence on moral issues—Monlau insists that 'el consorcio de la Moral con la Higiene es tan íntimo que casi forman un solo todo' (1868: 9)—should be seen in this context as a political strategy, and not simply as an inability to separate medical concerns from bourgeois values (though it was no doubt that as well).

In carving out a role for themselves as social regulators, the hygienists were, of course, consolidating their newly acquired professional status, as seen in the claim to 'know best' of the Comisión de Reformas Sociales' medical members. It was from the mid-1870s, coinciding with the Restoration's attempts to extend central State control, that medical experts started to play a significant role in Spanish public life (Rodríguez Ocaña in Huertas and Campos 1992: ii. 385; Álvarez-Uría 1983: 19). Here they were successfully fighting off the Church's attempt to curb their power with the 1875 Orovio Decree, which reimposed State control over the State school and university curriculum, effectively restoring traditional religious education and curbing scientific pursuit; scientific journals were also made subject to censorship (Kaplan in Lida and Zavala 1970: 261). The consequent mass resignation of Madrid professors was a defence of medicine as much as of Krausism; Madrid University was the centre for both. The medical experts' new public profile resulted directly from the new discipline of public hygiene, conceived as a branch of the social reform process: the teaching of public hygiene at Madrid University included treatment of the insane and prison management, as well as health legislation (Kaplan in Lida and Zavala 1970: 258; Santero 1885: ii. 160; Monlau 1868: 29–31).[12] The man responsible for the 1843 Education Reform Act which set up chairs of hygiene at Spanish universities, drawing up a centralized (in this case, modernized and secularized) syllabus and introducing the new subject of 'medicina legal', was Pedro Mata, who himself became Professor of Legal Medicine at Madrid University in 1844 (Kaplan in Lida and Zavala 1970: 256; López Piñero 1964: 84; Granjel 1983: 27–8). As will be seen in Chapter 3, Mata's medical theories are referred to in Galdós's *La desheredada*: he is also mentioned approvingly by Baldomero Santa Cruz in *Fortunata y Jacinta* (Pérez Galdós 1992: i. 144). In the latter novel, the use by a street vendor of the label 'turrón higiénico' (Pérez Galdós 1992: i. 395) to market his wares indicates that the concept of hygiene, and its positive connotations, were by the mid-1880s perceived to have percolated through to all levels of society.

The new discipline was divided into the twin branches of 'public hygiene' and 'private hygiene': both implied social control. 'Public hygiene' covered the sanitary aspects of town planning, which included the regulation of the non-individualized bodies of the urban masses and prostitutes; 'private hygiene' covered the regulation of individualized bodies within the bourgeois family, proposed as a model for other classes to adopt. The distinction was a class-based one rather than a strict division between public and private, since the two could not in practice be separated (hence the concern). Public hygiene included the intimate behaviour of the problem areas of the population; private hygiene stressed the social consequences of domestic

---

[12] Kaplan (Lida and Zavala 1970: 258) notes that 'from the Revolution on, empirical science was associated with the idea of public medicine'. Santero (1885: ii. 160–5) defines the purview of public hygiene as 'las leyes sanitarias', town planning (including 'paseos' and 'sitios de reunión' such as theatres), hospitals, penitentiary institutions, lunatic asylums, charitable institutions, factories, farms, slaughterhouses, markets—'y agréguese cuanto concierne á la agricultura, el comercio, á las vías y medios de comunicación, á la alimentación pública, á la habitación, en particular de las clases pobres, al abastecimiento de aguas, á la limpieza pública, al alumbrado y á la organización de la beneficencia, que es de suyo una institución higiénica, como la Higiene, si bien se advierte, es, á su vez, una institución eminentemente benéfica'. Public hygiene, Santero continues, is thus of interest to government, guardians of morality, philosophers, and legislators, as well as doctors.

life. Indeed, successive educational legislation from the 1840s to the 1880s kept changing its mind as to whether there should be a single Chair of Public and Private Hygiene, or separate chairs for each discipline (Granjel 1983: 27–31). Most hygienists wrote textbooks on both, dedicating separate volumes to each but in both cases adopting the same classificatory structure: for example, Pedro Monlau's much re-edited *Elementos de higiene privada* (1846) and *Elementos de higiene pública* (1847); Juan Giné y Partagás, *Curso elemental de higiene privada y pública* (1871); Benito Alcina, *Tratado de higiene privada y pública* (1882); Francisco Javier Santero, *Elementos de higiene privada y pública* (1885). Monlau was in 1865 appointed Director General de Beneficencia y Sanidad (Granjel 1983: 89), for charity (the term does not yet quite mean 'welfare') and health were twin prongs of the reform process. Medical journals proliferated in Spain from the late 1850s, most offering popularized medical advice to families; indeed, such journals helped construct the family on bourgeois lines. The foundation of the Sociedad Española de Higiene in 1882 stimulated the creation of new professional hygiene journals, notably the *Revista de la Sociedad Española de Higiene* (founded 1883). There was also a dramatic rise in books on health after 1868, again increasing after 1880 (Granjel 1983: 59). Dr López de la Vega's 1878 medical manual *La higiene del hogar*, in Galdós's library, insisted that every home should have one (1878: 7).

Most medical reformers were liberals who saw improvement of workers' unhygienic working and living conditions as a way of preventing organized social protest. In his 1871 *Curso elemental de higiene privada y pública*, written in response to the Paris Commune of that year, Giné y Partagás declared: 'Sólo la Higiene puede poner el fiel en la balanza en ese litigio entre el capital y el trabajo. [. . .] Nada se logrará reprimiendo; sólo higienizando se obtendrán efectos tan favorables como inesperados', going on to say that the nation had two options: Hygiene or the Guardia Civil (quoted by Rodríguez Ocaña in Huertas and Campos 1992: ii. 392). This makes it clear that 'social medicine' was an alternative form of policing; the term for public health regulations was 'policía urbana' (again, the rural areas were not included in the reformers' remit; Nazarín's taking of 'charity' to the neglected rural interior, in Galdós's 1895 novel of that name, is revolutionary). One should not underestimate, as Foucault often does, the genuine humanitarian concern with working-class misery of these reformers. Town planning and social medicine became inseparable since the aim of both was the avoidance of social conflict. Castro's 1860 plan for rebuilding Madrid, like that of Cerdà in Barcelona, was inspired by 'hygienic' principles, which included open green spaces to allow the circulation of fresh air; in both cases, speculators ensured that these never materialized. While Cerdá's modernization plan aimed to defuse class conflict by integrating the different social levels, Castro's plan opted for class segregation. The 1870s and 1880s saw an ongoing debate on the relative advantages and dis-advantages of class segregation versus integration with respect to housing, showing that the double aim was to integrate the 'alien' elements of the population while continuing to exclude them (Bahamonde Magro and Martínez 1994: 443–5; Fernández García 1993: 421; Bahamonde Magro and Toro Mérida 1978: 98). The few attempts to build workers' housing in the early 1870s—Rebolledo's 1872 proposal *Casas para obreros o económicas*, the 1873 cooperative El Porvenir del Artesanado, and the 1875–6 La Constructora Benéfica (Collins and Flores 1967: 31; Bahamonde Magro and Toro Mérida 1978: 99)—were all based on the principle of segregation. Arturo Soria's Ciudad Lineal project, publicized from the early 1880s, was radical in its uncompromising insistence on blending the sanitary advantages of the country with the economic advantages of the city (both based on the principle of free circulation), while insisting on mixing residential, commercial and industrial districts and, more importantly, the various classes. Each worker's family was to have its independent house and garden, to ensure individualization (Collins and Flores 1967: 35, 38). As Soria put it, the aim was 'la transformación de los sentimientos y las ideas de sus ciudadanos' enabling them to recognize 'la trascendencia de los derechos individuales', for how could one expect the propertyless to appreciate the principle of private property or, indeed, that of privacy? In an 1882 article, Soria proclaimed: 'Espero hacer la revolución HIGIENICA . . . limpieza general de personas, casas, calles, campos y ciudades; de los cuerpos y de las almas; de las costumbres y de las leyes, de las instituciones, de todo'; in short 'La revolución por el agua frente a la revolución por el fuego' (Collins and Flores 1967: 84–5, 106). An 1883 article contained the one-sentence paragraph: 'La policía apenas será necesaria' (Collins and Flores 1967: 193).

Soria's original backers were hygienists involved in improving Madrid's notoriously appalling sanitary conditions. These included the Austro-Hungarian Philiph Hauser who, after settling in Spain, became the leading Spanish public health expert; and the architect Mariano Belmás, author of an 1885 book on workers' housing tellingly titled *Mi casa*, and a leading figure in the Sociedad Española de Higiene. Hauser made his name with his report on the 1884–5 cholera epidemic (Huertas and Campos 1992: i. 152), awarded a prize by the Paris Academy of Science. It must be remembered that this epidemic, lasting eighteen months and claiming 120,000 lives, with particularly high casualties in the working-class districts of Madrid (Hauser 1979: 45), coincided with or immediately preceded many of the novels studied in this book. In his speech at the 1882 inaugural ceremony of the Sociedad Española de Higiene, King Alfonso XII made clear its goals:

> se trata de mejorar la sociedad, procurando en lo posible acrecentar la superioridad de nuestra raza, con lo que podríamos contar con soldados y trabajadores más útiles e inteligentes, consiguiendo con ello contribuir al desarrollo y engrandecimiento de nuestra industria y agricultura. (Rodríguez Ocaña 1987: 30)

The Society's debates were forwarded to the government to inspire interventionist legislation (in practice, they were rarely acted on). Medical and economic concerns explicitly come together here: Monlau's 1868 lecture course on public hygiene at the Universidad Central (never delivered but published) began with a visionary anticipation of how the new profession of 'médicos higienistas' would transform the nation-State by enabling every member of the population to attain the 'maximum de vitalidad y de valor representativo en el capital social efectivo', noting that contemporary economic arguments were 'pura Fisiología social y pura Higiene administrativa' (1868: 4, 9). We shall see later how the terminology of economic discourse invades that of medicine. This economic stress on augmenting and improving the workforce translated into a demographic concern with increased, healthy reproduction, making sexuality —the first recorded use of the word is 1859 (Corbin in Perrot 1990: 578)—the basis of private and public life (Foucault 1987:

25, 106–7), and specifically making women the key to the nation's 'ills', whether as cause or solution. In later chapters we shall explore the links between anxieties about Madrid's (and Oviedo's) atrocious sewage [Abwasser] problems and anxieties about prostitution in particular and women's bodies in general. The images of contamination, leakage, and blockage produced by such anxieties are central to the urban novels we shall study, providing a classic illustration of Mary Douglas's perception (1973) that constructions of the social body and of the physical body mirror and reinforce one another.

Alarm about prostitutes' transmission of syphilis—particularly with the discovery in the 1870s of hereditary syphilis, which increased worries about the contamination of the bourgeois family (Corbin 1990: 246–7)—led to the introduction of controls on prostitution in Madrid in 1858, 1865, 1877, and 1885, with similar controls introduced in other cities.[13] Corbin notes that the regulationism of the late 1870s and 1880s differed from the first wave in the mid-century in that it was driven by medical rather than moral arguments (1990: 256). These were concerned not with stopping prostitution but with containing it, requiring prostitutes to operate from licensed brothels in designated areas away from places of public concourse, and to undergo medical inspection twice a week by police medical inspectors—on the top floor of the Gobierno Civil Headquarters —and, if infected, enforced hospitalization; they were charged for this 'service' (Scanlon 1986: 109–10; Capel Martínez 1982: 282–7; Hauser 1979: 136–9).[14] As a point of intersection between the various classes, the prostitute becomes the symbol of the leakages in the system that threaten not only class distinctions but also the distinction between public and private. It is thus logical that the 1877 legislation on prostitution should have

---

[13] The Catalan hygienist Prudencio Sereñana y Partagás published *La prostitución en la ciudad de Barcelona, estudiada como enfermedad social* (1882) and *La sífilis matrimonial* (1887) (Rey González 1990: 18). The 6th issue of the Madrid journal *Revista Médico Social*, founded in 1886, has a long article on prostitution and syphilis by its founder, a member of the Sociedad Española de Higiene, which also held debates on prostitution and syphilis in the 1880s (Rodríguez Ocaña 1987: 39; Granjel 1983: 37).

[14] Controls in Spain seem to have been stricter than in France, where they were first introduced; according to Corbin (1990: 252–8), even under intensified regulationism in the 1880s, registered prostitutes in France were required to submit to police inspection once a week.

included wet-nurses in its provisions (Capel Martínez 1982; 286). The other social group that was the subject of repeated legislation from 1845 onwards was that of beggars and vagrants, since their mobility also represented a leakage in the system of social containment. The 1849 Penal Code made vagrancy a criminal offence. As with prostitutes, vagrants found not to have licences were rounded up and interned in 'asilos de beneficencia' or workhouses which effectively were jails; those not born in Madrid were 'deported' to their village of origin (Bahamonde Magro and Toro Mérida 1978: 47–50, 57; Bahamonde in Rodríguez Puértolas 1988: 163–82).[15]

That this medical involvement in social reform was part of a system of social regulation is evident from its close connection with penal legislation and criminology. From Mata's appointment as Professor of Legal Medicine in 1844, but particularly from the late 1870s on, 'medicina legal' became central to the study of medicine in Spain; its remit included forensic science but also the much broader issue of assessing criminal responsibility. Galdós's doctor friend Tolosa Latour—a founding member of the Sociedad Española de Higiene (Granjel 1983: 34)—was one of a number of medical experts who, from the early 1870s, campaigned for penal reform, intervening in trials to examine defendants physically, and pressing for a not guilty verdict on grounds of criminal irresponsibility due to cretinism or insanity. (Galdós's own attendance at trials as a journalist, personally interviewing the defendants and witnesses, has been documented (Andreu 1996–7).) In 1881 Dr Esquerdo—whom we shall later encounter as a hysteria specialist—attempted unsuccessfully to secure the reprieve of a serial rapist and woman-killer, Garayo el Sacamantecas, arguing that it took a medical expert to detect insanity in those who, to the untrained eye, might appear sane and therefore responsible (Maristany 1983: 370). The gender implications of this case are troubling, to say the least. The previous year Esquerdo had unsuccessfully intervened in the trial of Otero—the prototype for Mariano in Galdós's 1881 novel *La desheredada*—convicted and executed for attempted regicide (Gordon 1972). In his 1881 *Quemas y criminales*, another medical expert J. M. Escuder declared: 'El código del porvenir tendrán que hacerlo los médicos'

---

[15] For detailed study of these forms of social control, see Fuentes (1997*b*).

(Álvarez-Uría 1983: 244). In 1882 the Madrid Ateneo held a debate on 'Los locos delincuentes', in which Tolosa Latour participated with other health experts (Maristany 1983: 369–70). In their study of the 1886 trial of the priest Galeote, accused of murdering the Bishop of Madrid-Alcalá and found criminally irresponsible thanks to a report from the Real Academia de Medicina, Varela and Álvarez-Uría conclude that the case, which attracted great publicity, gave the medical profession the chance to 'llevar a la práctica un viejo sueño psiquiátrico consistente en negar las diferencias entre razón y locura con el fin de patologizar todo el campo social justificando así la intervención médica' (1979: 158). Galdós's novels of the 1890s, exploring the difficulty of distinguishing between 'normal' and 'abnormal' psychology, must be seen in this context, rather than as the sign of a rejection of materialism for spiritualism. In 1886, as a result of the Galeote trial, royal decrees ordered the setting up of three laboratories of 'legal medicine' plus an asylum for the criminally insane; the 1887 Penal Code made it a requirement for public health experts to be consulted at criminal trials. In securing a reprieve from the death penalty or a prison sentence and having such criminals confined instead to a lunatic asylum, medical experts were asserting their own right to control the socially deviant. To be declared criminally irresponsible also meant being declared ineligible for civil rights, since these could be held only by those capable of exercising free choice in the first place. As Álvarez-Uría puts it: the 'Estado tutelar' is based on the 'protección de animales, niños, mujeres, locos, criminales y obreros' (1983: 339), for all are conceived as legal minors. Interestingly, Varela and Álvarez-Uría (1979: 170) quote the hygienist Giné y Partagás as stating with regard to the criminally insane: 'La reaparición de los sentimientos de familia en la manía es el indicio más favorable que se puede desear.' They also note that one of these medical advocates of penal reform, Jaime Vera, was a founding member of the Partido Socialista Obrero Español in 1879, asking pertinently whether the acceptance by party intellectuals of this medicalization of social problems explains their adoption of reformist policies (171 n. 20).

Criminology was also the bridge connecting medicine with the new discipline of anthropology. Anthropology and social control have always been connected. Spain's early history shows this particularly well, for anthropology was effectively invented by the Inquisition's probing and recording of the most intimate details of private life, repeated in the New World by the Spanish friars who got the natives they were forcibly converting to document meticulously their customs and beliefs.[16] In both cases, the anthropological impulse served as a tool of homogenization; Hobsbawm notes (1990: 16) that here the Reyes Católicos anticipated the nineteenth-century process of nation formation (hence Isabel la Católica's co-option by late nineteenth-century historical painting and Francoist ideology). If Spain exported its nation-formation project to the New World, Anderson (1983: 50–65) and Pratt (1992: 6, 10, 140) have conversely argued that the nineteenth-century European nation-State was in many ways an importation of colonial models. In late nineteenth-century Spain, as elsewhere, discussion of social problems frequently incorporated the vocabulary of contemporary anthropology, whose aim was to survey, classify, and thus control 'other', 'primitive' races. We have seen how the Krausists' geographical expeditions, central to their nation-formation project, included forays into central Africa. Richards (1993) demonstrates that nineteenth-century empire-building was predicated on the compilation of an archive of anthropological information, made possible by the existence of a strongly centralized administration.[17] The same illusion that that which is written down becomes a 'fact', which in turn allows control, underlies nineteenth-century realism. Realist novels have to be long, because the greater the archive, the greater the control (in theory); and if the mass of detail threatens to get out of control, then the solution is to include some more. Galdós's longest novel *Fortunata y Jacinta*, a miscegenation narrative about the attempted incorporation of a 'savage', is a perfect example.

The realist novel must thus be seen as a manifestation of the same anthropological urge that inspired the Comisión de Reformas Sociales and the proliferation of public and private hygiene manuals to compile an archive of every aspect of national life regarded as a problem. Documentation implies

---

[16] See Ginzburg's essay 'The Inquisitor as Anthropologist' (1990: 156–64).
[17] Nead (1988: 150–1) notes that social reformers positioned themselves much like explorers investigating and reporting back on dangerous 'unknown territory'.

the aim of social reform/control. The largest compilation of statistics is Hauser's immensely impressive *Madrid bajo el punto de vista médico-social* (1902), the result of nearly twenty years spent documenting the city's sanitary conditions (with a long section on prostitution).[18] Unlike most of his Spanish contemporaries, Hauser proposed State intervention as the only way of guaranteeing reform, pleading for a 'socialismo de Estado', not in Cánovas's sense but in that of State controls implementing the recommendations of a civil society broadened to include the working-class elite (Hauser 1979: 32–3, 53–5). One can only speculate whether Hauser's support of State intervention owed anything to his familiarity with the highly centralized Austro-Hungarian imperial administrative model. Social reform was at the time referred to as 'missionary' activity, implying an analogy with empire. For the solution to the problem of how to incorporate the alien elements of the population without granting them civil rights was to colonize them; what in practice was called 'civilizing' them. Pick (1989) has studied the role played in late nineteenth-century nation formation by the medical discourse on degeneration, noting that it provides a model for classifying the nation's inhabitants into those fit and those unfit for incorporation. As Pick observes, the terminology of 'incorporation' and 'elimination' is that of a medical discourse concerned with 'improving' bodies through surveillance. Degeneracy theory, deriving from Bénédict Morel's 1857 *Traité des dégénérescences physiques intellectuelles et morales de l'espèce humaine*, leaves its traces on Spanish medical discourse from the 1860s onwards.[19]

Morel's chief concern was with what he called 'the dangerous classes'. Degeneracy theory's main impact in Spain, as elsewhere, was via criminology. In the 1880s the former discipline of legal

---

[18] Hauser published articles on public-health matters in the *Revista Contemporánea* and the *Revista de España* from 1884 on, as well as participating in the activities of Madrid's learned societies; he frequented Krausist circles. His involvement with the cholera epidemic gave him a high public profile (de la Calle in Hauser 1979: i. 20, 27–30).

[19] Monlau's 1853 *Higiene del matrimonio* talks of the 'decadencia' of the race (1865: 60), but his 1860 *Nociones de higiene doméstica y gobierno de la casa* (post-Morel) uses the term 'degeneration', significantly related to marriage: 'el matrimonio, que ha sido la fuente de la degeneración, ha de serlo de la regeneración' (1860: 14). Sanz del Río's *Ideal de la humanidad*, also written in 1860, similarly speaks of 'degeneration' (1860: 10).

medicine started to be referred to as criminal anthropology, under the influence of the Italian criminal anthropologist Cesare Lombroso, whose work on 'degenerate types' was first aired publicly in Spain at the 1881 trial of Garayo el Sacamantecas, giving rise to a public debate on the detection and classification of deviants that would peak 1889–95.[20] Pick (1989: 113–20) shows that Lombroso's anthropological documentation of Italian 'racial types' in the 'primitive' rural areas, whose inhabitants were seen by him as 'savages', was related to the contemporary nation-formation project accompanying political unification in 1860. Lombroso's reformist project, originally aimed at 'incorporating' the degenerate, seen as throwbacks to an earlier stage of evolution who could be 'civilized' through social intervention, became progressively more concerned with eliminating them, as degeneracy came to be seen as a sign of evolutionary failure whose effects would be perpetuated by hereditary transmission. Lombroso also became progressively more concerned with the 'savages within', in the form of anarchists and female delinquents and prostitutes, whom he described and photographed from every angle as if compiling a police archive. Ginzburg (1990: 96–125) has observed that the realist novel—based on the tracing of 'facts' from 'clues'—is connected to the development of forensic science, noting that the technique of fingerprinting originated in British colonial India; that is, as part of an empire-building project based on the enforcement of uniformity via individualization.

Nineteenth-century anthropology is inextricably linked with the development of photography (a key element in forensic science) and of the museum, since both document, classify, and contain. The pioneers of anthropology in late nineteenth-century Spain were doctors who saw the discipline as an instrument in their regulatory programme. Madrid's Museo Antropológico (known as 'el Museo Velasco') was set up in 1875 by the doctor Pedro Velasco who, in addition to creating the journal *El Anfiteatro Anatómico Español* (1873), founded the Sociedad Española de Antropología (1865) and the *Revista de Antropología* (1874). Velasco's assistant in these projects was his student Ángel Pulido, who succeeded him as the Anthropological Museum's Director. As Jagoe notes (Jagoe, Blanco, and

---

[20] His influence on Galdós's *Nazarín* is discussed in Labanyi (1993a: pp. xiii–xv).

Enríquez de Salamanca 1998: 330), these activities allowed Pulido to indulge a penchant for edificatory showmanship; in the late 1880s, like Charcot earlier, he staged public experiments in hypnotizing female hysterics. The Museo Antropológico had a Syphilitics' Gallery, whose regulatory function was all too evident: Pulido (1876: 137) records how a young man he was taking round it fainted. The Museum also contained jars with pickled female genitalia, and a model of a vagina with a speculum inserted in it. In addition to publishing various articles on hermaphroditism with Velasco in the first number of *El Anfiteatro Anatómico Español*, Pulido caused a sensation with a 1880 paper to the Sociedad Ginecológica (founded 1874), of which he was secretary, on 'Lactancia paterna' (Jagoe, Blanco, and Enríquez de Salamanca 1998: 314). These multifarious endeavours construct models of 'normal' sexuality through the sensationalist exposition of deviance. This involves warnings about degeneration through hereditary transmission (Pulido's Syphilitics' Gallery was set up at the time hereditary syphilis was discovered); and it involves the promotion of sexual difference as the norm. As a gynaecologist, concerned with female reproduction, Pulido had a professional interest in both matters. That Spain's first 'professional' publicizer of anthropology should have been a gynaecologist is significant: anthropology is conceived, not as the 'science of mankind', but as the 'science of men and women'.

As Foucault notes, nineteenth-century criminology, in inventing the 'delinquent', was applying the medical notion of the 'case history', for this was a form of 'bio-power' based on biographical knowledge, through observation not just of the crime but of the delinquent's life story (Rabinow 1984: 219). Álvarez-Uría (1983: 185) notes that degeneracy theory, stressing the importance of heredity, created the even broader notion of the medical 'family history': a concept central, of course, to Zola's *Rougon-Macquart* series as it was to criminology, another interest of Pulido's as author of the book *Locos delincuentes* (1883), based on the 1882 debates at the Madrid Ateneo. Pulido's widely read sex manual for bourgeois wives, *Bosquejos médico-sociales para la mujer* (1876), clearly influenced by degeneracy theory, has some lurid—but frank—pages on prostitution and syphilis, and keeps threatening to turn into novel form as Pulido describes his real and imaginary case studies in the minutest detail. It seems no coincidence that so many nineteenth-century Spanish medical experts—Monlau, Giné y Partagás, Pulido, Tolosa Latour—were, as Jagoe notes (Jagoe, Blanco, and Enríquez de Salamanca 1998: 306), also creative writers. The medical case study and the realist novel are similar in their biographical approach and in their anthropological illusion that knowledge (the archive) is control. The risk, however, in constructing the 'normal' through display of the 'abnormal' is that the gallery of deviants threatens to monopolize the space. Hence, as Jagoe observes (Jagoe, Blanco, and Enríquez de Salamanca 1998: 314), nineteenth-century Spanish medical manuals about women, whether written for them or for male experts, insist on the domestic, 'angelic' wife—a concept which, as Jagoe notes, came from non-medical bourgeois discourses of femininity—while painting a picture of a female body riven by uncontrollable desires.[21] The realist novel explores the space between these contrary representations.

The combined interest in deviancy and sexual difference found in Pulido is also evidenced in Pedro Mata's dual role as Spain's first Professor of Legal Medicine and as the man responsible for modernizing the university medical curriculum in the 1840s. For what this effectively means is a State-sanctioned break with the old Hippocratic and Galenic one-sex model which, as Laqueur (1990) has shown, between 1750 and 1850 gave way to a new model of sexual difference.[22] The Greek medical

[21] Of the many manuals written for women, the most popular were Monlau's much reprinted *Higiene del matrimonio* (1853) and Pulido (1876). In addition to Jagoe, Blanco, and Enríquez de Salamanca's magnificent anthology (1998), see Borderies-Guerena (Maquieira d'Angelo 1989), and Aldaraca (1992) who deals mainly with female conduct literature closely influenced by these medical manuals. Galdós's library possessed the following: *La mujer: apuntes para un libro* (1861) by Severo Catalina, a member of the Real Academia Española; and *La higiene del hogar* (1878) by Dr López de la Vega, published by the publishers of the women's magazine *La Guirnalda*, for which Galdós wrote in the 1870s and which published many of Galdós's own novels from 1875 (Jagoe 1994: 42–3). Catalina's book argues: 'Eduquemos á las mujeres, é, instruyámoslas después, si queda tiempo' (14), insisting that male infidelities 'son á lo más calaveradas' while female infidelities 'son á lo menos delitos' (117). Catalina also comments that 'Apenas hay ciencia moral y política que no destine al matrimonio un capítulo' noting that theology deals with its sacramental nature, jurisprudence deals with its contractual obligations, political economy deals with its 'consequences', and 'La literatura lo estudia todo' (100–1). As befits a medical expert, López de la Vega insists that every home should have a book on hygiene and ends by saying 'always consult a doctor'.

[22] López Piñero (1964: 89) notes that Mata rejected Hippocratic and Galenic medicine for positivism.

tradition which had dominated European science since the Renaissance supposed that women were the same but inferior, with the female reproductive organs an interior, undeveloped version of the male. As Laqueur convincingly argues, the new medical model whereby women were naturally equal but different, whose emergence coincided with that of political liberalism, provided a convenient justification for continuing to exclude women from civil rights while proclaiming the new doctrine of universal equality. The capitalist split between public and private spheres was thus legitimized on physiological grounds, sitting uneasily with contract theory's argument that women, in signing the marriage contract, had voluntarily abdicated their 'natural' rights. Although the Krausists were not positivists, one can see why the new two-sex medical model—which they all use in their arguments—should have appealed to them, for instead of justifying marriage as an 'improvement' on nature (Rousseau's model), it proposed marriage as a confirmation of women's 'natural' role (an idea also endorsed, contradictorily, by Rousseau). What was meant by women's 'natural role' was, of course, maternity, supposed to be their 'true' function because it was what made them different. Thus, in a classic circular argument, women's reproductive capacity made them different, while in turn their difference made their reproductive capacity their 'true' being. While the new medical model made the role of wife and mother virtually compulsory, it was, from the male point of view, an improvement on contract theory in that it provided a justification for refusing civil rights to all women, married or not. Jagoe (Jagoe, Blanco, and Enríquez de Salamanca 1998: 314–33) shows that traces of the Hippocratic and Galenic one-sex model survived among Spanish doctors for most of the century. Orovio's 1875 curbs on the medical curriculum, which remained in force till Sagasta reinstated freedom of expression in 1881, may have encouraged survivals of the old view, fundamental to Catholicism, that women had sexual drives as strong as, if not stronger than, those of men, justifying their subjection to male control for different reasons.

While the Krausists' endorsement of sexual difference was at odds with the Greek medical tradition, nevertheless they assimilated Krause's German Hellenism in their promotion

—through exercise, gymnastics, and the outdoors life—of a healthy acceptance of the body as natural by both sexes (Sanz del Río 1860: 89–92). The one work of Rousseau which the Krausists embraced was, as Pardo Bazán wryly shows in *La madre naturaleza*, his *Émile*, which advocates differential education for male and female youth, in both cases in a natural scenario. In founding a training school for women teachers, the Krausists were endorsing Rousseau's notion that woman was man's complement and helpmeet, since education of the young was seen as an extension in the public sphere of women's 'natural' aptitude for motherhood; that is, a 'naturally' female profession. The implication was also that training women to be teachers would train them for their future role as mothers; indeed, the trainees at the Krausist Escuela de Institutrices, founded in 1869, were expected to resign on marriage. Here the Krausists were echoing Rousseau's indecision as to whether femininity was 'natural' or the result of tutoring. Co-education was a basic principle of the Institución Libre de Enseñanza, though it never attracted as many female students as the Krausists' single-sex educational establishments for women (Jagoe, Blanco, and Enríquez de Salamanca 1998: 121). The Krausists expanded the female curriculum beyond domestic science to include the study of biology, geography, physics, and psychology. They also founded a highly successful Escuela de Comercio para Señoras in 1878, and in 1882 an Escuela de Correos y Telegrafos (less successful because of the lack of jobs for women in the public sector) and the journal *La Instrucción para la Mujer*. Although the Institución Libre's prospectus stated that girls should be educated 'con' and 'como' their male counterparts, practically all Krausists (the Institución's founder, Giner, among them) insisted that women were complementary to men (that is, equal but different) and should thus receive a specially tailored education (Scanlon 1986: 30–41, 52–3; di Febo 1976). Di Febo (1976: 75–6) notes that Giner de los Ríos's *Resumen de filosofía del derecho* (1898), while deploring legal discrimination against women, insisted they were especially suited for philanthropic work. Conversely Giner, echoing Rousseau and Hegel, insisted that women should not become judges because, being moved by personal emotion, they had no objective sense of justice; I shall return to this in Chapter 6.

Nevertheless, in encouraging women to deploy their 'maternal' talents in education and philanthropy, the Krausists effectively championed women's entry into the public sphere, at the same time labelling that part of the public sphere known as 'the social' female territory.[23] Female philanthropy allowed many women to gain a public voice (such as the reformer Concepción Arenal, active from the 1860s through the 1880s, with her journal *La Voz de la Caridad*) and to demonstrate their effectiveness as entrepreneurs (one thinks of Ernestina Manuel de Villena, the model for Galdós's Doña Guillermina, discussed in Chapter 5 of this book). Indeed Arenal, while insisting that reform was a largely moral matter, pressed for women to be allowed to hold State posts in 'Beneficencia', giving them the power to implement change; she herself held State posts as a women's prison visitor and, in 1868, inspector of women's reformatories (Scanlon 1986: 62–3). Riley (1988) has shown how philanthropy provided a platform for an incipient feminist movement, albeit one that was bourgeois in conception. The rise of 'the social' paradoxically remapped women as social identities precisely because of their separate 'feminine' role:

If the legacy of the eighteenth century had seen an intensification of a naturalised femininity, placed firmly in the family, then it's as if these very ascriptions were taken on in the nineteenth century, to be wielded as weapons of women's elevation. If women's sphere was to be domestic, then let the social world become a giant arena for domesticated intervention, where the empathies supposedly peculiar to the sex might flourish on a broad and visible scale. [. . .] If the subjection of women had been secured by their very designation as 'women', then let that be seized and refashioned, set to work. (Riley 1988: 46–7)

[23] For women's education in general, and women as educators, see Jagoe, Blanco, and Enríquez de Salamanca (1998: 105–45). For the role of State education in social regulation, see Varela and Álvarez-Uría (1991). For philanthropy in 19th-century Spain, see Álvarez-Uría (Seminario de historia 1988: 117–46); Shubert (1990: 52–6); Bahamonde Magro (Rodríguez Puértolas 1988: 163–82); Bahamonde Magro and Toro Mérida (1978: 45–7); and Bahamonde Magro and Martínez (1994: 478–80), who discuss State institutions for social control as well as private initiatives. Álvarez-Uría (Seminario de historia 1988: 144–5) observes that the notion that philanthropy was a 'maternal' activity constructed the poor as minors. Perinat and Marrades (1980: 215) note that Spanish women's magazines first discuss the possibility of women working in 1871, in relation to philanthropy. Hauser's monumental public health survey *Madrid bajo el punto de vista médico-social*, compiled from 1883 to 1902, ends by demanding government measures to raise the level of women's education.

In engaging in social reform, women were thus re-forming themselves as much as the objects of their labours. However, as Riley notes (1988: 51), the redefinition of women, through their involvement in 'the social', as overwhelmingly sociological entities allowed them to continue to be seen as operating outside the political, thus allowing demands for women's political rights (incipient in Spain) to be postponed. Indeed, women's involvement in 'the social' allowed reform to be construed as non-political, for its purpose was precisely—as liberals and conservatives declared—to defuse the threat of social revolution. One suspects that some of those who, in Spain, demanded that social reform be left to 'juntas de señoras' (Pérez Ledesma in Seminario de historia 1988, 161) were not just protesting against State control but trying to sabotage the reform process. At the same time, the moral concern of women reformers was seen by male politicians as a political threat: Riley cites the claim by an English Conservative MP, in an 1871 Commons debate (the year of the Paris Commune), that a 'women-chosen parliament' would be dangerous because of 'the increased importance which would be given to questions of a quasi social or philanthropic character' (1988: 72–3). In *Fortunata y Jacinta*, it is Jacinta's combination of political naivety and female empathy that allows her to perceive the injustice of class inequality. Her empathy, also, is for the female victims of working-class deprivation: she takes Pitusín because he is offered to her, but she chooses Adoración. As Riley notes (1988: 50–1), women's involvement in philanthropy could produce a cross-class female solidarity, fostering the study of 'women' as an object of enquiry. The mutual empathy of Jacinta and Fortunata, who meet only through the former's philanthropic involvement with the convent reformatory and the Calle de Toledo tenement, is an obvious illustration. At the same time, as the same novel shows so well, the gain in agency for the bourgeois female reformers was achieved at the expense of the working-class women they sought to 'improve'.

Regardless of who benefited, the key issue here is that 'the social' became constructed as a female area, since it meant the extension to the public sphere of the ideology of domesticity. This blurred the public/private division, not only because female 'improvers' entered the public sphere, but also because the stress on 'family values' was an attempt to 'privatize' the public arena of class relations. Thus the working-class home became the target of reform. Indeed, this reform process, which invaded working-class homes to 'moralize' the poor through the inculcation of domestic virtues, was referred to in Spain as a 'política familiarista': a term which makes clear the confusion of public and private.[24] The net result was a feminization of politics, whose aim was not to politicize women (though in practice it did) but to deny that social reform was a political matter. A further result was that the blame for social 'ills' was laid squarely on the family, and particularly on mothers who failed to fulfil their maternal duties. Foucault (1987: 38) has argued that the stress on 'normalizing' deviants meant that the 'normal' (that is, bourgeois) family was largely left alone; but the proliferation of medical manuals makes it clear that this was far from the case. Indeed, the medical experts' concern with preventing as well as curing social 'diseases' constructed even the most 'normal' family as potentially pathological and thus requiring scrutiny. The diffuse and ever broadening programme of social control was undertaken in the name of 'family values': Le Play's *L'Organisation de la famille* (1871, again the year of the Paris Commune) saw the working classes as a problem because of their lack of an organized family structure, and opposed State intervention precisely in order to make the family pre-eminent (Casey 1989: 12–14). Concern with regulating the family may have given increased power to mothers in alliance with the 'family doctor', but in the long run the process had the contrary effect of eroding the family's control over its own affairs. Pick comments that degeneracy theory converted reproduction into a problem that 'could no longer be entrusted to the self-regulation of the family' (1989: 72). As Habermas shrewdly observes: the family, having earlier been removed from production, was now stripped of its 'functions of control', with the result that its private autonomy was reduced to 'functions of consumption' (1989: 155–6). And consumption, seen as the wife's responsibility, meant women entering the market-place albeit as buyers. The result of this massive invasion of the family by the various social regulators was, to quote

---

[24] In her journal *La Voz de la Caridad* (1871), Concepción Arenal argued that 'la asistencia domiciliaria' was the cheapest and most humane, as well as the most effective, form of charity (Pla et al. 1987: 90).

Donzelot, that 'the family appears as though colonized' (1979: 103). As we shall see in the following chapters, the realist novel, in addition to exploring anxieties raised by women leaving the home for the street, provides a critique of the new techniques of social control that invaded the privacy of the home. But, in subjecting the everyday life of the family to scrutiny, the novelist also contributes to its pathologization as part of a surveillance programme based on the assumption that the key to social control is to make society describable.

PART II

The Urban Novel: Female Adultery and the Exchange Economy

3
Mapping the City: Galdós's *La familia de León Roch* (1879), *La desheredada* (1881), *Lo prohibido* (1884–1885)

ADULTERY and prostitution, both of which take women out of the home into the public sphere of exchange relations, form the subject matter of several of Galdós's novels, particularly those of the 1880s which focus on the middle classes and on money. Galdós called his novels of the 1880s his *novelas contemporáneas* not only to distinguish them from his historical novels (the *episodios nacionales*) but also to make the point that his subject matter is modernity; I shall here translate *novelas contemporáneas* as 'novels of modernity'. The last novel of what he called his 'early period'—*La familia de León Roch*, written in 1879 before the two-year silence preceding his *novelas contemporáneas*—is the first novel to deal with the financial world, the first set in Madrid, and the first to discuss adultery. To be more precise: it is set on the outskirts of Madrid, and it deals with relations that verge on the adulterous; location and subject matter, hovering on the edge of the city and adultery respectively, are connected. The first 'novel of modernity', *La desheredada* of 1881, plunges headlong into city life, taking prostitution as its emblem. As a commodity circulating among buyers of every social class, the prostitute figures the freedom and equality promised by the market. In the sequel novels *Tormento* and *La de Bringas*, both of 1884, prostitution blurs with marriage as Amparo accepts a marriage proposal—ending in concubinage—for money but also for love, while Rosalía commits adultery not for love but for money. The following novel *Lo prohibido*, published in two parts in 1884–5, deals with adultery and the world of high finance, showing what happens when the subjects broached in *La familia de León Roch* are seen through to a conclusion. Galdós's next and most important novel, *Fortunata y Jacinta*, published in four parts in

1886-7, deals with a prostitute who becomes an adulteress. The overall movement is, after preliminary exploration of an adultery which fails to materialize, from prostitution to adultery: that is, from the relatively straightforward case of the woman who abandons the private sphere for the public, to the trickier issue of the woman who moves in both spheres at once, blurring the boundary between them.

La de Bringas and *Fortunata y Jacinta* are the most complex novels because prostitute and adulteress merge in the same person. I shall take *Tormento* together with *La de Bringas* since, as sequel novels, they raise related issues. I shall not discuss the later sequel novels *La incógnita* (1888-9) and *Realidad* (1889) since, although their protagonist is an adulteress, by this stage Galdós is no longer concerned with the links between adultery and the market. Nor, except in passing, will I discuss *Miau* (1888), which relates the breakdown of the family to the all-pervasiveness of the State but is not a novel of adultery. I shall start by outlining the treatment of adultery and prostitution in *La familia de León Roch*, *La desheredada*, and *Lo prohibido*, in order to introduce the issues which Galdós develops more fully in *La de Bringas* and *Fortunata y Jacinta*.

LA FAMILIA DE LEÓN ROCH

Critical studies of this novel have concentrated on its relationship to Krausist views on the education of women (Lida 1967; López Morillas 1968; Gómez Martínez 1983; Jongh-Rossel 1985: 65-73; Jagoe 1992). My argument here is that, if the novel is concerned with the government of the household, it is because this is seen as an issue crucial to the government of the nation. The novel can be read as a problematization of Sanz del Río's proposal that the family is the basic unit of socialization—a 'personal society' or 'domestic State'—whose function is to mediate ('harmonize') relations between the individual on the one hand and civil society and the State on the other. As Sanz del Río insisted (1860: 208), in keeping with his individualistic, democratic model of the nation, civic virtues must be formed from the bottom up; if they are merely imposed from above by the law, they will be hollow. By instilling moral values in the individual, the family provides the foundation for the formation of a higher-level public morality. The family, in other words, is the model for society, understood in the new sense of an integrated body regulated through techniques of persuasion rather than through enforcement; that is, through the propagation of domestic values as a model for public behaviour. The Krausist insistence that reform should be effected by private initiative rather than by the State was the other side of an increasing concern about State interference in local and individual life. The Krausist organicist view of society attempted to strike a balance between regulation and free flow by advocating a graded hierarchy of social units (stretching up from the individual through the family, the municipality, and civil society to the State), each unit existing to facilitate the working of the others, while not interfering in one another's activities.[1] This blueprint for a society of separate but complementary 'bodies' is clearly difficult to achieve in practice. *La familia de León Roch* shows how the family fails to provide a model for 'the social' and how the privacy of family life is violated by a series of public intrusions.

The novel draws constant parallels between the 'gobierno de la familia' and the government of the nation. It opens with the 'trinity' dominating 'la vida nacional': the Marqués de Fúcar, Joaquín Onésimo, and Federico Cimarra, representing finance, the civil service, and the press respectively—that is, the State, and civil society in its double form of the market and the public sphere of critical opinion. Intertwined with these is the new sector of 'the social', in which private philanthropy furthers the task of State regulation. Fúcar illustrates the enmeshing of the various sectors: as a financier, he is a member of the parliamentary commission drafting the new anti-vagrancy law, and the patron of various philanthropic societies. The international dimensions of his financial activities show how nation formation depends on, yet is undermined by, foreign capital: for example, he is on the board of directors of an agricultural development bank backed by capital from an English fertilizer

---

[1] See Sanz del Río (1860); Azcárate (1877*a*, 1877*b*, 1885 in particular); Giner de los Ríos (1875, 1969); and Díaz's analysis of Krausist political thought (1973). Azcárate's 1883 essay 'Programa de Gobierno y de organización social' contains a section titled 'Sustraer la vida doméstica á las intrusiones del fisco, de la burocracia y de la curia'; the next section goes on to discuss the need for the juridical protection of women against seduction.

company (Pérez Galdós 1966: 786). In addition to being a journalist, Cimarra is a stock-market speculator and is given a post in the colonial administration in Cuba, bearing out Habermas's claim that, in the late nineteenth century, the independence of the public sphere of private opinion was eroded as civil society increasingly merged with the State. The extension of State control is illustrated through Onésimo: 'ese fanal luminoso de la Administración que, encendido en todas las situaciones, ilumina con sus rayos a una pléyade de Onésimos que en diversos puestos del Estado consumen medio presupuesto' (763). He is also referred to as 'un Diluvio administrativo' (826), anticipating Galdós's inundatory family of civil servants in the *novelas contemporáneas*, the Peces, whose most eminent member will be the object of Rosalía de Bringas's first adulterous assignation. Water imagery, as Tony Tanner notes, is frequently used in the realist novel to express the dissolution of the public/private boundary created by adultery (1979: 66–72, 171–8, 312–20). State expansion produces a parallel dissolution. The image of 'leakages'—'filtraciones', which the narrator notes is a term 'tomado por la Hacienda al arte de la fontanería' (805)—is used by the Marquesa de Tellería to describe the ruinous state of her family's domestic economy. Her vow to 'reformar radicalmente la administración' and 'hacer economías' borrows the language of the State because, as she says, 'el orden doméstico' is, or should be, the 'base de las virtudes privadas y públicas' (805). In practice, her family—like most others in the novel—mirrors the disorder of national life, particularly that of an economy geared to the national debt (mentioned throughout the novel).

Onésimo cynically dismisses León's claim to be a man of principles since the intellectuals who have governed the nation have been a disaster in both their public and private lives: 'Pues lo mismo gobiernan sus casas' (766). León too turns out to be incapable of governing his household and recognizes his inability to reform national life (956). The words he uses when admitting his double failure—'Me espanto de reconocerme incapaz de fundar nada sólido' (956)—are directly reminiscent of the phrase 'All that is solid melts into air' used in *The Communist Manifesto* to describe the dissolution of social forms produced by capitalism (Marx and Engels 1974: 83; Berman 1983). In this world where everything is put into circulation the question is not whether to maintain or blur the public/private boundary but, since everything is already in flux, how to distinguish between good fusions and bad confusions.[2] Which is a problem of distinguishing marriage from adultery. In *La familia de León Roch*, marriage (good fusion) has lapsed into adultery (bad confusion) because the Krausist ideal of the family as a mediation of the public and private spheres from the bottom up has been replaced by the top-down invasion of the family by the State, the market, and the new category of 'the social' (the last ironically owing its impulse in Spain to the Krausist reformers who championed individual privacy). León accuses his politician brother-in-law Gustavo Tellería, who eavesdrops on his intimate conversation with Pepa, of being a 'policeman' and 'customs official' in the pay of a prying State (923). Intimate relations are frequently described in economic terms: Pepa's marriage to Cimarra is an 'incautación' of her property in her person (827); she and her daughter Monina are for León a 'familia prestada' (902). Her father, the Marqués de Fúcar, extends his 'philanthropic' activities to the private sphere by maintaining three illegitimate households in addition to his family home (919). As an 'engendro del parlamentarismo y del *contratismo*' (875, Galdós's italics) whose title of nobility is a reward not for fighting the Moors but for 'felicísimas contratas entre fieles cristianos' (917), Fúcar is at least consistent in applying the same rules to his public and private life, as is Cimarra in his embezzlement of public funds and fraudulent use of his wife's money to keep mistresses (950). Cimarra's marriage to Pepa is so disastrous because it was from the start conceived as a business deal; he refers to women with the phrase 'En negocio de mujeres' (950). As Cimarra concludes, it is easy to be a 'distinguido hombre público' in a country where the civil service is a 'prevaricación pública', politics a 'pillaje', and 'la mitad de los matrimonios de cierta clase son *menages à trois*' (952–3). When Cimarra advocates total State control of the nation's wealth, he is endorsing the lack of morality that results from the invasion of the private by the public (770).

---

[2] In an 1872 article for the *Revista de España*, Galdós suggested that the remedy to current 'anarchy' or 'confusion' was 'reconciliation' or 'fusion': the blurring of distinctions is the problem and the solution (Pérez Galdós 1982: 41). Galdós's 1871–2 political articles for the *Revista de España* also insist on the national debt.

The novel shows the formally separate spheres of the State, private enterprise, and 'the social' to be inextricably confused with each other and with the domestic sphere because, in an economy based on the circulation of capital, where everyone is lending money to and borrowing money from everyone else, the key liberal concept of private ownership (including that of women) is threatened. In *La familia de León Roch*, the confusion of public and private property involves the whole economy, for the chief form of private investment is in 'la deuda pública'; that is, government bonds issued to pay off the national debt (such bonds were referred to as 'valores de Estado', making it clear that the credit of the nation-State was at stake). The circular nature of the flow of money is illustrated by the repeated loans to the government made throughout the novel by the Marqués de Fúcar, in exchange for credit enabling him to pay off his own debts. As Cimarra—right as usual—says: 'La bancarrota nacional es una fuente de riqueza' (787–8).[3] Or in the words of the society wit Nules: 'La riqueza [. . .] es un círculo' (913). The novel ends as it began, in a circle mirroring the circulation of money, as Fúcar yet again lends money to the government in exchange for an infusion of credit, 'con lo cual la operación se redondea aquí de un modo completo' (960).

The flow of capital also breaks down the boundary between city and country as 'propiedad inmueble' is converted into 'moveable property' or money. The Tellería family's country estates have passed to urban moneylenders; León's father made his money trafficking in land and urban property (and government bonds, like everyone else). We are told this at the start of the novel, set in a spa town—appropriately, given the conversion of the nation's wealth into 'liquid' assets—where Madrid high society reproduces 'en el campo la vida estrecha, incómoda y enfermiza de las poblaciones' (762). On the same page we are told that León is a natural scientist (geologist and botanist, both favourite Krausist professions), himself blurring the distinction between the natural and the cultural. A similar prefiguration of adultery occurs with Pepa Fúcar, whose adolescent whim was to have a conservatory built and then have it moved: an apt spatial instability for a construction blurring the distinction

---

[3] The economic historian Sardá (1948: 166) refers to the foreign debt as an 'ingreso'.

between the indoors world of home and outside world of nature. Pepa's upbringing as a little rich girl has made her into a hothouse plant—echoing J. S. Mill's description of the bourgeois female in *The Subjection of Women* (1988: 22)—as her natural spontaneity is warped by being allowed to express itself only through the artificial world of consumer commodities (whose monument, the Crystal Palace which housed the Great Exhibition of 1851, was built by a designer of greenhouses).[4] Pepa describes her upbringing as that of a 'savage' or 'kaffir' spoilt by the feathers and beads of civilization (861).

The house in which León installs himself after marriage to María, hoping harmoniously to combine natural science with family life and city with country (796), has a newly landscaped garden designed to divide the public from the private—'para separar la calle, que es de todos, de la casa, que es de uno solo' (791). In practice, it disturbingly turns nature into a consumer object: 'El jardín era nuevo, de esos que se traen de casa del horticultor como los muebles de casa del tapicero' (790). Situated 'en los bordes de la villa, bañado de aires saludables' (809), it is a theoretically ideal matrimonial home based on the harmonious balance between nature and culture, and on the circulation of air recommended in contemporary public- and private-health manuals. María's dying brother Luis Gonzaga is moved to her and León's house from the unhygienic Tellería home in the old centre of Madrid, whose lack of ventilation (809) mirrors his attempts as a priest to submit María's body to unhealthy religious constraints. Corbin (1986: 89–135) has shown the contemporary terror of stagnant water and air, epitomized by the cesspool, seen as the source of miasmatic infection. León accuses the Church of turning María from a running spring into a stagnant pool: 'Pero no la dejaron correr, la encerraron en un charco' (911). A problem arises here, for León's ideal of the healthy marriage as one which allows the wife to 'correr', in keeping with the Krausist stress on physical exercise and country excursions, is dangerously close to the economic ideal of circulation which blurs the public/private distinction. Both are expressed through water imagery; but if natural flow is healthy, economic flow is a threat. This invasion

---

[4] Galdós's library contained Ayguals de Izco's letters reporting on the Crystal Palace Exhibition (Berkowitz 1951: 221).

of medical discourse by the language of economics, which mirrors it but produces different effects, reproduces the ideological contradictions of the period.

In practice, as the narrator notes, the outskirts where León's matrimonial home is situated do not idyllically blend city with country, but are the site of Madrid's rubbish tips and the ragpickers' hovels:

> Al amparo del tejar vense chozas de adobes y esteras, obras arquitectónicas de que se reirían las golondrinas, los topos y los castores, y al amparo de estas guaridas de puntable, los especuladores de la basura analizan la recolección de la mañana, hurgando en los montones de trapos, barreduras, papeles, restos mil de lo que diariamente le sobra a una gran ciudad. (812)

As 'speculators', the ragpickers who recycle the waste products of a consumer society are putting into practice the capitalist ideal of the circulation of goods, but the result is a similar pollution to that which results, in the discourse of hygiene, from stagnation. Adultery and consumerist excess and waste are further connected in the Fúcar family mansion where Pepa lives with her father and daughter: a 'museum' of superfluous commodities (the Spanish 'gastar' means 'to spend' and 'to waste'). Pepa's house, situated in the country outside Madrid but a temple to capitalist over-accumulation, blurs city and country even more alarmingly than León's matrimonial home. The figures on its chapel's painted ceiling are interpreted allegorically as images of the national economy, with a depiction of Christ's multiplication of the loaves that is a 'copia gráfica de la entrega y recepción de algunos artículos de contrata' (896). This chapel is a stylistic mix of Gothic, German neoclassical, Roman, Chinese, and Greek, like a miniature World Exhibition. The house also has (in addition to another conservatory) its Arab and Japanese rooms, and a 'Sala Increíble' nicknamed 'el museo', lined with collector's items from the French Directory period when the revolution in thought produced a 'revolución del vestido', as the 'fiebre innovadora' was harnessed by industry in the form of fashion (938). In the capitalist system in which Pepa is inscribed through her banker father, the new is that which is designed to be obsolescent. The emphasis on consumerism as excess and waste is reinforced by the dining room's description as a 'palacio de la indigestión' (906). Here Galdós introduces for the first time the references to World Exhibitions and fashion that will become the dominant images, in his later 'novels of modernity', of capitalist consumerism.

León and Pepa's near adulterous relationship develops when he moves out of his matrimonial home to rent a house next to hers, in this ambiguous zone described by his wife María as 'ni ciudad ni campo, sino un conjunto irregular de palacios y muladares' (883). Initially, León seems to achieve a near perfect mix of city and country life, as he, Pepa, and Monina form the ideal Krausist family based on altruistic devotion (expressed through his and Pepa's nursing of her sick child), as opposed to the egoism of his marriage to María (in which each tries to turn the other into a mirror of the self). However, the narrator reminds us that this perfect 'marriage' is an adulterous 'familia prestada', based on his love for 'una madre que no era su mujer' and 'una niña que no era su hija' (836). Fittingly, it is set against bankers' discussions on their next loan to the government.

In the third and last part of the novel, the blurring of married and adulterous relations (all of them platonic, for no one is sleeping with anyone else, inside or outside marriage) escalates as León's wife, having collapsed in his rented house, is taken for reasons of geographical expediency to be nursed in Pepa's home. The result is an extraordinary confusion of roles, with everyone under the same roof simultaneously occupying the position of legitimate owner and illicit intruder. María, as León's legitimate wife, becomes an intruder in the home of the woman to whom he is adulterously attracted. When Pepa 'steals' into María's bedroom, disturbing her intimacy with León, she becomes an intruder in her own home: 'Estoy de más aquí' (916). This last phrase—relating adultery to the excess on which capitalism depends—is echoed when Pepa's husband Cimarra describes León as 'el que por la moral, por la ley, por la religión, está de más en este horrible encuentro de tres personas allí donde no debe haber más que dos' (954). Cimarra in turn is both legal owner and intruder when he returns to reclaim his position as Pepa's husband and 'steal' his daughter; he repeatedly lurks like a burglar outside her home to which, as her husband, he has right of access. At the end he signs an agreement banning him, as an 'intruso' and 'usurpador' (947, 949), from 'trespassing' on property to which he has a legal claim (955): not only does he, as husband, have property rights over Pepa's person but, since she is an only child, he will automatically inherit management rights over the family home and fortune on her father's death. Here we have a case of figurative adultery between husband and wife: adultery has crept into the heart of marriage. When Pepa tells León of Cimarra's reappearance, they are in the 'Sala Increíble' or 'museo': the collector's items displayed on its walls start to revolve around León in a 'confusa masa', linking the circulation of commodities to the confusion of familial and extra-familial roles (938). This blurring of the difference between marriage and adultery is conveyed by the characters' difficulty in knowing how to address one other: Pepa calls León 'Hombre, amigo, amante, esposo, o no sé qué' (944); León addresses her as 'querida amiga y esposa mía, esposa por una ley que no sé definir' (956–7). Cimarra's conversation with the priest Paleotti (overheard by León, the intruder in this instance) about his own marriage to and figurative adultery with Pepa, and about León's quasi-adultery with and figurative marriage to her, takes place in the 'Galería de la Risa' lined with political cartoons forming 'la historia del siglo escrita en carcajadas' (949), implying that this dissolution of boundaries constitutes the history of modernity.

The issue of the invasion of the private sphere by 'the social' is explicitly raised in the novel by the Church's intrusion into domestic affairs, the practice of the confessional having been extended by the Catholic Church in the course of the nineteenth century as a form of social regulation designed to compete with that exercised by lay reformers (Corbin in Perrot 1990: 549). María's confessor Paleotti challenges León's domestic authority by intervening in their private relationship, producing another figurative adultery. When Paleotti says to León, 'nos vive doña María', he casts himself in the role of duplicate husband, as León observes (908). León in turn accuses Paleotti of having made María into her husband's concubine: another case of adultery between husband and wife (929). In this novel where everyone is eavesdropping on everyone else—for its theme is the invasion of privacy—the confessor is the supreme eavesdropper. As Paleotti himself says, 'Es imposible que un sacerdote entre dos días seguidos en una casa sin saber todo lo que ocurre en ella' (952).

At the end of the novel León finds himself barred from his wife's body—lying in state in the chapel of Pepa's family home, in a shocking confusion of the familial and the extra-familial—both by Paleotti as her confessor, and by the statue of San Luis Gonzaga over the altar which is the spitting image of María's brother, Luis Gonzaga. As a trainee missionary, Luis represents the Church's role in social regulation; as noted previously, social reform, even in a lay context, was regularly referred to as 'missionary' activity. María's relationship with her brother is the most complex of all those in the novel, superimposing near incest on figurative adultery. León calls María's subordination to her brother's religious influence 'una especie de infidelidad' (798), for like her confessor he usurps León's role as head of the family. León challenges him: '¿Quién te ha llamado a gobernar el hogar ajeno?' (821). That María's and Luis's love for each other borders on the incestuous is clear: when Luis dies with his head on her shoulder, she covers him with 'ardent' kisses; when she dies, she asks to be buried next to him (822). If, in this novel, adultery represents the intrusion of an outside agent into the home, incest represents the threat of sameness resulting from rejection of the outside world: in both cases distinctions are eroded. Luis is an intruder into María's marriage, but as her brother—an identical twin in all but sex (even here the difference is slight, given his feminine features)—he is part of her family.[5] The definition of the family is breaking down because it is impossible to say where the boundary is between what is outside it and what is inside it. This problem is posed by the novel's title, for it is not clear what León's 'family' is. Is it the married couple he forms with María, the ideal but illicit family he forms with Pepa and Monina, or the Tellerías as his 'familia política'?

Luis's death from a wasting disease—the nineteenth-century female disorder of anorexia nervosa, in his case masked as religious asceticism—is linked with waste in its opposite sense of excess consumerism through the statue of his namesake San Luis Gonzaga that presides over the Fúcars' temple to capitalist

[5] The phrase 'hermanos del alma' used of María and Luis prefigures its use in Alas's *La Regenta* to refer to Ana's relationship with her confessor. The linking of mysticism and disease (anorexia) in the effeminate Luis is also repeated in Ana. Like Ana and her childhood figurative brother Germán, María and Luis imitate St Teresa and her brother by running away to fight the Moors.

over-accumulation. That María's funeral should, at her request, be held in this chapel, decorated with exotic pot plants from the conservatory, inscribes her in the imagery of consumerist excess and commodification of the natural associated with adultery. (Her reading of fashionable imported French devotional literature (871) also links her with the circulation of consumer goods that breaks down national boundaries.) The incestuous refusal of healthy natural flow, represented by Luis's unnatural 'cultivation' of disease (811), and the market model of circulation, which breaks down all boundaries, both lead to sameness and to waste: consumption in its two senses of consumerism and wasting away. Luis starves himself to death whereas in Pepa's 'palace of indigestion' everyone is overeating, but the results are similar. Indeed, María's and Luis's near incest/figurative adultery finds its inverted mirror-image in Pepa and León, bound together not only by near adultery but also by figurative incest: the text keeps reminding us that they were reared together as brother and sister. Ironically, it is this that allows them to constitute the ideal Krausist family, albeit adulterous: Sanz del Río repeatedly talks of the 'fraternal' nature of family love, which enables it to provide a basis for 'the brotherhood of man'. The novel poses the problem of distinguishing, in this world where all boundaries are being eroded, not only between marriage (good fusion) and adultery (bad confusion), but also between good forms of fraternal love (León and Pepa's mutually supportive but illicit relationship) and bad (the licit but mutually devouring relationship between María and Luis).

Although Catholic traditionalism, figured by incest, and the modern ethos of the market, figured by adultery, both lead in the novel to a breakdown of family boundaries, there is an important difference between the two. For, in the former case, the breakdown results from stagnation while, in the latter, it results from circulation; the second option is at least, in terms of both economic and medical discourse, healthy. Part I focuses on Luis Gonzaga's intrusion into León's and María's household, and parts II and III focus on the various combinations of marriage and adultery centred on the Fúcars' consumerist palace, implying that there has been a move from the religious to the economic model: progress of a sort. In both cases, women—María and Pepa—are the casualties. The emphasis throughout on intruders in the home shows that at this stage Galdós is principally concerned with the breakdown of the boundary between the public and private spheres that occurs when the former invades the latter. In his subsequent 'novels of modernity', he will become increasingly concerned with the breakdown that occurs when women start to leave the private sphere for the public. From now on, women will cease to be victims and will become agents.

LA DESHEREDADA

Like *La familia de León Roch*, this first of Galdós's 'novels of modernity' opens with a discussion of national life, this time set not in a watering hole but in a location that represents an even greater dissolution of forms: Madrid's municipal lunatic asylum, Leganés. Water imagery is still present: Isidora's father Rufete is being subjected to water therapy—the principal nineteenth-century treatment for insanity (Corbin in Perrot 1990: 660)— as she arrives to see him.[6] Leganés stands for the unmappable city: '¡Oh Leganés! Si quisieran representarte en una ciudad teórica [. . .] no habría arquitectos ni fisiólogos que se atrevieran a marcar con segura mano tus hospitalarias paredes' (Pérez Galdós 1966: 967). Galdós's novel is a parallel attempt to map the unmappable contours of modern city life, which dissolves the private in the public, just as the inmates of Leganés are subjected to public surveillance in the exercise yard. The latter is described as a 'bolsa de contratación de manías' (968), for it is above all the world of commerce that is shown to be responsible for the remapping of both public and private relations. As she waits in the asylum director's office, Isidora gazes at the map of Spain on the wall, with its statistics and boundaries and pictures of modern transport and industry (974–5), for the function of this official 'mapa gráficoestadístico'—like Madoz's mid-century *Diccionario geográfico-estadístico-histórico de España*— is to construct the nation as a bounded, compartmentalized unit under State surveillance and control.

---

[6] Pla et al. (1987: 106) quote an 1879 news report on Leganés, praising its modern 'departamento de baños' on the best foreign lines.

As a municipal institution, Leganés provides an image of State surveillance and control as deranged as Rufete's fantasies of national life. Indeed, the secretary running the director's office turns out to be one of its inmates. Rufete's madness consists in thinking that he is the State: that is, in having confused his private self with the public sector to the point that the former is wholly taken over by the latter. He had previously worked in 'Propiedades del Estado', and as secretary to three provincial governors (972): the agents of central control and homogenization after the 1833 local government reform which divided the nation into forty-nine provinces administered on the French centralized model (Artola 1973: 241). For Rufete, State business ('esas cosas de gobernar') is principally a matter of the national economy: his papers are filed under the headings 'National Debt', 'State Pensions', 'Customs', 'Banking', and 'Property Register'; another file, linking the State to the new form of social regulation that is town planning, is titled 'Urbanización de Envidiópolis' (973). The astronomical sums of pesetas which Rufete tots up in his head keep 'dissolving' into 'metal líquido' (968) for, when the role of State regulation is to guarantee the freedom of the market, facilitating the conversion of wealth into 'liquid assets', control and dissolution merge impossibly.

The novel contrasts the crazed mobility of modern society with the ordered, closed, but claustrophobic world of the *ancien régime*, represented by the palace of the Marquesa de Aransis, with Beethoven playing on the piano, dust sheets over the furniture, and the room where Virginia de Aransis 'murió de encierro' (1024): an inversion of Isidora's story, which charts her move from the private to the public sphere as she goes into circulation.[7] Isidora's first visit to the Aransis palace relates her demands for equality—'¿Somos iguales, sí o no?' (1029)—to her intrusion into its closed walls; appropriately, freedom being a function of the market, the doorkeeper who lets her in works as a broker dealing in 'fondos públicos': the 1868 Revolution's package of economic freedoms had removed previous restrictions on the use of financial intermediaries, allowing any (male) citizen to act in such a capacity (García Delgado 1985:

---

[7] Sieburth (1994) sees the Aransis palace as an image of high art, threatened by the new world of mass production represented by Isidora.

404). Her second visit, when the Marquesa disillusions her about her claim to the title, coincides with the masses taking to the streets on the declaration of the First Republic. The Marquesa's static social order, based on the inheritance of property, is doomed; the lesson Isidora has learned is that wealth is acquired through private initiative in the public sphere of the market. And the public sphere par excellence is the street, open (in theory) to all. Galdós is fond of using the phrase 'echarse a la calle' in its double meaning of 'to take to the streets' and 'to start a revolution', for revolutions are made by those staking a claim to the public sphere. It is made clear that Isidora's social aspirations are linked to the new political demands of the masses, given a national voice for the first time by republicanism which also for the first time attempted to mobilize women politically: 'Su apetito de engrandecerse no era un deseo tan sólo, sino una reclamación' (1039). Republican rhetoric used the term 'clases desheredadas' to refer both to women and to the masses (Hennessy 1962: 85; Scanlon 1986: 10; Carr 1966: 312). In proclaiming her equal rights, Isidora is not so much wanting to join the aristocracy as posing the question of what does the liberal principle of equality mean for those whom liberalism itself has excluded from citizenship: that is, vagrants and workers (deemed to have voluntarily alienated their freedom by entering into a relationship of dependence), and women (deemed 'naturally' dependent by virtue of their sex)? This triad is represented in the novel by Isidora's brother Mariano, the printer Juan Bou (a self-employed artisan who champions workers' rights),[8] and Isidora herself. Galdós's choice of Isidora as his principal focus shows his awareness that the problem of the 'disinherited' classes' access to the public sphere is posed particularly acutely by women. As vagrant and prostitute, Mariano and Isidora belong to a public sphere—the street— that is not recognized as part of civil society despite the fact

---

[8] The founding members of the Madrid section of the Workers' International, established in January 1869, included four printers and a lithographer, as well as a ropemaker (Mariano works briefly in a rope factory). This was the only Spanish section of the International where Marxism, strong among printing workers, predominated over anarchist tendencies, culminating with the foundation in 1879 of the Spanish Socialist Party by Pablo Iglesias, himself a typographer. Printing was the most modernized of Madrid's various industries, still largely artisanal in the Restoration period. See Bahamonde Magro and Toro Mérida (1978: 66); and Fernández García (1993: 508, 517).

that, in both cases, it integrates them into the market economy. Under current legislation on vagrants and prostitutes, Mariano would be liable to arrest; and Isidora could operate only if confined to a registered brothel that kept her off the streets and out of sight. The novel is a study of the problematic nature of the equation of freedom with the ability to enter the market.

The fact that Isidora, while embracing the new notion of social mobility via free enterprise, continues until late in the novel to cling to her fraudulent claim to an aristocratic title shows how, in Spain, the new liberal order coexists with relics of the old order based on birthright. Shubert (1990: 60–8) notes this overlap, with the nobility reinforcing its traditional landowning role by purchasing disentailed land, and the new bourgeoisie buying titles of nobility from the State; but nevertheless insists that this was a move to a bourgeois order in which ownership and rights are based, not on inheritance, but on entry to the market. The Marqués de Fúcar in *La familia de León Roch*, mentioned in *La desheredada* and later novels, is a perfect example. The Aransis palace, likened to a cemetery, represents the death of the old order based on birthright, similarly illustrated by the fraudulent nature of Isidora's claim to an inheritance. As a 'desheredada', she is not deprived of a rightful inheritance but a member of the 'clases desheredadas', theoretically equal but in practice denied entry to civil society, despite being enmeshed in the market. Once she abandons her claims to status based on inheritance, she is logically bound for a career as a prostitute, for how else could a woman enter the market as a 'free individual'? The problem, of course, is that the liberal 'free individual' is by definition a self-made man; the notion of the self-made woman is a contradiction in terms. Isidora can become a female entrepreneur only by making herself into a consumer object, thus—like the worker—'voluntarily' alienating her freedom.

The socialist doctrine of Juan Bou, in proclaiming 'los derechos del pueblo', poses the question: who is the 'pueblo'? That is, who constitutes the nation: all Spaniards, or only some of them? Sanz del Río's *Ideal de la humanidad* throughout used the term 'pueblo' to refer to the nation, the term 'nación' being used in its old sense of 'raza', though 'nacional' is used in its modern meaning of pertaining to the nation-State. Hobsbawm (1990: 14–16) notes that the Real Academia Española dictionary does not give 'nación' its modern meaning of 'nation-State' until the 1884 edition, three years after *La desheredada*; previous editions defined the term as a 'conjunto de habitantes de un territorio, país o reino' without any mention of attachment to a State. The narrator of *La desheredada* describes as 'egoísta' —lacking the Krausist virtue of reciprocity—Bou's notion of a workers' State, in which only workers are recognized as 'the people': 'Nosotros, los que no tenemos las manos llenas de callos, no éramos pueblo; vosotros, los propietarios, los abogados, los comerciantes, tampoco erais pueblo' (1078).[9] Who, in other words, constitutes the nation if only certain Spaniards have civil rights and therefore citizenship? Bou looks forward to a time when, under collective ownership, money and with it wages will have been abolished, and individuals will simply exchange their labour (1082-3). If labour and not property is the basis of citizenship, we still have the problem of a definition of citizenship that excludes some Spaniards; that is, unless labour is made compulsory for the whole population.[10] Indeed, Mariano and Isidora—as vagrant and prostitute—would fare worse under a system equating citizenship with labour than under a market economy, which at least allows Mariano to 'speculate' in the products of his scavenging—he is described as knowing more 'Economía política' than most university graduates (1100)—and

---

[9] The use of 'vosotros' in this sentence gives an insight into the social composition of Galdós's presumed readership, which is also constructed as male: at the start of the novel, madness in women is described as different from that in 'nosotros' (969).

[10] Bou's political ideas echo the insistence of the Republican Party (founded October 1868) during the *sexenio revolucionario* of 1868–74 that property should derive from labour (Bahamonde Magro and Toro Mérida 1978: 60). This was seen by conservatives and liberals—including the Krausist Giner de los Ríos (Díaz 1973: 148)—as a threat to the 'natural' right to property. Republican demands in 1868 for the 'right to work' were likewise seen as a threat to freedom of contract (Bahamonde Magro and Toro Mérida 1978: 61). However, Bou's utopia without money seems more in line with the International's insistence on the abolition of private property. See Bahamonde Magro and Toro Mérida (1978: 60-3), who note that parliamentary discussions used the terms 'socialist' and 'republican' interchangeably. Díaz (1973: 237) notes that at the time Spanish socialist demands for the abolition of property were based more on Proudhon than Marx. Bou's utopia based on the exchange of services echoes the anarchist concept of 'mutual aid'. In his 1871–2 articles in the *Revista de España*, Galdós attacked federal republicanism and the International for promoting the destruction of property, expressing repeated horror at the 1871 Paris Commune (Pérez Galdós 1982). When in the early 1900s Galdós became a republican supporter, he called the moderate liberals he had supported in the 1870s a 'disaster' (Pérez Galdós 1982: p. xi and *passim*).

Isidora to traffic in her property in her person. The issue of Isidora and Mariano's rights is set against the background of Amadeo I's resignation, the Federal Republic, and the Restoration of the monarchy under Alfonso XII, because it raises questions of legitimacy that concern not just their inheritance of the Aransis estate but the constitution of the nation. As mentioned in the Introduction, the 1869 Constitution placed sovereignty in 'the nation', introducing universal suffrage (meaning all males over 25). The First Republic's draft Constitution (which never reached the statute books), in addition to declaring Spain a federation of seventeen autonomous States, defined sovereignty as lying in 'the people'. Krausist reformers supported national sovereignty, with suffrage based on a limited property qualification, but were against popular sovereignty, implying universal suffrage, on the grounds that the masses needed to be educated before being enfranchised. The 1876 Constitution revoked universal suffrage by reintroducing a relatively high property qualification, dropping the notions of both national and popular sovereignty, and placing sovereignty in the joint hands of the monarchy and parliament (Solé Tura and Aja 1978: 57–9, 65–7, 70–2; Díaz 1973: 165). The issue of national sovereignty is implicit in Isidora's visit with Miquis to the Retiro and the Prado, both of which had been Crown property till the 1868 Revolution, which declared them the property of the nation and opened them to the public (Pla *et al.* 1987: 32, 63). Mariano's attempt to assassinate Alfonso XII can be seen as his inarticulate protest against the Restoration State apparatus which had reneged on the principles of national and popular sovereignty.[11]

The *sexenio revolucionario* of 1868–74 was also, as the novel notes, marked by the threat to national boundaries posed by cantonalist secession under the First Republic, and by the Carlist and Cuban Wars. Like Cimarra in *La familia de León Roch*, Melchor Relimpio, accused of embezzling public funds in his post as Provincial Governor under the Republic, is put in charge of customs and excise in Cuba: a key issue in the independence struggle, raising the issue of economic as well as political

---

[11] Gordon (1972) gives information on the 1880 trial of Otero, convicted and executed for his attempted assassination of the young Alfonso XII in 1879, on whom Mariano's story is clearly based; see also Dendle (1982).

boundaries. Joaquín Pez also takes up a government post in Cuba to get himself out of debt, while Sánchez Botín makes a fortune out of buying up credit slips ('abonarés') from soldiers returning from the Cuban War and trading them in for government bonds. The corruption associated with State administration in Cuba suggests that the threat to national boundaries—Cuba being constitutionally a province of Spain—is linked to the invasion of the State by the market.[12] As parliamentary deputy and former minister, Sánchez Botín also lines his pockets through involvement in election rigging, and the use of political influence to secure government subsidies for his railway company (reminiscent of the notorious abuse of political influence by the financier Salamanca in the 1840s and 1850s), fraudulently confusing public interests with his own (1090).[13] As Joaquín Pez comments, the only way to make a private fortune in Spain is through State business (1088). By making Isidora the mistress successively of Joaquín Pez, Sánchez Botín, and Melchor Relimpio, Galdós links the conversion of the State into a marketplace to her prostitution, for both threaten the public/private distinction.

The issue of national sovereignty is posed also by the novel's insistence on the internationalization of the economy, with its dependence on French capital, dominant till the 1870s when British interests began to compete (Carr 1966: 343, 391). Joaquín Pez is in debt to French credit companies (probably a reference to the Crédit Mobilier whose Spanish offshoot had such a hold over the Spanish economy). The world of fashion is depicted as a French import; the dressmaker Madame Eponina who seduces Isidora is French.[14] Like her successor Rosalía de Bringas, Isidora is seduced not so much by men as by consumerism, which promises freedom and equality to

---

[12] In an 1872 article in the *Revista de España*, Galdós described 'la cuestión de Cuba' as a threat to 'la integridad nacional' (Pérez Galdós 1982: 28). From 1886 to 1890 he was member of parliament for Guayama in Puerto Rico (like Cuba, technically a province of Spain), in Sagasta's administration.

[13] Carr (1966: 281) notes that Salamanca, who made his fortune through 'speculation in the borderlands of public and private finance', was the model for Galdós's treatment of national life. For the scandal over Salamanca's granting of government subsidies to his own railway company, see Vicens Vives (1969: 383).

[14] Aldaraca (1992: 111) quotes an 1875 article in the women's magazine *La Guirnalda*, for which Galdós wrote, which warns against fashion as a product of 'el industrialismo francés' whose 'novedades sirven para explotar a las familias'.

all—a social mobility described as a counterfeit equality: 'la moneda falsa de la igualdad' (1019). The advent of the First Republic, which promises the extension of civil rights to 'the people', is set against the background of carnival masks displayed in the shop windows as the city centre is turned into a consumerist spectacle: an 'abierto bazar, exposición de alegrías' seen by gaslight, with a 'river' of people 'flooding' the streets in a 'fluido magnético conductor de misteriosos apetitos' (1058–9). Continuing this imagery of dissolution, the Republican period will constitute a 'marea revolucionaria' (1064).

Water imagery is everywhere in this novel, conveying the fluidity and fluctuations of the market-place, as distinctions break down and goods flow in an unceasing stream. The 'inundation' of the State by the morality of the market is represented by the Peces 'coleando' in every sphere of the public administration, their 'principios líquidos' confusing public and private spheres, the former being a giant fish tank while the latter is leaking ('haciendo agua') (1034, 1066). Fashion, with its stress on the ever-new, is a sea in incessant motion: when Isidora tries on French fashions, she sees in the mirror 'las inmensidades movibles del mar' (1114). Her expenditure on fashion accessories makes her a 'liquidadora' (1135), whose end will inevitably be bankruptcy ('liquidación'). Her house, mirroring her own conversion into secondhand goods, is furnished with the proceeds from 'liquidaciones' as those higher up the social scale auction off their possessions to pay their debts (1064); Isidora in turn will pawn her property in the chapter titled 'Liquidación'. In the chapter titled 'Disolución', her intoxication with consumerism is explicitly linked to the alcoholic 'mareo' of José Relimpio (1152), who does the shopping and loves looking at himself in the mirror, and whose obsession with double-entry bookkeeping serves only to record the circulation of goods: that is, the 'liquidation' of his and Isidora's assets as the debit columns 'engulf' the credit columns like 'olas de un piélago tempestuoso' (1077).[15] José Relimpio had abandoned his treatise on accountancy at the sections titled 'Mi cuenta', 'Su cuenta', and 'Cuenta común', because the flow of money makes it impossible to tell what belongs to whom (1014).

[15] Berkowitz (1951: 15) notes that the margins of many of the novels in Galdós's library are covered with columns of handwritten accounts, showing that he kept redoing his sums always to end up with a negative balance.

The Paseo de la Castellana, where the members of Madrid high society turn themselves into a display of fashion exhibits, is also described as a 'torrent' producing a 'bonito mareo'. As Miquis notes, it is a 'noria' because the circulation of wealth makes today's creditors tomorrow's debtors (994). The image of the 'noria' recurs in the different sense of the 'treadmill' with the unstoppable 'rueda' in the rope factory where Mariano briefly works, the ever-turning handle of Emilia Relimpio's sewing machine, and the rotating plate on which Juan Bou carves his typographical designs, for consumption and production form an inseparable cycle. Despite his socialist ethos of production, Juan Bou is locked in the world of commodities by his printing of advertising copy, brand labels, and cheap mass-produced literature (1079).

The consumerist city described in *La desheredada* is one in which the streets have been invaded by the masses ('la muchedumbre'), for the world of mass-produced commodities creates a mass society. As Benjamin notes in his description of Baudelaire's Paris, the modern city is the public sphere of the street, which turns people as much as things into consumer exhibits, available to all—even those who cannot buy—in the form of the spectacle (1989: 50, 57, 173).[16] If consumption creates the public, it is advertising—the display of commodities—that creates the mass public. Galdós's 'novels of modernity' are concerned with appearances not in the sense that they are false, but because—as Simmel noted (1990: 122)—modern city life is based on visual display. In his 1913 preface to the French edition of *Misericordia*, Galdós described himself as a Baudelairean *flâneur* consuming the spectacle of the passers-by (Pérez Galdós 1972: 224). In practice, Galdós's novel depicts a female *flâneur*: Ledger (1995: 266–7) notes that women were a very visible presence in the public spaces of the modern city. Isidora sees the city centre—'aquel Madrid tan bullicioso, tan movible'—as a jumble of commodities whose 'infinitas variedades' resulting from the proliferation of brand names blur into the sameness of mass production (1011): what Benjamin called the sameness of the ever-new (1989: 172). The breathless catalogue of consumer objects that follows reads like a

---

[16] Sieburth notes that 'Isidora has been learning the laws of what Guy Debord calls the society of the spectacle' (1994: 37).

description of one of the nineteenth-century World Exhibitions which Benjamin proposed as an image of modernity (1989: 164–6): Galdós's first visit to Paris in 1867, before embarking on a literary career, not only introduced him to Balzac's novels but also took him to the Second Paris World Exhibition—a fitting double initiation for a novelist of modern city life. Corbin (1990: 204–5, 214) observes that the prostitute was an essential ingredient of the visual display that is the hallmark of the modern city, noting that the prostitute's self-exhibition at the same time indicated the failure of regulationism (aimed at enclosing prostitutes to keep them out of view) and generated increased regulationism (the debate around prostitution reached its height in Europe between 1876 and 1884). Corbin also observes that contemporary hygienists believed the level of 'sexual commerce' to be directly related to increases or decreases in commerce as such (1990: 247).

The appearances that are so important in this world of consumerist spectacle—the mirrors in which Isidora consumes her own image include shop windows (Fernández Cifuentes 1988: 309)[17]—are real enough, but their function is to create false needs: Isidora constantly justifies buying non-essential goods on the grounds that she 'needs' them. This creates a gap between exchange value and use value, mirroring the spiralling of credit whereby tokens of monetary value become detached from their referent. As Fernández Cifuentes notes in his perceptive article: 'Wherever [Isidora] looks in the city, she will only find signs for sale and the selling of signs' (1988: 310). Tsuchiya, developing these perceptions, relates Isidora's construction of herself as exhibition object to Baudrillard's notion of the simulacrum, noting that this problematizes representation by fusing the false with the real (1998: 204): an anticipation of concerns more commonly associated with postmodernism that we shall encounter in later chapters and to which I shall return in my conclusion. Laqueur (1990: 231–2; 1992: 213) proposes

---

[17] Fernández Cifuentes is, to my knowledge, the only critic to have related Galdós's depiction of the modern city in *La desheredada* to Walter Benjamin's writings on 19th-century Paris. Sieburth (1994: 90–1) draws on Benjamin's 'The Work of Art in the Age of Mechanical Reproduction' in her interesting discussion of what she sees as the novel's critique of a growing mass culture based on the notion of reproduction. On the changing relation of bodies to cities, and the importance of the visual, see Sennett (1991, 1994).

that prostitution is the embodiment of 'pure exchange' for, as in usury, nothing is produced. Citing Gallagher, he notes: 'what multiplies through her [the prostitute] is not a substance but a sign: money.' Thus '[p]rostitution becomes, like usury, a metaphor for the unnatural multiplication not of things but of signs without referents'. *La desheredada*, like the later *La de Bringas*, links prostitution and usury as emblems of this consumerist economy based on excess, in which value lies in appearance (signs) rather than in substance (things). Isidora's love of luxury items is not so much a sign of aristocratic distinction as of her seduction by the rhetoric of the market, which replaces the necessary with the superfluous. When Isidora's uncle from El Toboso (Dulcinea's birthplace in the *Quixote*, a sign that he lives in a world of delusion) insists that society is not marching towards equality and the loss of 'esos tabiques que separan a la Humanidad en compartimientos' (1062), he makes the mistake of equating social distinction with the fashion for French clothes, cooking, and other imports, oblivious to the fact that fashion is precisely what is creating sameness. But he has put his finger on a central paradox: namely, that—as Benjamin perceived—the function of fashion is to level distinctions by encouraging everyone to be 'distinguished'. Hence the problem of distinctions created by the fact that Isidora's 'distinguished' appearance makes her indistinguishable from a duchess (1087); the novel notes that this problem of distinctions is compounded by the introduction of increasingly cheap ready-made—that is, mass-produced—clothes (1019). In her 1889 essays 'La mujer española', Pardo Bazán noted that imitation of the latest fashions made it impossible to distinguish a magistrate's daughter from an aristocratic heiress, but that their likeness was 'counterfeit': that of 'la reproducción galvanoplástica a la moneda de viejo cuño' (1981: 56–7). In this society where value lies in appearance and not in substance, signs are everything.

Simmel (1990: 461) observed that fashion blurs differentiation with conformity because it is driven by the dominant social stratum's desire to differentiate itself from the other classes, but is then imitated by the subordinate strata, requiring the former constantly to invent new fashions to distinguish itself. Imitation—and its accompanying emotion, envy—was seen as the mark of modern consumer society by Gabriel Tarde in his theoretical work *Les Lois de l'imitation* (1890) (Williams

1982: 346–84).[18] Tarde saw this levelling process as a democratizing force; Galdós is closer to Benjamin in seeing the ever-same as a problem. Madrid is the city of envy—'Envidiópolis', as Isidora's father called it—because the market's promise of freedom and equality promotes 'cursilería', described as 'el prurito de competencia con la clase inmediatamente superior' (1035). In emphasizing 'lo cursi' in his *novelas contemporáneas*, Galdós is identifying Spain's insertion into capitalist modernity; indeed, into a global network of economic relations. In his 1897 speech on Pereda's election to the Spanish Royal Academy, Galdós noted that Spain had modernized by imitating other nations (Pérez Galdós 1972: 193). His choice of fashion as his emblem of modernity emphasizes that desire for the new is based on the imitation of foreign models: French *nouveautés*. In their desire for upward social mobility—to be 'like' the rich, which in this society based on visual spectacle is indistinguishable from 'being' rich—Isidora and Mariano are not rebelling but doing what is expected of citizens in a consumer society. They do not represent the demands of a budding socialism—that is Bou's role, motivated not by envy but by a desire to abolish the consumer economy—but the aspirations unleashed by the new capitalist mass society. Galdós's novel exposes the contradictions of the ideology of the market, whose unregulated competition promises freedom and equality while ensuring that only the 'big fish' get the pickings. This contradiction is articulated in Manuel Pez's slogan, coined at the Restoration's beginning, of 'el Orden armonizado con la Libertad, la Libertad armonizada con el Orden' (1066): a clear reference to Cánovas's equation of the defence of freedom with the defence of private property. There is nothing counterfeit about Isidora and Mariano's claims to be equal; the fraud, which offers them 'la moneda falsa de la igualdad', is perpetrated by their father, speaking in his madness as the voice of a State which exists to defend capitalism. Mariano's discovery that the mobility of the market offers equality only in theory leads him to express his envy by becoming an abortive regicide. As a child he had stabbed Zarapicos for having infringed 'los sagrados derechos de la propiedad' (1006) in appropriating his cardboard soldier's hat, acquired

---

[18] For information on Tarde's work and its reception in Spain, see note 1 to Chapter 6.

on the market in a toyshop stock clearance. He will kill those who deprive him of what liberal market theory says is his by right, or those who represent the system that promises him equality through the market but denies it in practice. Isidora's solution is 'suicidio': to kill herself metaphorically by becoming a commodity that circulates on the market, for goods, it seems, have greater social mobility than people. If she cannot have articles of commerce, she will become one.

The novel's setting against the declaration and fall of the First Republic makes the issue of property rights central. As Carr notes (1966: 327), federal republicanism—contrary to the frequent supposition that its major political exponent and leader, Pi y Margall, was 'the Spanish Proudhon'—supported the extension of property rights through cheap credit facilities, not the abolition of private property (that was the demand of the Workers' International). On the declaration of the Republic in 1873, Madrid traders, feeling threatened by the access to power of the lower middle classes and sectors of the masses, organized armed militias (Voluntarios de la Propiedad) to defend property; some Andalusian revolutionary juntas announced plans for land takeovers and in Montilla the Land Registry (Registro de la Propiedad) was burnt down. In September 1873 Castelar, taking over as Federal Republican President, calmed middle-class fears about property redistribution by dissolving the Republican popular militias (Voluntarios de la República), alienating lower-class Republican supporters (Bahamonde Magro and Toro Mérida 1978: 87–91). Isidora and Mariano are responding to this failure to incorporate the lower classes into a political system based on the ownership of property and, indeed, on the availability of credit.

La desheredada is a novel about property rights not only because of Isidora's claim to the Aransis estate but also because, as a prostitute, she claims her right to dispose of her 'property in her person'. If her lawsuit was an attempt to establish her 'verdadero estado civil' (1059), so, in selling herself, she not only becomes an object but asserts her right to enter the market which in liberal political theory constitutes civil society. In his study on Baudelaire, Benjamin (1989: 171) proposed the prostitute as the embodiment of modern consumerism because, in exchanging money for sex, she is both article of sale and seller. Critics—Vilarós (1993); Jagoe (1994); Sieburth (in Willem 1993: 27–40; Sieburth 1994); Tsuchiya (1998)—have disagreed over whether Isidora's final plunge into the street as a prostitute working in the public domain should be interpreted as a symbolic death or as an assertion of independence, for it is both. She will ask '¿Soy o no soy?' (1143) because the novel poses the question: what is the status of a woman who abandons the private sphere for the public? In abandoning her child, she forfeits the only status women have: that of motherhood. And in becoming a 'public woman',[19] she loses her individuality, dying as Isidora and becoming one of the anonymous masses (1154, 1157). But at the same time entry to the market is the membership ticket of civil society. Isidora will say 'Yo me he muerto', but also 'Yo me basto y me sobro' (1156) and 'No dependo de nadie [. . .] Soy dueña de mi voluntad [. . .] deseo ser libre' (1159). The novel's hesitations over Isidora's final decision—it is important that she chooses prostitution freely —reflect the contradictions in contract theory, which maintains that the individual who sells his labour asserts his freedom by freely disposing of his property in his person ('alienation' in the liberal sense of the free disposal of property as opposed to mortmain), when in fact he is alienating himself in the negative sense that Marx would stress. The inclusion in the novel of Juan Bou shows that Galdós is responding to the new dissemination in Spain of socialist ideas. In preferring to prostitute herself to Juan Bou rather than marry him, Isidora is maintaining her belief in the market model whereby freedom and civic status consist in the ability to sell one's property. Except that women, though eligible to work, are not legally able to make contracts: so what is the legal status of Isidora's selling of her property in her person?

This ambiguity is echoed by the contemporary legal position of prostitutes in Spain, tolerated provided they submitted to state regulation in the form of medical inspection and confinement to licensed brothels. It is not clear whether Isidora is going to work on the streets (as a non-regulated prostitute or 'insumisa') or in a brothel (in which case she is wrong to think that selling herself will give her autonomy). The latter seems likely

---

[19] Pulido's *Bosquejos médico-sociales para la mujer* (1876: 113–14) notes that the RAE dictionary gives the original meaning of 'prostitution' as 'exposición pública', adding that what makes it a health risk is 'la publicidad del pecado'.

since she has given her word to a woman who has been tempting her with finery (1158). In which case the threat is not so much that of a woman gaining individual autonomy, as that of women gaining autonomy by setting up in business together, in a 'public' house 'manned' entirely by women. Isidora declares her self-sufficiency—refusing Augusto Miquis's and José Relimpio's support, having come to despise men—in the name of a feminine first-person plural: 'Nosotras nos vengamos con nosotras mismas' (1156). Prostitution represents women collectively affirming their right to enter the market by trading in their own bodies: turning themselves into property but also, in the act of selling it, paradoxically affirming their ownership. Indeed, the prostitute's body is the one commodity that remains its owner's property after being sold and can be sold over and over again.

As a used body, infinitely recycled, the prostitute also highlights the problematic position of waste in the market system. Corbin (1986: 89–135) has shown how nineteenth-century treatises on town planning and public health were obsessed with the question of waste disposal, as the proliferation of goods and bodies in the modern city threatened to choke the system. Just as capitalist development depends on an ever-increasing spiral of surplus profit being ploughed back into the system, so the circulation of goods produces a surplus that requires further circulation in the form of the recycling of rubbish. If the circulation of commodities blurs distinctions with its flow, blockages to the system produce an overflow engulfing everything in a formless swamp. *La desheredada* deals with the problem of excess in the double form of 'lujo' and of waste. Both come together in the figure of the prostitute: a luxury in that she represents surplus sexuality, and a waste-disposal unit in that contemporary medical theory—obsessed with the healthy circulation of fluids in the body, just as contemporary economic theory was obsessed with the circulation of wealth (Shuttleworth in Jacobus, Fox Keller, and Shuttleworth 1990: 47–68)— insisted on the need for the efficient elimination of surplus flow, including semen, which if blocked would rot and pollute the system. Corbin's classic study of prostitution in nineteenth-century France (1990) notes that the major advocate of state regulation of prostitution, Parent-Duchâtelet, was also the leading expert on the municipal sewage system, and that registered brothels were referred to as a 'seminal drain' (Corbin in Gallagher and Laqueur 1987: 211; Corbin 1990: 53). Scanlon (1986: 107) points out that the first three chapters of Parent-Duchâtelet's *De la prostitution dans la ville de Paris* (1836) were translated in Amancio Peratoner's *El Sexto, no fornicar. Estudio tomado de los más eminentes teólogos, filósofos y higienistas sobre los estragos que la prostitución y los excesos venéreos acarrean al individuo, a la familia, a la sociedad*, published in 1880, the year before the publication of *La desheredada*. Pulido's 1876 *Bosquejos médico-sociales para la mujer*, the only Spanish medical manual for women to discuss prostitution fully and frankly, justifies it as a necessary 'llaga depuratoria del organismo social', referring to Parent-Duchâtelet and quoting St Augustine's comparison of the prostitute to 'esas cloacas construidas en los más suntuosos palacios para recoger los productos corrompidos y asegurar la salubridad del aire' (1876: 116). Drains are both necessary to hygiene and sources of pollution. Prostitutes are bound to be an essential ingredient of a society based on consumerist excess, like that of *La desheredada*. Isidora's lovers (with the exception of Juan Bou, who wanted to marry her) are those who represent surplus profit (Sánchez Botín), excess expenditure (Joaquín Pez), and economic excrescences of various kinds (Melchor Relimpio's fraudulent money-making schemes, Gaitica's gambling dens). They are, in other words, 'sanguijuelas del pueblo': excrescences in the sense of parasites or 'drains' on the system. In syphoning off their excess, Isidora in turn becomes a leech or drain: part of the city's sewage system. At the end of the novel, José Relimpio describes her as having fallen into the mire ('cieno'). She is swallowed up by the swamp that is the city: 'La presa fue devorada, y poco después, en la superficie social, todo estaba tranquilo' (1161).[20]

The recurrent image of the leech links the depiction of a city of economic parasites, consuming rather than producing, to the problem of waste disposal. Leeches are necessary to the health of the system; moneylenders, as 'bloodletters', facilitate the

[20] For the image of 'swamp-city' with reference to Paris and London respectively, see Corbin (1986: 114) and Wilson (1991: 26–46). Wilson notes that this image, created in relation to London by Dickens among others, was used as a pretext for controlling the working classes, and especially prostitutes, through the regulation of public health. On the 19th-century representation of the prostitute see also Bernheimer (1989); Walkowitz (1992); Matlock (1994).

circulation of capital. Augusto Miquis, the novel's exponent of medical discourse who tries to 'regulate' Isidora's behaviour, insists on the need for healthy flow: 'la fluidez de la sangre' (992–3).[21] By this he means a circular reciprocity: 'La Humanidad es como el agua [. . .] Los ríos más orgullosos van a parar al mar, que es el pueblo; y de ese mar inmenso, de ese pueblo, salen las lluvias, que a su vez forman los ríos' (991). This self-renewing system is based on a fixed-energy model of the universe, 'conservándose invariablemente en el conjunto de su efecto total' (989). As Russett notes (1989: 128), such a notion was central to Herbert Spencer's economicist view of society, based on the idea of the need to 'balance the books'. The term *equilibrio* recurs throughout Galdós's work, as it does in that of contemporary hygienists, where it has the meaning of 'stability'.[22] *La desheredada* suggests that Spanish society has become 'unbalanced' because foreign debt and foreign imports are draining the nation's resources, and because the 'pueblo' is being 'drained' by the rich. In this sense, Isidora's revenge in becoming a prostitute 'draining' off their ill-gotten gains could be seen as a healthy corrective. Mariano's desire to be a 'leech' is also logical; as a vagrant, he is a drain on society reciprocating the draining of its resources by 'la alta vagancia' (1064) or the idle rich. But the reciprocity set up here turns the nation into one big drain. Isidora's aunt, La Sanguijuelera, sells leeches in her shop that is a model of thrift and hard work, for leeches do contribute to healthy flow when they are offset by productivity. She has a notice on the wall saying 'No loans or credit' for, if she is selling leeches, she cannot allow her clients to be leeches too. For the socialist Juan Bou, all those who do not contribute to production are 'sanguijuelas del pueblo' or drains on the country's resources ('pueblo' in the double sense of the lower classes and the nation), including his late wife, the spendthrift daughter of a tax collector. If the State drains the nation's

---

[21] Tsuchiya (1998: 211–13) suggests that Isidora, in offering to sell herself to Miquis, is subverting his discourse of social control; she sees Miquis as just one example of the generalized male surveillance to which Isidora is subjected as consumer object.

[22] An example clearly relating the concept to the Restoration obsession with public order is Rubio Galí's 1890 speech to the Real Academia de Medicina. This stated that 'el estado sano de la sociedad resulta de la ponderación, esto es, del equilibrio. [. . .] Se expresa bajo la palabra *Orden*' and argued for the need to achieve an 'equilibrio en movimiento' (Rodríguez Ocaña 1987: 204–5).

resources through tax—Miquis calls it a kind of 'communism' (1064)—Joaquín Pez and Melchor Relimpio consider that they have a right as civil servants to drain the State's coffers: another reciprocal system in which everyone is draining everyone else. Joaquín and Melchor, like Cimarra in *La familia de León Roch*, are given State positions in Cuba which, being on the nation's edge, functions as a kind of dumping ground for the system's wastrels.

La desheredada gives a lot of space to description of the city's margins, where its refuse is dumped and where the lower classes scrape a living from the waste products of a consumer society. The images of waste go together with the images of leeches, which drain excess blood to normalize the circulatory system. The rubbish tips are 'una piltrafa de limpieza para que no corrompiera el centro' (978). Corbin (1986: 93) notes that nineteenth-century social reformers were concerned with 'evacuating' both sewage and vagrants, the latter being seen as a source of infection. For this reason the ragpicker, like the prostitute, occupied a special place in the nineteenth-century social imaginary, as Corbin (1986: 115–21) and Benjamin (1989: 19) note. Both Corbin and Benjamin observe that the ragpicker appears in the mid-nineteenth century as new industrial processes allow refuse to be recycled; the concern in the early nineteenth century with containing waste is now replaced by an obsession with how to make it productive.[23] *La desheredada* shows the city's ragpickers, who live off waste, to be efficient drains—much like prostitutes—despite their unsanitary living conditions, for they recycle the national wealth. Mariano will become an unproductive parasite only when he abandons scavenging for loitering outside the bullring. Galdós's description of the ragpickers Zarapicos and Gonzalete as 'comerciantes' who set the price of the commodities they trade in a makeshift version of the Stock Exchange (1004) is not entirely ironic, for they

---

[23] In Spain, Monlau (1868: 10) argued that bad smells were not only a health hazard but 'una pérdida para la fertilidad de los campos'. Hauser (1979: 234, 249–52), who started writing on public health issues in the Madrid press in the early 1880s, insists on the importance of recycling Madrid's rubbish and sewage, and gives detailed breakdowns of existing arrangements for doing so; he also uses the term 'los desheredados'. Santero's *Elementos de higiene privada y pública* (1885), in its lesson 119 on rubbish tips, describes these as a necessary evil since they allow the recycling of society's waste products (cf. the above discussion of prostitution as a 'necessary drain').

do keep the flow of goods moving.[24] They also demonstrate that even society's detritus is private property. But Galdós is clearly worried by a system that produces so much rubbish. The outlying slums where Mariano initially lives with La Sanguijuelera are described as a 'caricatura de una ciudad hecha de cartón podrido', running with industrial effluvia ('ríos de veneno') (977–8). La Sanguijuelera puts him to work in a rope factory, one of the industries denounced as a health hazard by public-health experts because of their use of 'despojos y grasas animales' (Huertas and Campos 1992: i. 162). The area south of the Rastro or flea market,[25] where El Majito's parents have their scrap metal business, is littered with 'basuras, escombros y residuos de carbón', and is 'cerca de donde, por fétidas bocas, arroja Madrid sobre el Manzanares lo que no necesita para nada' (998). Contemporary health experts were much concerned with Madrid's contaminated water supply (in 1879 it was estimated that the Canal de Isabel II supplying the city had water fit for drinking twenty-three days a year), and in particular with its inadequate drains: much of the city was without sewers, and all of its seven sewage outlets, producing an estimated 20 million litres of sewage a day, were channelled into the River Manzanares (Hauser 1979: 234; Magnien in Salaün and Serrano 1991: 115–16). The novel's descriptions of 'streams of poison' and sewage flowing into the Manzanares read as degraded versions of Miquis's vision of healthy natural flow. The shanty town among the rubbish tips in the Barranco de Embajadores—singled out by health experts because of its open sewer running into the Manzanares (Hauser 1979: 221–2) —is a 'forma intermedia entre la vivienda y la cloaca' and a 'ciudad movediza compuesta de ruinas', where even the surrounding hills look like 'montones de escombros y vertederos de derribos' (1004–5).[26]

---

[24] Hauser (1979: 319–20) quotes Mesonero Romanos's description of Madrid's flea market, the Rastro, as a 'lonja de contratación'.

[25] The Rastro was also criticized by health experts for selling secondhand clothes and mattresses from those who had died of infectious diseases (Hauser 1979: 320). Located in the Ribera de Curtidores, it was the centre of the leather industry, regarded as a health hazard because of the risk of 'miasmatic' contagion from the stench of skins being tanned in urine (Huertas and Campos 1992: i. 162).

[26] In an 1865 satirical article in *La Nación* on plans to widen the Manzanares (Pérez Galdós 1981: 32), Galdós praised 'este sucio y pacientísimo Job' for its 'caridad evangélica' in taking upon itself 'la lepra ajena'; his long list of Madrid's

This last area follows the 'línea de circunvalación' designated by the 1860 Castro Plan as the boundary of the new expanding city: the narrator notes that these outlying slums coincide with the future streets of the 'Ensanche' (991). (It was here that León Roch had his matrimonial home.) The city's margins are a polluted mix of the social and the natural—'Aquello no era aldea ni tampoco ciudad' (977)—as the waste products of a consumer society decompose in the open air and river, contaminating the countryside around. Isidora's and Mariano's position on the city's social fringes associates them with waste, Isidora becoming a prostitute-drain whose last lover Gaitica is described as a 'basurero animado' (1154), Mariano being rejected by society 'como se arroja al basurero un despojo inútil' (1147).

The discourse of hygiene used here is also the discourse of social reform: after Mariano's child murder, the press talks of the need for 'la curación del cuerpo social' (1010); Miquis—representing the new breed of professionally trained medical expert; by the start of the Restoration he has become director of one of Madrid's main hospitals (1068)—offers Isidora 'prescripciones higiénicas' and tells her to stay away from 'centros miasmáticos', meaning Madame Eponina's fashions (1113).[27] Santero's 1885 *Elementos de higiene privada y pública* (ii. 487) listed the following as 'social diseases': prostitution, alcoholism, vagrancy, gambling, crime, suicide; *La desheredada* contains them all in one form or another. Galdós's main personal connection with current reform campaigns was his doctor friend Tolosa Latour, a champion of penal reform and child health.[28] These

---

detritus carried away by the river includes the 'heces de hediondo perfume que quedan en los tocadores de esa ambulante prostitución que pasea las calles de Alcalá y de Sevilla'. During the *sexenio revolucionario*, Madrid city council—under popular control—debated the need to demolish the shanty town in the Barranco de Embajadores, described by a town planner as 'esas cloacas horribles [. . .] en donde viven, vegetan y duermen padres e hijos, lejos de toda noción de pudor y sin conocer el bienestar y encanto que a la familia añade un poco de luz, un poco de aire y un mucho de limpieza' (Bahamonde Magro and Toro Mérida 1978: 98–9).

[27] Pulido's *Bosquejos médicos-sociales para la mujer* (1876) warns women against reading novels on health grounds (51–71). He also suggests that, instead of writing 'novelas procaces, con las que contribuyen a fomentar peligrosos delirios en las muchachas de humilde condición', novelists should write about the need to widen job opportunities for women to save them from seduction and prostitution (127).

[28] Tolosa Latour published widely from 1880 onwards on children's diseases, childcare (including manuals for mothers), child labour, and legislation on child offenders, translating many foreign works. As editor of the *Diario Médico*, he

two concerns come together in the novel with Mariano. The question of penal reform is also raised with Isidora's stay in the women's prison in the Calle de Quiñones off the Calle de San Bernardo, where it had been relocated in 1842 (Répide 1989: 555). The chapter title refers to it as 'el Modelo' and the narrator talks of 'el vulgar y triste edificio llamado *Modelo* con descarada impropiedad' (1126), but the Cárcel Modelo for women—the 'cárcel de mujeres de Alcalá'—was not inaugurated till 1880, built precisely because of complaints about the shocking conditions in its predecessor in the Calle de Quiñones (Rivière Gómez 1994: 99). (In 1876, parliament also approved the building of the new Cárcel Modelo for men, which opened three years after the publication of *La desheredada* in 1884; built in the radial form of Bentham's Panopticon,

published chapter 1 of *La desheredada* and advertised Galdós's *Episodios nacionales*; he also founded the journals *Archivos de Ginecología y Enfermedades de la Infancia*, *El Hospital y el Niño*, and *La Madre y el Niño*—the last published extracts from *La familia de León Roch* and *El doctor Centeno* in 1883–4 (Jagoe 1994: 43). A founding member of the Sociedad Española de Higiene, Tolosa Latour headed the Natural Science section of the Madrid Ateneo, and was resident doctor at the Hospital del Niño Jesús and medical director of the Asilo de Huérfanos del Sagrado Corazón de Jesús, founded by Ernestina Manuel de Villena, the prototype for the philanthropist Guillermina in Galdós's *Fortunata y Jacinta*. In the 1890s he founded several seaside sanatoriums for children to combat scrofula and rickets (the disease deforming Isidora's child), and in 1904 was responsible for getting the Ley de Protección a la Infancia banning child labour through parliament. In 1879 he also translated from the French two works on water therapy: *Manual médico de hidroterapia* and *Hidroterapia*, the latter containing his own appendix 'El uso de los baños de mar en los niños'. He held the government posts of Secretario General del Consejo Superior de Protección a la Infancia y Represión de la Mendicidad—these two concerns are fused in Mariano as child vagrant—and Inspector del Cuerpo Médico Escolar, and Vocal del Consejo de Sanidad. In 1881—the publication date of *La desheredada*—he published the book *La protección médica al niño desvalido*. His statue in the Retiro describes him as an 'abnegado protector de la madre y del niño'. The information given here is taken from the Espasa-Calpe *Enciclopedia universal ilustrada europeo-americana* (1987–91) and Schmidt (1969).

In his essay 'Las españolas del porvenir' (1889: 205–14), Tolosa Latour praised the Krausist Escuela de Institutrices and Escuela de Comercio for saving women from dependence on 'algún *protector* de los que no pertenecen á ninguna Sociedad protectora'. In his prologue to the volume (pp. vii–viii), Galdós declares himself 'en continuo *flirtation* con la medicina [. . .] que considero llave del mundo moral' (p. viii). Galdós's library contained 28 medical texts (more than any other branch of science), plus 24 each on law and social science (including Rousseau's *Œuvres complètes* and Spencer's *Estudios políticos y sociales*, *Creación y evolución*, and *De la educación intelectual moral y física*), 29 on economics, 44 on political history, and 48 on political science (Berkowitz 1951: 18, 52, 182; Nuez 1990: 97). Ortiz Armengol (1996: 355) notes that from *La desheredada* onwards, Tolosa Latour provided Galdós with a professional source of information about medical matters.

it was the first in Spain to have an architectural design and organizational regime based on 'hygienic' principles[29]). Varela notes that Restoration bourgeois philanthropists were shocked by the communal existence in prisons and asylums, and kept pressing for a 'celular' division of space which increased surveillance while individualizing the inmates (Varela and Álvarez-Uría 1979: 234); even the 1884 Cárcel Modelo apparently offered such 'supervised privacy' only to those still awaiting trial (Santero 1885: ii. 561). The women's prison where Isidora is detained has private cells for those who can afford to pay, but subjects the poor to 'el bochorno de la sala común' (1139). The lunatic asylum at Leganés, which we are told is untouched by 'la administración reformista', heaps its inmates together in the common yard, the only form of 'privacy' being cages for the uncontrollable (967). As a result, both prison and asylum merely serve to contain society's rejects, doing nothing to reintegrate them into society as useful citizens. Indeed, Isidora's prison experience initiates her into the final stages of her descent into 'vice'.

The novel describes a society that has failed to produce a healthy balance between the natural and the social. Instead of civilizing the lower classes—Mariano, in addition to being described in terms of typically naturalist animal imagery, is a 'barbarian' and a 'kaffir' brought up in an 'estado casi salvaje' (1044–5, 1007)—it has turned them into human refuse. Miquis—the voice of public hygiene—takes Isidora for a walk in the Retiro Park, which—as 'un campo urbano, una ciudad de árboles y arbustos' (987)—seems to provide the ideal blend of city and country recommended by town planners: in 1882 Arturo Soria described it as 'El pedazo más grande y sano de

---

[29] Galdós praised the efficiency of the newly inaugurated Cárcel Modelo for men in an 1884 press article in *La Prensa* (Shoemaker 1973: 46–7); it is referred to in his 1895 novel *Nazarín* (Pérez Galdós 1895: 265) by its popular nickname 'el Abanico', so-called because of its Benthamite radial design. As Varela notes (Varela and Álvarez-Uría 1979: 234), its regulations—approved in 1883—laid down strict rules for the distribution of income derived from inmates' labour; most of that reverting to prisoners being placed in a savings bank until their release, thus inculcating habits of hard work and thrift. For a survey of Madrid prisons under the Restoration, see Iglesias Rodríguez in Bahamonde Magro and Otero Carvajal (1989: ii. 408–24). For Bentham's Panopticon, see Bentham (1995), including Božovič's excellent introduction.

nuestro pulmón' (Collins and Flores 1967: 163), allowing the circulation of fresh air. But the dominant image in the novel is that of the rubbish tip. Miquis's father-in-law, the lawyer Muñoz y Nones, is, jointly with his interest in public health, founding a reformatory to take child vagrants off the streets. His motto—'también la honradez es negocio' (1140)—implies belief in the possibility of a market system based on healthy flow and not on excess and waste. This is to be achieved by removing vagrants from the public sphere and putting them in a 'home': social regulation through the construction and enforcement of an institutionalized privacy. In a suggestive phrase, Tolosa Latour would in 1900 argue for legal reform to protect the young on the grounds that vagrant children were 'semejantes a monedas de cuño borroso que deben volver a la circulación y ser reacuñadas' (Varela and Álvarez-Uría 1991: 217). Muñoz y Nones's proposed reformatory, with its 'public privacy', is based on sound economic policy because it attempts to deal with the problem of waste—human refuse—by recycling it back into the system. Varela notes that the first Spanish law regulating child labour, passed under the Republic in 1873, was aimed at training them in a skill that would make them into useful citizens; throughout the Restoration, reformers complained that this law had never been implemented (Varela and Álvarez-Uría 1979: 221; Seminario de historia 1988: 155).[30] It has also been noted (Varela and Álvarez-Uría 1979: 163; Álvarez-Uría 1983: 134, 184, 245) that the 1870 Penal Code, under which Mariano would be tried, showed the beginnings of the influence in Spain of Morel's *Treatise on Degeneracy*, which viewed crime and madness as related lapses into a 'primitive' stage of human development. In describing the delinquent Mariano as a savage and an animal, and in raising the issue of hereditary transmission of degenerative traits (Rufete's 'monomanía' is passed on to Mariano and Isidora, and Isidora's child is deformed by rickets, suggesting that malfunctionings whose origin is socio-economic may be transmitted genetically), *La desheredada*, despite its positive depiction of Muñoz y Nones's reformism, is reflecting a growing concern that society is not

---

[30] The same Federal Republican legislation made it illegal for women to work, especially on becoming mothers (Tuñón de Lara 1976: 139).

progressing but regressing.[31] Indeed Leganés turns its inmates into animals by putting them in cages. Social reform, as well as consumerism, constructs citizens as individuals while undermining individuality.

The blurring of public and private through 'the social' will be further problematized in *Fortunata y Jacinta*, as Galdós moves from the treatment of those who abandon the private sphere of the family for the public world of the street—the vagrant and the prostitute—to the more complex case of the adulteress who occupies both places at once. Since it is normal for men to move in both public and private spheres—as opposed to Mariano's rejection of the private for the public—Galdós will, in order to deal with the problematic blurring of the two spheres, focus increasingly on—and give increased complexity to—his female characters.

LO PROHIBIDO

This novel—unlike *La de Bringas* and *Fortunata y Jacinta* which immediately precede and succeed it—focuses exclusively on adultery without mention of prostitution. It also deals exclusively

---

[31] Contemporary medical experts argued that 'monomanía' freed the criminal from responsibility for his acts. This issue was debated at the 1880 trial of Otero for his attempted assassination of Alfonso XII in 1879 (Varela and Álvarez-Uría 1979: 155–9). The theory of 'monomanía' was developed in Spain in the late 1850s and 1860s, under the influence of Morel, by the same Pedro Mata—favourably mentioned by Don Baldomero in *Fortunata y Jacinta*—who had modernized medical education in Spain in 1843, holding the Chair of Legal Medicine at Madrid University 1843–74. Mata was reluctant to accept Morel's belief that madness was hereditary but nevertheless insisted on the importance of knowing the criminal's family history (Álvarez-Uría 1983: 185, 187; Mata 1868). A friend of Prim (the liberal general responsible for the 1868 Revolution), he served on the Commission on the 1869 Constitution and was a parliamentary deputy in Serrano's revolutionary government, as well as being appointed Vice-Rector of Madrid University in 1869. In 1871 (just before *La desheredada* opens) he briefly served as Civil Governor of Madrid, banning gambling (cf. Isidora's last lover Gaitica), taking measures against crime and vagrants, and supporting charitable institutions (Toro Mérida and Prieto Alberca 1986: 17–18; Toro Mérida in Otero Carvajal and Bahamonde 1986: i. 285–98; Kaplan in Lida and Zavala 1970: 256). 'Monomanía' is also discussed by Pulido (1876: 358–73), who takes the reader round a lunatic asylum much like Galdós at the start of *La desheredada*, describing the case of a civil servant (kept on at his job because otherwise inoffensive) whose head was turned by the 1868 Revolution and who could be seen wandering the streets of Madrid muttering about his next political pamphlet.

with the world of high finance, in which the flow of capital echoes the circulation of women. Although it treats female adultery—Eloïsa and María Juana who succumb and their sister Camila who resists—this is relayed through the first-person narrative of their seducer, José María, unmarried but an adulterer since he is attracted only to married women. The novel is a failure because, in filtering its depiction of the female characters through José María's unreliable voice, it simplifies them.[32] The foregrounding of the male seducer, whose sexual transgressions do not problematize the public/private boundary except inasmuch as they turn women into adulteresses, is unable to compensate for this lack of complexity. Nevertheless, I wish to discuss *Lo prohibido* here, since it gives more information than any other novel about the impact of modernity on Madrid city life. Set in 1880–3, it is also the work which covers the period closest to the time when Galdós was writing his 'novels of modernity'. It thus helps us understand the cultural significance of adultery for his contemporary readers.

The narrator José María's arrival in Madrid from Jerez de la Frontera at the start of the novel, having given up his sherry business to live off invested capital, provides an excuse for a detailed description of the newly modernized, Europeanized city that had emerged from the second wave of 'urbanización' —a term used in the novel—after the 1868 Revolution. As a wealthy idler, José María is the *flâneur* 'consuming' the city, designed by town planners as a visual spectacle with its 'nuevas barriadas' and improvements to the façades of existing buildings, its 'expeditivos medios de comunicación', 'bonitísimos jardines' and theatres, and above all its 'variadas y aparatosas tiendas, no inferiores, por lo que desde la calle se ve, a las de París o Londres' (Pérez Galdós 1966: 1675). He moves house from one new district to another, for this is a city where—with improved transport, the circulation of capital, and the turnover of goods—things and people are on the move. His cousin Raimundo dreams he is Mayor of Madrid modernizing the city 'como un auténtico barón Haussmann', demolishing the existing Gran Vía in the name of 'arte, luz, higiene' to build a 30-metre wide avenue facilitating the flow of traffic (1698–9): plans for the building of a Gran

---

[32] For analysis of the novel's unreliable first-person narrator, see Terry (in Varey 1970: 62–89).

Vía on the lines of a Parisian boulevard were first mooted in 1862; a new plan, under discussion while Galdós was writing *Lo prohibido*, was approved in 1886, though building started only in 1910 (Fernández García 1993: 403, 438–9).[33]

By giving his narrator-protagonist a past in the sherry business in Jerez, Galdós is able to refer (1705) to the social agitation in that part of Andalusia; the reference is to 1882, the time of the so-called 'Mano Negra' unrest in the south, concentrated (as contemporary readers would have known) on the Jerez area—showing the underside to the capital's new affluence. It also allows him to stress the internationalization of the economy, with José María's Anglo-Spanish parentage and business interests, reflecting the influx of British capital since 1868. Varela Ortega (1977: 206) notes that Jerez wine producers (nicknamed 'angloandaluces'—that is, anti-nationalist—by protectionist Catalan industrialists and Castilian wheatgrowers) championed free trade in the 1880s. José María thus repeats the association of adultery with free trade made explicitly in the previous novel *La de Bringas*, as we shall see in the next chapter. We are told that, as a child, José María had lived in London at Sydenham, near the Crystal Palace that housed the first World Exhibition (1703). His friend Villalonga (principal informant to the narrator of *Fortunata y Jacinta*) is sent to England by the Ministry of Development to buy agricultural machinery (1694); Eloísa's husband Carrillo, with his 'manía anglopolítica', talks endlessly of English electoral reform and the English economy (1702, 1714); the narrator's English spinster friends are acquaintances of Herbert Spencer, whose works have been read by María Juana (1789, 1808). The erosion of national frontiers by the internationalization of the economy is matched by reference to Cuba, where the independence struggle was threatening national integrity. The adulterous Eloísa suggests solving the nation's economic problems by selling Cuba, and José María sells his Cuban shares for more reliable investments in urban property ('propiedad inmueble') (1745–6, 1749).

The novel goes into incredible detail about the narrator's buying and selling of shares on the national and international market. As before, the public and private spheres are blurred

---

[33] For details of the rebuilding of Madrid and the massive demolitions involved, see Navascués Palacio (in Fernández García 1993: 401–39).

by speculation in government bonds and loans to the Treasury, and through individuals—like the narrator's uncle—holding posts in both sectors. And again adultery is linked to both private and public debt, with the individual 'liquidaciones' of Carrillo, Eloïsa, and José María, and constant mention of the renegotiation of the national debt ('conversión de la deuda'). In 1881–2, the Finance Minister Camacho had negotiated a major 'conversion de la deuda'—the replacement of existing government bonds by new ones issued at a lower rate of interest or nominal value—to help deal with the State's inability to meet its foreign debt repayments, payable in foreign currency or gold, owing to the virtual halt of foreign investment in Spain and thus of imports of foreign currency. José María's final debt crisis takes place in 1883. This places it shortly after the Barcelona Stock Exchange crash of the winter of 1881–2 which abruptly ended the 'gold fever' or boom in banking shares of the early Restoration period;[34] and in the year when a dramatic fall in the Bank of Spain's bullion reserves (largely due to their exodus to cover foreign debt repayments) forced it to suspend the convertibility of its banknotes into gold, thus disconnecting the peseta from the now internationally accepted gold standard and 'floating' it on the market. This meant a big increase in the issue of paper money, which replaced metal coin as the standard form of payment, and severe 'fluctuations' in the exchange rate; the net result was inflation at home and depreciation of the peseta's foreign exchange value. The positive spin-off was the 'repatriation' of the foreign debt as Spanish speculators bought up government bonds payable in foreign currency which, with the peseta's falling exchange value, brought instant high returns. The negative side was that, even more than before, investment went not into industry (which would have stimulated production) but into the national debt (money making more money). It also meant the replacement of 'real' money by fiduciary (paper) money, whose value depended on the credit/creditability of the issuer (the nation). The rapid depreciation of the peseta showed that the nation's credit was at a low ebb (Sardá 1948: 175–93). It is against this

---

[34] Bahamonde Magro and Toro Mérida (1978: 140–1) note that share prices on the Madrid Stock Exchange rose steadily from 1877 till the late 1881 Barcelona Stock Exchange crash. Tortella (1974: i. 531) notes that this Stock Exchange crash made a strong impact on popular memory.

background of spiralling economic flow leading to loss of credit/ creditability that Galdós sets his novel about unfaithful wives going into circulation, seduced by a representative of capitalist modernity.

Eloïsa's adulteries are directly related to her passion for the circulation of money in the form of consumerism. As a child, she had loved shop windows and collecting (1680, 1707); she 'governs' her husband's and her father's home in the sense that she does all the shopping. Adultery with the wealthy José María allows her to fill her house with exotic commodities (acquired at home and in the 'grandes almacenes' and 'magasins de nouveautés' of Paris), turning it into a miniature Crystal Palace. Her dream is to put a glass roof over the patio, simulating the glass and steel structures that housed the World Exhibitions. As José María will say: 'te he enseñado a arrastrar tu fidelidad por los mostradores de las tiendas de lujo' (1775). José María has a nightmare in which he makes love to Eloïsa amid frenetic movement on the Stock Exchange (1701); what is threatening here is not just that her 'fanatismo de las compras' is getting him into debt, but that she is getting out of his control. The last straw will be when she starts to acquire a knowledge of the Stock Exchange ('cosas tan contrarias a la condición espiritual de la mujer'), presuming—ironically since she is breaking the marriage contract—to know all about 'las contratas' (1749). Her deranged brother Raimundo—perceptive like all Galdós's madmen—has a vision of how the nation's wealth depends not on the amount of money held but on the degree to which it circulates: 'corre, gira, pasa, rueda, y en este movimiento infinito, va haciendo ricos a los que la poseen' (1751)—an image of an inflationary economy out of control.[35] This vision is implicitly linked to Raimundo's 'Mapa moral gráfico de España', whose number-one vice is adultery (1800). Eloïsa will be punished

---

[35] In *The Philosophy of Money*, Simmel (1990: 139) notes that the relation of value to the rate of circulation of money, rather than to the amount of money, is basic to the modern capitalist exchange economy, observing that in 1890 the Bank of France had a turnover on current accounts of 135 times the amount deposited, while the ratio for the German Bundesbank was 1 : 190. It was the existence of national banks, backed by the State, that enabled the proliferating credit system to function. Vilar (1991: 19) notes that, in 1905, the statistician de Foville calculated that all the gold in the world extracted from the earth to that date could be fitted into a 10-metre cube, demonstrating dramatically that monetary value depended on circulation and not substance.

with a terrible illness in the form of a growth, linking her escalating career as an adulteress to the proliferation of money circulating on the market; her husband, who also spends excessively, dies of a circulatory disease. José María's punishment for seducing other men's wives will be a stroke: that is, congestion of the circulatory system, leaving him paralysed.

In addition to its increased financial detail, *Lo prohibido* also makes increased reference to the blurring of the public and the private through 'the social'. Philanthropy and finance are intertwined in the novel, not only because the wealthy bourgeoisie is involved in both, but because they represent two aspects of the same problem. Eloïsa's husband Carrillo gets into debt through financing philanthropic societies. These put child vagrants and prostitutes—the two problem categories in *La desheredada*—into institutions, and, more insidiously, go into the private homes of the poor (1721). Galdós's criticism of this invasion of privacy is implied by the fact that Carrillo is incompetent to manage his own household, and is blind to the problem of 'la alta vagancia' posed by his wife's lover José María, described as a 'vago' in the paragraph preceding mention of Carrillo's 'rescuing' of vagrants.

The second sister whom José María seduces, María Juana, is also linked both to the financial world and to 'the social'. Her home represents an adulterous intrusion of the market into the private sphere since it hosts her financier husband's 'tertulias económicas'—nicknamed 'nuestro Bolsín'—where discussion centres on 'liquidations' and 'fluctuating' exchange rates (1610). María Juana additionally represents a travesty of philanthropic initiative, in that she justifies committing adultery with José María on the grounds that she is trying to 'reform' him. Her claim to be concerned with his 'regeneración moral y física' (1816) involves her in the dubious self-gratification of trying to fix him up with a wife and prying into the intimate details of his affair with her sister Eloïsa. José María quickly tires of this 'amor filantrópico' which disguises titillation as altruism: 'Ni qué otra cosa sino mareo podía producirme aquello de amarme por salvarme' (1846). María Juana's 'amor filantrópico' is related to Eloïsa's consumerism through the obsession of both with imitation. María Juana interrogates José María about Eloïsa's house and acquisitions (including her plan to turn the patio into a miniature Crystal

Palace), even going through her wardrobe (1834). She also sees herself as imitating Madame de Warens 'saving' Rousseau (1846). Her 'reform' of José María takes the form of trying to get him to imitate her husband Medina: 'tómale por modelo si puedes, constitúyete en su imitador' (1848). In fact José María is already trying to imitate Medina by usurping his place; he seduces María Juana not because he is attracted to her, as he is to Eloïsa and Camila, but because he wants to give Medina his come-uppance. As an adulterer attracted to women only if they are owned by other men (hence the novel's title; he rejects Eloïsa when her husband dies), José María too is driven by the consumerist passion for imitation that Tarde saw as the major impulse behind the contemporary loss of social distinctions.[36]

María Juana's attempt to 'cure' José María from 'vice' and 'sickness'—to regenerate him morally and physically—links adultery with the medical discourse of degeneration that was always implicit, and became increasingly explicit, in the late nineteenth-century concern with social reform. The concern with degeneration first raised in *La desheredada* becomes a central issue in *Lo prohibido*. The novel mentions Herbert Spencer, the foreign author most translated in late nineteenth-century Spain after 1875, and especially after 1880 (Maurice and Serrano 1977: 22). Spencer's economistic vision of society was reinforced by his application to the social sciences of Darwin's evolutionary scheme for, as Bertrand Russell has noted (1980: 746), the latter's theory of natural selection was a transposition onto the natural world of the liberal doctrine of unregulated market competition, in which 'victory went to the animals that most resembled successful capitalists': what Spencer called 'the survival of the fittest'. Spencer became increasingly influenced by degeneracy theory, which in turn was reinforced by Darwin's suggestion that evolution could be accompanied by pockets of regression, manifested in genetically transmitted racial deterioration (Russett 1989: 63–77). José María's moral degeneracy expresses itself in his physical degeneration; both are linked to his excess consumerism. His affair with María Juana takes place mostly in the sick Eloïsa's palace of consumerism, and it is at this time that he starts to suffer from debt crisis and 'una gran

---

[36] Tarde's theory of imitation provides a productive way of rereading Girard's theory of triangular desire (1966) as the driving force of the 19th-century novel.

debilidad física' (1847). Financial and sexual over-expenditure makes both Eloïsa and José María 'degenerate' physically, but she recovers and he does not. Russett (1989) and Shuttleworth (in Jacobus, Fox Keller, and Shuttleworth 1990: 47–68) have shown how, in the late nineteenth century, the economic terminology central to Spencer's thought invaded medical discourse in the form of a terror of male physical, and particularly sexual, over-expenditure. José María's economic unproductiveness as a *flâneur* or 'vago' is matched by his physical sterility: it was assumed that the Don Juan, like the prostitute, was infertile as a result of excess expenditure. José María both fails to produce children and, as a parliamentary deputy who neglects his duties, is a 'padrastro de la patria' (1784).

José María's financial and sexual over-expenditure is linked to his nervous illness. This is clearly a case, not of male hysteria as critics have suggested (Aldaraca 1992: 213–8; Charnon-Deutsch 1990*a*: 177–81; Tsuchiya 1997), but of the newly invented disease of neurasthenia, affecting both men and women, and allegedly caused by the 'overtaxing' (another economic intrusion into medical discourse) of the nervous system by the excessive stimulation of modern city life.[37] In 1868 the hygienist Monlau described 'neurosismo' as 'la diátesis del siglo, la endemia de la civilización contemporánea', calling it a sign of degeneration resulting from loss of energy (18–20). Monlau contrasted this contemporary malaise with previous centuries when the problem was excess energy, requiring bloodletting to be prescribed as a cure; one is reminded of *La desheredada*, where leeches, although still sold by La Sanguijuelera, are no longer a cure but a drain. Interestingly, given José María's confirmed bachelor status, Monlau had in his much-reprinted *Higiene del matrimonio* (1865: 57–60) asked for government measures against 'celibato voluntario' because it led to dissipation of energies (adultery and prostitution) and 'la decadencia y ruina de los imperios'. In an 1884 article in the *Revista de*

---

[37] See Russett (1989: 112–29) who notes that 'neurasthenic collapse was frequently described in economic terms' as 'bankruptcy' (116); and Showalter (1987: 134–7). Although the term was used earlier, male neurasthenia was first defined by Beard in *A Practical Treatise on Nervous Exhaustion (Neurasthenia)* (1880), and female neurasthenia by Mitchell in *Lectures on the Diseases of the Nervous System, Especially in Women* (1881). Beard's and Mitchell's ideas were popularized in France by Huchard in 1883 (López Piñero 1985: 126–8).

España, at the time Galdós was writing *Lo prohibido*, the public-health expert Hauser noted a huge increase since the mid-century of 'padecimientos nerviosos' due to urbanization (Rodríguez Ocaña 1987: 24). The doctor Augusto Miquis, reappearing from *La desheredada*, calls José María's illness 'el mal del siglo, el cual, forzando la actividad cerebral, creaba una diátesis neuropática, constitutiva en toda la Humanidad' (1677), directly echoing Monlau's phraseology; later in the novel it is described as 'una manifestación del estado *adinámico*, carácter patógico del siglo XIX en las grandes poblaciones' (1695, Galdós's italics). The fact that this nervous condition is presented as a congenital defect running in José María's family does not necessarily contradict the notion that it is caused by modernity but, as in Zola's obsession with inherited neurosis, stresses the degenerative racial effects on successive generations. Augusto Miquis's optimistic belief in *La desheredada* that society is a fixed-energy system capable of self-regulation and self-renewal —a notion central to Adam Smith's classic liberal economics— seems to have given way to the notion of entropy—progressive exhaustion of energies—that, from the term's coinage in 1865 (Russett 1989: 128), increasingly dominated late nineteenth-century scientific and social thought. It was this fear that modern society was so draining its resources that the fixed-energy system would no longer be able to transfer spare capacity from elsewhere to repair the cumulative exhaustion of energies that led to Herbert Spencer's increasing obsession with degeneration (Russett 1989: 128).

In addition to leaving him paralysed, José María's stroke leaves him with the voice of a 'castrato' or a 'soprano' (1885–6): a feminizing castration. By the end of the novel, he is lacking all signs of virility (1899): as in degeneracy theory, exhaustion is equated with effeminacy. Darwin had seen progress as the move towards increased differentiation, including sexual differentiation (Freud would later build on this idea). In applying Darwin's theories to society, Herbert Spencer had equated social regression with the lapse into indifferentiation, including loss of sexual difference. *Lo prohibido* depicts a society where the proliferation of consumer goods has led to the 'sameness of the ever-new'. The Don Juan, whose repetition compulsion is motivated by a constant desire for the new, is an apt emblem of this phenomenon. But, above all, the novel suggests that

Spanish society is threatened with indifferentiation because, in neglecting his business affairs for consumerism, José María is entering a female domain: men are becoming like women. However, excess consumerism does not make women excessively feminine, for it takes them out of the home into the traditionally male public sphere of the street. Consumerism feminizes men and masculinizes women.[38] *Lo prohibido* takes further the association of adultery with loss of differentiation in the form of incest insinuated in *La familia de León Roch*, since José María is adulterously attracted to three sisters who are his cousins. Loss of sexual differentiation is now the chief concern. The interfering María Juana insists that women are the stronger sex and that men are 'todos de alfeñique' (1836), a belief confirmed by the fact that her brother Raimundo is more neurotic than any of his three sisters. As a neurasthenic, José María also maintains that women have stronger nervous systems than men (1679). José María's stroke and final paralysis are precipitated by his rejection by Camila, who overpowers him physically when he assaults her: 'Una mujer tenía más fuerzas que yo' (1851).

Camila is one of Galdós's strangest characters because she has all the qualities that, in Tanner's analysis, are possessed by fictional adulteresses—the narrator-protagonist initially takes her to be 'una mala mujer' (1683)—and yet she turns out to be the model wife.[39] Galdós seems here to be exploring the fine line that exists between the good fusion of nature and culture that is marriage, and the bad confusion between them that is adultery: a problem of distinctions that had exercised him in *La familia de León Roch*, and that will be explored further in the next novel, *Fortunata y Jacinta*. Apart from her physical strength, not a quality normally associated with the feminine ideal, Camila has no sense of propriety—nothing in her matrimonial home is in its proper place—and she represents an intrusion of untamed nature into society: 'una salvaje, una fierecilla indócil' incarnating 'todo lo incivil que la civilización contiene' (1709). But her association with the natural is a sign of health: she is 'saludable como una aldeana' (1684), and José

---

[38] Dijkstra (1986: 212–13) notes the contradiction in late 19th-century degeneracy theory, which supposes that the feminine is a lower stage of development from the masculine, but nevertheless sees 'masculine' women as a sign of regression.

[39] For discussion of Camila, see Scanlon (1984).

María's attempt to seduce her by taking her and her husband for a seaside holiday only makes her healthier than ever, as husband and wife frolic on the beach like a couple from 'la Edad de Oro, o las sociedades primitivas' (1786).[40] It is Camila's physical health that makes her morally healthy; the equation of civilization with moral and physical degeneration requires the converse equation of nature and the primitive with moral and physical health. José María 'sullies' Camila mentally by seeing her image on the 'sobado papel de los billetes de Banco' at the Stock Exchange and at Medina's 'Bolsín' (1843), for she represents the unspoilt by contrast with the 'used goods' of consumer society.

In other words, as the late nineteenth century comes increasingly to see civilization—based on excess, waste, and pollution—as a form of sickness, attitudes to nature undergo a change. Adultery no longer figures the loss of distinctions caused by the lapse back into, or intrusion of, the natural (as in the late eighteenth-century texts studied by Tanner), but that caused by the consumption of the natural (the last text examined by Tanner, *Madame Bovary* of 1857, illustrates this shift). We have already seen how, in *La desheredada*, water imagery represents the dissolution of distinctions caused not by natural flow but by the flow of money and goods. The contradictory juxtaposition in *La familia de León Roch* of the notions of hygienic circulation (good) and economic circulation (bad)—both represented by water imagery—develops in *Lo prohibido* into an opposition between Camila, whose obsession with 'agua fresca' represents hygienic flow, and Eloïsa, representing economic flow in the form of a spiralling cycle of 'liquidations'. The narrator was correct in his assumption that taking Eloïsa shopping would put her into circulation as an adulterous wife. Having tired of her excess consumerism, he falls for what he regards as an alternative model of adultery: that represented by Camila as an intrusion of the wild. Hence his supposition that taking her to the sea will precipitate her adultery. Camila teaches him that the threat to civilization comes not from nature but from

---

[40] The hygienist Monlau's last work (1869) was *Higiene de los baños de mar*. Santero's *Elementos de higiene privada y pública* (1885) has three chapters on 'baños' (seaside and otherwise). See n. 28 above for the creation of seaside sanatoriums for children by Galdós's friend Tolosa Latour, and his 1879 study on the subject.

civilization itself, whose excessive expenditure is draining its resources, turning the natural into waste. Galdós is not here setting up a simplistic opposition between nature (good) and culture (bad), but is showing the need for a healthy balance ('marriage') between the two, represented by Camila's passion for taking baths in her city home. Indeed, it is by introducing her husband—described as a 'kaffir' and 'donkey' (1786)—to the hygienic merits of running water that she 'civilizes' him. Camila's spontaneity provides a regenerating influx of natural energies that compensates for the excess consumption (in both senses of the word) of modern urban society: she insists on breastfeeding her first child, and at the end of the novel gives birth to twins. And, alone in this family of overspenders, she teaches herself accountancy for she represents Spencer's ideal of equilibrium achieved through 'balancing the books'. Eloïsa and María Juana become masculinized in a negative sense by their entry into the world of consumerism, finance, and philanthropy; in reading Spencer, María Juana also opts for books normally read by men. Camila, however, applies his theories instinctively. Her 'natural strength', which allows her to overpower her would-be male seducer, makes her not a masculine woman but the perfect wife and mother. José María's gesture of leaving his property to Camila is an attempt to counter the degenerative effects of the hereditary disease afflicting their family.

The logic of the Spencerian view of society as a fixed-energy system threatened with breakdown by the excessive strain on its resources requires that salvation—if it exists—must come from an infusion of new energies into the system. But how are energies to be transferred from 'outside' the system to 'inside', and where does one find an 'outside'? The answer to this problem is provided by woman, who being outside and inside society represents untapped energies already within the system at its disposal. And if consumerism, associated with women, is seen as the problem, it is logical to look to a woman for the solution. The corrective to the feminization of men is, it seems, strong women. One is reminded of John Stuart Mill's comment, in an 1867 House of Commons speech, that 'unless there are manly women, there will not much longer be manly men' (Riley 1988: 86). However, what Galdós seems to be arguing for is the need for women who are strong but still feminine: a fine balancing of what in the nineteenth century were seen as opposites. Fortunata, in the next novel, will die in the attempt to fulfil this impossible role, as she again raises the issue of social regeneration through an input of natural female energies, this time coming more clearly from outside the system since she is working-class. By making his later agent of regeneration not a perfect wife but a prostitute—in theory a social drain, here drained by society—as well as an adulteress—hitherto associated in his novels with consumerist excess—Galdós will complicate things to the maximum, both for his heroine and for the reader. Having sketched out the development of the association that Galdós establishes between prostitution, adultery, and modern city life, I should now like to turn to the first novel where all three issues come together: *La de Bringas*.

4
Excess and the Problem of Limits: Galdós's *Tormento* (1884) and *La de Bringas* (1884)

LA DE BRINGAS, the first of Galdós's novels to focus squarely on female adultery, is also the novel that deals most explicitly with the State bureacracy and with money. As a wife who commits adultery solely for money—possibly the only case in the European novel—Rosalía de Bringas brings together the concerns expressed in *La familia de León Roch* and *La desheredada*: namely, the invasion of the private sphere by the public, figured by adultery, and women's abandonment of domesticity for the market, figured by prostitution. Rosalía's adultery/prostitution represents the two faces of the liberal modernizing process—the extension of State control and the development of the exchange economy—which blur the public/private distinction. The novel shows the two processes to be inextricably entwined.

There is a sense in which Rosalía moves, with the 1868 Revolution whose package of liberal reforms opened the market up to private initiative, from a clientelist to a free-enterprise approach to adultery, as she abandons her initial expectations of support from representatives of the State (her first lover is a State functionary, like her husband) and embarks on the active pursuit of 'bigger fish' in the form of 'los Fúcares, los Trujillo, los Cimarra' whom we know from the earlier novels *La familia de León Roch* and *Tormento* to be financiers and speculators. In doing so she will become an entrepreneur in her own right, embracing adultery as a career that makes her the family's sole breadwinner. But, just as *La desheredada* illustrated the uneasy coexistence of the new market model with relics of the old model based on birthright, so in *La de Bringas* we do not have a simple passage from a monarchical favour system to post-revolutionary free enterprise. In a reversal of Emma Bovary, whose adulterous affairs get her into debt, it is Rosalía's debts, incurred as a result of excess consumption, that get her into adultery: immersion in the new consumerism pre-dates both her first adultery with a State bureaucrat and the Revolution that introduces new economic freedoms. The preceding novel *Tormento* shows how Rosalía had been initiated into consumerist pleasures by gifts from her cousin Agustín Caballero, an incarnation of free enterprise who had made his fortune in America: Agustín's gifts fuse the notion of wealth acquired through individual effort with that of dependence on favours from on high. And the State patronage system that characterizes the monarchy does not disappear with the Revolution, for the latter's enforcement of free enterprise through new liberalizing legislation creates a contradictory fusion of State control and market ideology: this 'supervised freedom' would be the hallmark of the Restoration. It is logical that Pez—whose blueprint for national regeneration consists in creating 'un sistema administrativo perfecto, con ochenta o noventa Direcciones generales. Que no hubiera manifestación alguna de la vida nacional que se escapara' (Pérez Galdós 1985: 187)—should continue to swim in the revolutionary 'waters' that intensify the dissolution of public/private distinctions begun in the earlier period. Immediately after the Revolution, Rosalía commits adultery with the narrator who, as State appointee of the new free-trade regime, combines the old State favour system with the new market model.

The complementarity of State control and free enterprise is shown by the connection of both with the concept of excess. Dependence on the State creates a nation of parasites draining its resources without replenishing them: as a social drain, the parasite turns excess into waste. Everyone is living on 'sobras' or leftovers handed down from above, whether it be Rosalía receiving unwanted dresses from the Queen—in *Tormento*, we are told that the Bringases' furniture also includes 'despojos' from the Royal Palace (Pérez Galdós 1966: 1460)— or the paupers at the Maundy Thursday royal banquet receiving food hampers, in a travesty of philanthropy incorporating the poor into the State favour system. The poor recycle their handouts back into the system by selling them; it is not they who are a social drain in this society based on 'el repartimiento de limosnas que hace el Estado' (1985: 106). The circular flow of goods that is the market facilitates the recycling of wealth, but it also requires excess in the form of surplus profits and the creation of false needs to stimulate consumption. These two factors are linked in the novel through Rosalía's recourse to moneylenders (who use money to make more money) in order to buy increasingly luxurious (superfluous) clothes. The novel shows how the capitalist economy blurs the distinction between need and excess because it needs surplus. Galdós's concentration on fashion illustrates this well, for it is hard to say at what point clothes cease to be essential items and become non-essential luxuries. Rosalía knows the shawl that is her first purchase is a 'lujo' her husband would not permit because it is not 'de necesidad absoluta' (1985: 99), but argues that dressing well is a 'deber ineludible' (1985: 126-7). Similarly she justifies her adultery (excess sexual activity) as 'need': 'Pecar, llámote necesidad' (1985: 266). Francisco Bringas has no 'needs'— '¡Dichoso hombre! El no tenía necesidades' (1985: 270)— because he is not guilty of excess expenditure: it is excess that creates needs. And yet Francisco Bringas is also inscribed in this economy of excess as a 'cesante'. Galdós's 'novels of modernity' are peopled with 'cesantes' because they highlight the problem of redundancy. As civil servants, they show that excess is as intrinsic to a proliferating State bureaucracy as it is to the consumer economy.

Critics (Varey 1966; Blanco and Blanco Aguinaga in Pérez Galdós 1985) have proposed that Rosalía and her husband Francisco represent the contrasting attitudes to money of the incipient capitalist order and the outgoing *ancien régime*. I shall argue that both are responding—in different, but not entirely different, ways—to the new order in its twin forms of state control and consumer capitalism. Both, initially at least, illustrate the problem of parasitism created by the extension of the centralized State. In first committing adultery with Manuel Pez, who as head of the Treasury controls the national budget, Rosalía is not yet 'floating' herself on the free market but 'angling' for financial favours from a representative of the State: 'Si Pez no hubiera sido empleado, habría perdido mucho a sus ojos, acostumbrados a ver el mundo como si todo él fuera una oficina y no se conocieran otros medios de vivir que del presupuesto' (1985: 170). It is Pez who encourages her to commit adultery by invading her domestic space, just as he fosters State encroachment in all areas of national life: 'me acostumbro a considerar como casa propia la casa de mi amigo' (1985: 189). As adulterer and as State representative, he is 'de más' in the Bringases' family home. Rosalía's belief that she has a right to financial favours from Pez mirrors her, and most of the characters', belief that they have a right to be parasites on the national wealth. This belief is encouraged by Pez, as a supporter of what the narrator ironically calls 'el socialismo manso' (1985: 107) or the aspiration to total State control. For, despite complaining that everyone tries to cheat the State by smuggling goods through the customs, Pez is happy to oblige with letters of recommendation letting his 'friends' off customs duty because this favour system extends his personal power at the expense of impoverishing the State (1985: 231). In a blurring of public and private that mirrors his role as adulterer, he regards the State as his personal fiefdom. Given the universal favour system operated by Pez as head of the Treasury, Rosalía has good reason to be indignant at not receiving the expected handout; that she sees this as a refusal of State support is implied by her description of Pez's rejection letter as being from 'el director de Hacienda' (1985: 272). Pez is, it seems, happy to grant favours provided they drain the State coffers and not his own purse (though the distinction between the two is hazy since the latter is filled from the former). Again we have the problem of how to distinguish between need and excess: Pez had offered Rosalía 'lo que me sobra' (just as the Queen gives her her cast-offs); now it seems that he 'needs' what before was presented as excess. Rosalía has learnt a major political lesson when she abandons this favour system, which puts her in a position of powerlessness, for the market, based on a 'free' exchange of contracts that has to be honoured by both parties.

In this initial belief that she has a right to live off the State, Rosalía is in agreement with her husband, who expects the State to provide him with free railway tickets and to pay him double salary when off sick (1985: 173), not to mention paying his son for a phantom job (1985: 57). Like Rosalía, he looks to Manuel Pez as his chief source of favours; his supposition that the State will provide for his private needs blurs public and private as much as his wife's adultery. Francisco Bringas's hair picture is a present to the Pez family in return for favours past and future. His insistence that he will not adulterate it—'me cree usted capaz de adulterar?' (1985: 60)—with hair from outside the Pez family is ironic, because it is part of the universal bribery system that—like adultery—blurs public and private. Bringas is explicitly inscribed in the equation of public and private represented by State control through his position as Primer Oficial de la Intendencia del Real Patrimonio. We are told in *Tormento* that the only books he possesses are the Bible and Madoz's *Diccionario geográfico-estadístico-histórico de España* (1966: 1475) whose attempt to map the nation was part of the project of extending State control. His confusion of public and private leads him to run his domestic economy as if it were a State department. In keeping control of the household budget, he is a 'legislator' (1985: 180, 214): an image of new central State control. In this sense he is a domestic version of Pez as head of Hacienda, wanting to submit everything to his vigilance. *Tormento* gives us a detailed description of his administrative regime: his desk is 'de las que llaman de ministro', and his system of little drawers with separate piles of coins for different forms of essential household expenditure, plus a basket for additional expenses, is described—not entirely ironically—as one which could usefully be imitated by the Treasury: 'Allí lo superfluo no existía mientras no estuvieran cubiertas todas las atenciones.' But Bringas's meticulous attempt to distinguish between essential and non-essential expenditure leads to absurdity: 'Los restos de lo necesario pasaban semanalmente a la partida y al cestillo de lo superfluo, y aún había otro hueco adonde afluía lo sobrante de lo superfluo' (1966: 1466). This last category of 'lo sobrante de lo superfluo' is the source of his erratic payments to Amparo, inscribing her in the system of 'sobras' that constitutes the State favour system. The problem of distinguishing between need and excess is as much part of this favour system as it is of the consumer economy illustrated by Rosalía's clothes.

When the narrator proposes Bringas's domestic regime as a model for the national economy, he is echoing contemporary demands by Krausist reformers to moralize the nation from the bottom up, applying family values to society and the State. In an 1870 parliamentary speech, Segismundo Moret, then Ministro de Hacienda, argued that public expenditure should imitate 'los principios de honradez y de orden que cada uno aplica a su propia casa y familia, que consiste en trabajar para aumentar las rentas y economizar para disminuir los gastos'

(Elorza 1973: 171). What Bringas is doing is the reverse: applying to the household the model of the State, where surplus capital, rather than being reinvested in the system to produce long-term benefits, is doled out in the form of 'sobras'. Both Moret and Bringas are eroding the public/private split which liberalism had originally instigated by splitting production (under male control) off from the household (under female control). In keeping hold of the domestic purse-strings—'la economía doméstica' is described as his speciality—Bringas is usurping the female role, supervising the various household removals as an 'amo hacendoso' (1966: 1459) and even helping in the kitchen. In this, he is not a typical bourgeois husband —the description of the Santa Cruz family in *Fortunata y Jacinta* shows that it was normal for the husband to put the household budget under his wife's control (Pérez Galdós 1992: i. 249)— but is interfering in what should be his wife's separate domain. This intrusion of the male public sphere into the female private realm does not lead to increased male control but to his feminization as a house-husband ('amo doméstico').

Bringas's State post in charge of Crown property puts him at the centre of a major contemporary row about the distinction between private and public spheres. *La de Bringas* twice mentions the 'rasgo' of Isabel II which in 1866 triggered the Noche de San Daniel riots, witnessed by Galdós as a student (1985: 13 n. 11), and in which Juanito Santa Cruz will take part in *Fortunata y Jacinta*: Isabel's gesture had been to offer to help pay off the national debt by putting Crown property on the market, keeping a quarter of the proceeds herself (Bahamonde Magro and Martínez 1994: 529; García de Cortázar and González Vesga 1994: 461). Despite this sop to liberal belief in the privatization of property, Isabel had made the mistake of supposing she was free to dispose of the 'patrimonio real' as her private property when it was public property (a confusion of public and private that was, of course, reflected in her notorious adulteries, raising the question of whether the monarch is free to dispose of 'his' person as 'his' private property, a question doubly problematic when 'his' is 'her').[1] Isabel's

---

[1] Carr (1966: 245) quotes an 1853 opposition paper which, at the time of the Queen Mother's involvement with the Marqués de Salamanca in a scandal over preferential railway deals, accused the royal family of being 'like prostitutes sell[ing] their honour for money'.

mistake is excusable given the ambiguous concept of sovereignty which, prior to the 1868 Revolution, lay in the monarchy as representative of the nation but not in the nation as such. As we have seen, the 1869 Constitution introduced the idea of national sovereignty, broadened by the Republic to popular sovereignty. The first act of the Revolutionary Guard at the end of *La de Bringas* is to pin a notice on the Palace railings claiming it as the 'Palacio de la Nación, custodiado por el Pueblo' (1985: 300). The role of 'the people' as custodians of a Palace owned by 'the nation' is far from clear. Are 'the people' part of, or separate from, 'the nation'? (They are certainly outside, and not inside, the palace.) Francisco Bringas naively thinks the revolutionaries would lay down their arms if the Queen said to them: '¡Todos sois mis hijos!' (1985: 297), for his belief in the State as a favour system supposes that the nation is the contradiction in terms of a public family. The fact that the Revolutionary Junta has forgotten to feed the popular militia guarding the palace shows that this paternalistic notion is a delusion. That the final eviction from the Palace of its previous tenants (civil servants and other beneficiaries) does not mean the end of this favour system is clear from the fact that the man put in charge of Crown property by the Revolutionary Junta is the novel's narrator, a crony of Pez who opened the novel by asking a favour from Bringas as then head of Crown property, and who ends it by granting favours to others, including Rosalía. In replacing Bringas in his job and (briefly) in his bed, he ensures the continuation of a system based on the adulterous blurring of public and private.

In between *Tormento* and its sequel, Galdós moves the Bringas family from their previous private accommodation into the apartment in the Royal Palace which comes with Bringas's new post: their private home is in a public building, a blurring of distinctions reinforced by their naming its rooms after the State apartments, plus naming their children after the royal couple and heir. The Palace is described as a hopeless confusion of public and private, causing the narrator and Pez to get lost. It is a city complete with neighbourhoods, squares, streetlamps, and fountains (1985: 66–8) not only because it is a microcosm of Madrid society but because its interior resembles the public space of the street. Particularly disconcerting is the conversion of solid walls into gaps and vice versa: 'Es que durante un siglo no se ha hecho más que modificar a troche y moche la distribución primitiva, tapiando por aquí, abriendo por allá [. . .], convirtiendo la calle en vivienda y la vivienda en calle, agujereando las paredes y cerrando huecos' (1985: 68). The Bringases' bedroom has a skylight letting in light from the 'corredor-calle de la ciudad palatina' (1985: 73), boding ill for the maintenance of marital privacy. In *Tormento*, Rosalía had particularly liked the fact that, in their previous home, you could hear the bustle of the street from the marital bedroom: 'parece que estamos en la calle' (1966: 1463). The Palace is a leaking edifice; indeed, the narrator and Pez feel seasick as if in a ship foundering on the high seas (1985: 70).

As in earlier novels, water imagery evokes the confusion of public and private produced both by State control and by consumerism. Galdós's description of the Palace, while explicitly illustrating the absorption of the private into the State, coincides uncannily with Walter Benjamin's description of the Paris shopping arcades as simultaneously street and interior, with their glass roofs (like the Palace 'claraboyas') and indoors gaslight (also like the Palace). Like Galdós's Palace, the arcade is for Benjamin a 'labyrinth', a 'stream', and 'a city, even a world, in miniature' (Benjamin 1989: 37, 50, 54–5). Bowlby (1985: 74) notes that the proprietor of the Bon Marché department store in Paris justified his 'illogical' reorganization of its departments on the grounds that 'What's necessary [. . .] is that they walk around for hours, that they get lost', as Pez and the narrator do in the Palace which has been refurbished—'refashioned'—so as to defy all logic. Benjamin also saw the arcades as smaller versions of the nineteenth-century World Exhibitions, whose commodity fetishism—what he nicely calls 'the sex-appeal of the inorganic' (1989: 56, 166)—created a 'state of religious intoxication' (Baudelaire's words). One is reminded here of Rosalía's fetishistic attraction not to men but to clothes, described as 'la acción intoxicante de una embriaguez de trapos' (1985: 104). As Aldaraca observes (1992: 133), her response to the shawl whose purchase initiates her into consumerism is akin to sexual orgasm. Marx used erotic imagery to describe the capitalist stimulation of false desires, accusing the entrepreneur of 'play[ing] the pimp' by exciting in consumers 'morbid appetites [. . .] all so that he can demand the cash for this service of love' (Harvey 1989: 102).

Excess and the Problem of Limits 147

In *Au Bonheur des Dames*, published in 1883 the year before *La de Bringas*, Zola compared his department store to 'those commercial houses of tolerance', the name for licensed brothels (Corbin 1990: 210). Benjamin (1989: 158) noted that the 'magasins de nouveautés', which the arcades were built to house, first emerged with the boom in the textile trade; Bowlby (1985: 67) similarly states that the first 'magasins de nouveautés' specialized in fabrics for dressmaking: Rosalía sees the shawl in the window of the 'almacén de novedades' Sobrino Hermanos. (*Fortunata y Jacinta* will, of course, make the draper's trade central to its study of modernity.) It was the window displays of the Paris arcades, signalling the new concern with marketing, that made Benjamin propose them as an emblem of the modern city, based on visual spectacle. *La de Bringas* is a novel about vision (Bly 1986) because it is a novel about modern urban life. And visual spectacle, requiring an audience, is the domain of the public. As Refugio notes, the Madrid middle classes 'viven en la calle' (1985: 283), for in a consumer society to be is to be seen. *La de Bringas* is concerned with visual appearances because, in this world of commodities, appearance and not use determines value. The eye specialist Golfín judges the Bringas family by their visual appearance in the street. His success as a doctor—of humble origin, he is a classic self-made man—is due to his ability to restore the faculty on which the modern city most depends: that of sight.[2]

Benjamin differentiates between two kinds of visual display, both intrinsic to consumer capitalism: the arcade and the World Exhibition on the one hand, and the private collection on the other. If the arcade and the World Exhibition construct the public sphere as a world of commodities in circulation, the private collection constructs an interior world in which objects are fixed and encased to create an illusory permanence and security compensating for the unceasing movement outside. Roughly speaking, the former corresponds to Rosalía's passion for clothes and the latter to her husband Francisco Bringas's collector's mania. Both attitudes are responses to consumer capitalism. Although the former celebrates economic flow and the latter tries to repress it, both the World Exhibition and the

---

[2] On the importance of the visual in modernity, see—in addition to Benjamin (1989) and Simmel (1990, 1997)—Crary (1990); Asendorf (1993).

private collection juxtapose objects that have been lifted out of their disparate historical and geographical contexts. In this sense, both represent the commodity fetishism that Marx defined as the attempt to suppress awareness of the social relations underlying the production and supply of commodities (Harvey 1989: 100–1). Rosalía's garments mix different styles ('con una sencillez verdaderamente pastoril', 'a lo jockey') and different materials (silks, satins, velvets, cottons, lace, feathers) from France, Africa, and India, making her creations miniature World Exhibitions displaying the de-historicized spoils of Empire (1985: 93, 119–20, 124). Bringas indulges in a similar kind of cultural pillage when he constructs his hair picture from a mixture of architectural styles lifted from disparate historical and geographical sources: 'a la manera viñolesca', 'a la usanza gótica', 'con ciertos atisbos platerescos', 'piramidal escalinata', 'zócalos grecorromanos', 'cresterías semejantes a las del estilo tirolés que prevalece en los quioscos' (1985: 53).[3] Benjamin notes that 'The highest, the ultimate mask of this totem-tree [of objects] is kitsch' (Frisby 1985: 246–7). Rosalía is accused of being a 'cursi' and Bringas's hair picture is kitsch incarnate. Both, with their fetishism of the object, are described as collectors.[4]

The difference between them is that Rosalía wants to display her collection of clothes in public, not just by inviting the public into her home—already in *Tormento*, Agustín notices that she

---

[3] Navascués Palacio (in Fernández García 1993: 434–5) notes that architectural style under the Restoration was marked by its 'eclecticism'. Ariza (1988: 70, 73, 79, 250) notes that the Retiro Park—described in the novel—contained, among other follies or 'caprichos', a 'Casa Persa' with a 'Salón Oriental', and a 'fuente egipcia' (both built in the Romantic period), plus (constructed under Isabel II) a 'Paisaje Español' consisting in a garden mixing the Italian, French, and English styles. The Retiro was from the 1850s used for exhibitions putting the world on display: Ariza mentions two which exhibited a group of Ashanti 'natives' and seven Eskimo families respectively; in 1880 a 'Renaissance pavilion' and an 'Arab pavilion' were built to house an international exhibition of plant and bird species. Under the Restoration, there were various unrealized large-scale projects for massive glass-and-steel pavilions in the Retiro on the lines of the Crystal Palace. Two of these were built and remain in existence: the Palacio de Velázquez to house the Exposición de Minería of 1883; the Palacio de Cristal to house the Exposición Colonial of 1887 (Simón Palmer 1991: 79).

[4] On collectors in this and other novels by Galdós, see Gold's excellent discussion (1988: 123–47) which includes some interesting comments on the kitsch (230 n. 23). On this last concept, see also Calinescu (1987: 225–62).

is starting to dress for public view indoors (1966: 1531)—but by parading it in the street; whereas Bringas's collection is kept at home under lock and key.[5] Nevertheless Rosalía's overaccumulation of clothes means that they are mostly shut away in her chest-of-drawers, and she gets a collector's pleasure from viewing them in private. When Pez says of Bringas's hair picture 'Esta obra debería ir a un museo' (1985: 130), he is highlighting the collector's mentality that has produced it. As Benjamin notes, the nineteenth century was the age of the private collector, whose 'phantasmagorias of the interior' (1989: 167) were assembled to suppress awareness of the traffic of goods outside, just as Bringas tries to shut out the coming Revolution based on demands for free trade:

The collector was the true inhabitant of the interior. [. . .] To him fell the task of Sisyphus which consisted of stripping things of their commodity character by means of his possession of them. But he conferred on them only a fancier's value, rather than use-value. [. . .] The interior was not only the private citizen's universe, it was also his casing. (1989: 168–9)

As Benjamin observes, the bourgeois found a casing for everything: 'for slippers and pocket watches, thermometers and egg-cups, cutlery and umbrellas. [. . .] For the Makart style, the style of the end of the Second Empire, a dwelling becomes [. . .] a kind of case for a person and embeds him in it together with all his appurtenances' (1989: 46). Benjamin notes that this was also an attempt to compensate for increasingly complex power relations which made the bourgeois feel no longer at the centre but a 'pensioner': Bringas's collector's mania can be seen as his response to the threat of redundancy represented by the Revolution's consecration of the capitalist economy. His hair picture, encased first in a frame and then in glass, is envisaged as an exhibit in one of Benjamin's private museums, whose function is to abstract commodities from the network of economic relations by turning them into 'art' (he sees himself as an 'artista'). The hair picture depicts a

---

[5] Corbin (in Perrot 1990: 487) notes that the construction of the bourgeois individual in the course of the 19th century was accompanied by the adoption of different forms of dress for home and street.

mausoleum.[6] Bringas also offers to build Rosalía a marble wardrobe like a tomb, in an attempt to contain her clothes in a deathly stasis, just as he locks his money in his moneybox. When the Marquesa de Tellería complains that, by withdrawing money from circulation, Bringas is responsible for the country's backwardness—'¡El dinero de manos muertas es la causa del atraso de la nación!' (1985: 138)—she is referring to the old system of mortmain which until the liberal disentailment laws of the mid-century prevented land from being put on the market. But Bringas does not represent the old view of wealth as unmoveable property in the sense of inherited land. His aim is the immobilization of moveable property (a contradiction in terms, doomed to failure), for it is banknotes that he keeps locked away. The precariousness of his attempt to deny economic circulation is illustrated by the episode when his new overcoat —a fashion garment which is also a form of encasement—is stolen. He is right to see this as a sign that the Revolution— ushering in free trade—is coming.

Bringas's attempt to enclose the flow of goods is a form of death in that it is unproductive, but there is a sense in which it can be seen as an advanced form of commodity fetishism; that is, the worship of money as a commodity in its own right, rather than (as in Rosalía's case) for the commodities it can buy (Harvey 1989: 102). As Marx noted:

> The boundless greed after riches, this passionate chase after exchange-value, is common to the capitalist and the miser; but while the miser is merely a capitalist gone mad, the capitalist is a rational miser. The never-ending augmentation of exchange-value, which the miser strives after by seeking to save his money from circulation, is attained by the more acute capitalist by constantly throwing it afresh into circulation. (Marx 1990: 149)

Simmel (1990: 238–47) also saw the miser as a greater commodity fetishist than the spendthrift since he worships money

---

[6] Ariès (1987: 461–2, 475–556) comments on how the 'privatization' of death in the course of the 19th century, as collective graves were replaced by individual tombs, was paralleled by increasing state regulation (the requirement to register deaths, municipal control of cemeteries). He also notes that the increasing beautification of death, with new landscaped cemeteries outside the city, turned cemeteries into a 'museum of tombs' or a 'tableau'; a tendency reinforced by the invention of the locket, containing a lock of hair. Bringas's hair picture illustrates all these concerns.

in and of itself. In practice, saving and consumerism were not opposed: Moret defended the 1868 Revolution's demands for free trade on the grounds that it would bring down prices, allowing the poor to 'economizar' while stimulating consumption (Elorza 1973: 170). Under the Restoration, saving was promoted as much as consumption: legislation of 1880 required savings banks to be set up in all major towns, and schoolchildren and trainee teachers were encouraged—sometimes required—to make weekly deposits (Varela and Álvarez-Uría 1979: 228–9; Pérez Ledesma in Seminario de historia 1988: 162–3).

Varey (1966) has argued that Bringas's nickname 'el buen Thiers' is ironic because he would have been appalled by the French economist's defence of the capitalist order in his book *De la propriété*, which Galdós owned in Spanish translation.[7] But Bringas and Thiers (difference in intellectual stature apart) have several things in common. Thiers was best known as a statesman dedicated to combating socialism and imposing law and order; as Galdós's readers would have remembered, he was the President responsible for crushing the Commune in 1871. As a historian—like Cánovas in Spain, who shared his conservative brand of liberalism—he helped construct a new sense of nationalism; Bahamonde Magro and Martínez (1994: 497) note that the translation in Spain of Thiers's historical writings helped encourage in Spanish historians of the second half of the nineteenth century the idea of historiography as a scientific discipline whose function was to systematize and recover 'un pasado cuyo protagonista sería la nación'. *De la propriété* was published in September 1848 in response to the revolutionary upheaval of July that year.[8] Its defence of private property is explicitly geared to refuting socialist ideas. Book 1 sets out the basis of capitalism in private property, arguing that civilization consists in the progression from nomadism to land settlement, reaching its height in imperial expansion (chapter 14).

---

[7] Elorza (1973: 134) sees the immediate translation into Spanish of Thiers's *De la propriété*, plus that of Bastiat's *Harmonies économiques*, as a defensive measure on the part of Spanish liberalism against an incipient socialism.

[8] The copy of *De la propriété* in the Biblioteca Nacional comes, in a nice irony, from the library of Pi y Margall, the main intellectual exponent in Spain of the ideas of Proudhon, known chiefly for his slogan 'property is theft' (though, as noted in Chapter 3, as Federal Republican leader Pi effectively championed the access to property of the lower classes through cheap loans, not the abolition of property).

Book 2, titled 'Du communisme', argues that the abolition of property means a return to barbarism; its inevitable consequence is 'la suppression de la famille' (143). Chapter 5 of book 2 is expressly titled 'Du communisme par rapport à la famille. Que la propriété et la famille sont indissolublement unies, qu'en détruisant l'une le communisme détruit l'autre.' Book 3 on socialism—meaning workers' associationism—argues against workers' demands for price controls and the right to work, since these would mean State interference in freedom of contract: here, remembering that Galdós called Pez's dream of State control 'el socialismo manso', Bringas might curiously find himself siding with socialism against Thiers. Varey notes (1966: 65–6) that Galdós earmarked the pages of book 1, chapters 3 and 4; these are titled 'L'Universalité de la propriété' and 'Des facultés de l'homme. Que l'homme a dans ses facultés personnelles une première propriété incontestable, origine de toutes les autres.' This last chapter, echoing the Lockean notion that freedom consists in the right to dispose of one's property in one's person, is crucial to understanding the significance of Rosalía's adultery. In the rest of book 1, Thiers argues that the natural inequality between different individuals' personal faculties justifies the unequal distribution of wealth, for the individual has the right to the fruits of his labour (in Spain, Giner defended this argument). It is Thiers's insistence on production as the basis of wealth that Bringas would have had difficulties with, for he argues that the purpose of capitalist accumulation is not just to increase private property but to further the circulation of wealth. The image of natural flow he uses is much like that of Miquis in *La desheredada*:

Souffrez donc ces accumulations de richesses, placées dans les hautes régions de la société, comme les eaux, qui destinées à fertiliser le globe, avant de se répandre dans les campagnes en fleuves, rivières ou ruisseaux, restent quelque temps suspendues en vastes lacs au sommet des plus hautes montagnes. (1848: 83)

In practice, Bringas does not totally deny the exchange economy, for his waste-not-want-not mentality makes him an advocate of recycling. His hair picture even recycles death in the form of Pez's dead daughter's locks, kept—in a further recycling—in an old sweet box; its frame is recycled from 'el perrito bordado de mi prima Josefa' (1985: 62). The drawers and baskets and boxes in which he keeps his money are an attempt to suppress movement, but he also joins his daughter Isabelita in her favourite game of taking her collection of objects out of their boxes to rearrange it and put it back 'colocado de otro modo' (1985: 255). Like Isabelita he collects used goods found in the street, such as corks, putting them in a drawer 'que era la sucursal del Rastro' in case they come in handy (1966: 1475). In this sense he is a bourgeois ragpicker. But he is an unproductive ragpicker because the objects he collects are so useless he can rarely find a new use for them. The start of *Tormento* allows him to deploy his talents for *bricolage* as he sets about fixing things in the new house, nailing down (immobilizing) the carpets and mending things so they can be reused. But mostly his collecting of second-hand goods compounds, rather than eliminates, the problem of waste, leading to a crisis of overaccumulation. Isabelita's repeated nightmares culminate in a feeling of congestion, relieved by vomiting up the food and images blocking her system.

The other two Bringas children, Paquito and Alfonso, are respectively obsessed with removal vans and revolutionary ideas: these two notions come together at the end of *La de Bringas* as, with the Revolution, the inhabitants of the Palace are forced to move house. The circulation of traffic produces a similar congestion to that created by Bringas's and Isabelita's attempt to 'box' commodities in: 'El día que salieron, la ciudad alta parecía una plaza amenazada de bombardeo. No había en ella más que mudanza, atropellado bombardeo de personas y un trasiego colosal de muebles y trastos diversos. Por las oscuras calles no se podía transitar' (1985: 305). Frisby, glossing Benjamin, notes that the bourgeois interior was filled with 'furniture that retained the character of fortification, embattlements against the outside world, against its transitory nature' (Frisby 1985: 247). The Revolution—'el diluvio' (1985: 294)—is an assault on Bringas's private 'citadel' of objects, expelling him into the flow of goods outside. But the movement was there before the Revolution: the earlier novel *Tormento* had opened with another household removal. The Revolution simply signifies public—legal—acknowledgement of the capitalist economy that had been developing since the mid-century. As we have seen, one of the Revolution's first acts was to demolish Madrid's old city walls to relieve the congestion caused by urban expansion and increased traffic.⁹ This final 'día de la mudanza' is associated with Rosalía's adulterous going into circulation through reference to the latter as a 'mudanza moral' (1985: 305).

Bringas and Rosalía represent different aspects of the overaccumulation that Marx had seen as the cause of the first crisis of European capitalism in 1848, triggered—like the 1868 Revolution in Spain—by a credit crisis resulting from excessive speculation in railway construction (Harvey 1989: 260, 264). Both his hoarding and her compulsive spending lead to overaccumulation and blockage of the system. Her solution to the paralysis produced by debt crisis is to take out further loans; this was also the solution adopted by the Revolution's Finance Minister, Figuerola (Tortella Casares 1973: 299–300). The problem produced by moving money around too much is solved, but also compounded, by moving it around some more. Circulation and congestion, as Marx demonstrated (1990: 181), go together, making capitalism inherently crisis-prone.

Rosalía obviously incarnates the capitalist economy since, in committing adultery for money, she puts herself on the market as a commodity. In *The Communist Manifesto*, Marx and Engels (1974: 101) had sarcastically commented that the bourgeoisie had no reason to be afraid that communist demands for collective ownership would lead to the abolition of the family since their predilection for wife-swapping made bourgeois marriage 'in reality a system of wives in common'. What needs stressing in this equation between adultery and the exchange economy is not just Rosalía's self-commodification but the fact that, as Thiers noted, the right to dispose of one's property in one's person is the basis of the liberal belief in individual freedom. Feminist critics (Charnon-Deutsch 1985*a*; Aldaraca 1992: 125–43; Delgado 1995) have read *La de Bringas* as a study in female emancipation, since adultery gives Rosalía financial independence. In terms of market theory, she is right to find it preferable to sell herself rather than give her services for free; that the

---

⁹ Bahamonde Magro and Toro Mérida (1978: 104–5) note that, with the introduction of trams from 1871 and especially in the 1880s when *La de Bringas* was written, the centre of Madrid was beset by huge problems of traffic congestion due to excess circulation, requiring the Ayuntamiento to impose safety measures. Corbin (1986: 115) notes that the shift in the later 19th century from concern about how to contain waste to concern with recycling it was a reaction to the problem of congestion.

latter leads only to servitude was demonstrated by Amparo's humiliating position in the Bringas household in *Tormento*. Galdós's equation of emancipation with adultery implies that he has serious reservations about women's independence and about a system that defines freedom in terms of the market. Rosalía's mistake is to apply market theory to her domestic life—her sewing room becomes 'una sucursal de Sobrino Hermanos' (1985: 119)—blurring public and private in a parallel confusion to that produced by her 'legislator' husband's interference in the domestic economy. In so doing, she exposes the contradictions in liberal theory which promises freedom to all while denying it to women by excluding them from the market. If Bringas becomes a feminized 'amo doméstico', Rosalía is masculinized by entering the market as an adulteress and as a consumer: Pez calls her a bull attracted not to men but to 'el trapo' (1985: 229). Her anger at discovering she has committed adultery for free and not for money highlights the twisted logic of commodity fetishism, according to Hartsock's definition of the term as 'the process by which people come to believe that social relations among people can take place only by means of things' (1985: 97). Bowlby (1985: 27–9) notes that the consumerist rhetoric of seduction destabilizes gender by positioning the shopper as a female seduced by the commodity —Marx also defined commodity fetishism as the inverted logic by which 'commodities appear as the purchasers of persons' (Hartsock 1985: 100)—but at the same time as its 'masculine' possessor. As Bowlby also notes (1985: 11), in buying rather than selling, the female shopper has more agency (in the sense of choice) than the prostitute who similarly enters the market. And, of course, female shoppers—unlike prostitutes—do not exist to service men's pleasure. Aldaraca (1992: 107) observes that women's consumerism was seen as threatening because it offered the possibility of an all-female pleasure, excluding men. Rosalía shuts herself up in her sewing room with Milagros and Emilia; on seeing the shawl that so excites her, she exclaims '¡Qué pieza!' (1985: 98) as if a man savouring a woman's attractions —in *Fortunata y Jacinta* (i. 688, ii. 40), the phrase 'buena pieza' is used of Fortunata by both Juanito Santa Cruz and Juan Pablo Rubín.

Unlike Bringas's hoarding, which attempts to deny capitalist flow, Rosalía's passion for clothes celebrates it: 'Emilia se puso a trabajar en medio de un mar de trapos y cintas, cuyas encrespadas olas llegaban hasta la puerta' (1985: 214). But she is still indulging in commodity fetishism—that is, denying the underlying reality of social relations—by creating a false impression of the family's economic situation, as do Milagros and Pez through their ostentatious self-display. The novel's demonstration that 'seeing is not believing' makes the point that, in a society based on commodity fetishism, the surface spectacle is designed to conceal an unacceptable economic reality. Although as a consumer Rosalía furthers the circulation of wealth, she is as unproductive as her husband; Aldaraca (1992: 101) notes that this was one of the chief objections to 'lujo'. Her dressmaking, like his hoarding, recycles used materials —'refund[iendo] lo viejo dándole viso y representación de novedad' (1985: 97)—in a way that compounds excess rather than eliminating waste. Her recycling of materials additionally confirms Benjamin's perception that fashion constitutes the realm of the new and the ever-same. As in *La desheredada*, fashion creates sameness also in that, being based on the imitation of models, it leads to uniformity. When Rosalía notices that Refugio is wearing a 'vestido [. . .] de novedad', this means that she has recognized it as an example of the latest mass-manufactured French models. It is Refugio's importation, as owner of an 'almacén de novedades', of the latest mass-manufactured French fashions that produces the loss of class distinctions that forces Rosalía into acting as her maid. Refugio will rub this in cruelly by telling her the Marquesa de Tellería called her a 'cursi': that is, that her apparent distinction is nothing but the secondhand imitation of models. Although Refugio's clothes are new, they are jumbled up in her flat in a 'masa caótica de objetos de moda' and 'ropas de uso' (1985: 276) for the imitation of models turns the new into the secondhand. Refugio is a trader in the latest French fashions and, as a high-class prostitute, in soiled goods. When Rosalía introduces fake banknotes into her husband's moneybox, she has to soil them to make them seem genuine—'sometió los trozos a una serie de operaciones equivalentes al traqueteo de los billetes en la circulación pública' (1985: 219)—for the circulation of goods and money makes everything secondhand. The money-lender Torquemada's house is furnished with secondhand goods acquired from defaulting debtors, in another adulterated mixture of styles figuring the exchange economy.

The moneylenders Torquemada and Torres, for all their crassness, genuinely facilitate the economic flow on which consumer capitalism depends. So, as shopkeeper and prostitute, does Refugio, who thereby gains a considerable degree of independence: 'no debo a nadie, y si debo lo pago; vivo de mi trabajo, y nadie tiene que ver con mis acciones' (1985: 286). Rosalía at this stage has not acquired independence because she has not yet freed herself from dependence on the State-controlled favour system and learnt to play the market. To do so requires her not to eliminate superfluous consumption, for the consumer economy requires the creation and satisfaction of false needs, but to stop overspending beyond her means. This controlled excess is figured by her future 'regularization' of adultery as a career. Another image of controlled excess is provided by Agustín Caballero in *Tormento*, whose lavish spending is backed by hard-earned capital: his servant Felipe describes his newly furnished mansion as an example of 'abundancia' without 'derroche' (1966: 1486). But Agustín's mansion nevertheless prefigures his abandonment of marriage for concubinage, for it becomes an object of public visual display. When Amparo goes on a guided tour of her intended marital home, she feels 'seasick' at the sight of so many commodities, and reflects that industry has so increased human needs that need and excess are indistinguishable. The visit is described as an 'exposición doméstica' and the dressing room, with its 'vitrinas', as a 'museíto muy mono' (1966: 1533), for this intended marital home is a miniature World Exhibition or museum of modern conveniences. And the museum—unlike Bringas's private collection—is the contradiction of an interior designed for public view. It is logical that Agustín's gift to Rosalía of the commodities in his museum should launch her on the road to adultery, making her already at the end of *Tormento* 'la misma señora de Bringas retocada y adulterada' (1966: 1564). In shopping for a wife to complete his ideal marital home, Agustín 'buys' a woman—he courts her with banknotes—who is 'soiled goods'—Amparo describes herself as a 'fraude de mujer' or 'counterfeit wife' (1966: 1529)—for in the capitalist exchange economy the new blurs with the secondhand. He is acting as a good capitalist when he accepts her nonetheless, so as not to 'waste' her. But, as secondhand goods, she cannot be his wife if marriage is to retain its definition as a private sphere distinct from the public sphere of the market.

In developing a passion for shopping, Agustín—the 'bear' from the Wild West, or the 'kaffir' as Rosalía calls him—is also 'feminized' by what he himself terms 'la afeminada sociedad' (1966: 1468). His former life on 'the frontier' poses the question of where the boundary lies between civilization and barbarism. His frontier outpost near the Mexican–US border is not a dividing-line between order and chaos but a nightmarish mixture of capitalism—'no había más que comercio'—and the law of the jungle, where the amassing of private fortunes coexists with concubinage, polygamy, and polyandry (1966: 1478): that is, forms of cohabitation that reject the notion of exclusive property rights. If civilization is capitalist circulation, then it is hard to distinguish from the lack of stable property rights that Thiers saw as the hallmark of savagery. In Spain, Agustín discovers that his ideal of reconciling 'las instituciones históricas con las novedades revolucionarias' (1966: 1513), meaning free trade, is a delusion because free trade subverts the individual ownership of property as much as it confirms it. In returning to 'la comarca fronteriza' (1966: 1562) to live in concubinage with Amparo at the end of *Tormento*, Agustín is not rejecting modern civilization and free trade—he goes to Bordeaux where he has business interests—but is recognizing that capitalism, by putting everything into circulation, is a form of anarchy.

Polo, who leaves Europe for the Philippines, makes an inverse journey. He starts from the premiss that civilization, himself included, is degenerate. Padre Nones sends him to the countryside near Toledo to be 'civilized' by returning to 'el estado salvaje' (1966: 1506): exercise, fresh air, and 'trabajo saludable' regenerate him by making him an 'hombre primitivo' (1966: 1524). In going to be a missionary in the Philippines he will no doubt secure his own regeneration by returning to natural savagery, but what of the 'kaffirs' whom Amparo imagines him civilizing? Vicens Vives (1969: 612) notes that the Philippines were 'the great market place, the open door from Europe to Oriental trade'; *Fortunata y Jacinta* (i. 151–2) tells us that in the mid-nineteenth century the commercial importance of the

Philippines was overtaken by that of the British trading post in Singapore, but that Spanish trade with the Far East picked up after 1868. This suggests that Polo's 'civilizing mission' is, like it or not, inseparable from the worldwide extension of the capitalist economic system.

If civilization is barbarism (Agustín's discovery), and savagery is civilization (Polo's lesson), we have a serious problem of distinctions. There is no frontier; or, to put it differently, everywhere is a 'comarca fronteriza' which, instead of separating opposing territories, marks their meeting point. The Palace is described in *La de Bringas* as a leaking ship because it is ambiguously positioned between the 'wild' Campo del Moro and the 'civilized' formal gardens of the Palacio de Oriente, planned on the French model by Joseph Bonaparte though not completed till the mid-century (Hauser 1979: 80). It is also invaded by pigeons, making it a 'salvaje república' (1985: 70). Rosalía's adulterous dalliances with Pez take place, as in the novels analysed by Tanner, in locations sited midway between city and country: the Palace terrace overlooking the Campo del Moro, and the Retiro Park whose 'Montaña artificial' and zoo reconstruct nature as a spectacle to be viewed by city-dwellers (1985: 124–5). In an 1865 article in *La Nación*, Galdós described proposals for embellishing the Retiro with fountains, statues, obelisks, and conservatories as its conversion into 'una especie de museo' (Pérez Galdós 1981: 15). At the time of Rosalía's walks with Pez, the Retiro was still Crown property though the public was allowed into parts of it; as wife of the head of Crown property, she has access to both public and private areas. We are told that some of the land is up for sale, thanks to Isabel II's *rasgo*, and that the railings round this area have been removed (1985: 128).[10] The Retiro provides an image of the blurring of private and public, as well as of the adulteration of nature. The latter is illustrated graphically by the Bringas

---

[10] In 1865 a third of the Retiro's original extension was put up for sale in what Navascués Palacio calls a 'torpe actuación especuladora'. After the 1868 Revolution, when the Retiro became a public park controlled by the Ayuntamiento, the walls round its perimeter were demolished, as were those separating the previous royal 'reservados' from the public areas. In 1876, the State formally conceded the Retiro to the Ayuntamiento in perpetuity, on condition it be used for public recreational purposes (Navascués Palacio in Fernández García 1993: 426–7; Pla et al. 1987: 33; Simón Palmer 1991: 73; Ariza 1988: 79–80, 243).

children swimming in the polluted River Manzanares, the stench of sewage—referred to as 'emanaciones nada balsámicas' (1985: 245)—being particularly strong in the summer months.[11] The association of this contagion with capitalism is reinforced by comparison of the moneylender Torres's unctuous smile to a 'fluido miasmático' (1985: 132). Even the seaside recommended by hygienists (Bringas's doctor recommends the spa waters of Cestona) has been adulterated since, as *Tormento* notes (1966: 1474), with the opening of the Ferrocarril del Norte in 1865 holidaying in San Sebastián has become a fashion. Curiously, swimming in the Manzanares does make the Bringas children healthy as they revert to the state of 'moros' (1985: 245). As befits an adulteress, Rosalía hates the real countryside (Navalcarnero, where Bringas took her for their honeymoon), preferring the adulterated variety resulting from capitalist modernization.

De Bolla (1989: 132) describes the capitalist system as 'institutionalized excess' or 'excess within limits'. But what are the limits and where, in this adulterated society, are they? If excess by definition exceeds limits, what might 'excess within limits' be? De Bolla notes (1989: 112) that the eighteenth-century English discourse on the national debt was based on an analogy between the circulation of capital in the nation and the circulation of blood in the body, which problematized the latter.[12] For if, as was argued, a healthy nation is one with a healthy debt (that is, with a healthy inflow and outflow of capital), what constitutes a healthy body? The logical answer is that the most healthy body is that of the prostitute: the body whose limits are open. *La de Bringas* is a novel about frames that do not hold. The Palace is leaking; Rosalía takes off her corset to the highest bidder; the frame to Bringas's hair picture fails to contain the objects he crams into it, straining perspective to breaking point. And the novel is framed by an unreliable narrator who, in evicting

---

[11] Magnien (in Salaün and Serrano 1991: 116) notes that in summer the water of the River Manzanares was 'fangosa, negra y nauseabunda'. In his *Elementos de higiene privada y pública* (1885: ii. 370), Santero says, 'Por decoro no hablo de los baños del río Manzanares'.

[12] Vilar (1991: 250) paraphrases John Law's *Money and Trade Considered* (1705): 'It was especially important that money should circulate like blood through the body, and the central bank should be conceived of as a heart constantly pulsing money into circulation instead of letting it lie stagnant.'

the Palace's inhabitants, is responsible for the final 'flood' of goods and people, and who additionally commits adultery with Rosalía. An unreliable frame cannot be a frame. As a sequel novel, whose opening chapter—as Bly notes (1981: 20–1)—must have happened some time in the middle of the novel, and whose final epilogue tells us what happened 'after the end', *La de Bringas* is the impossibility of a novel without a frame.[13] Its formal contradictions reproduce those of a society based on 'excess within limits', for limits that contain excess cannot be limits.

The novel's trick beginning also tricks the reader into confusing art (Bringas's hair picture) with 'reality' (Bringas in his apartment, which of course, being in a novel, is not reality at all). This novel of commodity fetishism is, of all Galdós's novels, the one that most problematizes representation because it depicts the conversion of reality into a mask and the riotous traffic of goods and women: as Refugio says, 'Esto es un carnaval de todos los días' (1985: 283). Seeing is not believing, not only because surface appearances are designed to deceive, but also because, when everything is in movement, the result is blurred vision. Bringas's temporary blindness is induced by his concentration on his 'work of art' so as to blind himself to the flow of goods outside, but what he is finally left with is a blurred vision that figures money in motion: 'la visión calenturienta de millares de puntos luminosos o de tenues rayos metálicos, movibles, fugaces' (1985: 156). Marx defined the capitalist exchange economy as 'value in motion' (Harvey 1989: 107). Visitors to the 1851 First World Exhibition described the mass of commodities as a blur that was too much for their eyes to take in (Richards 1990: 27, 31). Amparo felt a similar 'dizziness' at the sight of Agustín's 'museum' of commodities. As Richards notes (1990: 32), the vision of surplus created by the Crystal Palace 'both extended the sway of sight over all commodities and signalled the rise of a new imagistic mode for representing them'. Richards is referring to impressionism; the result in *La de Bringas* is a spatial distortion (Bly 1974) created by this impossible 'excess within limits'. Bringas's sight disorder is defined as 'congestión retiniana' (1985: 149), linking it to the congestion of objects swirling in Isabelita's

---

[13] For more detailed discussion of the problem of narrative framing, see Gold (1993: 23–47) and Labanyi (1990).

nightmares. De Certeau (in During 1993: 153–4) notes that the modern city is characterized by 'an opaque and blind mobility' because so much is going on it is impossible to see it all; this, he argues, produces a utopian urge—exemplified in town planning—to bring the city under control by subjecting it to a panoptical view. The impossibility of doing this is shown by the Bringas children viewing the Maundy Thursday paupers' banquet from the vantage point of a skylight in the ceiling: the panoptical view only compounds the distortion.

The emphasis in *La de Bringas* on commodification also challenges realism because it means that things are defined not by what they are (use value) but by what they are worth (exchange value). Monetary value is not fixed or inherent but shifts with the movements of the market. When metal coin, whose intrinsic value matches that of the object it represents, is replaced by fiduciary or token money (banknotes, bills of exchange, credit), whose intrinsic value is worthless, the relationship between the object and its monetary representation becomes entirely arbitrary. As Marx put it (Harvey 1989: 101), money in the capitalist system, which depends on fiduciary currency to speed up circulation, is an 'arbitrary fiction': words on bits of paper. Theoretically everyone can now 'write money'; but how then does one distinguish between 'real' money and counterfeit money? Originally, paper money was guaranteed by the issuer's promise to exchange it for its value in 'hard metal'. But when in 1883, the year before *La de Bringas*, the Bank of Spain ended convertibility of its banknotes into gold, that guarantee was lost. In 1881, *La desheredada* had started to chart the detachment of signs from things. In 1884, after Spain's abandonment of the gold standard, *La de Bringas* depicts a self-reflexive world where the relationship between signs and things has been lost and meaning lies entirely in the free-floating system of signs. Spain's abandonment of the gold standard some thirty years before other European countries helps explain why Spain's major realist novelist, also the one most concerned with money, should problematize realism in a more modern way than perhaps any of his European contemporaries. The other explanation is Spain's picaresque and Cervantine traditions, but their unreliable narration can in turn be linked to sixteenth-century Spanish monetary discourse which, as Vilar has shown (1991: 155–68), was ahead of the rest of Europe because it had to grapple with the problem of inflation (unstable value) caused by the influx of American metals.

In *La de Bringas*, everyone is writing money and defaulting on payment, showing the gap between representation and reality. Rosalía receives 'papelitos' (bills) from Sobrino Hermanos, a promissory note (deferred to 'one day') from Pez, payment reminders from the moneylenders Torres and Torquemada (with whom she had signed contracts, despite the fact that women were not legally entitled to do so without their husband's signature); she even makes a contract with Milagros lending her money (Milagros does honour half of it). In *Tormento*, Agustín's love letters to Amparo took the form of banknotes. For money can say everything (though it may prove worthless), and everything can function as money or 'symbolic capital' (to use Bourdieu's term): the food hampers for the poor, the bottles of wine and French capons with which the narrator bribes Bringas, Bringas's hair picture, the candlesticks which Rosalía pawns, Rosalía's body. Agustín Caballero hires José Ido as his bookkeeper, despite his flimsy grasp on reality as a writer of popular fiction, because he has beautiful handwriting: what matters is the sign rather than what is represented. Goux has related the modernist abandonment of representationalism to the general abandonment of the gold standard from around 1914 through his study of Gide's *Les Faux-monnayeurs* (1984). *La de Bringas* is also a novel about counterfeiting. Harvey (1989: 107) notes that the phrase 'the value of money', which we all understand, is a tautology meaning 'the value of value', for money is an arbitrary symbol that has no intrinsic value. Bringas, who values money for its own sake, is the author of the hair picture which provides an ironic self-reflexive comment on the problematic nature of artistic representation. In her classic study of collecting, Stewart notes that 'the collection represents the total aestheticization of use value. The collection is a form of art as play [...] unlike many forms of art, the collection is not representational. The collection presents a hermetic world' (1993: 151–2). One thinks here of Bringas's games with Isabelita, in which objects can be infinitely reshuffled because they form part of a closed, self-reflexive world: the point is to return the objects to their boxes at the end of the game. Simmel's analysis of the miser as the ultimate commodity fetishist shows him to incarnate an abstract understanding of money as a self-reflexive system of representation (Dodd 1994: 110). If as a miser Bringas is a capitalist gone mad, as an artist 'copiando indoctamente a la Naturaleza' (1985: 55) he is a realist gone mad; that is, a realist turned collector. *La de Bringas* is a self-reflexive novel commenting on its own status as an 'arbitrary fiction' because it is concerned with 'the value of money'; that is, with 'the value of value'.

5
The Consumption of Natural Resources: Galdós's *Fortunata y Jacinta* (1886–1887)

GEORG SIMMEL'S *The Philosophy of Money* (1900) argues that modernity is a product of the exchange economy. Simmel differs from Marx in focusing on consumption rather than production, for he is concerned with the ways in which capitalism is experienced by society at large; his book originated in an 1889 lecture 'The Psychology of Money'. His premiss is that socialization is exchange (1990: 175), and that money is 'nothing but the pure form of exchangeability' (1990: 130). Money is therefore 'entirely a social institution and quite meaningless if restricted to one individual' (1990: 162). Money is motion: 'There is no more striking symbol of the completely dynamic character of the world than that of money. The meaning of money lies in the fact that it will be given away. When money stands still, it is no longer money according to its specific value and significance.' Bringas's hoard of banknotes illustrates this well for it has no value, and can safely be replaced by blank sheets of paper, so long as it is kept locked away. In *Fortunata y Jacinta*, Maxi makes a similar discovery when he fills his replacement piggy-bank with worthless small change, and uses his savings to initiate himself into social relations. Simmel notes that, in the exchange economy, value is not fixed and inherent but fluctuating and based on the relationships between things. This mirrors late nineteenth-century science which 'has abandoned the search for the essence of things and is reconciled to stating the relationships that exist between objects and the human mind' (1990: 103). Money, in other words, generates modern relativism (1990: 126).

Simmel argues that the development of credit and paper money has increased this relativistic tendency, creating sophisticated forms of symbolic thought whereby things are seen in terms not of inherent worth but of what they represent. This representationalism requires the creation of triangular configurations, for in the exchange economy things are related to each other indirectly through the relation of each to a third term: money. Simmel calls this capacity for symbolization through appeal to a third term one of the greatest intellectual advances made by mankind, for it supposes a high degree of abstraction (1990: 146). Here again, one is reminded of Girard's analysis of the importance of triangular desire in the nineteenth-century novel (1966); *Fortunata y Jacinta* is a novel based on a network of interlocking triangular relationships (Fortunata, Juanito, and Jacinta; Maxi, Fortunata, and Juanito; Fortunata, Jacinta, and their 'joint' child; Fortunata, Guillermina, and Mauricia). The abstract, symbolic nature of money is seen by Simmel as the basis of the modern cultural trend towards the replacement of reality by forms of representation (1990: 148).[1] This, I shall argue, is the significance of nineteenth-century realism, in its desire to represent everything. If one accepts this view, the move towards more abstract representational forms at the end of the century marks, not a break, but an intensification of the process as, with the increasing use of fiduciary or token currency, 'money becomes more and more a mere symbol' (Simmel 1990: 152). Simmel's argument confirms Benjamin's insight that the seeds of modernism, as the expression of capitalist modernity, can be traced back to the mid-nineteenth century. Simmel notes that the replacement of reality by representation is made necessary by the increasing size and complexity of modern urban society, requiring the creation of representative symbols (money) and the delegation of power to representative agents (elected parliamentary deputies) (1990: 175–6). He also notes that, as money increasingly becomes a symbol with no intrinsic worth, it depends more and more on its validation by public institutions and authorities (1990: 184). An increasingly abstract system of monetary representation goes hand in hand with the growth of the State, conceived as a representative body.

Fortunata y Jacinta depicts a society dominated by the market and by the State. It is the first of Galdós's novels to explore in

---

[1] Simmel's insights on the importance of abstraction in modernity are developed productively by Asendorf (1993) in his discussion of changes in object relations and modes of perception in the modern city, and their cultural consequences.

detail the problem of *caciquismo*; that is, an adulterated system of political representation. The exchange economy depicted in the novel is similarly marked by a fear of being passed off with adulterated goods for, if value lies in what things cost rather than in what they are, the distinction between the fraudulent and the legitimate becomes problematic. The novel illustrates Simmel's contention that modernity, being mediated by money, is characterized by relativism. All the relationships in the novel, even the most selfless, are mediated by money. As Doña Lupe exclaims when Fortunata insists she keep her money after she has definitively left Maxi, 'Conservar el dinero era sostener una especie de parentesco' (Pérez Galdós 1992: ii. 388). Doña Lupe's business acumen makes her prefer compromise to principle, for money makes all things relative. The novel shows the impossibility of making clearcut distinctions in an exchange economy where everything is interconnected. It develops to the full the problem posed in *La familia de León Roch*: that of distinguishing between good fusions (marriage) and bad confusions (adultery, figurative incest). The parallels between private and public life have been read as political allegory (Ribbans in Varey 1970; and Ribbans 1977, 1993); they can also be read as an illustration of the inextricable confusion of that which should be separate. The relativism resulting from this blurring of distinctions is articulated by the novel's closing words: 'lo mismo da.'

The characters and narrator constantly comment on the complex interconnections behind disparate events: Juanito would not have met Fortunata if Estupiñá had not fallen ill; Nicolás Rubín would not have been made a canon if Fortunata had not been unfaithful to Maxi. The first part of the novel turns into a history and geography lesson, for the most remote events have public and private repercussions: the British establishment of a trading post in Singapore and the construction of a railway across the Suez Isthmus change the course of the Madrid textile trade and with it that of the Arnaiz family. Harvey (1985: 11; 1989: 261–5) notes that the global dimensions of the capitalist economy produce a sense of relative space, requiring artists to find a way of representing a world in which everything affects everything else. If *La de Bringas* was an attempt to express capitalist 'excess within limits', in *Fortunata y Jacinta* the excess is bursting out of limits. The spatial congestion of the earlier novel is replaced with a sprawling structure verging on formlessness. Part I (the story of the Santa Cruz family) is a novel in its own right but its end is the start of another one (that of the Rubín family, occupying parts II–IV). *Fortunata y Jacinta* is an attempt to write a 'novel about everything', for in the global exchange economy everything is relevant. The novel's apparent openness is the other side of a vast network of connections that traps the characters within its confines; the story of the Rubín family becomes inextricably entwined with that of the Santa Cruz family so that we come back to them full circle at the end: an end which, with the birth of Fortunata's son, is another beginning. As Fortunata says on discovering that Guillermina is now the owner of the house where she will die: 'Era como una red que la envolvía, y como pensara escabullirse por algún lado, se encontraba otra vez cogida' (ii. 398). The image of this interconnectedness is the family: the 'enredadera' (i. 241) of kinship relations which binds the different economic strata of Madrid, indeed of the nation, in an unintelligible tangle— an image not so much of unity as of hopeless confusion.[2] The novel poses the problem of knowing who does or does not belong to the family when everyone is related to everyone else. In addition to families constituted by marriage, it deals with extended families (whose servants and dependants are and are not part of the family unit), foster families, surrogate families (Guillermina's orphanage), and 'political families' (as political groupings were, and still are, called in Spain): this last a particularly hopeless tangle of what ought to be separate.

Chapters 2–5 of part I trace the process of nation formation that, since the late eighteenth century, has enveloped everything and everyone within its folds. In so doing, they articulate the anxieties underlying the novel as a whole. That Galdós should choose the drapery business as a cipher of the modernization process is not accidental for, as Hall observes (1992: 116), it was the first form of commerce to develop the characteristics of modern retailing, by introducing plate-glass shop windows, window displays, and the gas-lighting that turned the newly modernized city into a theatrical display. The original Santa Cruz draper's shop, built up from 1796 by Don Baldomero's self-made father, was inherited by him in 1848: the year of the

---

[2] Sinnigen, who productively applies Anderson's views on the nation as imagined community to Galdós's novels, notes that the latter illustrate the concept of the nation as one big family (1996: 23).

first Europe-wide capitalist crisis of over-accumulation. Don Baldomero maintained his father's practices unchanged, except that, with the tariff reforms of 1849, he started to import cloth from abroad. The firm did not advertise its products through the press or travelling salesmen, though in the mid-century it engaged Estupiñá to publicize its wares in Madrid; Vicens Vives (1969: 692) notes that advertising began in Spain around 1830. It did not use the standardized metrical system of weights and measures introduced in 1858; and prior to 1868, when the peseta was made the national currency, dealt in a variety of different coinages. In other words, an integrated national economy was not yet fully developed. Prices were stable and cash payments were encouraged, though after 1845 banknotes started to be used for wholesale payments only. The firm's speciality was cloth for army uniforms and men's capes: ready-made clothes did not yet exist, and menswear was more important than ladies' fashions. Above all, it was a family firm where the employees ate and prayed and went for walks with the owners: the capitalist split between household and business had not yet occurred. All this alters with the 1868 Revolution. Don Baldomero realizes the new economic climate will bring changes he is not suited to handle (despite having frequented the same political *tertulia* as Pascual Madoz, author of the 1855 Disentailment Law, he is opposed to free trade for nationalistic reasons) and sells the business off, instituting the private/public split. However the split is imperfectly realized, reflecting Spain's incomplete transition to modernity, for the firm's new owners are his nephews.

The novel stresses the incestuous tendency of pre-1868 Madrid commerce, both because the owners of different establishments were related and because the firm was not yet separated from the family. 'Todos somos unos,' says El Gordo Arnaiz (i. 125) who treats his business competitor Don Baldomero like a brother. Indeed the latter is married to Arnaiz's cousin Bárbara, who is additionally Don Baldomero's cousin. Bárbara's father's business also illustrates the lack of division between public and private spheres, with the family living over the shop, and the latter—like other Madrid commercial establishments—hosting a *tertulia* which provides a forum for public critical debate at a time when clubs (casinos) did not exist and patriotic societies were still exclusive (i. 162). Bárbara thus grows up with a knowledge of business and public affairs

—she remembers discussing the first banknotes (i. 164)—that Jacinta, also brought up over the family shop but a generation later, will not have. Bárbara's father (a partner in the Compañía de Filipinas, created in the eighteenth century and dissolved thanks to British competition in 1833) imports textiles from the Philippines, China, Japan, and India, showing that trade with the Far East developed before the existence of an integrated national or European market.[3] The narrator comments that the 'nacional obra de arte' (i. 128), the *mantón de Manila*, is an oriental product, for in the capitalist system the foreign contributes to the making of the national. In the mid-century, the *mantón de Manila* is replaced as the 'national costume' by new imported French ready-made fashions. In the 1850s Bárbara's sister-in-law, Isabel Cordero, effectively takes over running the family business, abandoning oriental imports for French, Belgian, British, and Swiss 'novedades', specializing in white linen as plans to supply Madrid with running water anticipate a time when people will wash and change their clothes regularly: work on the Canal de Isabel II, first proposed by the Marqués de Pontejos whose modernizing efforts are mentioned in the novel, started in 1848, with the first supplies starting in 1854 in response to the cholera epidemic of that year (Martín Muñoz in Otero Carvajal and Bahamonde 1986: 205; Hauser 1979: 213). Corbin notes that the construction of privacy in the course of the nineteenth century expressed itself in 'the extraordinary success of lingerie' (in Perrot 1990: 487). Isabel Cordero's commercial talents, sensing the new importance of ladies' fashions, feminize the business. There is no suggestion that she is exceeding her female role in running the firm, because business and family are still an indivisible unit: 'Lo mismo funcionaba en la cocina que en el escritorio' (i: 158). In saving the family firm as well as giving birth to seventeen children, she is acting as a model wife.[4] In the 1870s, after the public/private

---

[3] Vicens Vives (1969: 536–7, 570) notes that, in the 18th century, a series of protectionist royal decrees had banned the import and sale in Spain of textiles imported from China and South-East Asia. This prehistory meant that trade with the Far East was inextricably linked to demands for free trade.

[4] Ryan (1994: 46–7) notes that, prior to the 1840s, wives did play an active role in capitalist enterprise, mainly as overseers, but that after that date work came to be seen as 'paid' (that is, contracted) and wives were thus relegated to the private sphere of unpaid domestic labour. See also Davidoff and Hall (1987); and Hall (1992).

split has been effected, Aurora Samaniego—who manages several departments of a department store also specializing in white linen—will be made an adulteress, for women who occupy both public and private roles are now a problem.[5]

In introducing female fashions, Isabel Cordero is unwittingly ushering in a new age of free trade, when things are no longer kept in the family and women start to leave the home to go shopping. If the earlier period was incestuous, the new age will be marked by adultery. The change from a society based on the family unit to one based on free flow is figured by the generational shift from Don Baldomero and Doña Bárbara's common matrimonial bed to the separate beds of Juanito and Jacinta, in line with the recommendations of late nineteenth-century hygiene manuals that air should be allowed to circulate freely between bodies (Corbin 1986: 98–102). The narrator comments that the bourgeoisie's mid-century takeover of the public sphere has been called 'el imperio de la levita', but that it is more aptly symbolized by ladies' fashions:

lo más interesante de tal imperio está en el vestir de las señoras, origen de energías poderosas, que de la vida privada salen a la pública [. . .] ¡Los trapos, ay! ¿Quién no ve en ellos una de las principales energías de la época presente [. . .]? Pensad un poco en lo que representan [. . .] y sin querer, vuestra mente os presentará entre los pliegues de las telas de moda [. . .] toda la máquina política y administrativa, la deuda pública y los ferrocarriles, el presupuesto y las rentas, el Estado tutelar y el parlamentarismo socialista. (i. 153)

Here Galdós gives us an image of the exchange economy in which everything is related to everything else, not only because the whole economic and political development of the nineteenth century lies behind changes of taste, but also because women's entry into the market as consumers mirrors the blurring of the public and the private created by the traffic of money and goods, and by the State's increasing invasion of private life through legislation, tax, and social reform. By 'el parlamentarismo socialista' Galdós presumably means total State control, as in his reference in *La de Bringas* to Pez's 'socialismo manso'; if

---

[5] Corbin (1990: 210) notes how Zola's *Au Bonheur des Dames* depicts the lingerie department of his department store as 'a vast dressing room in which a multitude of women, in the grip of desire, abandon their underclothes'.

universal suffrage is also meant, women's entry into the public sphere is an even more appropriate symbol.

After 1868, the Santa Cruz firm too is feminized as it shifts from military uniforms and menswear to imported female fashions. The new free-market economy requires press advertising and a nationwide network of travelling salesmen, and credit facilities for female clients. The construction of a national economy includes the incorporation of women as consumers. We are reminded that these commercial changes could not have happened without railway construction, tariff reform, and the rebuilding of Madrid thanks to the disentailment of Church property (i. 148–50); things go into circulation and women follow. The demolition of the Iglesia de Santa Cruz, on the day the narrator first meets Juanito Santa Cruz (i. 108–9), formed part of the 1869 *ensanche* designed to facilitate the circulation of traffic and goods in Madrid; the event is mentioned in the same breath as Figuerola, the Finance Minister in the revolutionary government responsible for its package of free-trade reforms. Galdós's choice of the Plaza de Santa Cruz as the location of the Santa Cruz family home is significant, since it was a popular commercial concourse, functioning from the seventeenth century through to the late 1920s as the place where those seeking employment in domestic service would congregate to sell, not only the wares which those migrating from the countryside had brought with them to finance the journey, but their 'property in their persons'—that is, their labour (Sarasúa 1994: 61–2).[6] The Santa Cruz family quite literally inhabits Madrid's main labour market, which turns persons into economic resources or 'human capital'. Sarasúa (1994: 170–1) notes that the Mercado de Santa Cruz was especially known for its 'vendedores ambulantes de telas' and wet-nurses seeking employment; in both cases, those from Asturias were especially famous. Sarasúa also notes (1994: 263–4) that from the mid-nineteenth century, as production became separated from the household unit, domestic labour became increasingly 'feminized'—that is, restricted to unproductive domestic service

---

[6] Sarasúa (1994: 62) cites an article in the workers' press from as late as 1927 which states that unemployed workers have only two options in order to find work: to go from door to door, or to wait to be hired in the Plaza de Santa Cruz. See also Sarasúa's colourful citations from an 1846 description of the labour market in the Plaza de Santa Cruz (1994: 170–2).

in the form of housekeepers and maids—which changed the face of the human market in the Plaza de Santa Cruz. The significance of this context of market relations, which did not need spelling out for Galdós's contemporary readers, should be obvious.

Despite his opposition to free trade, Don Baldomero supports the general belief in progress, understood by him in terms of Bastiat's doctrine of *laissez-faire* and the hygienist Pedro Mata's view of the individual and collective body as a self-regulating, self-renewing system: 'La naturaleza se cura sola; no hay más que dejarla. Las fuerzas reparatrices lo hacen todo, ayudadas del aire' (i. 144).[7] The healthy body is one in which flow is unimpeded. Don Baldomero uses this argument to justify allowing his son to do what he likes, with the result that Juanito consumes without feeding anything back into the system. A generation later, the novel ends on a note of exhaustion and pessimism: belief in the body's capacity to renew its energies has been lost. This is not, as is commonly stated, the result of a change from production to consumption as Don Baldomero sells off the family firm: his draper's shop was always a retail outlet stimulating consumption, and in investing his money he is still contributing to the national wealth by facilitating the flow of capital. What has happened is that the capitalist dynamic initiated in the first half of the century has, with the removal of controls in 1868, overflowed the system's limits.

In dedicating chapter 3 to the 'corredor de géneros' Estupiñá, who claims to have witnessed every major political event of the century, Galdós gives us a walking lesson in national history. Estupiñá's love of the market-place—'la calle, el aire libre, la discusión, la contratación' (i. 172)—logically makes him a smuggler avoiding customs duties for he sees State control as a threat to individual freedom: 'Según él, lo que la Hacienda llama suyo no es suyo, sino de la nación, es decir, de Juan Particular' (i. 173). This points to the central contradiction in the liberal project, which furthers individual rights while extending the powers of the nation-State. Juanito's and Jacinta's honeymoon in 1871, made possible by the new national railway network, serves to construct an integrated image of the nation in the mind of Jacinta and the reader. The lessons in national

---

[7] For information on Mata, see Chapter 3 n. 31.

history which Juanito gives her replicate the topoi—Sagunto, Jaime de Aragón, Roger de Flor, Don Juan de Austria—treated by late nineteenth-century historical painters in their officially sponsored attempt to create a myth of national origins (Reyero 1989). Jacinta's uneducated comments undermine this myth-making, observing that Juanito's national 'heroes' were 'brutos' and their deeds 'una barbaridad' (i. 221). The conversion of the nation into representation is explicitly subverted later in the novel when the drunken lower-class braggart, José Izquierdo, becomes 'el gran *modelo* de la pintura histórica contemporánea' (i. 348, Galdós's italics), sitting for paintings of Jaime de Aragón entering Valencia and Cortés burning his boats (ii. 415).[8] The journalist Federico Ruiz's obsession with cataloguing every ruined castle in the nation (i. 412) shows the shaky foundations on which national history is constructed.[9] That the State has succeeded in turning even its most neglected citizens into Spaniards will be shown later in the novel at Mauricia's last rites, where the slum tenants pin up a national flag made from curtains that have been variously recycled (ii. 182): an illustration of the *bricolage* process whereby the image of a unified nation is constructed out of heterogeneous materials.

Juanito's and Jacinta's first major stop is Barcelona, where they visit the modern textile mills, giving Jacinta an insight into the reality that lies behind commodity fetishism: 'Está una viendo las cosas todos los días, y no piensa en cómo se hacen' (i. 214). She is the one who perceives the dreariness of the factory girls' machine-like existence: the first of many references in the novel to 'máquinas' that are exhausted rather than self-renewing. Her nascent philanthropic concern is that of a woman for other women: again the first hint in the novel of new all-female social configurations, bypassing men. Most of the rest of the journey takes them through fertile agricultural

---

[8] In Galdós's review of the 1884 National Art Exhibition, he exhorted artists to paint 'la época presente', following the example of Spain's Golden Age painters who 'cuando pintaban historia, es decir, Biblia o mitología, la modernizaban, trayéndola a la *vulgaridad* de su tiempo'. Galdós's critique here is in line with that of Krausist critics who attacked the grandiloquent school of official-sponsored historical painting for hiding behind a mythical vision of the national past as a way of avoiding a problematic present (Pena López 1990: 142; 1994: 226).

[9] See Hobsbawm and Ranger (1984: 64, 69, 183) for the role played by archaeology in 19th-century attempts to invent a national tradition.

land where nature and culture are in harmony; Valencia is a 'ciudad campestre', Seville harmoniously blends architecture and nature. Only Castile is arid, and the couple adds to Madrid's draining of the periphery's resources by consuming a '*montón de cadáveres* fritos' (fried birds) on the train (i. 219, Galdós's italics). This image of the nation as a harmonious 'marriage' of nature and culture is broken when in Seville they intrude into the wedding celebrations of an Anglicized Spanish couple from Gibraltar (implying their connections with commerce), and Juanito lets out the story of his 'devouring' of the uncultured Fortunata, from the start associated with the consumption of birds (Gilman 1966; Gullón 1974; Utt 1974) since when they met she was eating a raw egg in her aunt's poultry shop, whose rows of corpses showed that 'La voracidad del hombre no tiene límites' (i. 181). This problem of a consumption that has exceeded its limits, upsetting the harmonious 'marriage' of nature and culture, is central to the novel.

The novel's treatment of national politics from 1869 to 1876 is set against the consumption of food and drink, at the Santa Cruz table or in Madrid's many cafés. Despite the Santa Cruz family's origins in the draper's business, most of the consumption that takes place in the novel is not of fashions but of food, for the stress is on the exhaustion of natural resources.[10] The redundant civil servants who fill the cafés think they have a right to drain the State's coffers—as Feijoo puts it, 'sólo se trata de saber a quién le toca mamar y a quién no' (ii. 15)— because they see State property as their own: 'hablaban del país como de cosa propia' (ii. 14). Basilio Andrés de la Caña talks of the Treasury as 'mi ramo' (ii. 20), meaning that he has a right to a job, but his confusion of public and private also supposes that the State has a right to its citizens' wealth: his speciality is gathering fiscal statistics to improve tax collection (ii. 447). In Galdós's next novel *Miau* (1887) the *cesante* Villaamil, also obsessed with tax collection, will reappear as an incarnation of blindness to the public/private distinction. Though honest and less fanatical than Pantoja, who regards all private property as theft from the State, Villaamil is no different from his corrupt son-in-law Víctor in thinking he has a

---

[10] For discussion of digestion references in the novel, see Labanyi (1988).

right to live off the State, and in expecting his 'amigos' in high places to grant his requests for favours. The *cesante*, constantly migrating to different cafés in the hope of better pickings, is a bourgeois vagrant or beggar; Bahamonde Magro and Toro Mérida (1978: 57) note that the 1868 Penal Code extended the definition of vagrancy explicitly to include the unemployed, though of course it was the working classes that the law had in mind.

As we shall see when discussing the rural novel, *caciquismo*'s reduction of national politics to the securing of office through a network of 'amigos políticos' was a form of *compadrazgo* converting social relations into kinship ties: hence contemporary use of the term 'political families'. Galdós was familiar with this system, having been elected as an 'official' candidate for Sagasta's Liberal government in 1886 (at the time *Fortunata y Jacinta* was being written) on the shameful basis of a mere seventeen votes (Berkowitz 1948: 204): his lack of connections with his constituency in Puerto Rico, which he never visited, required his election to be 'fixed' by local government agents (*caciques*). In *Fortunata y Jacinta*, the 'sociedad de los vagos' (ii. 12) constituted by Madrid's political aspirants is a 'public family' that lives 'en la calle'; that is, in the café. The novel describes this café society as a 'feria' or market where ideas and jobs are exchanged (ii. 22): a kind of bourgeois—and considerably less socially useful—equivalent of the labour market for which the Plaza de Santa Cruz was famous. For Juan Pablo Rubín, the café is what the 'hogar doméstico' is to the 'buen burgués' (ii. 126); he lives with a 'mujer pública', Refugio, because he has no concept of privacy. The State is an extended family—not unlike the variegated habitués of the Santa Cruz table—which includes appendages related not by kin but through a favour system: Bahamonde has described the electoral loyalties of Madrid's servants to their masters' political affiliations as a kind of *caciquismo urbano* (in Fernández García 1993: 505). The extended family is an adulterated family, for its appendages—standing, like the adulterer, inside and outside the family unit—blur its boundaries.

The most noticeable feature of the 'political families' at the Santa Cruz table and in Madrid's cafés is their promiscuity, for the Restoration 'turno en el dominio' (ii. 15) was based on a politics of conciliation: 'Allí brillaba espléndidamente esa fraternidad española en cuyo seno se dan mano de amigo el carlista y el republicano, el progresista de cabeza dura y el moderado implacable.' In this 'universal brotherhood', everyone is an 'amigo particular de todo el mundo', regardless of political affiliation (ii. 15). The novel shows that this political promiscuity—a 'fraternity' based not on an incestuous keeping things in the family but on an adulterous bringing everyone in—goes back to the *sexenio revolucionario*: Juan Pablo Rubín and José Izquierdo oscillate between Carlism and republicanism. These changes of loyalty make it easy for the Restoration to 'unify' the nation; the result is a family of disparate, unfaithful bedfellows. Café society has ceased to be the public sphere of critical debate between private individuals that Habermas saw as the hallmark of the Enlightenment project (and which Galdós described in *La Fontana de Oro*, set in the Romantic period), because it no longer sees its function as that of an opposition; as Habermas notes (1989: 138), the proliferation of State employees was largely responsible for this loss of critical independence. Even the journalists Federico Ruiz and Basilio Andrés de la Caña take government posts as well as writing for the press.

Feijoo, the only member of this café society who is indebted to no one, conserves the critical spirit of Spain's major Enlightenment intellectual, Padre Feijoo, but he too makes use of the State favour system, albeit to help others. With the Restoration, in addition to getting Nicolás Rubín appointed canon (Church appointments being under State control since 1845), he persuades Villalonga to give Juan Pablo a job in the prison service, where he had worked (as well as in the secret police and police inspectorate) before the Republic (ii. 148). Galdós tells us that Villalonga—who holds a top post in the Ministerio de Gobernación, the super-ministry to which all other ministries responsible for home affairs were responsible, and whose brief was to bring the provinces under central control—is 'uña y carne de Romero Robledo' (ii. 46): the Ministro de Gobernación who was used by Cánovas to rig elections, particularly in the 1880s.[11] The ex-army chaplain Quevedo, one

---

[11] For Galdós's diatribe against Romero Robledo's electoral abuses, see Goldman in Labanyi (1993*a*: 142–3). For the centralizing function of the Ministro de Gobernación, see López Garrido (1982: 79).

of Juan Pablo's café associates, is the strongman who 'fixes' Villalonga's election to a mining village in Almería (ii. 128, 148). In 1876 Villalonga appoints Juan Pablo Provincial Governor of 'his' province, making it clear that his job is to subdue all opposition; we are told that Romero Robledo has given him *carte blanche* to use whatever methods are necessary (ii. 444). Juan Pablo instantly promises to make one of his café 'friends' his inspector of police. Juan Pablo had started his career as a travelling salesman in the provinces, helping construct a nationwide market. His later career in the prison service and in the violent enforcement of State authority shows how the other side of nation formation is centralized regulation and control: that is, the massive invasion of private life. Juan Pablo justifies this 'Estado tutelar' based on coercion since 'el pueblo español está ineducado y hay que impedir que cuatro pillastres engañen a los inocentes' (ii. 446). His incompatible mixture of 'socialismo sin libertad, combinado con el absolutismo sin religión' (ii. 29), acquired from his variegated political past, suits him admirably to the job of enforcing 'el espíritu conciliador' of the Restoration (ii. 446). He does not give up his mistress Refugio but keeps her out of sight in Madrid, for the Restoration is about having it both ways. Feijoo also engineers Fortunata's reconciliation with Maxi as 'otra Restauración' designed to help her have it both ways as a wife and adulteress; but there is a fundamental difference here, for Feijoo's golden rule is the inviolacy of privacy.

José Ido, obsessed with his own wife's supposed adultery, defines this 'adulterous' politics of reconciliation as 'libertad; pero [. . .] sin desmandarse, mirando siempre la Ley' (ii. 421). As a former teacher, Ido supports the project of national unification through State regulation: the function of the State education system introduced in 1857 was to create a 'supervised freedom' (Varela and Álvarez-Uría 1991). Ido corrects spelling mistakes found in the street, just as Maxi corrects Fortunata's non-standard speech. Galdós's refusal to standardize or correct his lower-class characters' speech can be seen as a protest against this homogenization; in a nice malapropism, José Izquierdo calls State education 'la Destrucción pública' (i. 347). When the narrator of *Fortunata y Jacinta* praises the 'dichosa confusión de clases' of modern Spanish society which has 'solved' class conflict by creating 'la concordia y reconciliación de todas ellas', he is setting out the political programme of the Restoration, rightly attributing this 'national unity' to the State bureaucracy, the State education system, and the levelling effects of money (i. 240). We must remember that the narrator is a friend of Villalonga, fully involved in enforcing the Restoration's 'supervised freedom'. In his 1897 speech on reception to the Spanish Royal Academy, Galdós called this homogenization a dissolution of forms (Pérez Galdós 1972: 177–80). The narrator comes closer to this view when he goes on to describe Spain's supposed social 'harmony' as a 'revoltijo', labyrinth, and 'enredadera' (i. 241).

That the Restoration's 'espíritu conciliador' is a bad confusion of things that ought to be separate is implied by the analogy drawn between the nation's changes of political allegiance and Juanito Santa Cruz's marital prevarications. The Restoration is the culmination of the *sexenio revolucionario*'s oscillation between order (monarchy/marriage) and anarchy (republic/adultery), 'reconciling' the two by fusing them simultaneously. It is not just that Fortunata's 'otra restauración' permits her to have it both ways (for a while); Juanito is reconciled with Jacinta, on the day Alfonso XII enters Madrid, because he is attracted to her as if she were 'la mujer de otro' (ii. 56). The relationship between husband and wife has itself become adulterous. As Jacinta comments, Juanito's marital caresses are 'sobras de otra parte' which 'vienen muy usadas' (ii. 58). To confuse things more, Fortunata's constant love for Juanito makes adultery a form of fidelity. When Fortunata asks which is the real marriage, Juanito's relationship with his wife or his adulterous relationship with her, she is asking an important question for marriage and adultery are becoming indistinguishable.

The vagaries of national politics and Juanito's sexual prevarications are both described as subject to fashion: 'En el fondo de la naturaleza humana hay también, como en la superficie social, una sucesión de modas' (i. 285). Juanito's new style of dressing betrays his affair with Fortunata (i. 187); the changes of political regime keep the drapers happy because the new incumbents and their wives update their wardrobes (ii. 125). Politics enters the novel in the form of gossip or news; as such, it becomes fashion (the term 'novedades' is used in the novel for both). Villalonga's account to Juanito of Fortunata's return is intercut with his news of Pavía's coup of January 1874, which ended the Federal Republic; Jacinta's confrontation with Juanito over his affair with Fortunata is delayed by gossip about the newly inaugurated Restoration. The Restoration is the culmination of the realm of fashion initiated in the mid-century because it is an attempt to harmonize modernization with stability; that is, the new with the ever-same. As in fashion, this signifies standardization (national unity) through the imitation of foreign models. Like the adulterous Don Juan of *Lo prohibido*, Juanito's relations with women are those of a consumer driven by desire for the latest model possessed by others; apart from being attracted to his wife as if she belonged to another, his desire for Fortunata is rekindled when he learns she is dressed in the latest Parisian fashions and with another man, and again when he hears she is married. He tires of her because, unlike his friends' mistresses, she fails to assimilate fashionable French manners and her constancy represents an imperviousness to fashion: 'Otras mujeres [...] cambian de ilusión como de moda. Esta no' (ii. 63). It is logical that he should replace Fortunata with Aurora: a Frenchman's widow and manager of the 'novedades' sections of a new department store.

Juanito does not go shopping like José María in *Lo prohibido*, but he is the *flâneur* consuming the city's pleasures: 'no tenía absolutamente nada que hacer más que pasear y divertirse' (i. 284). He rejects his father's suggestion that he make his money productive by investing it and devotes it entirely to consumption. His controlled dissipation is an image of capitalist 'excess within limits':

Gastaba, sí, pero con pulso y medida [...] como conocía tan bien el valor de la moneda, sabía emplearla en la adquisición de sus goces de una manera prudente y casi mercantil. [...] De la cantidad con que cualquier manirroto se proporcionaba un placer, Juanito Santa Cruz sacaba siempre dos. (i. 286–7)[12]

Feijoo comments on his meanness in 'buying Fortunata off': 'No se ha corrido que digamos' (ii. 90). The term 'correr' is

---

[12] This directly echoes the hygienist Monlau's advice to the married (1865: 191): 'economizar sus placeres será duplicarlos.'

used throughout the novel in a variety of forms to refer to both financial and sexual expenditure. The same Don Baldomero who is reluctant to introduce advertising ('corredores de género') insists that Juanito should have his fun in Paris: 'Déjale que se divierta y que la corra' (i. 114). Juanito hunts Fortunata down like a 'corredor que [...] recorre calles sin encontrar el negocio que busca' (i. 440). As a prostitute, Fortunata is 'muy corrida', while the prostitute Mauricia is a 'corredora de géneros'. Doña Lupe remarks that, despite her dissolute morals as a prostitute, Mauricia is an extremely efficient commercial representative—logically, for both activities signify entry to the market. Ido's ideal of supervised freedom supposes that stability is necessary because 'No corriendo el dinero, la plaza está mal' (ii. 421); this is much like Juanito's 'excess within limits'. The problem is how to make money flow without it flowing too much. Feijoo is similarly concerned with allowing sexual expenditure without overspending. His advice to Fortunata to reduce her excessive emotional output— 'recortar a usted el corazón para que haya equilibrio' (ii. 92)— is another version of Restoration compromise. But he devotes himself to restoring her energies: he is more concerned with her health than her morals, and he delights in watching her eat, whereas Juanito consumes her while conserving his own energies. It is not just a problem of limiting expenditure, but of making it flow reciprocally so that energies are renewed and not drained.

Fortunata may be uninterested in fashion, but she cannot escape the market economy that is all around her: her father was a market vendor and her mother had a poultry establishment, like her aunt (i. 484). Her habitation, at the start and end of the novel, of the Cava de San Miguel links her inextricably with the market economy in the form of the adjacent Mercado de San Miguel, described in an 1881 issue of the *Boletín de Beneficencia y Sanidad Municipal* as spilling out onto the surrounding streets (including the Cava de San Miguel), and as a health hazard because of its 'hacinamiento y confusión', 'poca ventilación', and 'mal olor' resulting from the accumulation of rotting fruit and vegetables and its total lack of drains or water supply (Hauser 1979: 399–402). This contemporary view of the Mercado de San Miguel as a source of putrefaction and contamination, invading the surrounding city centre, should warn us against interpreting Fortunata's association with it as a straightforward sign of natural health and vitality. Her association with the market links her in every sense with prostitution, as a form of economic trafficking and as a possible source of moral and physical contagion. Unlike Isidora in *La desheredada*, Fortunata became a prostitute out of necessity, not free choice. Her incorporation into the market as an exchange commodity thus makes her a victim rather than a free agent. Shopping, however, gives her a measure of freedom, not because she enjoys it, but because it provides an excuse to be absent from the marital home. Feijoo increases her independence by giving her some shares and some sound management advice: entry to the market does give freedom if one knows how to play it and if one has some start-up capital. Fortunata's first adultery with Juanito, like her original affair with him, was governed by blind instinct; her second adultery with him, after Feijoo's lessons, is consciously chosen. This second adultery, in which she freely disposes of her property in her person, culminates in what, for market theory, is the litmus test of individual freedom: the making of a contract freely disposing of her property, as she dictates a will leaving her child to Jacinta and her shares to Guillermina. Freedom of testament—signifying the freedom to dispose of one's property—was a key liberal demand. Wills were the only contract, apart from the marriage contract, that all nineteenth-century Spanish women were legally entitled to make; single women over 23 could sign contracts and conduct business—though not belong to a chamber of commerce or hold elected office or be a civil servant—but they lost these rights on marriage (Scanlon 1986: 124; Shubert 1990: 32).[13] As Fortunata says when Estupiñá objects that she needs authorization to put her shares in Guillermina's name, 'Pamplinas. Es mío, y yo lo puedo dar a quien quiera' (ii. 522); she is here asserting a fundamental right. Fortunata knows that Jacinta will take her child anyway when she dies; by making a contract giving her the child, she is not changing the outcome

---

[13] On the importance of freedom of testament, see the section 'Sobre la transmisión de la propiedad' in Giner de los Ríos's *Estudios judíricos y políticos* (1875: 33–50); and Azcárate (1881: 118–21). Spanish women were granted freedom of contract for the first time under the Second Republic, with the 1931 Constitution, a freedom rescinded by the Francoist State (Graham in Graham and Labanyi 1995: 101).

but is making the key point that she is a free individual.[14] True to the liberal definition of freedom, it is her ownership of property (some shares and a son inscribed in the property-owning system as the Santa Cruz heir) and her consequent ability to dispose freely of it that makes her a free individual. She thus achieves her aim of being recognized as the bourgeois, property-owning Jacinta's equal. Her will puts into effect her earlier proposition to Juanito of making a 'trato' with Jacinta, giving her a child in return for her husband. But the final 'deal' is one which Fortunata brings about on her own: she conceives her son with Juanito playing only an unwitting, instrumental role; and her will is a contract between three women, leaving Juanito out of the picture. It is this final contract between women that empowers Jacinta to dictate the terms of a *de facto* legal separation to Juanito (what at the time was called 'divorcio'). Jacinta hereby not only declares Juanito free, but establishes her own claim to freedom.

At this final point, Jacinta starts to develop adulterous fantasies about her former admirer, the now dead Moreno Isla, who as a London banker stands at the apex of the capitalist system.[15] Moreno knew how to manage money but died of a heart attack because he could not manage his bodily economy: his doctor's advice, like that of Feijoo to Fortunata, is to avoid 'overtaxing' himself emotionally. Contemporary hygiene manuals saw the passions as an illness excessively draining the body's reserves (Monlau 1860: lesson 12; Santero 1885: lessons 94–105). Moreno's death is caused by a circulation problem (high blood pressure), producing congestion and subsequent haemorrhage. Fortunata, also good at managing her finances but unable to manage her emotional expenditure, likewise dies of a haemorrhage after attacking her rival Aurora while recovering from childbirth; hygiene manuals singled this period out

[14] Under legislation of the time, ratified by the 1889 Civil Code, a woman was legally barred from investigating the paternity of her child, and the father was not obliged to recognize the child unless there was written evidence of his paternity in his hand, or unless he was already treating the child as his. If the father recognized the child, he could invoke *patria potestas* and remove it from the mother at the age of 3 (Scanlon 1986: 125–6).
[15] Moreno Isla's biography is reminiscent of that of the mid-century Prime Minister Mendizábal who lived for twelve years as a merchant banker in London, before returning in 1835 to implement the disentailment laws that incorporated the whole of the national territory into the market economy.

as one when women had to take special care to conserve energy, to allow the organism to repair itself (Monlau 1865: 514). Moreno dies because he dams his emotions up; Fortunata dies because she lets them out: the result in both cases is a fatal draining of reserves. These two contrasting failures to achieve balance signal an unbalanced economic system. As Jacinta puts it on visiting the tenement building: 'Falta equilibrio y el mundo parece que se cae. Todo se arreglaría si los que tienen mucho dieran lo que les sobra a los que no poseen nada. ¿Pero qué cosa sobra?' (i. 272). In this society of consumerist excess, this is a leading question. Moreno's emotional and physical congestion figures capitalist over-accumulation. Conversely, Fortunata represents the *pueblo* who feeds the system but does not consume.

The distinction between marriage and adultery is further complicated because consumerism, associated with female adultery because both take women into the public sphere, is in this novel also associated with marriage.[16] Maxi's adulterous mother was married to a goldsmith whose supposed Jewish origins further associate him with the exchange economy; Manolita, the adulteress in the Micaelas convent reformatory, is wife to a 'comerciante de novedades' and daughter of the state administrator in charge of the national debt (i. 622); the adulterous Aurora is a department store manager. But Fortunata commits adultery for love, refusing Juanito's offers of gifts. However, she marries for money. Bebel's influential *Woman and Socialism* (1879)—retitled *Woman in the Past, Present and Future* by Bebel in 1883 and translated by Pardo Bazán in the early 1890s— had denounced marriage as a form of prostitution in which the wife is 'sold' to the husband, whose embrace she could not refuse, unlike the prostitute who could choose her clients

---

[16] The standard association of adultery with shopping is shown in the pamphlet in Galdós's library—*¡Guerra al adulterio! Estudio de ciencia social por An. Engineer* (1878), published by the press of the woman's magazine *La Guirnalda* which also published Galdós's novels – which asks: '¿Hay muchos que mientras queden en su casa no recuerden con terror que su mujer ha salido *de compras*?' (1878: 57). The pamphlet curiously suggests that only the adulterous male lover should be punished (with death by the husband), since he is usually the active seducer (and also because women, being weak, cannot help it). The author, who talks throughout of 'la adúltera' with no mention of adulterous husbands, regards the need to curb adultery as a problem of national regeneration (though he notes that things are worse in France where, in 1877, there were 10,000 cases of adultery!) (1878: 12–14).

(Bebel 1988: pp. x–xi). The Krausist support for women's education was explicitly based on the need for unmarried women to be able to earn a living so they would not marry for economic reasons.[17] Maxi initially bought Fortunata's favours as a prostitute, and buys her as a wife by offering her respectability, as he himself recognizes: 'Haber comprado aquellos ojos' (i. 697). Doña Lupe is prepared to accept her back into the family after her first infidelity, in return for investing the money received from her other adulterous lover, Feijoo; and she continues to treat her as a member of the family even when pregnant with Juanito's child, because of the allowance expected from the Santa Cruz family. As Turner notes (1992: 284), Doña Bárbara is acting as a shopkeeper's daughter with an eye for a bargain when she arranges Juanito's marriage to Jacinta, the 'jewel' in the 'muestrario' exhibited by the 'negociante en hijas', Isabel Cordero (i. 158–60). This incestuous marriage between first cousins, who additionally have been brought up—like León Roch and Pepa—as brother and sister, is designed to bring the errant Juanito back into the family fold, conserving sexual and financial resources. Much like Engels in *The Origin of the Family, Private Property and the State* (1884), Galdós implies that bourgeois marriage is a commercial transaction. The chief shopper in the novel is the model wife Doña Bárbara. She cannot let a day go by without shopping even if she needs nothing, though—like Juanito—she never overspends, and she gives her surplus to charity. Shopping takes her literally into the market-place, where she checks the 'cariz [. . .] de las cotizaciones' (i. 256) as if a dealer on the Stock Exchange. Doña Lupe is also forever sending her servant Papitos out to buy food. The two families into which Jacinta and Fortunata marry are both firmly inscribed in the exchange economy, through the Santa Cruz family's past in the draper's trade and Doña Lupe's moneylending (as a widow, Doña Lupe enjoys her late husband's legal right to engage in business). Doña Lupe engages in moneylending, like Doña Bárbara in shopping, not out of need but out of obsession ('vicio'). She goes almost every day to the pawnbrokers' auctions of unredeemed goods advertised in the press,

---

[17] See, for example, Alas's 1879 essay 'El amor y la economía' (Lissorgues 1980–1: i. 126–31).

employing Mauricia to resell the goods for her, and her house —like Torquemada's—is crammed with furnishings acquired from defaulting debtors.

Both these marriages into bourgeois families are sterile, as was that of Doña Lupe, whereas outside marriage the working-class Fortunata is fertile. Shuttleworth (in Jacobus, Fox Keller, and Shuttleworth 1990: 59) notes that, in the nineteenth century, the lower classes' alarming fertility was contrasted with middle-class women's supposed barrenness, attributed to their idle lifestyle which obstructed free flow. It was commonly assumed that a high birth rate was a sign of a strong nation. Contemporary Spanish fears of declining bourgeois birth rates are only partly supported by statistics, not reliable till the 1870 creation of the Registro Civil.[18] The overall national birth rate, though lower than in the first half of the century and than elsewhere in Europe, was rising by 0.63 per cent per annum (Granjel 1983: 136–7), and the birth rate for Madrid remained steady throughout the Restoration (Fernández García 1993: 479–87).[19] Madrid's population was growing rapidly—from 282,635 in 1868 to 480,081 in 1888—but this was due to immigration since throughout the nineteenth century deaths outweighed births: Madrid's overall mortality rate was second in Europe only to St Petersburg, reaching over 40 per 1,000 inhabitants in the period 1880–7 (Hauser 1979: 51; Huertas and Campos 1992: i. 147–8). Infant mortality was appalling—in the period 1880–4, almost 50 per cent of children born died before the age of 5 and, according to 1899 figures, deaths in the munipical orphanage La Inclusa stood at 73.8 per cent (Magnien in Salaün and Serrano 1991: 117)— but this affected the lower classes far more than the affluent. Mortality rates in general were especially high in the working-class tenements or *casas de vecindad* (such as the one in the Calle de Toledo visited by Jacinta and Guillermina, or that which opens Galdós's 1895 novel *Nazarín*), which housed an average of

---

[18] Monlau (1865: 292–341), strongly in favour of a 'política poblacionista', devoted a long section to the 'tragedy' of sterility, noting (269–70) that the poor were more fertile than the well-off. Pulido (1876: 339) argued that the 'most stupid' races were the most fertile. Hauser (1979: 520) observed a decline in Madrid's birth rate since 1860.

[19] García Delgado (1985: 136) gives a population increase for Spain in the period 1857–1900 of 20%, compared to 50% for Europe overall. For information on demographic growth, see Vicens Vives (1969: 617–18).

1,200 people each. Gallagher has shown how Malthus, concerned with the difficulty of feeding a growing population, argued that Adam Smith was wrong to see the exchange economy as a self-regulating mechanism, for it turned food into money but did not convert money back into food; this supposed that workers' bodies were a problem both because they were reproducing too healthily and because they were enfeebled by malnourishment. Malthus insisted on the need to distinguish between productive and non-productive labour; only that which increased the food supply fell into the former category (Gallagher and Laqueur 1987: 83–106). As Nadal (1994: 68) and Vicens Vives note (1969: 648, 699), Spain had to start importing wheat from 1877 as a result of falling grain production; in 1883, 31 per cent of food was imported, giving rise to public concern.

In *Fortunata y Jacinta*, the bourgeoisie is producing money and goods (especially the former) but is consuming food. The sterility attributed to it in the novel is a symbolic projection onto itself of the depletion of resources which it is in fact creating elsewhere. Juanito does not give Jacinta a baby but plays at being a baby suckling at her breast; in addition to being sterile, she has a nightmare in which she is unable to breastfeed and hallucinates that babies are drowning in the drains. Doña Lupe —a foster (that is, non-natural) mother—has an artificial breast made of manufactured cotton. She is called 'la de los pavos' because her husband acted as middleman selling eggs from the provinces and transferring money back in return.[20] Her loans also drain wealth from the colonies: Cuba and the Philippines (i. 541). By contrast the lower-class Fortunata, associated with the Mercado de San Miguel, figures her own reproductive capacity through her love of raw eggs; contemporary medical discourse saw the ovaries as the key to the female bodily economy (Laqueur 1990: 166, 171–81).[21] She consequently provides the

[20] The radial structure of the railway network built from 1851 geared the national economy to supplying Madrid as a centre of consumption (Fernández García 1993: 529, 533). All of Madrid's food and drink, apart from beer, was imported from elsewhere in Spain or abroad.

[21] The 1847 discovery of 'spontaneous' ovulation (not linked to orgasm, as previously thought) meant the end of the old Galenic medical model whereby men were seen as responsible for procreation, with women being mere 'vessels' (Jagoe, Blanco, and Enríquez de Salamanca 1998: 316). Fortunata will, in fact, take the active role in procreation with her second pregnancy, reducing Juanito to the role of unwitting instrument.

nourishment demanded by the bourgeoisie: both sexual nourishment and an heir. As a result, she is drained and her fertility destroyed: her milk dries up and she bleeds to death. She thus combines Malthus's two categories of the healthy, fertile working-class body and the enfeebled working-class body. The hiring of a wet-nurse to replace her signifies the ultimate commodification of natural resources; Estupiñá reports on the selection of wet-nurses he has procured as if they were cheeses in the market (ii. 502).[22] The repeated maxim—articulated by Villalonga and Juanito, and by the narrator paraphrasing Juanito and Guillermina—equating Fortunata with the 'bloque del pueblo, al cual se han de ir a buscar los sentimientos que la civilización deja perder por refinarlos demasiado' (i. 693) supposes that regeneration for a consumerist society comes from the people, representing the natural resources at its base. But it also supposes that 'the people' exist as 'human resources' to be utilized by 'society'. Perrot notes that in the late nineteenth century the family was increasingly seen as 'genetic capital' (Perrot 1990: 147–8); what was meant here was, of course, the provision of productive labour by the lower classes. In his discussion of the liberal concept of 'property in one's person', Macpherson cites Locke's contemporary William Petyt on this point: 'People are [. . .] the chiefest, most fundamental and precious commodity, out of which may be derived all sorts of manufactures, navigation, riches, conquests and solid dominion. This capital material, being of itself *raw and undigested*, is committed into the hands of the supreme authority in whose providence and disposition it is to improve, manage and fashion it to more or less advantage' (1990: 228, my italics). This passage could almost have been written as a description of the plot of

---

[22] Contemporary hygiene manuals railed against the practice of hiring wet-nurses, seen as a source of contagion and degeneration because of their unhygienic lower-class habits (Pulido 1876: 25–41; Santero 1885: ii. 213–14, 489). Monlau (1865: 520) demanded State medical inspection of wet-nurses, three years later (1868: 14) noting that the Madrid Ayuntamiento had that year issued regulations controlling their hiring. Capel Martínez (1982: 286) notes that the 1877 regulations for the control of prostitution issued by the Madrid Ayuntamiento included obligatory medical inspection of wet-nurses; the association of the two was logical enough, since in both cases women were entering the market by putting their bodies up for hire. The new medical controls of wet-nurses are depicted in Galdós's *El amigo Manso* (1882), where Augusto Miquis reappears as head of this service, housed in the Diputación Provincial, which subjects the milk of prospective wet-nurses to chemical tests and inspects their 'herramientas'. Miquis comments that the best wet-nurses come from Asturias like the cows (Pérez Galdós 1966: 1245–6).

Fortunata y Jacinta, which shows a consumer society 'digesting' the 'raw egg' that is Fortunata and 'improving' her for its own profit. As a prostitute, Fortunata figures the commodification of the self that follows from the liberal concept of 'property in one's person'. While Fortunata's assertion of her freedom is demonstrated through her decision to dispose of her body and its 'produce' in accordance with her wishes, the novel is more concerned with the commodification that ensues from the 'improvement' process designed to 'feed' the poor into the system as 'human resources'. The novel shows that this feeding of natural and human resources into the system increases productivity—Fortunata does 'produce the goods' in the form of a male heir—at the expense of draining those same resources, leading to overall exhaustion of the system: that is, to degeneration.

Madrid is depicted as a city full of consumer products, particularly natural produce: the problem is not scarcity but congestion, excess, and waste. Jacinta can barely make her way through the crowds and stalls in the Calle de Toledo, the location of Madrid's newest glass-and-steel covered market, the Mercado de la Cebada built in 1870–5 (Pla et al. 1987: 84), and of the municipal slaughterhouse built in 1855 (Fernández García 1993: 525; Hauser 1979: 371). Fortunata has a nightmare in which the Calle de Toledo is blocked by 'una de estas obstrucciones que tan frecuentes son en las calles de Madrid' (ii. 256) as two delivery carts, one full of carcasses from the slaughterhouse, collide, upsetting the roadside stalls. This nightmare of over-accumulation is presided over by a monstrous image of degeneration 'que se ha quedado a la mitad del camino darwinista por donde los orangutanes vinieron a ser hombres' (ii. 256). Fortunata's other dream, recalling meeting Juanito outside a shop window full of 'tuberías', represents an opposing ideal of healthy flow: Freudian not because the pipes are phallic symbols but because Freud's notion of the bodily economy was a 'hydraulic' one, equating health with flow and sickness with blockage.[23] Both Doña Bárbara and Doña Lupe

---

[23] Ilie (1998) rightly rejects a Freudian interpretation of Fortunata's dreams, insisting that their content is often not sexual but social, and noting Galdós's interest in water supply and drainage systems. For Freud's notion of a 'bodily economy' regulated by free flow or blockage, see Freud (1991*b*: 39, 184, 264–5, 275, 413–16); also Still (1997: 7–8) who relates this to market theory in relation to gender. For analysis of economic conceptualizations in Freud and Marx, see Goux (1973).

are obsessed with fear of being passed off with rotten goods, for food goes rotten if market flow is not fast enough. They are also worried by the risk of buying fraudulent or adulterated goods: contemporary works on public hygiene discussed the problem of food adulteration at length.[24] The *pueblo* who sells the natural produce on which society relies is associated both with the 'fresh' and with the 'rotten' or 'contaminated'. Corbin (1986: 142–60 and in Gallagher and Laqueur 1987: 209–19) has shown how nineteenth-century fears of the working classes were expressed through emphasis on their 'rotten' smell, for miasmatic theory held that disease was transmitted by the smell of putrefying matter; such fears crystallized around the body of the prostitute, the French word *putain* (and the Spanish *puta*) deriving from the same root as 'putrid'. Doña Lupe's annoyance at being fobbed off with rotten cod is much the same as her worry over whether or not the working-class prostitute Fortunata is 'rotten'.[25] This urban novel is peopled with consumers and middlemen (shopkeepers, market vendors, 'corredores') for in the exchange economy, where things pass from hand to hand, nothing is really fresh. The new social mobility generated by the exchange economy also makes it difficult to pin the 'rotten woman' down. William Acton's *Prostitution* (1857) expressed special concern at the fact that most women who resorted to prostitution did so on an occasional basis, returning to 'regular' life, thus making it difficult to separate out the rotten from the pure (Wilson 1991: 41). The great French legislator on prostitutes and drains, Parent-Duchâtelet (described by Corbin as a 'veritable Linnaeus of prostitution'), expressed the same anxiety, noting that his proposals to 'enclose' prostitutes in licensed brothels were based on the model of the convent (Corbin 1990: pp. ix, 4–5): it is in the convent reformatory of

---

[24] Santero (1885: ii. lessons 94–105); Hauser (1979: i. 393–420). Huertas and Campos (1992: i. 169, 176 n. 3) refer to the contemporary publication E. Serrano, *La vida en Madrid: alimentos adulterados y defunciones* (Madrid, 1883).

[25] Fresh fish reached Madrid only from the 1860s, thanks to the new railway network (Fernández García 1993: 530; Artola 1973: 105). The association of prostitutes with the 'rotten' intensified as a result of the discovery in the 1870s of the hereditary transmission of syphilis, leading to intensified regulation of prostitution throughout Europe. For attempts to 'sanitize' prostitutes in Spain, see Hauser (1979: ii. 133–55). The transmission of syphilis by prostitutes was discussed in the 1880s by Spanish medical journals and the Sociedad Española de Higiene (founded 1882) (Granjel 1983: 37; Rodríguez Ocaña 1987: 39).

Las Micaelas that Fortunata will re-establish contact with the prostitute Mauricia, who reawakens in her the illicit sexual desires that she is ostensibly purging (i. 600–1, 641).

Jacinta does not shop for clothes or food, and she gives her surplus to her sisters and charity, but she too becomes a consumer when she buys a 'son' who turns out to be counterfeit goods. Her 'acquisition' of Pitusín is set against the orgy of consumerism leading up to Christmas. When he is deposited on a sack of gold coins in Jacinta's sister's shop, the latter's reaction is that he is a forgery; the 'recognition scene' with his supposed father Juanito is delayed by talk of the devaluation of government bonds (i. 412). From the start Pitusín is associated with the rotten: the patio of the tenement building where he lives is hung with stinking drying 'despojos' and skins; situated in the Calle de Toledo, it is near the slaughterhouse and the tanners' district round the Rastro, both singled out by all contemporary public health experts as sources of contagion. Pitusín cannot tell the difference between food and rubbish: he eats potato peel and orange peel, and tips the rice pudding on the floor. When Guillermina first sees Fortunata's child at the end, she inspects him 'como el numismático observa el borroso perfil y las inscripciones de una moneda antigua para averiguar si es auténtica o falsificada' (ii. 473). Although this child is the 'genuine' 'article'—'oro de ley' (ii. 458)—he is still taken to Jacinta by Estupiñá 'como ladrón o contrabandista' (ii. 523) for he is at the same time the product of an adulteration. Estupiñá's hesitations as to how to behave towards the child (taking off his hat but treating him as contraband) reflect the difficulty in this consumer society of distinguishing between the genuine and the adulterated.

Much has been written about the various characters' attempts to mould Fortunata: this needs to be put in the context of contemporary bourgeois concerns with reforming (re-forming) the lower classes to make them into citizens sharing middle-class values.[26] The need to educate the masses was central both to the Krausists' social reform project and to the Church which competed with them for control of the new modes of social

---

[26] Tsuchiya (1993) and especially Fuentes Peris (1996–7, 1997b) are major contributions here. Kronik (1982), concerned with the metafictional dimensions of the 'fabrication' of Fortunata, remains a classic study.

regulation (though only in the former case was education seen as a means to social advancement). The purpose of this reform programme was to recycle human refuse back into the system, making it socially useful. This raised the problem, not just of knowing whether recycled goods were 'fit for consumption' or remained 'rotten'; but of who defines what is rotten in the first place. The very notion of recycling rubbish back into the system supposes that it has been made into refuse by the system to start with. The attempted 'redemption' of Fortunata as 'soiled goods' raises all these problems of definition. The various Pygmalions who try to 'sculpt' her into acceptable shape need to perceive her as 'unhewn stone' since, just as nineteenth-century and earlier colonizers justified the colonization process by supposing that they were claiming 'virgin' or 'empty' territory, so the bourgeois improvers justified their interference by seeing the lower classes as 'savages' lacking in civilization. *Fortunata y Jacinta* can be read as an exercise in nation formation construed on colonial lines, since its vast documentary canvas incorporates into the nation those inhabitants (the working classes and women) whose position and allegiance are in doubt, both by compiling an anthropological archive that makes them knowable and by incorporating Fortunata (a working-class woman) into 'society' through her sexual liaisons with men of the bourgeoisie and petty bourgeoisie. Contemporary medical manuals (Pulido 1876: 339; Santero 1885: ii. 760) contained sections on demography and race, noting that the 'inferior' races were best adapted to healthy reproduction, and recommending miscegenation in the colonies as a way of 'improving the stock'. *Fortunata y Jacinta*, in constructing Fortunata as a 'savage' and superior breeder, takes the form of a miscegenation narrative: that is, a colonially conceived blueprint for the nation based on the 'improvement of the race' through the white man's fertilization of the 'native' female. This colonial concept of miscegenation, being based on the white man's coupling with the native female, supposes that female 'others' can be incorporated into the nation, but the reverse—the 'incorporation' of the native male via his coupling with the white female—is unthinkable. Thus Fortunata can be 'improved' (up to a point) while her uncle José Izquierdo has to be 'contained' within the frame of the historical paintings for which he becomes an artist's model. The ultimate goal of improving the male stock is achieved through the fruits of miscegenation: Fortunata's child has to be a male, and he will be fully incorporated into 'society' while Fortunata, having served her purpose, is denied full assimilation by being made to die.

However, the novel's representation of this colonially conceived nation-formation process is highly ambivalent. Guillermina may describe Fortunata as 'anterior a la civilización' (ii. 251), justifying her attempt to 'improve' her; but the narrative shows that Fortunata is not 'virgin territory' because she has been forced into prostitution by Juanito's irresponsibility. Nevertheless, the novel does on the whole propose a bourgeois view of the lower classes as primitives who 'lack culture' rather than having a culture of their own. Although the narrator revels in lower-class speech forms, he describes them as 'defective' (i. 482); and, when the lower classes are praised, it is usually for middle-class virtues (Fortunata's and Severiana's love of cleaning and skill in stocking the larder), though they do have the good sense to prefer the *mantón de Manila* to French bustles. Their negative qualities are presented as the result of lack of education or perversion by drink; this is reassuring because it supposes that they are reformable and that the bourgeoisie is doing them a favour by 'improving' them. Galdós clearly admires his principal female 'savage' (Fortunata) for her spontaneity and substantiality, represented by her solid, statuesque body which needs no Pygmalion to sculpt it into shape, though it does need a benevolent Feijoo to feed her well. Nevertheless, the novel does suppose that Fortunata has gained something from her introduction to middle-class life. It likewise seems to approve of the decision to put Pitusín in Guillermina's orphanage so he can learn a trade or 'even a profession' (i. 426), and of Jacinta's sponsoring of Adoración's education to be a teacher, despite the fact that neither child nor their relatives are consulted on the matter (ii. 67). Here the object of the reform process is clearly shown to be that of recycling human 'refuse' so as to make it productive by integrating it into the workforce. As Guillermina says of the apparently 'useless' José Izquierdo: 'no hay hechura de Dios que no tenga su *para qué* en este taller admirable del trabajo universal' (i. 376).

The novel makes it clear that, in practice, its bourgeois social reformers are motivated not by altruism but by the desire to enforce authority. Philanthropy is shown to be a key ingredient of the 'Estado tutelar' which, under the Restoration, blended State and private forms of social control into a nationwide programme of 'supervised freedom'. The last we hear of Villalonga is that he has been made Director de Beneficencia y Sanidad (ii. 418). Doña Lupe's attempt to reform Fortunata is explicitly referred to as a 'tutela enojosa' (i. 661). The involvement of the Church in this programme of 'supervised freedom' is especially singled out for criticism: the reform efforts of the priest Nicolás Rubín and the nuns in Las Micaelas fail because they ignore the realities of their working-class protégées' lives. Galdós's opposition to Nicolás Rubín's programme for 'disinfecting' Fortunata is made clear by the text's insistence that it is he who smells bad: 'Y a propósito de espliego, a él, físicamente, tampoco le vendría mal' (i. 719). His inability to distinguish the rotten cod Doña Lupe serves him mirrors his inability to judge human refuse. The convent reformatory of Las Micaelas, although well intentioned, subjects its fallen women (prostitutes and adulteresses) to a regime of labour and supervised privacy, recycling them by fitting them for domestic employment; in fact, contemporary surveys stated that a majority of late nineteenth-century Madrid's estimated 17,000 prostitutes (the figure is for 1872) were former domestic servants who had been forced into the 'trade' after being seduced by their masters (Magnien in Salaün and Serrano 1991: 117; Hauser 1979: 143, 146). Rivière Gómez's fascinating study (1994) of the 'expedientes' of 1,118 prostitutes interned between 1844 and 1865 in the convent reformatory of the Adoratrices Esclavas del Santísimo Sacramento, nicknamed 'Las Micaelas' after its founder and director Micaela Desmaisières, Vizcondeza de Jorbalán, shows that half of these women had formerly been domestic servants. She notes the case (1994: 126) of a particular internee put in domestic service by Micaela Desmaisières, who returned to a brothel because she wanted a salary (domestic service was normally paid with free board and lodging but not money); regardless of the medical and other risks, prostitution clearly was seen by those who 'opted' for it as an enabling entry into the market. Rivière's study (1994: 111) also shows that the reformatory's regime, based on French models, functioned by classifying its internees into different groups: the Micaelas (categorized by their religious devotion and quickness to learn) and the Filomenas (the uneducated and recalcitrant) (Rivière Gómez 1994: 111).[27] Galdós's two groups, the Filomenas and the Josefinas, do not correspond to these categories but nevertheless show the importance of classification as a surveillance method that constructs the individual as 'subject' in every sense; we see how the reformatory individualizes its rebellious internees by literally putting them in cages. Individualization means standardization and obedience: the creation of 'free citizens' who have learnt to use their free will to curb their desires. Mauricia rejects the nuns' 'cleanliness-is-next-to-godliness' regime by installing herself on the rubbish tip; when the nuns throw her out as rubbish, she makes her exit triumphally escorted by a troupe of street-cleaners. This connection is apt, for just as prostitutes were simultaneously seen as cleansing agents and sources of putrefaction, so Madrid's municipal 'servicio de limpieza' included the licensing of 10,000 'traperos' or ragpickers who—just as prostitutes were required to keep out of public view—were allowed to 'circulate' only at night (Hauser 1979: 248).

Most of the philanthropic Pygmalions in the novel are—like their late nineteenth-century counterparts—women. I would not include Feijoo in this catetgory since, although he sees Fortunata as a 'diamante en bruto' (ii. 95) and recommends a regime of 'freedom with limits', he does not want to reform her but to give her freedom of manœuvre. He loves her as she is, and is genuinely altruistic to the extent of giving her up to another man. He is right to think that society would find his advice to her immoral. The chief male Pygmalion is Maxi, whose masculinity is in doubt. Maxi's philanthropic 'mission'—which makes him a missionary or reformer (i. 513)—confirms his feminine disposition. He articulates his 'campaña virtuosa' (i. 491) in the language of social reform, with the result that Doña Lupe has moral scruples about dissuading him. In 'buying'

---

[27] See Rivière Gómez (1994) for detailed information about the Adoratrices Esclavas del Santísimo Sacramento and prostitution in 19th-century Spain in general. The original 1845 Colegio de María Santísima de las Desamparadas was governed by a Junta de Señoras (mostly with aristocratic titles); Micaela Desmaisières decided to found a new religious order to run her institution in 1856 because of the difficulty of keeping staff, a problem also palliated by making the better-educated internees responsible for training those less educated, who in turn were put in charge of those with no education at all. From 1854, the reformatory was subsidized by the Junta Provincial de Beneficencia, showing the entanglement of public and private welfare systems (Rivière Gómez 1994: 104–6).

Fortunata so as to 'redeem' her (an economic as well as religious term, of course), Maxi is another bourgeois ragpicker recycling refuse. He at least recognizes that she was not inherently 'rotten' but was made into 'rubbish' by the bourgeois Juanito: 'El la arrojó a la basura ... yo la recogí y la limpié ... él me la quitó y la.... volvió a arrojar' (i. 707). His medical career as a chemist inscribes him in the discourse of public and private hygiene, with its reformist implications, which he is using here (although pharmacy and medicine were taught in separate faculties, he has studied at Madrid's Central University, known for its Chair of Hygiene). Ballester compares pharmacy to music since, in 'tuning' the human organism, the chemist is a 'compositor del cuerpo' (ii. 286). But Maxi gets his mixtures wrong in the pharmacy and at home, nearly poisoning clients and living off drugs rather than food. It is clear that in redeeming Fortunata he is not thinking of her but working out (in practice, compounding) his own complexes about having an adulterous mother and being thought incapable of relations with women. What he really wants to prove is that he owns her; he discovers that the only way to own her completely is to have her dead.

The chief female Pygmalions in the novel are (apart from the nuns in Las Micaelas) Doña Lupe and Guillermina. Doña Lupe—another bourgeois ragpicker—found Papitos begging on a rubbish tip and re-forms her into a productive member of society (of personal use to herself) by training her as a domestic servant. Papitos is a virtual prisoner in the house for supervised privacy is what makes model citizens. In recycling Papitos, Doña Lupe is obeying the same urge that makes her darn and mend old clothes—her priest son Nicolás is described as a 'zurcidor moral' for attempting to 're-form' Fortunata (i. 561) —and resell her pickings from the pawnbrokers' auctions. Her reforming activities are, like her moneylending, undertaken 'por pura afición' and not out of a sense of altruism:

Poseía doña Lupe la aptitud y la vanidad educativas, y para ella no había mayor gloria que tener alguien sobre quien desplegar autoridad. Maxi y Papitos eran al mismo tiempo hijos y alumnos [...]. El mismo Jáuregui había sido también [...] tan discípulo como marido. [...] La pasión de domesticar se despertaba en ella delante de aquel magnífico animal [Fortunata] que estaba pidiendo una mano hábil que la desbravase. (i. 583)

She is pleased to see Maxi develop a 'personalidad árbitra de sí misma' (i. 555) but cross when he asserts his independence too much. Fortunata's evasion of her surveillance mortifies her; she can tolerate her infidelities but not her insistence, tutored by Feijoo, on maintaining her right to privacy. When she searches Fortunata's drawers, her bunch of keys is described as worthy of a 'compañía de ladrones' (ii. 301). The reader is forced to ask who is guilty of the greater violation of privacy: Fortunata as an adulteress or Doña Lupe as a reformer?

Doña Lupe has masculine features, like Mauricia and like Guillermina, for all three women reject privacy: Mauricia as a prostitute and 'corredora de géneros', whose realm is the street; Doña Lupe and Guillermina as reformers. Guillermina's reforming zeal is exercised in the public sphere: she is always 'walking the streets'. She is not only a bourgeois ragpicker—building her orphanage from assorted 'sobras'—but a bourgeois beggar and pickpocket, shamelessly knocking on doors (including the Palace) and taking money out of her friends' and relatives' purses. Her invasion of privacy is total; she calls the police to take prostitutes off the streets against their will (i. 628), and gets the Civil Governor to override the 1868 Constitution's ruling on religious freedom (as the novel notes) by having Mauricia forcibly removed from the Protestant pastor's care. Given her lack of respect for the law and her 'street-walking', it is not surprising that Fortunata gets her mixed up with the rebellious prostitute Mauricia. Nevertheless, Guillermina's energy and her ability to get others working are admirable in this society devoted to the consumption of resources and 'la alta vagancia'. Her achievement in founding, maintaining, and building a new edifice for her orphanage is a modern miracle.[28] One of her main benefactors is Moreno Isla, who sees the beggars who ply their trade on Madrid's streets—'estos industriales de la miseria humana' (ii. 344)—as a sign of Spain's lack of civilization, for civilization consists in

---

[28] Bahamonde (in Rodríguez Puértolas 1988: 187–8) cites an 1891 press article praising the soup kitchen (Comedor de la Caridad) run by Ernestina Manuel de Villena (the real-life model for Guillermina) at her Asilo del Sagrado Corazón orphanage, staffed for the three months of winter by aristocratic ladies and even royalty. The article notes that children in the queues for the soup kitchen were divided according to sex and age, and given edifying instruction as well as bread and soup. On Guillermina, see Braun (1970, 1977); and Quispe-Agnoli (1998).

putting human refuse in a home (supervised privacy) and denying them access to the public sphere (that is, until they have been recycled as model citizens).[29] Guillermina's answer to Jacinta's question '¿Pero qué cosa sobra?' is that 'Todo sirve' (i. 269): nothing is excess or waste provided that it is redistributed and recycled to produce social equilibrium.

Guillermina is difficult to evaluate because she uses the rhetoric of the market—the need for circulation—as the basis of her reformist project. Her utilitarian notion that the rotten can be recycled as fertilizer—an image literalized in Fortunata's trajectory from prostitute to producer of the Santa Cruz heir —puts into practice the crass moneylender Torquemada's view of money as *guano*. The ground floor of her home is a bank, formerly owned by her family. The new, fully compartmentalized edifice she dreams of building for her orphanage (i. 268) is not unlike the modern department store with its specialized departments where Aurora works, for, like fashion, her orphanage-reformatory aims to produce individualized but standardized citizens. Galdós describes the religious charitable institutions springing up on the northern edge of the Ensanche (including the Micaelas and those of the religious orders expelled from France) as 'obras de contrata', adulterating the liturgy with 'novedades' resembling the sentimental tunes inserted as broadsheets in fashion magazines (i. 590–2, 594).[30] Doña Lupe is driven by a desire for imitation that is more consumerist than Christian when she offers to spend the night with the dying Mauricia: she wonders whether she should wear her new coat, and is disappointed not to find the fashionable

---

[29] Bahamonde puts the number of licensed beggars in Restoration Madrid at 10,000 (Fernández García 1993: 506).

[30] The same passage (i. 590–2) also describes these new religious buildings as characterized by an 'execrable' mix of architectural styles (i. 590–2); one thinks of Bringas's 'adulterated' mix of architectural styles in his hair picture, making it a miniature World Exhibition. One of the best examples of Restoration 'eclectic' architecture was, in fact, the Asilo de Huérfanos del Sagrado Corazón de Jesús built in 1880 by Guillermina's real-life counterpart, Ernestina Manuel de Villena (Fernández García 1993: 434). For the new religious orders that established themselves in Madrid's northern *ensanche* during the Restoration, see Penedo Cobo (in Bahamonde Magro and Otero Carvajal 1989: i. 251–65), who notes (262) that the architect for Villena's orphanage, Francisco Cubas, who built several other convents at the time, in some cases donating the freehold, was in 1886 given the pontifical titles of Marqués de Cubas and Marqués de Fontalba by Pope Leo XIII, on Villena's request.

ladies she imagined assisting Guillermina in her charitable acts. In elaborating his theory that imitation was the basis of modern consumer society, Tarde borrowed heavily from Thomas à Kempis's *The Imitation of Christ*, which he greatly admired (Williams 1982: 352–3). Fortunata's desire to imitate Jacinta, as in Tarde's theory, combines both kinds of imitation: she wants to follow her virtuous example and to order a skirt just like hers (ii. 193). She is also excited by the prospect of entering the reformatory as if by 'una moda que empieza' (i. 586). Fortunata is 're-fashioned' by the novel's various philanthropic Pygmalions; in this sense, they are not behaving so differently from Juanito who, in encouraging her to dress and behave fashionably, is wanting her to conform to an acceptable bourgeois model. Indeed, Juanito disguises his search for her in Madrid's brothels with 'razones filantrópicas' (i. 442). Guillermina is the opposite of a consumer in that she harnesses and creates energy, but her female invasion of the public sphere parallels that effected by women's entry into the market as shoppers. Just as Doña Bárbara haggles with the market vendors, so she bargains with tradesmen and industrialists. Even her 'socorros a domicilio' turn the privacy of the home into a public spectacle, as seen most notably in her 'staging' of Mauricia's death for public edification.[31] Her philanthropic motives, although altruistic in a material sense, give her a public role beyond that normally enjoyed by women:

La llama vivísima que en su pecho ardía no le inspiraba la sumisión pasiva, sino actividades iniciadoras que debían desarrollarse en la libertad. Tenía [. . .] un tesoro de dotes de mando y de facultades de organización que ya quisieran para sí algunos de los hombres que dirigen los destinos del mundo. (i. 264)

---

[31] Pérez Ledesma (Seminario de historia 1988: 165–6) quotes the Madrid Ateneo's reply to the Comisión de Reformas Sociales on such female home visitors: 'Es admirable, señores, ver *el espectáculo* de esas mujeres que, abandonando la atmósfera tibia de sus aristocráticos salones, se acuerdan un momento de que [. . .] hay hijos de Dios a quienes les falta lo más indispensable; y ante esta idea no les hace retroceder ni el viento, ni la lluvia, ni el lodo, y llegando a miserable albergue, suben y suben hasta el cielo, y entran en la habitación del pobre, y consuelan, y alientan, y fortifican aquellas almas heridas por la desgracia; y lo que es más importante, socorren espléndidamente, *aunque no con exceso*, en la medida sólo de las necesidades que sus ojos contemplan' (my italics).

Guillermina is, of course, a spinster. The narrator quashes the rumour that she turned to philanthropy when jilted by a fiancé, making it clear that she chose the freedom of the public sphere in preference to marriage. Her hundred odd orphans are a surrogate family that allows her to exercise her feminine maternal function while rejecting privacy: her own and that of others.[32] Doña Lupe, a widow who adopts a foster family and various 'savages', is likewise called a 'gran diplomática y ministra' (ii. 441) for these female reformers, like the agents of the State, represent the invasion of individual citizens' privacy.

It is made clear that the overall beneficiary of this philanthropic recycling of human refuse is bourgeois society because, in making waste useful, it incorporates social outcasts into the 'supervised freedom' of the 'Estado tutelar'. The terror of class war unleashed by the Paris Commune and the First Republic made the Restoration look to cross-class solutions: whether philanthropy, Catholic unions, or the 'asociaciones mixtas' of employers and workers advocated by the Krausists (Seminario de historia 1988: 140). Doña Lupe compares her pragmatism in admitting Fortunata into her middle-class family to that of a government which, faced by a revolution it cannot defeat, accepts it in order to 'dirigirlo y encauzarlo' (i. 539). The final alliance established between Fortunata and Jacinta is another attempt at a cross-class solution, but Fortunata's death shows that the reformers' attempt to incorporate the lower classes into a unified nation benefits the bourgeoisie at the expense of 'bleeding' the *pueblo*. In showing how the bourgeoisie regenerates itself by regenerating the lower classes, the novel asks which needs regeneration more: a consumer society exhausting its resources or the 'uncivilized' masses? Two concepts of degeneration are involved here: that which arises from arrested development, allowing relics of earlier stages of evolution to persist in the modern age, and that resulting from entropy or exhaustion of resources, aggravated by the accelerating spiral of capitalist development which needs to increase circulation to solve the problem of over-accumulation. The novel's description of the lower classes as 'salvajes' and 'fieras' supposes that they are a degenerate throwback to lower, less complex

---

[32] See Riley (1988) for the ways in which late 19th-century philanthropy empowered women.

evolutionary forms. But their very lack of complexity gives them a certain moral integrity, as seen in Fortunata's inability to dissimulate; even the braggart José Izquierdo is disarmingly transparent. Most of the moral problems explored in the novel —notably the invasion of privacy, whether by philanthropy or by the 'Estado tutelar'—stem from the bourgeoisie. The novel makes it clear that the *pueblo*'s moral degeneracy is attributable not only to its lack of civilization, but also to its incorporation into bourgeois society; for example, through prostitution. This hesitation as to whether Spain's decadence is caused by excess or insufficient civilization would continue to vex the writers of the so-called 1898 Generation, for the problem is accelerated and uneven development: that is, the coexistence of modernization and underdevelopment. The question of whether Spain is civilized or uncivilized is debated by Moreno Isla and Don Baldomero (ii. 69–72). Moreno holds that the race is deteriorating because of malnutrition (ii. 272); what he does not point out (but the novel does) is that the exhaustion of natural resources is the fault of the capitalist development which he, as a banker, promotes. The novel suggests that the distinction between civilization and backwardness is breaking down because both are producing degeneration.

The naturalistic aspects of *Fortunata y Jacinta* should—like those of *La desheredada* and *Lo prohibido*, and, as we shall see later, those of Alas's and Pardo Bazán's novels—be seen as a reflection of contemporary concerns with degeneration. The chapter titled 'Naturalismo espiritual' deals with Mauricia's death: her moral degeneracy is indicated by her masculine features and voice—developed only after her 'backsliding' into prostitution and alcoholism (ii. 235)—for earlier stages of evolution were supposedly less sexually differentiated (Russett 1989: 130–54).[33] It is impossible to tell the sex of the children in the working-class tenement, and those covered in black ink look like 'caníbales', 'mandingas', 'cafres', and 'caribes' (i. 324–5). This 'war paint' also associates the children with the Paris Commune—they form a 'barricade' (i. 324)—which encouraged representations of the working classes as degenerate 'savages'. Jacinta is so struck with Adoración because her immaculate dress makes

---

[33] Fuentes Peris (1996, 1997*a*, 1997*b*) studies the association of the working classes with drink in Galdós's novels and in Restoration Spain.

her clearly feminine, like herself. The 'masses' in the tenement are undifferentiated because there is no privacy or division between home and work; the women do piecework at home. And it is the women who work and rule the roost.

However the novel shows the 'civilized' bourgeoisie to be afflicted by a similar reversal of gender norms. Not only are Doña Lupe and Guillermina 'masculinized' by their public activities; Maxi 'regresses' into effeminacy and infantilism. Women and children were, like savages, held to be at a lower stage of human development than men, though this did not prevent women's masculinization from also being seen as a regression (Russett 1989: 54–7). This does not necessarily imply that Maxi is homosexual, though others take him to be so (i. 709), but he is impotent and starts to preach a doctrine of collective suicide, illustrating fears that a decadent mankind would cease to reproduce. The doctor Augusto Miquis says he would have advised Maxi not to marry; the hygienist Monlau insisted that those suffering from debilitation should consult medical experts before marrying (1868: 15), noting that permanent impotence before marriage provided grounds for annulment (1865: 107). Maxi's weakness is due to his 'poca y mala sangre' (ii. 213)—described by Monlau (1868: 19–20) as a pathological condition currently 'de moda'—causing a nervous disorder manifested in constriction of the epigastrium, obstructing the windpipe. This was the classic symptom of hysteria, which contemporary Spanish health experts, like Freud later, saw as a feminine disease but one that could occur in men. Interestingly, from Monlau's 1853 *Higiene del matrimonio* on (Monlau 1865: 35), they unanimously rejected the traditional recommendation of marriage as a cure for hysteria since those entering marriage needed to be well balanced. Ballester (ii. 323) proposes sending Maxi to see Dr Esquerdo, a hysteria specialist who, in an 1889 article (6–9, 337–40), not only warned against hysterics marrying but took a male hysteric (a doctor, in fact) as his first case-study.[34] In her indispensable study of nineteenth-century Spanish medical discourse, Jagoe

---

[34] Esquerdo was head of the mental section of Madrid's Provincial Hospital and in 1877 funded a private lunatic asylum at Carabanchel. Heavily influenced by Morel's theories of degeneration, he campaigned for mental health experts to be involved in assessing criminals (Rey González 1990: 56–7); see Chapter 2 above for his involvement in trials in the early 1880s.

(Jagoe, Blanco, and Enríquez de Salamanca 1998: 33–67) notes that neurological explanations of hysteria appear already in the seventeenth century, freeing it from the traditional Galenic medical model whereby it was seen as an exclusively female disease resulting from a 'wandering womb' which needed stabilizing through pregnancy. Jagoe observes that, at the end of the eighteenth century, as the notion of sexual difference started to develop, theories regarding hysteria as a disease of the womb (or of the ovaries) re-emerged, but now continence and not pregnancy was seen as the cure. In other words, hysteria becomes linked to nymphomania. Charcot's experiments with hypnotizing hysterics in the 1870s and 1880s demonstrated definitively that the causes and symptoms of hysteria were psychological and not physiological; Charcot also worked with male hysterics. A Spanish translation of Charcot's famous study of hysteria *Lecciones sobre enfermedades del sistema nervioso* was published in 1882. Jagoe notes that the Spanish Gynaecological Society debated the origins of hysteria in 1876, concluding that it was caused by a lesion of the womb or ovaries which subsequently affected the nervous system. Ángel Pulido, the Society's secretary, was the only doctor present who argued for its psychological origins; he briefly dabbled in hypnotizing female patients, which caused a scandal. Jagoe notes that the contemporary discourse on hysteria was a compendium of the contradictions in contemporary views on women, and that, although it was accepted that men could be hysterics, the symptoms of hysteria (instability, emotional excess, mimicry) constituted a caricature of prevailing misogynist definitions of femininity. Jagoe also notes that infertility, no longer seen as the cause of hysteria, was now posited as its result or 'punishment'. Freud and Breuer's first paper on hysteria of 1893 was translated into Spanish in the same year, earlier than in any other country.[35] Maxi's hysteria is connected with both psychological and physical disorders, the latter in the form of impotence. This can be taken as implying either that hysteria can be tied to the male as well as female reproductive systems, or that Maxi's reproductive organs have remained at a 'female' stage of arrested development. He has

---

[35] On hysteria outside the Spanish context, see Evans (1991), Beizer (1994), Matlock (1994), Kahane (1995), Micale (1995), David-Ménard (1989), Showalter (1987).

a 'cutis de niño con transparencias de mujer desmedrada y clorótica', and no facial hair (ii. 384). Fortunata has to treat him like a baby and in the later stages of his madness his speech reverts to infantile stutters (ii. 384); when he fights Juanito and later agrees to shoot him, his voice regresses to a treble (i. 707–8; ii. 499). Doña Lupe says, 'A ti hay que tratarte siempre como a los niños atrasaditos que están a medio desarrollar' (i. 521). By contrast, Fortunata's reversions to childhood, primitivism, and animality in her encounters with Jacinta (ii. 208, 252) give her increased strength, because regression masculinizes women but feminizes men.

The incestuousness of Maxi's mother–son relationship with Fortunata is mirrored by Juanito's baby talk and behaviour with Jacinta. Juanito is a physically perfect masculine specimen; he is however feminized by idleness, consumption, and his susceptibility to fashion. The mother–son figurative incest that characterizes the post-1868 period is different from the endogamous marriage, designed to keep business in the family, of pre-1868 society, for it is caused by men's regression to infantilism. The earlier form of incest figures the pre-capitalist period before the public/private split; the later form figures its threatened breakdown as women are masculinized by entry to the public sphere, and men are feminized by fashion (Juanito) and depleted resources (Maxi). The rapidity of this switch points to the accelerated and incomplete modernization of post-1868 Spain: the public/private split is at risk because it is recent and imperfectly realized. The superimposition of the earlier and later forms of incest in the marriage of Juanito and Jacinta—first cousins and figurative brother and sister, plus figurative mother and son—points to the coexistence in Restoration Spain of the pre-modern and the modern. The linking of incest with both economic orders further suggests that degeneration is caused by backwardness and progress in combination.

The novel repeatedly describes the individual and social organism as a 'máquina'; that is, a fixed-energy system that runs down if energy loss is not replaced by a transfer of resources from elsewhere in the body. This Spencerian view is reflected in Juan Pablo's ill-digested readings about an evolutionary universe ruled by natural law (ii. 42) and in the Parsons generator running the water-pump of the Micaelas reformatory, on which Maxi—so pitifully devoid of energy—fixes his attention. Most of the time, there is not enough wind to make the Parsons generator work. Shuttleworth notes that Spencer's two main organizing categories were those of waste and repair. As he put it, 'What in commercial affairs we call *profit*, answers to the excess of nutrition over waste in a living body' (Jacobus, Fox Keller, and Shuttleworth 1990: 58; original italics). *Fortunata y Jacinta* describes a society in which waste (over-accumulation) exceeds nutrition; as a result, the social organism is not capable of repairing itself but requires human intervention. The same Feijoo whose motto is 'no descomponerse' recognizes that the universal machine is in need of fixing: 'este mundo es una gaita con muchos agujeros, y hay que templar, templar para que suene bien' (ii. 92). What is being reproduced here is the debate, central to late nineteenth-century liberalism in Spain as elsewhere, over whether the role of the State is simply to remove obstacles to society repairing itself through free flow, or whether more drastic forms of State intervention are required. The novel shows that the consumer economy is increasingly exhausting resources, but that the 'Estado tutelar' and private reform initiatives are adding to the process. References to individual and collective 'máquinas' that cannot be repaired proliferate in the last third of the novel. Despite the birth of Fortunata's child, it ends on a note of regression, exhaustion, and death. Moreno dies with his 'tubería descompuesta' (ii. 336). In the chapter titled 'Disolución', the attempt to 'patch up' Fortunata's marriage fails, despite Doña Lupe's talent for 'arreglos y composturas' (ii. 161). Fortunata returns to her childhood home and bleeds to death. Feijoo regresses to childhood and dies. Maxi opts for living death as preferable to life. Another 'máquina del matrimonio' (i. 573) breaks down irretrievably as Jacinta 'divorces' Juanito. We, like him, are left with 'esa sensación de las irreparables pérdidas [. . .], sensación que en plena juventud equivale al envejecer [. . .] y marca la hora en que lo mejor de la existencia se corre hacia atrás, quedando a la espalda los horizontes que antes estaban por delante' (ii. 533).

The novel ends with a trip to the Cementerio del Este, built on the outskirts of Madrid in 1841 in accordance with mid- to late nineteenth-century hygienic concerns, which Ariza (1988: 265–6) notes was the only one of Madrid's cemeteries to have been conceived on a lavish scale with its formally landscaped terraces and plants and trees chosen for their pleasant smells and purificatory qualities.[36] As Ariès demonstrates (1987: 18–19), the 'modernization' of death was also a privatization, as families buried their dead in privately owned plots of land marked with individualized monuments, which at the same time converted the private into public display. The description of Fortunata's splendid funeral shows that even in death she cannot escape commodification by the bourgeoisie; it has been noted (Burns 1993) that the development in the late nineteenth century of funeral companies, offering a choice of differently priced 'packages', matched the rise of the department store. As Harvey notes (1989: 182), the capitalist system—based on investment and credit—signifies living off borrowed time: tomorrow's resources are consumed today. The end of *La de Bringas* was marked by temporal acceleration as Rosalía just managed to meet the deadline to pay off her loans. In *Fortunata y Jacinta*, as the references to death and dissolution accumulate in the novel's concluding pages, the sense of running out of time has increased: acceleration has given way to exhaustion.

This loss of substance leaves a society where all that exists is 'las formas': imitation and representation. This is another way of saying that society is ruled by fashion and money, particularly when the latter increasingly takes the form of paper money whose value is symbolic rather than based on substance. The novel repeatedly refers to 'papeles' in the double sense of 'roles' and 'paper'. The moneylender Doña Lupe imitates Guillermina in order to 'no hacer un mal papel' (ii. 203) and has a strongbox full of 'papeles' in the guise of promissory notes and banknotes. Even food has become paper with the 'bonos' Guillermina distributes to the poor (i. 328). As a system of representation, money is real but its value is unstable: the devaluation of government bonds makes Moreno decide he will buy no more 'papel de la querida patria' (i. 276)—the nation is signified by increasingly worthless bits of paper. Individual identity too is signified by paper, with the documents required by the Registro Civil (established 1870): Guillermina observes that Pitusín's birth certificate is just 'papeles, que tampoco prueban nada' (i. 374). Don Baldomero automatically buys a

---

[36] For the history of cemeteries in Madrid, see also Martínez Sanz (in Otero Carvajal and Bahamonde 1986: 485–517), who notes that it was only after the cholera epidemics of 1855 and 1865 that previous regulations banning burials in churches were enforced.

Christmas lottery ticket each year just as he annually renews his 'cédula de vecindad u otro documento que acredite la condición de español neto' (i. 379): without 'identity papers' purchased from the State one has no identity, for in the modern nation-State one's individual identity is one's national identity; the comparison with a lottery ticket, also issued by the State, implies that the value of such papers is highly uncertain.[37] This is a problem both of a token (fiduciary) system of monetary representation, and of a centralized State which represents its citizens in theory only: the fluctuating 'valor nominal' of government bonds (i. 412) is matched by the equally nominal value of a parliamentary system in which government posts are 'carne de nómina' (i. 451). When Villalonga, as parliamentary deputy, is described as 'el representante del país' (i. 431) and Juan Pablo, in his new post of Provincial Governor, calles himself 'el representante del Estado' (ii. 448), it is clear that representation is unreliable.

Feijoo insists that 'las formas' are 'casi todo' because they keep the social machine in working order (ii. 143). But he is mistaken in believing Fortunata's marriage can be repaired because marriage too has become a piece of paper: what Fortunata calls 'latines' (ii. 409) and what Doña Lupe recognizes as 'la ley escrita' or 'las ficciones de la ley' (ii. 440). Both Fortunata's and Jacinta's marriages are legal fictions contradicted by 'la Naturaleza' in the form of adultery. Here Galdós is not just criticizing marriage as an institution, but signalling the gap between sign and signified that occurs when the centralized nation-State attempts to subject all forms of private as well as public life to legal codification. But if Fortunata's marriage is 'un engaño [...] como lo que sacan en los teatros' (ii. 246), adultery has also been made into a hackneyed literary motif by a commercialized system of literary representation: the 'novelas por entregas' which Ido advertises (i. 297–8) and composes on paper and in life.[38] The characters' behaviour and accounts of

---

[37] The entry on 'Deuda' in the Espasa-Calpe *Enciclopedia universal ilustrada europeo-americana* notes that State lotteries are one of the various forms taken by the national debt.

[38] White (in White and Segal 1997: 123–33) argues that in the French 19th-century novel (including Zola as well as Flaubert), adultery is treated self-consciously as a hackneyed literary motif. In his 1884 'Dedicatoria' to his novel *Sotileza* (1884), Pereda (1959: ii. 188) complained that, to be taken seriously, novels nowadays had to depict 'el problema del adulterio y el problema de la prostitución'.

their lives are constantly compared to commercial literature and theatre, because the modern city, based on consumerist spectacle, unavoidably turns life into representation. Fortunata 'no hace papeles' (ii. 158) but she is still a 'traidora de melodrama' (i. 710). Aurora's department store consciously introduces sophisticated modern display techniques (ii. 290)—Bowlby (1985: 3) notes the use by the new department stores of theatrical forms of lighting and display—but the ingenuous market stalls in the Calle de Toledo are just as much a form of living theatre (i. 316–18, 394–5). Ballester and Ponce disagree over a play depicting marriage and over how to write Fortunata's story, the former wanting 'unadorned reality' and the latter an 'artistic' version. Galdós leaves their argument unresolved because, when reality is representation, the distinction between their two positions becomes meaningless. Realism problematizes the relationship between representation and reality, not—as in modernism—by insisting on the difference between the two, but by blurring the boundary between them while at the same time making it clear that representation is unreliable. This, I would argue, is more disturbing. Galdós's insistence on appearances is much more than a critique of social hypocrisy; it demonstrates his awareness that representation is the necessary condition of modern life. Modernity is constituted by paper money and legal fictions.

6
Pathologizing the Bodily Economy: Alas's *La Regenta* (1884–1885)

LA REGENTA is as much an urban novel as those of Galdós but its focus is very different. Its setting—the provincial capital Oviedo, fictionalized as Vetusta—is a modernized city integrated into the centralized political system but conscious of lagging behind the national capital: unbroken rail links with Madrid were established only in 1884 (Ruiz 1975: 22), after the novel's ending in the late 1870s/early 1880s and the year its first part was written. Its intermediate position as a modern but not modern city brings to the fore the tensions created by the modernization process: 'modern Vetusta' ('Vetusta' meaning 'ancient') is a contradiction in terms. The dual experience of rapid change and immobilism is reflected in the novel's temporal scheme, which quickens its pace (part I covering three days, part II three years) while increasingly getting enmeshed in a spiral of overlapping temporal loops: time is speeding up and getting nowhere; at the end we are back where we started, in the cathedral in October. Vetusta's inhabitants have internalized the capitalist rhetoric of flow and circulation but modernity is experienced by them as frustration and stagnation. As Benedict Anderson noted (1983), the modern nation is an imagined community 'invented' through print culture before it becomes a political and economic reality: Vetusta's sense of being part of the modern nation is derived from reading the national (and international) press and the same cosmopolitan diet of books (largely French) that is read in the capital. In *La Regenta*, as in an 1879 article (Lissorgues 1980: i. 154), Alas mocks the 'literary centralization' of the habitués of Oviedo Casino but, as Lissorgues notes (1980: ii. 19), it was only by himself reading the national press every day in Oviedo's Casino that he was able to be one of Spain's leading journalists while living in the provinces. In his 1890 study of capitalist modernity *Les Lois de l'imitation*, Tarde observed that modernity is created through the power of attraction of the metropolis, which provides a model radiating outwards: 'Paris reigns [. . .] over the provinces. [. . .] Every day, by telegraph or train, it sends into all of France its ideas, its wishes, its conversations, its ready-made revolutions, its ready-made clothing and furniture. [. . .] This hypnotism has become chronic' (Williams 1982: 355). As Tarde put it, the modern nation is 'imitation on a large scale'. Tarde's major contribution is his perception that imitation is first and foremost a psychological reality: the 'reproduction of desires' (Williams 1982: 360).[1] This idea was derived from Thomas à Kempis's principle *ab interioribus ad exteriora* (Williams 1982: 353): Kempis's *The Imitation of Christ* figures in *La Regenta* as a book recommended to Víctor by Ana and through the novel's parallel depiction of religious and consumerist imitation. In his later work *La Psychologie économique* (1902), Tarde insisted that the principal object of economic enquiry is not material goods but desire (Williams 1982: 361). Modernity figures in *La Regenta* not so much through consumerism as through the characters' contradictory desires. The novel shows that modernity, especially in a provincial capital, exists primarily in the head.

Although the novel's focus is psychological, it provides the reader with a large amount of information about recent urban transformation. *Vetusta transformada* is the last in Saturnino Bermúdez's series of local historical monographs, which parallel at provincial level the construction of the nation through archaeology undertaken by Federico Ruiz in *Fortunata y Jacinta*. The opening 'anatomy' of the city (Alas 1981. i. 109–16) shows us the remains of the old city wall, whose demolition had already been completed by 1855, allowing the urban expansion that took place from the 1850s through to the late 1870s when the novel is set (García Delgado 1992: 154–5). We are given a panoramic view of the building to the north and west

---

[1] Tarde's ideas were known in Spain through his articles from 1880 for the *Revue philosophique*; these included an 1881 article 'La Psychologie en économie politique'. From 1883 he became known in Spain especially for his writings on the Italian criminal anthropologist Lombroso, which Alas reviewed favourably (Maristany 1973: 34); in 1894 Adolfo Posada, like Alas a Krausist professor at Oviedo University, translated Tarde's *La criminalidad comparada*. *Les Lois de l'imitation* was translated into Spanish in 1907. See the entry on Tarde in the Espasa-Calpe *Enciclopedia universal ilustrada europeo-americana* (1987–91).

of residential districts for the new rich, who have made their money in national trade and in Cuba, where Asturias had the third largest colony (after the Canaries and Pontevedra) of emigrants of any Spanish province (Ruiz 1975: 65); and to the south of new industrial outskirts (processing coal and iron) and workers' estates. Between 1836 and 1877, Oviedo had grown by 330 per cent (compared to Madrid at 175 per cent): the second biggest population increase of any provincial capital (Artola 1973: 75); in 1887 its population stood at 20,100 (García Delgado 1992: 149).[2] The Calle de Traslacerca (now Calle Jovellanos), from which Mesía threatens to 'infiltrate' the garden of Ana's mansion, followed the line of the old city wall (Palacio Valdés 1991: 306 n. 35): Ana lives up against the boundary separating the old town from the new.[3] With urban expansion, the city centre has become a contradictory mix of palaces inhabited by aristocrats too traditional to move to the new outlying residential districts, and slums inhabited by those members of the proletariat too poor to move to the new workers' estates. Alvargonzález, Fernández, and Tomé (in García Delgado 1992: 155) state that the ruling classes of Oviedo had vetoed approval of a 'plan de Ensanche' to rebuild the centre on modern lines, fearing the changes in power relations that would follow; consequently modernization is patchy and mostly restricted to the outskirts. The old town—cramped, damp, dirty, with inadequate ventilation or sewage facilities—is everything denounced by contemporary public health experts. The only exceptions are the State buildings (police headquarters, municipal offices, and prison) occupying the space of the monasteries and convents demolished after disentailment; the Marqués de Vegallana has further plans to demolish a church to build a modern covered market (i. 490). By contrast the new outlying bourgeois residential districts are spacious, conforming to standardized town-planning regulations (and with the same kitsch stylistic eclecticism noted by Galdós as the hallmark of modernization), with wooded parks surrounding the private mansions and impressive new institutions being built by the

[2] Jutglar (1971: 57) puts the population of Oviedo at 14,156 in 1857, rising to 48,103 in 1900: a nearly fourfold increase.
[3] This is made clear by the map of Vetusta, with Alas's street names superimposed on a late 19th-century map of Oviedo, included in Amorós's and Martínez Cachero's exhibition catalogue (1985).

religious orders (back in vogue with the Restoration) which, as in Galdós's Madrid, coexist with the shanty towns ringing the city. The religious revival to the north is matched by the growth of anticlericalism and republicanism in the southern industrial outskirts: throughout the Restoration the Republicans won two out of Oviedo's three parliamentary seats, with a solid working-class vote (shifting to the Socialists in the 1890s) and strong support at Oviedo University; Alas was himself a lifelong republican (Varela Ortega 1977: 395–6; Ruiz 1975: 16). Urban expansion has created a new class segregation, with some explosive juxtapositions of social extremes.

In the course of the novel, this opening sketch is fleshed out with chapters describing the Church hierarchy and aristocracy —both, according to Ruiz (1975: 62-3, 79–80), disproportionately influential in Oviedo, mostly supporting Cánovas's Conservative Liberals rather than the Carlists—and the public sphere represented by the Casino. Ana's long walk takes us down the new tree-lined Boulevard, whose wide pavements allow the masses access to the city, and the Calle de Comercio—the real-life Calle Cimadevilla[4]—with its 'tiendas de novedades'; Alvargonzález, Fernández, and Tomé (in García Delgado 1992: 154) identify the commercial district around the Calle Cimadevilla as the only modernizing spillage outside the old centre prior to demolition of the city wall. After the building of the Calle Uría in 1878 as the city's main artery linking the centre with the railway station and forming the nucleus of the new-rich residential districts described in the novel (García Delgado 1992: 155), Oviedo would build some of the finest shopping arcades in Spain; Magnien (Salaün and Serrano 1991: 121) cites these, linking the Calle Uría with the Calle Pelayo, as a key example of the glass and metal structures that turned the street into a showcase.[5] Santos Barinaga's civil burial provides Alas with

---

[4] Identified tentatively by Sobejano (in Alas 1981: i. 353 n. 12) and confirmed by the map in Amorós and Martínez Cachero (1985). Sobejano's doubts are on account of the disparity between the luxury shops in the Calle Cimadevilla and the working-class strollers described in the novel; but the point of the modern city was that it created a new public space (the street) open to all, regardless of class. This scene in the novel shows precisely that the working classes in the street cannot afford the luxury items behind the plate-glass windows.

[5] Sobejano (Alas 1981: i. 112 n. 36) gives 1874 for the building of the Calle Uría. Magnien does not say whether Oviedo's shopping arcades were built by 1884 when part I of *La Regenta* was written.

an excuse to stage a demonstration of factory workers, small traders, and artisans, led by a schoolteacher (ii. 266). And the Magistral's rural origins allow inclusion of the coal mines that, with increased demand resulting from the new national railway network, had by the 1880s become Asturias's defining characteristic; by that date the availability of coal had also made the province the country's leading iron producer (Ruiz 1975: 69; Schwartz Girón 1970: 228).[6]

Alas's social canvas is more systematically comprehensive than that of any work by Galdós. But few readers would describe *La Regenta* as a social novel. Almost all the above information is relayed through the characters' minds: what interest Alas are the mental constructs that constitute a society in the process of modernization. The opening 'anatomy' of Vetusta takes the form of the Magistral's panoptical survey from the cathedral tower: the modern city is a mental construct because it exists as an object of social regulation. Álvarez-Uría (1983: 133–4) notes that the 'política familiarista' promoted by Restoration reformers, as by their counterparts elsewhere in Europe, paved the way for the turn-of-the-century development of psychoanalysis. The novel's psychological focus, anticipating so many of Freud's insights, needs to be seen in this context. The premiss of this 'política familiarista' was that reform should be implemented not by legislation but by improving the individual: hence the targetting of the private sphere of the family—indeed, the invention of privacy—as the means of regeneration. The novel shows how this policy—designed to avoid State intervention, seen as a violation of liberal freedoms—in practice led to massive interference in the family by what the Krausists called 'intermediary bodies': that is, private social initiatives constituting the public sphere of 'the social'. It also shows how this 'política familiarista' recast social and economic problems in moral terms, sidestepping the need for social restructuring. The aim was to create deserving citizens who would help themselves. But to moralize the lower classes, the bourgeoisie must themselves be moral. Corbin (1986: 163) notes how, in the late nineteenth century, concern with the 'stench' of the working classes gave way to worries about the odours emanating from

---

[6] Ruiz (1975: 15) notes that the Asturian miners' long-standing tradition of political activism dates back to the 1881 demonstration in the Cuenca de Nalón.

within the bourgeois home, girls' bedrooms being a special cause for concern. Galdós's trajectory from *La desheredada* to *Fortunata y Jacinta* likewise shows an increasing conviction that it is the bourgeoisie that is 'rotten'.[7] The bourgeoisie's concern with regulating the lower orders starts to be directed against itself. The rise of the all-bourgeois discipline of psychoanalysis at the end of the century coincides with the decline of 'social medicine' as the lower classes increasingly became subjected to State welfare programmes and regulation.

The Krausists who promoted reform via education also pioneered the study of psychology in 1880s Spain; Alas was a close friend of the leading Krausist psychological theorist, Urbano González Serrano. Ripamilán alludes to this new trend when he says 'psicológicamente, como dicen los pedantes de ahora' (i. 154); the society doctor Somoza, who used to attribute everything to indigestion, now calls everything a '*cuestión de nervios*' (i. 427). Krausist educational reform was aimed at creating responsible individuals capable of critical thinking within acceptable parameters. This goal of standardization through individualization was especially clear in 'social medicine', which established a distance between bodies by insisting on the hygienic circulation of air, turning the 'masses' into individuals (the most unhygienic state was the 'hacinamiento' of the working-class slums), while at the same time laying down rules for what constituted the 'healthy' and the 'sick'; that is, the 'normal' and the 'abnormal' (Corbin 1986: 98–102). The most individualized body is the most 'normal' body. 'Normal' here does not mean 'that which is the norm' but 'that which conforms to prescribed norms'. Indeed, the 'normal' is posited as the opposite of that which is the norm, for belief in the need for regeneration supposes an existing state of sickness.[8] We have seen in previous chapters how contemporary Spanish 'social medicine' was influenced by degeneracy theory. As Álvarez-Uría puts it (1983: 186), 'la medicalización de la

---

[7] This point is made by Fernando García Arenal (son of the reformer Concepción Arenal) in his detailed 1885 report to the Comisión de Reformas Sociales on sessions held with Asturian workers in 1884 in Gijón. Noting that the bourgeoisie criticizes the working classes for drunkenness and immorality when the boulevards are lined with the idle rich drinking and showing off their courtesans, he concludes: 'La reforma debe empezar por arriba' (1980: 149).

[8] Gilman (1979: 58) notes that the term 'decadence' came into use before the term 'progress'.

sociedad [. . .] sólo es posible mediante su patologización'. The social regulators construct the individual as sick in order to make him or her healthy: that is, a 'proper' individual. Restoration reformers attacked the Church for giving money to the 'undeserving poor', arguing that, in creating an army of spongers, they were producing the problem they claimed to alleviate (Fuentes Peris 1997*a*, 1997*b*: 196–212). But the regulators who aimed to help the poor help themselves equally needed to construct them as a 'problem'.

The two areas constructed as problems in the late nineteenth century were, as we have seen, the lower classes (the 'social question') and women (the 'woman question'). Krausist educational initiatives and medical experts' manuals were targeted largely at women since they were responsible for the family's moral education and health. This may have given women a position of increased importance, but it also placed all sorts of strictures on them. As in psychoanalysis, everything became the mother's fault. And not to become a mother was to fail in one's social duty. The construction of the 'normal mother' became the key to the construction of the 'normal family', which in turn was the key to social regeneration. *La Regenta* is full of 'abnormal' families where the mother, or lack of a mother, is to blame (in the Vegallanas' case, the father is equally wayward). Doña Paula tyrannizes her son to satisfy her greed; Rosa Carraspique fanaticizes her husband and daughters; Visitación is always in other people's houses, leaving her husband at home with the children; the motherless Olvido Páez is insufferably spoilt by her father; Ana is marked for life by not having known a mother, and will destroy her own marriage as a result of not becoming a mother. The only 'normal' family is so thanks to the 'religión del hogar' of its atheist father, Guimarán (ii. 340).

Shuttleworth (Jacobus, Fox Keller, and Shuttleworth 1990: 47–68) has shown how late nineteenth-century women were placed in a series of double-binds as their bodies became the site of unresolvable social anxieties. Whatever they did, they were defined as 'ill'. Charnon-Deutsch notes that Ana 'is perceived as ill by all the men in her life, who all try to cure her' (1994*a*: 71). The mysteriousness of her illness is due to the contradictory perceptions of what constitutes normality held by the various regulators competing for control of her body. Freud was honest enough to admit he did not know the answer to the question 'What does a woman want?' but Ana's confessor and doctor both claim to know what she 'needs' (ii. 72, 404). Her doctor tells Víctor she is not ill but tells Frígilis her apparent return to health is another symptom of disease: even when she is healthy, she has to be constructed as sick. As Shuttleworth (Jacobus, Fox Keller, and Shuttleworth 1990: 47–68) and Russett (1989) point out, late nineteenth-century medical discourse was based as much on economic theory as on biology, for both sciences borrowed from each other, Darwin's debt to Adam Smith being reciprocated by Herbert Spencer's debt to Darwin. The Spanish hygienists Monlau, Pulido, and Santero, like the Anglo-Saxon health experts discussed by Shuttleworth and Russett, constantly refer to the body as an 'economy' whose resources must be 'properly managed'. Both Monlau (1860: pp. v, 9) and Santero (1885: ii. 165, 173) insist that hygiene is a branch of political economy, both because a disturbance in one area of the bodily economy will, as in the national economy, affect the other areas, and because the goal of social medicine is to maximize citizens' productivity. The childless wife is thus a special problem. Pulido (1876: 14) warns that female sterility can cause serious physical and mental disturbances requiring medication or internment. For this bodily economy is strictly gendered: men's problem is over-expenditure of resources but women's problem is blockage, impeding natural flow. Blocked bodily fluids and energies, particularly those linked with women's reproductive function, were liable to fester and go rotten; women have to take care to 'sluice out' their 'dark drains' regularly. As Shuttleworth observes (Jacobus, Fox Keller, and Shuttleworth 1990: 56): 'The rhetoric of drains and sewers was not reserved for [...] prostitutes.' Shuttleworth points out that this rhetoric projects anxieties about the circulation of goods onto its analysis of the circulation of bodily fluids: the body mirrors a capitalist economy threatened by the related problems of accumulated waste and stockpiling (projected onto the female) and exhaustion of resources (projected onto the male). This view of the bodily economy as flow and blockage is illustrated in *La Regenta* by Víctor's notion of the circulation of the blood as 'una cosa como el depósito de Lozoya [Madrid's new modern waterworks, in operation since 1851], con canales, compuertas en el corazón' (ii. 117), an image which makes Víctor feel nauseous for he has his own problem of blockage.

Many critics have remarked on the novel's anticipation of Freud, but Freud's own 'hydraulic' conception of the bodily 'economy' emerged out of the worries about excess flow and blockage going back to the mid-nineteenth century. It is worth noting that the regenerationist Joaquín Costa started to advocate a 'política hidraúlica'—with irrigation projects producing a free flow of goods—from 1880, the date of his famous speech at Madrid University, 'Misión social de los riegos en España' (Maurice and Serrano 1977: 49; Costa 1911). Given Ana's own definition of herself as a hysteric (ii. 534), it is also worth noting that J. S. Mill, in *The Subjection of Women*, described hysteria as 'the mere overflow of nervous energy run to waste' (1988: 65), which would vanish if that energy were directed to an end. As Mill notes, working women did not suffer from hysteria. Ana's tragedy is, quite simply, that of the bourgeois wife who has nothing to do, aggravated in her case by the 'blocked' energies resulting from childlessness.

In the individual as in the social body, good management (the Spanish term 'buen gobierno' makes the political parallel clear) consisted in getting the balance right: too much flow was as bad as too little. Women whose 'flow' was obstructed were seen as likely to go insane, but those who 'let themselves go' were also liable to be declared insane. Indeed, as Shuttleworth observes, female blockage was more threatening than male overexpenditure for the latter could be controlled by exercise of the will, whereas women's bodies were seen as self-regulating yet pathological mechanisms beyond control. Men had bodies but women were bodies. If women could not control themselves, they needed male experts to regulate them: the phrase 'husbanding of resources' used in Anglo-Saxon medical discourse (Russett 1989: 115) makes it clear that control is male. One of the signs of Visitación's flightiness in *La Regenta* is that she prefers traditional female healers to modern male health experts, to the doctor Somoza's disgust (ii. 112). Laqueur (1990: 184–92, 207–27; Gallagher and Laqueur 1987, 27–8, 31–2) has shown how the discovery in 1847 of 'spontaneous ovulation' (tied to the menstrual cycle and independent of orgasm) was interpreted as meaning that women were not in control of their bodies but victims of its 'periodicity'. The obsession in late nineteenth-century hygiene manuals with menstruation supposed that women were biologically unstable, even when periods were regular. As Poovey notes, women were liable to be diagnosed as hysterical when their organic cycles were normal as well as when they were not, for in both cases their 'uterine economy' was out of control (Gallagher and Laqueur 1987: 146–7). Poovey quotes an 1847 obstetrics manual: 'The uterus is altogether removed from the direct influence of voluntary motion.' An 1892 childbirth manual cited by her asserts that it is 'as if the Almighty, in creating the female sex, had taken the uterus and built up a woman around it'. The Spanish health expert Monlau (1865: 152) similarly stressed: 'La matriz es el órgano más importante en la vida de la mujer [. . .]. En la matriz retumban indefectiblemente todas las afecciones físicas y morales de la mujer: el útero hace que la mujer sea lo que es. *Uterus est animal vivens in muliere, decían los antiguos; propter solum uterum mulier est id quod est.*' This last Latin dictum is also cited by Santero (1885: i. 406). As the medical writer A. Jimeno put it in 1882: 'De tal manera influye, de tal manera manda, de tal manera impera ese delicadísimo centro, siempre y a todas horas sin tregua ni descanso en la mujer, que no hemos vacilado en declararlo [. . .] su segundo cerebro.'[9] Ana's 'illness' consists in an organic instability that makes her oscillate between extremes. Her doctor's hesitations as to whether she is or is not ill articulate anxieties about a female bodily economy that is uncontrollable in sickness and in health. It is not surprising that she comes to feel that her self is inherently sick: 'aquella maldita enfermedad [el histerismo] que a veces era lo más íntimo de su deseo y de su pensamiento, ella misma' (ii. 534).

The men who variously define and try to cure Ana's 'illness' are her doctor (Benítez), her confessor (the Magistral), her seducer (Mesía), and her husband's naturalist friend Frígilis. Mandrell (Valis 1990: 23) notes that 'Ana is subjected to the perversely proprietorial scrutiny of men.' Despite the fact that he is a former judge, her husband, too involved with his hunting and pet birds, is not a regulator: he simply administers the advice received from others.[10] His abdication of his social responsibility by taking early retirement from the lawcourts is

---

[9] From *La mujer* (Zaragoza, 1882), 35; cited by Rodríguez Sánchez (1994: 266).
[10] Sinclair (1993: 189) has noted that the husbands of 19th-century fictional adulteresses tend to be administrators, cf. Galdós's Francisco Bringas. The theme of female adultery thus implies a critique of increased State regulation. The husbands of Emma Bovary and Fortunata—doctor and chemist respectively—are also failed regulators.

paralleled by his 'egoism' in not paying his wife enough attention. As a result, the task of regulating Ana's bodily economy is left to intruders in the family. Ana's illness is not a metaphor for a particular social disease afflicting Vetusta, but the various regulators' prescriptions project onto her body a series of social discourses which relate to the city's social, economic, and political life. In so doing, they make her body the site of discussion and struggle between competing philosophies: that of liberal political economy (Mesía); that of medicine (Benítez), closely allied to that of natural science (Frígilis); and that of a Church competing for control with the lay regulators by poaching their discourses (the Magistral). It is logical that Ana should feel her self fragmenting, because it is constructed as an impossible mix of contradictory prescriptions. Adultery makes Ana 'como todas'; that is, morally sick. But it also makes her physically healthy as, for the first time in her life, the obstructions to 'free flow' are removed. In equating the 'normal' with the healthy, nineteenth-century medical discourse constructed it as 'natural': the 'abnormal' was 'unnatural' or 'perverted'. *La Regenta* depicts a society in which the questions 'What is the normal?' and 'What is the natural?' have become unanswerable. The novel is also about the instability of a self created from the outside through a series of conflicting discourses: the self is trapped in a proliferation of representations. This leads to the alarming suggestion that there is no 'natural' self.

Critics differ in their views on Alas's relationship to Krausism but his political and legal writings make it clear that, whatever his religious hesitations, he shared its social tenets. The centrepiece of Krausist thought was its organicist view of society, based on an analogy between the individual body and the social body. It is this analogy that allows Ana's body to become the site of a series of social discourses. Krausist organicism supposed that society's component 'organs' were interdependent and that a malfunctioning in one area would affect the others. As Villacorta Baños notes (1980: 82), this organicism was easily able to absorb Spencerian thought, whose increasing concern with the inability of the social organism to regulate itself, and conversely with increasing State interference, was so influential in late nineteenth-century Spain. Krausist organicism was an attempt to strike a balance between the old-style *laissez-faire* liberalism, which prioritized the individual good, and increasing

State interventionism, in which the State put its own good before that of its citizens. Both extremes were denounced as 'particularist' or 'egoistic'. Sanz del Río (1860: 8) insisted that 'desde el punto en que [una tendencia particular] se aisla y pierde la forma social de servir en comercio positivo y recíproco a las demás tendencias y personas sociales, desde entonces esta tendencia y su persona se hace ilegítima, interiormente enferma, perturbadora y anti-humana'; on the previous page, he had added 'estéril' to the list. 'Egoísta' is one of the most frequently used words in *La Regenta*, especially in relation to Ana, who is childless, 'interiormente enferma', and has an illegitimate relationship. Giner de los Ríos (1875: 224) similarly saw such 'intereses egoístas, subjetivos y bastardos' as the source of decadence. The ideal Krausist society was based on 'reciprocity'; that is, the mutual concern of all social 'organs' for the well-being and autonomy of the others. The Krausists championed individual freedom and local autonomy against the incursions of the centralized State, while insisting that the individual and the municipality and province had responsibilities to the nation as a whole. They thus supported decentralization while rejecting separatism, and insisted that reform was the business of 'society' and not of the State. This ideal of a plural society, whose 'organs' respect each other's difference while working 'harmoniously' together, is an attractive one but one which refuses to acknowledge the very real existence of conflict and contradiction. As Díaz notes (1973: 21–6, 31, 41), Sanz del Río's reason for preferring Krause to Hegel was, in addition to his dislike of Hegel's subordination of the individual to the State, his unhappiness about the centrality of contradiction to Hegel's dialectical method. Krause's 'armonismo', based on the reconciliation of opposites, was felt to be a more productive philosophy for Spanish society, throughout much of the nineteenth century torn between political extremes. The Krausist-educated intellectuals of the Second Republic of 1931–6 would discover that this dream of a harmonious, plural society failed to take into account the importance of conflicting interests. *La Regenta* shows that egoism, on the part of the regulators and the regulated, triumphs over the best of intentions.

The leading Krausist intellectual Giner de los Ríos defended this organicist view of society against liberal contract theory, as represented by Locke and especially Rousseau. In his 1873

Principios de derecho natural,[11] Giner attacked Rousseau's supposition that man is 'naturally' asocial, and that society comes into being only when men pass from an original 'natural' state into the social contract by which they agree to curb their 'natural egoism' and work together for the common good. Giner insisted that men are 'naturally social' and that ethics are founded in natural law, which does not mean legitimization of an existing 'natural' state of things but the 'natural' existence in man of a sense of justice. For this reason the Krausists, while being among the first in Spain to accept Darwin's evolutionary theories, were unable to accept his principle of 'natural selection' which effectively subordinates nature to the free competition central to liberal contract theory (Bahamonde Magro and Martínez 1994: 520). The extent to which women are also 'naturally social' is not discussed by Giner, but throughout his work he maintained that their contribution to the whole was through the family (or, if unmarried, through the caring professions), since women were more 'particularist' than men and lacked a fully developed sense of justice. The contradictions in Krausist views on women are made explicit in an 1898–9 education report by Giner, which on the one hand recognizes that women's suitability for the caring professions suits them for a career in law, but on the other hand insists that they should be allowed to take on only minor responsibilities since:

La característica natural del temperamento femenino no es favorable para el tratamiento judicial de una cuestión. El sentimiento y el impulso predominan en su espíritu sobre la investigación fría y deliberada [...] El interés por las cuestiones legales es más probable que figure como una característica masculina más que femenina. (cited in Maquieira d'Angelo 1989: 286)[12]

---

[11] For an excellent discussion of Giner's political ideas based on this 1873 work, see Díaz (1973: part II).

[12] Such contradictions are echoed in the work of Simmel, who in his writings on women (1984) recognizes that their 'innate' incapacity for abstraction and 'particularism' makes them largely inadaptable to modernity, but also asks whether a different kind of 'feminine modernity' might be possible, counterbalancing the alienation produced by the increasingly abstract ('masculine') forms of modern life. It might be possible to read Alas's depiction of Ana, and Galdós's depiction of Fortunata, both seen in terms of the body (substance) and driven by entirely particularist emotion, in this light. But on the whole these novels, like most of those discussed in this book, seem to be concerned primarily with the construction of the female self by contemporary discourses of social control and by modern consumerism, rather than with 'the feminine' as an alternative form of modernity.

Alas echoed this belief in women's inability to get beyond the particular and to think in terms of objective principles in his 1894 article 'Psicología del sexo' (1894: 343), to which I shall return. The opposition between a masculine capacity and feminine incapacity for abstraction is illustrated in *La Regenta* by Ana's failed marriage to a former high court judge, showing her inadaptability to the abstractions of the law. Conversely, Víctor's incompetence at human relationships and especially in love can perhaps be related to his legal career, which has accustomed him to dealing with life in abstract terms; in the end, however, it is his ability to think in terms of an abstract principle of justice that enables him to rise above particularism in his extraordinarily altruistic response to Ana's adultery. The family was the cornerstone of Giner's special hostility towards Rousseau, for, if Locke held that society was constituted by contract but the family by natural law, Rousseau argued that both society and the family were constituted by contract. Giner insisted that marriage is not a contract but an 'organic state' in which the parts become a single 'body'.[13] This issue was made critical by the introduction of civil marriage in Spain in 1870, rescinded by Cánovas in February 1875, for if marriage was sanctioned by the State and not by the Church it was hard to see it as anything other than a contract. In 1883, the year before the publication of part I of *La Regenta*, the Radical Party had put civil marriage back on the political agenda by asking for a parliamentary debate on the matter (Varela Ortega 1977: 170). The Krausist refutation of contract theory's supposition that society and nature are in opposition, and its insistence on the harmonious fusion of the two in natural law, are crucial to *La Regenta*: if the social is rooted in the natural but nonetheless is sick, definitions of the natural become fraught with problems.

Giner's *Principios de derecho natural* was recommended by Alas as a textbook for his own courses on natural law. Appointed to the Chair of Roman Law at Oviedo University in 1883, he moved in 1888 to the Chair of Natural Law which he held till his death. His first appointment in 1882 had been to the Chair of Political Economics at Zaragoza, his earlier appointment

---

[13] This point is also stressed in Giner's essay 'Concepto de la persona social' (Giner de los Ríos 1969: 202–3).

to the Chair of Political Economics at Salamanca having been blocked for political reasons. Alas was professionally familiar with contract theory, the foundation of political economics. It is also clear from his political journalism that he was well versed in theories of the State. His constant defence of local autonomy versus centralization, and of national unity versus separatism, reminds his readers that local government is part of the State, although its function is to defend local interests, and that society (the public sphere) and the State are two different things (Lissorgues 1980–1: i. 172–4, 195). Although in favour of private social initiatives, in the course of the 1880s he came increasingly to accept the need for State-sponsored reform (García San Miguel 1987: 301). In his writings on law, he consistently followed Giner in rejecting contract theory for a concept of society—and marriage—grounded in natural law. In articles of 1878 and 1880 (García San Miguel 1987: 326; Lissorgues 1980–1: i. 127), he lamented the similarity of the wedding service to a contract, and insisted on the indissolubility of marriage. He also argued against the penalization of adultery, since the husband's honour depended on his own acts: this last point is acknowledged by Víctor, in a critique of the law which he had administered as a judge, when he reflects that he has no right to condemn Ana's infidelity when he has been pursuing Petra (ii. 484).

Alas's doctoral thesis 'El derecho y la moralidad' (1878), supervised by Giner de los Ríos, consisted in a critique of Rousseau (García San Miguel 1987: 124–5). In his 1881 preface to Ihering's *La lucha por el derecho*, he argued that the social contract has been a 'useful fiction', allowing the fight for individual freedom to be won by falsely supposing that the natural state is one of total individual independence. Alas is here picking up the contradiction in liberalism, which claims to be based on contract law but also justifies itself through appeal to the biological 'struggle for life', thus grounding itself simultaneously in the law and in nature. In this preface, Alas criticizes the appeal to Darwinistic theory, noting that the argument that social change must obey evolutionary laws has been used to justify liberalism's increasing drift towards conservatism (pp. xi, li). Alas insists that 'la vida humana comenzó siendo colectiva' since men had to club together to combat nature (pp. li–lii): man's social 'nature' is based on the improvement of nature. Alas's Krausist understanding of natural law does not mean acceptance of immutable biological laws, but belief in essential, universal ethical norms: for this reason he was able to accept Zola's naturalism while rejecting determinism.[14] The social contract can, he clarifies, give voice to these ethical norms, but it does not create them for they exist independently of historical contingency. He goes on to lament the oppositional thinking that sees the natural and the social as being in conflict (pp. liv–lvi). But his notion that man's social 'nature' is expressed by combating nature creates all sorts of problems of definition. As Díaz notes with regard to the identical theories of Gumersindo Azcárate, the leading Krausist social reformer of the 1880s, also from Oviedo and a close friend of Alas: the main flaw in the Krausist belief in natural law is that it fails to specify who is entitled to decide which rights are 'natural' and which are not (1973: 121).

This problem resurfaces in Alas's writings on women. While arguing for social change to allow them to earn a living (so they can marry for love and not for money), he consistently opposed women's emancipation, which he understood to mean women becoming like men, on the grounds that there were 'natural' differences between the sexes. Marriage was still women's 'natural' role because they were not constitutionally suited to the public sphere (Lissorgues 1980: i. 119–35). His major article 'Psicología del sexo', published in *La Ilustración Ibérica* in seven instalments in 1894 and never subsequently reprinted, is a compendium of all the biological theories of sexual difference analysed by Russett (1989) and Shuttleworth (Jacobus, Fox Keller, and Shuttleworth 1990, 47–68). Although it post-dates *La Regenta*, it corroborates many aspects of the novel's treatment of gender. The 'masculinization' of women is seen as a regression to an original state of bisexuality; Alas insists that this regression is not 'natural' because it goes against the natural evolutionary process of increasing sexual differentiation. He argues against Darwin's and Spencer's notion that females are incomplete males, whose development has been arrested at a lower evolutionary stage, insisting that both men and women have evolved out of an original indifferentiation:

---

[14] See Alas's introduction to the book version of Pardo Bazán's *La cuestión palpitante* (Alas 1972: 149–53).

this allows him to see both masculine women and feminine men as degenerate backslidings, rather than having to regard masculine women as more highly developed. It also allows him to affirm women's equality with men while justifying their subordinate position on the grounds of sexual difference, substantiating Laqueur's claim (1990) that theories of sexual difference were developed at the same time as political doctrines of equality because, if all humans were equal, new justifications of women's lack of access to the public sphere were needed. Natural sexual differences, Alas argues, underlie every aspect of human life, even 'la vida más espiritual y libre'; human beings are more than physiology but there is no 'barrera insuperable' separating mind and body (38, 231).

In this article, Alas cites scientific 'evidence' that what determines whether the embryo becomes masculine or feminine is the relationship of 'gasto' to 'ahorro': predominance of 'gasto' makes the embryo male, predominance of 'ahorro' makes it female (231). The female is based on a deficit of energy, hence the need to accumulate; the male is based on a surplus which requires expenditure. Thus men are active and outgoing, while women are passive and egoistic. Women have more fat on their bodies because they are busy 'hoarding' energy (they need to eat less because they store up energy through inactivity), while men are lean because they expend it (and therefore need more nourishment). He cites evidence that when bees are better fed they produce more female offspring, and that after epidemics more male children are born. This produces a nightmare scenario of devouring women and emaciated men. Indeed, Alas describes the sexual act as physical loss ('death') for the man and physical gain (pregnancy) for the woman (262): women get fat at the expense of men. Interestingly, he cites a French woman journalist's use of the same argument to explain why men feel a need to humiliate women (262). Economic and political discourse spills over into Alas's discussion of sexual difference throughout:

> La hembra, puede decirse, es *conservadora*; el hombre *liberal*. La hembra, más *rica*, algo así... como *capitalista* que acumula con avidez la propia sustancia, ahorra y crece, mientras el género masculino dilapida lo poco que tiene, es el verdadero *proletario*, en el sentido etimológico de la palabra (*prole* y *ginnere*), se dedica a engendrar, sin miedo á su propia pobreza. (259, original italics)

This constitutes the Don Juan—the man who most spills his seed —as the ultimate in generosity. The language of loss and profit used here merges with the language of social reform: 'El macho es reformista, innovador; las variaciones en la especie se le deben a él. La hembra es más *misoneísta*, guarda la tradición' (262, original italics).[15] Although Alas insists that both are necessary to create balance, the picture he paints of femininity is deeply threatening to someone who, like himself, supports social change. If women are regressive and men progressive, the former are to blame for the current lapses into sexual indifferentiation which Alas so decries. The energies which women need to store up are the 'peso muerto' which feeds future generations, for their 'hoarding' is needed to compensate the expenditure of energy in pregnancy (262). Women, defined by their reproductive function, are dominated by their viscera and nervous systems: that is, they are ruled by their bodies. The child is the extension of the mother, not of the father; the woman loves her child more than her husband because, in so doing, '*se ama a sí misma*' (262, original italics). Even when women seem to be altruistic, they are being selfish. Social reform must be left to men, first because women are incapable of 'ensayos desinteresados' or 'tentativas que no son negocios'; and secondly because active women 'gastan en esfuerzo innecesario las *reservas*, el capital de vida acumulado por la asimilación', thus creating racial degeneration (343, original italics). He particularly attacks 'la gran influencia de la mujer en la vida religiosa moderna' (343), presumably a reference to women's philanthropic activies, which he sees as a feminization of the Church. He concludes:

lo justo consiste en tratar de *modo desigual* las cosas desiguales. [. . .] Ni al niño le conviene que le traten como á hombre, ni al salvaje como á hombre de cultura refinada, ni al sano como al enfermo, ni al criminal como á santo, ni á la mujer como al hombre. La mujer no es menos que el hombre, es otra cosa. (343)

We have here a complete list of society's exclusions. Interestingly, when Alas's comparison gets to the sick and the healthy, there is a stylistic reversal putting the positive term first, so that

---

[15] Darwin's *Origin of Species* (1859) supposed that male reproductive cells were responsible for mutation and female cells for the constancy of the species (Coward 1983: 78–9).

—as in Benítez's hesitation about Ana's condition—it is not clear whether woman is healthy or sick. Alas's suggestion that women 'naturally' accumulate and that men 'naturally' spend does not, I think, contradict late nineteenth-century medical experts' obsession with correcting women's blockages and men's excess flow. For Alas's description of 'natural' sexual difference is a pathological one in which the natural is simultaneously healthy and sick. Men are needed to counter women's hoarding, and women are needed to check men's expenditure. This hesitation as to whether the 'natural' is sick or healthy is found throughout *La Regenta*.

In accordance with the above theory that men are 'naturally' liberal, Alas makes Ana's seducer Mesía the head of the provincial Liberal Party, 'Muy entendido en Hacienda y eso que llaman economía política' (i. 265). Mesía is a Don Juan who so overspends his sexual energies that he has to go into physical training to prepare himself for adultery with Ana. Monlau (1865: 145–6, 186–90) had insisted that sperm was the most precious product of the 'animal economy' and that it must therefore be released sparingly, calculating that loss of an ounce of sperm was equivalent to loss of forty ounces of blood. Santero (1885: i. 411) likewise stressed: 'De todas las causas de debilidad que pueden actuar sobre nuestro cuerpo, ninguna lo es en tan alto grado, por la enervación que produce y por lo rico que es el humor que sale de la economía, como las pérdidas del semen.' In accordance with such theories, Mesía is 'bankrupted' by his summer with the minister's wife, even though this takes place at an 'invigorating' seaside resort; a healthy holiday away from the city leads the minister's wife to adultery, as will happen with Ana. To repair his energies, Mesía reads hygiene manuals and takes to 'gimnasia de salón', horse-riding, and early nights (ii. 327). Sexual expenditure with Ana makes Mesía's bodily economy suffer an internal 'crac' (financial crash), requiring him to 'economizar' his sexual favours to Petra (ii. 450–1, 460). He is relieved when the affair with Ana is over because his energies are running out (ii. 513–4). The economic discourse of loss and profit that Mesía uses so cynically cannot be dismissed as a critique of his materialism, for it is the same language that Alas uses in his discussion of sexuality and the language of contemporary medical discourse. Although Mesía has ulterior motives for giving Ana 'hygienic' advice (ii. 420), his analysis of her is proved right: religion does make her ill and sexually blocked, and the countryside does make her healthy and open to sex. The only time in the novel when Ana is healthy is during her adulterous affair with Mesía, when she achieves an 'equilibrio' between her former extremes of obsession with religion and obsession with health, as Víctor observes (ii. 445); that is, a regularized release of energy.

As a supporter of free trade, Mesía logically has to favour the free flow of sexual energy; but his over-expenditure shows the need for freedom to be tempered with constraint. This reflects the increasing acknowledgement in Restoration Spain, even among Sagasta's Liberals (Mesía's party), that a measure of State control is necessary. As the local *cacique* (Alas's word), Mesía represents the abuse of central State power.[16] His intrusion into Ana's home—as he ingratiates himself with Víctor, usurps his role as head of the household by dismissing the maid, and installs himself in Ana's bedroom (adultery on the premises of the matrimonial home was a criminal offence even for the husband)[17]—mirrors his usurpation of political power in the province, as he manipulates the Marqués de Vegallana (*cacique* for Cánovas's Conservative Liberals), controlling the political fortunes of the latter's party as well as his own. Valera's private correspondence makes it clear that one of the keys to electoral success was to get the Regente of the local Audiencia to replace hostile justices of the peace with favourable ones (Romero 1992: 101). Mesía's seduction of 'la Regenta' (meaning wife of a Regente) is the private equivalent of such public abuses. The electoral leverage implicit in the post of Regente is shown by the fact that, in the case of Valera's contested election for Archidona (Málaga) in 1863, the Regente of the Audiencia in Granada (responsible for the whole of southern Spain) issued

---

[16] In a 1901 article, Pardo Bazán (1972: 140) noted that, around the time of German Unification in 1871, Bismarck became a favourite name for dogs and horses in Spain. One wonders whether, in giving the name Bismarck to the boy bellringer who opens the novel, Alas is making a gibe at the Prussian concept of the strong central State promoted by Bismarck. In Restoration Spain, Bismarck's name came to be associated especially with the State national insurance schemes he introduced in Germany (Habermas 1992: 146), admired by Cánovas's Doctrinaire Liberals as a way of palliating social conflict, but seen by many Krausist reformers as unwarranted State intrusion in welfare matters that ought to remain in private hands.

[17] It is worth noting that Ana's adultery also fits the one other circumstance in which the husband's adultery was deemed a criminal offence: that of causing 'public scandal'.

a writ against one of the local *caciques* for rigging the elections in Valera's favour. Valera describes his own and ministers' efforts to get the Regente to retract the writ (Romero 1992: 200–2, 215–16, 222). Víctor had, of course, before his early retirement been Regente of the Audiencia in Granada: the importance of the position he has held in the State administration must not be forgotten. Varela Ortega (1977: 369) notes that one of the main ways in which *caciques* secured influence over the State administration was by cultivating the friendship of judges and magistrates who could fix court rulings. Varela Ortega's definition of the *cacique* as 'el jefe local de partido que manipula el aparato administrativo en provecho propio y de su clientela' (369) is a perfect descripion of Mesía. Krausist attacks on *caciquismo* were aimed precisely at its 'particularismo' or 'egoísmo' in defending personal, rather than collective, interests.

In an 1878 article, Alas defined economics as 'la ciencia de los bienes materiales y de los servicios para el cuerpo, de la propiedad, en una palabra' (Lissorgues 1980–1: ii. 198). As a Don Juan with a strong interest in political economics, Mesía is concerned with property in people's persons. But his theoretical political role as defender of private property (the explicit objective of both Cánovas's Conservatives and Sagasta's Liberals) in practice takes the form of his control of the property of others. Political life in the novel has become a market-place, consisting in the granting of sinecures and the buying of votes. The latter is the Marqués's speciality: he is not afraid of the extension of suffrage when all the villagers are his 'colonos' (i. 321). This anticipates Cánovas's prediction that Sagasta's reintroduction of universal suffrage in 1890 would lead to more, rather than less, election rigging since the central State would have less control over the local *caciques*; here Cánovas was right for electoral fraud became notorious in the 1890s, fuelling the Regeneracionista movement which grew out of the earlier Krausist campaigns for political reform (Varela Ortega 1977: 421–2).[18] In 1879 Alas had himself embarked on a journalistic campaign against electoral fraud in Asturias (Lissorgues

---

[18] Varela Ortega (1977: 417) comments that Krausist attacks on *caciquismo* often overlooked the fact that the real problem was not central State interference but the reduction of politics to private interests which prevented the formation of a public sphere of critical debate. *La Regenta* is precisely concerned with this latter issue.

1980–1: i. p. xxxiii). Kern (1974: 67) notes that the years 1884–5 (when *La Regenta* was being written) were marked by heated criticism of Cánovas's abuse of *caciquismo*, via his Ministro de Gobernación Romero Robledo, to procure a massive majority for his Conservative Party in the 1884 elections.[19] Varela Ortega (1977: 404, 406) singles out 1884 as the highpoint of central government interference in elections under the regime of restricted suffrage operating from the elections of 1879 to those of 1886: in 1884 the electoral register was reduced from 33,000 to possibly as few as 12,000. Additionally in 1884, Romero Robledo used intimidation to remove Liberal mayors and councillors who refused to resign when Cánovas called elections on Sagasta's resignation. Alas consistently attacked *caciquismo* in his articles, particularly that notoriously exercised in Asturias for Cánovas's Conservatives by Alejandro Pidal y Mon, whose strongman was a local marquis (Lissorgues 1980–1: i. 23–40). Varela Ortega (1977: 394) describes how the Marqués de Canillejas, acting for Pidal as 'el zar de Asturias', could, when the Conservatives were calling the elections, guarantee victory for his candidates in eleven out of Asturias's total of fourteen seats, 'reserving' the remainder for the Republicans or Liberals; even when the Liberals were calling the elections, he could guarantee the *pidalistas* from four to seven seats. Pidal's speciality as president of the Unión Católica was manipulating the support of the clergy, susceptible to pressure because their salaries had since 1845 been paid by the State, as *La Regenta* reminds us (i. 389).[20] The Liberal strongman in Asturias was also a marquis: the Marqués de Avilés (Varela Ortega 1977: 395). Alas saw *caciquismo* as a manifestation of 'la absorción y tiranía del poder central', turning the provinces into colonized territories, though he also rejected separatism as a form of local *caciquismo* (García San Miguel 1987: 250, 279; Alas 1881: p. lix): in his view, a balance between central and local power was needed so each could check the other. Mesía's *cacicazgo* represents the usurpation of local autonomy by the centre, mirrored in his violation of the autonomy of the family. His long-term

---

[19] In an 1885 article, Galdós attacked Romero Robledo for rigging the 1884 elections (cited by Goldman in Labanyi 1993*a*: 142).

[20] See Varela Ortega (1977: 394–5). Pidal also got his brother appointed as ambassador to the Vatican, where he influenced the appointment of bishops, including that of Oviedo.

plan of achieving a position of power in Madrid through his seduction of the Minister of Justice's wife shows that his interests lie at the centre. Mesía's choice of minister is significant: Valera's correspondence further shows that it was vital for electoral candidates to secure the complaisance of the Minister of Justice or his Under-Secretary, responsible for appointing the judges who controlled the electoral process at a local level (Romero 1992: 76, 96, 178). Mesía gets the brutish Ronzal elected as provincial deputy for the Conservatives, knowing that the latter's envy is a sign of his wish to be like him, thus neutralizing political opposition; indeed, Ronzal will later join Mesía's Liberals (i. 271). Ronzal is so much an advocate of State control that he thinks the Diccionario de Autoridades is 'el diccionario del Gobierno' (i. 286) and cannot tell the difference between the State and the public sphere of critical debate that is the Casino (ii. 277). His mistake here is excusable since in practice the Casino, far from providing a forum for critical debate, is a school of imitation where the locals learn to mimic those with connections in Madrid. Varela Ortega (1977: 370) notes that *caciquismo*, which like Alas he insists is a sign of dependence on the central State, took the form of a 'club' of 'amigos' frequently meeting informally in the local Casino. Mesía, as local *cacique*, is also president of the Casino (i. 250). As Varela Ortega observes (418): 'Lo esencial en las elecciones españolas no eran las trampas violentas; lo más frecuente era precisamente la falta de lucha y el pacto entre *caciques* que la hacía posible.' *La Regenta* shows how the result is the elimination of political difference: 'Así era el turno pacífico en Vetusta, a pesar de las apariencias de encarnizada discordia' (i. 302).[21]

The political 'conciliación' of the Restoration is the opposite of the Krausist ideal of 'harmony' because it is based not on the various parties' reciprocal respect for each other's autonomy but on envy. The result is that political rivalries translate into the imitation of one's rival in order to usurp his place. This

---

[21] Varela Ortega (1977: 428 and *passim*) insists that the 'turno pacífico' was not, as is often said, an agreement between Cánovas and Sagasta to fix elections so that their parties alternated in power, but rather—as *La Regenta* shows—a complex bargaining process whose function was to mediate central and local interests through the reduction of the political to the private, producing a depoliticization of the electorate.

political system, rather than stimulating critical debate and a healthy intellectual pluralism, leads to a lethal kind of sameness in which everyone hates everyone else and difference cannot be tolerated. Hence the importance of Ana's efforts to resist the general desire for her to be 'como todas'. Everyone has their personal spy system gathering information that can be used against the envied. Power is gained through knowledge of people's private lives; that is, through the invasion of privacy.[22] Mesía gets his mistresses to confess to him the abject behaviour of their husbands and former lovers, so as to gain power over other males (i. 493). He is a social regulator not because he is interested in improving others but because, by invading and gathering knowledge about their private lives, he gains public influence, whether directly as with his seduction of the minister's wife, or indirectly by inspiring envy and thus consecrating his position at the top of the ladder of imitation: this is his motivation in succeeding with Ana where all other men have failed. When he calls himself an 'hombre político', he means that his actions are calculated for personal gain (i. 294). Unlike the Magistral and Benítez, he does not tell Ana what she needs because he is concerned only with what he wants. His vision of himself as a 'máquina eléctrica de amor' 'con conciencia de que puede echar chispas' (i. 358) is based on a view of the male body as liberal expenditure of energy controlled for egoistic ends. One is reminded of Giner's description (Giner de los Ríos 1969: 203) of excessive indidivualism as a kind of 'atomismo sensualista'. Mesía's liberality in seducing women parallels his brand of political liberalism.

Mesía's moral degeneracy is linked to degeneracy theory, not only because his sexual over-expenditure is exhausting his virility, but also because he is feminized by his obsession with fashion: as a sexual 'overspender', he logically has to be associated with consumption. To remain at the top of the ladder of imitation, Mesía himself has to imitate the latest fashions: if the lower ranks imitate those who order their clothes from Madrid, the latter imitate Mesía who buys his in Paris. Adultery is linked with consumerism in *La Regenta* not through the adulteress (Ana has no interest in fashion or shopping) but

---

[22] Valis (1992*b*: 266) notes that gossip 'turns the private into the public, the public into the private'.

through her seducer: her first major encounter with him in the novel is in the Calle del Comercio with its 'tiendas de modas', where 'Todo es movimiento' and the gaslight creates a sense of the new and the ever-same: 'Los vetustenses gozan la ilusión de creerse en otra parte sin salir de su pueblo. Todo se vuelve caras nuevas, que después no son nuevas' (i. 356–7). By taking us down the Calle de Comercio at nightfall, Alas can show how the gaslight turns the street into a theatrical display where the strollers are both spectators and spectacle. Just as the bourgeoisie imitates the aristocracy, so the working classes imitate the bourgeois custom of the 'paseo' (i. 350). In this novel, it is the men who are the chief imitators and consumers of fashion. Obdulia's clothes are flamboyant, Olvido Páez went through a phase of turning herself into a tailor's dummy, and Visitación (referred to as 'la del Banco', associating her with the exchange economy) consumes not fashion but food, invading other people's kitchens and private affairs as a substitute form of adultery (i. 486). But almost all the men in *La Regenta* are 'slaves of fashion' (i. 269). It was on his trip to the 1867 Paris Exhibition that Mesía learnt that religion was 'chic' (i. 360). He lives at an inn because he has no concept of the private. His materialist philosophy is described as that of a travelling salesman (i. 493); his concern with his public image makes him a self-advertiser. His materialist ideas (which he believes) and his professions of idealism (which he does not) are both copied from books, mostly French novels, for he exists only as a self-representation. The male consumers of fashion in *La Regenta* are also avid consumers of commercial fiction, which creates standardized images of social desirability. The male members of the Casino who constitute Vetusta's civil society turn themselves into commodified public images; one of the chief ways of doing this is by consuming women. Sexual relations are a market in which the men marry the richest women, take other men's hand-me-downs for their mistresses—Mesía hands Paco Vegallana his cast-offs 'como una dama rica y elegante deja vestidos casi nuevos a sus doncellas' (i. 291)—or resort to prostitution. The novel points to the hypocrisy of the almost daily tirades against prostitutes in the local paper when most of the local men are 'compradores de carne humana' (i. 261, ii. 39). In this society value derives from what one represents, which in turn derives from what one consumes, as grossly illustrated through the orgy of consumption that is the Marques de Vegallana's table. In falling for the local *cacique* and Don Juan, Ana shows that she too is inscribed in this value system. As the Magistral says, 'se había enamorado [. . .] de la ropa del sastre, de los primores de la planchadora, de la habilidad del zapatero, de la estampa del caballo, de las necedades de la fama, de los escándalos del libertino' (ii. 495). The Magistral is also right to think that Ana could not fall in love with him because of his priest's robes; that is, because of what he represents.

However the Magistral is equally obsessed with his self-representation. He is Mesía's direct rival for control of Ana's body because he too regards her as a public trophy. The Church is, like the Casino, a social body ruled by envy in which power is gained through knowledge: Gloucester and the Magistral both have their 'policía secreta' prying into the private affairs of others (i. 396; ii. 266). Weber (1966*b*) and Nimetz (1971) have argued that the parallels in the novel between religion, sex, and money illustrate the degradation of the spiritual by the material. I would read them rather as showing how the various social discourses of Restoration Spain infiltrate each other in the process of invading private life. This is particularly evident in the case of the Magistral, who represents the Church's attempt to 'modernize' its discourse by borrowing from medicine and economics, in order to compete with the new secular forms of social regulation. In his study of nineteenth-century Spanish sermons, Portero (1978) notes how in the mid-century the Catholic Church came closer to Protestantism in defending the acquisition of wealth as a reward for labour, the latter being seen as a way of redeeming original sin. 'Codicia' and 'avaricia'—the worship of money for its own sake—were still condemned, but came increasingly to be associated with the lower classes who were losing their 'sentido cristiano de la pobreza' (1978: 219). The Church's attitude to poverty becomes split: the old charity, based on the giving of alms, continued but Catholicism increasingly internalized the new lay philanthropists' belief that help should be restricted to the deserving poor or those who could be recycled as productive citizens.[23] Corbin

---

[23] For an excellent analysis of the conflicting discourses of charity and philanthropy in Restoration Spain, see Bahamonde Magro and Martínez (1994: 478–80), and Bahamonde Magro in Rodríguez Puértolas (1988: 163–82). On the notion of the 'deserving' and 'undeserving' poor, see Fuentes Peris (1997*a*, 1997*b*).

(Perrot 1990: 549–57) describes the nineteenth century as the golden age of the confessional. The confessional as physical object —first introduced around 1551 (Tambling 1990: 69)—came into widespread use around 1800, with confessors increasingly delving into intimate behaviour: the attempt to maintain social control in the face of new lay competitors creates the concept of the private in the process of invading it. Tambling (1990: 2) —echoing Foucault's definition of western man as a 'confessing animal' (1987: 59)—notes that the practice of the confessional produces a narrative of the self at the same time as making sexuality central to its understanding and control. The narrative of *La Regenta*—whose female protagonist is defined entirely by her sexual desires—is triggered by her general confession.[24] As Corbin notes, this practice caused widespread concern about priests' control of women 'whom they resembled in dress and sensibility': 'To the husband jealous of his authority, the priest became a rival' (Perrot 1990: 557). Even though the Magistral does not try to seduce Ana physically, his control of her through the confessional makes him Mesía's direct rival. Ana feels that her desire for Mesía is a betrayal of her fidelity not to her husband but to her confessor (ii. 56–7). Víctor complains that his home has become a Paraguay ruled by the Jesuits (ii. 205, 242); in fact, only the Magistral's early training was with the Jesuits but the latter, expelled from Paraguay in 1769 by an Enlightenment-influenced Spanish State, were the traditional enemies of liberalism. It is the Magistral's knowledge of the most intimate details of Ana's life that gives him power over her; her previous confessor Ripamilán represents an earlier stage in the history of the confessional less concerned with private life (i. 149). The Magistral's obsession with controlling others is shown not only in his opening panoptical survey of Vetusta, but also in his championing of the doctrine of papal infallibility, newly declared in 1870: he is the 'pontífice infalible' in the Carraspique home, where he abuses his power over the wife and daughters to assert it over the husband who is the region's chief Carlist supporter. Appropriately, the doctrine of papal infallibility is Víctor's major stumbling block to accepting Catholicism (ii. 217).

---

[24] Bauer (1993) notes that in fact the novel is framed at start and finish by two failed confessions, as well as by references to the homosexual Celedonio; here she notes, following Foucault, that homosexuality was the product of the 19th-century obsession with confession.

The Magistral's modern discourse, appealing to the medical and economic ideals of free flow, produces a clash with the traditional Catholic concept of morality as the containment of a body marked by original sin. Jagoe (Jagoe, Blanco, and Enríquez de Salamanca 1998: 321) notes that in the course of the nineteenth century the Christian ideal of male chastity (and to a lesser extent that of female chastity) came to be seen as 'unhygienic'. The Church was, like *laissez-faire* economics and Krausism, based on a concept of natural law, but a very different one in which patriarchal authority was needed, in both public and private spheres, to subdue an intrinsically evil nature incarnated in woman (Eve). The Magistral reverts to this view at the end when he calls Ana a 'prostituta como todas las mujeres', whose rotten body has contaminated him because he has failed to keep it under control (ii. 493–4). Alas's stress, at the start and end of the novel (i. 119, ii. 534), on the anaemic appearance of the statue of Christ in the cathedral figures Catholicism as an unhealthy religion of death, in opposition to the natural world. The simple-minded Bishop's love of nature (his house is full of songbirds) is kept under control by Doña Paula, repeatedly compared to a corpse. The St Augustine whom Ana reads had, in addition to sanctioning property for the first time in the history of the Christian Church (Attali 1989: 195), justified prostitution as a necessary evil like a drain, as Pulido's 1876 health manual for women pointed out (116). In obliging Ana to bottle up her physical and emotional impulses, Christianity does not allow her to 'drain them off' but produces an internal blockage which goes rotten. Here she is grotesquely mirrored by Saturnino Bermúdez, whose failure to relieve himself sexually causes stomach cramps and constipation (i. 122, 126). Ana constantly compares her inner self to a 'pozo negro' (cesspool) or 'subsuelo'. Contemporary public-health experts were obsessed with leakages of sewage into the water supply, and of miasmatic 'emanations' from the contaminated subsoil in streets that were not paved. Ana experiences Mesía's presence in the muddy, unpaved Calle de Traslacerca as a 'filtración' seeping into her mind and home.[25] She tries

---

[25] For a perceptive analysis of mud imagery in the novel, see Sinclair (1998: 45–58). Mandrell (Valis 1990: 16) comments that the role of Don Juan imitated by Mesía represents the 'power of infiltration'.

to resist the contamination of adultery by idealizing her non-physical relationships with her husband and her confessor: the former in practice a father–daughter relationship; the latter theoretically that of father confessor and spiritual daughter, in practice that of brother and sister ('hermanos del alma'). The alternative to adultery is figurative incest: another form of contamination based—as in Galdós's *La familia de León Roch*—on containment rather than leakage. Both uncontrolled flow and blockage make the body rotten. This double-bind is reflected in Ana's childhood escapade with her figurative brother Germán (his name coming from the same Latin root as 'hermano'): a genuinely innocent pre-pubescent adventure where the flow of the river in which they set sail turns to blockage as they get stuck on a mudbank. Ana's cloacal dream, in which she imagines herself pursued through stinking sewers by putrescent ecclesiastical figures, anticipates Freud's 'hydraulic' notion of the unconscious as that which is repressed: that is, not allowed to flow freely.[26] She sees her dream as an image of hell, but the novel makes it clear that it is the Church which makes her go 'rotten' inside by blocking her natural impulses: hence the ecclesiastical figures in the dream. The Magistral is also to blame for Rosa Carraspique's death from tuberculosis in the convent unhygienically situated next to Vetusta's rubbish tips, with sewage leaking through the walls: Valis (1992a: 207) notes that Oviedo did not have running water till 1879. The narrator reminds readers that the healthy practice of washing is an Islamic virtue (i. 127), a point made by contemporary public-health experts (Santero 1885: ii. 367–8, 820). The novel opens with the image of the city engulfed by rubbish as it digests 'la olla podrida'; in an 1882 article 'Anatomía urbana', comparing the architectural make-up of a city to the various organs of the human body, the town planner Arturo Soria repeatedly described the sewage system as 'el aparato intestinal de una ciudad' (Collins and Flores 1967: 169, 182).[27] This

---

[26] Valis (1992a) notes the imagery of circulation and blockage (and the related images of leakage and seepage) in this dream and elsewhere in the novel, citing historical evidence of fears of contagion—by sewers, by the working classes—in late 19th-century Oviedo. Valis relates such images to the notion of the inchoate, represented in Ana's body and in the 'body' of the novel.

[27] In the same article (Collins and Flores 1967: 184), Soria reports cases of typhoid in Madrid houses affected by 'gases subterráneos' from leaking sewage.

emphasis on Vetusta's lack of adequate sanitation constructs the city as suffering from the double problem of blockage and leakage, leakage being 'bad flow' caused by over-accumulation, as opposed to the 'good flow' permitted by free circulation. The 'humedad sucia' which seeps through Vetusta's 'tejados y paredes agrietadas' (ii. 83) represents a concern with the unhealthiness of modern urban society that is projected onto Ana's body through the discourses of religion and hygiene, both of which in different ways associate the female body with putrefaction.

Ana's first mystical/hysterical attack occurs on reading St Augustine at puberty.[28] Contemporary health manuals insisted that intellectual expenditure was particularly dangerous for girls at this point since it deprived the 'uterine economy' of the extra resources needed for this vital transformation. Santero states alarmingly:

> Cuando la mujer llega a la edad de doce años, esto es, cuando entra en la pubertad, un pequeño órgano situado en el hipogastrio, el útero, [. . .] despierta de su letargo funcional, para desplegar una actividad inusitada; centro de todas las sinergias, sojuzga á los demás órganos; se contituye [sic] asiento de nuevas y trascendentales necesidades, y, en una palabra, es el pequeño déspota que domina lo físico y lo moral de la mujer, y la constituye tal cual es. (1885: i. 405–6)

He goes on to warn against the reading of books (1885: ii. 84) which can interfere with the onset of menstruation. Pulido (1876: 105) likewise insists that the slightest upset can adversely affect the 'revolución profunda, radical' that is puberty, inducing (as in Ana's case) near fatal illness. Like Monlau, he describes girls' reaching of sexual maturity in nightmarish terms: 'Un órgano hasta entonces dormido, al parecer indiferente, la matriz, sacude su letargo, despliega su potente inervación y envuelve a la mujer toda en su esfera de actividad' (105). St Augustine is depicted as a negative influence on Ana, confirming the regime of enclosure and fasting imposed on her by her English-educated governess, who, since her escapade con Germán, had regarded her as marked by original sin: 'una flor podrida ya por la mordedura de un gusano' (i. 193). This earlier episode was crucial in making Ana regard her natural impulses as evil:

---

[28] For Ana's hysteria/mysticism, see Aldaraca (1990), Saillard (Lissorgues 1988), Labanyi (1991).

the priest who forces her to 'confess' put ideas into her head that had never occurred to her. As a result, 'contradiciendo poderosos instintos de su naturaleza, [. . .] contuvo los impulsos de espontánea alegría' (i. 195). This delayed her puberty till 15, making the mental effort of reading St Augustine at such a critical moment especially dangerous: his insistence that carnal love is sinful and that 'los niños son por instinto malos' (i. 203) instils in her an unhealthy religiosity based on rejection of the physical.

Sanz del Río (1860: 89–93) had insisted that the body must be given as much attention as the mind, approving of Krause's Hellenism; Mosse (1985) notes that the Hellenism of the German Enlightenment provided the ideal against which degeneracy theory measured modernity's 'sickness'. Ana's previous reading of the Greeks in her atheist father's library had given her an ideal of an unfettered life 'al aire libre' (i. 199). Her vision of the Greeks as 'un pueblo joven, sano en suma' (ii. 392) fits with her father's increasing belief that Spain is 'un pueblo gastado' and that the New World is 'devouring' a decadent Europe (i. 196). Ana's 'conversion' to St Augustine contrasts violently with this earlier nature worship. The narrator criticizes her father for letting her read the Greeks, for their 'healthy' open-air ideal is one that does not know the private world of the home. Her revolutionary father's failing is to put the public good before that of his family. The Greek cult of the healthy body—as filtered via Germanic Hellenism—was, of course, also a cult of the virile: something that Ana could relate to only with an implied loss of femininity. Ana's second mystical/hysterical attack results from her attempt to reconcile the contradictory ideals of Catholicism and Hellenic nature worship; a reconciliation achieved in the Song of Songs and St John of the Cross, also in her father's library, but rendered problematic by the religion of containment instilled in her. The Magistral, who also had a country childhood, similarly comes to experience religion, in the form of his priest's garments, as a shackle (ii. 321). Alas does not go so far as Mesía in supposing that not even priests can resist their natural urges, but he shows that priests have natural urges and that, if these are blocked, they become a 'cloaca de inmundicias' choked with 'basura corriente y encauzada' (ii. 494). The Magistral profits from this religion of containment by manipulating the repressions of those he confesses: 'El Magistral conocía una especie de Vetusta subterránea [. . .] "Era aquello un montón de basura." Pero muy bien abono, por lo mismo: él lo empleaba en su huerto' (i. 398–400).

The problem is not just that the blockage of natural impulses makes them fester inside, but that the Church's combination of this traditional rhetoric with its modernizing adoption of the discourses of hygiene and economics subjects the individual to contradictory messages. The causal link between late nineteenth-century social regulation and the later discipline of psychoanalysis is shown by the Magistral's insistence that the confessional is a hospital for sick souls: 'el alma tiene, como el cuerpo, su terapéutica y su higiene; el confesor es médico higienista' (i. 343).[29] To qualify for entry to this 'hospital' one has to be sick: 'toda alma que viene aquí está enferma' (i. 342). Ana's case shows that the traditional religion of containment creates the sickness that makes people turn to the Church for their 'curación moral' (ii. 22). The Magistral insists that virtue is 'el equilibrio estable del alma'; that is, containment and flow in the right proportions (i. 345). In his own attempt to get the balance right, he does gymnastics like Mesía (i. 410) and works off his unspent sexual energies with his maid (ii. 244). When he and Mesía pass each other out walking, the narrator comments that one is repairing 'fuerzas perdidas' and the other spending 'fuerzas inútiles' (ii. 328). When the Magistral tells Ana to go to El Vivero because exercise is 'higiénico' (i. 495), he is dangerously echoing the advice Mesía will give her. His first confession with her, expounding the need for 'hygienic flow' through the image of bathing in the river (i. 342), sent her out on a country walk to the 'fuente de Mari-Pepa', leading to an encounter with Mesía. The Magistral's language, when he speaks as a 'médico del alma', is perceived by Ana as 'un arroyo que corre entre flores y arena fina' (ii. 66–7); this is dangerously like the sensation of dissolving which Mesía produces in her.

The problem of establishing a balance between free flow and control is related via the Magistral to contemporary economic discourse. He has replaced the Bishop as the 'predicador de moda' because he is a 'Bastiat del púlpito' who presents salvation as a 'negocio', and charity as an investment producing

---

[29] The hygienist Monlau (1865: p. vi) called priests 'médicos del alma'.

Pathologizing the Bodily Economy 241

interest; he insists that this business operation is, as in Bastiat's mid-nineteenth-century notion of laissez-faire, 'mecánico' or self-regulating (i. 443, 451-2). Hirschman (1977) has noted that the attraction of Adam Smith's theories lay in their suggestion that passion and interest were the same thing. The Magistral's forte as a preacher is his description of the wasted body of the youth who 'overspends' his sexual energies (i. 453): a description reminiscent of contemporary health manuals' warnings about the effects of masturbation—a dissipation of resources which is an attempt to relieve sexual frustration. For both overspent and unspent energies turn the body to waste. The inverted parallel between Mesía (excess expenditure) and the Magistral (blockage) shows that the 'business' of 'salvation' is not as 'automatic' as the Magistral claims for some fine tuning of the system is needed. When we are told that Mesía sees himself as a 'máquina de amor' (i. 358), the implication is that —as in the many references in *Fortunata y Jacinta* to machines breaking down—he is a fixed-energy system liable, if resources are not properly managed, to exhaustion.

The Magistral resorts to this economic rhetoric so as to reconcile his own interests, in the form of his passion for domination, with those of his post as Provisor: that is, administrator of the Church's material concerns (i. 99 n. 17). He resolves Church business 'como por máquina con el criterio de su ganancia' (i. 469), showing that this 'automatic' system is skewed. The Magistral is called 'el jefe'—the term used of Mesía as political boss—by his subordinates in 'el mercado singular de la curia eclesiástica' (i. 467, 469). He runs the diocese like a *cacique*, dispensing favours and getting people out of jail or threatening to put them in it; he is also rumoured to have links with Carlism (i. 415, 464). His catechism class comprises his 'museo de beatas', the girls being 'aquellas rosas que eran suyas y no del Ayuntamiento como las del Paseo Grande' (ii. 202-3), making clear his rivalry with the State in the battle for social control. Indeed, catechism was one of the forms of social control intensified by the nineteenth-century Church to combat secularization; Vetusta's religious charitable organizations include the Santa Obra del Catecismo as well as the Escuelas Dominicales (i. 455). Used to being 'el amo espiritual de la provincia' (i. 397), the Magistral sees Ana as his by right: 'un tesoro descubierto en su propia heredad' (i. 401). If Mesía abuses his political influence to get rich, the Magistral abuses his ecclesiastical authority by forcing local priests to equip their churches from the store run by a front-man on his and his mother's behalf: the novel notes that this violates the Code of Commerce as well as canon law (i. 393). The counting of its takings in the basement is perceived by the Magistral as 'un gran foco de podredumbre, aguas sucias estancadas' (i. 564) for what should be free flow has become the stockpiling of wealth; as in the bodily economy, blockage of flow leads to putrefaction.

Both the Magistral and the narrator put the blame for this accumulation of wealth onto his mother: women are the 'natural' hoarders; the Magistral's youthful expansive urges have been constrained by the Church, into which Doña Paula has forced him to satisfy her material ambitions. Her behind-the-scenes presence rules the Bishop's palace and the Church administration, infiltrating the male public sphere (i. 469, 530). Like Ana, the Magistral has never known a proper home because he was brought up by a single parent who has no concept of privacy: Doña Paula employs an informer to follow him and 'sniffs' his rooms with her eyes (i. 423–4). Doña Paula's view of her son as her 'capital outlay' on which she has a right to claim 'interest', or if not to claim breach of contract (i. 546), is a perfect illustration of the notion of charity as interest that he propounds from the pulpit. His unhappiness makes it clear that economic rhetoric does not work when applied to the private sphere.

Despite the view expressed in Alas's 1894 article that hoarding is a female characteristic (the miners whom she exploits are equally avaricious but spendthrifts),[30] Doña Paula's conversion of her private life into a business masculinizes her. Conversely, the Magistral's position as a Church dignitary satisfies his masculine ambition but feminizes him by making him a hoarder unable to spend his energies: he sees his priest's robes as an 'afeminamiento carnavalesco' (i. 526); his immaculately manicured hands and buckled shoes (i. 101, 103) are like those of a woman. The Magistral's concern with his appearance echoes

---

[30] In his 1885 summary of information provided to the Comisión de Regormas Sociales by Asturian workers, García Arenal noted that drinking was particularly high among miners. Unlike Alas, he attributes working-class drinking not to 'codicia' but to the need to supplement a deficient diet (1980: 42–3, 52).

that of the Casino's members, for religion under the Restoration is the latest fashion. This creates a feminization since it is the women who oblige their menfolk to 'imitar en religión, como en todo, las maneras, ideas y palabras de la envidiada aristocracia' (i. 115). In particular, women have taken over the running of charity, as the Church sets up its own lay-administered philanthropic societies to compete with or infiltrate its non-religious rivals: the 'junta agregada de damas protectrices' headed by Visitación has taken over La Libre Hermandad, founded by the atheist Guimarán (i. 458).[31] The fashion-conscious Obdulia is one of the principal organizers of 'rifas católicas', 'bailes de caridad', and 'novenas' (i. 131); the Marquesa de Vegallana's religiosity consists in 'presidir muchas cofradías, pedir limosna con gran descaro a la puerta de las iglesias' (i. 305)—that is, in making a public spectacle of herself. The fashionable Jesuit preacher invited, for an exorbitant fee, to preach at the 'novena de los Dolores' is accompanied by 'las damas de más alcurnia, las más guapas y las más entrometidas' selling devotional objects by the high altar (ii. 333). Just as in his 1894 article Alas saw women's entry into the public sphere as a masculinization but lamented women's increased involvement in Church activities as a feminization, so in *La Regenta* bossy women (whether Doña Paula or the society ladies rattling tins at the cathedral door) are feminizing the Church while masculinizing themselves. The masculine Doña Petronila, known as El Gran Constantino because of her religious patronage, leads the Catholic charitable contingent that disputes the atheist Guimarán's right to supervise Santos Barinaga's last moments; as rival philanthropists, they argue as to which are the more 'entrometidos' (ii. 251). None of those who deplore Santos Barinaga's death on philanthropic grounds takes him any food; the Church has turned his daughter against him; the local freethinkers use his burial as a publicity stunt; and the council has so neglected the plot of land it is required to provide for civil burials that it is a rubbish tip.

Guimarán and the Bishop (both men) are the only Vetustans whose charity is altruistic, given regardless of the recipients'

[31] García Arenal, in his summary of Asturian workers' responses to the Comisión de Reformas Sociales in 1884 (1980: 69, 120), noted that they unanimously dismissed the Church as 'cosa de las mujeres', and that the charity offered by the Sociedad de San Vicente de Paúl encouraged begging rather than helping to make the poor useful members of society.

beliefs; Guimarán stands down from chairmanship of La Libre Hermandad and lets the Church-linked ladies' committee take over, since his atheism is keeping donations away. But even Guimarán succumbs to egoism in monopolizing Santos Barinaga's death; his conversion out of guilt is an exemplary act of social reconciliation, healing the rift with his enemy, the Magistral. As with Santos Barinaga, his funeral is made into a propaganda exercise, this time by the Church, officialdom, and the press. The battle for social control between rival philanthropists has turned even death into a public spectacle.[32] Through Doña Petronila, charity is associated with prostitution: she is forever counting the takings from her public 'soliciting'. In her obeisance to the Magistral, she becomes a procuress prostituting Ana to him, echoing Ana's aunts whose 'philanthropic' adoption of her had made them into procuresses putting her up for 'public auction' on the marriage market (i. 229–30). The Magistral's recommendation that Ana involve herself with charity, going into circulation rather than shutting herself up at home, is sound hygienic advice but it takes her into the public sphere, where he can have easier access to her. It also involves her in the commercialization of the Church: in her cloacal dream she sees herself handing out coins to the rotting ecclesiastical figures (ii. 126). When she walks barefoot as a penitent in the Holy Week procession, '*dándose en espectáculo*' in a '*cuadro vivo*', she feels her 'publicidad devota' is 'una especie de prostitución' for her naked feet 'habían sido del público' (ii. 359, 366, 383–4). Doña Petronila gives instructions to the 'modista' making Ana's costume as if designing an outfit for a fashion parade (ii. 355).

Ana's horror of 'la calle' and 'el culto público'—the only charitable activity she enjoys is visiting the private homes of the poor (ii. 228)—clearly redeems her in the narrator's eyes. At the same time her mystical phase is criticized because it is a self-absorbed passion that cuts her off from her social obligations: she and the narrator describe it as 'egoísta' (ii. 213), the supreme Krausist sin. But if Krausism insisted on the need for the individual to contribute to society, women were expected to do so through the family. Ana, with no children and a husband

---

[32] As Ariès notes (1987), before the capitalist public/private distinction death had taken place in public. Once the public/private split has been effected, public death comes to be seen as a violation of privacy.

who prefers to sew on his own buttons (ii. 326), is forced to look for an 'objeto para la sed de sacrificios' 'fuera del centro natural de la vida, fuera del hogar' (ii. 283). (It can be noted in passing that Víctor shares with another house-husband Francisco Bringas a mania for collecting and ordering miscellaneous objects.) The Magistral is right to remind Ana of her duties to others but, in discouraging her mysticism, he is thinking of himself; he is jealous of St Teresa (ii. 207) because Ana's mystical dialogue with her makes her unavailable for him (he is perhaps also jealous of the intimacy she is able to enjoy with another woman). His relationship with Ana lacks the Krausist virtue of reciprocity because both are thinking only of their own needs; the word 'egoísta' is used as much about them—particularly Ana—as it is about Mesía. Alas places Ana in an impossible position, making her guilty of female egoism but giving a negative depiction of her attempts to make herself useful in the public sphere. Her philanthropic phases are implicitly criticized also because they are a form of imitation: 'imitaré a estas señoras' (ii. 108). But her mysticism too is based on an 'espíritu de imitación', turning St Teresa into her 'modelo inmortal' (ii. 191, 194). Víctor sees her mysticism as a form of death for she develops an 'horror al movimiento, [. . .] a la vida' (ii. 208–9); she encourages him to imitate her by reading Kempis's *Imitation of Christ*, which temporarily instils in him the notion that the world is 'un montón de escorias' (ii. 215). Víctor sees her self-prostitution in the Holy Week procession as another form of death: 'se le figuraba ya que llevaban a su mujer al patíbulo' (ii. 365). Here too Ana is imitating a female penitent she had seen in Zaragoza (ii. 356). Whether her devotion is public or private, she cannot escape the Restoration's conversion of religion into a form of representation.

Ana describes her doctor Benítez, up to date with the latest medical theories, as 'también un confesor. Yo le dicho secretos de mi vida interior como quien revela síntomas de una enfermedad' (ii. 383). In regarding her inner life as a source of medical symptoms, Benítez constructs it as sick. Benítez's presence evokes literary naturalism in the sense that this, as Zola stated in *Le Roman expérimental*, represented the application to literature of current medical theory, with its stress on social regulation; Zola explicitly advocated the medicalization of the novel in order to make it a tool of social reform. Ana has seen pictures of the brain in the books of Henry Maudsley and Jules Luys: the former, influenced by degeneracy theory, was notorious for his belief in women's congenital inferiority because of their disposition to sickness (Showalter 1987: 101–20; Russett 1989: 67–8; Pick 1989: 208); the latter specialized in hypnotism at La Salpêtrière, where Charcot's experiments with hypnotizing hysterics allowed Freud to develop his theories of the unconscious (ii. 376 n. 14).[33] In her letter to Benítez (just before writing to her 'other confessor', the Magistral), Ana insists she will be 'esclava de la higiene' just as before she had sworn to be the Magistral's slave, obeying his medical instructions 'con religiosa escrupulosidad' (ii. 377). Benítez has told her not to indulge in *psicologías*, not because he does not believe in such things, but because the mind—particularly intellectual effort in women, detracting from the energies needed by their unstable 'uterine economy'—is sick. He probes Ana's 'vientre' daily for that is the seat of women's sickness, and interrogates her about the most basic bodily functions (ii. 119); as Poovey (Gallagher and Laqueur 1987: 147) and Shuttleworth (Jacobus, Fox Keller, and Shuttleworth 1990: 62–3) note, nineteenth-century women were not kept ignorant of their bodily functions but subjected, like Ana, to obsessive monitoring. Ana's periodicity is implied not only by her swings from one extreme to another, but also by the fact that her illness follows a seasonal pattern, triggered by the release and subsequent blockage of 'new sap' each spring.[34] This seasonal pattern implies that she is not in control of her 'bodily economy'; it regulates itself by repairing itself with time ('new sap' at springtime) but this is a pathological self-regulating mechanism whereby renewed vigour produces renewed congestion: Ana's final return to health produces an 'estrangulación deliciosa' (ii. 533) which sends

---

[33] Pick (1989: 212) notes that Maudsley's views on women were linked to his view of the body as the key to the nation's progress. Aldaraca (1990) has related Ana's hysteria to contemporary Spanish medical theory. For Charcot's work on hysteria, its Spanish translation, and contemporary Spanish debates on hysteria, see Chapter 5 above. Ana's mention of Maudsley's and Luys's pictures of the brain suggests that Alas was aware of the contemporary view of hysteria as a mental ailment; however, in making Ana childless and sexually deprived, he is continuing the traditional view of hysteria. For a study of hysteria in the novel, and of the novel as a hysterical text, see Sinclair (1998).

[34] The concept of 'periodicity' could be related productively to the novel's structure whose progression, as Gold perceptively notes (1995), is undermined by a 'feminine' principle of digression.

her back to the enclosure of the cathedral. Benítez's favourite expression is that the body should work like a clock (ii. 377): a self-regulating mechanism but one that needs the doctor to rewind it when it runs down and to repair it if it gets over-wound. His maxim *ubi irritatio ibi fluxus* is a belief in naturalist determinism but, more importantly, it refers to a bodily economy governed by flow and to women's supposed suggestibility. In his medical manual for women, Pulido (1876: 5, 172–6) stressed that woman's superior sensitivity 'eleva su irritabilidad á un grado sorprendente', and that the fine tuning of the female bodily economy made any internal or external upset liable to trigger a nervous disruption; conversely 'perturbaciones' of the imagination could produce fatal physical disruptions. Benítez echoes this view of women's hyper-impressionability when he tells Frígilis that a shock could kill Ana (ii. 486). It was women's impressionability that made them imitators, incapable of originality, reserved for men (Poovey in Gallagher and Laqueur 1987: 146). While convalescing in the country under Benítez's 'regime', Ana decides that people had been right to criticize her early attempts at writing poetry (ii. 383): in another double-bind, she had been criticized both for being a 'masculine' Georges Sand (since writing supposed entering the public sphere through publication) and for being a 'feminine' imitator.

Benítez does allow Ana to write private letters and a diary (in small doses). Corbin notes that the nineteenth-century practice of diary writing accompanied the confessional in constructing a private self—one that, in this case, does not have to be exposed to scrutiny by a social regulator but rather encourages self-regulation; that is, the individual's taking of responsibility for the construction of the self (Perrot 1990: 498–502). More specifically, the switch to Ana's first-person narrative for part of her period in the country illustrates Nicholas Green's examination of the ways in which trips to the countryside allowed nineteenth-century city-dwellers to construct a sense of a private self through their descriptions of nature in diaries and letters, directed at other city-dwellers (1990: 128–52). Green notes that the sense of privacy created by the solitude of nature was an illusion, for natural retreats were built and landscaped as commodified spectacles for city-dwellers, following the recommendations of hygienists and town planners, whose ideal was *rus in urbe et urbs in ruris*. Cerdá's 1867 *Teoría de la urbanización* bore the epigraph 'Rurizad lo urbano: urbanizad lo rural'; from 1882, through articles published largely in the same Republican paper *El Progreso* for which Alas was a columnist, Arturo Soria promoted his blueprint for 'la ciudad lineal' with the motto 'Ruralizad la vida urbana; urbanizad el campo' (Collins and Flores 1967: 28–9). As Corbin notes (1986: 154–5), this new city-dweller's vision of the country was a sanitized one, excluding the smells and lack of hygiene which earlier periods associated with rural life; the Spanish hygienists Monlau (1868: 25) and Santero (1885: ii. 556), despite recommending trips to the country, noted that villages were unsanitary places. In sending Ana to convalesce in a country retreat with all the latest modern conveniences, Benítez is putting into practice Arturo Soria's recommendation of a 'return to nature' which rescues the latter from its 'prostitution' in the city by applying to it the prescriptions of modern town planning. In an 1882 article published in *El Progreso*, Soria called this 'medicina' of open spaces, blending the advantages of city and country, a cure for 'los organismos caducos de *vetustas* capitales' (Collins and Flores 1967: 111, 160; my italics). Green's observation that the nineteenth-century French vogue for country retreats was a commodification of the countryside for the city-dweller's benefit is illustrated in Spain by Giner de los Ríos's famous 1885 essay 'Paisaje', which extols the regenerative effects of the Castilian countryside for the exhausted city-dweller: 'Rompamos un minuto los vínculos de la servidumbre cortesana y vámonos al campo, que está mucho más cerca de Madrid de lo que tantos se figuran' (1915: 367). Like Ana, Giner associates the countryside with the Hellenic ideal: an ideal of virile energy that is likely to create problems when the city-dweller seeking regeneration is a woman. Javier Barón notes that the Asturian countryside in particular was prized by late nineteenth-century landscape painters and wealthy collectors, its very 'remoteness' making it a consumer commodity (Pena López 1994: 351–2).

Green points out that nineteenth-century natural retreats were advertised as being within easy reach of the city: Vetusta's cathedral clock can be heard from El Vivero (ii. 371), the Marqués de Vegallana's country retreat where Ana goes to convalesce on Benítez's instructions. Its name, The Nursery, shows that this is artificially cultivated nature. Everything there is designed for comfort; the maid Petra dresses up as an 'aldeana fingida' (ii. 398); Ana and Víctor and their guests play at being country-dwellers: 'se recorrían aquellas aldeas pintorescas, se oían aquellos cánticos [. . .] de la danza indígena, y se volvía al oscurecer, comiendo avellanas y cantando, entre labriegos y campesinas retozonas, confundidos señores y colonos' (ii. 432). Víctor has always believed that in the country one has to put on fancy dress (ii. 134). Green (1990: 73) notes that the vogue for country excursions turned nature into a backdrop for entertainment: Ana sees El Vivero as the 'escenario' for a play or novel, with their guests from Vetusta acting out the parts (ii. 391). Her cult of nature while staying there is a literary imitation, derived from her father's books of Greek mythology, from Rousseau, and from a picture in an illustrated magazine (ii. 384, 438-9). Pugh (1988: 140-1) observes that landscape gardening was closely related to theatre design: the designer of the English landscaped garden which Pugh analyses (Rousham, designed in 1750) worked as a theatre designer as well as having trained in Rome as a historical painter; as we have seen, the genre of historical painting was explicitly concerned with 'constructing the nation'. Pugh (1988: 9-13) also notes that the landscaped garden was a 'utopia' in the sense of a 'nowhere', since its conversion of the countryside into a site for leisure and pleasure —the English term 'country retreat' is apposite—permitted a controlled release from the real world that was excluded: 'What we permit ourselves "in the garden" is what we refuse to permit in real life.' As Pugh nicely observes: 'Tasting pleasure without succumbing to bliss is a trick that is institutionalized in the garden'; one thinks of Ana's tasting of a single cherry from the basket destined for Mesía. Thus, Pugh notes, the parks of country houses were 'game reserves' in every sense of the term: the same Víctor who feels obliged to wear fancy dress in the countryside is addicted to hunting (and to the theatre, one may add), not out of need but for his city-dweller's pleasure. Pugh (1988: 62) notes that the enclosure of land—taking place in Britain from the late seventeenth century through to the mid-nineteenth century—turned 'wild life' into 'game'; the loss of communal land rights with the mid-nineteenth-century disentailments in Spain, converting all land into private property, similarly turned woodland and moorland areas into 'cotos de caza' or 'game reserves'. The episode in *La Regenta* where Víctor finds his wife's garter—passed to her maid Petra, who drops it in her dalliance with the Magistral—in the woodland hunting lodge on the Vegallanas' country estate illustrates the existence of an unsavoury reality beneath the 'fun and games'. El Vivero is designed precisely to edit out the reality of the Marqués de Vegallana's exploitation of his tenant farmers ('colonos') and of the region's flora and fauna which exist to turn his table into an image of excess consumption. Pugh notes that the landscaped garden's commodification of nature, which represses capitalist property and labour relations by aestheticizing them, is 'a paradigm of "improvement"' (1988: 13); that is, of the contemporaneous discourses of social control which were similarly concerned—particularly in the case of women—to disguise the repressive aspects of regulation by presenting it as a form of 'beautification'.

Just as El Vivero's 'armonía íntima del lujo y del campo' (ii. 390) is a fashionable imitation of nature constructed for urban consumers, so the seaside resort where Ana subsequently goes to clinch her return to health (and where Mesía joins her) is 'vestida muy a la moda' (ii. 433). What Ana most likes at El Vivero is the glass-covered balcony running round the house. Tanner (1979: 113–20, 154–61, 199–206) notes that scenes of adultery in the European realist novel tend to occur in country houses, parks, gardens, and on balconies, where culture and nature blur. Ana meets the Magistral in the park to her family mansion. At El Vivero, she talks to Mesía from her bedroom, leaning out of the window onto the glass-covered balcony, from which he peers intrusively into her marital privacy (ii. 432). Their adultery finally takes place on the glass-covered balcony to the Marqueses' house back in Vetusta, newly inaugurated that day as a conservatory built on the latest Parisian lines (ii. 440).[35] Tanner (and Labanyi 1986, following Tanner's suggestions) saw such images as figurations of an adultery feared as an intrusion of the natural into the social. I would now argue that *La Regenta*, like Galdós's novels, figures adultery as the blurring of city and country that occurs when the country has been 'adulterated' by being turned into a commodity for urban consumption. As Giddens

---

[35] Paul Johnson (1991: 456) notes that the new 19th-century art of interior decoration, as a kind of interior landscaping, was based on the ideal of blending house and garden, the conservatory being an essential ingredient.

notes (1985: 22), the construction of the nation-State, by turning the whole nation into one big market, necessarily supposes the elimination of the countryside. There is no going back to nature: both Ana and the Magistral lament the irreversible loss of their country childhood.

Nature figures in the novel largely in adulterated form: in Ripamilán's neoclassical pastoral poetry; in the Vegallanas' larder, an 'exposición permanente de lo más apetecible que cría la provincia' transformed by the cook's 'química culinaria' (i. 321); in Víctor's 'museo' of birds and insects; in the adulterated drink and food sold by Doña Paula to the miners who are turning natural resources into money (i. 556). Doña Paula is 'una aldeana que no veía en el campo más que la explotación de la tierra' (i. 536) for only city-dwellers idealize the country; in reality, they too are consuming it. Ana's imminent adultery with Mesía is explicitly symbolized by her consumption of a cherry from the basket being sent to him. Frígilis alters nature with his horticultural experiments, grafting trees and adapting eucalyptus to new environments,[36] but he does not consume it. He becomes the last of Ana's regulators when, after Víctor's death at Mesía's hands, she is subjected to a *cordon sanitaire* by the rest of Vetusta; that is, declared contagious and beyond cure (ii. 527). She subjects herself to 'las prescripciones de aquel médico frío, siempre fiel, siempre atento, siempre inteligente' (ii. 522). He is to Víctor's park what Mesía is to his house (ii. 132) in that he has usurped possession of it, but he is not an intruder because he has Víctor's and Ana's welfare at heart, as well as that of nature. His love of nature is 'más de marido que de amante, y más de madre que de otra cosa' because he nurtures it. His cult of nature is 'nada romántico' and entirely practical (ii. 136); it is not that of a city-dweller—Frígilis knows all Vetusta's gardens but shuns their owners—but that of an agriculturalist. Russett (1989: 87) has noted that Darwin's theory of natural selection, whereby those best suited to their environment survive, is a breeder's model for it supposes progressive improvement. Frígilis's 'manía de la aclimatación' transforms nature to improve it, like Darwin's doctrine of 'transformismo' which he espouses (ii. 151).

---

[36] Johnson (1991: 282) observes that the new 19th-century vogue for gardens was triggered by the importation of new species from Europe's colonial possessions.

But this poses the problem of who decides what constitutes improvement. Frígilis made a mistake in trying to graft Ana onto Víctor (just as he did with his experiment in interbreeding Spanish hens with English cockerels), for they do not grow into one organism as in the Krausist ideal of marriage. The reason is Víctor's egoism in not giving her the sexual satisfaction to which she has a 'natural right' as his wife: '[Ana] quería [. . .] algo más, aunque la avergonzaba vagamente el quererlo, [. . .] a que tenía derecho' (ii. 285). The novel makes it clear that it is his 'blockage' that creates hers. Appropriately Víctor dies because of a form of congestion: his full bladder, ruptured by Mesía's bullet (ii. 518–19). Frígilis's success with plants but failure with animals and humans suggests that the 'higher' forms of biological development do not obey the same natural laws as the 'lower'. Out hunting after discovering Ana's adultery, Víctor reflects on the 'egoism' of a nature for which morality and justice are irrelevant (ii. 483) and of Frígilis who, as a natural scientist, equates goodness with health (ii. 490, 492; i. 239). The egoism found everywhere in *La Regenta*—even in nature, according to Víctor—is in striking contradiction to the Krausist concept of natural law elucidated in Alas's legal writings, which supposes that ethics are inherent in the state of nature and that humans have a 'natural' ethical sense and sociability based on reciprocal concern and respect for the well-being and autonomy of others. Víctor respects Ana's autonomy but does not stop to think about her needs. Nor do Mesía and the Magistral, who additionally fail to respect her autonomy. Ironically, the only person who both nurtures her and respects her autonomy is the unsociable Frígilis, who believes only in biology. This implies that ethics may be inherent in nature after all; the novel notes that the only inhabitant of Vetusta with a genuine sense of religiosity is the atheist Guimarán, whose rejection of Darwin mirrors the Krausist critique of Darwin's market model of evolution, ruled by competition rather than by a Hegelian ethical principle. However, Frígilis makes Ana healthy but he cannot make her happy: under his care 'se le figuraba que lo mejor de su alma dormía' (ii. 527). Frígilis's natural science has no place for psychology; he is an enigmatic character because he has no psychology himself. It is because the concept of privacy is irrelevant to nature that the latter is indifferent to the invasion of Víctor's privacy by Mesía. The inner self is the construction of the social regulators who need to construct it as sick in order to justify their invasion of it. Alas's critique of the late nineteenth-century 'technologies of the self' (Foucault's term) which massively invaded privacy in the process of constructing it ends up dealing a death-blow to the Krausist belief that ethics are inherent in 'nature', which at the same time manifests itself in the novel as the value system against which the characters' egoism is to be measured and found wanting. Just as Alas's political writings of the 1880s reflect his increasing pessimism about society's ability to repair itself without State intervention (García San Miguel 1987: 301), so *La Regenta* suggests that, if ethics are not immanent in nature, then the forms of social regulation which the novel exposes may after all be necessary. Hence the novel's oscillation between sympathy for Ana as the object of social regulation, and its simultaneous depiction of her as unable to regulate herself and needing male direction. It must be said here that, while the novel gives a much more sympathetic depiction of its medical regulator than of its clerical regulator, medical regulation is not proposed as an answer for Ana's restoration to health leads her to adultery. Put crudely, the novel shows that religion makes you ill but medicine makes you immoral. But both the religious and medical regulators create in their subjects a sense of self, albeit a highly problematic one. Both are thus in the end necessary to—while simultaneously undermining—a liberal system based on the concept of the individual.

With the exception of the female philanthropists, criticized for their entry into the public sphere but minor characters, all the social regulators in *La Regenta* are men. But there is another category of invaders of privacy: female servants, whose ambiguous status as part but not part of the household puts them in an analogous position to that of the adulteress, simultaneously inside and outside marriage. Like adulteresses, all the insidious female servants in the novel—Doña Camila, Doña Paula, Petra, Teresina—indulge in illicit sex; what is worse, they do so for material gain, confirming the equation of female sexuality with egoism: the accumulation of resources at the expense of male bodily and financial expenditure. Doña Camila tries to seduce Ana's father and fleeces him financially. Doña Paula gets pregnant so as to blackmail the priest who has tried to seduce her, also fleecing him financially. Petra, in addition to using her mill-owner cousin as a kind of sexual insurance policy, accepts sexual favours from Mesía, and sexual and financial favours from the Magistral, in return for betraying Ana. Teresina is happy to cater for the Magistral's sexual and other needs in exchange for a future advantageous position. What is presented as worrying about these women is their desire for social advancement: Petra is especially reprehensible for preferring sexual to material payment from Mesía so as to put herself on the same level as Ana and the other bourgeois women he has seduced. If the Magistral's climb from cowherd to Church dignitary is presented as the realization of a 'natural', if ruthless, male ambition, the female servants' ambitions are presented as 'unnatural'.

The much reprinted hygienist Monlau (1865: 162–3) stated that women were biologically defined by their capacity for love, and men by ambition. *La Regenta* bears out this view, except that the female servants are refusing to behave like 'proper women'. Doña Camila and Doña Paula look physically masculine, as does the philanthropist Doña Petronila who similarly usurps the masculine role through her public activities. Conversely, the novel is worried by men who possess 'unnatural' feminine features and qualities: the homosexual acolyte Celedonio (i. 110–1; ii. 537); the 'adamado' priest Don Custodio (i. 119); Visitación's soprano-voiced husband, left at home with the children (ii. 100–1); Víctor in his insistence on doing his own housework; indeed, virtually the whole male population of Vetusta in its obsession with imitation (a female characteristic) and fashion.[37] The Magistral is an especially interesting case: his mixture of strong masculine facial features and thorax with feminine manicured hands and fashionable shoes illustrates the fact that his masculine ambition is realized through his priestly adoption of 'feminine' skirts. But even as a youth he was marked by an athletic masculinity and a feminine sensitivity. As Russett notes (1989: 55), the contemporary notion that women were at a lower stage of evolutionary development than men supposed that men went through a feminine stage before attaining masculinity. Although Alas refutes this notion in his later essay 'Psicología del sexo', the Magistral's recollection of his adolescent 'feminine'

---

[37] In his 1891 review of Galdós's *Ángel Guerra*, Alas stated: 'siempre será verdad que el afeminamiento es un peligro. Se cuenta que los romanos de la decadencia se vestían de mujer' (cited by Jagoe in Charnon-Deutsch and Labanyi 1995: 177).

sensitivity supports it. The Magistral is imprisoned not only by his 'feminine' skirts but also by a masculinity which requires him to strive for public eminence at the cost of private emotional fulfilment. He recognizes that his redeeming quality is his childlike devotion to his mother, from whom he has never emancipated himself (Sinclair 1998: 179–95; and in Charnon-Deutsch and Labanyi 1995). The novel also suggests that his tragedy is his inability to realize the feminine capacity for love which his relationship with Ana brings to the surface. *La Regenta* depicts a sexual instability that in most cases is an 'unnatural' perversion of biologically prescribed gender roles; Valis (1981: 31–2) has rightly related this to contemporary worries about decadence. But the Magistral's case suggests another subtext pleading for men to be freed from the straitjacket of masculinity.[38] The novel does, after all, provide an explicit critique of two key traditional Spanish models of masculinity: those of Don Juan and the Calderonian honour hero.

This sexual instability complicates the novel's depiction of 'the natural'. The emphasis on feminized men and masculinized women implies that modernity is constituted by loss of the natural. But the gender ambivalence of the Magistral suggests that 'the natural' is inherently unstable. It is not just a matter of correcting decadence by returning to a lost 'natural' sexual difference. Indeed, the male character who most approximates to the natural world in his behaviour—Frígilis—is a nurturing 'mother': another reason why his presence produces a disturbance in the novel. It has to be said that the novel's questioning of the notion of inherent masculinity is not matched by a similar sensitivity to women's predicament: the female characters who show masculine drives are unanimously condemned. In empathizing with his heroine, Alas is able to express his own feminine as well as masculine sensibility.[39] But Ana is not given a similar latitude. Her plight as an adulteress is not that of a

---

[38] Sinclair (1993: 244) perceptively notes that several 19th-century novels of adultery could be read as a critique of the new bourgeois model of sexual difference that required men to suppress 'feminine emotion'. Sinclair singles out as a notable example Karenin's extraordinary devotion to his unfaithful wife's baby by another man in Tolstoy's *Anna Karenina*.

[39] In his review of Galdós's 1891 novel *Ángel Guerra*, Alas, while lamenting the current 'feminization' of art, nevertheless recognized: 'No hay por qué renegar de lo mucho que tiene el arte de femenino. No está mal sentirse en el alma un *poco hembra*' (cited by Jagoe in Charnon-Deutsch and Labanyi 1995: 177).

wife unable to realize herself outside the private sphere of the family, but that of a wife unable to realize herself within the family as a woman. If men contain the feminine within themselves as an earlier stage of evolution, women are simply feminine.

Or are they? It could be argued that, if the feminine is an earlier stage of evolution, women's acquisition of masculine qualities is a sign of historical maturity. As we have seen, to avoid this conclusion Alas argued in 'La psicología del sexo' that both masculinity and femininity were derived from an earlier bisexuality, and that masculine women were thus a historical backsliding. Either way, women contain latent masculine tendencies. In *La Regenta* we do not find young girls displaying masculine tendencies which later are outgrown, as in Freud (Ana's country childhood did not make her a tomboy); the females who show masculine tendencies are adult women, most notably Obdulia in her desire to be a man when ogling Ana's naked feet. Despite Alas's arguments in 'La psicología del sexo', *La Regenta* presents masculine women as an 'unnatural' departure from an original femininity. This contradiction echoes degeneracy theory's hesitations as to whether loss of sexual difference is a regression or the result of excess civilization. Such hesitations reflect an increasing uncertainty as to what constitutes 'the natural'; it is no doubt precisely this uncertainty that explains degeneration theory's obsessive attempt to classify human behaviour as either 'natural' or 'unnatural'.

La Regenta opens and closes with the 'perverted' homosexual Celedonio because it depicts a society where nothing is 'natural'. The final description of Celedonio kissing Ana in a 'perversión de la perversión' (ii. 537) poses a riddle: is the perversion of a perversion doubly perverse, or does the second perversion cancel the first out? The impossibility of deciding whether heterosexuality in a homosexual is perverse or natural matches the novel's suggestion that the self is plural and unstable. Despite its condemnation of characters who depart from gender norms, it portrays a high degree of gender instability. Its depiction of the ways in which the self is constructed from the outside—through the various discourses of social regulation (including gossip) and through the characters' self-representations—does not set up an opposition between a genuine inner self and inauthentic impositions, but creates a conflict between a proliferation of personae all of which have to be accepted as constituent elements of the self.⁴⁰ The self is inseparable from representation. Corbin notes that the emergence of the bourgeois concept of the individual self in the course of the late eighteenth and nineteenth centuries was accompanied by an increasing identification of the subject (especially the female subject) with the body, creating the notion that appetites stemmed from the self rather than being responses to external stimuli (Perrot 1990: 479). This makes it possible for the first time to ask the question: 'What does a woman want?' But if the female body is itself constructed via the various male discourses of social control, there can be no answer to the question. Ana is condemned to be a void, not because she has not realized her full physiological femininity through maternity, but because the construction of her as a desiring subject is itself the product of competing social discourses, which she vainly tries to internalize. The novel's cyclical structure, taking her back to her point of departure and leaving her emerging from unconsciousness, is appropriate. As the product of a plurality of representations, the self must always be fissured and fragmentary; that is, sick.⁴¹ It is significant that Ana should feel her genuine self to be her 'histerismo', a disease which creates an inner instability because it is characterized by mimicry. The fact that imitation is endemic to all of Vetusta's inhabitants, male and female, raises the issue of whether modern society is by definition hysterical.

The inclusion in the novel of Zorrilla's *Don Juan Tenorio* not only makes Ana's life the imitation of what is already a representation, but also shows that the main function of the theatre is to allow the audience—Vetusta—to represent itself.⁴² The leading actor Perales imitates the Madrid actor Calvo and prescribes models for his leading actress to mimic, but being married to him

---

⁴⁰ Durand's discussion of multiple point of view in the novel (1964) could usefully be reread in the light of this observation.

⁴¹ In a suggestive passage of his essay 'Concepto de la persona social', Giner de los Ríos notes that the self is knowable only as an abstraction, since it is never apprehended as a totality but only 'en sus estados temporales, internos o externos, materiales y dinámicos, siempre en perdurable mudanza' (1969: 205). It would be interesting to explore Ana's sense of inner fragmentation, and the breakdown of linear time in part II of the novel, in this light.

⁴² Mandrell (1990: 13–15) relates the novel's use of *Don Juan Tenorio* to Girard's notion of 'mimetic desire', which I have related to Tarde's theory of capitalist modernity as imitation in my discussion of *La desheredada* in Chapter 3 above.

she is playing the love scenes for real (i. 365, ii. 47): performance and reality merge on stage as in the audience. The lines that Ana experiences as expressions of genuine emotion are seen by Mesía as fit only 'para hacer parodias', for they have been sullied by 'la necedad prosaica, pasándolos mil y mil veces por sus labios viscosos como vientre de sapo' (ii. 49, 51–2). This image of the toad recurs at the end of the novel because Ana's attempt to live out her inner emotions has made her into a stereotyped representation: the literary cliché of the fallen woman.[43] The image of the toad's slimy belly is itself both natural image and literary cliché. In figuring Celedonio's kiss—a homosexual's mimicry of a supposedly natural heterosexuality—its viscosity represents the impossibility of making distinctions between what is natural and what is imitation.

Like *Fortunata y Jacinta*, *La Regenta* shows a constant awareness that its depiction of female adultery is re-enacting previous literary models. The multiple examples of intertextual imitation in the novel have been listed elsewhere.[44] The most extreme case is Bedoya, who not only publishes plagiarized scientific articles and military biographies but steals the original sources so as to make them physically his. What is important here is that, like Flaubert's Bouvard and Pécuchet, he cannot tell the difference between what is his own work and what is copied: 'ya se le antojaba obra suya todo aquello' (i. 260–1). Alas's main debt to Flaubert is his exploration of the impossibility of originality. I would suggest that, in both writers, this demonstrates not just the impossibility of articulating experience in words without reducing it to clichés, but that modernity, as provincial society shows especially well, is constituted by the imitation of hegemonic models. The most disturbing feature of the imitations in *La Regenta* is that they are often unconscious, with the result that the genuine and the inauthentic become inseparable. Even when the representation is conscious, it becomes a part of the self which cannot be dropped at will. Víctor, in his hurry to embrace his sick wife, unthinkingly

---

[43] Sieburth (1990) argues interestingly that the novel's tendency to fall into melodrama undermines its narrator's repudiation of the genre.

[44] Freeland (1993) relates the novel's stress on imitation to Spencer's fear of regression into indifferentation. The characters' imitations of literature are discussed by Mandrell (1992 and in Valis 1990: 1–28), Sieburth (1990), and Brent (1951) in particular.

throws his cloak on the floor like Manrique in Act I of *El trovador* (ii. 113); even when devastated by her adultery, 'se entregaba a los arranques mímicos de su dolor' (ii. 503). The ingenuous Bishop is accused by the Magistral of imitating his counterpart in *Les Misérables* (i. 442), and the more he gets carried away by emotion in his sermons, the more the public regards him as a 'cómico' (i. 449). The Magistral feels his public persona as a priest is a 'comedia' that makes him a 'monedero falso' (i. 470, ii. 316), but he is here trying to dissociate himself from a self-representation which has to be acknowledged as part of himself. Conversely, his confession to Ana of the 'real' private self underlying his public façade constitutes a 'novel' (ii. 225). Ana similarly preserves her 'inner self' by composing novels in her head (i. 190, 192). She is convinced that the 'logomaquias' of her inner voice are based on genuine feeling: 'no hablaba así en sus adentros sino en vista de lo que experimentaba' (ii. 523). But to convey her inner emotions adequately to the Magistral, she needs the 'rhetoric' of written language (ii. 191–2). The impossibility of distinguishing between what is real and what is representation is experienced by Víctor when he finds himself living out a Calderonian honour drama at the same moment that he discovers their falsity, and by Mesía when he finds himself emotionally involved despite his conscious acting out of the Don Juan role. Conversely, the natural is shown to be a cultural representation when Ana has an ecstatic sensation of fusion with nature at Midnight Mass as a result of the organ playing popular melodies both traditional and fashionable (ii. 273–5). Even in the wilds, when Víctor goes hunting after discovering Ana's adultery, the moon is like 'una luna de teatro hecha con un poco de aceite sobre un papel' (ii. 483). Pugh notes that the most insidious feature of the landscaped garden, as a paradigm of the bourgeois ethos of 'improvement', is that it does not so much suppress nature as simulate it. Thus '[t]he garden is a repression of nature that masquerades as a mimesis of what it represses'. Representation, in other words, 'is confused for the real thing' (Pugh 1988: 12, 127). I would go further to argue that representation has in effect become the real thing.

Adulteration is thus unavoidable for what we have is not a confusion of the 'real' with the 'false'; much more disturbingly, representation constitutes the real. Words in the novel are shown to have a reality too devastating for the characters to bear. The narrator reminds Ana that the temptation she never admits to in her confessions is called 'adulterio' (ii. 19). The Magistral similarly does his best to avoid recognizing that what he is feeling for Ana is called love, insisting on referring to it as 'aquella pasión innominada' and 'su deliquio sin nombre' (ii. 196–7, 226, 240, 244, 257). It is his realization of the name given to deceived husbands that brings home to Víctor the enormity of his tragedy (ii. 475, 478, 504). The Magistral realizes that his most effective 'sword' is 'la lengua' (ii. 499) for words can kill: Frígilis tells Víctor that he could kill Ana 'con una palabra' (ii. 506); the Magistral's exhortations, although they get the wrong victim, send Víctor to his death. The importance of gossip in the novel shows that words, true or false, constitute reality. As Foja says with reference to the Magistral's renewed public credit thanks to Guimarán's conversion: '¡El papel Provisor sube!' (ii. 349). For, as with stocks and shares, the value of words is determined not by the inherent value of what they represent but by the credibility they enjoy with the public: Ana's adultery and Víctor's cuckoldry become inescapable realities once the words have entered the public domain.

Ana, in the empty cathedral, experiences the sensation of 'la fatiga de los reyes, la fatiga de los monstruos de ferias, la fatiga de cómicos, políticos, y cuantos seres tienen por destino darse en público espectáculo' (ii. 332), both because religion, as an organ of social control, is one of the forms of representation that constitute modern society and indeed the modern individual; and because the increasing spiral of representations is wearing thin with repetition. In his journalism, Alas repeatedly described national politics as representation in the sense of a theatrical performance, likening the opening of parliament to a première (García San Miguel 1987: 275; Lissorgues 1980–1: i. 41–5). He likewise argued that national life was a 'vida ficticia' (Lissorgues 1980–1: i. 150) since 'con el procedimiento civil el derecho se vá en papel y pluma' and 'toda la soberanía se reduce á una papeleta en que el ciudadano escribe el nombre de un representante'. He saw this reduction of public life to representation as endemic of modernity, contrasting with the more tangible exercise of democracy in ancient Rome:

Si hoy el derecho parece al vulgo algo que está en el papel sellado, para el plebeyo de Roma el derecho era algo con que se hacia [*sic*] el pan, [. . .] el derecho no estaba en los libros ni en las tablas del edicto tan sólo; andaba por las calles, al aire libre, se movía, se le veia [*sic*] ir y venir de la consulta al foro, estaba en el mercado y en los comicios. (1881: pp. lxii, lxx–lxxi)

Rome, in other words, had a public sphere that functioned as a critical forum. *La Regenta* shows how the parliamentary system of representation, rather than encouraging a public sphere of private critical debate, has converted local life into imitation and sameness. For Giner, representation was the key to citizenship since the individual should act not in 'his' own interests but as representative of the group, whether at national, municipal, or family level, engaging in a dialogue with representatives of other groups in a reciprocal system based on respect for political and cultural difference. Giner makes it clear that the husband represents the family in public life, but nevertheless insists that, since the family is an indissoluble whole, each family member should act as representative of the others (Giner de los Ríos 1969: 208,1875: 264). As an adulteress, Ana is acting in the interests of her own body (no matter how 'natural' her need for sexual fulfilment) rather than in the interests of the family 'body'. She is thus contributing to the breakdown of the system of representation constituting national life that more obviously results from the putting of private before public advancement of Mesía and his fellow local politicians. Her adultery simultaneously illustrates the invasion of the private sphere by the public, and the neglect of the public good for private benefit, both of which are figured by Mesía's role as *cacique*. An 1884 newspaper article, commenting on that year's fraudulent elections, asked: '¿De quién es la culpa?, todos: del gobierno que prostituye al cuerpo electoral y del cuerpo electoral que se deja prostitutir. ¿Dónde está el remedio?, abajo, en el pueblo, en el revivir de la opinión' (Varela Ortega 1977: 438). *La Regenta* suggests that the violation of Ana's body is as much Mesía's fault as her own, but it also implies that the answer lies in the moralization of women.

In depicting a society constituted by representation, Alas is not arguing for its abandonment but for genuine representation: acting in the interests of the whole rather than egoism. There is no going back to nature in the modern world, not only because the countryside has become a consumerist spectacle, but because the inner self is constituted by the proliferation of representations imposed on the individual, and particularly on women, by the late nineteenth-century social regulators who invented privacy in order to violate it (or, one could equally say, violated privacy in order to invent it). It is not surprising that so many of the great psychological novels of the late nineteenth century should be novels of female adultery since the new concern with social control, particularly of women, in this period made the creation of the inner self dependent on the violation of privacy. Neither is it surprising that these novels should be urban novels. As shown by Frígilis's lack of self, the return to nature means the abandonment of psychology. In the rural novels that we shall now examine, the journey from city to country requires the surrender of inner self. This, for some writers, is the attraction.

PART III

The Rural Novel:
Husbandry or Keeping it in the Family

7
Making *Caciquismo* Respectable: Valera's *Pepita Jiménez* (1874)

IN his edition of the novel (Valera 1989: 24–7), Romero demonstrates that *Pepita Jiménez* was written not, as commonly stated, from 1872 to 1874 in the Cordoban villages of Doña Mencía and Cabra where the Valera family owned wine- and oil-producing estates, but in Madrid in 1874, the year of the novel's publication in serialized and book form.[1] In January 1874, one month before Valera announced that he had started on the novel, the Spanish Federal Republic was dissolved by a military coup and replaced by a conservative centralist Republic under General Serrano, a long-standing family friend who had sponsored Valera's political career. In December, another military coup restored the Bourbon monarchy under Alfonso XII. The precise dating and location of the novel's composition are important because they destroy the myth that the novel reflects Valera's retreat from national politics, under the Republic, to the 'haven' of his native Andalusia; in other words, that it is an apolitical rural idyll.[2] In fact, Valera's stay in Doña Mencía and Cabra, to sort out the inheritance of the family estates on his mother's death, was in the summer of 1872, before King Amadeo's resignation and the declaration of the First Spanish Republic in 1873 which threw him out of political office (he was closely associated with Amadeo, having been

---

[1] It was serialized in the *Revista de España* in four instalments from March to May 1874.

[2] Of the many critics who argue for the novel's apoliticism, the best is Resina (1995), who reads it as an attempt to suppress awareness of contemporary political worries. My argument coincides in many respects with his, except that I see the novel's suppression of class conflict, not as a rejection of politics, but as part of an overall nation-formation project that is in itself political. Muñoz Rojas (1956: 19, 21) rightly stresses that Valera's representation in his novels of landowners and bailiffs who are involved in politics charts a specifically modern phenomenon, which is shown to coexist with relics of the pre-modern such as popular *fiestas*.

a member of the deputation that had accompanied him to Spain). The novel is written from the standpoint of the capital by an absentee landowner of the kind deplored in the novel's conclusion (1989: 390): Valera's visits to Doña Mencía and Cabra to administer his estates were never more than occasional and ceased after 1883.[3]

Despite Valera's sporadic protestations that he would like to retire from politics and spend the rest of his days on his Cordoban estates, his journalism and correspondence show him to be a political animal through and through.[4] His father was appointed Provincial Governor of Córdoba in 1833, the year in which the nation was divided into provinces on the French centralized model, with provincial governors as the agents of central control.[5] Valera's early career was dominated by the desire to become a parliamentary deputy, to which end he versed himself in the study of political economics, a subject he entertained hopes of teaching at university (Bravo Villasante 1974, 52, 63, 78). Galera Sánchez (1983: 226) notes that his interest in political economy was lifelong; his refutation of the economic demands of the First International during the 1871 parliamentary debate on its banning shows him to be familiar with current economic theories. Apart from his many diplomatic posts (attaché in Naples 1847–9 and Lisbon 1850–1; ambassadorial secretary in Rio de Janeiro 1851–3, Dresden 1854–5, and St Petersburg 1856–7; ambassador in Frankfurt 1865–6, Lisbon 1881–4, Washington 1884–6, Brussels 1886–8, and

---

[3] The last letter sent from Doña Mencía or Cabra in his lifelong regular correspondence with Menéndez y Pelayo is dated 1883 (Valera and Menéndez Pelayo 1946: 190). Bravo Villasante (1974: 298) states that in 1897 he had been absent from his estates for nearly twenty years. In Valera's essay 'El regionalismo literario' (1900), he reiterated his concern at 'el empeño que todos solemos tener de vivir en la capital y de abandonar los campos'; his use of the first-person plural is telling (1942: ii. 1043).

[4] See Romero (1992); Valera (1929, 1966, 1968); Valera and Menéndez Pelayo (1946). In 1860, on starting a political column in the *Revista de Ambos Mundos*, he stated that he was particularly concerned to make his mark as a political journalist. In 1863, three years after accepting the post of chief editor of the conservative liberal Albareda's paper *El Contemporáneo*, he declared, 'desde entoncs me metí de veras en la vida política' (Bravo Villasante 1974: 140, 142).

[5] Further information on the political activities of Valera's father, two uncles, and stepbrother is given in Galera Sánchez's excellent *Juan Valera, político* (1983). She notes (28) that Valera's father was defeated in the 1836 elections by the real-life prototype for Luis in *Pepita Jiménez*, who married Valera's father's sister (the prototype for Pepita) on her widowhood.

Vienna 1893-5), he held various positions in the Secretariat of State 1855-8, was a member of parliament 1858-63, Director General of Agriculture, Trade and Industry 1864, Under-Secretary of State in General Serrano's revolutionary government of October 1868, member of parliament again in 1869 and in 1871, Director General of Public Instruction and Senator for Córdoba in 1872, Private Secretary to the Minister of State in the first Restoration government of 1875, Senator for Málaga in 1876 and for the University of Salamanca in 1877, appointed Senator for life in 1881, and Consejero de Estado 1889-90 (Galera Sánchez 1989: 34; Bravo Villasante 1974; Jiménez Fraud 1973: 85-107, 163; Romero 1992: 28). This list does not include the times he unsuccessfully sought election to parliament. Jiménez Fraud (1973: 21) links Valera with the 'generation of 1868' whose prime concern was 'la urgente creación de una nueva conciencia nacional'. His government positions, particularly those in the Ministry of State, associate him firmly with the extension of central State control.

The fact that the novel was written in 1874 sets it in the context of the contemporaneous reconstruction of the central State after the federalist experiment which had ended in peasant revolt and attempted cantonalist secession in Valera's native Andalusia and the Levante. In his prologue to the 1888 American edition of *Pepita Jiménez*, Valera stated that he wrote it:

cuando todo en España estaba movido y fuera de su asiento por revolución radical, que arrancó de cuajo el trono secular y la unidad religiosa. Yo la escribí, cuando todo en fusión, como metales derretidos, podía entrar en el molde y amalgamarse fácilmente. Yo la escribí cuando más brava ardía la lucha entre los antiguos y los nuevos ideales. [. . .] Si yo hubiese procurado dialéctica y reflexivamente conciliar opiniones y creencias, el desagrado hubiera sido general; pero como el espíritu conciliador y sincrético se manifestó de modo instintivo, en un cuento alegre, todos la aceptaron y aprobaron. (Valera 1927: 250)

In misleadingly implying that the novel was written at the time of the political disruptions of 1873, Valera makes it clear that it was conceived in response to the threat to national unity posed by political disaffection in the rural south. In an 1872 article in the *Revista de España*, before the declaration of the Federal Republic, Valera has talked of 'el federalismo andaluz' as a characteristic of the rural south (Dendle 1982: 79). Just as General Serrano's unitarian Republic of 1874 paved the way for the Restoration by reasserting central control—indeed, Pavía's coup of early 1874 had called on Serrano to form a 'national' government—so *Pepita Jiménez* sets out in advance the Restoration's agenda of creating a modern, integrated nation-State through the palliation of conflict. Even if the novel's 'espíritu conciliador y sincrético' was unconscious at the time of writing, in 1888 Valera pointed to such a reading. The Restoration's chief tool for incorporating the rural majority into the modern nation was *caciquismo*. Luis's father and rival for the hand of Pepita is, as he is quick to tell us, 'el cacique del lugar' (149). Luis notes that one of his reasons for deciding to become a priest is that he does not want to inherit the estate of the father who spawned him illegitimately (166–7). In abandoning his planned ecclesiastical career, Luis not only wins his father's bride-to-be but accepts his inheritance of his father's land and position. Marriage to Pepita has political consequences for Luis and for the community. In his classic study *Los amigos políticos: partidos, elecciones y caciquismo en la Restauración*, Varela Ortega insists that *caciquismo* was not a feudal relic but a specifically modern phenomenon: the 'reacción defensiva del campo en un esfuerzo de adecuar a su código de valores la ofensiva modernizante de la ciudad' (1977: 462). In other words, *caciquismo* was an attempt to deal with the problem of uneven development in a rapidly modernizing society. First and foremost, it made the abstract transactions required by the central State explicable and manageable for those unused to the high degree of abstraction required by modern society, by recasting them in terms of personal (client–boss) relationships. As was said at the time, the *cacique* was 'el único vínculo que ligaba el campo con la ciudad y el pueblo con el Estado'. *Caciquismo* was thus, to quote Varela Ortega: 'la traducción—y respuesta—rural de una administración y normativa ciudadanas'; it was seen by contemporaries as 'el ruralismo de Estado o el triunfo de la provincia'.[6] Its translation of abstract into personal relationships also produced what

[6] Bahamonde Magro and Martínez (1994: 440) note that the liberal revolution was an urban phenomenon which needed *caciquismo* to impose itself on an overwhelmingly rural country (the 1869 census put the percentage of the working population in agriculture at 63%, compared to 13% in industry and 24% in the service sector).

Varela Ortega calls a 'privatization of politics'. In contemporary words, echoing the Krausist critique of egoism or particularism, *caciquismo* was the subordination of the State apparatus to 'los intereses egoístas de parcialidades o de individuos determinados' (Varela Ortega 1977: 355–6). As Varela Ortega stresses, the *cacique*'s influence depended on his ability to manipulate the State apparatus in order to grant personal favours; *caciques* were not necessarily those with land or money but those— usually local government officials—who understood how the State apparatus worked. On the other hand, the *cacique* served the State by ensuring that central government authority was enforced (the favour system guaranteed obedience by reinforcing indebtedness), particularly by ensuring that government-backed candidates were elected. The *cacique*'s essential function, both in granting favours and in enforcing authority, was as an agent of the central State. In Galdós's *Miau* (1887), the corrupt Víctor Cadalso—a member of 'la clase de aspirantes, con 5.000 reales, engendros recientes del caciquismo'—describes himself as a 'mediador entre el contribuyente y el Estado', and also as a defender of the State, in which he includes himself as a local government official (Pérez Galdós 1970: 582, 588). The origins of the term *cacique* in the enforcement of imperial authority make clear this centralizing role: *cacique* was the term for the Carib chiefs whose local power was tolerated by the Spanish conquerors in return for securing the native population's obedience (Varela Ortega 1977: 353–4). Luis talks of his father's *cacicazgo* as a 'mero y mixto imperio' (Valera 1989: 194): a phrase commonly used at the time in relation to the *cacique*'s domain. The term *cacique* came into use in Spain in the late eighteenth century, contemporaneous with the beginnings of the modern central State; it was only under the Restoration, whose 'fiebre codificadora' attempted to extend State control to every area of national life, that the term acquired prominence as *caciquismo* came to be seen as the root of the nation's problems.

Varela Ortega (1977: 417) notes that such complaints came from the cities which suffered *caciquismo* via election rigging, since the results in the urban constituencies were always drowned by those in the much larger number of rural constituencies where *caciquismo* was rife. However, in the countryside it was perceived to have a useful function in providing a direct connection with an otherwise remote central administration in Madrid.[7] As Varela Ortega also observes (1977: 417), *caciquismo*'s most negative effect was not, as contemporary critics alleged, that it prevented the exercise of representative government, for the *caciques* did represent their local clients' interests (their power depended on it), and the countryside's electoral dominance genuinely reflected the reality of a still overwhelmingly rural country. The problem was that, in making politics a matter of personal favours rather than of public issues, *caciquismo* depoliticized the rural electorate, preventing the development of a healthy, critical public sphere. In the second half of the nineteenth century, there were frequent complaints about the sway over national politics of Andalusia, where *caciquismo* was notoriously strong, particularly in Valera's native Córdoba where *Pepita Jiménez* is set. Despite the fact that Cánovas and his electoral henchman Romero Robledo were from Málaga and Córdoba respectively, the high proportion of politicians originating from Andalusia was not directly caused by *caciquismo* for, as Varela Ortega notes (1977: 358), members of parliament were rarely themselves *caciques* and almost always outsiders to the area; hence their dependence on a *cacique* with the local influence they lacked. Varela Ortega also stresses that *caciquismo* should not be seen as a right-wing phenonemon for it was as much a part of Liberal as of Conservative politics (1977: 390). Varela Ortega notes that the elections of 1871 and 1873, free from government interference, produced unworkable results; the rigging of elections through *caciquismo* thus came to be seen as necessary to ensure viable government (1977: 403–4). Valera, a Cordoban liberal writing in 1874, after these two problem elections and before the Restoration's abuse of *caciquismo* became a major concern, uses the term *cacique* in a positive sense, though with an awareness that it has negative connotations in the city. Luis, returning to his native village after his city education, is impressed by the seriousness of 'La dignidad de cacique, que yo creía cosa de broma' (148–9).

Valera's personal familiarity with the workings of *caciquismo*, and his vested interest in showing it in a positive light, are shown by his recently published correspondence with his brother concerning their 1858 and 1865 electoral campaigns in Málaga

---

[7] Carr (1966: 368–9) also comments that *caciquismo* served a useful purpose.

province (Romero 1992).[8] What is extraordinary to the modern reader is the matter-of-fact manner in which Valera refers to the procuring of electoral influence through the following variegated activities: letters to assorted 'amigos políticos' and influential relatives; the canvassing of ministers, under-secretaries, the Provincial Governor, the Regente of the regional Audiencia, and other assorted 'grandes electores'; the fixing of appointments of local judges and mayors; and the procurement of jobs for constituents' relatives (taken for granted as a politician's first duty). In accordance with Varela Ortega's observation that public policies were not an issue since voters supported whichever candidate granted their personal requests (1977: 242, 359), so Valera is willing to get electoral backing from political enemies (including the Carlist leader Nocedal), and to switch political allegiance to and from the governing party. In the whole of this electoral correspondance, policies are not once mentioned. Valera candidly lists the sums of money he owes his brother for buying support during the 1858 elections, when he won—after violent electoral irregularities (Galera Sánchez 1983: 36)—against the government candidate backed by Cánovas and his electoral henchman Romero Robledo. Throughout he refers to his election campaigns as a 'negocio' and, like Galdós's *cesantes,* talks of the 'turrón' (government salary) expected by himself and his constituents. His victory in the 1863 elections was annulled following a parliamentary investigation, headed by Romero Robledo and Cánovas, into fraudulent manipulation of the ballot boxes by one of the *caciques* supporting him. The other *cacique* supporting Valera was a liberal lawyer, confirming that *caciques* tended to be those who understood the legal ins-and-outs of an increasingly abstract centralized system. Although fearing (and showing) himself to be 'tan bellaco como los otros', Valera had the intelligence to see that 'Todas estas cosas que suceden en España tendrían remedio si verdaderamente hubiese una opinión pública independiente, enérgica y autorizada' (Romero 1992: 44). Galera Sánchez (1983, 63) notes that, with the increase of suffrage to 24 per cent of the population in 1869, with the introduction of universal manhood suffrage, the need to form public opinion was perceived to be crucial. Nevertheless, she also notes (1983:

---

[8] See also Galera Sánchez (1983).

64–5) that, on all his electoral campaigns, Valera never visited the district but just wrote letters to his 'amigos políticos'.

Valera was born into a well-connected, landowning, aristocratic but debt-ridden family: the title Marqués de Paniega, granted in 1765, was inherited by his elder stepbrother; his sister Sofía was a close friend of Eugenia de Montijo, into whose Parisian entourage she married through a brilliant society wedding to the elderly Marshal Pélissier (Duc de Malakof), who had recently won the Battle of Sebastopol (Azaña 1971: 21). Valera's electoral correspondence shows that he resented his political dependence on men whom he regarded as his social and intellectual inferiors. At the same time, the Valera family's title was a relatively recent creation, not tied to landowner-ship. As landowners, the Valera family belonged to the new class—predominantly bourgeois but, in Córdoba in particular, including many aristocrats—who rose to prominence with the mid-nineteenth-century disentailment laws that put the old *señoríos* on the market. Although aristocrats, the Valera family's relationship to their rural estates—devoted, like those of Luis's father, to agricultural production—was that of a new entre-preneurial bourgeoisie.[9] García de Cortázar and González Vesga (1994: 469, 475), who insist that 'la desamortización extendió por el agro la cultura capitalista' since even the traditional oligarchy now became agricultural producers, note that after 1860 viticulture became the spearhead of agricultural modern-ization, followed by olive-oil production; the estate which Luis inherits from his father is devoted to both of these forms of agricultural production. In making Luis's wealthy landowning father a respected local *cacique* who has obtained and managed his property 'con ingenio y trabajo' (377), Valera is not only vindicating the political institution on which the Restoration would depend, but is putting political influence and wealth in the hands of a class (effectively his own, despite Don Pedro's lack of a title) that already in the 1870s was losing both these

---

[9] Rueda (1986: 43) notes that Córdoba was one of the provinces where dis-entailed land was largely bought up by existing aristocratic landowners, increasing *latifundismo*; his information is based specifically on the municipality of Cabra where the Valera family held estates. Rueda (1986: 163)—like Shubert (1990: 1–6)—stresses that the fact that much disentailed land passed into aristocratic hands does not mean that Spain did not enjoy a bourgeois revolution, for the system of landowner-ship had changed from one based on privilege to one governed by the market.

things to the new officials and professionals created by State centralization.[10] In so doing, he is also tacitly replying to the political disturbances in Montilla, 16 kilometres away from his estates in Cabra and Doña Mencía, in the previous year 1873, during which peasants burnt down the Land Registry (Bahamonde Magro and Toro Mérida 1978: 89). In 1869 Valera had been parliamentary deputy for Montilla, Doña Mencía being in the Montilla constituency (Galera Sánchez 1989: 34, 1983: 64). Historians coincide in seeing the February 1873 events in Montilla as the key example of peasant revolt against private property. *Pepita Jiménez* anticipates the Restoration's declared aim, in response to the threat of social revolution unleashed by the Paris Commune and the Spanish Federal Republic, of making political influence and the ownership of property coincide.[11] The privatization of politics effected by *caciquismo* is paralleled by the novel's use of marriage to represent Luis's acquisition of political influence and land.[12] The novel also vindicates a system of landownership based on inheritance, as if attempting to reconcile the old aristocratic concept of inherited land with the new bourgeois order whereby landownership is governed by market forces: Luis 'deserves' to inherit his father's land because he helps him increase its productivity.

According to Varela Ortega (1977: 402), direct government interference in elections through the nomination of government-sponsored candidates, whose lack of contact with the local constituency made *caciquismo* necessary, began in 1850 with what were called the 'Cortes de familia'. He also notes (1977: 357) that non-government candidates were called 'candidatos naturales', as in the phrase 'hijo natural' (bastard). The notion that

[10] Muñoz Rojas (1956: 17–19, 22) notes that Don Pedro is an example of 'la nueva burguesía labradora', both because of his 'modern' involvement in national politics and also because he has bought his land and is concerned to maximize its output. He rightly stresses the novel's depiction of a society undergoing transformation in which wealth is changing hands as a result of new, complex political structures.

[11] It should be pointed out that, true to his lifelong liberal defence of freedom of expression and worship, Valera supported freedom of association for the First International during the 1871 parliamentary debate considering its banning in the wake of the Paris Commune, while attacking it for its destruction of the family and of private property, and for its atheism. Valera abstained in the final vote (Galera Sánchez 1983: 142–62, 220–33).

[12] Galera Sánchez (1983: 101–2, 105) notes that Valera's aunt, Dolores Valera y Viana (the prototype for Pepita), coordinated her son's electoral campaign in Cabra.

election rigging is an incestuous attempt to keep things 'in the family' is present in nineteenth-century political terminology. Luis makes the passage from illegitimate 'hijo natural' to heir of his father's mantle as *cacique*, by founding a family that will keep his father's status intact. But in passing the role of *cacique* from Don Pedro to Luis, Valera, while keeping political power tied to the inheritance of (productive) land, is also recognizing the need for a new variety of *cacique* linked to the modern city: Luis's return to his father's village home after his city education fulfils both requirements. Varela Ortega (1977: 358) observes that *caciquismo* was based on personal friendship between unequal partners, as in the social relations created by *compadrazgo* with which it frequently overlapped: in marrying a social inferior, whose wealth is acquired and not inherited (this requires Pepita to be a widow), Luis cements the superior position of the city in its role as 'protector' of the countryside.[13]

In making Luis a city-educated trainee priest, rather than a lawyer or other professional, Valera (apart from creating a dramatic impediment to his marriage) is arguing for a new brand of *cacique* with a moralizing mission. The family which Luis founds with Pepita is explicitly seen by his father, in a shockingly racist passage, as a domestic version of the missionary activities he had planned to undertake overseas (379).[14] This notion of marriage as the basis for collective moral improvement —'fundando en el lugar que le vio nacer un hogar doméstico, lleno de religión que fuese a la vez asilo de menesterosos, centro de cultura y de amistosa convivencia, y limpio espejo donde pudieran mirarse las familias' (362)—is, I suggest, the novel's chief link with Krausism, rather than the alleged pantheism so stressed by critics.[15] Valera was himself responsible, in his

---

[13] Azaña (1971: 215–16) notes that, as a widow, Pepita can be allowed personal independence.

[14] In an 1869 parliamentary speech, Valera had declared that the countries of Europe were 'la raza privilegiada del mundo, [. . .] llamados a dominar la tierra y llevar la civilización por todas partes' (Valera 1929: l. 256).

[15] For Valera's statements on Krausism, see Cate-Arries (1986), who points out the novel's debt to the Krausist idea of marriage based on the dignification of woman and the merging of husband and wife in a single body and soul; I would stress the importance of the body here. Galera Sánchez (1983: 224–5) notes that in the 1871 parliamentary debate on the First International, Valera attacked civil marriage (instituted in 1870), passionately defending the family against free love. The notion of Valera's alleged Krausist mysticism is perpetuated by Montesinos (1957) and López Morillas (1956).

prologue to the US edition, for starting this red herring, arguing that the novel derived from his reading of the Spanish mystics when preparing an 1873 article defending the Krausists against allegations of religious heterodoxy: allegations to which Valera, as a well-known religious sceptic and champion of intellectual freedom, knew himself to be vulnerable.[16] In opting for the Church, Luis represents the institution that was the State's major rival for nationwide social control; López Garrido (1982: 17) argues that in the mid-nineteenth century the Church was the only Spanish institution which functioned effectively as a national body. Luis's final abandonment of the priesthood for marriage allows him to put his civilizing mission into effect in a secular context, as did those Krausist educators who left the Church.[17]

Luis's realization that moralization of the rural masses at home is more urgent than missionary work in the Far East is a patriotic recognition of the importance of nation formation.

---

[16] See Jiménez Fraud (1973: 165–9), who wrongly identifies Valera's defence of the Krausists' supposed pantheism as his 1862 article defending the Krausist professors at Madrid University for their championship of freedom of expression. Romero (Valera 1989: 89) identifies it as his philosophical dialogue 'El racionalismo armónico' published in the *Revista de España* in 1873, but finds no Krausist influence on *Pepita Jiménez*. In 1877, Valera taught a course on contemporary foreign literature at the Institución Libre de Enseñanza (Jiménez Fraud 1973: 120). His relation to Krausism is discussed by Azaña (1971: 236–7), Pérez Gutiérrez (1975), Gil Cremades (1975: 127–246), and Cate-Arries mentioned above (1986: 221–36). During the debate on the 1869 Constitution, Valera had argued for the wording of the clause on religious freedom to be strengthened, changing its tentative reference to 'foreigners and Spaniards, should there be any' to the phrasing: 'Todo español tiene el derecho de sostener y difundir las opiniones religiosas que más conforme halle con la verdad; de dar culto a Dios con los ritos y ceremonias de la religión en que crea, y de reunirse y asociarse con otros hombres para realizar tan altos fines' (Bravo Villasante 1974: 173). In this debate, Valera had argued for retaining Catholicism as the State religion since this gave the State control over Church appointments; while seeing Christianity as a mark of European civilization, he noted that the Spanish Church had been especially intolerant, particularly in its expulsion of the Jews (Valera 1929: l. 256–77). Valera described his temperament as 'piadosa y optimista, aunque no sea cristiana' (Jiménez Fraud 1973: 105). In his 1888 prologue to the American edition of *Pepita Jiménez*, Valera defended the Spanish mystics because of their practical concern to be useful to society (Valera 1927: 252).

[17] In his political speeches, Valera argued that primary education should be under State rather than local control to ensure that it was enforced; Luis's bringing of education from the city to the country represents this top-down model (Valera 1929: l. 28–30). His abandonment of the Church for a secular model of 'improvement' also illustrates Valera's lifelong defence of freedom of expression, not only attacking the Church for its intolerance of dissidence but also rejecting the idea of a single official model of State education (Valera 1929: l. 333–4).

Alas was not the only contemporary Spaniard to note that the nineteenth-century extension of central State power reduced the provinces to the status of colonies.[18] The parallel drawn in the novel between overseas missionary activities and the provinces, if paternalistic, at least involves recognition of the fact that all is not well in rural Spain. As Luis comments, 'me doy a pensar que tal vez sería más difícil empresa el moralizar y envagelizar un poco a estas gentes, y más lógica y meritoria que el irse a la India, a la Persia o a la China' (168).[19] He insists that it is ridiculous to blame the nation's problems on the pernicious influence of modern ideas when in the countryside no one has ever read a book, and suggests that the clergy is at fault in failing to carry out its missionary role at home (169). Here Valera shows himself to be squarely in favour of modernization. Although the novel makes no reference to the chronic material deprivations of the rural south,[20] it does not depict the countryside as a repository of innocence: the locals have no respect for religion and their jokes are bawdy and uncouth (168), Pepita's housekeeper Antoñona is separated from her drunken husband (386), and Don Pedro is a profligate, unbelieving Don Juan (201).[21] Morality is equated with the modernizing influence of the city, incarnated in Luis who, as future *cacique* combining education with the ownership of land, will bring improvement while consolidating existing social structures. The novel's idealization of country life consists not in the defence of tradition but in the construction of a model for the future. Unlike Galdós's and Alas's novels, which focus on the breakdown of marriage as a way of exploring the problems created by modernity, *Pepita Jiménez* follows the romance format concluding in marriage, figuring a modernization process desired

---

[18] For example, the mid-century Liberal politician O'Donnell described the Civil Guard, created in 1844 to enforce central authority and break the power of the local councils, as 'una ocupación verdaderamente militar de todo el territorio' (López Garrido 1982: 163–4).

[19] Carr (1966: 286) notes that in the mid-century, Padre Claret—who in 1857 became Queen Isabel II's confessor—had started a domestic evangelizing movement undertaking highly successful 'missionary' tours of the nation.

[20] Resina (1995: 180) rightly notes that, in depicting the local peasants only on festive occasions, the novel creates the impression of a superabundance of food.

[21] In a letter from his country estates written in 1883, Valera commented that the locals' songs and performances of ballads were 'de una verdura subidísima, por lo cual no se cantan hasta que los niños se acuestan y duermen' (Bravo Villasante 1974: 224).

but not yet achieved. For Valera, writing in 1874, modernity is a fictional happy end.

And yet there is a sense in which the novel offers a critique of modernity. The femininity of the city-educated Luis implies that modern civilization is decadent. Charnon-Deutsch (1985*b*) has noted that, in the course of the novel, the originally feminine Luis is masculinized while the originally 'Amazonian' Pepita is feminized: a process culminating in Luis's display of horse-riding skills, in which he brandishes the whip previously held by Pepita. Luis's feminine sensibility is relayed via his own first-person narrative; the implication is that his 'sickly' femininity (184) consists precisely in his possession of an inner self. He is feminized not by modern city life (of which he has little experience as a seminarist) but by education: as Ong (1982) has shown, the extension of reading in the nineteenth century was one of the ways in which a new sense of private self was constructed. This link between reading and the construction of the inner self is shown by the literary references with which Luis litters his autobiographical narrative—autobiography being the literary genre most instrumental in creating a new subjectivity. The countryside is 'masculine' because its inhabitants do not read. Luis equates masculinity with a lack of interiority when he describes his father as 'tan varonil y poco sentimental' (201). As in Ana Ozores's case, Luis's private self is constructed through the practice of confession: his autobiographical private letters to his uncle, comprising the first part of the novel, are literal confessions. It is thus inevitable that his inner self should be sick, for the institution of the confessional is designed to construct, in order then to be able to relieve, sick souls. If the countryside helped Ana construct a private self through her private letters and diary, Luis is forced by his encounter with nature to abandon the inner self he had acquired through education. The tension between the construction of the inner self and the urge to abandon it is dramatized through Luis's use of the private letter format to describe his discovery of nature. For his loss of inner self takes the form of acceptance of the body. His repeated references to the Greek ideal of serene physical beauty when describing Pepita and nature are in keeping with Krausism's Hellenistic stress on the need to respect, and enjoy, the body and the countryside. Valera was well versed in Greek literature and in the German neoclassical literature from which Krause derived his Hellenism.[22] Critics, including Valera in his above-mentioned 1873 article, who have tried to reconcile Krausism with Catholicism by arguing that its Hellenic cult of bodily health and nature was a form of Neoplatonic mysticism have gravely misrepresented it.[23] If *La Regenta* depicts as insoluble the conflict between the Hellenic ideal and an inner self constructed as sick, *Pepita Jiménez* presents Luis's sacrifice of his inner self as the passage from a sick femininity to a healthy virility, expressed through his possession of Pepita's body. This Hellenic virility contrasts with the Catholic concept of masculinity implicit in the Dean's praise of Luis's 'virile' struggle to subdue his carnal appetites (213). Just as critics have misrepresented Krausism in the attempt to defend it, so too those who have tried to reconcile Valera's novel with Catholic orthodoxy have done him a disservice. Luis describes his attraction to Pepita as a death of the self: 'El amor y la muerte son hermanos. [. . .] Ansío confundirme en una de sus miradas; diluir y evaporar toda mi esencia en el rayo de luz que sale de sus ojos; quedarme muerto mirándola' (251). When he first kisses her, he feels a 'desmayo fecundo' (263). This is not a mystical death-unto-the-self and rebirth-in-God, but the surrender of a sick, feminized inner self to a healthy, virile acceptance of the body.

At this point, Luis's first-person narrative ceases and an unknown omniscient narrator takes over the narration of his final surrender to Pepita: the narrative point of view, in which Luis passes from subject to object, echoes the loss of inner self that is his acquisition of masculine sexuality. Luis's immersion in nature prior to surrendering to Pepita prepares him for this loss of inner self; as he enters the open countryside, the narration of his inner thoughts ceases: 'Don Luis se sintió dominado, seducido, vencido por aquella voluptuosa naturaleza, y dudó de sí' (319). His experience of 'la tierra toda entregada al amor' and of the erotic village festivities on the Noche de San Juan (320–1) inserts his private experience of love into the collective: 'Las calles estaban llenas de gente. Todo el pueblo estaba en las calles' (322). When he enters Pepita's bedroom, the narrative cuts out for reasons of decorum but also because

---

[22] See Bravo-Villasante (1974: 17, 73, 197, 208). In his prologue to his 1879 translation of Longus' *Daphnis and Chloe*, he felt obliged to apologize for the 'crudity' of the love scenes (which he nevertheless chose to translate).

[23] Díaz (1973: 55–6) makes this point.

the loss of the self can be represented only by 'la obscuridad' (345). Their definitive commitment to each other is sealed with a wordless kiss as body language takes over from the self that has been surrendered: 'La contestación de don Luis no cabía ya en el estrecho y mezquino tejido del lenguaje humano. Don Luis rompió el hilo del discurso de Pepita sellando los labios de ella con los suyos' (348). Their subsequent marital life, in which the self is dissolved in the family and the community, is narrated at even greater distance through the extracts from Luis's father's letters which form the epilogue. This return to the epistolary format paradoxically confirms the loss of the self for the letters of Don Pedro, being 'tan varonil y poco sentimental', talk only about others. The genre most associated with subjectivity is converted into a form of reportage.

The fact that Luis's acquisition of virility consists in the surrender of the inner self he has constructed in the city complicates things, for this posits a model of masculinity based on surrender. Like *La Regenta*, *Pepita Jiménez* constitutes a Krausist critique of egoism, arguing for a model of selfhood based on service to others, through marriage and the community. Valera has traditionally been praised as a psychological novelist,[24] but his novel shows the need to abandon a sick inner self for altruism. This is a convenient form of altruism in which both hero and heroine are granted love, wealth, and status; but the point is that the family, ownership of land, and the position of *cacique* involve responsibility to the collective. The word 'egoísmo' is repeatedly used of both Luis and Pepita. Luis recognizes, after lengthy debate, that his desire to become a priest is a form of egoism because it entails living in an inner spiritual world. He sees in Pepita a parallel egoism in her rejection of all suitors to date: in cutting short her speech with his kiss, he forces her also to surrender her self. Having abandoned control of the narrative, Luis speaks relatively little after the renunciation of his 'egoism'. His surrender of inner self makes him a man of action, now able—as he was not before—to confront the Conde de Genahazar. In this confrontation he distinguishes his brand of masculinity—acting in the service of others, specifically Pepita—from that of the Conde de Genahazar and his

---

[24] See Azaña (1971: 52) and his prologue to the 1927 edition of *Pepita Jiménez* (Valera 1927); also Jiménez Fraud (1973: 141).

gambling associates, concerned only with personal gain: 'Pues lo mejor es que no tengo sólo macho el entendimiento, sino también la voluntad; y con todo, en el conjunto, disto bastante de ser un macho, como hay tantos por ahí' (365). Although Luis needs to surrender his feminine inner self, his newly learnt ethic of service is a practical application of his 'feminine' education as a trainee priest; in bringing civilization to the countryside, Luis is also feminizing it. Armstrong (1989) has shown how emphasis on the bourgeois subject's moral values and sensibility endowed it with qualities conventionally regarded as feminine; indeed, she goes so far as to claim that 'the modern individual was first and foremost a woman' (1989: 8). Valera's attitude to both civilization and femininity is ambivalent: Luis needs the countryside to masculinize himself, just as it needs to be feminized by him.

Pepita's relationship to civilization and femininity is similarly complex. She is 'naturally distinguished' (170)—we are told that she is untypical of Andalusian village women—and combines the feminine qualities of charitableness and domestic economy —'Tiene la casa limpísima y todo en un orden perfecto' (171) —with horse-riding skills and an expert knowledge of agricultural processes.[25] If Luis's masculinization involves his passage from subject to object, Pepita's progressive feminization gives her a new inner self. Her speech is not represented directly till near the end of the novel when she confesses her love, first to her confessor, then to Luis. Again the self is constituted via confession; but Pepita's confession does not construct her inner self as sick for it is unapologetically based on love, not for a subjective mental image of Luis, but for the objective reality of his body (343). Her inner self consists in an altruistic love that is a death of egoism: 'he muerto en mí y sólo vivo en usted y para usted' (341). Despite the conventionalism of this feminine altruism, her (and Valera's) refusal to see her attraction to a male body as a sign of inner sickness is startlingly subversive of

---

[25] In his contribution 'La cordobesa' to a book on Andalusian women, Valera defined the Cordoban village woman ('lugareña') as 'en extremo hacendosa' and 'toda vigilancia, aseo, cuidado y esmerada economía', noting however that things had changed with modernity and that some Cordoban women were extremely cosmopolitan (Valera 1953: iii. 1297–9). Interestingly he commented that, although there was such a thing as national identity, provincial identity did not really exist since provinces were artificial man-made creations.

Catholic norms. From this moment on, she becomes extraordinarily eloquent and love becomes the sole subject of her speech (no more discussion of viticulture). The implication is that it is 'natural' for a woman to have an inner self, for woman's role is love; the surrender of egoism in her case means serving the collective through love for a husband. This paradoxical acquisition of self through ego-loss consists, of course, in acceptance of her female role as body and object of beauty offered to Luis for his pleasure. But it must not be forgotten that this also allows Pepita to accept her own body and sexuality; she does, after all, seduce Luis and not vice versa. In an interesting 1902 essay 'Meditaciones utópicas sobre la educación humana', Valera (many years later) insisted that, although 'el alma de la mujer difiere esencialmente de la del hombre' and women should not therefore enter the public sphere, nevertheless women were equal and could work in 'suitable' professions so as to be economically independent; here he also pointed out that men too have a role in the home. In particular, Valera continues, women should have the same primary education as men, and after that should be educated to be good housekeepers and to look after their bodies. By this, Valera meant both education in hygiene and physical education; he criticizes the 'mal entendido pudor' that keeps women ignorant and ashamed of their bodies. Valera's insistence that women should care for the body God has given them directly echoes Sanz del Río's writings; interestingly, given Pardo Bazán's use of the same writer in *La madre naturaleza*, he supports his arguments with extensive quotations from Fray Luis de León (Valera 1958: iii. 1397–420). Valera, however, goes further than the Krausists in arguing that it is wrong to expect total purity in women and to ridicule chastity in men; girls should not be kept ignorant of sexuality and there should be more tolerance for their 'extravíos amorosos'. Women should not be idolized as madonnas and denigrated as whores: 'Procuremos, pues, el justo medio entre tanta adoración y tanto estrago' (Valera 1958: iii. 1416–17). It must be remembered that Pepita, quite exceptionally for a late nineteenth-century novel anywhere, is allowed to sleep with Luis before marriage with total impunity and the author's evident approval.

Pepita's 'natural distinction' suggests that she does not need civilizing by Luis, though his combination of 'natural distinction'

(280) with education marks him out as her superior. Luis describes Pepita as a Galatea—an example of serene Hellenic physical beauty explicitly opposed to the spiritualized Christian feminine ideal—but one that is already perfectly formed (260). In the previously mentioned 1902 essay, Valera reverses the Pygmalion and Galatea myth, arguing that women's 'civilizing mission' is so important because, without their positive influence, men would not realize their potential:

En suma: yo me inclino a veces a sospechar que sin el benéfico influjo de las mujeres y sin la inclinación *irresistible* que hacia ellas sentimos, los hombres valdrían muchísimo menos de lo que valen: serían descuidados en el vestir, sucios, descorteses, feroces y rudos, más crueles que benignos y más tímidos que valerosos. (Valera 1958: iii. 1411)

This, of course, assumes that women exist for the benefit of men but it also assumes that women form men, who in their 'natural' state are inferior. As he puts it, women are essential to 'el progreso y la cultura' (Valera 1958: iii. 1411). Luis and Pepita represent town and country respectively but this is not a simple opposition between civilization (male) and nature (female). Pepita's function is to reveal to Luis the civilizing role he can play in his native village by founding a model family and assuming his position as *cacique*: it is the community and not Pepita that he will sculpt into shape. As his father says:

La gente de Madrid suele decir que en los lugares somos gansos y soeces, pero se quedan por allá y nunca se toman el trabajo de venir a pulirnos; antes al contrario, no bien hay alguien en los lugares que sabe o vale, o cree saber y valer, no para hasta que se larga, si puede, y deja los campos y los pueblos de provincias abandonados.

Pepita y Luis siguen el opuesto parecer, y yo los aplaudo con toda el alma. Todo lo van mejorando y hermoseando para hacer de este retiro su edén. (390)[26]

This last sentence is revealing. It shows, first, that paradise has to be constructed: it is not natural but the product of modernization. Second, that both Pepita and Luis contribute to the civilizing process: she, through the private sphere of the family; he, through both private and public spheres (the family and

---

[26] Shubert (1990: 81) notes that absenteeism among Andalusian landowners increased dramatically in the mid-century with the lure of the newly modernizing city and peasant unrest.

his inheritance of the position of *cacique*). And third, that this civilizing process consists in moral and aesthetic improvement: there is no suggestion of changing social and economic structures. Valera's work has been connected with *costumbrismo*; his early literary and political mentor was Estébanez Calderón, author of the *Escenas andaluzas* (1847). As we have seen, Estébanez Calderón's literary stance was congruent with his role as national statesman since the *costumbrista* construction of the regional, despite its exaltation of traditional social forms threatened by modernization and centralization, was part of the process of incorporating the rural areas into the nation. When acknowledging his debt to Estébanez Calderón, Valera stressed that the latter's Andalusian sketches had taught him how to be a *castizo* Castilian writer (Jiménez Fraud 1973: 94–5; Valera 1882: i. 91). In his essays on regionalism written in the 1890s, Valera dissociated the regional novel from all forms of political and cultural separatism, praising the 'inocente y pacífico regionalismo' that is provincial literary activity since this, together with studies on 'regional literature', forges links between centre and periphery, strengthening political ties (Valera 1942: ii. 798–800, 899–902, 1030–7). Luis's appropriation of Pepita's body similarly figures the incorporation of the abandoned rural south into the modern nation. This is a marriage in which everyone—including Luis's father as his rival—is a willing participant, thus glossing over the tensions between local interests and those of a modernization process conceived from the standpoint of the city. Although it is a marriage of unequal partners, the love is mutual because each has something to offer the other.

Valera's countryside is not a wilderness but is highly cultivated: the novel stresses its economic productivity. The family estates flourish after Luis's marriage to Pepita—'Todo prospera en casa. Luis y yo tenemos unas candioteras que no las hay mejores en España, si prescindimos de Jerez. La cosecha de aceite ha sido este año soberbia' (388)—but the city-educated Luis has to learn the art of agriculture from his father. Indeed, Pepita is his mentor here too, teaching him the importance both of being a husband and of husbanding the land. Both Don Pedro and Pepita are depicted as administrators, going through the accounts with their bailiffs. Despite the discussion of modern agricultural methods, economic production is in this rural environment still based on the household unit. The fact that Pepita's sessions with her bailiff take place in her dressing room illustrates this lack of public/private division. The ideal of the household as productive unit is illustrated in the 'perfect match' of Antoñona's father-in-law's skill in manufacturing and mending agricultural implements with her own culinary arts (261). In marrying Pepita, Luis joins her estate to that of his father, keeping economic production as well as political influence in the family.

The novel's construction of the countryside as cultivated nature also fits with the Krausist insistence that there is no divide between the natural and the social because the drive to improve on nature is inherent in natural law. By setting Luis's and Pepita's marriage against the background of this cultivated nature, Valera creates a typically Krausist organicist concept of the family as the integration of individual and community, and of society and nature. It can also be argued, in keeping with the Barthesian notion of 'naturalization' as a ploy for presenting bourgeois structures as universal (Sontag 1982: 93–149), that, in so doing, both Valera and Krausism are passing off as 'natural' conceptions of the family and society which are the product of specific political structures.[27] In proposing the family as the basis of a perfected ideal community, Valera is suggesting that social structures are immutable: a matter of natural, blood relationships. In his correspondence, he calls parliamentary deputies 'padres de la patria' (Romero 1992: 183); Varela Ortega uses the phrase 'padre o padrastro de la provincia' for the *cacique* (1977: 355). *Pepita Jiménez* equates the role of *cacique* with that of the father; it is only by renouncing celibacy and becoming a father in turn that Luis can inherit his father's political role. Indeed, he improves on it by fathering offspring inside rather than outside marriage, ensuring that he is a 'proper' father rather than a 'padrastro'. His oedipal rivalry with his father, who monopolizes the local women as well as the land, makes the

---

[27] Tierno Galván (1977: 16–17) criticizes Valera for arguing that the artist's moral aim should be to 'no perturbar el orden natural de las cosas, sino a conservarle y a mejorarle', on the grounds that what he means by 'orden natural' is 'el orden burgués interpretado por un aristocratizante'. In an 1864 essay, Valera claimed that the social order could not be changed without changing the natural order, according to which 'Necesario es que dominen los pocos, en quienes se halla la inteligencia [. . .]. El reinado de la clase media no tendrá fin sino con la civilización del mundo' (1884: i. 24).

point that, in marrying, he is assuming the father's place. As in Freud's theory of the Primal Horde, defeat of the father leads not to the rejection of patriarchal authority but to its confirmation. The incestuous nature of Luis's love for Pepita is highlighted through comparison with Hippolytus' love for his stepmother Phaedra, and—less appropriately—Amnon's love for his sister Tamar (244, 248, 255); Luis describes his love for Pepita as 'como a hermana' (206). Luis's father, unlike Freud's father of the Primal Horde, colludes in the incest because, in so doing, he reclaims Luis as his successor, thus perpetuating his role. As Luis notes, somewhat undermining the novel's equation of patriarchy with service to the community, fatherhood is another form of egoism since the father loves in the son a continuation of himself (166). Don Pedro's voluntary acceptance of a backseat role as benign grandfather also conveniently defuses his previous disruptive role as sexual predator, allowing Luis to replace him as a new, improved patriarch whose morals are guaranteed by his religious training.[28]

What Luis finds most striking about village life is its lack of privacy, particularly in his father's house which, since he is the *cacique*, is open to all: 'teniendo la honra de ser hijo del *cacique*, es menester vivir en público' (209).[29] In privatizing the political, *caciquismo* conversely makes private relations a public affair. For this reason, too, Luis has to abandon the inner self constructed by his city education. The Casino is the only genuinely public space in the village that is not centred on the household; it does not function as a public sphere of critical debate because—like that in Vetusta—it is devoted to gambling and private gossip; we are told that it houses the national press (209) but we never see anyone reading it. The village authorities gather, under Don Pedro's aegis, in Pepita's house: 'La gente formal de la tertulia es la de siempre. Se compone, como si dijéramos, de los altos funcionarios; de mi padre, que es el *cacique*; del boticario, del médico, del escribano y del señor Vicario' (232). According to Rueda (1986: 167–9), the *escribano*—mentioned by Luis as one of those having access to his private bedroom (209)—had responsibility for local legal transactions, including the registration of property; every

---

[28] Cammarata (1976) argues that, in blessing Luis's oedipal rivalry, Don Pedro is sanctioning anti-patriarchal desires.

[29] Resina (1995) notes the ubiquity of public space in the novel.

municipality that could afford it contracted a doctor, teacher, and one or more *escribanos*, whose status was 'algo intermedio entre el funcionario público y el profesional privado'. The public/private divide is blurred not, as in Galdós's and Alas's novels, through an adulterous intrusion of the public into the private (perceived as negative) but through an incestuous incorporation of the public into the private (perceived as positive), for the local public authorities, meeting in Pepita's home and with free access to the bedroom, are subordinated to the 'hogar'. Like many others at the time, the village in *Pepita Jiménez* seems not to be able to afford a teacher; at least, there is no mention of one. Valera's omission of any reference to the lamentable state of rural education is surprising since his last public office before writing *Pepita Jiménez* was as Director of Public Instruction (1872); indeed, in an 1861 article he had insisted that what he understood by democracy was not 'el dominio del populacho ignorante y grosero, sino su desaparición, ó dígase su transformación en gente culta y urbana' (1884: iii. 217–18). Though it could also be argued that Valera's omission here is consonant with his novel's defence of *caciquismo*, given that the main aim of the latter was the enforced depolicization of the electorate. Pepita's exercise of charity—palliating the political problem of poverty through a private favour system that reinforces subordination—is the female equivalent of this paternalistic if benevolent brand of *caciquismo*. The boss–client structure of local relationships is stated explicitly: Luis is not used to people contradicting him 'porque durante su niñez le rodeaban criados, familiares y gente de la clientela de su padre' (301–2).[30] The position occupied by servants, relatives, and 'clients' is indistinguishable. Varela Ortega stresses that *caciquismo* functioned as a cross-class network, affording a degree of social cohesiveness based on inequality (1977: 356–8). It is appropriate that Luis's and Pepita's marriage should be cemented by her former wet-nurse Antoñona, demonstrating the closeness of these unequal family bonds. After their engagement, they get Antoñona reconciled to her drunken husband, setting them up in a tavern in the provincial capital as a 'satellite' family tied to theirs through the favour system (386–7).

---

[30] Muñoz Rojas (1956: 18) observes that the servants in the novel 'son todavía familia'.

What Luis brings to this economic and social structure based on the household is—as his father intimated when talking of the need for the capital to 'pulirnos'—external embellishment. For, in the overwhelmingly agricultural Spain of 1874, substance—economic production—is provided by the countryside. This reduction of modernization to 'polish' creates a degree of ambivalence about the value of the 'urbanity' brought by Luis from the city. After the birth of their son, the family goes on a European tour and brings back 'lindos muebles, muchos libros, algunos cuadros y no sé cuántas otras baratijas elegantes que han comprado por esos mundos, y principalmente en París, Roma, Florencia y Viena' (389). In Don Pedro's view, 'la elegancia y el buen gusto con que acabarán ahora de ordenar su casa servirán de mucho para que la cultura exterior cunda y se extienda' (390). This newfound civilization is 'exterior' because it will be imitated by the collective but also because it is imported and consists in external trappings. In his private letters, Valera stressed the uncouthness of the countryside. In an 1875 letter to his wife from Cabra, he wrote: 'Esto es un país pobre, ruin, infecto, desgraciado, donde reina la pillería y la mala fe más insigne. Yo me finjo otra Andalucía muy poética, cuando estoy lejos de aquí' (Valera 1989: 30). In another 1862 letter, complaining of 'las enojosas y prosaicas ocupaciones de hacer cuentas y de ir al campo a ver las labores', he insisted:

Ahora, más que nunca, estoy convencido de que los poetas bucólicos se han inspirado del recuerdo idealizado del campo y no de la presencia del campo mismo, y de que la poesía de las églogas [. . .] ha nacido del contraste, en el seno de populosas ciudades y en épocas de civilización refinada y de una vida en extremo artificial. [. . .] Los rústicos no comprenden ni sospechan siguiera la hermosura de la naturaleza. Sólo aprecian su utilidad. [. . .] Horacio lo entendió al poner el elogio de la vida rústica en boca de Alfio el usurero. (Valera 1989: 146–7)[31]

Luis brings to the village the aesthetic sense lacking in country-dwellers concerned only with use value. In the process he introduces the concept of exchange value: his 'baratijas elegantes'

---

[31] See also Valera's 1863 letter to his brother written in Doña Mencía (Romero 1992: 132–3), and his 1880 letter to Menéndez Pelayo, also written in Doña Mencía (Valera and Menéndez Pelayo 1946: 72), which iterate the same sentiments.

have no use value for his practical father, who admires them (as he is supposed to) not for what they are but for what they represent: civilization. The fact that the final description of Luis's and Pepita's aesthetic improvements to their house and grounds is put in the country-bred Don Pedro's mouth introduces a sceptical note. As Valera observed in the above letter, the bucolic is attractive to city-dwellers in times of 'una vida en extremo artificial'. In transforming the orchard into a garden with imported trees and a 'pequeña estufa, llena de plantas raras' (392), Luis and Pepita change it from a productive unit into an exotic simulation of nature constructed for the city-dweller's eyes, much like El Vivero in *La Regenta*.[32]

Pugh (1988) has analysed the political implications of the English landscaped garden as a depoliticizing aestheticization of the natural, that—in a repeat of the process of commodity fetishism—edits out the economic relations (labour, private property) behind capitalist modernization. In this sense, Luis's final construction of a landscaped garden encapsulates the novel's 'embellishment' of *caciquismo*. As Pugh comments, 'pastoral is really a recipe for canny husbandry' (1988: 26). As in Pugh's description of the garden at Rousham, Valera constructs a pastoral 'utopia'—the village has no name—where 'the curse of labour' (Pugh 1988: 18) is edited out. The novel's only mention of the local labourers is when they attend Luis's and Pepita's wedding, converting labour into an image of leisure, pleasure, and celebration. In similar fashion, the talk of agricultural production takes place at a picnic during an 'excursion' to the country. Pugh notes (1988: 136) that the landscaped garden converts the countryside into a place of retirement and leisure for the city-dweller, constructing rural life as a permanent holiday. The novel's aestheticization of *caciquismo* constructs Luis as a 'gentleman-farmer'. As Pugh notes (1988: 128), 'the garden, surplus to agricultural needs [. . .] demonstrates that there is land to spare'. In this sense, Luis's and Pepita's garden can be read as a symbol—and concealment—of the new agricultural relations based on capital accumulation and surplus value which is Luis's contribution to modernization.

[32] Muñoz Rojas (1956: 15–16) notes that Valera's concentration on rural village life rather than the countryside proper represents 'una cultura de gentes asentadas en grandes pueblos que viven del pueblo y no lo habitan', observing that Valera betrays his city attitude by calling the labourers 'rústicos'.

Pugh (1988: 62) notes that the old *hortus conclusus* walled nature out, whereas the new landscaped garden eclipses the boundary between culture and nature, giving the impression that there is no 'outside' or 'raw nature' left, in a delusion of total civilization. If, in 1884–5, *La Regenta*—via its description of El Vivero—presents this phenomenon as an adulteration of the natural, in *Pepita Jiménez*, written ten years earlier, it represents a utopian dream of civilization as the perfect marriage, erasing the troublesome 'outside' of contemporaneous rural rebellion.

Pugh's comments on the mock Greek temple and statue of Venus—a copy of the Medici Venus—at Rousham could almost have been written as a response to Luis's and Pepita's garden, whose crowning embellishments are a little Greek temple with 'muy cómodos muebles' and a marble copy of the Medici Venus. These artefacts, whose description ends the novel, are as kitsch as Bringas's hair picture: it is hard to think that Valera meant them to be taken seriously. Pugh (1988: 40) notes that Rousham is 'a paradigm of the site where the original has no status'. The mock temple, 'made old in a new style that purports to be an ancient style', is an attempt to 'marry' modernity and tradition. As Romero notes in his edition of *Pepita Jiménez* (94), their mock Greek temple and other imported knicknacks turn the house and garden into a kind of museum. Valera visited the Paris Exhibition of 1855 (Romero 1992: 23); whether consciously or not, *Pepita Jiménez* anticipates the critique of modernity as spectacle and imitation that we have discussed in Galdós's and Alas's novels of the 1880s. Valera's articles and letters, despite their repeated insistence that Spain's backwardness is due to its past isolation from modern European intellectual currents, bemoan the importation of foreign models (Valera 1882: i. 222, 1884: ii. 218, 1989: 27; Jiménez Fraud 1973: 122–8; Bravo Villasante 1974: 174). Pepita is praised, before her and Luis's final European shopping spree, for having the 'buen gusto, inaúdito, raro, casi inverosímil en un lugar de Andalucía' to decorate her dressing room with Spanish lithographs instead of the usual bad French prints (273–4). The novel's equation of modernity with the imitation of foreign models is by implication a critique of modernity as feminization. Valera demonstrated his adherence to the contemporary belief that imitation was a feminine quality in his 1886 letter to Menéndez Pelayo, qualifying his praise of Pardo Bazán's literary talents on the grounds that 'como toda mujer, tiene una naturaleza *receptiva*' (Valera and Menéndez Pelayo 1946: 297, original italics) and should therefore not be taken seriously (like Luis's cultural imports?). Despite Luis's masculinization as he learns to husband Pepita and the land, the novel ends with an imported, reproduction statue of Venus. As we have seen, evolutionary theory was used to argue that the female represented an earlier stage of evolution from the male; in *Pepita Jiménez*, the countryside (nature) is represented by a woman and the city (culture) by a man. But Luis and civilization are also feminine, and it is Pepita who conquers him. The final statue of Venus represents not only modernity as cultural imitation, but also the Hellenic ideal of enjoyment of the body (nature), incarnated in Pepita. However, Pugh's analysis of the reproduction Medici Venus at Rousham suggests a more negative reading. He sees such statues as another kind of commodity fetishism, masking power relations through the male gaze's conversion of possession into aesthetic pleasure. For Pugh, the Medici Venus' concealment of her *pudenda* with her hands embodies pastoral's concealment of 'the real relations of power, of men over women and over other men, of the human subject over nature' (1988: 116). While this analysis seems pertinent to *Pepita Jiménez*, it must not be forgotten that Pepita seduces Luis, even if she thereby constitutes herself as a 'prize' for his possession. However one reads the novel's concluding image of the status of Venus, the fact remains that it figures modernity as the triumph of the feminine.

The relationship between a countryside concerned with use value and a modernity based on exchange value is also raised by the novel's discussion of debt. Luis notes (159–60) that money is even more important in the country than in the city because it is the only indicator of status (he will introduce other related indicators with his 'baratijas elegantes'). This shows that money in the country already has exchange value as the source of personal credit: indeed, Pepita's rich, elderly uncle bought her as his bride. Again, we have a marriage keeping property in the family. Pepita's uncle made his fortune from moneylending: credit in the financial sense gives him social credit or 'symbolic capital'. As Varela Ortega notes (1977: 363), private usury was endemic in the rural areas owing to the lack of agricultural credit facilities; this gave moneylenders, many of whom functioned as *caciques*, considerable political clout. Elections were often held in winter, the season of maximum peasant indebtedness, to ensure electoral obedience (Kern 1974: 33). In noting that Horace puts the praise of country life in a usurer's mouth, Valera puts moneylending on the side of civilization. In marrying Pepita, Luis not only inherits his father's land (itself devoted to capitalist production) but also becomes the administrator of her moveable wealth acquired through business transactions.[33] Their marriage thus joins the old and modern financial orders based on unmoveable and moveable property respectively. However, the novel shows a certain unease about the credit system, not only in Luis's insistence that Pepita's uncle charged low interest rates, but in the fact that his first act after committing himself to Pepita is to get the Conde de Genahazar to repay his debt to her: that is, to replace his promissory note or 'papelucho' (351) with hard cash. To achieve this, Luis stakes 'todo su oro' against the Conde's entire moveable wealth (365, 367); the fact that Luis's money is in gold coin means that its nominal value is based on its intrinsic (metal) value. The gambling Conde de Genahazar represents the traditional landowning nobility, but also a corrupt modernity, showing Valera's awareness of the complex alignments of old and new in late nineteenth-century Spain: he is from the city, wears the latest fashions, and has twice been a parliamentary deputy (298–9). His failure to honour his debts is linked both to his decadent aristocratic status and to a fraudulent system of parliamentary representation. The Conde de Genahazar figures the unacceptable face of representative government, whose nominal value is not matched by intrinsic worth, by contrast with the *cacique* Don Pedro and his heir, backed by land and gold.[34] In an extraordinarily interesting

---

[33] Valera was well aware of the legal position of the husband in administering his wife's property, since he was estranged from his own young wife because of her complaints about his using her estate to pay off his debts. To give him credit, in 1872 he agreed to put the management of her property in her hands (Bravo Villasante 1974: 178–81). Throughout his life Valera borrowed money, mainly from the Bauer banking family, long-standing family friends (Bravo Villasante 1974: 223, 261). *El comendador Mendoza* (1876) was dedicated to Bauer's wife.

[34] One cannot help but observe that the Conde de Genahazar, as an elegantly dressed, city-dwelling, debt-ridden member of parliament, bears a closer biographical resemblance to Valera than either Don Pedro or Luis.

article of 1865, titled 'Del dinero en relación con las costumbres y a la inteligencia de los hombres' (DeCoster 1965: 571–88), Valera had argued, apparently without irony, that 'el ser rico significa y tiene que significar que vale más quien lo es, en lo moral y en lo intelectual, que el que es pobre' (581–2), continuing: 'El dinero se puede asimismo afirmar que da mérito intrínseco, como el no tenerlo, le quita' (585). The article concludes by insisting that we should not lament the present century's love of money for '¿Qué otra cosa ha de amar en la tierra, si no ama el dinero que las representa todas, las simboliza y las resume?' (586). Valera has here perfectly understood the abstract representative value of money in the modern market system, but nevertheless continues to equate such value with inherent moral value.

Luis represents a modernizing influence in moral and aesthetic terms, but in economic terms he stands in a halfway position between the old and the new: helping boost agricultural output but as part of a system of production based on the household unit; uniting his father's land with Pepita's moveable wealth but backed by gold rather than a 'papelucho'. When Luis's uncle compares Pepita to a 'fiel contraste' or municipal office of weights and measures that will test whether Luis is 'oro puro' or a base admixture (376), he is showing belief in gold as the ultimate measure of value but also expressing anxiety about possible adulteration. The Finance Minister Figuerola's reduction of the metal content of both gold and silver coin in October 1868 and March 1869 had triggered a polemic between supporters of the new 'nominalist' monetary system and defenders of the old 'criterio metalista' based on intrinsic worth. The Bank of Spain's and the public's reluctance to accept the new coins as equivalents of the old ones led to an 1871 decree allowing gold coins to be minted according to pre-1868 specifications, which produced an even bigger gap between sign and signified since these bore the head of a now dethroned Isabel II. This absurdity was halted in 1873—the year before *Pepita Jiménez* was written—when the minting of gold coin was temporarily suspended altogether owing to falling gold prices and a public run on gold, as political crisis led to lack of confidence in the value of paper money. As Sardá notes (1948: 155–62), this temporary suspension of gold minting (resumed in 1876) put Spain at odds with the international monetary system, based at the time on adherence to the bimetallic system (gold and silver) by the Latin Monetary Convention (France, Belgium, Switzerland, and Italy), plus Scandinavia's and the United States' adoption of the gold standard in 1872 and 1873 respectively. The discourse of land, gold, and debt in *Pepita Jiménez* parallels the current debate in Spain over nominal versus intrinsic value.

In this respect it is worth contrasting *Pepita Jiménez* with Valera's later novels *Doña Luz* and *Juanita la Larga*, whose plots are again constructed around *caciquismo* and money. *Doña Luz*, serialized in the *Revista Contemporánea* in 1878–9 just four years after *Pepita Jiménez* but three years into the Restoration, depicts *caciquismo* in far more negative terms and connects it directly with worries about an increasingly fiduciary monetary system. Like Luis, Luz is the illegitimate child of a landowner, a marquis in this case. Her mother, unlike that of Luis, is not a local woman but an adulterous countess from the capital. Luz's neglect is thus blamed on a combination of 'uncivilized' rural machismo and female adultery associated with the modern city. Luz grows up under the tutelage of her late father's bailiff Don Acisclo, who in 1860 decides to 'meterse en' national politics as *cacique* for the government's electoral candidate, challenging the power of the leading *cacique* Don Paco, 'el grande elector de este distrito' (Valera 1970: 130–1). It is made clear that there is no difference between the *caciques* of the two parties: indeed, Don Acisclo sets about imitating Don Paco, buying political influence with money and offers of government posts ('turrones'). It is also made clear that Don Acisclo's fortune has been acquired, through years of pilfering from the Marquis's estate, by means that are legal in name only. The government candidate Don Jaime, a Madrid resident who has never before visited the district, is sarcastically described as a 'diputado-modelo' because of the huge number of 'turrones' he gives away. He is supported by 'el Cincinato electoral' Don Juan Fresco precisely because he will not interfere in local affairs and will rid the district of the 'plague' of job-seekers who, once they have their government posts in the city, will never return to the village. The narrator makes it clear that, as a result, the country is left with no one to make the land productive. Chapter 12 'El triunfo' provides a veritable glossary of the terminology of election rigging, in which both *caciques* are clearly involved.

It is crucial that the successful electoral candidate's reliance on political fraud should be accompanied by his seduction of Luz in order to acquire, through marriage, the fortune he knows she is about to inherit from her mother in the form of government bonds held in Paris, London, and Frankfurt banks: fraudulent political representation is thus linked to the issue of fiduciary monetary representation. The *escribano* who informs Luz of the inheritance stresses that the 'valor nominal' of this paper fortune bears a purely arbitrary relationship to its 'valor en efectivo' (230). Don Acisclo dreams of converting this paper fortune into land, by using it to lend money at an exorbitant rate in the form of 'hipotecas', so that the mortgaged land will fall into his hands (237). The narrator's reluctance to condemn Don Acisclo outright is perhaps due to the fact that he regards value as lying not in a fiduciary monetary system but in land, whereas Jaime, as Luz caustically comments, was enamoured by a 'flecha de oro' in the form not of her substance but of what she represented; that is, her value in government bonds. Metal coin, with the reduction of its metal content, is also by implication part of this fiduciary system of monetary representation. Luz describes the future child of her union with Jaime as a coin, for he is indeed born of money, hoping that he will have the 'material impresión' not of Jaime—whom she sends back to the capital—but of the priest Enrique—a former missionary, like the seminarist Luis in *Pepita Jiménez* representing an alternative model of civilization based on inherent moral values—who loved her for what she was rather than what she represented (245). When the child is born, she names him Enrique for, like a coin, he can be given a nominal value that bears a purely arbitrary relationship to his material substance as Jaime's child. As in *Pepita Jiménez*, Valera here retains a nostalgia for a value system based on intrinsic value, but recognizes that modernity is irremediably governed by a fraudulent system of political representation and a fiduciary system of monetary representation, both of which are based on the gap between nominal and intrinsic value.

In *Juanita la Larga*, published some twenty years after *Pepita Jiménez* in 1895, a *cacique* again earns the female protagonist's love. But she now has neither land nor moveable property but only credit, in the form of her reputation and the promissory note she writes to restore the money stolen by her figurative brother Antoñuelo.[35] Fiduciary value has become accepted to the point that it can be represented as positive. The *cacique* has also changed. If in *Pepita Jiménez* he was the local landowner and in *Doña Luz* his bailiff, now he is no longer linked to the land. For although the landowner—who, like Don Pedro in *Pepita Jiménez*, acquired his land through initiative and not birthright—is still the official *cacique*, in practice his role is filled by the Secretario del Ayuntamiento, Don Paco, whose function as agent of the central State is made clear by his comparison to Bismarck and Cavour: the architects of German and Italian Unification. Don Paco resolves all lawsuits for the local lawyers, draws up all legal documents (wills, property and marriage contracts) for the local *escribano*, fixes the local taxes, and oversees the rubbish collection, conservation of public buildings, and food supply (Valera 1985: 72–4). The *cacique* is now the local government official who understands, and monopolizes, the workings of the State. And, as in *Pepita Jiménez*, the *cacique* is again depicted as a positive political influence. By the 1890s, Valera seems to have moved towards acceptance of more abstract forms of economic and political representation, except that *Juanita la Larga* ends with Juanita's delinquent figurative brother Antoñuelo making a fortune in Cuba, just as *Pepita Jiménez* ended with the information that Pepita's good-for-nothing brother has prospered in Cuba as an 'hombre de negocios'. Valera was concerned with the colonial administration of Cuba, first through his post in charge of American affairs in the Ministry of State in 1855 (Romero 1992: 25), and later as ambassador in Washington 1884–6, where he reported back to Madrid on US moves to intervene in the independence struggle (Bravo Villasante 1974: 226). *Pepita Jiménez* was written against the background of the first Cuban War of 1869–79; the issue was on the agenda again at the time of *Juanita la Larga*'s composition in 1895, Maura's proposal for Cuban autonomy having been rejected in 1893, provoking the outbreak of war in 1895 (Tuñón de Lara 1976: 208). The implied contrast in both novels between colonial Cuba and provincial Spain suggests that enlightened *caciquismo* at home has brought national unity

---

[35] For a brilliant Lacanian analysis of letters, bills, banknotes, and promissory notes in *Juanita la Larga*, as well as in Galdós's *La de Bringas*, see Smith (1989: 69–104). Smith notes that the value of money depends on circulation rather than inherent worth (81), relating this to Lacan's notion of lack, particularly in relation to women.

(the incorporation of the countryside into the modern nation), while in Cuba unscrupulous entrepreneurs have caused political disaffection. The chemist in *Juanita la Larga* gives a brilliantly clear exposition of the capitalist financial system: money is 'el objeto que vale por sí y representa además y mide con exactitud lo que valen los otros objetos, facilitando la circulación y los cambios, sobre todo si se le añade cierto descubrimiento más sutil aún, o sea, la virtud representativa de todo lo que vale por algo que por sí vale poco o nada y que se llama crédito' (294). Pepita's brother and Juanita's figurative brother personify this exchange economy whereby that which has minimal or zero intrinsic value can come to be worth a fortune.

Valera's hesitations in *Pepita Jiménez* between a value system based on inherent value (land and gold, albeit integrated into a bourgeois system of production) and a modernity characterized by representation (the consumerist aestheticization of nature that ends the novel) are paralleled by the same novel's ambivalent attitude to fictional representation. On the one hand, the shifts of narrative perspective—from Luis's first-person confessions to an unknown third-person narrator and finally to Don Pedro's reportage—mark the passage from subjective to objective narration. Ruano de la Haza's attempt to identify the narrator of the middle section (1984) seems to me a mistake. He is right to note that the fictional editor, while suggesting the Dean as possible author, leaves the issue open; but the point is surely that the narrator of this section (titled 'Paralipómenos' because it fills in the key 'facts') does not have a self. The fictional editor praises him for concealing 'su yo' like the classical historians, and correspondingly suppresses his marginal comments and glosses as irrelevant personal intrusions (355–7). But there is a typically Cervantine double game going on here, because the existence of the unknown narrator's marginal comments and glosses shows that the self persists on intruding.[36] The obtrusive classical references of both the editor and the unknown narrator of the 'Paralipómenos' section show them to be as much the product of a city education as their male protagonist who has to learn to abandon the inner self constructed by reading

---

[36] Valera wrote three essays on the *Quixote* in 1862, 1864, and 1905 (Jiménez Fraud 1973: 141–53). His use of a fictional editor simultaneously to reinforce and undermine narrative reliability is clearly indebted to Cervantes's novel.

(and writing). Indeed, these literary references are our main clue in trying to establish the unknown narrator's identity, for they constitute the only biographical information we have about him (they clearly constitute him as male, since only men were given a classical education). *Pepita Jiménez* is a literary text which argues for the abandonment of the self while also showing that reading and writing—that is, literature—are what constitute the self. Thus Luis wonders at the end of the novel if his present bucolic life is not more 'egoísta' than his former missionary dream (392) for, in his new role of art collector, he is more than ever relying on culture to provide him with both a private self and a social identity: his future political role as *cacique* consists in setting himself up as a model for the rest of the village to admire and imitate. His final importation of 'muchos libros' and other cultural artefacts purchased in Europe's major cities shows the impossibility, and ultimately undesirability, of abandoning the modern city for nature, for representation is what constructs both the individual and the community. Valera's bookish depiction of the countryside should, I suggest, be seen not as a failure to achieve realism but as making the point that representation is both inescapable and necessary.

Nevertheless, Valera is a difficult writer to place since he seems to be wanting to have it both ways; that is, to have representation and substance at the same time. His protagonist Luis abandons the traditional Christian Neoplatonic notion of nature as book or sign—'debo amarla como signo, como representación de una hermosura oculta y divina, que vale mil veces más' (183)—for an appreciation of nature as material reality: Pepita's body and the land, whose worth consists in their use value to Luis as husband and husbandman. In an attempt to evade moral criticism, Valera created the myth—perpetuated by critics—that he was an idealist and not a realist writer. It must be remembered that, at the time, the term 'idealism' was used in the philosophical sense of a belief in essences, as in the Platonic notion of mimesis, whereby the work of art is a secondhand imitation of a material world which itself is the imitation of a higher essential reality. In rejecting the Neoplatonic notion of nature as book or sign, Luis is rejecting idealism for philosophical realism: belief in the ultimate reality of the material world. But he is still clinging to a belief in stable, inherent value, albeit now located in matter: the body and land.

This rejection of the Neoplatonic view of reality as representation in some ways curiously parallels Luis's challenge to the credit system incarnated in the Conde de Genahazar, in the name of a monetary system based on gold. In converting the Conde de Genahazar's 'papelucho' into gold coin, Luis is trying to make sign (representation) and signified (substance) coincide. But, in incorporating the countryside into the exchange economy by improving agricultural production and importing foreign consumer goods, he shows that he cannot —and does not want to—escape the abstract system of representation that is the capitalist monetary system. And, as future *cacique*, his role as personal representative of the State will be to palliate the abstract nature of a newly centralized political system of representation, which the Conde de Genahazar's example additionally shows to be commonly fraudulent. The implication is that Luis may be permitted to enjoy the modern consumer luxuries that replace nature with simulacra, and can be trusted to counter the Conde de Genahazar's political unreliability, because he is backed by intrinsic value in the form of land and gold. The novel's marriage of city to country is an attempt to give substance to an urban modernity characterized by representation, and conversely to provide an uncouth rural Spain with the external trappings of civilization in the form of aesthetic embellishment. Its optimistic supposition that it is possible to 'marry' modernity (representation) to nature (substance)—contrasting with Galdós's and Alas's conviction that nature has everywhere been replaced with representation —reminds us that Valera is writing at a time when, despite the temporary suspension of the minting of gold coin, the principle of convertibility into gold has not yet been abandoned as it would be in 1883.

8
Patriarchy without the State: Pereda's *Peñas arriba* (1895)

WRITTEN in 1892–4 and published in January 1895, *Peñas arriba* provides a link between the realist novel and the regenerationist literature of the turn of the century, as has been noted: 1895 is the date of Unamuno's *En torno al casticismo*.[1] I hope to have shown in the chapters so far that concern with national decadence, attributed both to underdevelopment and to modernization, and the use of medical analogies, derived from the contemporary discipline of social medicine and encouraged by Krausist and Spencerian organicism, date back to fiction of the early and mid-1880s; while worries about the 'feminizing' effects of modern urban civilization are found as early as *Pepita Jiménez* (1874). The fiction of the so-called 1898 Generation is generally seen as marking a break with realism, both in its impressionistic techniques (Baroja, Azorín) and in its metafictional experimentalism (Unamuno). The 1890s were marked by spiralling inflation and devaluation of the peseta, dramatically opening up the gap between nominal and intrinsic value (I shall return to this at the end of this chapter). The 1890s were also the decade when protests about unrepresentative government reached their height: *caciquismo* was a prime concern of the regenerationist movement, culminating in Joaquín Costa's classic enquiry *Oligarquía y caciquismo* (1901). The 'break' with realism of the 1898 writers can be seen as an intensification of the concern with the problematic nature of representation that characterizes, and defines, the realist novel. Pereda's relationship to realism is still more complex than that of Valera for, while arguing for modernization (of a kind) through the maintenance of traditional rural structures, he (mostly) rejects

---

[1] Lucas Mallada's *Los males de la patria* had already been published in 1890; as we have seen, Costa's 'regenerationist' writings date back to 1880.

urban modernity and the central State. His repudiation of the modern system of economic and parliamentary representation, based on fluctuating, abstract relationships, leads him to propose an alternative system of representation based on stable, inherent value. But, as we shall see, the result occasionally borders on impressionism in its juxtaposition of elements linked not to each other but to a common source: nature and, beyond that, God. It is worth noting that the 1898 writers also attempt to turn nature—but not God—into a legitimizing source.[2]

Regenerationism was concerned with *caciquismo* as an erosion of local autonomy, preventing the exercise of genuine representative government. As previously noted, the problem was not so much that the *caciques* did not represent their constituents' interests, as that they prevented the creation of a public sphere of critical debate by privatizing the political. Although he rejects *caciquismo*, Pereda proposes a form of local autonomy based on the private; that is, on the family. Like Valera, but more radically, he proposes the family as a unit which fuses the private with the public, in a return to pre-capitalist structures prior to the public/private split. In its attempt to overcome what is seen as an unhealthy divorce between the public and the private, Pereda's novel frequently presents as 'natural' situations that in the urban novel, concerned with erosions of the public/private divide, would be disturbing. If Krausism wished to make the family the basis for developing a sense of citizenship while maintaining the family's autonomy as a private sphere, Pereda privatizes politics by making the family public: an abolition of privacy that asserts communal values while maintaining private property (transmitted through inheritance and not through the market), in this way keeping both land and power within the family.

In their defence of local autonomy, regenerationist thinkers undertook an investigation of common law, based on local *fueros* handed down by tradition, which enshrined communal rights while being based on the family unit: the village *concejos* were elected bodies whose members were elected from among the local *vecinos*, meaning male married heads of household who worked the land (Shubert 1990: 190). The fact that the

---

[2] See Labanyi (in Millington and Smith 1994: 127–49). I would now argue that the 1898 writers show an awareness of the impossibility of their attempt to ground 'truth' in nature.

rights upheld in the *fueros* were communal and unalienable had made them suspect to liberalism, bent on 'freeing' property up to individual ownership through the market. Their local nature, differing from region to region, was also seen as an obstacle to creating a unified nation. Hence the liberal politician and Krausist Segismundo Moret's 1863 study *La familia foral y la familia castellana*, which highlighted the centrality of the family in local customary law, had seen the pre-modern extended family as an obstacle to the free disposal of property, consequently recommending the modern patriarchal family as a means of economic modernization (Casey 1989: 111).[3] In the early stages of nineteenth-century liberalism, the imposition of central control was also seen as a way as breaking the power of the traditional rural oligarchy. The purpose of the local government reform of 1833, which divided Spain into forty-nine provinces controlled by centrally appointed provincial governors, had been to abolish the traditional communities and historical kingdoms. This same reform law made municipal councils elected bodies so as to provide a check on abuses resulting from the new centralization of power. In this way, both provincial and municipal tiers of government were able (in theory) to bypass the large landowners. As the electorate broadened to include a new class of professionals, traders, and artisans, mid-century Moderate governments sought to curb the power of the municipalities. The local government law of 1845 made mayors and deputy mayors in all municipalities with over 2,000 *vecinos* Crown appointments, with those in smaller municipalities appointed by the Civil Governor (himself a central State appointment); the number of elected councillors was also drastically cut to one half plus one, the rest being Crown appointments. Shubert notes that this system 'whereby the mayors were transmission belts for the authority of the central government' was retained during the Restoration by its municipal law of 1877 (Shubert 1990: 171). Key local affairs were put under central or provincial control (notably policing, with the 1844 creation of the Civil Guard); at the same time, 2,000 municipalities of under 100 *vecinos* were abolished (Bahamonde Magro and Martínez 1994: 263–5; López Garrido 1982: 38–9, 130–2). Provincial control of taxation, plus

---

[3] Co-authored with Luis Silvela, this study was awarded a prize by the Academia de Jurisprudencia (Elorza 1973: 156–7, 169).

the sale of common lands with the mid-century disentailments, deprived the municipalities of their major sources of income. As Álvarez Junco notes (in Graham and Labanyi 1995: 47, 83), their financial inability to carry out the lesser administrative tasks allocated to them placed them in a permanent situation of illegality, 'tolerated' by the central authorities in exchange for political favours. This provided a breeding-ground for *caciquismo*. It was in the rural oligarchy's interests to collude, through *caciquismo*, with the central State in its attempt, from the midcentury, to break the power of the *municipios*. Varela Ortega's observation that many *caciques* were local government officials, notably Secretarios del Ayuntamiento (the villains in Pereda's novels of the 1870s), does not contradict this picture for these, like mayors, were central appointments. In this climate, the restoration of local *fueros*, based on a system of grassroots representation through heads of family, could be seen as a democratic check on a central State which had exceeded its brief. Such an agenda had appeal for both progressives and rural traditionalists (but not for urban conservatives committed to free enterprise, except in those regions where local nationalism was strong); hence the notorious political ambiguity of regenerationism. Varela Ortega (1977: 246) reminds us that it was not till the early twentieth century that regenerationism started to advocate anti-democratic forms of government; in its beginnings in the 1880s and 1890s, it was a plea for increased local autonomy. It thus dovetailed with the contemporaneous growth of regionalist movements: in 1892, Sabino Arana published his *Bizkaya por su independencia*, and Prat de la Riba called the Manresa Assembly to discuss Catalan autonomy.[4] In the same year, just before Pereda started writing *Peñas arriba*, the Galician regionalist Alfredo Brañas sent him a signed copy of his book *La crisis económica en la época presente y la descentralización regional* (Madariaga de la Campa 1991: 389).[5] Also in 1892, Pereda was invited to the Jocs Florals in Barcelona, where his defence

---

[4] Madariaga de la Campa (1989) has documented the Cantabrian regionalist press from the 1860s; Santander and Asturias are referred to as 'las dos Asturias', rejecting the 1833 division of 'las Asturias' into two provinces.

[5] Like Pereda, Braña supported decentralization but not separatism, arguing for dual allegiance to 'las dos patrias' (Spain and Galicia). Also like Pereda, his brand of regionalism was strongly Catholic and traditionalist. In 1891 he founded the Asociación Regionalista Gallega (Bahamonde Magro and Martínez 1994: 504).

of traditional local rights was welcomed by the Catalan industrial bourgeoisie, despite their divergent attitudes to the capitalist system, since it could be co-opted in support of their attempt to harness Catalan nationalism to a conservative agenda (Bonet 1983). Regenerationism's defence of local autonomy was a product of the Krausist concern with creating a plural society based on active grassroots participation. Although it held appeal for rural traditionalists, its major participants were linked with Krausism. Despite the vast political differences between them, Alas was able to praise the regenerationist project set out in *Peñas arriba* in his March 1895 review:

Con ciertos distingos y reservas, el aspecto del regionalismo y de la *autarquía* municipal que Pereda ahora defiende no puede menos de parecer aceptable a cuantos consideren que en la excesiva concentración de las fuerzas vivas de un país hay graves peligros, muy parecidos a los de la apoplejía. (González Herrán 1983: 429–30)

This point of contact between Krausism and rural traditionalism helps explain Galdós's surprising friendship with Pereda. Giner de los Ríos, along with Unamuno, contributed to the two-volume *Derecho consuetudinario y economía popular de España* (1885 and 1902); the first volume consisted in Costa's *Materiales para el estudio del derecho municipal consuetudinario en España*. Costa started writing on such matters in 1879 when he published the replies to his questionnaire on customary law in Alto Aragón (Costa 1984: 15). Costa's links with Krausism were close, having been taught by Giner and Azcárate (Díaz 1973: 184), and himself contributing some teaching to the Institución Libre de Enseñanza (editing its journal 1880–3) as well as contributing to Azcárate's courses in comparative law at Madrid University in 1874–5 (Pérez de la Dehesa in Costa 1973: 8; Maurice and Serrano 1977: 49). Like Azcárate, he argued in the early 1880s for the current centralized legislation based on the Napoleonic Code to be replaced by an English model of civil liberties based on common law. In his 1885 *Materiales para el estudio del derecho municipal consuetudinario,* Costa argued for the abandonment of all foreign models in favour of a legal system based on native local customary law, seen as 'emanating directly from the sovereignty of the people'. This volume is a detailed study of family councils and property rights, stressing the sovereignty of the family.[6] Among the institutions singled out were the Leonese *esponsales*, which arbitrated village contracts, and the *desposorio* of Ciudad Real, which judged young people's behaviour: both use the terminology of marriage. Costa argued for the re-establishment of the old *concejos*, made up of local heads of family, which had been dominant across northern Spain, including Pereda's Santander. He additionally proposed that a large percentage of local tax revenue be retained for local development purposes, in the form of agricultural credits and technical support. Kern (1974: 61–4) notes that volume ii, by a variety of contributors including Unamuno, argued that customary law provided a 'natural' basis for local government, stressing its concern with the conservation of natural resources, particularly of woodlands, and suggesting that this could be adapted to promote agricultural development, harnessing tradition to modernity. As Kern puts it (1974: 6), this investigation 'proved that Spain had a usable past'. However some contributors, including Unamuno (whose contribution was written in 1895, although the second volume was not published till 1902), were uneasy about basing modernity on tradition; Altamira (Professor of Law at Oviedo University from 1897, and previously at the Institución Libre de Enseñanza) observed that modern society had achieved individual freedom by ridding itself of corporativism. Azcárate, in his *El regimen parlamentario en la práctica* (1885), attacked this 'return to the past' as a return to ignorance and apathy, arguing in favour of modern European democratic structures based on genuine political representation, through the creation of an active civil society (Kern 1974: 61–4). The varied responses listed here illustrate the attractions and dangers of using the past to build the future: the *desposorio* of Ciudad Real, in which heads of family judged young people's behaviour, exemplifies the repressive potential of such traditional local institutions, no matter how representative of the community. Clavero (1982: 14) notes that foral law could be used to defend 'posiciones realmente atávicas en temas tan importantes como los de derecho de familia'. In this respect *Peñas arriba* produces mixed feelings: its advocacy of an autarkic, vertically structured corporativism uncomfortably

---

[6] Alonso Martínez, the architect of the 1889 Civil Code which attempted a compromise with customary law, noted in his study *El código civil en sus relaciones con las legislaciones forales* (1883) that the *fueros* related the organization of land to that of the family (Elorza 1973: 153).

anticipates early Francoism, but its passionate plea for local autonomy—something the Francoist State was bent on destroying—is likely to appeal to readers of most persuasions.[7] It is worth noting that left-wing models of local autonomy could also be based on a deeply conservative view of the family: the former President of the Federal Republic Pi y Margall's *Las nacionalidades* (1876), which argued that the *municipio* was the 'natural' social unit, insisted that the family did not provide a model for social structures since the 'obvious inferiority of women' (Hennessy 1962: 264) meant that it was not based on reciprocity and thus could not be governed by contract.

One of the contributors to volume ii of *Derecho consuetudinario* was Gervasio González de Linares, whose 1882 book *La agricultura y la administración municipal*, originally published in the *Revista de España*, had been hailed by the conference of Aragonese lawyers which set up the research project leading to the two volumes of *Derecho consuetudinario*. González de Linares's book is a study of local government in the Cabuérniga district of Santander, undertaken when he was Mayor of Cabuérniga 1873–7. *Peñas arriba* is set in the village of Tudanca (fictionalized as Tablanca) in Cabuérniga district, during the period 1870–1. González de Linares (1882: 18–19) mentions the Tudanca landowner Francisco de la Cuesta on whom Pereda's Don Celso is based, praising him for 'guiding' the villagers 'con un desinterés no común por desgracia en nuestros pueblos'. When Pereda met Don Celso's prototype (whose niece was married to Pereda's cousin) in 1871, he was Mayor of Tudanca.[8] Pereda's patriarch has no connection with any form of local government for this, particularly if he were a Crown-appointed mayor, would link him with the central State apparatus. Despite the impression given that we are introduced to the whole community of Tablanca, there is no reference to its mayor anywhere in the novel, though the 'ayuntamiento' is briefly mentioned for its success in balancing its books and its prevention of alcoholism through its monopoly ownership of the only tavern (Pereda 1988: 216,

---

[7] The contradictory political appeal of *Peñas arriba* is nicely captured by Mariano Cavia's review of January 1895 in *El Liberal*, which saw the novel as an amalgam of traditionalist regionalism, Pi y Margall's federalism, Tolstoy's Christian 'socialist' patriarchy, and Randolph Churchill's intellectual elitism (Madariaga de la Campa 1991: 389).

[8] For information on Francisco de la Cuesta (who died in 1883), see Madariaga de la Campa (1991: 142, 374–6); and Cossío (1973: iii. 269, 273).

271). We do, however, meet Don Pedro Nolasco who had been an elected village representative in 1825, Deputy Mayor in 1827, *regidor* in 1830, and Mayor in 1832 (Pereda 1988: 173): appointments all held prior to the reorganization and centralization of local government in 1833. In marrying his granddaughter, the city-bred Marcelo inserts himself into the pre-liberal system of local representation.

González de Linares's book was written in response to 'el caciquismo político local' (1882: p. vi) and 'la tutela funesta de los partidos' (1882: p. xi) which thwarted his attempts at reform, particularly in agricultural development, when Mayor. Throughout he bemoans 'el freno de la centralización', which he blames (rightly) on liberalism, defining himself as a conservative because of his opposition to liberal centralizing policies. He notes that the current 'tendencia a la unidad', which has produced 'resultados desastrosos' (1882: 336), in fact started with the Catholic Kings, whose precocious creation of a unified nation-State killed local life (1882: pp. xvii–xviii). He stresses the need for an active local public sphere, for more schools (including technical schools), and for reform from the bottom up, with the local population given adult responsibilities. The 'municipio', he insists, is the 'base de la vida política' (1882: p. ix) since it is the local population's only access to power, transactions with the central State being too remote and abstract. His book is impressive in its concrete proposals for conserving and improving livestock, crops, orchards, and woodland, combining an ecological concern with a desire for economic modernization. To achieve his proposed 'regeneración, partiendo de los municipios' (1882: 363) he calls for a return to the traditional *concejos*, governed by an elected *regidor*, with responsibility for 'todos sus bienes propios y comunes', for a local police force (abolished in 1844 with the creation of the centrally controlled Civil Guard), and for 'beneficencia' (1882: 223–33). Although he supports private property (land enclosure), he praises the former communal forms of organization (including communal landownership and labour) which encouraged active local participation, as opposed to the current 'tutela gubernamental' which creates inertia by taking responsibility away from the local population, additionally failing to implement the needed changes because of centrally appointed officials' ignorance of local matters.

González de Linares's note on the prototype for Pereda's Don Celso singles him out for his defence of Tudanca's commonly owned 'prado de concejo', whose communal mowing provides the climax of *Peñas arriba*. González de Linares notes that communally worked 'prados de concejo' still existed in Tudanca and two other nearby villages under the same Ayuntamiento: perhaps the only ones to escape disentailment in the province; he also notes that the 'prado de concejo' of Tudanca was one of the biggest ever to have existed in 'el país' (presumably in the sense of 'region'), producing ten cartloads of hay for each of the village's eighty *vecinos*. His description of the allocation of labour for its annual communal mowing coincides exactly with that of Pereda: 'Es muy interesante la operación de dividir en suertes el prado, cuyo sorteo se hace en presencia de todos los vecinos, quienes, después de terminado, empiezan a la vez la siega y siguen haciendo juntos la recolección' (1882: 18–19).[9] Carr notes that the profits from such communally owned and worked lands had paid for the village schoolmaster and doctor, allowing the municipality to exercise a tutelary function (1966: 273); with the loss of this income with the enforced disentailments and privatization of property, most villages were unable to provide such services, despite their legal responsibility for primary education since 1857. It is thus not surprising that González Linares should conclude that centralization is to blame for the backwardness of the rural areas and the underdevelopment of the agricultural economy on which the nation depends.[10]

The differences between González de Linares's analysis and that of Pereda are as striking as the obvious similarities. Unlike other regenerationists, González de Linares barely mentions the family as the basis of traditional local government structures, for his stress is on communal rather than patriarchal forms of organization. Nor does he mention moral or religious matters, except to note that State inspectors refused to listen to villagers' insistence that local education could not, and should not, be left to the Church. In *Peñas arriba*, Don Celso's will leaves a special bequest to the local municipally run school (367)—in

---

[9] Shubert (1990: 191–2) gives further information on such communal forms of land usage, distributed by lot ('suerte'), and on the accompanying communal forms of labour, noting that participation in the latter was often obligatory.

[10] González de Linares's work is discussed by Kern 1974: 58–60.

1877 Pereda's family had paid for a primary school to be built in his native village Polanco, in Santander province, where he lived till his death (Madariaga de la Campa 1991: 176)—but the village doctor Neluco, the novel's major regenerationist spokesman, argues against educating the locals above their station, insisting paternalistically that the educated should 'descend' to their level (236).

Most of the geographical and anthropological information in *Peñas arriba* is based on Pereda's 1871 visit to Tudanca during his election campaign as parliamentary candidate for Cabuérniga district, representing the Carlists whose defence of local freedoms was accompanied by a strongly Catholic moral conservatism and nostalgia for a pre-modern stable, hierarchical rural order. This election campaign also formed the basis of Pereda's 1879 novel *Don Gonzalo de la Gonzalera*, not set in the mountain highlands but constituting a diatribe against central government interference through *caciquismo* in the wake of the 1868 Revolution. We deduce that *Peñas arriba* is set in 1870–1 from Don Celso's vague reference to the 'políticas nuevas' which, two years before, disturbed the village in *Don Gonzalo de la Gonzalera* (363): the precise references to time are to months, not to years, creating the impression of an ahistorical calendar ruled by natural cycles. This vagueness, plus the fact that Marcelo is writing his memoirs 'algunos, bastantes años' after the events narrated (574), allows Pereda to introduce regenerationist concerns more appropriate to the 1890s; at the same time, the dating of events to 1870–1 puts the blame for the decay of local life on the 1868 Revolution: that is, on progressive liberalism.[11] In reality, centralization was largely the product of mid-century Moderate governments (López Garrido 1982) and of the drift towards conservatism under the Restoration. The draft constitution of the 1873–4 Federal Republic (never passed) proposed a Spanish nation divided into seventeen autonomous 'Estados', as a way of pre-empting separatist reactions to increased centralization (Bahamonde Magro and Martínez 1994: 592–3). But the Federal Republic's concern to construct national unity via grassroots democratic participation was not acceptable to rural traditionalists. In 1876, the new Restoration government

---

[11] Montesinos (1969: 248) notes that Pereda only starts to idealize the Cantabrian countryside after the triumph of liberalism with the 1868 Revolution.

rescinded the Basque *fueros* on ending the third Carlist War, and introduced draft legislation, passed in 1878, reorganizing local government: all posts in local and provincial government were now made Crown, rather than elected, appointments, except for councillors in municipalities with a population under 30,000; however, these elected councils could be abolished by provincial civil governors on instructions from the Ministerio de Gobernación. Artola describes the question of whether mayors should be elected or appointed as 'el gran debate político de la España decimonónica' (in Gortázar 1994: 97–8). Property valuation, on which taxation and suffrage were based, was also taken out of municipal hands and put under provincial control. The 1876 Constitution effectively subjected the whole nation to unified legal codification, though some safeguards for foral 'differences' were conceded, in keeping with Cánovas's policy of rule by compromise (García Delgado 1985: 381–2). The King's speech on 'Municipal Life' of 1882, written by Sagasta and his Ministro de Gobernación, deplored the previous Cánovas administration's centralizing measures but insisted they would stay on the books. However, the 1889 Civil Code made concessions to foral rights (Clavero 1982: 132–6), and in 1889 Sagasta introduced a bill (passed in 1890) restoring the 1869 Constitution's introduction of universal manhood suffrage for municipal councils, provincial assemblies, and the national legislature. The King's speech on 'Local and Provincial Affairs' of 1891, written by Cánovas's dissident conservative Ministro de Gobernación, Silvela, promised 'curtailment of the centralism which for fifty years has caused nothing but corruption and tutelage'; and later that year Silvela tabled a local government reform bill, proposing to divide Spain into thirteen regions, each governed by an elected council, abolishing the artificially created provinces and 'returning administration to its natural centres'. In November 1891, Cánovas forced Silvela's resignation and replaced him with his long-standing electoral henchman Romero Robledo, giving rise to anti-centralist demonstrations in the north-west, Catalonia, and Andalusia (Kern 1974: 37–8, 44, 75, 77–80). In displacing resentment against the Restoration's (and particularly Cánovas's) centralizing measures onto the 1868 Revolution, Pereda shows that his real fear is the universal manhood suffrage introduced by the 1869 Constitution and restored by Sagasta in 1890, which—while maintaining the centralized system—broadened the electoral basis of local, as well as national, government.

Pereda's links with Carlism were lifelong. In 1870, as a member of the provincial Carlist Junta, he visited the Carlist pretender to the throne, Don Carlos, in Vevey (Switzerland). He was a Carlist parliamentary deputy from 1871 to January 1872, before the outbreak of the third Carlist War of 1872–6, during which his brother Manuel and several close friends had their property confiscated by the Ministerio de Gobernación for their involvement (Madariaga de la Campa 1991: 138, 148).[12] In *El sabor de la tierruca* (1882), the village Mayor, while not assisting the Carlist guerrillas, refuses to take action against them (Pereda 1959: i. 1294). Carr (1966: 354) notes that after the end of the third Carlist War in 1876, Carlism, under the leadership of Vázquez de Mella, became a 'doctrine of regional revival under a strong patriarchal Catholic monarchy'. Although he did not participate in public Carlist meetings, Pereda was a member of the Santander Carlist Círculo Tradicionalista, founded in 1891; in 1892 invited the Carlist leader, the Marquís de Cerralbo, to his house in Polanco; in 1893 attended the funeral service for Don Carlos's wife; and on the suicide of his eldest son in 1893, while he was writing *Peñas arriba*, received a personal letter of condolence from Don Carlos (Madariaga de la Campa 1991: 149). This traditionalist background was combined with active involvement in local industry and banking. The family factory in Santander, manufacturing candles, soap, and sulphuric acid, placed them among the province's top twenty industrial taxpayers; Pereda became its co-owner (with his brother Manuel) in 1882 and on his brother's death in 1890 took over its management.[13] In 1875, Pereda joined the Junta Rectora of the Banco de Santander (one of the first to issue paper money, till 1874 when currency issue was restricted to the Bank of Spain), with which he was associated till his death; later, in 1898, he was

---

[12] Bahamonde Magro and Martínez (1994: 576) note that the 1871 elections marked the height of the Carlists' electoral success, with 51 deputies and 28 senators in 26 provinces, in a curious alliance with the Republicans. What both parties had in common was their rejection of the modern central State.

[13] Madariaga de la Campa prints an advertisement for the company's soap, which—nicely, given his rural novels' exaltation of marriage and his urban novels' (*Pedro Sánchez* (1883) and *La Montálvez* (1885)) denunciation of adultery—proclaims it to be 'duro sin adulteraciones'. The factory's products won a gold medal at the 1888 Barcelona World Exhibition (Madariaga de la Campa 1991: 171, 173).

appointed to the Consejo de Administración of the newly created Santander Monte de Piedad y Caja de Ahorros. As a member of the top Santander industrial bourgeoisie, he participated actively in local philanthropic associations, in 1892 helping set up the Escuelas Salesianas in Santander, staffed by French friars (Madariaga de la Campa 1991: 172–6). The rural patriarchy advocated in *Peñas arriba* needs to be put in this perspective: like early Francoism, it is a rejection of the cultural and social implications of modernity but not of economic modernization.[14] As Varela Ortega notes (1977: 244–5), it was not till the early twentieth century that regenerationism turned into a protest against industrialization. In the late nineteenth century, everyone was in favour of economic modernization; the protests of rural producers were directed not against industry or modern agricultural methods, but against the subordination of the economy to the interests of city consumers.

Pereda's fictional Tablanca is seen through the eyes of the city-bred Marcelo not only because Pereda is trying to convert his urban readers to his plea for rural regeneration (Pereda 1988: 84), but because the country needs the city to modernize it. Unlike Luis in *Pepita Jiménez*, Marcelo is not a native of the village (though his father was) but of Madrid. His ancestry, with an Andalusian mother, makes him a fusion of the northern and southern rural provinces. A more muted combination of north and south and of country and city is found in the village girl he marries: of local parentage but with a father who had emigrated to Andalusia; never having left Tablanca but with the mannerisms of a 'señorita de ciudad' (252) and making her dresses from patterns in a fashion magazine received by post (376). Like Valera, Pereda laments the tendency to abandon the country for the city—we are given several examples of families, including Marcelo's own, broken up by emigration to the city and to America (225, 251)—but he is in favour of temporary emigration allowing the importation of new skills and knowledge.[15] Marcelo, an emigrant's son, brings material

---

[14] For this view of early Francoism, see Richards (in Graham and Labanyi 1995: 173–82).

[15] Pereda's eldest brother emigrated to Cuba, as did many young men from Santander province, in 1822, prospering in business and helping support the family. In 1852 he returned to Europe, first to England, settling in Santander in 1855 and acting as the young Pereda's mentor.

improvement; Neluco brings medical expertise acquired in Madrid. In depicting the city's improvement of the country, *Pepita Jiménez*—written in 1874 against the background of recent cantonalist secession—implies the need to incorporate the regions into the nation. *Peñas arriba*—written in 1892–4 when the problem is viewed as over-centralization—sees the city's improvement of the rural areas as a way of making them self-sufficient. But Pereda is still arguing for an integrated nation—not so different from the Krausist organicist model—in which the various organs fulfil their individual function while contributing to the whole. As the novel's other regenerationist spokesman, the Señor de Provedaño, says in basic agreement with Costa:

yo le diría al Estado desde aquí: 'Tómate [. . .] lo que en buena y estricta justicia te debemos de nuestra pobreza para levantar las cargas comunes de la patria; pero déjanos lo demás para hacer de ello lo que mejor nos parezca: déjanos nuestro bienes comunales, nuestras sabias ordenanzas, nuestros tradicionales y libres concejos; en fin (y diciéndolo a la moda del día), nuestra autonomía municipal.' (308)

In 1891 the Grupo Regionalista Cántabro, in an article in the conservative regionalist paper *El Atlántico*, founded with Pereda's backing, claimed that their programme was based on that expounded in Pereda's novels: 'Nada de separatismos [. . .] españoles y muy españoles todos, amantes de la unidad nacional' (Madariaga de la Campa 1991: 390). In his 1900 study *Centralización, descentralización, regionalismo*, Moret—now converted to the idea that centralization and not local customary law was the problem—argued that decentralization was needed to palliate regionalist demands, which he saw as leading to 'el absoluto *divorcio* de una parte del país con el resto de la nación' (Elorza 1973: 189–90). Throughout the 1890s, with the growth of peripheral nationalisms, it became common to refer to separatism as the 'divorce' of one part of the nation from the rest; hence Pereda's novel will propose local regeneration through the marriage of centre and periphery. In his 1897 speech on reception to the Spanish Royal Academy, Pereda pleaded for a regional novel that was '*nacional, española neta*' (Pereda 1897: 5–28, original italics); in his reply to Pereda's speech, Galdós praised him as a *castizo* Castilian writer, arguing that the national novel had, by definition, to be regional in order to reflect the cultural variety of a nation lacking in unity 'fuera del orden político, cuyos artificios [...] no se ocultan a nadie' (Pereda 1897: 39). From his early *costumbrista* sketches, the *Escenas montañesas* (1864), onwards Pereda's work is concerned with combating a centralizing modernity by creating national awareness of the local; that is, constructing a nation based on regional variety. His early work coincides with *costumbrismo* in assuming that local customs are doomed to succumb to the centralizing impulse, but from the early 1880s he starts to propose them as a model for the future. His speech to the Real Academia Española states explicitly that, by 'regional novel', he does not necessarily mean 'rural novel' but the representation of those elements of the nation that are 'truly Spanish' because they refuse the imitation of foreign models which comprises modernity (Pereda 1897: 5–28). (Throughout his speech, Pereda refers to modernity and its supporters as 'modernismo' and 'modernistas', showing that the restricted use of these terms to refer to a specific poetic movement—based on the imitation of French models, of course—was not the only current usage.) In *Peñas arriba*, the Señor de Provedaño—based on the historian, journalist, and lawyer Ángel de los Ríos, a Catholic Monarchist who belonged to Sagasta's Liberal Party[16]—declares his belief in progress provided that 'esas modificaciones de las costumbres y de las leyes se deriven [...] de la naturaleza de las cosas mismas; que las leyes se acomoden al modo de ser de los pueblos, no los pueblos a las leyes de otra parte' (307). This belief in national unity based on regional variety is matched by the novel's depiction of a local community whose 'organic' unity is based on the preservation of class differences: here Pereda's organicism differs from that of Krausism, concerned to 'elevate' the masses through education.

Marcelo's first task on taking over Don Celso's patriarchal role is to familiarize himself with the 'organism' comprised by the 'tratos y contratos' under which the local sharecroppers and tenant farmers have usufruct of his newly inherited land: the 'organic' nature of these contracts suggests that they are *censos*, unalienable leases and sub-leases transmitted through inheritance, which in many areas, particularly north-west Spain,

---

[16] Madariaga de la Campa (1991: 391), noting that he attended meetings of the local council with a loaded gun, calls him a 'liberal a su modo'.

survived the disentailment laws (Clavero 1982: 83–154). Contract law is subsumed into an organic concept of landownership, whose permanence—being unalienable on the market—'solves' the 'problema social que dan por insoluble los "pensadores" de los grandes centros civilizados' (552). The only other contract mentioned in the novel—marriage—is also permanent and institutes 'natural' ties: hence its function as a model for social structures. The changes which Marcelo introduces, earning him the title of 'reformador' (554), confirm the existing social and moral order while facilitating economic modernization. This contrasts with *Pepita Jiménez* where Luis brings moral and aesthetic improvement while leaving social and economic structures untouched. If Luis made purely cosmetic improvements to his house, taking land out of cultivation, Marcelo—in addition to laying out a garden—reorganizes the orchard, brings new land under cultivation, improves the road from the house to the village, and rebuilds the house. To do so, he contracts a Madrid architect and uses a mixture of local raw materials and modern accessories imported from the capital; he also imports the contents of his former Madrid home. The house Pereda had built in his native Polanco in 1872 was famous for its modern conveniences and garden designed by a French landscape architect (Madariaga de la Campa 1991: 33).

However, Marcelo leaves the kitchen untouched, for its hearth serves as a communal village forum—'allí y sólo allí era donde exponían y ventilaban los asuntos más importantes de su vida' (332): a subordination of the public to the private sphere similar to that in *Pepita Jiménez* except that it takes the form, not of polite card-playing presided over by a young lady, but of hearty meals—with all social classes (including the servants) eating together—presided over by a down-to-earth though courteous patriarch. This local civil society is effectively all male, since the female servants do not speak. We are told that the tax collector does his business in this 'casa de todos', subordinating even the collection of State revenue to the hearth (333). But in practice we see the members of this *tertulia* discussing only private matters. What little we are told about Don Celso's role as public benefactor—mainly through his will—implies that, apart from the bequest to the school, it is restricted to private donations and the writing off of debts. His patriarchal example is explicitly opposed to *caciquismo*, for it upholds local autonomy rather than the interests of the State. But it consists in a similar privatization of the political, both in basing the community on the family—in addition to ensuring his own family's continuity and pre-eminence by leaving his land to his nephew Marcelo, his will permits Pito Salces and Chisco (if he chooses) to marry—and in reducing local affairs to questions of individual welfare. Don Celso's 'protection' of the community is repeatedly described as an 'obra benéfica'. If, in the urban novels of the 1880s studied above, philanthropy—carried out by women— was seen as an unwelcome public invasion of the private, here —carried out by a man—it is a welcome privatization of 'the social'. Indeed, Don Celso's beneficence corresponds more to the old-style charity than to the new philanthropy aimed as 'improving' the poor.

In choosing the doctor Neluco as his spokesman, Pereda is able to articulate his organic concept of the national 'body'.[17] But as a social regulator Neluco shows no interest in issues of public health: a one-line mention of his conversation with Marcelo about 'las condiciones higiénicas de la valle' (227) quickly turns into a discussion of Don Celso's personal illness. Elsewhere Marcelo comments that 'La raza es de lo más sano' because of 'la continua gimnasia del monte, la abundancia de la leche y la honradez de las costumbres públicas y domésticas' (218), linking public health—as did many contemporary health experts—to private morality. Marcelo's 'reformas' serve chiefly to enhance his own status and comfort as leading landowner, though they do provide labour for the community. His cultivation of the orchard brings to mind Candide's discovery of the need to 'cultiver son jardin', here in the sense of bettering his own property and providing a model of practical improvement that will allow the community to be economically self-sufficient (though relying on Madrid for modern manufactured goods and expertise). But the dominant image is that of the house: its rebuilding by Marcelo embodies the 'andamiajes de proyectos' (538) which Neluco encourages him to undertake on the land. The building of the community is a rebuilding for it is a modernization based on tradition: the new house is an improved

---

[17] The Krausist political philosopher Azcárate had already in his 1876 *Resumen de un debate sobre el problema social* seen the nation as a 'sick body' (Díaz in Lida and Zavala 1970: 239–53). As repeatedly stressed throughout this book, concerns with degeneration/regeneration date back to well before the 1890s.

version of the old, Marcelo is a Don Celso 'refundido y hasta mejorado' (554).[18]

To turn this round, the rebuilding is also a building because the novel undertakes what Hobsbawm and Ranger (1984) have called the 'invention of tradition'. We are told that Tablanca is exceptional in its patriarchal bliss, for the other local villages having been disrupted by modernity in the form of new political ideas, brought by outsiders (271, 305). In his *Oligarquía y caciquismo*, Costa commented that Pereda's fictional patriarch and his real-life prototype were, sadly, not typical of the Spanish rural oligarchy (Costa 1973: 25). It has been noted that Pereda invents his own version of local dialect (Rey in Pereda 1988: 137 n. 28, 140 n. 36, 379 nn. 271 and 273; López Biada in Bonet et al. 1985: 197–222; Penny 1980; Montesinos 1969: 148),[19] and that his geography is a mixture of the real and the imagined (Clarke 1969: 55; Cossío 1973: iii. 269–71; Rey in Pereda 1988: 85, 275 n. 187). He decided to write a novel about the Cantabrian highlands precisely because it was the one part of the region he had never written about, being unfamiliar with it except for his brief 1871 trip twenty years previously (Madariaga de la Campa 1991: 363; Cossío 1973: iii. 269).[20] Before embarking on the novel, he made two excursions: to the Sejos Pass (abandoned because of fog) and from Cabuérniga over the Palombera ridge to Campóo. In a November 1892 letter to Menéndez Pelayo, he complained that he was finding the novel hard going because of 'el poco conocimiento que tengo de aquellas regiones', and interrupted it till 1893 when Ángel de los Ríos visited him and helped him with geographical information, taking him on a further trip (again fog-bound) to the Sejos Pass, the Valley of Campóo, and Proaño, after which he rewrote chapter 2 and other passages. Pereda's topographical descriptions also reproduce whole paragraphs from de los Ríos's introduction to his book *De Cantabris*; Pereda acknowledged

---

[18] Madariaga de la Campa (1991: 375) prints Pereda's sketch of Don Celso's house.

[19] Pereda was one of the informants for the Spanish Royal Academy's 1875 inquiry into regional linguistic variety: an inquiry which illustrates how the mapping of the regions formed part of the project of constructing the nation. According to Montesinos (1969: 46–8), Pereda's reply shows that at that date he still had a largely negative view of popular speech as a 'corruption' of standard Castilian (see also Cossío 1973: iii. 123–4); but he singled out the area of western Asturias, where *Peñas arriba* is set, for its linguistic 'bellezas'.

[20] Cossío (1973: iii. 123–4) notes Pereda's negative dismissal of 'la insípida Montaña' in an early letter of 1853.

him as his fictional 'collaborator' (Pereda 1988: 146 n. 44; González Herrán 1983: 406–8; Madariaga de la Campa 1991: 368–9). Nonetheless, de los Ríos pointed out geographical inexactitudes on the novel's publication. The novel's detailed mention of de los Ríos's publications and manuscripts (attributed to his fictional incarnation, the Señor de Provedaño) shows that the past has to be 'invented' through writing. These publications and manuscripts include: an etymological study of Castilian surnames (i.e. the transmission of identity through the father); a historical study of the 'behetrías, primitivas libertades castellanas' (a form of fiefdom originating in Cantabria at the start of the Reconquest, terminable by the serf at any point, allowing freedom of movement); two novels and a 'leyenda' based on local history; plus a technical plan for a local irrigation project (as noted in a previous chapter, Costa had since 1880 been advocating the need for hydraulic schemes) (300–2). The recuperation of the past is combined with the construction of the future; and the reconstruction of both local and national past sit side by side. The Señor de Provedaño's house is littered with relics from his local archaeological explorations (299), the nineteenth-century vogue for archaeology being one of the principal ways of inventing a national tradition. Marcelo exclaims: 'Entonces comprendí lo que valían los libros y las investigaciones arqueológicas de aquel hombre, destinados a reivindicar para su "patria chica" las glorias que se le negaban en la grande' (307). The Señor de Provedaño regales Marcelo with a series of lectures on local history, from the ancient Cantabrians' supposed Greek origins (giving them a Hellenic virility opposed to current decadence), their fight for independence against a series of centralizing invaders (Romans, Arabs), the early medieval 'Hermandades' (a hierarchical model of democratic participation based on the natural—male—bond of 'brotherhood'), to the destruction of local freedoms by the Catholic Kings, Carlos V—the former lord of the Señor de Provedaño's ancestral manor allegedly having been punished for his participation in the Comuneros' revolt, a favourite subject of nineteenth-century historical painting (Reyero 1989: 134–6)—and modern liberal politicians.[21]

---

[21] Montesinos (1969: 254) comments that the Señor de Provedaño represents a kind of Spanish traditionalism which 'coincidió sorprendentemente con los supuestos del federalismo'.

All this is reproduced in Marcelo's dream, which turns the past into a prophetic vision of the future, with the Señor de Provedaño leading the defence of 'la santa libertad de los pueblos y los fueros sagrados', repelling the century-old flood of invaders with his pitchfork: an image of regeneration through work and agriculture (306–19). Pereda's construction of a tradition of 'independencia y tenacidad cántabras' makes him see as negative those elements of Spanish history—the 'yugo romano' (126) and the Catholic Kings—glorified by proponents of State nationalism from the late nineteenth century through to early Francoism. Neluco also recounts how the Señor de Provedaño saved the mountain rescue team he was leading from freezing to death by making them perform local songs and dances: folklore is literally a life-saver (327). Marcelo had previously (126) been sceptical about his father's tales of the ancient Cantabrians—referred to as 'we', connecting them with their contemporary descendants—and casts doubt on the veracity of the Señor de Provedaño's historical reconstructions. But he finds them none the less attractive for that (311): the point of this 'invention of tradition' is to create a usable myth for the future. The novel's plot traces the birth and maturation of a plan for constructing the future, stopping at the moment when it is time for Marcelo to put it into effect: his postscript 'many years later' gives us no information about what has happened since. This postscript, written in the city, also tells us that Marcelo has maintained his links with modern urban civilization. The Señor de Provedaño is (like Marcelo by training) a lawyer, has held top State posts in various provinces (304), and ends his local history lesson with the image of the railway line linking Madrid with Santander (312): this construction of a regional tradition forms part of the construction of the nation, in which the railway was so instrumental. At the end of the novel, Don Celso reveals that his wealth in fact comes mainly from his estates in other provinces (360, 368).[22]

Pereda's justly famous landscape descriptions (Clarke 1969 and 1997; Akers 1982) are likewise part of a project for 'inventing the regions', as José-Carlos Mainer has aptly said of late nineteenth-century Spanish landscape painting (Pena

---

[22] The prototype for Don Celso, Francisco de la Cuesta, had studied law at Valladolid University (where his brother was Rector) and frequently visited the outside world (Cossío 1973: iii. 273).

López 1993–4: 26–39). The influx of Madrid holidaymakers to Santander province with the new railway line, a phenomenon mentioned in Pereda's early novels, was matched by a vogue for paintings of northern mountain scenery as city-dwellers discovered the wilds.[23] According to Javier Barón (Pena López 1993–4: 382), several Cantabrian painters studied with Carlos de Haes, the first incumbent of the Cátedra de Paisaje at the Academia de San Fernando (created 1844), who had instituted the practice of *plein air* painting and himself painted in Cantabria, including several views of the Picos de Europa.[24] Reviewers of *Peñas arriba* compared its landscape descriptions to those of Haes and of the contemporary Cantabrian painter Casimiro Sainz (González Herrán 1983: 436). One of these local students of Haes, Fernando Pérez de Camino, was a *contertuliano* of Pereda and illustrated several of his novels. Pereda encouraged the formation of a group of local landscape painters, and wrote the prologue for the 1889 volume of sketches *La Montaña: paisajes, costumbres y marinas de la provincia de Santander* by Pérez de Camino and another Haes student, Victoriano Polanco, praising their sketches as a 'patriotic' project.[25] One local painter, Agustín Riancho, talked of walking for miles in Cantabria in search of 'el paisaje primitivo' (Barón in Pena López 1993–4: 382), much like Marcelo in the novel. Marcelo's 'excursions', like those of Pereda when writing the book, echo those undertaken by Giner de los Ríos in Castile as part of a project for forming a national consciousness (as well as regenerating unhealthy city-dwellers): the novel's panoramic views from the Cantabrian peaks look out over Castile to the south as well as Santander to the north, just as the local landscape artists mentioned above toured and painted other areas of Spain.

Travel literature was, of course, a genre developed by the 1898 writers, notably Unamuno who in his *Por tierras de España y Portugal* (1911) accused Pereda of viewing the landscape as

---

[23] Montesinos (1969: 248) notes that, when Pereda started writing, the urban bourgeoisie despised the countryside, particularly mountains, but that by the 1890s this had changed.

[24] Reproduced in *Carlos de Haes* (1996: cover and plates 11–13); and in Litvak (1991: plate V).

[25] Many of these sketches are narrative in form; for example, 'Una carta de Ultramar' or 'La hierba' (on mowing the communal meadow, so important in *Peñas arriba*). The volume includes a sketch of 'Casas de Pereda en Polanco', comprising 'La casa antigua' and 'La moderna'; the latter, several storeys high, is vast.

an outsider; Pereda apparently told him that he did not like the countryside (Pereda 1988: 103; Clarke 1969: 229–33). But travel literature is, by definition, written from the tourist's point of view: *Peñas arriba* has the classic format of the travel book—written in the city by an outsider recording his impressions on first visiting the area—except that, unlike most travel writers, Marcelo decides to settle there. The novel's conservationist slant—unlike that of González de Linares, concerned with agricultural practicalities—is that of the outsider who wants to preserve the wilds—what Marcelo calls 'aquella naturaleza virgen' (213)—so that he can invade and 'possess' it. The counterproductive logic whereby tourism violates that which it wishes to keep inviolate is demonstrated in the bear hunt episode, where Marcelo is torn between excitement at taking part in the massacre, and guilt at destroying innocent creatures who he has been told attack only when provoked (157, 383). The night before, he dreams that the bears put him on trial (383) and, throughout the hunt, they are referred to as a 'familia' in their 'domicilio' (385); the she-bear protecting her cubs in the cave is a 'señora con su prole' in her 'salón de recibir' (394), and the returning male looks at Marcelo 'como si a mí solo quisiera pedir cuentas de los horrores cometidos allí con su familia' (397). The male bear dies with its head on its mate's neck, in a touching *Liebestod* (398). The chapter ends by describing the exploit as 'nuestra bestial hazaña' (401), suggesting that, if the bears are 'human', the humans are beasts. That this should be Marcelo's last excursion before he himself founds a family with Lita introduces an uncomfortable note.

This episode constructs Marcelo as a frontiersman, bringing civilization to the wilderness but also receiving his own initiation into masculinity from it (confirmed by the bearskins he is awarded as trophies).[26] Stephen Kern notes that, with the conquest of the American frontier in the late nineteenth century, a new concern developed to conserve the wilderness through the creation of National Parks (1983: 166). Pereda's novel betrays an ambivalent desire both to conserve the wilds—the village priest, although a good hunter, is respectful of animal life and hunts only 'alimañas' (211)—and to abolish the frontier

---

[26] This point is made by Valis (1979) who sees the novel as 'a nineteenth-century princely enchiridion or prince's manual of instruction'.

between the civilized and the wild by conquering the wilderness that still exists in Spain's remote rural areas. Despite Pereda's rejection of the centralization which led the Spanish State to view the provinces as colonies, Marcelo's 'discovery', 'settlement', and future 'population' of the highland village constitute a kind of colonization. Marcelo corrects Neluco's description of Don Celso's patriarchy as an 'imperio', preferring to see it as a 'family' (337), but he perpetuates this family by marrying a 'reina indígena' (572). He prepares himself for his expedition with travel literature on 'montañas', 'selvas', and 'salvajes', 'lo mismo que si proyectara una excursión por el centro de un remoto continente inexplorado' complete with 'osos' (153). He also sees himself as a Julius Caesar crossing the Rubicon (134). There is an implied criticism here of his city-dweller's attitude; but in crossing the *cordillera* he is genuinely crossing a Rubicon into another world, and he really does pass a bear on his way to the village, confirming his role as great white explorer. The later bear hunt demonstrates the savagery of the local men, represented by Chisco—initially seen as an ancient Cantabrian barbarian (153)—and Pito Salces, whose exploits throughout are referred to as 'barbaridades' admirable for their virility but deplorable for their brutality. Marcelo has to translate his educated speech for the locals' benefit and vice versa, as if in a foreign country. His description of the valley, even at the end, as a 'salvaje comarca' implies that it is primitive as well as wild. Chisco and Pito are depicted as inscrutable natives, the former being an 'impenetrable continente'; like a colonial explorer in darkest Africa, Marcelo makes an effort to 'descender con mi razón, más luminosa, a las tenebrosidades de aquellos hombres' (531–2). *Peñas arriba* ends, like Valera's *Pepita Jiménez* and *Juanita la Larga*, with a reference to Spanish America through Marcelo's sister, married to an 'americano' in what is probably Cuba (sugar mills and coffee plantations are mentioned), who promises to come home to see him installed in Tablanca. *Peñas arriba*, like *Juanita la Larga*, was written as war was threatening to break out in Cuba after the rejection of Maura's 1893 proposal for Cuban autonomy, and it is set during the first Cuban War of 1868–79. Given that Cuba was constitutionally a province of Spain, the mention of Cuba would have suggested to readers that the consequence of denying a measure of local control was likely to be separatist conflict; alternatively it could be taken to imply that, if Spain was losing its last colonies, Spaniards should turn their attention to improving the neglected 'colonies' at home. One is reminded of Luis's abandonment, in *Pepita Jiménez*, of his overseas missionary plans for a 'mission' in the provinces: Don Celso's protection of his 'flock' is referred to as a religious 'ministerio' matching that of the local priest (481).

As befits a frontier society, Tablanca is a community where all-male relationships are paramount, with women providing food and, in the best of cases, pleasant decoration—plus children, to make the settlement permanent. Pardo Bazán repeatedly noted that, in the rural areas, women worked in the fields alongside men (1981: 69–70, 1972: 121–2) but in Tudanca the women are almost always indoors; going to fetch water from the spring leads to Facia's disastrous encounter with her criminal husband. The emotional impact of Marcelo's engagement to Lita, though fundamental in demonstrating that the capital should 'espouse' the country, is undermined by his awareness that he is narrating an 'escena sempiternamente cursi a los ojos de un espectador desapasionado y frío' (571). By contrast, he feels no inhibitions about describing his friendship with Neluco, his admiration for the Señor de Provedaño, or even his closeness to the servant Chisco. Pito Salces's heroism in saving Chisco's life and the priest Don Sabas's embrace with the dying Don Celso are the most moving episodes in the novel. One feels that it is only the emotion released by Marcelo's sorrow at his uncle's death that allows him subsequently to recognize his love for Lita.

Like José María in Galdós's *Lo prohibido*, Marcelo is a decadent city bachelor but he is not a Don Juanesque seducer of women. His problem is that his life of artifice has deadened his sensibility; he recognizes that he has never felt strong feelings for women nor, it seems, for anything else except travel (128). He loves and leaves places rather than women. His Baudelairean *spleen* is a version of the neurasthenia afflicting Galdós's José María; he is prone to nightmares, listlessness, and depression, and suffers from claustrophobia when not in open spaces.[27] As with that of José María in *Lo prohibido*, his

---

[27] Pereda himself suffered from neurasthenia, despite living in the country (Rey in Pereda 1988: 15; Cossío 1973: iii. 111–12).

bachelorhood is presented as sick and unnatural. The bears show that families exist in nature; this additionally refutes the modern idea of marriage as a contract. Lita and her mother comment on the 'unnaturalness' of Marcelo's city habits (443); he is attracted to Lita because of her 'naturalness' (444). This 'naturalness' includes her capacity for expressing emotion: it is her grief at Don Celso's death that allows Marcelo to acknowledge his own and, in so doing, to admit to the love—the 'corrientes misteriosas' he had never believed in (544)—he feels for her. When Neluco talks of the 'gangrene'—described as a form of neurasthenia: 'gastada su sensibilidad con el roce de tantos y tan continuos sucesos'—devouring the nation's centre (Madrid), he refers to the latter as both a 'head' and a 'heart' (237): emotional as well as intellectual regeneration is needed. Marcelo lays the first stone of the 'monumento de regeneración' (572) by committing himself to the village, but this is above all a personal regeneration. Neluco talks of the need to cultivate the health of the nation's 'extremities' in order to regenerate its sick centre (238), but in practice it is those individuals who leave the capital for the rural periphery who are regenerated. How the capital itself can be regenerated, without ceasing to be a city, is not clear: a problem Marcelo is aware of when, back in Madrid, he laments the fact that it is not possible to build the city in the country (559).

Like *Pepita Jiménez*, *Peñas arriba* describes regeneration through the marriage of the city, represented by a man, to the country, represented by a woman. Pena López has noted that Giner de los Ríos exalted the Castilian landscape as masculine and the northern landscape as feminine, the nation thus being based on a perfect complementarity (1982: 94–7, 1990: 143–7). The tendency in *Peñas arriba* to view the landscape from a height has been noted (Clarke 1969: 133–4): the viewers are always male, 'dominating' the implicitly feminine panorama spread before them. But Marcelo, like Luis in *Pepita Jiménez*, has to be masculinized by the country. Unlike Luis, Marcelo's city life has feminized him not by making him excessively emotional but because it lacks emotion, being based on external spectacle and display: he collects 'artículos de lujo', especially works of art; frequents high society and the theatre; and takes an interest in politics and literature only to keep up with fashion (128–9). Though he does not get into debt, he has dissipated a substantial amount of the fortune inherited from his businessman father, never having worked: his life is feminine because it is idle (128). When the novel opens, he has just returned from a fashionable spa town and Paris, his luggage packed with the latest 'novedades' in the form of clothes and books, and is feeling 'cierta languidez de espíritu, cierta inapetencia moral' (131). He decides to take up his dying uncle's invitation to visit him in the 'wilds' in order to prove that:

> o es uno hombre, o no lo es; o tiene entrañas de humanidad, agallas [...]; o sirve o no sirve para algo más útil y de mayor jugo y provecho que pisar alfombras de salones; engordar el riñón a fondistas judíos, sastres y zapateros de moda; concurrir a los espectáculos; devorar distancias embutidas en muelles jaulas de ferrocarril, y gastar, en fin, el tiempo y el dinero en futilidades de mujerzuela presumida y casquivana. (132)

Civilization is here seen as a feminine love of spectacle, fashion, and consumerism, and decadent sensuality (associated with Jews). Interestingly, masculinity is associated not only with becoming productive but also with 'humanity': emotion. Immediately after deciding to go to Tablanca, Marcelo feels a 'virilidad desconocida' and sense of physical and moral health (132). But he becomes a 'true man' not only by taking on Don Celso's patriarchal role but also by learning the value of emotion from Lita, a woman. Even Don Celso, presiding over the kitchen hearth, is a kind of masculine 'mother' to his 'children': he is described as having 'escasas letras y excelente corazón' (124). Marcelo starts the novel with 'letras' but no heart; by the end he has learnt to combine the two. The model of masculinity proposed by Pereda is tempered with femininity: an inevitable consequence of proposing the family as the model for social relations. Marcelo's participation in the bear hunt was to put the animals out of their agony by giving them the 'tiro de gracia': like Luis's confrontation with the Conde de Genahazar in *Pepita Jiménez*, the hunt represents his initiation into masculinity as well as proposing a gentler (more genteel) form of masculinity as an improvement on the 'rude', 'brutish' virility of Pito and Chisco. Marcelo is regenerated, and will regenerate the village, because he has abandoned a negative model of femininity (consumerism) for a positive one based on emotion. In both cases, he is a feminized man.

At the end he describes this transformation as his conversion from a 'cortesano muelle, insensible y descuidado' into an 'hombre activo, diligente y útil' (572–3). The destructive lure of a non-productive consumerism is illustrated by the cautionary tale of Facia, whose head is turned by the confidence trickster selling useless baubles. Here too consumerism is associated with women: 'Para las mujeres, sobre todo, tenía el charlatán un anzuelo irrestible' (203). The trickster, who has been in America and will go back there after abandoning Facia, represents modern mobility: the 'torrente circulatorio de las insaciables ambiciones' unleashed by politics and the Stock Exchange (237). He claims to have been ruined on the Stock Exchange and, like Marcelo at the start, 'Le gustaba correr el mundo' (203). He is by implication associated with the 'charlatanes y traficantes políticos' who come from the 'absorbentes centros políticos y administrativos del Estado' claiming to offer cures when they are concerned only with lining their own pockets (239–40). Pereda coincides with Galdós in accusing the city of draining the countryside by consuming and not producing. But Pereda differs from Galdós in proposing as a remedy to the excess circulation of modernity a stability expressly opposed to freedom of movement.[28] When Marcelo first arrives in the 'wilds', he sees the mountains as 'barreras' imprisoning him; he learns to value their stability and permanence, and opts for marriage to Lita as a 'tie' to bind him to the village for ever (533). When he returns to Madrid, he now experiences the city streets, with their straight lines, as a 'jaula' (558–9).

Marcelo also initially describes the mountain wilderness in terms of disease and waste: 'una inmensa piel de leproso' (149), 'aquella escombrera de montes dislocados' (152). But he comes to realize that it is he who is sick because he is useless. Without the distractions of the city he literally does not know what to do, having no practical skills: 'Yo no era cazador [. . .] ni entendía jota de ganados, ni de labranzas, ni de arbolados, ni de hortalizas' (195–6). On his first attempts at hunting, he is

---

[28] Pereda's speech to the Real Academia Española is similarly structured around the opposition between the 'torrente circulatorio' of modernity—referred to by Pereda through the language of the market ('precio', 'mercado', 'moneda corriente')—and the stability and permanence of nature: an opposition central, of course, to Unamuno's theory of 'intrahistoria' elaborated in *En torno al casticismo*, written the same year as *Peñas arriba*.

a 'cazador de figurín' (198). After his uncle's death, he does not know 'en qué invertir las horas' (535): an intrusion of the discourse of the Stock Exchange, but also an indication that activity should bring a return. Neluco provides him with a programme of activities—inspecting his land to see what reforms are needed—designed to bring personal and collective improvement. As Neluco says, 'para qué se quiere el dinero' if not to put it to work? Neluco also encourages him to marry Lita: regeneration means becoming productive by husbanding the land and husbanding a wife, making both bear fruit. The final rebuilding of the house—'Aquel traqueteo de herramientas y bullir de obreros' (563)—is an image of practical activity. Neluco reminds Marcelo that he cannot make a useful contribution in Madrid where he is one of the crowd (561). On arrival in the village he had been struck by the uniformity of its houses and inhabitants (215–16). At the end, it is the uniformity of the city that is rejected for he is included in it; in the village, his education, as well as his inheritance of his uncle's land and position, makes him stand out above the rest (including Lita, superior to the other village women but seeing herself as his inferior). The activity represented by the rebuilding of the house, which stands above the village, confirms this pre-eminence. Marcelo's superiority allows him to be useful as the village's benefactor, but one has to ask who is benefiting most. He describes the village as a 'patriarcal y mínima república' (337) but, in founding a 'dinastía' (572), he establishes himself as sovereign ruler.

What attracts Marcelo to Lita is her—and her mother's—constant activity. When he first meets her, she is making bread; on other occasions she is dusting; when she and her mother come to help while Don Celso is dying, they bring their knitting and crochet and frantically clean and tidy, reorganizing the household for the last rites and cooking the banquet for the funeral guests. Marcelo is masculinized by learning to become useful, but his model in doing so—as in his acquisition of a heart—is a woman. The difference is that Lita is concerned with the domestic economy while he is concerned with becoming useful on the land and in the community. But, although the women are confined to the house, the distinction between private and public does not in practice hold. Marcelo's main activity consists in making the house into a family home, concerning himself particularly with that most private of places, the bedroom. And Lita's activities in baking bread and dressmaking for other girls in the village, although feminine, constitute the household as a unit of production. Almost all the men at Don Celso's hearthside *tertulia* bring some form of work, whether it be carving milking bowls or clogs from wood (333-4). The parallel female *tertulias*—mentioned but not depicted—are called 'jilas' because everyone is spinning (336). We are told that all the villagers make items of clothing or farm equipment (218). When Marcelo visits the home of Neluco's sister, another whirl of activity, he notes the mixture of household and farm implements and products (273). Most notably, on arriving at the Señor de Provedaño's manor, he finds the distinguished historian busy forking hay and next morning mowing at the crack of dawn (295, 316). For this is a pre-capitalist world prior to the public/private split instituted by the separation of production from the household, limiting the latter to consumption. The rural periphery represents the nation's regeneration because, in a reversal of the capital, it has no place for consumption (other than of essential items) but is devoted entirely to production.

The novel presents the village community as one big family—an 'hermandad' with Don Celso, and later Marcelo, as its father or head (271)—because there is no distinction between public and private. Marcelo prefers the analogy of the family to that of empire because the former is based on 'natural' relationships (336): everyone in Tablanca is figuratively 'sangre de nuestra sangre' (345) and treats everyone else with a 'familiaridad cariñosa' (336); indeed, they are literally all related (267). When Marcelo first meets Lita it is pointed out that he is her mother's cousin, though sufficiently distant for them not to need a papal dispensation to marry, and thus her uncle (250). The figurative incest which in the urban novel figures a disturbing refusal of the public/private division is here presented as exemplary. The nearest thing in *Peñas arriba* to figurative adultery is El Tarumbo's obsession with other people's affairs, always out repairing their property and neglecting his sick wife and his own ruinous home (219-20): a negative confusion of public and private interests which consists in abandoning the latter for the former. Although private affairs in Tablanca are a public matter, the stress is on the privatization of the public achieved by bringing everything into the home. The tradition of hospitality is stressed throughout. There is thus no problem, other than minor embarrassment, about Marcelo inviting Lita and her mother to move into the house while Don Celso is dying. Not only do they take over the running of the household but Marcelo vacates his bed for Lita to sleep in (409–501): this, in the urban novels concerned with maintaining boundaries, would be shocking (548). The whole village is invited in to witness Don Celso's death which, as was the case prior to the bourgeois privatization of death (Ariès 1987: 18–19), constitutes a public event; Shubert (1990: 129) notes that under customary law villagers were required to attend funerals. Marcelo invites notables from the whole province to the funeral as 'huéspedes míos', turning his bedroom ('gabinete') into a public 'estrado o sala de honor' (516). The kitchen hearth in Don Celso's house, which symbolizes the incorporation of the public sphere into the home, is significantly the first place Marcelo is taken to on arrival. The climax to the novel, immediately preceding Marcelo's engagement to Lita, is the mowing, through a traditional system of communal labour, of the village commons or Prao-Concejo, whose name keeps alive the pre-liberal community organization based on elected heads of family (566).[29] One is reminded of Tolstoy's *Anna Karenina*, whose most moving moment is when Levin—his concern with agricultural husbandry and with husbanding Kitty serving as a contrast to Anna's adultery—mows a field together with his peasants. In *Peñas arriba* Marcelo, despite his newly discovered interest in husbandry and in husbanding Lita, does not join in but watches the 'patriarcal faena' from his superior position as village benefactor. Communal organization for Pereda is modelled on the family, as a body of shared interests governed by the father as (superior) head. In describing Don Celso and the nation's capital as both head and heart of the organisms they respectively govern, Pereda is perhaps not so much feminizing patriarchy as proposing a masculine model that usurps the female function, leaving women with nothing to do. A warning about the repressive potential of the patriarchal order is provided by Facia's husband who abuses his *patria potestas*, blackmailing Facia into giving him her hard-earned

---

[29] For information on this system of communal labour and on the pre-modern *concejos*, see Colina de Rodríguez (1987: 206–14). The Ley Camacho of 1888 had put up for sale on the market those common lands which had survived the mid-century disentailment legislation.

savings by threatening to claim his daughter who, like her earnings, is legally his (458).

In rejecting bachelorhood for marriage, Marcelo is abandoning egoism for collective responsibility. As with Luis in *Pepita Jiménez*, this involves the surrender of a sick inner self, but Marcelo's inner self is sick in the sense that it constitutes an inner void or numbness. In acquiring a heart, Marcelo gains a new inner self which is healthy because it is immersed in the collective (family, village). Pereda has been accused of unconvincing characterization (Montesinos 1969: 259) but his concept of a public self has no place for deep psychology. Marcelo's first-person narrative, although a conversion narrative, is not so much autobiography as travel literature, telling us about the self only insofar as it reacts to the outside world, which is the chief focus. In *Pepita Jiménez*, Luis is not in control of the narrative since his letters are written in the course of the action whose denouement he ignores, and he finally abandons it to an unknown third-person voice. Marcelo, writing with hindsight and responsible for the whole account, retains narrative control throughout. Rather than a loss of the self, we have an initial split between the narrating self (informed by hindsight) and the self narrated (deluded), which disappears as the latter comes to coincide with the former. There is no Cervantine problematization of the narrative (the discovery at the end that some years have elapsed between the time of events and the time of writing only confirms that nothing has happened since to contradict the account given); simply a move towards the fusion of subject and object that parallels Marcelo's merging of private and public.

However, in basing the novel on the opposition between Marcelo's initial city-dweller's vision and his final appreciation of the countryside's 'true' value, Pereda is not simply contrasting artifice with nature. Throughout, nature is described in terms of painting (the word 'cuadro' recurs constantly), sculpture, architecture, theatre (an 'anfiteatro' or outdoors theatre), music, or as a book. This can partly be explained as Marcelo's city-dweller's view of nature: he tells us at the start that he only likes mountains 'como decoración' (130). But this view of nature as art if anything increases as Marcelo comes to appreciate its worth. Pereda seems to be going out of his way to show that all the cultural forms that give civilization value exist in nature too: there is no need to go to the city to find art (just as families exist in nature as well as in society). Nature, too, is spectacle and representation. Implicitly echoing Plato, Neluco opposes the contemplation of a painting copying nature to contemplation of the 'original' artwork that is nature itself: 'en este valle mínimo [. . .] encuentro yo cada día, cada hora, cada momento, el himno sublime, el poema, el cuadro, la armonía insuperables, que no se han escrito, ni pintado, ni compuesto, ni soñado todavía por los hombres [. . .]: el arte supremo en una palabra' (232-3). Pereda's 'panoramas'—as he calls them— stress the play of light, the juxtaposition of planes and patches of colour, and the framing of the whole by the surrounding mountains (144-5, 187-9), for nature is an artistic composition —that is, the work of God. This religious sense of nature reaches its climax in Marcelo's excursion with the priest Don Sabas to the peak from which they dominate all the points of the compass (258-63): a panoramic 'cuadro' which, with the rising mist, creates optical illusions and simulates 'el templo ojival, el castillo roquero, la pirámide egipcia, el coloso tebano'—a compendium of world art. The contrast with the kitsch juxtaposition of heterogeneous styles in Francisco de Bringas's hair picture, copied from books that themselves are copies, could not be greater. This 'arte sobrehumano' produces in Marcelo a sense of the sublime as Don Sabas, 'con voz solemne y varonil', chants a hymn to God's glory. Kant notoriously defined the sublime as a masculine category (Lloyd 1984: 75-6) because of its transcendent quality (by contrast with 'feminine' beauty, grounded in the material). This virile, sublime art of nature is implicitly contrasted with the city's feminization of culture through consumerism: Marcelo knows the value of art as a wealthy connoisseur and collector, but here is a painting that cannot be bought. Its value, in other words, is inherent, rather than residing in its price on the market.

In *Pepita Jiménez*, Luis abandons his earlier religious notion of nature as book and becomes a collector of art objects; Marcelo moves from being an art collector to an appreciation of nature as sacred text. Initially he needs Don Sabas to translate for him 'las páginas de aquel inmenso libro tan cerrado y en griego para mí' (212). The uncultured Chisco and Pito cannot 'leer' the book of nature; nor can those who are so immersed in culture that they can appreciate 'el natural' only when reproduced on canvas (213). Marcelo, because he is midway between these two extremes, is able with Don Sabas's help to begin to 'read' in Nature things he had never before read in paintings or books (213). On their culminating excursion, he learns to read the book of nature 'solo, de corrido y muy a gusto'; they stand side by side 'leyendo el gran libro en la misma página' (263). The spectacle of nature is just as much a form of representation as that offered by the modern city, but one based not on the fluctuating, arbitrary value system of consumer culture but on inherent, stable value as a reflection of its eternal Creator. The Platonic definition of mimesis, whereby the work of art is a secondhand copy of a material reality which itself is a 'reflection' of a hidden truth, is not appropriate to modernity. Modern life is representation but the representation—based on exchange value and not on inherent value—reflects no hidden truth. Modernity lacks depth because it is what it seems: appearances are everything. The fact that the moon, as the last rites are brought to Don Celso, imitates effects which Marcelo has seen 'pintados en lienzos y cartulinas' (486) does not devalue the scene for these stock artistic effects, produced by nature, illuminate God's presence. Indeed, these optical illusions created by nature reinforce the notion of mimesis as the surface reflection of a hidden truth. The last chapter ends with a hymn of praise to nature as a sign of God's magnificence (573). When Marcelo temporarily returns to Madrid, he cannot always detect God's presence when he looks up at the partially hidden sky (559). Modernity is 'godforsaken' because it is a copy that imitates only itself. On Marcelo's return to Madrid, he asks himself: '¿quién soy yo, qué represento, qué papel hago [...]?', and feels increasingly uncomfortable with his 'desairado papel de comparsa anónimo [...] en el montón decorativo de esa incesante farsa de la vida' (560). Modern city life is an empty —purely decorative—representation.

Peñas arriba also describes nature as a 'language' which 'speaks' to man through its sounds (232). Galdós, in his prologue to Pereda's 1882 novel *Sotileza*, was the first of many critics to praise Pereda for his representation of speech. Pereda's stress on orality—particularly the speech of the illiterate or minimally educated—suggests a desire to return to an 'original' plenitude of meaning prior to literacy, of the kind which Derrida (1976) traces as a constant in the western Platonic tradition. Pereda's delight in regional speech forms helps explain his hostility to educating the rural masses. He compares the cadences of the local dialect to the 'classical' rhythms of the *Romancero* or oral ballad tradition (216). But Pereda is not proposing the abandonment of writing: Marcelo needs it to communicate his story to the modern urban reader. However, Pereda makes us aware of the inadequacy of written language for conveying his characters' speech, and for conveying the sublimity of Don Celso's last rites (489). The 'naturalness' of the villagers and especially of Lita and her mother—the three books which Lita has read did not much impress her, and the only books in their home are St Teresa's letters, two devotional texts, and the *Quixote* (377)—is conveyed by their association with speech, contrasting with the city-bred Marcelo's association, as narrator, with writing. The customary law which *Peñas arriba* proposes as a model is also unwritten, unlike the 'códigos' of a modernizing, centralizing liberalism in its attempt to 'write the nation'. In his 1892 speech at the Barcelona Jocs Florals, Pereda had insisted that the 'unidad de Patria' needed to take account of the regions, rather than be confined to 'un puñado de cláusulas estampadas en un libro bajo el rótulo de *Leyes de Estado*' (Madariaga de la Campa 1986: 54); his 1897 speech on admission to the Real Academia Española similarly pleaded for an 'organic' State rather than one that derived from 'unas cuantas leyes estampadas en el papel' (Pereda 1897: 11). In *Peñas arriba*, Neluco attributes the failure of the Señor de Provedaño's fight against State intrusion to a legal system which exists only on paper and punishes those who try to put it into practice 'al pie de la letra' (322). His sketch of a typical corrupt State official takes the form of an 'arbitrista' skilled in manipulating the law who knows 'el valor que esas habilidades representan en el derecho flamante, y la manera de negociarlas' (323). Varela Ortega notes that *caciquismo* was a complex bargaining process based on 'cuasi-contratos' in which central and local interests were traded against each other (1977: 427). Pereda sees modernity's sickness—'el mal nuevo' (323)—as the subordination of politics to a legal system that exists on paper and is ruled by the market: that is, a value system based on contract and exchange relationships and not on inherent worth.

Varela Ortega also notes that the political system operating under the Restoration whereby, instead of elections being held to decide which party would form a government, the Crown appointed a government which then called elections to get itself elected (calling on the local *caciques* to rig the election of government-nominated candidates), was at the time described as the conversion of power into the 'representante de sí mismo' (1977: 368). Again we have the idea of modernity as a fiction which represents itself; that is, a self-referential system. The scene in *Peñas arriba* where the various provincial patriarchs —victims or antagonists of *caciquismo*—come to pay homage to the dead Don Celso brings in a metafictional dimension since, apart from the Señor de Provedaño, they are returning characters from Pereda's earlier *Los hombres de pro* (1876) and *Don Gonzalo de la Gonzalera* (1879). *Caciquismo*—as a fraudulent, self-referential form of political representation—makes its appearance in the novel via characters whose fictionality and intertextuality is highlighted. Don Recaredo, although he gave the electoral candidate Simón his come-uppance in *Los hombres de pro*, is described in terms that suggest that he is himself a *cacique*, albeit one opposed to liberalism: he is 'bien relacionado con los hombres del ajetreo político de la capital y sucursales de ella; muy solicitado de aspirantes a la representación en Cortes del distrito' (519). (The Señor de Provedaño had held government posts but is not described as a 'gran elector'.) Some contemporary reviewers saw the spectre of *caciquismo* lurking behind *Peñas arriba*'s advocacy of patriarchy (González Herrán 1983: 430–1); they were wrong, for Don Celso and the visiting patriarchs who congregate at his funeral oppose a centralized system of representation divorced from its regional base. But Don Recaredo's presence gives reason for doubt. The subsequent climactic episode of the mowing of the communal Prao-Concejo contrasts with the self-referential fictional status of *caciquismo*'s intrusion. The whole community (meaning the male peasants) takes part under the 'presidency' of an elected *regidor*, who designates the 'partidores' who, for that day, have responsibility for dividing the commons up equitably between groups of villagers, who in turn appoint a delegate to mow it for them; each day for a week, new representatives are nominated in a rota system that gives everyone responsibility (566). Here, by contrast with the artifice of the earlier intertextual references, we have a scene of genuine representation inserted into a natural scenario. In his speech to the Real Academia

Española, Pereda interestingly argued that regionalist sentiment reinforced State nationalism since allegiance to a concrete local reality made intelligible the abstract concept of allegiance to 'the nation' (1897: 14).

Marcelo notes that the village is governed by a largely premodern economy in which natural produce is used as a form of exchange alongside money: 'eran moneda corriente los frutos de la tierra, como en los pueblos primitivos' (217–18). Paper money does not exist. Marcelo's initial tips to his local guides are paid in silver coin: 'hard metal' but, for Pereda's readers in 1895, effectively token money since the metal value of silver fell on the international market throughout the period 1873–1900 (Tortella Casares 1974: i. 473, 476, 480–1). The fortune which Don Celso keeps in his safe is in jewels (precious metals and stones) and in old-style gold coin (359–60): the minting of gold coins, halted 1873–6 but in 1876–81 comprising 37 per cent of the total coinage minted, was definitively ended in 1882 due to declining gold reserves, with gold coins virtually disappearing from circulation by 1894 when the novel was being written, and disappearing from circulation altogether in 1896 (Tortella Casares 1974: i. 460, 479). In the case of both jewels and gold coin, exchange value matches intrinsic value (slightly less so in the case of gold coin, owing to the reduction of its metal content). In the later part of the novel, having accepted the mantle of patriarch, Marcelo takes to tipping the locals in gold coin. Don Celso's will (505–6) rewards his servants in land and gold coin (the male servant, Chisco, gets twice as much as Facia). This contrasts with the stories of Facia's criminal husband, a fraudulent gold prospector (289), who had corrupted the village women with his worthless trinkets, whose inherent value did not match their exchange value; and of Don Celso's renegade relatives who had traded their ancestral home against their debts to the local tavern (282–5), in a blatant underselling of the family manor's inherent worth. Chisco refuses the overtures of Tanasia's family, happy for him to marry her now he has inherited wealth, because he wants to be valued for his intrinsic and not his monetary worth (567): a little parable in its own right. Don Celso's dead wife 'valía un Potosí de oro puro' (222) and Lita is 'limpia como los oros' (245) for their value is inherent. Marcelo checks Lita's 'carat-value' ('calidad') by confronting her with a book of theatrical prints (509): her insistence that she would like to see such a spectacle but not be part of it confirms that her value is not just surface appearance.

Don Celso's safe does contain three papers: his will, an inventory of his possessions, and a *Memoria* listing the charitable donations he wishes Marcelo to continue. These are the only bits of paper in the novel presented as having value for they are private legal documents, not part of the State's legal apparatus, and they transmit the inheritance of the past. They are also 'naturalized' by being written in ink that Don Celso has made himself from natural substances collected in the mountains (357). The novel's descriptions tend, like these documents, to take the form of inventories, listing items rather than—as in Galdós's and Alas's descriptions—stressing the connections between them. For *Peñas arriba* constructs a world held together by family ties—which, being natural, 'just are'—outside the network of interrelationships established by the modern exchange economy. In particular, the novel's landscape descriptions verge on the impressionistic in their listing of heterogeneous elements viewed from the standpoint of a spectator but not always subordinated to the laws of perspective. On Marcelo's climactic excursion with Don Sabas (210), he notes that the 'faja azul' of the sea appears to be higher than the coastline, forming a disconcerting continuum with the 'otras [fajas] mucho más blancas' of the mist enveloping the hills. The mist clears to reveal a motley collection of 'notas difusas'—'las manchas verdosas de las praderas, los puntos blancos de sus barriadas, los toques negros de las arboledas, el azul carminoso de los montes, las líneas plateadas de los caminos reales, las tiras relucientes de los ríos'—with no indication of their relative distance from each other or from the spectator. As Marcelo discovers, the 'book of nature' does not immediately make sense but needs a 'translator', like the priest Don Sabas, capable of revealing the hidden source that gives it meaning. The occasional impressionism resulting from Pereda's rejection of a value system based on the relationships between things coincides surprisingly with the beginnings of the move towards abstraction in late nineteenth-century painting, in its attempt to convey the increasingly abstract nature of modern forms of representation. There are moments when Pereda's inventories threaten to break up beneath the weight of disconnected detail: as, for example, in the narration of the preparations for Don Celso's last rites, consisting in a disjointed list of phrases with no main verbs lasting for nearly a page (484–5). It is as though Pereda can risk incoherence at this point because the meaning of his chaotic enumeration of contiguous but disparate actions is guaranteed by the fact that they are making ready for the presence of God in the house. The landscape description which comes closest to abstraction is the one where Marcelo and Don Sabas experience the mirage-like atmospheric effects as a revelation of God's glory.

Ong (1982: 16–30, 79–81) has suggested that the Platonic concept of mimesis as the reflection of a hidden truth marks—and coincides with the beginnings of—the move from orality to literacy, since writing consists of signs representing an underlying, invisible, absent meaning. Writing has to be deciphered, just as Don Sabas 'translates' the 'book' of nature. Ong also notes that modernist writers' attempts—as in stream-of-consciousness—to return to the 'fullness of meaning' of orality, where there appears to be no gap between signifier and signified, differ fundamentally from the orality of pre-literate communities, for such 'secondary orality' depends for its effect on readers' sense of its difference from written norms. Pereda's rejection of modern exchange value for a pre-modern value system based on inherent worth is part of the realist project because it derives its meaning from his urban readers' acceptance of modernity as the norm. Both realism and modernism are as concerned with restoring 'fullness of meaning' to the empty signifiers of modernity as they are with expressing the conversion of reality into representation: hence the appeal of both to writers of reactionary as well as progressive persuasions. Pereda is as much a modern writer as Alas or Galdós—the latter also fascinated with the 'superior' expressiveness of the speech of the illiterate or semi-literate (the lower classes and women)—because even the most progressive writers construct modernity as a problem. If the defining characteristic of modernity is its rejection of value systems based on inherent worth, it can be nothing else.

9
Problematizing the Natural: Pardo Bazán's *Los Pazos de Ulloa* (1886) and *La madre naturaleza* (1887)

I HAVE taken *Los Pazos de Ulloa* and its sequel *La madre naturaleza* last, out of chronological sequence, since they do not fit the relatively tidy schemes proposed by either Valera or Pereda. In these novels the setting is not a village but the countryside proper, for their major concern is the question of what constitutes 'the natural'—an issue crucial to a period which used the distinction between 'natural' and 'unnatural' forms of behaviour as its major tool of 'normalization'. I suggest that Pardo Bazán was attracted to naturalism because it threw into focus, as the Church realized when it attacked it, the contradictions inherent in the contemporary appeal to 'nature' as a means of social legitimization. For the equation of 'the normal' with 'the natural', as in the concept of natural law which underlies naturalism and so much nineteenth-century thought, supposes that it is not just habitual but inevitable; in which case 'normalization'—making 'normal' that which anyway is inevitable—is a contradiction in terms. We are back to the nineteenth century's hesitations as to whether nature, and by extension society, are self-regulating mechanisms or whether there is a need for human intervention. This hesitation is expressed by Gabriel when, at the end of *La madre naturaleza*, he asks whether nature is a 'mother' (mother knows best) or a 'stepmother' (negligent if not malignant). In the same novel, Gabriel notes the illogicality of his momentary desire to undo progress and return to nature for, if evolution is a natural law, how can progress be 'unnatural' (Pardo Bazán 1985: 215)? His contradictions here are those of contemporary society in defining 'the natural' simultaneously as the opposite of civilization and as the socially acceptable, while also viewing degeneration as the result of excessive progress and of retarded development.

These contradictions run through Zola's work, heavily influenced by degeneracy theory, in its opposition of a neurotic degenerate modernity to healthy natural instinct while at the same time showing the latter to be degenerate in the sense of brutish ('la bête humaine'). Pardo Bazán's treatment of the city/country divide highlights this ambivalence. *La madre naturaleza* is based on Zola's *La Faute de l'abbé Mouret* only in a limited sense, for the latter's simple lament for lost natural innocence is not typical of the normally complex view of nature found in his work. In *La cuestión palpitante*, Pardo Bazán questioned Zola's uncritical acceptance of modern scientific theory (Pardo Bazán 1966: 39–41). I shall argue that her critique of naturalism is based not so much on a Catholic defence of free will (for *Los Pazos de Ulloa* shows that belief in this principle did not prevent the Church from restricting the free will of women) as on her objection to the contemporary use of biological argument to 'naturalize' women's subordination. Her two sequel novels show how their city-educated male characters construct nature in the image of their own beliefs or fears, in order to legitimize 'normalizing' notions of 'natural' femininity. In particular, they show how nature and woman are equated through the identification of both with motherhood: the first novel focuses on constructions of woman as mother; the second on constructions of 'mother nature'. Critics have seen Pardo Bazán as a writer riven with contradictions, notably that between her espousal of naturalism and her professed Catholicism (Osborne 1964; Pattison 1971). I shall argue that her two sequel novels, although they do contain contradictions, are more usefully read as a critique of the contradictory appeal to theories of 'the natural' by the various contemporary discourses regulating women: those of medicine (the science which provided Zola's model) and the Church, and in the second novel also that of liberal political theory. In assembling their spokesmen—Juncal, Julián, and Gabriel—at Manuela's bedside at the end of the second novel, Pardo Bazán is not so much revealing her own indecisions as exposing the contradictions between, and within, their various positions. As a woman, on the receiving end of such controlling discourses as well as a member of the social establishment, she was well placed to perceive such contradictions. *Los Pazos de Ulloa* and *La madre naturaleza* not only point to the inconsistencies in the various male discourses of social

Problematizing the Natural 339

control depicted, but also show some surprising coincidences between apparently incompatible positions.

The relationship between city and country in Pardo Bazán's rural novels is considerably more complex than that proposed by Valera and Pereda. Instead of the straightforward abandonment of city for country by a male protagonist, we have multiple two-way movements between city and country by male and female characters. In the first novel, Julián arrives in the country from the provincial capital Santiago; goes back to the city taking Don Pedro with him, allowing the city to be viewed through a countryman's eyes; and returns to the country followed by Don Pedro and the city-bred Nucha. It ends with Julián and Nucha attempting, but failing, to escape the countryside. The second novel starts with Gabriel's arrival at the Pazos de Ulloa from the national capital Madrid, and ends with his return to it; Perucho flees the country for Madrid, and Manuela chooses to leave for a Santiago convent so he can return (but we do not know if he will). Both novels end with the characters in places they do not want to be in, whether country or town, for neither is a satisfactory option.

Although questions of husbandry and husbanding are raised, Pardo Bazán—unsurprisingly for a writer who in the 1890s would become one of Spain's leading feminists—gives much more prominence to the position of the female (and of the feminine man). I hope to show how Pardo Bazán's sequel novels anticipate many of the arguments enunciated in her later essays. The marriage of city male to country female found in Valera and Pereda appears in *La madre naturaleza* with Gabriel's proposed marriage to Manuela. But it is reversed in the marriage of rural male (Pedro) to city female (Nucha) in the first novel, which posits an equation between man as 'brute' nature and woman as civilization, inverting normal suppositions.[1] Both of these marriages of city to country are based on the man's egoism in projecting onto woman a reverse image of himself intended to redeem him. That of Pedro to Nucha goes horribly wrong; that of Gabriel to Manuela fails to materialize because she rejects the role in which he casts her.

---

[1] Charnon-Deutsch (Millington and Smith 1994: 82–3) notes that, in *Los Pazos de Ulloa*, the feminine (Nucha, Julián) has no affinity with nature but is overwhelmed by it, whereas the masculine characters are entirely at home in it.

Like Valera's and Pereda's protagonists, Pedro and Gabriel opt for endogamy (marriage to a first cousin and niece respectively) as a 'civilizing' measure designed to combat the invasion of the lower classes (Sabel and Perucho). But in both cases the attempt to 'keep it in the family' fails, for social mobility, which Pardo Bazán clearly deplores, has to be recognized as the price of modernity. The most extreme case of incest—that between Manuela and Perucho as half-brother and half-sister—represents a contrary abandonment of civilization for nature, proclaiming the right to cross-class alliances (mitigated here by the fact that they are legitimate and illegitimate offspring of the same landowning father), and to a 'fraternal' relationship between the sexes which defies the 'civilized' notion of 'natural' sexual difference. Pardo Bazán uses the fact that incest is both 'unnatural'—unacceptable— and 'natural'—pigs and birds do it (1985: 241, 299)—to expose the slipperiness of the terms: Gabriel calls it 'natural' and 'una monstruosidad' in virtually the same breath (1985: 241–2).[2] Additionally, multiple figurative incest occurs in the bond between the city-bred Gabriel and Nucha, who is his figurative mother as well as sister and wears his ring (a marriage gift from her 'amante hermano') next to her wedding ring (Pardo Bazán 1986: 235). That Gabriel should be shocked by the incest of Nucha's daughter Manuela with her half-brother Perucho when he finds 'natural' his own wish to marry Manuela as the 'living portrait' (1985: 97) of his dead sister and as his figurative sibling is just one of his inconsistencies. Incest, actual or figurative, occurs across the full range of combinations: country male–country female (Perucho–Manuela), country male–city female (Pedro–Nucha), country female–city male (Manuela–Gabriel), city female–city male (Nucha–Gabriel), undermining the city–country opposition on which the novels are ostensibly based. The situation is further

---

[2] The difficulty of deciding whether incest is or is not unnatural no doubt explains why it was not till a relatively late stage in the social regulators' attempt to categorize human behaviour as 'normal' or 'deviant' that incest was criminalized. Twitchell (1987: 130) notes that incest was one of the last crimes to be codified in English criminal law (in 1908). Previously it was seen as a crime against God and handled by the ecclesiastical authorities—as it is in *La madre naturaleza*.

complicated by the fact that the incests between first cousins (Pedro–Nucha) and between literal uncle and niece and figurative siblings (Gabriel–Manuela) are shown to be socially acceptable but bad matches, while that between half-brother and -sister (Perucho–Manuela) is universally condemned but comprises the 'perfect couple'. The novels' refusal to fit into tidy categories is, I suggest, the point. Valera and Pereda propose solutions; Pardo Bazán depicts a world where there are only problems for if 'the natural' can mean both good and bad, and is and is not in opposition to society, no solution—natural or otherwise—can be wholly satisfactory.

Given Pardo Bazán's interest in the contradictory discourses of a male-defined modernity which uses nature as a way of talking about itself, it is not surprising that *Los Pazos de Ulloa* should combine the incest found in Valera's and Pereda's rural novels with the adultery depicted in Galdós's and Alas's novels of modern urban life. Pardo Bazán's focus is, however, on the male adulterer, dissociating adultery from the 'woman question': here, men are the problem. Like incest, adultery functions as an unstable signifier: in its figurative version (Julián's love for Nucha), it represents the social regulator's intrusion into the home, found in so many urban novels; in its literal version (Pedro's return to the peasant Sabel), it represents a converse regression to nature. Incest and adultery blur—as they do in some urban novels—not only because the regression to nature is figured by both but also because Julián and Pedro are adulterously attracted to women who are part of the family, Julián having been brought up in Nucha's household as the housekeeper's son, and Sabel being Pedro's servant. Incest occurs across the board because in these novels almost everyone, for different reasons, is trying to keep the outside world of modernity out. Although *Los Pazos de Ulloa* and *La madre naturaleza* are rural novels concerned predominantly with the resistance to, or rejection of, modernity, they have much in common with *La Regenta*, which Pardo Bazán read in the course of writing the first of her two sequel novels. She herself was alarmed to discover that her quasi-adulterous priest had been partially anticipated by Alas's Magistral (Mayoral 1989: 18–19). But there is a more fundamental similarity in both writers' depiction of the contradictory messages inscribed on women by the various discourses of social control.³ Indeed, Pardo Bazán's novels can be seen as a feminist reply to Alas's seeming agreement with his social regulators in their construction of woman as sick. Alas is concerned with a world in which nothing is natural any more. Pardo Bazán depicts the natural world of Galicia but shows how even the backward rural areas are incorporated into modernity.

By setting her two novels in 1866–70 (with an epilogue in 1880) and 1885 respectively,⁴ Pardo Bazán is able to trace the development of modernity from the period around the 1868 Revolution to the start of the Regency (both mentioned). Her decision to set the first novel around 1868 associates the onset of modernity with the 1868 Revolution which opened Spain up to modern ideas; it is no coincidence that so many novels written under the Restoration return to this time. The second novel takes us further into the Restoration than any of the texts studied so far. Both novels follow their openings with chapters outlining the key features of modernity: *Los Pazos de Ulloa* with Julián tracing in the Ulloa Manor library the legal and economic changes comprising the family's recent history, and with the banquet at Naya outlining the political scenario; *La madre naturaleza* with the biography of Gabriel Pardo, comprising an intellectual biography of the modern nation. The section of *Los Pazos de Ulloa* devoted to the 1869 election campaign is similarly crucial, showing how the extension of democracy—this was the first election held in Spain under universal manhood suffrage—has brought politics to the remotest backwaters. Critics have tended to dismiss the chapters dealing with politics as

---

³ In the first of her four essays 'La mujer española' (1889), Pardo Bazán notes husbands' fears of 'la negra sombra del director espiritual, un rival en autoridad, tanto más temible cuanto que suele reunir el prestigio de una conducta pura y venerable al de una instrucción superior [. . .] Así que de todas las prácticas religiosas de la mujer, la que el hombre mira con más recelo es la confesión frecuente [. . .] no sabré ponderar la impaciencia y enfado con que los hombres ven este influjo, ni las insinuaciones malévolas y hasta calumniosas con que disputan a los Jesuitas el dominio del alma femenil' (1981: 36–7).

⁴ Manuela is born in October 1869 and is 11 in the epilogue to *Los Pazos de Ulloa*, dating it in 1880. *La madre naturaleza* takes place 'around 18 years' after the first novel's start in 1866 (1985: 125). The date must be 1885 rather than 1884, since Juncal mentions the Regency (1985: 111): Alfonso XII's mother María Cristina was appointed Regent in 1885 on his premature death. We are told that Perucho is 'four or six' years older than Manuela (1985: 211), which makes him 20–2 in 1885; nevertheless he is described at not yet having facial hair.

costumbrista local colour or unnecessary parentheses (Mayoral 1989: 27); they are neither, for they show the incorporation of the regions into the modern central State.[5]

What Julián discovers in the library is, on the one hand, the intellectual background to modernity (the Enlightenment texts of Pedro's liberal forebear) and, on the other, the conversion of the family's land into a 'caos de papeles' (1986: 157). We are given a detailed account of the traditional Galician system of land tenure, based on the leasehold *foro*, further sublet into *subforos*. Pardo Bazán describes this as a 'maze' (157): Rueda (1986: 128–31) has shown how, in Galicia, *foros* originally leased to peasants frequently passed back into the hands of the landowning nobility through secondary leases or as security on loans, then being further sublet back to the peasantry. In customary law the Galician *foro* was unredeemable, passing on the leaseholder's death to his heirs. The system largely survived the mid-nineteenth-century disentailments, despite successive legislation attempting to subject it to contract law by giving leaseholders the right to buy the land, for few peasant leaseholders had the money to do so. Those leases that were redeemed passed into the hands of a new class of intermediaries (businessmen, State employees, and members of the liberal professions, especially lawyers) who continued to sublet the land but had the power to evict the original tenants. Clavero (1982: 83–154) has shown that successive centralizing legislation, in its attempt to reach some compromise with foral law, produced an inextricable tangle of hereditary and contractual principles. Rueda notes that, in Galicia, the disentailment laws did not lead to major changes in landownership as such, for what changed hands was, in almost all cases, not the freehold but the leasehold or usufruct.[6] This creates a complex situation in which the old

---

[5] Henn (1988: 15–33) is the only critic who treats the novel's representation of national politics seriously.

[6] For discussion of liberal legislation's attempt to solve the anomaly in a market system of the Galician *foros*, see Clavero (1982: 83–154). Clavero (126–32) notes that, after the 1873 Federal Republic's law making all leaseholds redeemable by their peasant tenants, quickly rescinded in 1874, the *censos* (the generic term for the many local forms of leasehold) became a major subject of public debate and monographs, including *El Código civil en sus relaciones con las legislaciones forales* (1883) by Alonso Martínez, the architect of the 1889 Civil Code which fudged the issue by facilitating landowners' eviction of tenants without making it easier for tenants to buy out their leases.

squirearchy retained nominal landownership but effective land rights passed to a new middle class. This turns land, like money, into a piece of paper whose value is nominal and not intrinsic. The precariousness of this conversion of land into paper is shown by the lamentable state of the title deeds and leases, half devoured by vermin, in the Ulloa Manor library. Don Pedro owns the land but not the money and the power that comes with it. His ownership of the land is made even more nominal by the fact that it is mortgaged (1986: 161). The title of Marquis has also become divorced from ownership of the land, though the peasants, respecting customary law, continue to see the title as 'inherent' in the land (1986: 163). This can have happened only as a result of the mid-century disentailment laws that made it possible to 'free' land from the *mayorazgo* system of inheritance from father to eldest son; we are told that the title passed to its present incumbent in Madrid 'por rigurosa agnación' (patrilineal male-only descent). The second novel tells us that Pedro's ancestors protested against the abolition of seigneurial rights by keeping a scaffold on their territorial boundary till the mid-century (1985: 227): Bernaldo de Quirós's classic 1907 study (1975: 100–1) describes how former local systems of justice were abolished in the late eighteenth and early nineteenth centuries with the national codification of the penal system. The selling of disentailed land on the market in the mid-nineteenth century completed this process by bringing land formerly under seigneurial control under the control of the State. Pedro's ownership of the land through the market signifies his loss of seigneurial rights (which he continues however to exercise through his 'ownership' of Sabel's body).

The novels show the old aristocratic order to be based on male privilege in the form of a system of male-only inheritance. Ironically, the same system of 'agnación' responsible for the family title passing to another branch of the family is upheld by Pedro, contravening the abolition of the *mayorazgos* by mid-century liberal legislation, when he rejects Manuela as heir.[7] In

---

[7] In 1885—just before Pardo Bazán wrote her two novels—Cánovas, on the death of Alfonso XII, declared the pregnant Queen María Cristina Regent, rather than give the throne to their daughter, fearing a dispute over the succession to the throne (as had occurred in 1833, triggering the first Carlist War) should María Cristina subsequently give birth to a son (which she did in the form of the future Alfonso XIII) (Carr 1966: 359).

La madre naturaleza, Juncal tells us that Pedro plans to leave his whole estate to the illegimate Perucho, totally disinheriting his legitimate daughter (1985: 102). Nucha's city-bred aristocratic father also leaves the whole family estate to his only son Gabriel, despite the fact that he is the youngest child (1986: 233).[8] Nucha's father is a civilized version of Pedro (1986: 207) not just physically but because both, as traditionalist aristocrats, privilege the male. Indeed, in marrying Nucha to Pedro while knowing about his concubinage with Sabel (1986: 247), and in failing to intervene despite the rumours in Santiago that Pedro is physically abusing Nucha (1986: 407), her father condones Pedro's behaviour. In lamenting the aristocratic order's replacement by one based on the market while criticizing its defence of male privilege, Pardo Bazán is being less contradictory than it might seem for, as we shall see, she shows how modernity disguises—and indeed exacerbates—women's traditional subordination with new arguments.

Clavero (1982: 119–20) notes that the debate on the erosion of local customary law (*fueros*) by liberal centralizing legislation was in Galicia largely limited to the question of land tenure (*foros*). Pardo Bazán's criticism seems directed at the new economic order, not at central government interference in traditional local rights. The theft of the gold coins hoarded by Pedro's mother (1986: 159–60) shows that even gold cannot be kept exempt from the new economic mobility, while constructing the latter as illicit. The illegitimate Perucho is throughout *Los Pazos de Ulloa* associated with money (not gold but copper); he is an 'hijo natural' but he is not simply a 'child of nature'. His grandfather Primitivo (a moneylender) bribes him with a coin in the kitchen at the start, as does Nucha later. It is in order to earn the coins Primitivo has promised him that Perucho betrays Julián and Nucha, who as a result stand accused of adultery. This implicitly associates the new money economy with illegitimacy and adultery. The coins that really attract Perucho are not those he has been promised but the 'ochavos roñosos' which, though they have less value, seem more valuable to him because 'Las adquisiciones y placeres de Perucho los representaba

---

[8] Bahamonde Magro and Martínez (1994: 465) note that a kind of 'mayorazgo encubierto' continued to operate after the mid-century, with wills leaving most of the 'tercio de mejoras' (the one-third of property that could be allocated freely) to the eldest son.

generalmente un ochavo' (1986: 392). In his appreciation of money not for its metal content but for what it can buy (what it 'represents'), Perucho has perfectly assimilated the lessons of the modern exchange economy. He steals the eggs from the chicken-run not for their use value but for their exchange value, selling them on the market (1986: 262).

The fall of the house of Ulloa is due not to the invasion of nature (that is the result), nor even entirely to Pedro's uncle's mismanagement, but to the transition from an economic system based on inherent value (represented by the aristocratic equation of worth with birth) to one based on nominal value (where status derives from money and what it can buy). The new order is incarnated in Primitivo, who despite his name is not a straightforward symbol of rural backwardness since his 'astucia salvaje más propia de un piel roja que de un europeo' (1986: 32) makes him a '*cacique* subalterno' (1986: 348). His 'barbarism' resides in the economic and political power he wields as a result of the transition to a modern capitalist system based on the exchange economy and parliamentary democracy: his power increases dramatically after the 1868 Revolution, particularly with the 1869 elections (1986: 255–6). He fits Varela Ortega's description of the *cacique* as a modern phenomenon, often of humble origins,[9] frequently a moneylender able to put pressure on his debtors, and almost always an administrator. We see Primitivo in his office as unofficial administrator of Don Pedro's estate, surrounded by mountains of coins and papers (1986: 390–1). Varela Ortega cites complaints about *caciques* 'sin posición ni nombre' controlling districts 'sin propiedad en ellos, sin fortuna', and coming to Madrid in peasant dress and *alpargatas* (1977: 365–6). Although Primitivo does not own land yet, he is set to do so: he supports Pedro as electoral candidate in order to lend him money for his campaign, with his land standing as security (1986: 357); it is in his interest to betray him for, if Pedro does not win a parliamentary salary, he will default on his debt. The money which Primitivo lends Pedro is in fact stolen from him in the first place: another image of the new circulation of wealth as illegitimate usurpation, in which it is impossible to say what belongs to whom. By making

---

[9] Sagasta's Ministro de Gobernación (or 'gran elector' as the post was popularly known) was the son of a Toledo peasant (Varela Ortega 1977: 365).

Pedro's illegitimate son Perucho Primitivo's heir, Pardo Bazán ensures that the latter's ill-gotten gains will return to their 'rightful' owner; she also kills Primitivo off before he can claim Pedro's land as his. In so doing, she is shoring up her own landowning class's threatened position.[10]

The banquet at Naya introduces us to the local public figures. In addition to the clergy (more interested in politics than religion) and the aristocracy (the anachronistic Carlist Ramón Limioso and Don Pedro), these comprise: the doctor Máximo Juncal, the notary, the judge, a law student, and the Conservative *cacique* Barbacana who is a lawyer. The preponderance of legal representatives is noticeable: the law was the State's centralizing tool. Varela Ortega (1977; 388–9) states that Orense province, where the novels are set, was a Conservative nucleus though Liberal Party organizations generally predominated in Galicia and republicanism was strong in La Coruña and El Ferrol.[11] Republicanism is represented at the banquet by Juncal,[12] and the conversation informs us about the Liberal *cacique* Trampeta. The latter is the Secretario del Ayuntamiento; as his nickname indicates, he wields power by threatening his enemies with legal proceedings. Both *caciques* are linked with the law, whose function is to 'empapelar' (1986: 346): again power is exercised through paper. Varela Ortega notes that the complex nature of the Galician land tenure system lent itself to legal

---

[10] The Pardo Bazán family manor, the Pazo de Meirás, was purchased by popular subscription and donated to General Franco by the Civil Governor of La Coruña in 1938 (Preston 1993: 316–17). Pardo Bazán campaigned insistently for her father's pontifical title to be converted into a hereditary peerage, entitling her to call herself Countess; this was granted in 1908. Being of recent pontifical origin, her title was not attached to landownership as in the case of the traditional nobility; hence perhaps her evident regret at the separation of the Ulloa family title (described as one of the oldest in Spain) from the land (Schiavo in Pardo Bazán 1981: 10).

[11] Pardo Bazán had shown the strength of federal republicanism among women cigarette-makers in La Coruña in her 1882 novel *La tribuna*. 'La mujer española' mentions the strength of republicanism among working-class women in general (Pardo Bazán 1981: 65).

[12] In making Juncal a Republican, Pardo Bazán is reflecting current political fears of a Republican resurgence. A failed Republican coup took place in 1883, and another in 1885 whose leaders were sentenced to death; the 1885 municipal elections were won with a big majority by the Liberals in alliance with the Republicans. Varela Ortega suggests that the main reason for Cánovas's 1885 Pacto del Pardo with Sagasta, committing the latter to support the Regency on Alfonso XII's death, was to break this electoral alliance which threatened the monarchy (1977: 171, 193, 195, 284).

blackmail; as in *Los Pazos de Ulloa*, the typical Galician *caciques* were 'El picapleitos de capital de provincia y el secretario de ayuntamiento, experto en trucos legales' (1977: 389).[13] In her perceptive reply (the only one by a woman) to Costa's 1901 questionnaire *Oligarquía y caciquismo*, Pardo Bazán noted that the uneducated peasant is not afraid of physical violence against individual representatives of the law but 'tiembla ante el papel sellado'; his inability to fathom the abstract nature of the State means that in his eyes 'es terrorífica la organización del Estado' (Costa 1902: 370). In this reply (Costa 1902: 373–81), Pardo Bazán saw *caciquismo* as endemic in Galicia given the peasantry's lack of education; the *cacique* had a crucial function because he enabled the rural populace to relate to the State through an individual representative who made its abstract nature manageable by personalizing it. Unamuno's reply to Costa's questionnaire (Costa 1902: 486–93)—probably the most insightful of all the replies received—makes this point explicitly. He rejects the current idea that *caciquismo* is a disease, proposing that it is the logical consequence of the rural masses' lack of education, without which the system would not function (a 'mal necesario' and 'la única forma de gobierno posible, dado nuestro íntimo estado social'). For, if the law is a 'cosa abstracta y escrita', by contrast 'El cacique es la ley viva, personificada, es algo que se ve y se toca y á quien se siente' (Costa 1902: 487–8).

The most obviously fraudulent exercise of power through bits of paper is the 'trueque de papeletas' (1986: 369) that takes place at the 1869 elections, when Trampeta switches the voting urns. This, plus the accompanying forms of intimidation described in the novel, is included in Varela Ortega's list of common types of fraudulent electoral practice (1977: 411–12). Varela Ortega also notes (403) that the 1869 election was one of the few not marked by government interference, giving the local *caciques* a free hand. In *Los Pazos de Ulloa*, however, we see Trampeta in close consultation with the Provincial Governor who in turn is acting on instructions from the revolutionary government in Madrid, who have imposed a *diputado cunero* (as government-appointed candidates were called) from Madrid

---

[13] Velasco Souto (1987: 146) notes that Pardo Bazán's *caciques* are *funcionarios* or wealthy peasants who function as intermediaries between the dominant social groups and the rural masses.

who never visits the district. It was, of course, the remoteness of central government that made *caciquismo* necessary. The system of *encasillados* whereby the government was responsible for nominating candidates, allocating a proportion of places to the opposition, was criticized at the time on the grounds that elections were not contested through the ballot box but 'written' (Gortázar 1994: 184).

This imposition of a candidate from the capital is Pardo Bazán's one explicit criticism of political centralization. In essays of 1899, she lamented the suppression of Basque foral rights (1981: 67) but made it clear that she did not support Galician regionalist aspirations (1972: 79–81). Although she includes some *galleguismos* in these two novels,[14] including a song in Galician (1985: 257), she refers to Galician throughout as a 'dialect', not a 'language'. We are told that Manuela speaks to Perucho 'en dialecto' (1985: 13) and to Gabriel in Castilian with a strong local accent (1985: 148), but in both cases her speech is given in standard Spanish. In *La madre naturaleza*, Perucho and Manuela commit incest on the site of what we are told was probably an ancient Roman fort where the Romans were routed by the native Cantabro-Galician hordes, though it may have been a pre-Roman stronghold built to preserve 'la independencia gallega' (1985: 203, 206). The ambiguity as to whether or not we should approve their incest is reflected in the ambiguity as to whether this ancient battleground represents the defence of local freedoms against centralizing modernizers or the defeat of civilization by barbarism; in effect, the novel shows civilization and barbarism to go hand in hand. In both novels, educated characters are consistently presented as sympathetic while the villains are uneducated. It is Gabriel's education and reading that make him concerned with the state of the nation; his project for 'civilizing' Manuela includes teaching her standard Spanish (1985: 128). But Pardo Bazán is clearly worried by the ideological centralization produced by the national press—another conversion of politics into paper. As Goros says, 'Los papeles son la perdición de hoy en día' (1985: 291). Despite his education, the doctor Juncal uncritically assimilates the jargon of the anticlerical republican papers to which he subscribes; the satire of the semi-literate El Gallo's

---

[14] For a list of *galleguismos* in *Los Pazos de Ulloa*, see Casares in Mayoral (1989: 129–39).

ill-digested readings of the political press is vicious. The problem is the combination of local ignorance with the influx of new political ideas: politics is described as an 'hechicera' even more powerful than the local witch María la Sabia, whose superstitions are also deplored.[15]

The advent of politics leads to the expulsion of María la Sabia and her all-female *tertulia* from the kitchen; by the time of *La madre naturaleza* (1885), it has been replaced by the all-male 'ateneo' of El Gallo and his fellow peasants, where the national newspapers are read out loud for the benefit of the illiterate, and moral and political science are discussed (1985: 254). It is not clear that this is an improvement. Hall (1992: 159) notes that, in the course of the nineteenth century, with the rise of male clubs which gave middle-class men a social and political identity, civil liberty came increasingly to be associated with 'manliness'.[16] Women were not admitted as members of the Madrid Ateneo, the major national forum for public debate, until Pardo Bazán was admitted as its first female member in 1895 (Pardo Bazán 1981: 13). In her openly feminist essays and speeches of the late 1880s on, Pardo Bazán repeatedly stressed that liberal democracy, in extending civil rights to the male populace, had disadvantaged women by creating a previously non-existent gap between public (male) and private (female) spheres.[17] The pre-modern world is not idealized in her novels but at least it does not confine women to the private sphere: Sabel enjoys a freedom of movement that Nucha and her city-bred sisters never have. This class distinction is also a distinction between the pre-modern and bourgeois orders: the de la Lage family, though arrogant about its aristocratic status, has assimilated bourgeois norms of domesticity based on the confinement of women to the house, where the daughters

---

[15] Pardo Bazán's depiction of the influence of federal republican ideas on women cigarette-makers in La Coruña in *La tribuna* (1882) had similarly implied that the uneducated were led astray by the political press. However, in a 1901 article 'Feminismo' she also noted that the bourgeoisie's refusal to grant women political rights forced feminists to look to socialist parties whose position on women was much more positive (Pardo Bazán 1972: 120-1).

[16] Ryan (1994) also notes that by the 1830s a new 'brotherhood' of all-male clubs was forged.

[17] See, for example, 'La mujer española' (1889) in Pardo Bazán (1981: 30-1, 33, 50-1); 'La educación del hombre y de la mujer' (speech at 1892 Congreso Pedagógico) in Pardo Bazán (1981: 75-7); 'Feminismo' (1901) in Pardo Bazán (1972: 121).

amuse themselves with caged birds figuring their own entrapment (1986: 213, 1985: 70–1). El Gallo's gentrification takes the form of a male supremacy 'ruling the roost' not through brute force like his father-in-law Primitivo, but by parading in fashionable clothes while he keeps his daughters shut up at home (1985: 132). Pereda's *tertulia* in the kitchen in *Peñas arriba* is presented as a welcome return to a pre-capitalist class harmony prior to the public/private split, a harmony also represented by the lack of separation between agricultural and domestic production. In Pardo Bazán's novels the kitchen *tertulia*, whether female or male, is seen as an invasion of the domestic hearth by the lower classes; the servants also spy on their superiors in their private apartments. And the storage of agricultural produce inside the home—like the cohabitation of humans and animals in the peasant cottages (1985: 18, 161)—represents the decline of the Limioso household in the first novel and of Don Pedro's household in the second (1986: 271, 1985: 136–7). Despite her critique of the sexual inequality exacerbated by the public/private division, Pardo Bazán still regards the latter as the measure of civilization.

It is because it blurs this division by privatizing the political that *caciquismo*, although a product of modernity, is seen in *Los Pazos de Ulloa* as barbaric. As the narrator notes, in a perfect illustration of the privatization of politics that Varela Ortega sees as *caciquismo*'s most negative legacy: 'Las ideas no entran en juego, sino solamente las personas' (1986: 343).[18] The government-imposed candidate in this 'Cortes de familia' is the Ministro de Gobernación's cousin (1986: 359). Pedro is expected to win the elections for the Carlists despite his total lack of political ideas—apart from a vague hope that the return to absolutism will restore the old seigneurial entailments and *mayorazgos* (1986: 349)—simply because the voters know him personally as a local man. The Carlists originally imposed a candidate who, though a Galician from the provincial capital Orense (another lawyer), was not known locally. Unlike the Liberal candidate from Madrid, Pardo Bazán implies that he was a good choice because he was educated and had solid political beliefs (1986: 347); the fault here lies with an electorate who votes for the

---

[18] In an 1891 interview with a German woman journalist, Pardo Bazán likewise insisted that in Spanish politics what counts is persons, not ideas (Pardo Bazán 1981: 206).

person and not for a political programme. Varela Ortega observes that the 1886 elections, when *Los Pazos de Ulloa* was being written, were notable for the amount of house-to-house canvassing by local candidates, taking politics not just to the remote rural areas but into the home (1977: 420–1). Pedro's home is invaded by strangers during his campaign, to Nucha's displeasure; in a thoroughly modern tactic, Pedro takes his baby daughter, dressed in a new frock, with him on his canvassing (the only time he pays her any attention). *Caciquismo* is directly associated with adultery, as a parallel erosion of the public/private boundary, through Primitivo's spreading of rumours about Julián's adultery with Nucha to undermine Pedro's electoral support. The *cacique* Primitivo—himself an outsider who invades the house—is, of course, responsible for his daughter Sabel's continued presence in the Pazos, against her will, as Pedro's adulterous mistress.

Pardo Bazán shows both political factions to be barbaric. The 'Apuntes autobiográficos' published with *Los Pazos de Ulloa* inform the reader that she had Carlist sympathies in the 1870s, but that her father was a parliamentary deputy for the liberal Progressive Party from 1869 (the election described in the novel) to 1871. Although we are told that the Liberal Trampeta more frequently resorts to violent methods, it is the Carlist Barbacana who uses the convicted murderer El Tuerto— described as especially sinister because he is an urban thug; that is, a modern degenerate (1986: 374)—to kill Primitivo for his electoral disloyalty. The mention of the Carlist *partidas* preparing to take to the hills in the third Carlist War of 1870–5 (1986: 283, 292) makes it clear that national unity is under threat from the extreme right as well as the extreme left in the form of federal republicanism, among the new ideas discussed by the locals (1986: 344). Given her professed Catholicism, Pardo Bazán's depiction of the local priests' blatant involvement in Carlist electoral manipulation—including the Arcipreste de Loiro's 'winning' an election by smashing the ballot box, for which he receives the 'gran cruz de Isabel la Católica' (1986: 360)—is a savage indictment. Politics, like the economy, is ruled by an exchange system—the exchange of favours and money, the replacement of one Carlist candidate by another (Pedro), the *cacique* Primitivo changing sides, and the final switching of voting urns—which makes both parties interchangeable in their barbarism. The start of *Los Pazos de Ulloa* is generally interpreted as a symbolic representation of Julián's 'descent' from civilization into barbarism, in the sense of a natural world untouched by civilization. It is more accurately read as a descent into the barbarism resulting from the attempt to implant a modern central State apparatus in a backward rural country. The first paragraph tells us that the road which plunges Julián into this 'fallen' world has been built by engineers knowingly flouting State regulations, bribed by a nearby political personage with electoral influence; we later learn that this is the *cacique* Barbacana. In *La madre naturaleza*, Gabriel quotes a politician's comment that maybe democracy will make us happy in 700 years' time: Spain's current barbarism is the result of over-hasty modernization, creating a 'país imposible' because it is an incompatible mix of the modern and the backward, in which modernization reinforces backwardness (1985: 101). Given this entanglement of opposites, it is not surprising that Julián and Nucha fail to put the house in order.

The novels' treatment of the class mobility that accompanies economic mobility is highly ambivalent. Nucha's father is criticized for refusing his daughters' middle-class pretenders, who represent the new liberal professions: a law student and a medical student, the latter a village blacksmith's son. And Gabriel finds it just that the illegimate Perucho, born to a peasant mother, should inherit part of his father's estate (1985: 103). Despite the legal rights enjoyed by illegitimate offspring in certain circumstances,[19] Casey notes that 'When the household and its property became the basic unit of society, there was really little place left for bastards' (1989: 112): Perucho's expulsion from the house in the course of *Los Pazos de Ulloa* signifies the transition to bourgeois modernity. In sending Perucho off to Madrid to be a shop assistant (1985: 302), Gabriel implies that it is acceptable for him to be raised to petty bourgeois status

---

[19] The 1889 Civil Code confirmed earlier legislation whereby illegitimate children born to parents where there was no legal impediment to their marriage were automatically entitled to inherit the father's property (assuming, of course, that the father recognized his paternity); such children were called 'hijos naturales'. Where there was a legal impediment to the parents' marriage (for example, if either was already married), there was no such entitlement; such children were called 'hijos no naturales' (Scanlon 1986: 134). Perucho's case is complicated since there was no legal impediment to his parents' marriage when he was born, but there is now since, although Pedro is a widower, Sabel has married El Gallo.

but no more. Perucho is redeemed by the fact that his love for Manuela is not motivated by desire for superior status or wealth. Sabel, too, is redeemed by wanting to marry a man of her own peasant class. And Julián's promotion from the servants' quarters to the family table as chaplain is no threat because of his reverence for the nobility (1986: 153). The desire for social advancement of the peasants Primitivo and El Gallo is, however, presented as intolerable. Primitivo is a kind of Gothic monster, emerging from the shadows or from the subterranean realm of the kitchen, whose domestic hearth has been invaded by peasants and turned into a witches' coven.[20] El Gallo's gentrification in the second novel is grotesque rather than Gothic, for by 1885 the lower classes have come out of the closet and are openly climbing the social ladder. Considerable attention is paid in *La madre naturaleza* to the kitsch trappings of El Gallo's apartment in the Pazos, reflecting the modern spatial relativism that allows an uncouth peasant home to boast an imitation Japanese porcelain lamp, an American calendar, a newspaper called *El Globo* with pictures of a Russian village on the Volga or Constantinople viewed from the Bosporus, and gilt or inlaid furniture aping the latest international chic: examples of 'el falso bienestar y el lujo de similor que hoy penetra hasta en las aldeas' (1985: 132–3). It is in El Gallo's parlour, where everything is an imitation, that Gabriel confronts Perucho over his violation of class boundaries in loving Manuela, which seems forgivable by contrast (he is, of course, a 'natural' aristocrat by birth). Although acknowledging modern mobility, Pardo Bazán betrays a hankering for a world in which personal status is based on birth or innate worth, and not on imitation. If Don Pedro's mother, prior to the 1868 Revolution, was obsessed with hoarding gold, now, in the 1880s, El Gallo's concern with status takes the form of a penchant for gilt and for changing his furniture. The novels contradict El Gallo's modern belief that status depends on 'apariencias' (the 'things' purchased or 'represented' by money) by suggesting that the 'distinction' that is a sign of 'true class' is innate and cannot be acquired. The judge's wife's grotesque overdressing (1986: 266), and the advent of progress to Cebre in the form of a pretentiously titled

---

[20] Goitre—the monstrous 'bocio' of the witch María la Sabia—is discussed as a public-health concern by Santero (1885: ii. 566–7), grouped together with cretinism: a major concern of degeneracy theorists.

'Círculo de instrucción y recreo, artes y ciencias' and 'algunas tiendecillas' claiming to be 'bazares', suggests that the new bourgeoisie can do no more than mimic the trappings of civilization (1986: 410–11).[21] El Gallo's attempts to speak standard Spanish only betray the 'extracción indeleble que le retenía en su primitiva esfera social', while his efforts at reading and writing confirm that 'el pueblo no sabe leer y escribir jamás, aunque lo aprenda' (1985: 127–8).

Charnon-Deutsch (Millington and Smith 1994: 81, 84, 87–90) argues that Pardo Bazán's class prejudice interferes with her destabilization of sexual difference in *Los Pazos de Ulloa*, since she depicts the female peasants Sabel and the wet-nurse as 'human cows' (1986: 171, 280, 285; 1985: 287), uncomfortably echoing contemporary views that women were defined by their 'natural' function as mothers.[22] Medical discourse, which was largely responsible for this 'naturalization' of women's confinement to the private sphere, is represented in both novels through the doctor Juncal, a social regulator whose authority is backed by his professional status.[23] He is throughout referred to by the modern term 'higienista', and we are told that he is well read in the latest medical theory, including Darwin; indeed, he is newly graduated from the University of Santiago de Compostela (1986: 279), which three years later in 1872 would become the first Spanish university to introduce Darwin to the curriculum (Glick 1982: 16).[24] The fact that Darwin's second book *The Descent*

---

[21] Artola (1973: 75) notes that the growth of towns in Galicia, as in Cantabria, was 'spectacular', with Orense—the provincial capital of the province in which *Los Pazos de Ulloa* and *La madre naturaleza* are set, and where Perucho is sent to school in the second novel—enjoying the biggest population increase 1837–77 of any provincial capital (with Oviedo in second place at 330%, as we have seen).

[22] The hygienist Pulido (1876: 48), a gynaecologist by profession, states that the best wet-nurses come from 'lugares montañosos' like the best cows, anticipating the identical comment by Augusto Miquis in Galdós's *El amigo Manso* (Pérez Galdós 1966: 1245–6).

[23] Pardo Bazán's ambivalent attitude to Juncal is discussed by Hemingway (in Mayoral 1989: 61–71), who sees him as a spokesman for naturalist ideas.

[24] The 1875 Orovio Decree, in addition to ordering rectors to ban lecturers from criticizing Catholic dogma, provoking the resignation of the Krausist professors at Madrid University, also intervened to ban the teaching of Darwin's theories at the University of Santiago by Augusto González de Linares (a student of the Krausist Giner de los Ríos) under the October 1868 Freedom of Education Act. Orovio ordered the deportation of several well-known lecturers; others resigned in solidarity. Cánovas consequently sacked Orovio, and the decree was revoked. See Glick (1982: 15 and in Lida and Zavala 1970: 270); Bahamonde Magro and Martínez (1994: 520); Varela Ortega (1977: 104–5).

of Man, and Selection in Relation to Sex (1871), which highlighted the female's role in reproduction and genetic inheritance, was translated into Spanish in 1876, before the translation the following year of the earlier *Origin of Species* (1859), is important, since from the start Darwin's reception in Spain was tied to his biological theories of sexual difference. Pardo Bazán's critique of Darwin in her early 1877 essay 'Reflexiones científicas contra el darwinismo' (mentioned in the *Apuntes autobiográficos* published with *Los Pazos de Ulloa*) has to be read in this context. *Los Pazos de Ulloa* shows how childbirth has been taken over by the male professional, whose decisions are unquestioningly obeyed. He subjects the wet-nurse to a medical examination, in line with contemporary health experts' recommendations (Monlau 1865: 515–20; Pulido 1876: 47–9; Santero 1885: ii. 489).[25] Nucha protests at Juncal's refusal, as a 'fanático de la higiene', to allow her to breastfeed, not even letting her try (1986: 295, 279); indeed, he takes the decision before she has given birth (1986: 280). He is here complying with current medical opinion that for frail, nervous women breastfeeding represented a dangerous loss of bodily fluids (Monlau 1865: 507; Pulido 1876: 46; Santero 1885: i. 404). The narrator makes it clear that the blockage of natural flow caused by her unused milk, and the consequent psychological distress, is a major cause of Nucha's post-partum illness (1986: 293). Prior to the actual childbirth, pregnancy had made her more healthy (1986: 273). Contrary to the traditional medical view that hysteria was caused by the failure to achieve maternity, Nucha becomes hysterical after giving birth, as she notes (1986: 317), for she understands her mental and physical condition better than Juncal thinks. Here Pardo Bazán's views are in line with contemporary medical theory which, as we have seen, had by the 1870s, in Spain as elsewhere, rejected the Galenic notion that hysteria was the result of a failure to conceive, instead viewing it as psychologically induced (Jagoe, Blanco, and Enriquez de Salamanca 1998: 339–48). While the novel could be seen as still linking hysteria with childbirth, it is clear, as Charnon-Deutsch observes (Millington and Smith 1994: 81–2) that her

---

[25] Perinat and Marrades (1980: 120) cite an 1875 article in the women's magazine *La Moda* giving advice on how to 'dirigir la higiene de la nodriza' since village women have no idea of hygiene.

condition is exacerbated by her doctor's refusal to let her breast-feed and her husband's neglect and physical abuse. In the second novel, her daughter Manuela has similar 'convulsiones' and 'soponcios' after discovering that she is Perucho's sister and that he has left (1985: 284, cf. 1986: 277). Juncal attributes this to her 'herencia materna' combined with puberty, implying a congenital feminine debility (1985: 285), but he does so before knowing about the emotional trauma which is clearly responsible for disrupting Manuela's habitual physical and psychological stability, previously stressed. Juncal's statements on Nucha's unsuitability for childbearing agree with current medical recommendations that frail, nervous women should consult doctors before marrying and having children (Monlau 1865: 33–5; Pulido 1876: 46; Santero 1885: i. 404), but he also insists that nature has equipped women with extra reserves of energy enabling them to recover from childbirth (1986: 291). Pardo Bazán would make this point in an 1892 review and in her speech to the 1892 Congreso Pedagógico, insisting that pregnancy was not an illness but a natural bodily function, and that, in a healthy body where childbirth was followed by breastfeeding, 'la normalidad se afirma, el cuerpo se robustece, la vida llega a su plenitud. Yo en esto hablo por experiencia' (having married at 15, she had a son and two daughters). She further argued that women were far from the weaker sex since they lived longer than men, despite the unhealthy sedentary regime to which bourgeois women were subjected (Pardo Bazán 1981: 77–9, 150–1). In maintaining that it is Nucha's 'unhygienic' city upbringing that has made her unsuitable for childbearing by contrast with 'healthy' peasant women (1986: 278–9), Juncal is echoing contemporary anxieties about the degenerative effects of city life, but he is also arguing that women are not 'naturally ill'. The novel shows the unfairness of contemporary assumptions that city women are sick, for the sedentary city life makes the male (Nucha's father) deteriorate physically too, and Nucha's city-bred sister Rita is a perfect healthy specimen.[26] Juncal notes that sickly, neurotic women are also found in the country (1986: 287).

In other essays of 1889 and 1901 (1981: 47–50, 69–70, 165; 1972: 121–2), Pardo Bazán combated the notion that women

---

[26] Pardo Bazán's speech to the 1892 Congreso Pedagógico criticized the notion that exercise was 'improper' for young ladies (1981: 150).

were physiologically incapacitated by pointing out that peasant and working-class women undertook the most strenuous forms of physical labour: 'Verdad es que en el terreno económico, ¿cuándo ha existido la desigualdad de los sexos? [. . .] la mujer ha trabajado siempre; las labores más duras, más penosas, nunca se le han vedado en nombre de la debilidad y delicadeza de su organismo' (1972: 121–2). She notes that in Galicia she has seen pregnant women and nursing mothers working in the fields, and women working as dockers, porters, and stone-breakers, but that women are denied access to white-collar jobs and the professions (1981: 69–70, 1972: 122). Carr (1966: 9–10) notes that Galicia was seen as 'primitive' in the rest of Spain because its women worked as farm labourers, railway porters, and roadmenders; Pardo Bazán points out that this is not a sign of a supposed primitive lack of sexual differentiation, but of economic necessity on the part of the poor (1981: 69–70). Shubert (1990: 38) points out that the high level of emigration in Galicia led to exceptionally high numbers of women working in agriculture especially; in 1887 (the date of *La madre naturaleza*), women made up 43 per cent of the workforce in the region. *La madre naturaleza* shows the local women doing the harvesting at night, and Manuela stacking hay alongside the men (1985: 15, 124). However, the novel also shows that this regime of physical labour, plus the demands of motherhood, makes peasant women deteriorate rapidly; Sabel may be a model of natural health in the first novel, but eighteen years later she is more of a wreck than any 'decadent' city-dweller. Pedro's purely physical existence also ages him more drastically than his prematurely balding and greying city cousin Gabriel. 'Nature' makes you healthy and unhealthy; in both cases, this is due to social and not innate physiological factors. Just as in her later essays Pardo Bazán stressed that peasant women worked out of economic necessity, so in *Los Pazos de Ulloa* the narrator explains how male emigration turns the women of the Castrodorna valley into 'Amazons' (1986: 299): this social history explains the wet-nurse's 'Amazonian' physique. The narrator also notes that, after marriage, these local 'Amazons' are 'tan honestas como selváticas' (1986: 298–9).[27]

[27] This point is made by Pardo Bazán in 'La mujer española' (1981: 69), where she notes that most Galician peasant women marry after having had children. The health expert Pulido (1876: 145) noted that Galicia had the highest rate of illegitimate births in 19th-century Spain, closely followed by Madrid; see also Carr (1966: 10).

Problematizing the Natural

Nevertheless, the 'savage' wet-nurse's imperviousness to Nucha's attempts to educate her into civility suggests a belief in innate lower-class inferiority. The narrator agrees with Nucha's description of her as a 'tonel de leche' (1986: 298), implying that peasant women have no function other than childrearing. It could, however, be argued that Pardo Bazán is here demonstrating that the biological aspect of motherhood is a natural function that, first, does not determine a woman's value and, secondly, does not need to be taught by men because the most inferior women can do it. In her 1892 Congreso Pedagógico speech (1981: 81), she insisted that women did not need to be educated to be mothers because they were programmed with maternal instincts; as early as *La cuestión palpitante* (1882), she had commented ironically on the generations of women who breastfed their children out of obedience to Rousseau (1966: 77). Juncal is undecided as to whether the wet-nurse's 'natural' approach to childrearing is good or bad (1986: 299), anticipating the second novel's indecisions as to whether nature is a mother or a stepmother. He is here recognizing the contradiction between his belief in 'la acción bienhechora de la naturaleza' (mother nature knows best) and his belief in the need for the medical expert to intervene (father scientist knows best); he delays intervening surgically in Nucha's difficult childbirth as long as possible. By the time of *La madre naturaleza*, he has forgotten his medical textbooks and become convinced that 'la naturaleza, así como es madre, es maestra del hombre, y el instinto y la práctica obran maravillas' (1985: 65, 95). His belief that nature is a mother supposes that the doctor's role is to be as non-interventionist as possible.

Juncal refers Gabriel to the superior skills of the local healer, whose fame has spread even to Madrid (1985: 25), noting that most doctors are hostile to traditional medicine not only because its practitioners are not professionals but also because they make no distinctions between men and beasts. What this means in effect is that the traditional healer does not regard medicine as a form of moral policing, like the contemporary medical experts who busied themselves writing manuals for women. The picturesque figure of Antón *el algebrista* on the one hand shows that Darwin's demonstration of the unity of creation is anticipated in traditional medicine, drawing on pre-Christian knowledge and beliefs (1985: 25). But he also makes no distinctions between male and female, seeing both as fulfilling the laws of nature through procreation (1985: 28). This implies that women are defined by their reproductive capacity but does not turn motherhood into a restrictive 'spiritual mission'. In an 1892 reply to a member of the Real Academia de Medicina (1981: 158–9), Pardo Bazán noted the illogicality of medical experts' simultaneous insistence that women were determined by physiology and that they were superior spiritual creatures: an illogicality which doctors resolved by constructing the female body as 'naturally sick' for it was difficult to argue that a woman determined by a healthy physiology needed containing (hence the threat posed by Rita). Shuttleworth (Shires 1992: 31–51) has shown how, in order to make them conform to a spiritual ideal, doctors subjected nineteenth-century mothers to a restrictive physical regime and then criticized them for not being models of 'natural' health. The injustice of this is shown in Pedro's desire to have a pious wife and subsequent rejection of Nucha because she cannot compete with Sabel's healthy, 'natural' performance in childbirth. It must be remembered that it is Pedro, and not Pardo Bazán, who reduces Sabel to her reproductive function here. We see that Pedro's preference for Sabel as superior childbearer submits her to a servitude as great as that of Nucha, the difference being that she is a sexual slave while Nucha is confined to the sickbed. Pedro has in many respects got the wife he wanted, for the logic of his view of the wife as pure yet defined by her physiology is that she be sick. Juncal reminds us that the wet-nurse, defined by her physiology, is also a slave (1986: 280–1). Earth mothers and sick mothers are equally condemned to servitude by their reduction to anatomy.

However, Juncal agrees with Pedro that 'el gran combate de la gestación y el alumbramiento [. . .] al cabo es la verdadera función femenina' (1986: 279), showing that the pre-modern belief in lineage and modern medicine coincide in reducing women's role to that of reproduction. Where they diverge is in Pedro's pre-modern belief that a girl child is inferior, contrasting with Juncal's modern belief that a girl child is equal but that females are 'naturally different': a perfect illustration of Laqueur's analysis (1990) of the pre-modern and modern orders which construct women as 'the same but inferior' and 'equal but different' respectively. Juncal all too easily writes Nucha off as sick but, as an atheist materialist who comes increasingly to question the medical expert's interventionist role, at least he does not give her moral prescriptions. And he marries a wife who is a picture of health but does not become a mother and has chosen to go on working after marriage (1985: 62). The narrator points out that Juncal does not apply the maxims of medical science to himself (1986: 279), meaning that he ignores its moralizing implications by continuing to drink and indulge in illicit sexual relations (at this stage he has not yet married his baker). His equation of morality with physiology—'Para Máximo Juncal, inmoralidad era sinónimo de escrofulosis, y el deber se parecía bastante a una perfecta oxidación de los elementos asimilables'—is immediately undermined by making it clear that he appeals to physiological argument to justify his moral weaknesses (1986: 279, 281, 285). Here Pardo Bazán is not just satirizing naturalist use of medical terminology; her critique of the reduction of morality to physiology has crucial implications for gender. Charnon-Deutsch (Millington and Smith 1994: 69–95) has argued convincingly that Pardo Bazán's depiction of Nucha as a 'born' mother despite her difficulties in childbirth, and of Sabel as a negligent mother despite the ease with which she gives birth, destabilizes the equation between motherhood as moral mission and motherhood as biological process.

As Charnon-Deutsch notes (Millington and Smith 1994: 90), the equation of biological and moral parenthood is further destabilized by the 'exercise in cross-dressing' constituted by Julián's role as surrogate father and co-mother to Nucha's baby. This shows not only that fathering is—or should be—a moral and emotional, and not just biological, matter, but also that gender roles are not wholly determined by biological sexual difference. Indeed, as Charnon-Deutsch points out (Millington and Smith 1994: 85, 90), it is because he 'mothers' Manuela that Julián is a good father: the only one in the novel. This unhinging of gender from biology is Pardo Bazán's most radical disagreement with naturalist physiological determinism. However, this unhinging is only partial since Julián is physiologically as well as psychologically androgynous: the brutish rural males' view of him as a 'niño', 'niña', or 'mariquitas' is confirmed by the narrator's insistence on his 'temperamento linfático-nervioso, puramente femenino' (1986: 146), which grounds temperament in physiology, and reference to his almost total lack of facial hair (1986: 198). The point Pardo Bazán seems to be making here is that theories of sexual difference do not function even at the biological level: the novel shows that, just as not all women are constitutionally frail and sickly, so conversely not all men are constitutionally tough. The hygienist Monlau (1868: 19–20) had seen 'linfatismo', described in terms similar to Galdós's description of Maxi (another sexually ambiguous 'saint') in *Fortunata y Jacinta*, as a major contemporary sign of degeneration. However, Pardo Bazán legitimizes Julián's femininity through her use of Christian references: just as St Joseph (whose role Julián is aware of occupying) provides a biblical precedent for the non-biological father, so the androgynous effigy of his patron saint, St Julian, provides a model for his conception of the priest's moralizing mission in terms of the feminine mission of 'ministering angel'. As 'ministering angels', both Nucha and Julián are not only childrearers but also household managers; in this latter capacity, Nucha's competence is noticeably greater.

There is, however, an important difference between the roles of Nucha and Julián as 'ministering angels' for, as priest, Julián is inscribed in the institutional apparatus of social control. Juncal and Julián are presented in the novel as parallel social regulators, the former caring for the body, the latter for the soul (1986: 285). But the moral advice imparted by Julián has important consequences for the body: in its name, he washes Perucho, advises Pedro to marry Nucha, and turns Nucha into the Christian image of 'la perfecta casada', echoing Fray Luis de León's famous 1583 conduct book of that name. *La perfecta casada* was still a recommended text for women in nineteenth-century Spain, as it would be under the Franco regime. In her 1889 essays 'La mujer española' (1981: 32)—written for the *Fortnightly Review* and reprinted in *La España Moderna*—Pardo Bazán commented that the modern bourgeois wifely ideal largely coincided with Fray Luis's recommendations and those of Juan Luis Vives's *Instrucción de la mujer cristiana* (1524), noting however in her 1892 Congreso Pedagógico speech that at least Vives defended women's education (1981: 78). The failure of Julián's moralizing mission is a comment not so much on his personal inefficacy as on a Church which invades the home by imposing gender norms on women. *Los Pazos de Ulloa* ends with a satire of the Church's targeting of women as an instrument of moralization as Julián founds 'una congregación de hijas de María' (a typically late nineteenth-century pious institution) to stop the local girls from dancing on Sundays (1986: 408), in the absurd supposition that this will moralize the rural masses. Julián's position inside and outside the home—'como de la familia', as Nucha says (1986: 341)—makes him a figurative adulterer regardless of his feelings for Nucha: he is the only one of the novel's social regulators who lives on the family premises. Unlike Galdós and Alas, Pardo Bazán professed to be a Catholic, but her criticism of the Church's prescription of a male-defined image of femininity is if anything more devastating than their critique of the confessor's interventionist role. If *Los Pazos de Ulloa* shows the tragedy caused by the implantation of the orthodox Christian ideal of marriage recommended in *La perfecta casada*, *La madre naturaleza* attempts a rehabilitation of Fray Luis as heterodox mystic, demonstrating the subversiveness of his translation of, and commentary on, the Song of Songs by putting it into practice: Manuela is a sister-bride, and her lips taste of the milk and honey with which Perucho has fed her. Gabriel reads and comments on Fray Luis's text at the very moments that Manuela and Perucho leave the house and finally commit incest, noting that it is not surprising that Fray Luis was imprisoned by the Inquisition when his text proposes as an ideal 'fraternal' love, based on equality between partners (1985: 240–1).[28]

Julián's feminine qualities may make him ineffectual but they are the best part of him, making him caring, nurturing, and—despite his failure to see his own role in causing it—empathetic to women's suffering (he identifies with Nucha's labour pains to the extent of experiencing them in his own body). He serves as focalizer for much of the first novel because his feminine temperament gives him an inner self sensitive to what is going on.[29] Interestingly, in her 1892 Congreso Pedagógico speech Pardo Bazán noted that Christianity had contributed to the advancement of women through its creation of the individual moral conscience: that is, the notion of the inner self. The

---

[28] In an 1892 review, Pardo Bazán attacked the Krausist psychologist González Serrano for insisting that friendship with women was impossible because male/female relations were based on difference and not equality (Pardo Bazán 1981: 143–53).

[29] For an excellent analysis of the sexually ambivalent nature of the narrative voice in *Los Pazos de Ulloa*, see Bieder (1990).

implication of this perception is that western individualism is grounded in a sense of subjectivity exemplified par excellence by the feminine. Here Pardo Bazán anticipates Nancy Armstrong's argument that the first bourgeois subject, being defined by a subjectivity traditionally associated with the feminine, was a woman (Armstrong 1989). Pardo Bazán further notes that, if Christianity thereby emancipated women '[n]o en la familia, sino en el santuario de la conciencia', today priests, instead of encouraging women's spiritual independence, tell them to be obedient wives (1981: 83–4). Julián is an example of this 'feminine' Christian inner sensibility, but as a priest he does nothing to advance the development of Nucha's inner self. Indeed, the only moment in the novel when we are made aware that she has an inner self is when she rebels against the role of long-suffering Christian wife he has imposed on her. Nucha's lack of inner self prevents readers from identifying with her, but it is the necessary consequence of her assimilation of the wifely self-denial promoted by the Church in its modern bourgeois version.

Indeed, Julián not only fails to nurture Nucha's inner self; he is directly responsible for her bodily mortification. He insists on casting her in the role of virgin, even after marriage and motherhood, because he cannot accept the body, especially the female body. In an 1892 essay, Pardo Bazán stated that she had lost her respect for the Christian feminine ideal incarnated in Dante's Beatrice, realizing that this spiritualization of woman was the other side of a revulsion for women in the flesh (1981: 122–3).[30] The novel shows how the Church derives its models of femininity from 'horror stories' of female virgin-martyrs: in reading the story of the virgin-wife St Cecilia to Nucha, Julián creates a Gothic atmosphere perceived by both of them (1986: 296–7). Nucha's assumption of the role of Christian wife turns her into a martyr: the consummation of her marriage is anticipated by her as a sacrificial death; she bears the marks of Pedro's physical abuse on her wrists like stigmata. The use of the Gothic occurs most obviously in Nucha's descent with Julián into the locked cellar.[31] In one sense this scene represents

[30] Anticipating late 20th-century feminist criticism, Pardo Bazán invited literary critics to analyse Don Quixote's idealization of Dulcinea in this light.

[31] In his analysis of this scene (in Charnon-Deutsch and Labanyi 1995: 216–29), Hart sees the Gothic as a destabilizing feminine space exclusive to Nucha and Julián.

her attempt to confront the terrors of male domination, represented by the iron ring to which a black slave was chained in former times: the 'woman question' was less often linked to the anti-slavery movement in Spain than in Britain (the Cuban-born Gómez de Avellaneda's 1841 novel *Sab* is a notable exception) but, in her 1892 translation of John Stuart Mill's *The Subjection of Women,* Pardo Bazán rendered the title as *La esclavitud femenina.* However this scene can perhaps also be read as Nucha's attempt to confront the horror of the female body that has been instilled in her; the episode produces a hysterical emotional release. It is clear that Julián's suppression of his bodily urges is responsible for his own hysterical tendencies, which find an outlet in dreams and in his spasms on Nucha's grave. His Christian embarrassment at washing his own body and that of Perucho (he limits himself to hands and face), having been taught that nakedness is sinful (1986: 146, 169), contravenes the nineteenth-century medical maxim that cleanliness is next to godliness. We are clearly meant to be disgusted by the brutish local males' lack of personal hygiene; the worst offenders are the priests in whom rural abandon joins hands with the Christian scorn of the body. Juncal and Julián are rival social regulators because what medicine proscribes as unhealthy is prescribed as a virtue by the Church. In learning to enjoy bathing the baby Manuela, after she has 'melted' his physical inhibitions by urinating on his lap (1986: 302), Julián discovers happiness because it is his first—and only—experience of the body other than that achieved through self-mortification. The implication is that being a mother—even if you are a man—makes you healthy while Christianity makes you ill. The reversals effected here are startling. The unhealthy hysterical aspects of Julián's femininity are the result of his enforced 'virginal' chastity, but surrogate motherhood allows him to develop a positive femininity based on acceptance of the body.

Julián dimly comes to perceive that Pedro prefers Sabel to Nucha because of, rather than despite, the latter's Christian chastity (1986: 307). But he never sees that, by encouraging a Christian model of femininity based on self-denial and particularly on denial of the body, he is partly responsible for Nucha's death; the furthest he gets is the obvious conclusion that a virginal woman would be better off in a convent. He is at least consistent in applying to himself the same denial of the body he expects of women. In finally agreeing to help Nucha escape the matrimonial home, Julián is not rejecting the virginal ideal but trying to restore her to virginal status. Punished with 'exile' by the Church authorities for his complicity with a wife's disobedience—tantamount to the actual adultery of which he is wrongly accused[32]—Julián devotes the rest of his life to an ascetic mortification of the body which, by the time Gabriel meets him in the second novel, has turned him into a living corpse. His necrophiliac worship of Nucha's grave is a cult of death. But his inhuman 'impasibilidad estoica' is no more than a 'mask', 'veneer', or 'shield' (1985: 303), for the body's reality cannot be denied: the mere mention of Nucha brings the blood flowing back into his face. His attempt to implant a model 'Christian marriage' in the Pazos is doomed, regardless of his personal inefficacy, because it denies the fact that human beings have bodies. When, at the end of the second novel, Manuela decides to go into a convent, it is not to conform to the virginal ideal which Julián tries to impose on her having to failed to do so with her mother, but so that Perucho can come back. In sending Manuela to the convent, Pardo Bazán has been accused of imposing an artificial Christian solution.[33] But the novel ends with Gabriel's anger at Julián's Christian view of the natural as sick, made explicit in the latter's statement that Christ came to 'sanar a la naturaleza enferma' (1985: 316). Indeed, Julián contradicts his recommendation of retreat from the world as a solution for Manuela by admitting that his own 'mística indiferencia' is to blame for her incest since, in eradicating his human love for her in the name of an abstract love of mankind, he has neglected her (1985: 304).

Julián's final denial of his own body can be achieved only because he hires Goros to look after the material side of existence. He chooses a male housekeeper so as to keep women's bodies off the premises. In a sense he is also attempting to keep his own femininity at bay: he becomes more 'varonil' during

---

[32] Monlau (1865: 5) declares that 'la mujer que quiere una cosa diferente de la que quiere su marido, ó el marido que tiene una voluntad diversa de la de su mujer, comete un adulterio moral', since they are legally one body. Although he puts the wife's disobedience first, he at least includes the husband in his strictures.

[33] Bieder (1987: 111–12) rightly sees the end as an affirmation of self by Manuela as well as an act of self-denial, noting that she is opting out of patriarchy by choosing to go to a community run by women.

his years in the wilds (1986: 412). But he cannot eliminate the feminine because Goros performs all the feminine domestic functions from cooking to darning (1985: 167–9). It is made clear that Goros's androgyny is based not on an acceptance of femininity but on a misogyny which makes him take over women's role to make them unnecessary. His 'manía de misógino [...] siempre echando la culpa a las hembras' is explicitly related to 'la santa indignación que inflamó a tantos padres de la Iglesia contra las mujeres que hacen prevaricar a los ordenados y contra el sexo femenino en general' (1985: 172). Ironically, Goros's and Julián's Christian horror of the female body leads to a subversive destabilization of sexual difference since, as the narrator comments, they form a perfect 'hogar' based on the 'marriage' of complementary opposites. Again, gender roles are shown to be independent of biology.

La madre naturaleza brings in a third social regulator, Gabriel. If Juncal and Julián represent a clearcut opposition between views of women (in both cases repressive) based on the supremacy and denial of the body respectively, Gabriel embodies the much more messy philosophical trajectory of post-1868 Spain. Politics intrudes here in the form of political philosophy, particularly in its liberal variants (Krausism and Rousseau). The emphasis is on modernity as instability and contradiction. During the *sexenio revolucionario*, Gabriel was obliged as artillery officer to fight for a national unity he passionately supported, represented by a Liberal government he deplored, against his Carlist fellow-Spaniards whose valour he admired. The only difference between himself as an 'amadeísta' and the Carlists is a name: politics is just a matter of words (1985: 77). Under the Federal Republic he turns to Madrid high society, including an affair with an aristocratic widow who refuses marriage. There are incestuous implications here since his lover is his cousin's wife's sister. Disillusionment with the fickleness of modern city woman sends him back to politics in the form of pro-Restoration conspiracy and Krausist philosophy, the latter contradicting the former. He is attracted to the Krausist reformist stress on ethics as the basis of national life. When the Republic calls on the artillery to restore national unity, Gabriel returns to the Carlist front, now as a 'republicano teórico' (1985: 81). Finding his theories contradicted by military activism and by Pavía's coup ushering in the Restoration, he throws himself into natural science, studying under a Krausist geology professor. But this does not offer him firm ground either, only fragments of rock (1985: 82). The organicist doctrine, shared by Krausism and natural science, of a universal harmony binding all creation together in a network of 'relaciones lógicas' fails to offer stable certainties (1985: 82) for, as Simmel noted, a world in which meaning lies in relationships is one in which value is relative.

Gabriel's zigzagging between different options is more than a conflict between idealism and materialism. It illustrates the problem of modern relativism: there is no one answer. It is appropriate that Gabriel should be the character whose relationships are the most complex, Nucha simultaneously being his sister, mother, and bride (and, if he marries Manuela, mother-in-law); Pedro his cousin, brother-in-law, and would-be father-in-law; and Manuela his niece, figurative sibling, and hoped-for bride. In this novel everyone is related to everyone else in several ways at once—Manuela is Perucho's half-sister and lover; Nucha is Pedro's cousin and wife; Sabel is his servant and mistress; Julián is Nucha's figurative brother and husband, being figurative father to her child but also its surrogate mother—with the result that it is impossible to say who is what. No one is sure what word to use for the relationship between Manuela and Perucho: she is 'su . . . [. . .] su hermana'; he is 'su . . . amigo' or 'su . . . , ¡lo que sea!' (1985: 108–9, 240, 287). And this proliferation of relationships leads to the impossibility of Manuela having two fathers (Pedro, Julián), Pedro having two fathers-in-law (Señor de la Lage, Primitivo), and there being two 'jefes de familia' (Pedro, Primitivo) (1986: 303, 357, 367). This labyrinth of multiple relationships figures the uncertainties of modern relativism: in such a world, incest (sexual attraction to a relative) and adultery (having two wives or husbands, without committing oneself 'absolutely' to either) seem unavoidable.

After an adulterous affair where the woman again refuses absolute commitment, Gabriel returns to military science, manufacturing explosives. His foreign travels compound his relativism because when abroad he finds Spain superior, but when in Spain he finds it inferior (1985: 83–4). He consequently becomes a 'gran reformador' mounting 'una campaña actívisima, especie de coalición de todos los elementos intelectuales del país a fin

Problematizing the Natural 369

de civilizarlo', stressing the need to build roads and canals (1985: 84). Here he echoes Costa's regenerationist campaign, also originating in Krausism, which from the early 1880s argued for a 'política hidráulica' (Costa 1911; Maurice and Serrano 1977: 49). The disillusionment with parliamentary democracy implied by Gabriel's supra-party alliance of intellectuals anticipates the direction regenerationism would take after 1900. The 'misterio' which Gabriel perceives at the end of his failed search for 'certidumbre' (1985: 85) is, I suggest, not so much a religious concept as an awareness that, in a relativistic world, there are no fixed, absolute truths.

Gabriel's 'mystical' tendencies are, like those of Ana Ozores, a symptom of the sickness of modernity: in his case, in the form of neurasthenia—the disease of urban man exhausted by over-stimulation. Like Ana, Gabriel swings between opposing options because he is over-impressionable. His 'sick' tendency to let his fantasy run away with him is stressed throughout:

> Era una especie de eretismo de la imaginación, que al caldearse desarrollaba, como en sucesión de cuadros disolventes, escenas de la existencia futura [...]. En la fantasía incorregible del artillero, los objetos y los sucesos representaban todo cuanto el novelista o el autor dramático pudiese desear para la creación artística. (1985: 107)

It is Gabriel's habit of turning reality into representation that makes him an 'hombre moderno en toda la extensión de la palabra' (1985: 122). In deciding to abandon Madrid for the countryside, he is adopting the remedy for neurasthenia prescribed in contemporary health manuals. As a neurasthenic, he is degenerate: because of his adulterous affair, because he is mentally exhausted and prematurely aged, and because his hypersensibility has feminized him. In this sense he is an androgynous focalizer, like Julián in the first novel.

Gabriel's decision to go to the Pazos and marry his niece Manuela is an attempt to escape from modern mutability, returning to roots in the form of 'mother nature' and the memory of his 'mamita' Nucha (1985: 85). He expects to achieve this stability by founding a family: 'La esposa, el hijo, la familia [...] Jordán en que se regenera y purifica el alma', an action conceived as 'el cumplimiento de una ley natural' while contributing to 'la regeneración de la sociedad' (1985: 86, 88). Again we have the Krausist view of the family as an organic unit providing the basis of social regeneration. What this involves in Gabriel's case is not the colonization and settlement of nature itself, as in *Pepita Jiménez* and *Peñas arriba*, but the 'civilization' of a bride who is seen as an embodiment of 'the natural'. Charnon-Deutsch (Millington and Smith 1994: 81) notes that the concept of mother nature, while seemingly idealizing the feminine, casts man in the superior role of civilizer. It thus perfectly embodies the nineteenth century's contradictory construction of 'the natural' as that which is desirable and that which must be tamed, that which 'knows best' and that which needs 'cultivating' or reforming (re-forming): that is, 'husbanding'.

The concept of 'mother earth' is introduced in the first novel through the related notion of woman as 'earth mother'. When Nucha's city-bred father expresses his desire to 'ingertar' [*sic*] the 'retoños de tan noble estirpe' that are his daughters on to a suitable 'tronco' (1986: 209), he is conforming to the same breeder's model of the female used by the rural Pedro when he describes Rita as a 'magnífico patrón donde injertar el heredero', like a farmer valuing 'un terreno fértil' for 'la cosecha que podrá rendir' (1986: 212). In showing that this view of woman as 'land' to be 'cultivated' by the male cuts across the city/country divide, Pardo Bazán demonstrates that it is not 'natural' but a cultural construction. In practice, men's claim to be the 'cultivators' is undermined by the fact that Nucha's father has been civilized by living in a household of women: 'cinco hembras respetadas y queridas civilizan al hombre más agreste' (1986: 247). Pedro explicitly seeks a wife to civilize him. In the second novel, Gabriel even suggests that marriage would moralize the clergy by subjecting them to women's civilizing influence (1985: 93). Pardo Bazán here exposes the contradiction whereby men were seen as 'cultivators' of women, while at the same time women were entrusted with the domestic mission of transmitting moral—i.e. civilizing—values. Men domesticate and women domesticize; a difference which translates as that between man as hunter and woman as hunted, both frequent images in *Los Pazos de Ulloa*. Pedro's choice of a bride takes the form of his 'hunting' of the 'hermosa res' he thinks is Rita but who turns out to be Nucha, in which the sisters subvert his stereotypical notion of sexual difference by dressing themselves and Pedro up. Rita subverts class rather than gender roles by dressing as a servant, confirming Pedro's taste for women beneath his station. But the 'masculine' Manolita dons the colonel's uniform worn by her great-grandmother when riding 'a horcajadas' like a man ('según costumbre de su época, autorizada por el ejemplo de la reina María Luisa', as the narrator notes), and they dress Pedro in a sexually hybrid mixture of three-cornered hat, garlands of flowers, and a 'chupa' which, as Mayoral's note explains, could be an item of military uniform or a woman's jacket (1986: 226–30).[34] It is by 'trapping' Nucha that Pedro reaffirms his masculinity. Nucha asks what she has done to deserve her husband's maltreatment, for in trying to 'domesticize' the Pazos she has done what was expected of a wife. What she discovers is that the wife's civilizing mission constructs her not as superior but as slave: the rings round her wrists from Pedro's physical abuse directly echo the ring to which the black slave had formerly been chained. Whether earth mother or civilizer, woman's subordination is the same.

In *La madre naturaleza*, the equation of woman and nature occurs in a different form. Gabriel casts himself in the Rousseauesque role of male tutor to Manuela, seen as embodying a 'virgin nature' that is both the remedy to a decadent urban civilization and in need of tutoring.[35] By introducing this Rousseauesque topos in the second novel, Pardo Bazán is able to show that it is merely the modern 'civilized' equivalent of the cruder notion of woman as earth to be fertilized found in the first. It is also, of course, a modern secular version of Julián's idealization of woman as virgin. Indeed, in his contradictory supposition that woman represents a 'virgin nature' but also needs to be educated for motherhood, Rousseau echoes Julián's impossible ideal of the wife as 'virgin mother'. Gabriel's philanthropic desire to educate Manuela fits with his former role as Krausist regenerationist reformer; as we have seen, women's education was the centrepiece of the Krausist reform programme. Although Krausist political philosophy rejected Rousseau's notion of the social contract, its simultaneous belief in women's 'natural' femininity and in the need to educate them to be

---

[34] The androgynous effigy of St Julian also wears a 'chupa' (1986: 175).
[35] For Rousseau's views on women, see Lloyd (1984: 75–8) and Kennedy and Mendus (1987: 78–105).

'true' women essentially reproduced Rousseau's theories.³⁶ In regarding Manuela as a 'terreno virgen' because she has been reared by 'mother nature' (1985: 140, 239), Gabriel is casting nature in the dual role of virgin and mother. Just as the concept of 'mother nature' supposes that nature knows best but needs cultivating by man, so 'virgin territories' represent a lost authenticity but exist to be colonized. In both cases, the equation of woman with nature legitimizes male 'husbandry' rights. The paternalism of Gabriel's proposal for 'civilizing' his young niece is stressed. His decision to marry her is based on the argument that he cannot be her tutor unless he can appropriate the *patria potestas* currently held by her father (1985: 98). He conceived this plan in his dead father's bedroom, making it clear that it represents his assumption of the paternal role. Indeed his father, in what is described as a modern city-dweller's attitude, had in the first novel fantasized about retiring to the countryside to lay out a garden and cultivate an orchard (1986: 247), echoing Rousseau's *La Nouvelle Héloïse*.³⁷ This novel and Rousseau's *Social Contract* and *Confessions* are among the books Gabriel finds in the Pazos de Ulloa library, moth-eaten and defaced by Perucho's and Manuela's childhood scribblings (1985: 156): a warning that Perucho and Manuela will rewrite Rousseau's texts in their own way.³⁸ It is made clear that the Rousseauesque scenario Gabriel constructs before he has even met Manuela—as she and her father note (1985: 139, 147)—is the product of his urban male fantasy, exacerbated by his neurasthenia: the product of over-stimulation of the brain by modern city life. He candidly imagines her 'inocencia selvática' and himself 'educándola, formándola, iniciándola en los goces y bienes de la civilización'. His fantasy ends with an overtly Rousseauesque image of her breastfeeding their future child in the open air, watched of course by him (1985: 108).

---

³⁶ Pardo Bazán had a lifelong friendship with the leading Krausist thinker, Giner de los Ríos, who encouraged her to write and published her first book of poems. In the obituary she wrote on his death in 1915, she praised his work for women but dissociated herself from Krausism as a philosophical movement (1972: 336–41). For their correspondence, see González Arias (1992).

³⁷ Tanner (1979: 113–20, 143–65) has brilliantly analysed the relationship between gardening, marriage, and adultery in Rousseau's novel.

³⁸ Noted by Urey (1987a), who reads the novel through Derrida's discussion of the 'supplement/origin' aporia in Rousseau's *Essay on the Origin of Languages*.

Problematizing the Natural

Gabriel's 'cultivation' of this 'terreno virgen' allows him to affirm his masculinity, sapped by modernity, because it consists in the construction of a supposedly 'natural' scenario based on sexual difference. By restoring Manuela to her rightful status as 'señorita' he is also attempting to re-establish class distinctions. There is a contradiction here, since the restoration of class distinctions means a return to the pre-modern order, while the 'natural' sexual difference which Gabriel aims to impose on Manuela is a modern product designed to justify women's continued subordination while paying lip-service to the liberal doctrine of universal equality. If Don Pedro and Primitivo illustrate the pre-modern order that sees women as 'subordinates because inferior', the social regulators Juncal and Gabriel illustrate the new liberal view of women as 'subordinates because equal but different': the two men instantly empathize when they meet. Pardo Bazán noted that modern legal theorists, in basing women's subjugation on a 'metafísica sexual' of 'natural' sexual difference, had legitimized it by presenting it as a duty and virtue rather than the result of force; as she observes, a brilliant sleight of hand since such moral argument, unlike the rule of force, institutionalizes subordination on a permanent basis (1981: 75–6). Here Pardo Bazán shows herself to have understood perfectly the link between political liberalism and the new medical theories of sexual difference that Laqueur would later (1990) 'discover'. Pardo Bazán's rejection of political liberalism may be partly based on class snobbery, but her reasons for opposing it on grounds of gender are impeccable. In *Los Pazos de Ulloa*, Nucha's marriage to Pedro coincided with the 1868 Revolution: the new liberal view of marriage as a social contract in which the wife voluntarily alienates her freedom only puts a civilized gloss on what is enforced submission, just as the introduction of universal (male) suffrage with the 1869 elections is shown to be a cover for primitive thuggery. Pedro's despotic rule over Sabel and Nucha represents the coexistence in a newly modernizing but still largely rural Spain of the pre-modern system of subordination of women through the 'droit de seigneur', based on inherited land rights, and its modern bourgeois version justified through a new belief in 'natural' sexual difference, which requires women to acquiesce to their subordination. As readers, we cannot help asking whether there is that much difference between the primitive rule of force whereby Primitivo can oblige his daughter Sabel to be Pedro's mistress and Pedro can beat her, and the 'civilized' legislation that requires Nucha to obey her father by marrying Pedro, and makes it a crime for her to leave the matrimonial home despite his physical abuse and his concubinage on the premises: a circumstance which made male adultery a criminal offence (Scanlon 1986: 127–8, 131). In the second novel Gabriel, being a 'civilized' liberal, will not force Manuela into submission but wants her—as in Rousseau's social contract—to opt for it voluntarily by agreeing to be a 'young lady' and wife.

The illogicality of supposing that sexual difference is 'natural' but needs to be instilled by a tutor is exposed when Gabriel accuses Manuela's father of neglect in allowing her to grow up as a 'marimacho' (1985: 137): her natural upbringing has not made her 'naturally' feminine. The subtext to Gabriel's Rousseauesque agenda emerges when he describes Manuela as 'un terreno inculto, virgen, lleno de espinos, ortigas, zarzales [. . .] ¡Cuánto tengo aquí que enmendar, que enseñar, que formar [. . .]!' (1985: 140–1): his idealization of a 'feminine nature' is an idealization of his male civilizer's role. Alternatively he sees her as a wild gazelle ('cierva') who needs taming (1985: 165); as Pardo Bazán noted in 'La mujer española' (1889), women's education as practised at the time would be better called a 'doma' or 'breaking in' (1981: 92). Gabriel's self-important view of himself as Rousseauesque tutor is ironized by the narrator on his first excursion with Manuela as, in a reversal of his theoretical scheme, he follows her as leader 'rumiando aquello del terreno virgen', 'muy encariñado ya con su oficio de preceptor' (1985: 140–1). On their second excursion he congratulates himself that she is 'domesticada ya' and fantasizes about his 'tierno protectorado', an 'obra de caridad' in which he plays the role of multiple social regulator: father, teacher, even doctor (1985: 154). In her speech at the 1892 Congreso Pedagógico, Pardo Bazán criticized Rousseau for regarding woman's destiny as that of man's helpmeet, commenting that if Émile is allowed to progress, Sophie is condemned to remain a minor (1981: 75–6). Gabriel talks of respecting Manuela as a companion, but also of playing with her as a 'chiquilla' (1985: 216), illustrating the liberal view of woman as 'equal but different'; that is, a minor. Rousseau—whom she calls a 'retrógrado más o menos disfrazado'—is the chief target of Pardo Bazán's criticisms throughout her later feminist writings, both because of his views on women's education in *Émile*, and also because of his notion of the social contract which passes subordination off as free choice (1981: 75–6, 84, 94–5, 114).[39]

Manuela disproves and rejects Gabriel's model of 'natural', 'virgin' femininity from the start. In refusing the marriage contract he offers her, she is also refusing the social contract which, as Pateman suggests (1989), would be better called the 'sexual contract' since it is based on the fiction that women choose their subordination. Free from the gender constraints of a bourgeois education, Manuela from the start refuses to submit voluntarily to Gabriel's 'superior' male control, in an intuitive rejection of her mother's aquiescence to the role of sacrificial victim. Gabriel is taken aback when she fails to receive him with the expected deference and enthusiasm. When he tells her that a young lady's duty is to please, she glowers by way of reply (1985: 143). As the text points out, he needs to be taught about nature by her and not vice versa (1985: 150–1). And she refuses his symbolic offer of an arm because, as she retorts, she has two perfectly good ones of her own (1985: 140). He protests that he is not a 'damita' too delicate for a major excursion, but compared to her he is the weaker sex (1985: 157). Always outdoors, as befits a 'child of nature' but contradicting 'natural' feminine domesticity, Manuela's physical strength is stressed: in the novel's opening episode, we see her replace a peasant girl in holding down a cow while it is operated on (1985: 21, 124). Gabriel hopes to 'conquer' her because of her 'nervous' temperament and suggestibility—a view of her immediately contradicted when she fearlessly pursues a snake and brandishes its newly shed skin (1985: 152–3); indeed, her earlier participation in the operation on the cow showed her to be totally lacking in 'feminine' squeamishness.

Throughout these scenes Gabriel is ironically described as 'el comandante' (referring to his previous army career); in practice, it is he who is conquered and who is suggestible. During his sleepless night before the incest takes place, his neurasthenic imaginings are comically undercut by the mosquitoes divebombing him. He falls asleep imagining Manuela guiding him

---

[39] In 1915, Pardo Bazán revealed that when young she had thought of writing a political tract 'inspirado por la lectura del *Contrato social*' (1972: 337).

through the fields in biblical submission, already tutored to speak perfect Castilian, at precisely the moment she is stealing out of the house with Perucho (1985: 215–17, 222). By narrating Gabriel's sleepless night after the following day's events, Pardo Bazán exposes his Rousseauesque scenario as a delusion. The incest will shatter his view of Manuela as 'virgin territory' because he is forced to accept that she is in every sense not a virgin. The novel seems remarkably unworried by her premarital sex with Perucho, a problem only because he is her half-brother.[40] In offering at the end to marry her despite the fact that she is not a virgin, Gabriel shows that he has progressed considerably. However, when he also tells Julián that he will be 'padre, madre, hermano, protector, esposo amantísimo' to her (1985: 306), the only encouraging note is the inclusion of 'madre' and 'hermano' in the list.

Manuela does accept Perucho's 'natural' leadership—they are a 'perfect couple' because he is 'cuatro o seis años' older than she (1985: 211)—but their 'fraternal' relationship is based on his nurturing her as well as leading and teaching her.[41] As Pateman notes (1989: 77–115), the liberal slogan of 'liberty, equality, fraternity' meant fraternity in its literal sense of 'brotherhood' for women were excluded. In *La madre naturaleza*, Pardo Bazán redefines the notion of fraternity as a brother–sister relationship allowing equality and freedom to both sexes by unsettling the 'natural' differences between them. Perucho had 'mothered' Manuela as a baby, as he reminds her when taking off her shoes on their climactic excursion (1986: 400, 1985: 108, 190), during which he also feeds her. As he insists to Gabriel, he has been everything to her: mother, father, nanny, teacher, brother, lover (1985: 262). For their 'fraternal' relationship allows both of them to occupy masculine and feminine roles. It is this that allows them to be equal and free while being one body—'El bulto se acercó . . . Era doble' (1985: 251)—contrasting with the Krausist ideal of marriage as the creation of a single 'body' made up of complementary opposites. In a notable gender reversal, Manuela adores

---

[40] In her prologue to her translation of J. S. Mill's *The Subjection of Women*, Pardo Bazán justified his premarital relations with his future wife. Pardo Bazán's own affairs after separating from her husband in 1883 are well known (Pardo Bazán 1975).

[41] Mayoral (1989: 49) observes that their relationship is fraternal in the sense of equal.

Perucho for his physical beauty and he adores her despite her plainness. According to the *Apuntes autobiográficos* published with *Los Pazos de Ulloa* (Pattison 1971: 32), the first modern Spanish novel that Pardo Bazán read (in 1879) was *Pepita Jiménez*, which also showed that women are sexually attracted to men's bodies: the descriptions of Perucho's beauty are mostly focalized through Manuela's gaze.

La madre naturaleza subjects the Pygmalion myth to an ironic twist. Gabriel wants to sculpt Manuela into shape, seeing her as a 'diamante en bruto' (the words used by Feijoo of Fortunata) and as 'cera virgen' waiting to be given 'los deliciosos relieves que un hombre como él sabría imprimirle' (1985: 165, 214). In 'La mujer española', Pardo Bazán pointed out that 'los defectos de la mujer española [. . .] en gran parte deben achacarse al hombre, que es, por decirlo así, quien modela y esculpe el alma femenina' (1981: 26). In offering to sculpt Manuela into shape, it is clear that Gabriel is looking to his own salvation as a prematurely aged neurasthenic; as with Fortunata and her various Pygmalions, we have to ask who needs regenerating more. Indeed Gabriel starts to wonder whether Manuela would not be better left uncivilized, but he is still thinking of how she can best serve him (1985: 214). Perucho is an anti-Pygmalion because he does not want to make Manuela conform to an ideal: he loves her for what she is. As he takes her shoes off, her legs are described as like those of a Greek statue 'acabada de esculpir en mármol' (1985: 191): she does not need 'forming' (the marble is described as unpolished only because the natural transformation from girl to woman is not yet complete). And in a radical inversion of the Pygmalion scheme, Manuela worships Perucho as classical statue: one that again is already perfectly made.

The repeated descriptions (1986: 168; 1985: 122, 210, 259, 268) of Perucho as Greek statue—an Apollo or 'joven deidad olímpica'—make him an embodiment of the 'virile', Apollonian ideal of serene physical beauty posited by degeneracy theory as the antidote to an effeminate, decadent, neurasthenic civilization (Mosse 1985). His blond locks (contrary to Galicia's dark-haired Celtic ethnic origins) make him the perfect Aryan type. In making Perucho the perfect racial specimen, Pardo Bazán may be showing that the eugenic concerns of degeneracy theory logically imply the need for miscegenation between the upper classes and the masses; this however supposes adherence to the breeder's model of woman which elsewhere is criticized. The fact that Manuela, though not beautiful, is like Perucho strong and healthy and compared to a Greek statue, despite being born to a sickly city-bred mother and being the product of incestuous inbreeding between aristocratic cousins, suggests that what matters is not genetics (nature) but upbringing (nurture). The male writers studied so far echo degeneracy theory in seeing the blurring of sexual difference as a symptom of regression to a primitive lack of differentiation.[42] Pardo Bazán reverses this scenario by depicting Manuela's and Perucho's incest as a regressive lapse from civilization into a gender indeterminacy which makes them healthy examples of the classical ideal. The comparison of Manuela to a Greek statue also subverts degeneracy theory's latent and often overt misogyny in equating the healthy with the 'virile' (Dijkstra 1986). Classical imagery is, however, mostly associated with Perucho. It is his 'virility' that wins him the respect of Gabriel, also described as 'varonil', particularly towards the end of the novel. Two different models of virility are in operation here. Both are contrasted with the 'brute masculinity' of the local men, based on careless dress, a scorn for washing, and a lack of emotional sensibility: a lack, that is, of an inner self. Perucho's natural virility is based on the authenticity and singlemindedness of his emotions; Gabriel's civilized virility consists in his patrician 'nobility' in sacrificing his egoism to the good of others. To maintain his virility, Gabriel has to combat the feminizing effects of neurasthenia; or is his 'virile' capacity for self-sacrifice itself an assimilation of feminine values? Perucho's natural virility includes the 'feminine' capacity for true love and steadfast devotion; one is reminded of Fortunata. When Gabriel tells him to pull himself together and 'be a man', Perucho insists on his right to weep on his breast, in the process forcing Gabriel into a maternal position (1985: 270). Gabriel, whose ideas fluctuate between opposing poles because they are second-hand borrowings from books, envies Perucho his unwavering conviction, exclaiming, 'Quisiera tener el cerebro virgen' (1985: 296–7).

---

[42] Pardo Bazán shows a knowledge of French degeneracy theory in her 1882 *La cuestión palpitante* (1966: 182).

Although Gabriel contrasts Manuela's uninhibited 'natural self' favourably with the artifice of fashion-conscious city *señoritas*, he nevertheless concludes that civilization is necessary to 'reprimir la bestialidad humana' (1985: 214–15). Despite the sympathetic depiction of Manuela and Perucho, we are clearly not meant to approve their incest. When Gabriel swings between the contrary views that progress is the result of natural evolution and that it is based on the repression of natural urges (1985: 215), he is hesitating between the mid-century Darwinian model and Freud's twentieth-century view, expressed in *Civilization and its Discontents*, which coincides with degeneracy theory in regarding civilization as sick. But Freud also insisted that repression was necessary. In supposing that nature is a stepmother, the end of *La madre naturaleza* implies that nature is in need of remedial treatment. But the critique in the two novels of the social regulators' attempts to 'improve' women also implies that civilization is sick (based on repression). Neither nature nor civilization offers a definitive answer. The convent Manuela opts for at the end does at least save her from the subordination to men represented by the three social regulators at her bedside; it is made clear that her intention is not to become a nun but to find a 'retiro y descanso' (1985: 314) allowing her to decide what she wants to do. But Julián's role in approving this decision reminds us that, even in this all-female space, she will still be subordinated to a male confessor. Of the three male social regulators hovering over her, all basing their advice on a theory of 'the natural', only Juncal believes that nature should be left to follow its course. Julián's view that nature is sick and Gabriel's final suggestion that it is a stepmother imply that the social regulators will always find excuses to intervene.

Nature cannot provide an answer to the sickness of modernity because any view of nature that proposes it as an antidote to civilization by definition constructs it as an inverted mirror-image of the disease it is supposed to heal. When degeneracy theory talks of 'the natural', it is 'reading' nature in the light of its cultural obsessions. Pardo Bazán's use in both novels of male city focalizers who journey to the country allows her to make the point that 'the natural' is a cultural construct, and that both culture and nature are defined by men. In *The Subjection of Women*, which Pardo Bazán translated in 1892, John Stuart Mill famously observed that 'what is now called the nature of women is an eminently artificial thing' (Mill 1988: 22). In making her three social regulators hesitate and disagree over what nature is and what, if anything, should be done about it, she is exposing the arbitrariness of their definitions. Only the city-educated characters theorize about nature, for theories of nature are a cultural product. The one rural exception, Antón *el algebrista*, derives his proto-Darwinistic ideas mainly from observation of nature rather than from his few Enlightenment texts (1985: 26, 29). His notion that there is no difference between humans and animals—'todo lo mismísimo' (1985: 30) —positions him inside nature; he, like it, lacks an inner self. Manuela's and Perucho's discovery of their incest expels them from their natural paradise because it forces them to reflect for the first time on what nature is, thus positioning them within culture and giving them an inner consciousness, in both cases created through their 'confession' of their 'sin'. The second novel's mention of Rousseau's *Confessions* reminds us of the interdependence between the construction of the inner self and the construction of a theory of nature, and the role of confession as a vehicle for both. Confession implies a desire to remedy what is perceived as sickness; as *La Regenta* stated, and as Pardo Bazán's novels imply with their similar pairing of doctor and priest, the confessional is a 'hospital for sick souls'. As principal focalizers, requiring an inner consciousness and the ability to theorize about nature, Julián and Gabriel have to be neurotic. They also have to be readers for, as Ong has argued (1982), literacy creates the inner self.

Los Pazos de Ulloa and *La madre naturaleza* show how the characters'—and narrators'—visions of nature are readings of it. Manuela and Perucho are described in terms of natural imagery and of classical references, for degeneracy theory's appeal to the regenerative effects of nature was also a demand for a return to classical civilization: it 'read' nature through classical texts. The river crossed by Manuela and Perucho evokes 'las urnas, las náyades, concepción clásica y encantadora del río como divinidad' (1985: 188); the foliage they traverse is like '*ex-votos* de faunos que inmolaron su pelaje rudo al capricho de una ninfa' (1985: 202). Their incest in the grass covering the graves of slain Roman soldiers similarly equates the return to nature with a classical revival: in an image worthy of Frazer or Spengler, their copulation represents the rebirth of the

Problematizing the Natural 381

classical warrior-heroes whose blood fertilizes the oak beneath which they lie. Both Julián and Gabriel are shown reading books and projecting their readings onto nature. We have seen how Julián's reading of the lives of Christian martyrs turns the landscape into a Gothic fantasy. Gabriel 'reads' nature through Rousseau's and Fray Luis's readings of it; indeed Fray Luis's translation is a reading of a reading. Gabriel explicitly comments on Fray Luis's Neoplatonism (1985: 156, 221): his glosses on the Song of Songs exemplify a conception of nature as a sign of an underlying divine truth (1985: 156, 221); the title of his *Nombres de Cristo*, which Gabriel also reads, enunciates a Neoplatonic view of the word as cipher for a hidden divine essence. When Gabriel interprets the natural world around him through Fray Luis's texts, it is clear that he is not revealing any essential truth but projecting onto nature a cultural reading that is not inherent in it. Gabriel's indecision as to how to interpret nature results from his projection onto it of the conflicting texts he reads, as well as his projection onto it of his emotions, whose changeability in turn derives from the fact that his self is the product of reading: '¡A fuerza de lecturas, de estudiar y de ejercitar la razón, me he acostumbrado a ver el pro y el contra de todas las cosas!' As Gabriel observes, 'La naturaleza de asemeja a la música en esto de ajustarse a nuestros pensamientos y estados de ánimo' (1985: 108).

Nature is in *La madre naturaleza* repeatedly compared to a symphony (1985: 34, 118, 320) and to a painting (1985: 13, 108, 150, 209, 244): both narrator and characters are unable to avoid projecting cultural representations onto it. Such comparisons make the point that nature is a state of mind. Critics have observed how Pardo Bazán's descriptions betray the influence of contemporary French impressionism, a musical as well as artistic movement (Mayoral in Pardo Bazán 1986: 21).[43] In *La cuestión palpitante* Pardo Bazán praised Zola most for his impressionistic descriptions, singling out the Goncourt brothers' talent in this respect (1966: 66, 105–9, 138–45).

---

[43] From 1906, Pardo Bazán's *tertulias* at the Pazo de Meiras were attended by the Galician landscape painters Francisco Llorens and Ovidio Murguía de Castro (the latter the son of Rosalía de Castro and the founding father of Galician nationalism, Manuel Murguía). Pardo Bazán's patronage of the painters Jenaro Carrero and Joaquín Vaamonde (neither a landscape painter) is well known (Pena López 1993–4: 316–17, 327–8).

Significantly, she notes that the Goncourt brothers' impressionistic descriptions are the result of their 'simpatía por la vida moderna' encapsulated in (citing one of their characters) '[l]a sensación e intuición de lo contemporáneo, del espectáculo con que tropezamos a la vuelta de la esquina' (Pardo Bazán 1966: 108–9). What makes Pardo Bazán's descriptions impressionistic is their insistence on the changing play of light and the fact that they are always viewed through a character's eyes. Nature is shown to be mutable because of the passage of time: the second-by-second mutation of the rainbow which opens *La madre naturaleza* (1985: 13); Manuela and Perucho's day-long excursion which permits description of the same landscape as the sun rises, peaks, and falls; the contrasting gloomy and peaceful visions of the Pazos in the first novel, as the seasons rotate. But, in a much more unsettling way, it is shown to be mutable also because it looks different to different people or even to the same person looking at it at different moments. Perspectives are shifting because they are, precisely, points of view. This may be a simple matter of physical positioning: Manuela, lying in the grass looking at Perucho, perceives the wild flowers to be taller than the mountains (1985: 209). But more importantly, as in impressionist music and painting, Pardo Bazán shows nature to be defined by changing mood. If the same landscape is described as predominantly Gothic in the first novel and radiant in the second, it is not just because the former takes place mostly in autumn and the latter entirely in summer, but because the emotions which Julián and Nucha project onto nature are very different from those of Gabriel. And it is Julián's shifting emotions as well as the passage of the seasons that make the scenery in the first novel mostly Gothic but sometimes beautiful. Nature is real enough but it lacks stable, inherent meaning.

Critics have noted that Pardo Bazán's use of characters as focalizers gives her novels a psychological slant (Hemingway 1983 and in González Herrán 1997: 389–403; Varela Jácome in Mayoral 1989: 81–101; Mayoral in Pardo Bazán 1986: 44–5). This is so, not because her characters' psychology is especially complex, but because she shows reality to be a psychological projection. This has important consequences for an understanding of her realism. Her novels anticipate artistic modernism in expressing a modernity in which value is not stable and inherent but relative. Villanueva notes that her use of psychological perspectivism anticipates the modernist novels of Henry James (Mayoral 1989: 32–3).[44] She is the only one of the writers studied in this book who went on, in the early 1900s, to write *modernista* novels (*La quimera* (1905), *Dulce dueño* (1911)). Gabriel is aware that he is projecting ideas and emotions onto the natural world. He notes that the 'no sé qué de arcaico' which attracts him to the Pazos is the product of 'las cansadas imaginaciones modernas' (1985: 130). During his sleepless night, he observes that in the dark 'todo se abulta y transforma' and, in an embodiment of modern relativism, has the sensation of constantly changing size. He compares his 'representaciones' to the 'cuadros disolventes' of a revolving 'cromátropa', for he is seeing reality through a modern distorting lens (1985: 218, 221).[45] His contemplation of Nucha's grave turns into a shortlived Gothic hallucination because he is looking at 'objetos en los cuales, como en cifra, vemos representado nuestro destino', additionally projecting onto them 'todo lo que en lugares semejantes evocan, sueñan y forjan los creyentes y los medrosos, los nerviosos y los alucinados' (1985: 247). He falls in love with Manuela before meeting her because 'en esta chiquilla he cifrado yo muchas cosas' (1985: 135): what matters is not what she is but what she represents. By contrast Manuela, as a 'child of nature', does not 'read' anything into the natural world but sees it for what it is: 'La flor, que era una margarita, le contestó "mucho", pero la muchacha, que nada tenía de romántica, no le había preguntado cosa alguna' (1985: 144). Gabriel concludes:

¡Empeñarnos en que la naturaleza tiene voces, y voces que dicen algo misterioso y grande! [. . .] ¡Voces! . . . ¡Voces! ¡Unas voces que están hablando hace miles y miles de años, y a cada cual le dicen su cosa diferente! Deduzco que ellas no dicen maldita la cosa . . . , y que nosotros las interpretamos a nuestra manera . . . [. . .] Las voces están dentro. . . . (1985: 239)

---

[44] Villanueva (in Mayoral 1989: 23) also notes that Pardo Bazán's sequel novels are contemporaneous with those of Huysmans and Dujardin (the 'inventor' of stream of consciousness). For Pardo Bazán's sympathetic reaction to literary decadentism, see Kronik (in Mayoral 1989: 163–74).

[45] In an interesting article, Fernández (in González Herrán 1997: 97–112) documents Pardo Bazán's positive response, rare among writers at the time, to the early cinema.

And yet Gabriel cannot help reading meaning into nature. His readings of Fray Luis immediately return to his mind 'como en placa fonográfica' (1985: 239): a modern version of Plato's cave where the brain does not reflect a hidden divine truth but is a man-made reproductive device. It is not that reality has ceased to function as a sign but that, with the loss of fixed, inherent truths, it is an empty sign onto which one can, and will, project one's own cultural and emotional baggage. Gabriel's relativism is not necessarily that of a religious sceptic; he does not talk of having lost his faith. It is that of a modernity whose forms of economic and political representation are arbitrary. Pardo Bazán did not have to be a freethinker to perceive the resulting loss of absolute values. El Gallo's initiation into culture is 'muy relativa' because 'saber leer y escribir no es conocer los signos alfabéticos, nombrarlos, trazarlos; es, sobre todo, poseer las ideas que despiertan estos signos' (1985: 127). Here Pardo Bazán, while mocking the extension of literacy to the masses, is recognizing that words are not containers of inherent truths, available to all who possess their material representations, but empty signs waiting to be filled with meaning. This lack of 'innate' value dissociates class from birth, as she notes with distaste, but it also dissociates gender from biology. As the various nineteenth-century discourses on women insisted, sexual difference is 'natural' in the sense that it is real; but, as the multiplication of discourses itself demonstrates, the 'natural' has no stable, inherent meaning. In turning reality into representation modernity turns sexuality into gender (that is, a social construct), subjecting women to a proliferation of contradictory norms whose very arbitrariness allows the possibility of alternative mappings.

Conclusion
Modernity and Representation

IN all the major realist novels studied in the preceding chapters, we have seen how modernity is constructed as representation, whether in the form of the increasingly abstract systems of monetary and political representation that come with capitalist modernization and liberal nation formation, or in that of the related imitation and mimicry resulting from consumerism and from the discourses of social control that attempt to mould individual (especially female) identity. We have also seen how this perception of modernity as representation introduces a self-reflexive dimension, as the mechanisms whereby reality is converted into representation are subjected to critical scrutiny. Two things must be noted here. First, that the critique of modernity as representation is common to writers of all political persuasions. And second, that these novels, as fictional representations and consumer products themselves, contribute to the conversion of national life into representation that they are concerned to expose. The critique of representation is self-reflexive because, in commenting on the representation process that 'constructs' the nation, the realist novel is commenting on its own procedures.

It must be stressed that the realist novel's concern with appearances is not a straightforward exposure of social hypocrisy but, much more fundamentally, an examination of this modernizing process whereby reality is converted into representation. Appearances are not contrasted with an underlying 'truth'; they are false in the sense that they are not based on inherent value but they constitute reality. Contrary to early twentieth-century modernism's insistence on the irreconcilable gap between reality and representation, realism collapses the two into a single entity; that is, a reality constituted by representation. Realism can thus simultaneously provide an objective depiction of reality and a critique of representation, without the latter contradicting the former. Indeed, the purpose of the increasingly complex forms of monetary and political representation on which late nineteenth-century consumer capitalism and liberal democracy depended was to provide an objective measurement of value and opinion: for the nation-State to function, both needed to be represented in an abstract form that transcended subjective partiality. Similarly, the aim of consumerist standardization and social regulation was to encourage individuals to identify with abstract models of identity, allowing the construction of a homogeneous 'society'—as when Don Baldomero, in *Fortunata y Jacinta*, takes it for granted that the function of his personal 'cédula de identidad' is to accredit him with a national identity as a 'Spaniard'. This is an accreditation process because, as with financial credit, it depends on a process of abstraction whereby identity is defined, not by what one is as a person, but by what one represents in public terms. Indeed, the object was to construct citizens as individuals who freely chose to merge their personal identity with the socially prescribed role-models held out to them for imitation, thus maintaining the liberal fiction of the social contract. The nineteenth-century realist novel is concerned with the inevitable conflicts arising from this contradictory construction of the private self through the assumption of a publicly defined role. A devastating example is Ana Ozores's reduction to the status of being 'como todas', through an act of her own volition which involves her conversion into a public spectacle through exhibition and gossip, as well as the converse intrusion into the home of the public figures who are her social regulators and/or adulterous seducers. It is not surprising that critics should disagree over whether Ana or environmental pressures are to blame, for liberal democracy requires individuals to choose homogenization. In so doing, Ana freely opts for the stock fictional role of the fallen woman which the public does its best to impose on her: the novel's self-reflexive dimension forcefully makes the point that the modern nation-State requires individuals to make their private identity coincide with public representations. In the various urban novels discussed in the preceding chapters, the critique of homogenization is figured by the invasion of privacy or the woman's abandonment of the home for the public realm of the street: in both cases, the result is adultery, in the latter case overlapping with prostitution. The only alternative—illustrated in the rural novels discussed—seems to be to resist modernity's conversion of the self into representation by opting for a different kind of loss of self figured by incest: whether in the form of Valera's and Pereda's refusal of the public/private split for a pre-modern concept of society based on the household, or in that of Pardo Bazán's attempt in *La madre naturaleza* to replace gender 'normalization' with fraternal sexual relationships. In all of these last examples, the attempt to resist modernity is either partial or unsuccessful.

The last three writers set their novels against rural backgrounds also because their critique of modernity's conversion of reality into representation requires them to ask what, if any, might be the place of nature in this scheme. In opting for urban locations, Galdós and Alas are suggesting that 'the natural' no longer exists, for it too has been commodified and consumed. It seems not to be coincidence that all the rural novels studied here include discussion of the Neoplatonic notion of nature as a book, reflecting a hidden divine essence, for Neoplatonism—like modernity but in a different way—raises the issue of reality as representation. The large number of references to Plato in Simmel's *The Philosophy of Money* shows an awareness of this similarity. The difference, of course, is that, for modernity, reality is a representation of values that are arbitrary, relative, and shifting whereas, in Neoplatonism, reality reflects underlying essential values. Valera and Pardo Bazán reject this pre-modern view: Valera for a notion of stable, inherent meaning based on the materiality of the body, land, and gold (with a degree of acceptance of the new consumer economy); Pardo Bazán so as to explore the diverse and contradictory cultural constructions of 'the natural' which the various social regulators in her two novels attempt to impose on women for their own ends. Pereda's very different answer to the question of the place of nature in modernity is that, if modernity is an empty representation devoid of essential truth, then nature is a superior Platonic representation of God's glory.

In arguing that the abandonment of convertibility into gold destroyed the notion that signs have a stable referent, Goux (1984) suggests that modernist writers reacted by investing the sign itself with a Platonic absolute value. I would argue that this is merely one kind of modernist response to modernity's replacement of the concept of underlying essential truth by the notion that value is constructed by fluctuating, arbitrary market relationships. Specifically, it is the response of those who are hostile to modernity: Goux's example of Mallarmé's attempt to construct a world of Platonic absolutes in language can thus curiously coincide with Pereda's rehabilitation of Platonism which, although it exalts nature as sacred book, at the same time produces nature descriptions which verge on abstraction. Another response, represented by all the other writers studied in this book, is to accept (willingly or reluctantly) that value is arbitrary, relative, and shifting, and to explore the possibilities and problems for representation that ensue. It would, of course, be absurd to argue that nineteenth-century realism is no different from modernism. My argument is, rather, that modernism should be seen, not as a radical break with realism—an 'aesthetics of rupture' as it is so often called—but as an intensification of the problematization of representation found already in realism. Such a view helps us understand why so many nineteenth-century realist writers—particularly in Spain, for reasons that this conclusion will suggest—ironically undermine the representation of reality which they at the same time construct. Critics have mostly reacted to this phenomenon by suggesting that realist novelists are in practice not really realist novelists at all; if this is the case, it seems likely that something is wrong with the definition of realism being used. My aim in this conclusion is to propose a redefinition of realism which allows it to contain the self-reflexive critique of representation found in so many realist texts.

I have used Walter Benjamin's theories in this book because of his perception that cultural modernity can be traced back to the mid-nineteenth century. Goux's otherwise brilliant analysis is flawed by his conventional supposition that nineteenth-century realism corresponds to a period which believed in the inherent value of 'things' and saw money as the transparent sign of that value.[1] Such a belief corresponds, in fact, to the period of classical economics from the mid-eighteenth century to around 1840 when, as Dodd has shown (1994: 8–9), money

[1] See, with reference to the United States, Michaels (1987). For monetary and literary concepts of value in the 18th century, see Thompson (1996). Goux's earlier book (1973) examines the parallels between psychoanalytic and monetary discourse as theories of symbolic representation. On money and desire, see also Buchan (1997).

was seen as a neutral medium facilitating the exchange of goods: that is, a purely instrumental sign, lacking value in its own right but serving to determine the value of things. Realism in the conventional sense of the belief that language, as a sign system, can 'faithfully represent reality' would thus coincide with classical economists' belief that value lies not in money but in things. Curiously, of all the Spanish novelists studied here, Valera comes closest to fitting this description. But, in practice, this view of both 'classic realism' and classical economics is a simplification, for money has never been a purely neutral sign but has always had a value in its own right: that of its metal content. Gold and silver were adopted as currency in the western world precisely because of their value as precious metals: a value which has always fluctuated according to demand but whose instability only began to be perceived with the development of the exchange economy. Thus, as we have seen, the awareness in sixteenth-century Spanish monetary discourse that the value of silver and gold fluctuates on the market can be related to the questioning of representation found in the Spanish picaresque novel and the *Quixote*.[2] The *pícaro* was associated with the Seville underworld produced by the scramble for 'easy wealth' in the New World, and the protagonist of Quevedo's *El buscón* leaves for the Indies. Cervantes twice applied for positions in the Indies (in 1582 and 1590) and, as is well known, a high proportion of the printed copies of the *Quixote* found a ready market in the New World. It is also worth noting that Cervantes's various positions in the State bureaucracy included that of itinerant tax collector, giving him an understanding of the relationship between an unstable monetary system and an incipient State apparatus (Byron 1979: 258, 347–9, 372). The insistence on appearances that characterizes the whole of Spanish Golden Age literature, as it does the novels of Galdós, can be seen as the expression of a sophisticated appreciation of the arbitrary relation of value to things in an economy which the traffic with the New World had subordinated to the laws of the market.

In *The Order of Things*, Foucault proposed that the seventeenth- and eighteenth-century 'classical order' broke with the previous

---

[2] Shell (1995: 133) notes suggestively that Felipe II, unable to understand why the influx of gold and silver from the New World was not producing more wealth, called it 'ghost money'. Shell (1978, 1994, and 1995) explores the relation between monetary and artistic concepts of representation through the centuries.

Neoplatonic notion that meaning lay in things inasmuch as these were a representation of a divine essence, introducing the new idea that meaning lay in the relationships between things. In a suggestive chapter titled 'Exchanging' (1970: 166–214), Foucault linked this epistemological shift to the rise of mercantilism. Foucault's key examples are Velázquez's *Las meninas*, with its self-reflexive perspectivism; and the *Quixote*, which demonstrates that only a madman can still believe in a world of stable essential values, represented by the Neoplatonic notion of the world as book which Don Quixote takes literally by reading it as a romance of chivalry. The fact that Foucault's key examples are both Spanish suggests that this major shift in the European world view had its origins in the sixteenth-century Spanish discourse on inflation, which Foucault seems not to know. Vilar —a European economic historian familiar with the Spanish context—insists that this Spanish monetary discourse (largely by theologians who had a professional concern with the erosion of stable values) should be afforded a major place in the history of economic philosophy (1991: 157). He also reminds us that paper money and credit have existed in some form from the early mercantilist period (1991: 157). Indeed Giddens (1985: 156) notes that the deferment of payment intrinsic to the exchange economy is itself a form of credit. In dramatizing Rosalía de Bringas's frantic but successful attempt to 'buy time', Galdós is capturing what Giddens sees as the key feature of the money economy. Vilar (1991: 250) cites early eighteenth-century monetary theorists who, whether favourable or hostile to paper money, explicitly described it as a 'fictitious' symbol. And, although Adam Smith insisted that wealth lay in industry (the production of things) and not in the possession of money as such, from the start capitalism was based on the notion of surplus value: that is, money making more money. This, indeed, is Marx's definition of capital. Vilar also notes (1991: 286) that 'far from being in opposition to one another, the move towards gold coin as the universal standard, and the development of banking and credit, took place simultaneously'; that is, in the second half of the nineteenth century. Harvey (1989: 260–53), following Benjamin's lead, traces modernist awareness of the arbitrary relation between sign and signified back to the Europe-wide credit crisis of 1847 which, in addition to triggering the revolutions of 1848, created anxieties about credit as 'fictitious capital' (Marx's term). If realism in the conventional sense of 'the faithful representation of reality' has ever existed, it is best situated in the period of classical economics—though here too one has only to think of *Tristram Shandy*; indeed, in Britain the period of classical economics (starting around 1760, when the first part of *Tristram Shandy* was published) coincided with intense debate about the national debt (de Bolla 1989); it was only in 1821 that Britain adopted the gold standard. The period dealt with in this book—that of Spain's imperfect transition to modernity—is so interesting because it is characterized by a residual belief that money has an inherent value (that of its metal content, which however fluctuates on the market like the value of everything else), plus an escalating awareness that it is an arbitrary sign whose value is purely relative. The same tension between a residual belief in inherent value, and a dominant belief that value is arbitrary, relative, and unstable, underlies both the social critique and the theory of representation (implicit or explicit) in nineteenth-century realism—especially, though not only, in the later part of the century.

In this book I have also drawn, as did Benjamin, on the work of Simmel since his analysis of modernity shows a particularly keen awareness of such complexities. Simmel's ideas are suggestive for various reasons. First, because he—like Tarde, to whom I have also referred—is concerned with the psychological impact of capitalist modernity, and specifically with its privileging of money as a system for channelling, and expressing, desire. *The Philosophy of Money* (1900) grew out of Simmel's 1889 essay 'The Psychology of Money'. As Simmel argues (1990: 78–103; Dodd 1994: 43), in the modern market economy the value of things, determined by exchange value and not by use value, has nothing to do with their 'nature' but is a sign of their desirability. This perception of money as the marker of desire is fundamental to the nineteenth-century realist novel's treatment of psychology. Just as human desires are, in the realist novel, based on unstable, shifting relationships (hence the repeated theme of the breakdown of marriage), so Simmel insists that monetary value, determined by exchange relations, is relative: that is, arbitrary and fluctuating. In the same way Ana Ozores's desires are based on the relative desirability of Mesía and the Magistral, which fluctuates in her eyes according to the degree of public credit enjoyed or needed by each at any one moment; in opting for Mesía, whose public desirability is not backed by personal 'substance', Ana is succumbing to a market concept of value. Indeed, as a Don Juan figure, Mesía incarnates a market concept of value whereby desirability is commensurate with demand. The tragic gap between Ana's desire for Mesía and his lack of inner worth is, I suggest, the point. As previously noted, it must be remembered that in the nineteenth century idealism meant belief in essential values. As its opposite, realism logically implies belief that value is arbitrary, shifting, and relative. The revised definition of realism that I propose is thus 'the representation of a reality constituted by exchange relations'. Such a relativist outlook, based on a market model of human relations, by definition supposes a lack of absolute, inherent values. It is worth noting that the word 'comercio' is the standard term for social relations used throughout Sanz del Río's *Ideal de la humanidad*. This revised definition of realism does not preclude nostalgia for inherent, essential meaning but involves recognition that it is at best only part of the picture. Simmel himself noted (1990: 160) that the monetary concept of value which characterizes modernity contains a residual belief in inherent value in the form of the gold or bimetallic standard, which ties money to an intrinsic value (albeit one that fluctuates on the market). The advantage of defining realism as 'the representation of a reality constituted by exchange relations', by contrast with standard dictionary definitions of the term as the faithful representation of reality,[3] is that, while not precluding a residual belief in (or nostalgia for) inherent value, it allows realism to contain within it the questioning of representation found in its major practitioners.

We also may recall here Anderson's perception that the realist novel, in constructing a complex web of social relations (which, like market relations, are often transitory, indirect, and arbitrary in that they are the product of chance), mirrors and indeed constructs the new concept of the nation as 'imagined community'. The development of the capitalist exchange economy—which, as Marx and Simmel observed, makes money a form of social exchange (Marx 1990: 436–8; Simmel 1990:

---

[3] *OED*: 'close resemblance to what is real; fidelity of representation, rendering the precise details of the real'; *RAE*: 'sistema estético que asigna como fin a las obras artísticas o literarias la imitación fiel de la naturaleza.'

130, 162)—is inextricably linked to the more abstract social networks that characterize the nation-State. For, as Giddens comments (1985: 128), the capitalist system is 'the form of production on which everyone becomes dependent'. 'Everyone' here means what it says, for the point of money is to provide a 'universal equivalent of exchange' (Frisby in Simmel 1990: p. xxxi). At the same time, the national monetary systems which became tightly defined in the course of the nineteenth century with the imposition of standardized national currencies construct the users of money first and foremost as members of a national community. The State had always imposed its presence on its citizens via taxation (Simmel 1990: 316; Giddens 1985: 157), but the extension of a centralized administrative system in the nineteenth century turned this fiscal relationship into a form of social control embracing all areas and members of the population. This is nicely illustrated by Valera's cautionary tale, in *Doña Luz*, of the Andalusian villager who boasted to a visitor about the fabulous sums of money he had made from his agricultural activities, only to discover that the visitor was a tax inspector (1970: 197–8). Bahamonde Magro and Martínez (1994: 377) note that, in the mid-century, the undeclared taxable income in Valera's province of Córdoba exceeded the amount declared; this failure to pay taxes (*contribuciones*) effectively means a failure to contribute to the nation. Giddens notes that fiduciary money could not have developed without the nation-State's 'monopoly of the certification (not necessarily the direct production) of money, via legally accredited means'. In particular: 'The centralization of state power was the necessary condition [. . .] making it possible to detach money in circulation from its convertible bullion value.' Fiduciary money can thus be called 'national money' since 'the limits of its general acceptability as the medium of circulation are determined by the domain of exercise of the political power on which the fiduciary money is based' (Giddens 1985: 154–5). Historians of capitalism and the nation-State place the transition from the *ancien régime* to modernity somewhere between 1750 and 1850. As Giddens insists: 'The social order [. . .] initiated by the advent of modernity is not just an accentuation of previous trends of development. In a number of specifiable and quite fundamental respects, it is something new' (1985: 33). If one reads the realist novel as the expression of the new representation systems constituted by the capitalist monetary economy and the nation-State, both based on increasingly abstract networks of social relations, it becomes clear that the decisive cultural shift also occurs in this period; that is, with the development of, rather than after, realism.

Simmel's argument that the central role played by money in modernity is an indication, not of materialism, but of an unprecedented capacity for abstraction led critics at the time to see him as the theorist of impressionism (Frisby in Simmel 1990: pp. xxiv–xxv). For impressionism figures the beginnings of the artistic move towards abstraction that would culminate in early twentieth-century modernism. As in Simmel's analysis of money as a sign system based on relative, arbitrary, shifting value, impressionism creates a sense of 'the real' through the relationship to each other of individual patches of colour that have little direct relationship to the object represented; impressionist painters were also, of course, fascinated with showing how colour is not inherent in objects because it changes at different times of day. I hope to have shown how Pardo Bazán's impressionistic descriptions relate to her wider questioning of the conversion of reality into representation through the discourses of social control. The blurred vision of Galdós's Francisco Bringas when he is left with 'la visión calenturienta de millares de puntos luminosos o de tenues rayos metálicos, movibles, fugaces' goes beyond impressionism, or even *pointillisme*, to near total abstraction, for he can no longer see 'things' but only the frenetic circulation of unstable metal signs that have lost any referent. This is an appropriate vision for a miser who, as we have seen, fetishizes money as a commodity in its own right. As Marx put it in the first nine chapters, titled 'The Theory of Value', of the only volume of *Das Kapital* published in his lifetime: when the development of the banking system leads to the use of money not to increase production but to make more money, capital 'enters now, so to say, into private relations with itself' (1990: 450); that is, capitalism enters into a self-reflexive phase. The formula with which Marx represents the earlier industrial phase of the capitalist economy—$M>C>M_1$ (money buys a commodity which is sold for a larger sum of money)—is, in the banking era, replaced by the formula $M>M_1$ (money makes more money without the exchange of any commodity) (1990: 445–51). In other words, 'things' disappear as a middle term and we are left—like Bringas—with the circulation of pure signs with no referent.

Galdós's insistence on money has traditionally been seen as a sign of his realism in the sense of a concern with the material world. It has been assumed that the self-reflexive dimension of his work, so stressed by recent critics, makes him a modern rather than a realist writer.[4] I hope to have shown that the monetary references in Galdós's work make him a realist writer in the different sense that he is responding to the increasing abstraction and self-reflexivity of the modern capitalist monetary system, which detaches value from 'things'. It is logical that Galdós, as the novelist who most mentions money, should also be the one whose work is the most self-reflexive. It is no coincidence that his first 'novel of modernity', *La desheredada*, should have been written in 1881 at the height of the Barcelona boom in banking shares, which in reality was a 'paper fever' rather than a *febre d'or*. Tortella (1974: i. 474) notes that the dramatic increase of paper money in circulation in 1880–1 produced public alarm about the harmful effects of 'dinero barato': that is, money whose value was cheapened by the lack of correspondence between nominal and inherent worth, and also, by implication, because increasing circulation allowed it to fall into the hands of those who themselves did not have inherent financial or moral worth. We have seen how, already in 1881, *La desheredada* depicts a consumerist modernity in which what counts is not things but signs; thus, as Fernández Cifuentes observes (1988: 310), the only way Isidora can get her value recognized is 'to put it up for sale'. Richards (1990: 16) notes that nineteenth-century advertising 'is not the distorted mirror of production: it is the capitalist mode of production. What it produces so deliriously are signs, signs taken for wonders, signs signifying consumption.' The socialist Juan Bou is well placed to appreciate that money is a 'mere formula'—anticipating Marx's insights in *Das Kapital* which Galdós cannot have known in 1881[5]—because he is a

---

[4] See in particular Kronik (1977, 1981, 1982); Urey (1982, 1989); Tsuchiya (1990).

[5] Volume i of *Das Kapital* (the only volume published before Marx's death in 1883) was published in 1867. A serialized Spanish translation of the first four sections appeared in 1886; the first complete Spanish version appeared in 1897–8. But Marx's ideas in *Das Kapital* were popularized in Spain through summaries, especially that produced in French in 1883 by Deville (translated into Spanish 1887). The first Spanish translation of *The Communist Manifesto* was published in 1886 (Artola 1973: 345).

printer who manufactures advertising material and product labels. Realism is not so much a mirror or window onto the world as a window display, like those in which Isidora looks not only at the goods for sale but also at her own image reflected back at her; that is, a world of signs or abstract values conferred by a price label, which represents itself—and the consumer—as a representation. It is logical also that Galdós's extraordinarily self-reflexive novel *La de Bringas* should have been written in 1884, directly following Spain's abandonment of the gold standard the previous year. For, as Marx notes in 'The Fetishism of Commodities', monetary value 'converts every product into a social hieroglyphic' or 'cabalistic sign' (Marx 1990: 436; Harvey 1989: 101). Thus, in fetishizing consumer goods for their appearance value rather than their use value, Rosalía is turning 'things' into signs while, in doing the same with money, Francisco Bringas is, as we have seen, replacing 'things' with signs altogether.

Critics have noted Galdós's move away from realism (in the sense of concern with the material world) in his novels of the 1890s; it was in the 1890s that the peseta, no longer tied to gold, entered a downward spiral of depreciation on the international markets. Galdós's most self-reflexive novel after *La de Bringas*, *Nazarín*, was written like Pereda's *Peñas arriba* in 1895, the year before gold coin completely disappeared from circulation in Spain. Like Pereda's Marcelo but more radically, Nazarín rejects urban modernity and engages in contemplation of nature as a Neoplatonic sign of God's glory. His search for essential meaning requires him to forgo all forms of private ownership of goods, for participation in the monetary system involves acceptance of a system of arbitrary, unstable values. It also requires him to reject the conversion of reality into representation effected by the proliferation of print culture: a latter-day Don Quixote, he takes literally the Neoplatonic metaphor of the world as book, reading it as if it were the Gospels; the only books he keeps are religious ones, representing—if not authored by—the voice of God. Like that of Don Quixote as interpreted by Foucault, Nazarín's quest for stable values in the capitalist era is shown to be, if not that of a madman, that of a saint who cannot be accommodated in modernity. His refusal to compromise represents his rejection of the relativity of value that characterizes the exchange economy. But, inasmuch as he is reacting against the modern monetary system, it could be argued that the capacity for abstraction required by it has, in a curious way, facilitated his ability to conceive of an abstract entity (albeit one of a very different kind) such as God. Simmel (1990: 236–9) notes the appropriateness of the commonplace that money is the modern God: 'In reality, money in its psychological form, as the absolute means and thus the unifying point of innumerable sequences of purposes, possesses a significant relationship to the notion of God [. . .] In so far as money becomes the absolutely commensurable expression and equivalent of all values, it rises to abstract heights way above the whole broad diversity of objects; it becomes the centre in which the most opposed, the most estranged and the most distant things find their common denominator and come into contact with one another' (Simmel 1990: 236–7). Thus, Simmel argues that there is a direct link between the development of monotheism and that of a money economy (Simmel 1990: 237). It could similarly be argued that modernity's conversion of reality into representation makes possible Nazarín's confusion of world with book that, in a more obvious sense, signifies his attempt to return to a pre-modern belief in Neoplatonic essences. Nazarín's quixotic attempt to live out the Scriptures should perhaps be seen not so much as a rejection of modernity—which he cannot escape anyway since the Guardia Civil, as agents of the nation-State, bring him back to Madrid by force—but as what happens when a residual Neoplatonism meets modernity. It is not so surprising that Galdós's 'mystical' novels of the 1890s should coexist with his *Torquemada* series, about a moneylender who makes money out of money and whose first son is a mathematical genius: that is, brilliant at abstraction.[6] As is well known, Torquemada dies with the word 'conversión' on his lips, in what may be a reference to religious conversion or to the practice of debt conversion whereby the national debt was reduced by issuing new government bonds at a lower interest rate or lower nominal value. The passage from an increasingly fiduciary monetary system to belief in God is a giant leap from belief in relative value to belief in absolute, essential value, but both have

---

[6] The use of economic discourse in the *Torquemada* series is studied by Urey (in Labanyi 1993*a*: 181–98) and Delgado (1999: 31–47). Delgado notes the importance of the increasing gap between signifier and signified opened up by the proliferation of paper money.

in common the replacement of things by abstraction. Indeed, as Marx noted (Harvey 1985: 5), both are based on 'faith'.

Although Galdós is the writer who most questions representation and who is most concerned with money, I hope to have demonstrated that both these features figure in all the Spanish realist novels discussed. I hope also to have shown that all the writers studied are equally concerned with the increasingly abstract forms of political representation required by the modern nation-State. If the Spanish realist novel questions representation more than that of any other country it is, I would argue, because public discussion of the problematic nature of both monetary and political representation was particularly acute in Spain in the 1880s, continuing through the 1890s. We have seen how the realist novel anticipates the concern with decadence of the so-called 1898 Generation; the continuum between the realist novel's questioning of representation and the impressionism of Baroja and Azorín or the fictional games of Unamuno can be linked to their common concern with the malfunctioning of the representation systems on which capitalist modernity and liberal democracy depend. The 1898 writers are chiefly concerned with the fraudulent nature of parliamentary representation—here, their critique of *particularismo* directly echoes that of the late nineteenth-century Krausists —but their mistrust of a monetary system characterized in the 1890s by spiralling depreciation is implied by their dismissal of economic modernization for a return to the land (albeit described in impressionist terms as lacking a stable essence). The *regeneracionista* theorists who did argue for economic modernization (Costa, Mallada) were unanimous in rejecting urban consumerism for agricultural production. In the realist novel, discussion of the problematic nature of monetary and political presentation go hand in hand. It is logical enough that a country in which modernization was problematic should have a keener sense of the arbitrariness of the representation systems which constitute modernity than countries where modernization was more successfully implemented. The crisis of monetary and political representation is directly linked to the critique of linguistic representation found in the Spanish realist novel since it led to repeated expressions of concern, which I will now briefly trace, about the fact that Spain existed as a modern nation only on paper.

In 1865 Galdós wrote a satirical article in *La Nación* in which 'un título de la Deuda' and 'un billete del Banco de España' commiserate about the fact that no one wants them any more since both are worthless 'papeletes'. The crumpled banknote laments: 'Todos me rechazan y dándome el infamante apodo de *papel mojado*, me cierran sus cajas poniéndome de patitas en la calle. El envanecido oro se niega á cambiarse por mí y la plata me mira con horror.' The parable ends with the government bond looking forward to a mythical future when he will be worth millions, and the banknote lamenting the premature death of his progenitor, Credit (Pérez Galdós 1981: 66). This article was provoked by the 1865 credit crisis that triggered the 1868 Revolution: in many ways a replay of the 1847 credit crisis, sparking Europe-wide revolution, that Harvey has proposed as modernism's starting point. This 1865 crisis caused, and in turn was aggravated by, mass public demands for banknotes to be reimbursed in metal coin (Sardá 1948: 148). The collapse of financial credit was a collapse of national credit since government bonds were 'papel de Estado' and banknotes were guaranteed, though not at this stage exclusively issued, by the Banco de España. Financial crisis was thus bound to end in political crisis (the overthrow of the monarchy); conversely, the revolutionary government's proclamation of national sovereignty was accompanied by the replacement of the monarch's head on coinage by the national insignia. Galdós's 1865 perception that the nation's credit was based on worthless 'papeletes' anticipates the ongoing public debate on the monetary system that would take place throughout the Restoration, in response to the peaking of the national debt in its early years, the Barcelona Stock Exchange crash of late 1881, the debt conversions of December 1881 and May 1882, and abandonment of the gold standard in 1883: all of which were caused by, and in turn prompted, what Tortella calls an 'avalancha de papel'. The supply of bank notes had been spiralling since the ceiling on their issue was raised in 1874; it was raised again in 1881, and yet again in 1883 to five times its 1881 level (Tortella Casares 1974: i. 141–2, 158, 276; Artola 1973: 306–7). The sense that the apparent increase in wealth was not backed by substance was exacerbated by a chronic trade deficit, a problem throughout the nineteenth century but peaking in 1883–7 (Vicens Vives 1969: 697): the period when many of the novels studied here were written. Camacho's spectacular debt conversions of 1881–2 made evident the arbitrary nature of monetary value by reducing the national debt's 'valor efectivo' (as cash value is significantly called in Spanish) by 50 per cent, compensated by guaranteed payment in francs or sterling.[7] Debt conversion was effectively a way of 'writing down' or 'writing off' the national debt. The 1883 decision to abandon convertibility into gold was an emergency measure to curb the consequent massive outflow of metal holdings from the country (García de Cortázar and González Vesga 1994: 462). Although the Spanish monetary system remained tied to silver after 1883, it was effectively entirely fiduciary given that throughout the period 1873–1900 silver prices were falling, which meant that silver coin's metal value fell progressively below its nominal value (Tortella Casares 1974: i. 476, 480–1). Not only was the gap between signs and 'things' widening, but the value of signs was becoming progressively greater than that of 'things'. As early as 1876, a parliamentary monetary commission had found that silver coin was based on 'una relación ficticia de valores' (Sardá 1948: 177).

The national debt was a problem throughout continental Europe, but Spain was unique in abandoning the gold standard at a time when the other major nations had recently abandoned the bimetallic system for a single standard based on gold.[8] England had effectively moved to the gold standard in the mid-eighteenth century, doing so officially in 1821: one wonders

---

[7] The first 'conversión de la deuda' was effected by Garay in 1818; other major 'debt conversions' were those of Mon (Villaamil's former boss in Galdós's *Miau*) in 1841 and of Bravo Murillo in 1851. The practice was first introduced in England in 1715; France also effected several conversions between 1825 and 1888. See the helpful entries on 'Deuda pública' in the Alianza *Diccionario de historia de España*, ed. Germán Bleiberg, vol. i, and that on 'Deuda' in the Espasa-Calpe *Enciclopedia universal ilustrada europeo-americana*.

[8] The gold standard was adopted by practically all western nations (following the line set by Britain in 1821) in the course of the 1870s: by a newly unified Germany in 1871, by the Scandinavian countries in 1872, by the United States in 1873. In 1885 the Latin Monetary Union (France, Belgium, Switzerland, Italy), having abandoned the issue of silver coin in 1878, formally ended its adherence to the bimetallic system and moved to a system tied exclusively to gold. The international gold standard was maintained until the start of the First World War, and after the war was re-established by most countries by 1928 but collapsed in the wake of the 1929 Wall Street crash. By 1937, no nation continued to adhere to the full gold standard. See Sardá (1948: 153, 160, 175–6) and entry for 'gold standard' in the *Encyclopaedia Britannica*.

whether this has some connection with the relative lack of self-reflexive awareness in the nineteenth-century English novel, by when the national debt, a major problem at the time of *Tristram Shandy*, was under control. Given the development of the Russian novel, it is worth noting that Russia was in a similarly anomalous position to Spain, with a *de facto* fiduciary system till 1897 when it (unlike Spain) moved to gold (Tortella Casares 1974: i. 475–6, 483). Spain's anomalous position with regard to the gold standard, pointed out by contemporary observers, helps explain why Spanish realist novelists in particular should have had such a sophisticated understanding of the problematics of representation. As Tortella puts it (1974: i. 487), using a terminology that invites application to literary realism: 'España se adelantó al resto de Europa en desembarazarse del mito del dinero de pleno contenido', opting for 'el dinero signo'. In abandoning the 'mito del dinero de pleno contenido' in 1883, at the time of the realist novel, Spain made the same major intellectual leap that the other major western powers would make around 1914 and again—definitively—after 1929, coinciding with the major period of production of literary and artistic modernism. Athough this move was much criticized by Spanish contemporaries, worried about the increasing depreciation (chronic in the 1890s) of a free-floating peseta no longer tied to gold, recent economic historians have congratulated Spanish politicians on their foresight, noting that depreciation of the peseta effectively reduced the national debt and relieved a chronic balance of payments deficit (Tortella Casares 1974: i. 533).[9]

We have seen that, in the novels studied, a discourse—explicit or implicit—about money accompanies what in every case is an explicit discourse about *caciquismo*, almost always accompanied by concern at the extension of the central State of which *caciquismo* was a manifestation. Like the discourse on money, this political discourse is specifically concerned with a malfunctioning of representation, for liberal political theory is the theory of representative government. Hobsbawm (1990: 19) notes that the modern notion of 'the nation' that developed

[9] The only Spanish contemporary work I have found that approves the decision to abandon gold is Vicente Ortí y Brull, *La cuestión monetaria* (Madrid: Imprenta y Litografía de los Huérfanos, 1893), which shows a sophisticated awareness of the symbolic nature of money.

in the late nineteenth century was inseparable from the notion of representative government. Carr (1966: 367-8) observes that the opening session of every Restoration parliament discussed electoral abuses. It is important to remember that liberal democracy does not mean government by the people, but government by elected 'deputies' who represent civil society (the criteria for membership of the latter having varied in different periods). Habermas (1989: 5-14) traces the evolution of the western concept of political representation since the High Middle Ages. If under feudalism the Crown and the nobility represented their own power to a public constituted as an audience, with the Renaissance the nobility's function came to be that of representing the monarch. The emergence of the notion of the divine right of kings gave the monarch the right to rule, not because of his own worth, but because he represented God, and initiated a major reversal since, as Giddens notes (1985: 93-4), instead of the nobility representing the monarch, the latter now came to be seen as an embodiment of the State, which under the *ancien régime* started to separate off from the Crown (Giddens 1985: 93-4). With the consequent emergence of civil society, a new notion of sovereignty developed according to which citizens (that is, those enjoying civic rights) agreed, via the social contract, to place legislative power in the Crown and State jointly, as their representatives. As the concept of universal human rights emerged with the French Revolution, this evolved into the notion of national sovereignty whereby legislative power resided in the nation, on whose behalf the members of civil society elected parliamentary representatives to govern via delegation. There is here a double process of representation, whereby parliamentary deputies represent the interests of the members of civil society who have chosen them, and the latter represent what they deem to be the interests of the rest of the populace, which has no say in the matter. In periods when suffrage is not universal (and in the nineteenth century even universal suffrage excluded women), such a system of representation is clearly fraught with difficulty. Casey (1989: 138) notes that, with the conservative backlash to the 1848 revolutions, the concept of democracy lost the egalitarian connotations it had had in the immediate post-1789 period and acquired the restricted sense of political representation outlined here. This coincided with the mid-century extension of an increasingly centralized State bureaucracy, relying more and more on the exercise of power via delegation at exactly the same historical moment that larger sectors of the population were starting to demand a political voice. As Habermas shrewdly comments (1989: 87, 136), the function of the mid-nineteenth-century liberal notion of representative government was precisely to make belief in universal freedom compatible with restricted membership of civil society: only those who were autonomous, independent individuals could adequately represent a society based on the principle of individual freedom. Thus J. S. Mill's *Representative Government* (1861), much cited by the Krausists and translated into Spanish in 1878, argued that the enlightened must represent the uninformed multitude, who should however be helped via education to become enlightened citizens.

Bahamonde Magro and Martínez (1994: 65) note that Spain's first Liberal Constitution of 1812 'estableció por primera vez en la historia del país la representación nacional en contraposición al privilegio histórico'. This Constitution was, of course, never implemented, creating a situation where representation existed only on paper. The effect of the 1876 Restoration Constitution, which reneged on the *sexenio revolucionario*'s proclamation of universal manhood suffrage and national (under the Federal Republic, popular) sovereignty, introducing a high property qualification for suffrage and relocating sovereignty in the Crown and parliament, was to reduce drastically the number of the nation's inhabitants entitled to elect a parliamentary representative. Martínez Cuadrado (1973: 57) estimates the percentage of the population eligible to vote at general elections under the Restoration, prior to Sagasta's 1890 re-establishment of universal manhood suffrage, at 5.7 per cent in 1879, 4.9 per cent in 1881, 4.6 per cent in 1884, and 4.5 per cent in 1886–7: a progressive reduction of a dismal figure (Martínez Cuadrado 1973: 57). Solé Tura and Aja (1978: 73) suggests that in 1886, 'perfeccionado el sistema censitario' (restricted suffrage based on a property qualification), only 2.1 per cent of the population could vote. Most contemporary complaints, notably from the Krausists, were about the relocation of sovereignty in the Crown and parliament. In a sense this followed logically from the curtailment of voting rights for if only a tiny fraction of the population could vote, it was hard to argue that the legislature represented the nation (and much less 'the people', a term which made explicit the inclusion of the lower classes). But the placing of sovereignty in the Crown and parliament eroded political representation still further, since it meant that the tiny body of voters, rather than delegating legislative powers which nominally remained theirs, had by the fact of voting placed power fully in the hands of the legislature. Technically this meant that the latter could do what it liked, regardless of any notional obligation to represent the interests of the electorate (and regardless of the even vaguer obligation to represent the interests of the wider populace supposedly represented by the electorate). Thus, in effect, the placing of sovereignty in the Crown and parliament meant that the legislature represented itself. In other words, political representation—like the advanced capitalist economy—becomes self-reflexive. This was aggravated by the 1876 Constitution's extraordinary provision that, in the event of a parliamentary vote of no confidence and consequent government dissolution, the King, rather than call elections to determine which party should form a government, should appoint a new head of government who would be invited to hold elections to procure a majority and thus form a government. Again we have a self-reflexive form of political representation whereby the government holds elections to elect itself: as we have seen, a contemporary commentator explicitly described this process as the conversion of power 'en representante de sí mismo' (Varela Ortega 1977: 368). The system that ensured that this always happened was, of course, *caciquismo*.

The centrality of the concept of representative government to Krausist political theory is a gauge of contemporary concern at the Restoration's reneging on the principles of the 1869 Liberal Constitution. Galdós's 1871–2 political articles for the *Revista de España* persistently defended the liberal monarchy of Amadeo I (chosen as king because of the House of Savoy's role in Italian Unification) against Carlist absolutism on the one hand and federal republican demands for popular access to power on the other, on the grounds that Amadeo's acceptance of the 1869 Constitution made the monarchy a 'sistema representativo' enshrining the principle of 'la representación nacional' (Pérez Galdós 1982). Under the Restoration, Galdós and Alas were among the many political journalists who repeatedly attacked successive governments, those of Cánovas in particular, for making a mockery of the principle of political representation. For example, in his 22 May 1884 article 'Régimen representativo' (1923: 19–26), Galdós insisted that Spain had not assimilated the 'admirable organismo sajón [. . .] del self-government'; Alas's press campaigns against electoral abuses and the erosion of local autonomy have been discussed in Chapter 6. It must be remembered that the Krausist defence of political representation was always conceived in terms of J. S. Mill's understanding of the term as government by an enlightened minority on behalf of those less capacitated. Conservatives and Liberals all claimed to be adhering to the principle of representative government but they disagreed hugely about the extent of the representation. Even though Sagasta conceded to Cánovas in dropping the principle of national sovereignty in 1883, in 1890 he restored universal manhood suffrage. A Krausist political text in Galdós's library, Miguel Moya's *Conflictos entre los poderes del Estado* (1879), prefaced by the Krausist political theorist Azcárate, makes it clear that the Krausist theory of political representation was a way of reconciling restricted representation with universal human rights: its final chapter, titled 'El gobierno representativo', justifies representative government on the grounds that it allows all classes to participate in society each in their own capacity.[10] Enríquez de Salamanca (1993) notes that, under the Restoration, voting rights were held not just by those paying tax above a certain amount but also by members of the liberal professions, called 'capacidades', making it clear that they were seen as society's 'betters'. Elorza (1973: 187–8) comments that Segismundo Moret's typically Krausist concept of representative government as the political parties' 'mediation' between the individual and the State, expounded in his 1884 book *La representación nacional: teoría del sufragio*, was a way of preventing the masses from swamping the enlightened minority. As we have seen, *caciquismo* was felt to be a problem at the time, not because it restricted political representation to a minority, but because it allowed the mass of rural votes to swamp those of an educated urban bourgeoisie. Azcárate's *El régimen parlamentario en la práctica* (1885) attacked both the extension of central State

---

[10] Galdós's library also contained Spencer's *Estudios políticos y sociales* (in a 1904 translation), the first section of which is on 'El gobierno representativo'.

power and *caciquismo* as a 'degeneration' of the principles of 'representación y delegación' (title of a section in Chapter 5). As his 1877 book *El self-government y la monarquía doctrinaria* makes clear, Azcárate was here arguing for self-government in the sense of government on behalf of the people, as opposed to *caciquismo*'s fraudulent practices which allowed the government to elect itself through manipulation of the votes of the ignorant rural masses (Azcárate 1877a). The brutish parliamentary deputy Trabuco in *La Regenta* illustrates this concern with the uneducated usurping the educated's rightful role in government.

The Krausists' rejection of female suffrage was consistent with their belief in representative government since, as we saw in Chapter 2, it was based on the notion that the husband legally and politically represented the wife (and children). Despite the Krausists' rejection of Hegel's subordination of the individual to the State, they were here echoing his argument that the husband did not own his wife and children but represented them (Landes in Elshtain 1982: 131–2). Consequently, women asserting their independence was seen by them as an abuse of political representation not entirely dissimilar to *caciquismo*'s threat to the rule of an enlightened minority: Ana Ozores's adulterous liaison with the local *cacique* Mesía thus constitutes a double adulteration of the representation process. We have seen how the cardinal sin for the Krausists was *particularismo* or egoism: putting one's own interests before those of the body one represents. Translated into the terms of liberal political theory, this means representing oneself. *Particularismo*, whether that of Ana Ozores as a woman who puts herself before the family or that of Mesía as local *cacique*, is another form of self-reflexivity.

The flagrant abuses of *caciquismo* made it abundantly clear to contemporary commentators that political representation —in the sense of rule by an enlightened minority—was not working. Apart from the frequent use of 'electores ficticios' (whole cemeteries in some cases), municipal councils frequently existed on paper only, never meeting (Varela Ortega 1977: 410, 412). In his 1891 essay *La administración local*, awarded a prize by the Real Academia de Ciencias Morales y Políticas, Bartolomé de Vera y Casado noted that local councils, unable to produce the written reports required of them by the central

State, hired agencies in the cities to produce fictitious documents ('estas ficciones') (Vera y Casado 1893: 56). Force mostly did not need to be used to rig elections because the election results were simply 'written', sometimes published in the local press several days in advance (Varela Ortega 1977: 123, 423). As Varela Ortega comments, and as everyone at the time knew: 'los resultados oficiales, no representaban lo que decían representar' (1977: 422). In fact, only about a quarter of the already tiny electorate used their right to a vote, with the result that candidates were sometimes elected on the basis of 1,000 votes; in the overseas territories, the number of votes cast ranged from 1 to 500 (one thinks of Galdós's 1886 election to represent a district of Puerto Rico) (Varela Ortega 1977: 424). Parliamentary representatives concentrated their efforts, not on parliament as a representative body (Galdós never made a parliamentary speech), but on the various ministries that could grant favours to their clients (Varela Ortega 1977: 360). Varela Ortega (1977: 435) puts the blame for this political abuse squarely onto the Liberal Party's abandonment of the principle of national sovereignty, which made representative government into a fiction, in practice replaced by a self-reflexive system whereby elections were not held but written —or staged. Indeed, the 1883 majority Liberal vote in favour of dropping the principle of national sovereignty had split the Party, leading to a decree of dissolution and the King's invitation to Cánovas to hold elections to vote his Conservative Party into power—which it duly did in 1884 in the dirtiest elections in the history of *caciquismo*. It was in the wake of these elections, which patently showed political representation in Spain to be a fraudulent, self-reflexive system, that *La de Bringas, Lo prohibido, Fortunata y Jacinta, La Regenta,* and *Los Pazos de Ulloa* were written.

The use of theatrical imagery to describe contemporary politics found in the novels of Galdós and Alas is a commonplace in the Restoration press.[11] Costa's *Oligarquía y caciquismo*, summarizing the replies to his 1901 Ateneo-sponsored questionnaire on the subject, described the 1868 Liberal Revolution as an

---

[11] This commonplace of course dates back to Larra's sarcastic claim, in his 'Tercera carta de un liberal de acá a un liberal de allá', that 'no sólo vivimos bajo un régimen representativo sino que esto no es más que una pura representación' (1951: 1125–6).

'aparato teatral' and 'simulacro de revolución' because it had failed to eradicate the *cacique*; in fact, it was the Restoration that brought the *cacique* to prominence. Costa reports Macías Picavea's reply that 'Monarquía, partidos, Constitución, Administración, Cortes son puro papel'. Costa himself insists throughout that there were two nations: one that existed in 'las leyes de papel', and one that existed in practice, based on custom. Given the 'creciente multiplicación del papeleo' (Jutglar 1971: 83) produced by the extension of central State power, particularly with the Restoration's codification of all areas of public and private life, the State's replacement of representative government by a self-reflexive system was also a problem of legal misrepresentation. Costa—a lawyer by training like so many Krausists— denounced the State's 'fe ciega en la virtud del papel impreso, en la eficacia de la Gaceta' (the State newspaper which published new legislation, whose contents Costa described as 'engañosas ficciones'), for it had produced a country where 'la libertad se había hecho papel, sí, pero no se había hecho carne' (Costa 1973: 19, 20–2, 26, 43). Here Costa directly echoes Alas's 1881 lament, discussed in Chapter 6, that the law is generally perceived as 'algo que está en el papel sellado', unlike the Roman *res publica* where it was a tangible presence. Fiestas Loza notes that legal misrepresentation deriving from the Restoration's privileging of the written document was aggravated by Cánovas's 1875 abolition of the 'juicio oral y público' (public trial by jury, based on oral evidence from witnesses) introduced by the 1869 Constitution; the 1881 Civil Justice Act specifically stated that all evidence must be in writing. As a result, there was practically no communication between judge and defendant, particularly, of course, when the latter was illiterate. Sagasta reintroduced oral evidence in 1882, and trial by jury in 1888 (García Delgado 1985: 420, 425, 428, 430). Interestingly, Costa's political demands in *Oligarquía y caciquismo* included a return to the gold standard (1973: 43): the failure of political and monetary representation are seen as part of the same problem, for both contribute to the loss of credibility of a nation constituted by paper representations.

Regardless of the political abuses and spiralling of fiduciary money which so exercised Restoration public opinion, the perception that Spain as a modern nation existed only on paper was in a sense inevitable, since modernity by definition consists in the construction of ever higher degrees of political and monetary abstraction. As we have seen, *caciquismo* did help Spain's vast rural majority deal with an increasingly abstract centralized administration which was omnipresent yet remote. If Galdós, in his 1892 novel *Tristana*, talked of 'nuestra edad, de más papel que hierro y de tantas fórmulas hueras' (Pérez Galdós 1970: 1537), it was not only because of problems specific to Spain's imperfect modernization, but also because the modern nation-State is based on a 'theory of abstract community', to cite the title of a recent book (James 1996). Indeed, the modern nation-State is necessarily self-reflexive in that it first defines itself as such on paper, and then proceeds to turn that definition into reality through a process of centralization and homogenization. Even if the State genuinely represents the nation, and not itself as in Restoration Spain, it represents an entity that it is at the same time creating. This is made possible by political liberalism's rejection of inherent worth, based on birthright, for a belief in universal freedom based on the radically new concept of the self-made man, whose worth derives not from what he is but from what he does. The seeds of destruction of the humanist concept of the self are sown by the same political theory that proclaims itself to be based on the individual subject.

In *The Order of Things* Foucault argued that, at the end of the eighteenth century, the 'classical order' was replaced by a new belief in underlying, organic causes located in things and beyond direct human control and representation, which for that very reason became the object of human investigation. Thus the double concept of 'man' as investigator and as object of study was created, separating being from representation (1970: 235, 239, 308, 312). Foucault notes that this paved the way for the discovery that 'man' was historically determined, indeed—as Foucault stresses—invented (371, 387). In his later work, Foucault went on to show how nineteenth-century organicism, in postulating the existence of underlying 'natural' causes, provided an alibi legitimizing the new discourses of social control that accompanied (but were not necessarily part of) an increasingly centralized State apparatus, and which were engaged in constructing the 'selves' they claimed to be 'normalizing'. In a circular argument, 'the natural', located in the human (particularly female) body, is posited as a pre-existing essence so that the 'normalizers' can step in to manufacture it. As

Bhabha notes: 'The productivity of Foucault's concept of power/ knowledge lies in its refusal of an epistemology which opposes essence and appearance' (1994: 72), for Foucault demonstrates that 'essences' are not inherent but constructed. Laqueur (1990: 150) comments that the body is the 'gold standard' of nineteenth-century discourse, meaning that it is posited as an underlying 'essence'. His metaphor is more appropriate than he realizes for worries, particularly acute in Spain, about the increasingly free-floating nature of monetary value coincide with a growing awareness that bodies, especially those of the working classes and women, are refusing to comply with the supposedly inherent – that is, 'natural'—norms prescribed for them. Simmel, acute as usual, notes that the 'money principle' is linked to 'the development and valuations of inner life' because it allows the concept of a self that is measured by a universal standard while at the same time being 'free-floating' (1990: 54), thus making it possible to reconcile the notion of standardized norms with the notion of the 'self-made' man. In his foreword to the English edition of Donzelot's *The Policing of Families*, Deleuze argues that the new area of 'the social' is constituted by a 'system of regulated flotation' whereby 'relationships between public and private, state and family, law and medicine, and so forth' cease to be 'pegged to a standard', in the same way that in the economy 'a currency is said to be floating when its value is no longer determined by reference to a fixed standard but in relation to the price of a hybrid variable market' (Donzelot 1979: p. xvi). Deleuze is here picking up Donzelot's suggestion (217–34) that psychoanalysis refined the discourses of social control developed in the late nineteenth century so as to reconcile the concept of the individual with the concept of society, much as Keynes did in the economic sphere through his hybrid blend of individual freedom and functional adjustment. What this effectively did was collapse the public/private distinction by making the individual responsible not just for 'self-correcting' his or her behaviour but for articulating the problem and the remedy in the first place, thus disguising as maximum individualism what in effect was social regulation. This process whereby the individual is made responsible for 'discovering' the rules, rather than having pre-defined norms imposed from outside, is what Donzelot calls 'flotation' (211).

Tambling (1990: 179–82) gives a more sympathetic view of psychoanalysis, arguing that, if one the one hand it encourages individuals to construct a self through narrative, on the other hand it exposes the processes through which that self is constructed; thus psychoanalysis provides a basis for contesting the regulatory confessional discourse promoted by institutionalized religion and medicine. The same could be said of the novels by Galdós, Alas, and Pardo Bazán studied here, for they show how such 'techniques of individualization' (Foucault's term) fail, either because they are resisted or because, when accepted, they produce disastrous results. In so doing they expose the liberal concept of the self as an 'arbitrary fiction' (to quote Marx's definition of money). It should be noted that contemporary public debate, so alarmed by the arbitariness of monetary and political representation, mostly deemed it necessary to impose behavioural norms on women and the working classes (the latter chiefly via the moralization of wives and prostitutes). Indeed, as noted in Chapter 2, the new non-State forms of social regulation step in precisely because the legislature is felt to be incapable of serving as a system of representation (Foucault 1987: 89). Despite public complaints—echoed by Galdós and Pereda—about the ways in which social standardization was causing the loss of traditional popular 'types', and about the State's invasion of privacy (private philanthropic agencies were seen as less invasive precisely because they were private), there was no generalized public awareness that this prescription of supposedly 'natural', but in fact invented, behavioural norms was another conversion of reality into representation.[12] As seen in Chapter 9, Pardo Bazán's journalism of the 1890s would make this point forcefully, echoing John Stuart Mill's point that what is called 'natural' femininity is the product of cultural moulding. But it is a point already made in Galdós's, Alas's, and Pardo Bazán's novels of the mid-1880s. In these novels, the regulators are mostly male (or masculinized women) and the objects of control are all female for, if liberal man is self-made, liberal woman is made. Jagoe (1992) and Charnon-Deutsch (Willem 1993: 173–89) note the frequency in Galdós's novels of the Pygmalion motif in which a male regulator attempts to

---

[12] Pointon (1990: 23–4) suggests that the Pygmalion myth was so popular with 19th-century painters because it raised issues about mimesis and representation.

sculpt a woman into shape (*Doña Perfecta, Gloria, La familia de León Roch, Elamigo Manso, Fortunata y Jacinta, Tristana*; Charnon-Deutsch also includes Miquis's attempts to shape Isidora in *La desheredada*, Agustín Caballero's misjudgement of Amparo in *Tormento*, and José María's negative moulding of Eloïsa and failed moulding of Camila in *Lo prohibido*.). This motif also occurs with the multiple male regulators in Alas's *La Regenta* and in Pardo Bazán's *Los Pazos de Ulloa* and *La madre naturaleza*. Ana Ozores is seen by the men of Vetusta as a statue of Venus: Saturnino Bermúdez corrects Ronzal's comparison of her to the Venus de Milo (misrendered as the 'Venus del Nilo'), saying the Medici Venus is a more flattering comparison, but Ronzal's slip is apt since, as the blank object onto which the local men project their various fantasies of 'Woman', she is analogous to a limbless torso (Alas 1981: i. 224–5). One thinks here of the amputation that Galdós's Tristana will undergo as the symbolic expression of Don Lope's and Horacio's combined attempts to mould her in their image of 'Woman'. Tristana is described as a 'figurilla de papel' (Pérez Galdós 1970: 1536) for in the 'edad de papel' one is, particularly if one is female, a construct; if Don Lope objects to the State and the Church it is, one suspects, because he regards them as competitors threatening his monopoly control over women. The reproduction of the Medici Venus that ends *Pepita Jiménez* reminds us that the feminine ideal is, precisely, a reproduction. Rogin notes that the nineteenth-century American vaudeville tradition of blackface coincided with an emphasis on 'self-making' in the market-place (for men) and in the parlour (for women). What he does not point out is that the 'parlor games and theatricals, tableaux vivants, shadow pantomimes and burlesques' (1996: 50) through which bourgeois women constructed themselves were cases of self-making only in the sense of acting out male-prescribed gender roles. (Bourgeois men's roles were, of course, also prescribed but by themselves.) One thinks here of the games played at the Marqués de Vegallana's houses in Vestusta and in the country, which construct sexual difference through the gaze and the chase, as does the fancy dress episode in *Los Pazos de Ulloa* which ends with Nucha's 'capture'. Bahamonde Magro and Martínez (1994: 466) comment that the nineteenth-century bourgeois mansion was an 'espacio interior de representación social', blurring public and private. It must be noted that this theatrical scenario served above all to demarcate gender divisions; in the gender-segregated Santa Cruz home, even the masculine, streetwise Guillermina sits knitting or sewing in Doña Bárbara's dressing room (Pérez Galdós 1992: i. 263).

As noted in Chapter 2, this construction of individualized citizens who will take on responsibility for regulating themselves was a form of colonization. Bhabha has noted that the colonized are forced to mimic the behaviourial norms of the colonizer, but that this mimicry offers scope for subversion (1995: 85–92). Manuela in *La madre naturaleza* rebels simply by refusing to play the game, but Fortunata learns to use to her advantage the bourgeois norms she has internalized by following Feijoo's advice to perfect the art of 'play acting', as perhaps Tristana does with the role of wife in the later novel. In Ana Ozores's case the subversion is less clear, but her retreat into hysterical illness, seen at the time as a form of mimicry, could be seen as her internalization of the multiple contradictory discourses projected onto her body by her male regulators in such a way that the consequent fragmentation of the self allows her to evade their various attempts to confine her to a particular image of woman. In imitating St Teresa she is clearly obeying the Magistral's instructions in such a way that she evades his power, replacing him with a female role-model. Poovey (Gallagher and Laqueur 1987: 15) notes that nineteenth-century doctors accused their female patients of being actresses (Freud's dismissal as fantasies of his female patients' stories of seduction by the father is a classic example); in fact, as Charcot's stagings of female hysteria at La Salpêtrière make evident, doctors were forcing women into the role of performer by requiring them to fit male models of female behaviour which, given that women were seen as constitutionally ill, effectively meant performing the role of hysteric; that is, performing the role of performer. Ana plays the role of perfect patient for her doctor, just as she plays the role of penitent for her confessor. Butler (1990) has argued that the fact that identity is performative rather than innate allows one a measure of freedom in selecting which of the various socially prescribed models to imitate, crossing genders and combining or moving between different models if wished, though one does not have the freedom to move outside the range of options available. In her uncoupling of gender from biology, Pardo Bazán comes close to Butler's position, though the results in a society based on the regulation of sexual difference are tragic. However, in most of the novels studied in this book one does not feel the female protagonists have much latitude, for the stress is on the negative effects of the social regulators' invasion of privacy.

Butler is, of course, a major theorist of postmodernism. The novels discussed in this book frequently anticipate postmodernism in their perception that reality is constituted by representation; indeed, in collapsing reality and representation they are closer to postmodernism than to the modernist stress on the gap between the two. Harvey (1989: 10–29) notes that the origins of postmodernity, like those of modernity, can be traced back to the mid-nineteenth century when capitalism started, with the growth of consumerism, to move into its post-industrial phase. Frisby points out that Simmel's stress on a consumer capitalism constituted by the circulation of signs detached from a stable referent has much to offer theorists of the postmodern 'society of the spectacle' (Simmel 1990: p. xxxii). The stress on imitation in the urban novels of Galdós and Alas, especially, comes close to the postmodern 'loss of the real' and its replacement by simulacra. Interestingly, Dodd singles out as an anticipation of postmodernism Simmel's analysis of the miser, who loves money purely for its sign value (1994: 108–12). It seems appropriate that Bringas, who becomes trapped in a world of circulating signs without a referent, should create a classic piece of postmodern kitsch, with his hair picture indiscriminately combining a heterogeneous mix of different architectural styles copied, not from 'nature' as he claims, but from books. Bringas's hair picture is pure postmodern pastiche: style self-reflexively imitating itself. Bringas can indiscriminately mix different architectural styles because, once signs have become detached from their referent and become free-floating, anything can be combined with anything else. Bringas the postmodern kitsch artist is also Bringas the collector.

I have described Bringas, in his mania for collecting, assembling, and reassembling miscellaneous trivia, as a bourgeois ragpicker. Frisby notes that Benjamin's critical method as a cultural historian of modernity is that of the 'refuse collector' who excavates 'the trivia, the refuse' of the past, lifting it out of the 'encrusted surface' in which it has become embedded, and reassembling its fragments through a montage process into a new configuration (1985: 189, 215–16, 225, 227; the quotes are from Benjamin). I hope in this book to have played something approximating to the role of cultural ragpicker, excavating heterogeneous textual and historical detail (much of it appropriately concerned with waste and sewage), and reassembling it to create a kind of archaeology of the anxieties of late nineteenth-century Spain. I do not want to suggest a mechanical causal link between contemporary economic, political, and social concerns and the realist novel, but I hope to have shown how a series of public discourses, of which the novel is one, converge in their concern with the loss of stable, inherent value and the consequent conversion of reality into representation. Butler (1990: 2) notes that the term 'representation' by definition supposes that what is created pre-exists. The realist novel's claim to be depicting what it is constructing obeys the same trope whereby the liberal State claims to represent politically the citizens it sets out to construct through the law; or whereby money purports to represent the value of things which it in fact determines; or whereby late nineteenth-century social reformers claimed that the behaviour they were imposing was natural. The fact that, in late nineteenth-century Spain, the flawed nature of the modernization process made glaringly apparent the arbitrariness of monetary and political representation allowed the Spanish realist novel to claim to be documenting a reality which it was effectively constructing, while at the same time exposing the representation process—its own included—for what it was. Liberal man, being self-made, demonstrated that, with the modern abolition of inherent worth, reality is representation. Liberal woman, being made yet 'natural', highlighted the contradiction whereby representation constructs what supposedly pre-exists. Thus, even though the arbitrariness of gender norms was not widely challenged in public debate, woman functioned as a cipher of the problems inherent in modernity's conversion of reality into representation. Woman's conversion into representation via the social regulators' invasion of privacy or via consumerist imitation highlighted the further contradiction of modernity's erosion of the public/private division which it had itself created. Consumerist imitation additionally raised the threat of women not only ceasing to be 'natural' but also ceasing to be made since, like men, they were starting to make themselves. Hence the realist novel's urgent need to construct its gallery of female protagonists—whose name often appears in the title in the form of a social label or representation (*La desheredada, La de Bringas, La Regenta; Fortunata y Jacinta* is subtitled *Dos historias de casadas*)—while at the same time exposing the representation process by which they are constructed: whether by other characters, by themselves, or by the author. The alternative solution, adopted by Pereda in his attempt to undo modernity, is virtually to eliminate women from the text altogether.

References

ABRAHAMSON, MARSHA R. (1991). 'Krausism, Pepita Jiménez, and the Divinization of Life', *Letras Peninsulares*, 4: 225–43.

AGUADO, ANA MARÍA, et al. (1994). *Textos para la historia de las mujeres en España* (Madrid: Cátedra).

AKERS, JOHN CHARLES (1982). 'José María de Pereda and the Craft of Literary Regionalism', Ph.D. dissertation, University of California (Los Angeles).

ALAS, LEOPOLDO (1881). 'Prólogo' to R. von Ihering, *La lucha por el derecho*, trans. Adolfo Posada (Madrid: Victoriano Suárez).

—— (1894). 'Psicología del sexo', *La Ilustración Ibérica*, 12: 3, 6, 38, 231, 259, 262, 343.

—— (1972). *Teoría y crítica de la novela española*, ed. Sergio Beser (Barcelona: Laia).

—— (1981). *La Regenta*, ed. Gonzalo Sobejano, 2 vols., 5th edn. (Madrid: Castalia).

—— (1984). *La Regenta*, trans. and introd. John Rutherford (London: Penguin).

ALDARACA, BRIDGET (1983). 'The Revolution of 1868 and the Rebellion of Rosalía Bringas', *Anales Galdosianos*, 18: 49–60.

—— (1990). 'El caso de Ana O.: histeria y sexualidad en *La Regenta*', *Asclepio*, 42: 51–61.

—— (1992). *'El ángel del hogar': Galdós y la ideología de la domesticidad en España* (Madrid: Visor).

ÁLVAREZ-URÍA, FERNANDO (1983). *Miserables y locos: medicina mental y orden social en la España del siglo XIX* (Barcelona: Tusquets).

AMIGONI, DAVID, and WALLACE, JEFF (eds.) (1995). *Charles Darwin's 'The Origin of Species': New Interdisciplinary Essays* (Manchester: Manchester University Press).

AMORÓS, ANDRÉS, and MARTÍNEZ CACHERO, JOSÉ MARÍA (eds.) (1985). *Clarín y 'La Regenta' (1884–1994)* (Madrid: Ministerio de Cultura).

ANDERSON, BENEDICT (1983). *Imagined Communities: Reflections on the Origin and Spread of Nationalism*, 2nd rev. edn. (London: Verso).

ANDREU, ALICIA G. (1982). *Galdós y la literatura popular* (Madrid: SGEL).

—— (1989). *Modelos dialógicos en la narrativa de Pérez Galdós* (Amsterdam: John Benjamins).

—— (1996–7). 'Benito Pérez Galdós, Higinia Balaguer, y el "Crimen de la calle de Fuencarral"', *Anales Galdosianos*, 31–2: 65–74.

ANON. (1906). 'La geografía perediana', *El Diario Montañés* (1 May), repr. in *Homenaje a Pereda* (Santander: Ediciones de Librería Estudios, 1983), 38–43.
ANTHIAS, FLOYA, and YUVAL-DAVIS, NIRA (1989). *Women and the Nation-State* (London: Macmillan).
ARENAL, CONCEPCIÓN (1974). *La emancipación de la mujer en España*, ed. Mauro Armiño (Madrid: Júcar).
—— (1993 [1868]). *La mujer del porvenir*, ed. Vicente de Santiago Mulas (Madrid: Castalia/Instituto de la Mujer).
ARIÈS, PHILIPPE (1973). *Centuries of Childhood: A Social History of Family Life* (Harmondsworth: Penguin).
—— (1987). *The Hour of our Death* (London: Penguin).
ARIZA, CARMEN (1988). *Los jardines de Madrid en el siglo XIX* (Madrid: Avapiés).
ARMSTRONG, JUDITH (1976). *The Novel of Adultery* (London: Macmillan).
ARMSTRONG, NANCY (1989). *Desire and Domestic Fiction: A Political History of the Novel* (Oxford: Oxford University Press).
—— and TENNENHOUSE, LEONARD (eds.) (1987). *The Ideology of Conduct: Essays in Literature and the History of Sexuality* (New York: Methuen).
ARNOLD, MATHEW (1960). *Culture and Anarchy* (Cambridge: Cambridge University Press).
ARTOLA, MIGUEL (1973). *La burguesía revolucionaria (1808–1869)* (Madrid: Alianza).
ASENDORF, CHRISTOPH (1993). *Batteries of Life: On the History of Things and their Perception in Modernity* (Berkeley and Los Angeles: University of California Press).
ASÚN, RAQUEL (1985). *La España de la Restauración* (Madrid: Siglo XXI).
ATTALI, JACQUES (1989). *Historia de la propiedad* (Barcelona: Planeta).
AZAÑA, MANUEL (1971). *Estudios sobre Valera* (Madrid: Alianza).
AZCÁRATE, GUMERSINDO DE (1877*a*). *El self-government y la monarquía doctrinaria* (Madrid: Librerías de A. de San Martín).
—— (1877*b*). *Estudios filosóficos y políticos* (Madrid: Imprenta de Manuel M. de los Ríos).
—— (1879). *Ensayo sobre la historia del derecho de propiedad y su estado actual en España* (Madrid: Imprenta de la Revista de Legislación).
—— (1881). *Resumen de un debate sobre el problema social* (Madrid: Gras y Compañía).
—— (1883). *Tratados de política: resúmenes y juicios críticos* (Madrid: Imprenta de Enrique de la Riva).
—— (1885). *El régimen parlamentario en la práctica* (Madrid: Imprenta de Fortanet).
BAHAMONDE MAGRO, ÁNGEL, and MARTÍNEZ, JESÚS (1994). *Historia de España: siglo XIX* (Madrid: Cátedra).

—— and OTERO CARVAJAL, LUIS ENRIQUE (eds.) (1989). *La sociedad madrileña durante la Restauración, 1876–1931*, 2 vols. (Madrid: Comunidad de Madrid).
—— and TORO MÉRIDA, JULIÁN (1978). *Burguesía, especulación y cuestión social en el Madrid del siglo XIX* (Madrid: Siglo XXI).
BAKER, EDWARD (1991). *Materiales para escribir Madrid: literatura y espacio urbano de Moratín a Galdós* (Madrid: Siglo XXI).
BARRETT, MICHÈLE, and MCINTOSH, MARY (1982). *The Anti-Social Family* (London: Verso).
BARROSO, FERNANDO V. (1973). *El naturalismo en la Pardo Bazán* (Madrid: Playor).
BAUDRILLARD, JEAN (1968). *Le Système des objets* (Paris: Gallimard).
BAUER, BETH WIETELMANN (1993). 'Confession in *La Regenta*: The Secular Sacrament', *Bulletin of Hispanic Studies*, 70: 313–23.
BEBEL, AUGUST (1988). *Woman in the Past, Present and Future* (London: Zwan).
BÉCARUD, JEAN (1964). *'La Regenta' de Clarín y la Restauración* (Madrid: Taurus).
BEER, GILLIAN (1985). *Darwin's Plots: Evolutionary Narrative in Darwin, George Eliot and Nineteenth-Century Fiction* (London: Ark).
BEIZER, JANET (1994). *Ventriloquized Bodies: Narratives of Hysteria in Nineteenth-Century France* (Ithaca, NY: Cornell University Press).
BENJAMIN, MARINA (ed.) (1991). *Science and Sensibility: Gender and Scientific Enquiry 1780–1945* (Oxford: Blackwell).
BENJAMIN, WALTER (1989). *Charles Baudelaire: A Lyric Poet in the Era of High Capitalism*, 3rd edn. (London: Verso).
BENTHAM, JEREMY (1995). *The Panopticon Writings*, ed. Miran Božovič (London: Verso).
BERKOWITZ, H. CHONON (1948). *Pérez Galdós: Spanish Liberal Crusader* (Madison: University of Wisconsin Press).
—— (1951). *La biblioteca de Benito Pérez Galdós* (Las Palmas de Gran Canaria: El Museo Canario).
BERMAN, MARSHALL (1983). *All That is Solid Melts into Air: The Experience of Modernity* (London: Verso).
BERMINGHAM, ANN (1987). *Landscape and Ideology: The English Rustic Tradition, 1740–1860* (London: Thames and Hudson).
BERNALDO DE QUIRÓS, C. (1898). *Las nuevas teorías de la criminalidad* (Madrid: Biblioteca Jurídica de Autores Españoles y Extranjeros).
—— (1975). *La picota, Figuras delincuentes*, ed. José Antón Oneca (Madrid: Turner).
BERNHEIMER, CHARLES (1989). *Figures of Ill Repute: Representing Prostitution in Nineteenth-Century France* (Cambridge, Mass.: Harvard University Press).
—— and KAHANE, CLAIRE (eds.) (1985). *In Dora's Case: Freud-Hysteria-Feminism* (London: Virago).

BHABHA, HOMI (ed.) (1990). *Nation and Narration* (London: Routledge).
—— (1995). *The Location of Culture* (London: Routledge).
BIEDER, MARYELLEN (1987). 'The female voice: gender and genre in *La madre naturaleza*', *Anales Galdosianos*, 22: 103–16.
—— (1990). 'Between Genre and Gender: Emilia Pardo Bazán and *Los Pazos de Ulloa*', in Noël Valis and Carol Maier (eds.), *In the Feminine Mode: Essays on Hispanic Women Writers* (London: Associated University Presses), 131–45.
—— (1993*a*). 'Emilia Pardo Bazán and Literary Women: Women Reading Women's Writing in Late Nineteenth-Century Spain', *Revista Hispánica Moderna*, 46: 19–33.
—— (1993*b*). 'Plotting against the Reader: Strategies of Subversion in Stories by Emilia Pardo Bazán', *Indiana Journal of Hispanic Literatures*, 2.1: 137–57.
BLANCO, ALDA (1993*a*). ' "But Are They Any Good?" ', *Revista de Estudios Hispánicos*, 2: 463–70.
—— (1993*b*). 'The Moral Imperative for Women Writers', *Indiana Journal of Hispanic Literatures*, 2.1: 91–110.
BLY, PETER A. (1974). 'The Use of Distance in Galdós' *La de Bringas*', *Modern Language Review*, 69: 88–97; repr. in Jo Labanyi (ed.), *Galdós* (Harlow: Longman, 1993), 103–15.
—— (1977). 'Fortunata y no. 11, Cava de San Miguel', *Hispanófila*, 59: 31–48.
—— (1981). *Pérez Galdós, 'La de Bringas'* (London: Grant & Cutler).
—— (1983). *Galdós's Novel of the Historical Imagination: A Study of the Contemporary Novels* (Liverpool: Francis Cairns).
—— (1986). *Vision and the Visual Arts in Galdós: A Study of the Novels and Newspaper Articles* (Liverpool: Francis Cairns).
—— (ed.) (1988). *Galdós y la historia* (Ottawa: Dovehouse).
—— (1991). *Pérez Galdós, 'Nazarín'* (London: Grant & Cutler).
BONET, LAUREANO (ed.) (1972). *El naturalismo* (Barcelona: Península).
—— (1983). 'Pereda entre el regionalismo y la lucha de clases: crónica de un viaje a Cataluña', in *Literatura, regionalismo y lucha de clases* (Barcelona: Universidad de Barcelona), 117–218.
—— et al. (1985). *Nueve lecciones sobre Pereda* (Santander: Institución Cultural de Cantabria).
BONET CORREA, ANTONIO (ed.) (1978). *Plan Castro* (Madrid: Colegio Oficial de Arquitectos de Madrid).
BOTREL, JEAN-FRANÇOIS (1988). *La Diffusion du livre en Espagne, 1868–1914: les libraires* (Madrid: Casa de Velázquez).
—— (1993). *Libros, prensa y lectura en la España del siglo XIX* (Madrid: Fundación Germán Sánchez Ruipérez).
—— and SALAÜN, SERGE (1974). *Creación y público en la literatura española* (Madrid: Castalia).

BOURDIEU, PIERRE (1996). *Distinction: A Social Critique of the Judgement of Taste* (London: Routledge).
BOWLBY, RACHEL (1985). *Just Looking: Consumer Culture in Dreiser, Gissing and Zola* (London: Methuen).
BRAUN, LUCILLE V. (1970). 'Galdós' Re-creation of Ernestina de Villena as Guillerina Pacheco', *Hispanic Review*, 38: 32–55.
—— (1977). 'The Novelistic Function of Mauricia de Dura in Galdós's *Fortunata y Jacinta*', *Symposium*, 3: 277–89.
BRAVO, MARÍA ELENA (1995). 'La Revolución de 1868 y el feminismo español', *La Balsa de la Medusa*, 35: 87–106.
BRAVO VILLASANTE, CARMEN (1973). *Vida y obra de Emilia Pardo Bazán* (Madrid: Editorial Magisterio Español).
—— (1974). *Vida de Juan Valera* (Madrid: Editorial Magisterio Español).
BRENT, ALBERT (1951). *Leopoldo Alas and 'La Regenta': A Study in Nineteenth-Century Spanish Fiction* (Columbia: University of Missouri Press).
BROWN, DONALD FOWLER (1957). *The Catholic Naturalism of Pardo Bazán* (Chapel Hill: University of North Carolina Press).
BUCHAN, JAMES (1997). *Frozen Desire: An Inquiry into the Meaning of Money* (London: Picador).
BURGUIÈRE, ANDRÉ, KLAPISCH-ZUBER, CHRISTIANE, SEGALEN, MARTINE, and ZONABEND, FRANÇOISE (eds.) (1992). *History of the Family*, ii: *The Impact of Modernity* (Cambridge: Polity).
BURNS, MICHAEL (1993). 'Post-mortem', *London Review of Books* (18 Nov.): 19.
BUTLER, JUDITH (1990). *Gender Trouble: Feminism and the Subversion of Identity* (New York: Routledge).
BYRON, WILLIAM (1979). *Cervantes: A Biography* (London: Cassell).
CACHO VIU, VICENTE (1962). *La Institución Libre de Enseñanza* (Madrid: Rialp).
CALHOUN, CRAIG (ed.) (1992). *Habermas and the Public Sphere* (Cambridge, Mass.: MIT Press).
CALINESCU, MATEI (1987). *Five Faces of Modernity: Modernism, Avant-Garde, Decadence, Kitsch, Postmodernism* (Durham, NC: Duke University Press).
CALLEY, LOUISE NELSON (1961). 'Galdós' Concept of Primitivism: A Romantic View of the Character Fortunata', *Hispania*, 44: 663–5.
CAMMARATA, JOAN (1976). 'Luis de Vargas: An Oedipal Figure in *Pepita Jiménez*', in Lisa E. Davis and Isabel C. Tarán (eds.), *The Analysis of Hispanic Texts: Current Trends in Methodology* (New York: Bilingual Press), 206–25.
CÁNOVAS DEL CASTILLO, ANTONIO (1884). *Problemas contemporáneos*, 2 vols. (Madrid: Imprenta de A. Pérez Dubrull).

CAPEL MARTÍNEZ, ROSA MARÍA (ed.) (1982). *Mujer y sociedad en España: 1700–1975* (Madrid: Dirección General de Juventud y Promoción Sociocultural).

Carlos de Haes: un maestro del paisaje del siglo XIX (catalogue of exhibition held at the Centro de Exposiciones y Congresos, Zaragoza, 28 May– 28 June 1996) (Zaragoza: Centro de Exposiciones y Congresos), 77–101.

CARPINTERO, HELIO (1994). *Historia de la psicología en España* (Madrid: Eudema).

CARNERO, GUILLERMO (1994). 'Cultura y literatura en la vida española del siglo XIX', in *El mundo literario en la pintura del siglo XIX del Museo del Prado* (Madrid: Ministerio de Cultura), 19–65.

CARR, RAYMOND (1966). *Spain 1808–1939* (Oxford: Clarendon Press).

—— (1980). *Modern Spain 1875–1980* (Oxford: Oxford University Press).

CARRERAS ARTAU, TOMÁS (1952). *Estudios sobre médicos-filósofos españoles del siglo XIX* (Barcelona: CSIC).

CASADO, SANTOS (1994). 'La fundación de la Sociedad Española de Historia Natural y la dimensión nacionalista de la historia natural en España', *Boletín Institución Libre de Enseñanza*, 2nd series, 19 (Apr.): 45–64.

CASEY, JAMES (1989). *The History of the Family* (Oxford: Blackwell).

CASTRO, AMÉRICO (1987). *La realidad histórica de España*, 9th edn. (Mexico City: Porrúa).

CATALINA, SEVERO (1861). *La mujer: apuntes para un libro* (Madrid: A. de San Martín).

CATE-ARRIES, FRANCINE (1986). 'El Krausismo en *Doña Luz* y *Pepita Jiménez*', in *Homenaje a Luis Morales Oliver* (Madrid: Fundación Universitaria Española), 221–36.

CAUTER, LIEVEN DE (1993). 'The Panoramic Ecstasy: On World Exhibitions and the Disintegration of Experience', *Theory, Culture and Society*, 10.4: 1–23.

CHAMBERLAIN, VERNON, and HARDIN, RICHARD F. (1990). '*Pepita Jiménez* and the Romance Tradition', *Anales Galdosianos*, 25: 69–75.

CHARLTON, DONALD (1984). *New Images of the Natural in France: A Study in European Cultural History, 1750–1800* (Cambridge: Cambridge University Press).

CHARNON-DEUTSCH, LOU (1985*a*). '*La de Bringas* and the Politics of Domestic Power', *Anales Galdosianos*, 20: 65–74.

—— (1985*b*). 'Gender-Specific Roles in *Pepita Jiménez*', *Revista de Estudios Hispánicos*, 19: 87–105.

—— (1987). 'Speech and the Power of Speaking in *La Regenta*', *Crítica Hispánica*, 9.1–2: 69–85.

—— (1989*a*). 'Voyeurism, Pornography and *La Regenta*', *Modern Language Studies*, 19.4: 93–101.

—— (1989b). 'La Regenta and Theories of the Subject', Romance Languages Annual, 1: 395–8.

—— (1990a). Gender and Representation: Women in Spanish Realist Fiction (Amsterdam: John Benjamins).

—— (1990b). 'On Desire and Domesticity in Spanish Nineteenth-Century Women's Novels', Revista Canadiense de Estudios Hispánicos, 14: 395–414.

—— (1993). 'The Social Masochism of the Nineteenth-Century Domestic Novel', Indiana Journal of Hispanic Literatures, 2.1: 111–35.

—— (1994a). 'La Regenta and the Sutured Subject', Revista de Estudios Hispánicos, 28.1: 65–78.

—— (1994b). Narratives of Desire: Nineteenth-Century Spanish Fiction by Women (University Park: Pennsylvania State University Press).

—— and LABANYI, JO (eds.) (1995). Culture and Gender in Nineteenth-Century Spain (Oxford: Oxford University Press).

CHOAY, FRANÇOISE (n.d.). The Modern City: Planning in the Nineteenth Century (London: Studio Vista).

CIPLIJAUSKAITÉ, BIRUTÉ (1984). La mujer insatisfecha: el adulterio en la novela realista (Barcelona: Edhasa).

CIRUJANO MARÍN, ELORRIAGA, PLANES, PALOMA TERESA, and PÉREZ GARZÓN, JUAN SISINIO (1985). Historiografía y nacionalismo españoles 1834–1868 (Madrid: CSIC).

CLARKE, ANTHONY (1969). Pereda paisajista: el sentimiento de la naturaleza en la novela epañola del siglo XIX (Santander: Institución Cultural de Cantabria).

—— (1984). 'El regreso a la tierra natal: Peñas arriba dentro de una tradición europea', Boletín de la Biblioteca de Menéndez Pelayo, 60: 213–69.

—— (ed.) (1997) 'Peñas arriba', cien años después. José María de Pereda: crítica e interpretación (Santander: Sociedad Menéndez Pelayo).

CLAVERO, BARTOLOMÉ (1982). El código y el fuero: de la cuestión regional en la España contemporánea (Madrid: Siglo XXI).

CLEMESSY, NELLY (1981). Emilia Pardo Bazán como novelista (de la teoría a la práctica) (Madrid: Fundación Universitaria Española).

COLINA DE RODRÍGUEZ, LUZ (1987). El folklore en la obra de José María de Pereda (Santander: Institución Cultural de Cantabria).

COLLINS, GEORGE R., and FLORES, CARLOS (1967). Arturo Soria y la Ciudad Lineal (Madrid: Revista de Occidente).

COLLINS, MARSHA S. (1990). 'Sliding into the Vortex: Patterns of Ascent and Descent in La desheredada', Anales Galdosianos, 25: 13–23.

VI Coloquio de Historia de la Educación (1990). Mujer y educación en España 1868–1975 (Santiago de Compostela: Universidade de Santiago).

COOK, TERESA (1976). El feminisimo en la novela de la Condesa de Pardo Bazán (La Coruña: Diputación Provincial de La Coruña).

COPLEY, STEPHEN, and SUTHERLAND, KATHRYN (eds.) (1995). *Adam Smith's 'Wealth of Nations': New Interdisciplinary Essays* (Manchester: Manchester University Press).

CORBIN, ALAIN (1986). *The Foul and the Fragrant: Odor and the French Social Imagination* (Leamington Spa: Berg).

—— (1990). *Women for Hire: Prostitution and Sexuality in France after 1850* (Cambridge, Mass.: Harvard University Press).

CORDONES-COOK, JUANAMARÍA (1990). '*Lo prohibido*, narrativa narcisista', *Anales Galdosianos*, 25: 35–43.

CORNELL, DRUCILLA, ROSENFELD, MICHAEL, and GRAY CARLSON, DAVID (eds.) (1991). *Hegel and Legal Theory* (New York: Routledge).

CORRIGAN, PHILIP (ed.) (1980). *Capitalism, State Formation and Marxist Theory: Historical Investigations* (London: Quartet).

—— and SAYER, DEREK (1991). *The Great Arch: English State Formation as Cultural Revolution*, 2nd edn. (Oxford: Blackwell).

COSSÍO, JOSÉ MARÍA DE (1973). *Estudios sobre escritores montañeses*, vol. iii (Santander: Diputación Provincial de Santander).

COSTA, JOAQUÍN (1902). *Oligarquía y caciquismo como la forma actual de gobierno en España* (Madrid: Imprenta de los Hijos de M. G. Hernández).

—— (1911). *Política hidraúlica* (Madrid: Biblioteca J. Costa).

—— (1912). *El arbolado y la patria* (Madrid: Biblioteca J. Costa).

—— (1973). *Oligarquía y caciquismo, colectivismo agrario y otros escritos*, ed. Rafael Pérez de la Dehesa, 3rd edn. (Madrid: Alianza).

—— (1984). *Teoría del hecho jurídico individual y social*, ed. Juan-José Gil Cremades (Zaragoza: Guara Editorial).

COWARD, ROSALIND (1983). *Patriarchal Precedents: Sexuality and Social Relations* (London: Routledge & Kegan Paul).

CRARY, JONATHAN (1990). *Techniques of the Observer: On Vision and Modernity in the Nineteenth Century* (Cambridge, Mass.: MIT Press).

CROSBY, CHRISTINA (1991). *The Ends of History: Victorians and the Woman Question* (New York: Routledge).

CUBITT, GEOFFREY (ed.) (1998). *Imagining Nations* (Manchester: Manchester University Press).

DARWIN, CHARLES (1901). *The Descent of Man and Selection in Relation to Sex* (London: John Murray).

DAVID-MÉNARD, MONIQUE (1989). *Hysteria from Freud to Lacan: Body and Language in Psychoanalysis* (Ithaca, NY: Cornell University Press).

DAVIDOFF, LEONORE, and HALL, CATHERINE (1987). *Family Fortunes: Men and Women of the English Middle Class, 1780–1850* (London: Hutchinson).

DAVIES, RHIAN (1996). '*La España Moderna*: The Cultural Review and Spain', 2 vols., D.Phil. thesis (University of Oxford).

DAVIS, GIFFORD (1975). 'Catholicism and Naturalism: Pardo Bazán's Reply to Zola', *Modern Language Notes*, 90: 282–7.

DAVIS, LISA E. (1977). 'Max Nordau: degeneración y la decadencia de España', *Cuadernos Hispanoamericanos*, 326-7: 307-23.
DE BOLLA, PETER (1989). *The Discourse of the Sublime: Readings in History, Aesthetics and the Subject* (Oxford: Blackwell).
DECOSTER, CYRUS (ed.) (1956). *Correspondencia de don Juan Valera (1859-1905)* (Madrid: Castalia).
—— (ed.) (1965). *Obras desconocidas de Juan Valera* (Madrid: Castalia).
DE LA CALLE, MARÍA DOLORES (1989). *La Comisión de Reformas Sociales 1883-1903: política social y conflicto de intereses en la España de la Restauración* (Madrid: Ministerio de Trabajo y Seguridad Social).
DELGADO, LUISA ELENA (1990). '"El interés del relato": estrategias narrativas en la serie de *Torquemada*', *Anales Galdosianos*, 25: 59-67.
—— (1995). '"Más estragos que las revoluciones": detallando lo femenino en *La de Bringas*', *Revista Hispánica Moderna*, 48: 31-42.
—— (1999, forthcoming). *La imagen elusiva: lenguaje y representación en la narrativa de Galdós* (Amsterdam: Rodopi).
DENDLE, BRIAN (1965). *Obras desconocidas de Juan Valera* (Madrid: Castalia).
—— (1980). *Galdós: The Mature Thought* (Lexington: University of Kentucky Press).
—— (1982). 'Isidora, the *Mantillas blancas*, and the Attempted Assassination of Alfonso XII', *Anales Galdosianos*, 17: 51-4.
DERRIDA, JACQUES (1976). *On Grammatology* (Baltimore: Johns Hopkins University Press).
DESMOND, ADRIAN (1989). *The Politics of Evolution: Morphology, Medicine and Reform in Radical London* (Chicago: University of Chicago Press).
DÍAZ, ELÍAS (1973). *La filosofía social del krausismo español* (Madrid: EDICUSA).
DÍEZ, JOSÉ LUIS (ed.) (1992). *La pintura de historia del siglo XIX en España* (Madrid: Museo del Prado).
DÍEZ DE BALDEÓN, CLEMENTINA (1986). *Arquitectura y clases sociales en el Madrid del siglo XIX* (Madrid: Siglo XXI).
DÍEZ DEL CORRAL, LUIS (1943). *El liberalismo doctrinario* (Madrid: Instituto de Estudios Políticos).
DI FEBO, GIULIANA (1976). 'Orígenes del debate feminista en España: la escuela krausista y la Institución Libre de Enseñanza (1870-1890)', *Sistema*, 12: 49-82.
DIJKSTRA, BRAM (1986). *Idols of Perversity: Fantasies of Feminine Evil in Fin-de-Siècle Culture* (New York: Oxford University Press).
DODD, NIGEL (1994). *The Sociology of Money: Economics, Reason and Contemporary Society* (Cambridge: Polity).
DONZELOT, JACQUES (1979). *The Policing of Families: Welfare versus the State* (London: Hutchinson).

DOUGLAS, MARY (1973). *Natural Symbols: Explorations in Cosmology* (Harmondsworth: Penguin).
—— (1984). *Purity and Danger: An Analysis of the Concepts of Pollution and Taboo* (London: Routledge).
—— and ISHERWOOD, BARON (1979). *The World of Goods: Towards an Anthropology of Consumption* (London: Allen Lane).
DREYFUS, HUBERT L., and RABINOW, PAUL (1982). *Michel Foucault: Beyond Structuralism and Hermeneutics* (Brighton: Harvester Press).
DURÁN, MARÍA ANGELES (ed.) (1993). *Mujeres y hombres: la formación del pensamiento igualitario* (Madrid: Castalia-Instituto de la Mujer).
DURAND, FRANK (1964). 'Characterization in *La Regenta*: Point of View and Theme', *Bulletin of Hispanic Studies*, 41: 86–100.
—— (ed.) (1988). *La Regenta* (Madrid: Taurus).
DURING, SIMON (ed.) (1993). *The Cultural Studies Reader* (London: Routledge).
ELEY, GEOFF, and SUNY, RONALD GRIGOR (eds.) (1996). *Becoming National: A Reader* (Oxford: Oxford University Press).
ELORZA, ANTONIO (1970). *La ideología liberal en la ilustración española* (Madrid: Tecnos).
—— (1973). 'El liberalismo en la Restauración', in *La utopía anarquista bajo la Segunda República española* (Madrid: Ayuso), 121–208.
ELSAESSER, THOMAS (1987). 'Tales of Sound and Fury: Observations on the Family Melodrama', in Christine Gledhill (ed.), *Home is Where the Heart is: Studies in Melodrama and the Women's Film* (London: British Film Institute), 43–69.
EL SAFFAR, RUTH (1987). 'Mother Nature's Nature', *Anales Galdosianos*, 22: 91–102.
ELSHTAIN, JEAN BETHKE (1981). *Public Man, Private Woman: Women in Social and Political Thought* (Oxford: Blackwell).
—— (ed.) (1982). *The Family in Political Thought* (Brighton: Harvester).
ENGELS, FRIEDRICH (1988). *The Origins of the Family, Private Property and the State* (London: Lawrence & Wishart).
ENGINEER, AN. (1878). *¡Guerra al adulterio! Estudio de ciencia social* (Madrid: La Guirnalda).
ENGLER, KAY (1977). *The Structure of Realism: The 'Novelas contemporáneas' of Benito Pérez Galdós* (Chapel Hill: University of North Carolina Press).
ENRÍQUEZ DE SALAMANCA, CRISTINA (1993). 'Calidad/capacidad: valor estético y teoría política en la España del siglo XIX', *Revista de Estudios Hispánicos*, 27: 449–61.
ESQUERDO, JOSÉ MARÍA (1889). 'De la locura histérica', *Revista Clínica de los Hospitales*, 1: 1–9, 274–81, 337–40.
EVANS, MARTHA NOEL (1991). *Fits and Starts: A Genealogy of Hysteria in Modern France* (Ithaca, NY: Cornell University Press).

EWEN, STUART (1988). *All Consuming Images: The Politics of Style in Contemporary Culture* (New York: Basic Books).
FAUS SEVILLA, PILAR (1972). *La sociedad española del siglo XIX en la obra de Pérez Galdós* (Valencia: Imprenta Nacher).
FEAL DEIBE, CARLOS (1971). 'Naturalismo y antinaturalismo en *Los Pazos de Ulloa*', *Bulletin of Hispanic Studies*, 48: 314–27.
—— (1984). '*Pepita Jiménez* o del misticismo al idilio', *Bulletin hispanique*, 86: 473–83.
—— (1987). 'La voz femenina en *Los Pazos de Ulloa*', *Hispania*, 70: 214–21.
FERNANDEZ, JAMES D. (1992). *Autobiography and the Rhetoric of Self-Representation in Spain* (Durham, NC: Duke University Press).
FERNÁNDEZ CIFUENTES, LUIS (1988). 'Signs for Sale in the City of Galdós', *Modern Language Notes*, 103: 289–311.
FERNÁNDEZ GARCÍA, ANTONIO (ed.) (1993). *Historia de Madrid* (Madrid: Editorial Complutense).
FINNEY, GAIL (1984). *The Counterfeit Idyll: The Garden Ideal and Social Reality in Nineteenth-Century Fiction* (Tübingen: Niemeyer).
FOLGUERA, PILAR (ed.) (1988). *El feminismo en España: dos siglos de historia* (Madrid: Editorial Pablo Iglesias).
FOUCAULT, MICHEL (1970). *The Order of Things: An Archaeology of the Human Sciences* (London: Tavistock Publications).
—— (1971). *Madness and Civilisation: A History of Insanity in the Age of Reason* (London: Tavistock Publications).
—— (1973). *The Birth of the Clinic: An Archaeology of Medical Perception* (London: Tavistock Publications).
—— (1987). *The History of Sexuality: An Introduction* (Harmondsworth: Penguin).
—— (1991). *Discipline and Punish: The Birth of the Prison* (London: Penguin).
FOX KELLER, EVELYN (1985). *Reflections on Gender and Science* (New Haven: Columbia University Press).
FRAISSE, GENEVIÈVE, and PERROT, MICHELLE (eds.) (1993). *El siglo XIX*, vol. iv of Georges Duby and MICHELLE PERROT (eds.), *Historia de las mujeres en occidente* (Madrid: Taurus).
FRANKLIN, JILL (1989). 'The Liberty of the Park', in Raphael Samuel (ed.), *Patriotism: The Making and Unmaking of British National Identity*, iii: *National Fictions* (London: Routledge), 141–59.
FRASER, NANCY (1990). 'Rethinking the Public Sphere: A Contribution to the Critique of Actually Existing Democracy', *Social Text*, 25–6: 56–80.
FREELAND, ALAN (1993). 'Evolution and Dissolution: Imagery and Social Darwinism in Eça de Queirós and Leopoldo Alas', *Journal of the Institute of Romance Studies*, 2: 323–36.

FREUD, SIGMUND (1977). *On Sexuality*, vol. xii of *The Pelican Freud Library* (London: Penguin).
—— (1991a). 'Femininity', in *New Introductory Lectures on Psychoanalysis*, vol. ii of *The Penguin Freud Library* (London: Penguin), 145–69.
—— (1991b). *On Metapsychology*, vol. xi of *The Penguin Freud Library* (London: Penguin).
FRISBY, DAVID (1985). *Fragments of Modernity* (Cambridge: Polity).
FUENTES PERIS, TERESA (1996). 'Drink and Social Stability: Discourses of Power in Galdós's *Fortunata y Jacinta*', *Bulletin of Hispanic Studies* (Liverpool), 73: 63–77.
—— (1996–7). 'The Control of Prostitution and Filth in *Fortunata y Jacinta*: The Panoptic Strategy in the Convent of Las Micaelas', *Anales Galdosianos*, 31–2: 35–52.
—— (1997a). 'Drink and Degeneration: The "Deserving" and the "Undeserving" Poor in Galdós's *Ángel Guerra*', *Romance Studies*, 29: 7–20.
—— (1997b). 'Visions of Filth: Deviancy and Social Control in the Novels of Galdós', Ph.D. thesis (University of London).
FURST, LILIAN (1995). *All is True: The Claims and Strategies of Realism* (Durham, NC: Duke University Press).
FUSS, DIANA (1989). *Essentially Speaking: Feminism, Nature and Difference* (New York: Routledge).
GALÁN GARCÍA, MARÍA ISABEL (1993). 'La medicina en la novela de escritores médicos españoles (1882–1913)', Ph.D. thesis (Universidad Autónoma de Madrid).
GALE, JUDITH (1990). *El regionalismo en la obra de Pereda* (Madrid: Pliegos).
GALERA SÁNCHEZ, MATILDE (1983). *Juan Valera, político* (Córdoba: Diputación Provincial de Córdoba).
—— (1989). 'Don Juan Valera y las elecciones en Estados Unidos', in *Don Juan Valera y Doña Mencía* (Córdoba: Diputación Provincial de Córdoba), 33–9.
GALLAGHER, CATHERINE (1985). *The Industrial Reformation of English Fiction: Social Discourse and Narrative Form, 1832–1867* (Chicago: University of Chicago Press).
—— and LAQUEUR, THOMAS (1987). *The Making of the Modern Body: Sexuality and Society in the Nineteenth Century* (Berkeley and Los Angeles: University of California Press).
GARCÍA ARENAL, FERNANDO (1980). *Datos para el estudio de la cuestión social*, ed. Ramón María Alvar González (Gijón: Silverio Cañada).
GARCÍA DE CORTÁZAR, FERNANDO, and GONZÁLEZ VESGA, JOSÉ MANUEL (1994). *Breve historia de España* (Madrid: Alianza).
GARCÍA DELGADO, JOSÉ LUIS (ed.) (1985). *La España de la Restauración: política, economía, legislación y cultura* (Madrid: Siglo XXI).

—— (ed.) (1992). *Las ciudades en la modernización de España: los decenios interseculares* (Madrid: Siglo XXI).
GARCÍA SAN MIGUEL, LUIS (1987). *El pensamiento de Leopoldo Alas 'Clarín'* (Madrid: Centro de Estudios Constitucionales).
GARCÍA SARRIÁ, FRANCISCO (1975). *Clarín o la herejía amorosa* (Madrid: Gredos).
GAY, PETER (1984–6). *The Bourgeois Experience: Victoria to Freud*, 2 vols. (New York: Oxford University Press).
GELLNER, ERNEST (1987). *Culture, Identity, Politics* (Cambridge: Cambridge University Press).
GIDDENS, ANTHONY (1985). *The Nation-State and Violence* (Cambridge: Polity).
GIL CREMADES, JUAN JOSÉ (1975). *Krausistas y liberales* (Madrid: Seminarios y Ediciones).
GILLOCH, GRAEME (1996). *Myth and Metropolis: Walter Benjamin and the City* (Cambridge: Polity).
GILMAN, RICHARD (1979). *Decadence: The Strange Life of an Epithet* (New York: Farrar, Strauss & Giroux).
GILMAN, STEPHEN (1966). 'The Birth of Fortunata', *Anales Galdosianos*, 1: 71–83.
—— (1971). 'The Consciousness of Fortunata', *Anales Galdosianos*, 5: 55–65.
—— (1981). *Galdós and the Art of the European Novel 1867–1887* (Princeton: University of Princeton Press).
—— (1982). 'Feminine and Masculine Consciousness in *Fortunata y Jacinta*', *Anales Galdosianos*, 17: 63–70.
GINER DE LOS RÍOS, FRANCISCO (1875). *Estudios jurídicos y políticos* (Madrid: Victoriano Suárez).
—— (1876). *Estudios de literatura y arte* (Madrid: Victoriano Suárez).
—— (1915). 'Paisaje', *La Lectura*, 15: 361–70.
—— (1969). *Ensayos*, ed. Juan López Morillas (Madrid: Alianza).
GINZBURG, CARLO (1990). *Myths, Emblems, Clues* (London: Hutchinson Radius).
GIRARD, RENÉ (1966). *Deceit, Desire, and the Novel: Self and Other in Literary Structure* (Baltimore: Johns Hopkins University Press).
GLICK, THOMAS F. (1982). *Darwin en España* (Barcelona: Península).
GOLD, HAZEL (1986*a*). 'Francisco's Folly: Picturing Reality in Galdós's *La de Bringas*', *Hispanic Review*, 54: 47–66.
—— (1986*b*). 'Problems of Closure in *Fortunata y Jacinta*: Of Narrators, Readers and their Just Deserts/Desserts', *Neophilologus*, 70: 227–38.
—— (1988). 'A Tomb with a View: The Museum in Galdós's *Novelas contemporáneas*', *Modern Language Notes*, 103: 312–34.
—— (1990*a*). 'Show and Tell: From Museum to Novel in Clarín's *La Regenta*', *España Contemporánea*, 3.1: 47–70.

GOLD, HAZEL (1990*b*). 'Back to the Future: Criticism, the Canon, and the Nineteenth-Century Spanish Novel', *Hispanic Review*, 58: 168–204.

—— (1993). *The Reframing of Realism: Galdós and the Discourses of the Nineteenth-Century Spanish Novel* (Durham, NC: Duke University Press).

—— (1995). 'Literature in a Paralytic Mode: Digression as Transgression in *La Regenta*', *Revista Hispánica Moderna*, 48: 54–68.

—— (forthcoming). 'El nomadismo urbano y la crisis finisecular en Misericordia', *Actas del 6° Congreso Internacional de Galdosistas* (Las Palmas de Gran Canaria: Cabildo Insular de Grana Canaria).

GÓMEZ MARÍN, JOSÉ ANTONIO (1972). 'Pardo Bazán: el paisaje como ideología', *Triunfo*, 28. 527 (4 Nov.): 47.

GÓMEZ MARTÍNEZ, JOSÉ LUIS (1983). 'Galdós y el krausismo español', *Nuera Revista de Filología Hispánica*, 32.1: 55–79.

GÓMEZ MENDOZA, ANTONIO (1982). *Ferrocarriles y cambio económico en España (1855–1913): un enfoque de nueva historia económica* (Madrid: Alianza).

—— (1989). *Ferrocarril, industria y mercado en la industrialización de España* (Madrid: Espasa Calpe).

GONZÁLEZ ARIAS, FRANCISCA (1992). *Portrait of a Woman as Artist: Emilia Pardo Bazán and the Modern Novel in France and Spain* (New York: Garland).

GONZÁLEZ DE LINARES, GERVASIO (1882). *La agricultura y la administración municipal* (Madrid: Est. Tip. de El Correo).

GONZÁLEZ HERRÁN, JOSÉ MANUEL (1983). *La obra de Pereda ante la crítica literaria de su tiempo* (Santander: Ayuntamiento de Santander).

—— (1985). 'Pereda y el fin de siglo (entre modernismo y noventa y ocho)', in Laureano Bonet et al., *Nueve lecciones sobre Pereda* (Santander: Institución Cultural de Cantabria).

—— (ed.) (1997). *Estudios sobre Emilia Pardo Bazán: in memoriam Maurice Hemingway* (Santiago de Compostela: Universidade de Santiago de Compostela y Consorcio de Santiago de Compostela).

GONZÁLEZ HIDALGO, JOAQUÍN (1872). *Nociones de fisiología e higiene para uso de los alumnos de segunda enseñanza*, 5th edn. (Madrid: Imprenta de Miguel Ginesta).

GONZÁLEZ MARTÍNEZ, PILAR (1988). *Aporías de una mujer: Emilia Pardo Bazán* (Madrid: Siglo XXI).

GONZÁLEZ SERRANO, URBANO (1883). *Cuestiones contemporáneas* (Madrid: Tipografía de Manuel G. Hernández).

GORDON, M. (1972). 'The Medical Background to Galdós's *La desheredada*', *Anales Galdosianos*, 7: 67–77.

GORTÁZAR, GUILLERMO (ed.) (1994). *Nación y estado en la España liberal* (Madrid: Noesis).

GOUX, JEAN-JOSEPH (1973). *Freud, Marx: économie et symbolique* (Paris: Seuil).
—— (1984). *Les Monnayeurs du langage* (Paris: Éditions Galilée).
—— (1988). 'Banking on Signs', *Diacritics*, 18.2: 15–25.
GRAHAM, HELEN, and LABANYI, JO (eds.) (1995). *Spanish Cultural Studies: An Introduction. The Struggle for Modernity* (Oxford: Oxford University Press).
GRANJEL, MERCEDES (1983). *Pedro Felipe Monlau y la higiene española del siglo XIX* (Salamanca: Universidad de Salamanca).
GREEN, NICHOLAS (1990). *The Spectacle of Nature: Landscape and Bourgeois Culture in Nineteenth-Century France* (Manchester: Manchester University Press).
GULLÓN, AGNES MONCY (1974). 'The Bird Motif and the Introductory Motif: Structure in *Fortunata y Jacinta*', *Anales Galdosianos*, 9: 51–75.
GULLÓN, GERMÁN (ed.) (1983). *Fortunata y Jacinta* (Madrid: Taurus).
GULLÓN, RICARDO (1970). *Técnicas de Galdós* (Madrid: Taurus).
—— (1973). *Galdós, novelista moderno* (Madrid: Gredos).
HABERMAS, JÜRGEN (1989). *The Structural Transformation of the Public Sphere: An Inquiry into a Category of Bourgeois Society* (Cambridge: Polity).
HALL, CATHERINE (1992). *White, Male and Middle Class: Explorations in Feminism and History* (Cambridge: Polity).
HALL, STUART (1993). 'Ethnicity, Race and Nation: Narrating Cultural Identities', plenary lecture to conference 'Empire, Nation, Language' held on 3 December at School of Advanced Study, University of London.
HARTSOCK, NANCY C. M. (1985). *Money, Sex, and Power: Toward a Feminist Historical Materialism* (Boston: Northeastern University Press).
HARVEY, DAVID (1985). *Consciousness and the Urban Experience* (Oxford: Blackwell).
—— (1989). *The Condition of Postmodernity* (Oxford: Blackwell).
HAUSER, PHILIPH (1979). *Madrid bajo el punto de vista médico-social*, ed. Carmen del Moral, 2 vols. (Madrid: Editora Nacional).
HEILBRONER, ROBERT L. (ed.) (1986). *The Essential Adam Smith* (New York: Norton).
HEMINGWAY, MAURICE (1983). *Emilia Pardo Bazán: The Making of a Novelist* (Cambridge: Cambridge University Press).
HENN, DAVID (1988). *The Early Pardo Bazán: Theme and Narrative Technique in the Novels of 1879–89* (Liverpool: Francis Cairns).
HENNESSY, C. A. M. (1962). *The Federal Republic in Spain: Pi y Margall and the Federal Republican Movement 1868–74* (Oxford: Oxford University Press).
HERR, RICHARD (1969). *The Eighteenth Century Revolution in Spain* (Princeton: Princeton University Press).

HERZBERGER, DAVID K. (1985). 'Narrative Self-Awareness in Pereda's *Peñas arriba*', *Hispania*, 68: 22–9.

HIBBS-LISSORGUES, SOLANGE (1995). *Iglesia, prensa y sociedad en España (1868–1904)* (Alicante: Instituto de Cultura 'Juan Gil-Albert').

HIDALGO MONTEAGUDO, RAMÓN, RAMOS GUARIDO, ROSALÍA and REVILLA GONZÁLEZ, FIDEL (1992). *Madrid Galdosiano* (Madrid: Fundación Caja de Madrid).

HIRSCHMAN, ALBERT O. (1977). *The Passions and the Interests: Political Arguments for Capitalism before its Triumph* (Princeton: Princeton University Press).

HOBSBAWM, ERIC (1990). *Nations and Nationalism since 1780: Programme, Myth, Reality* (Cambridge: Cambridge University Press).

—— and RANGER, TERENCE (eds.) (1984). *The Invention of Tradition* (Cambridge: Cambridge University Press).

HORIGAN, STEPHEN (1989). *Nature and Culture in Western Discourses* (London: Routledge).

HUERTAS, RAFAEL, and CAMPOS, RICARDO (eds.) (1992). *Medicina social y clase obrera en España (siglos XIX y XX)*, 2 vols. (Madrid: Fundación de Investigaciones Marxistas).

HUTCHINSON, JOHN, and SMITH, ANTHONY D. (eds.) (1994). *Nationalism* (Oxford: Oxford University Press).

HUYSSEN, ANDREAS (1986). *After the Great Divide: Modernism, Mass Culture and Postmodernism* (London: Macmillan).

IGLESIAS, MARÍA DEL CARMEN, and ELORZA, ANTONIO (1973). *Burgueses y proletarios: clase obrera y reforma social en la Restauración (1884–1889)* (Barcelona: Laia).

ILIE, PAUL (1998). 'Fortunata's Dream: Freud and the Unconscious in Galdós', *Anales Galdosianos*, 33: 13–100.

JACKSON, ROBERT M. (1987). 'The Gardens in Nineteenth-Century Spanish Fiction: *La de Bringas*', in Gene H. Bell-Villada Antonio Giménez and George Pistorius (eds.), *From Dante to García Márquez: Studies in Romance Language and Linguistics* (Williamstown, Mass.: Williams College), 182–90.

JACOBUS, MARY, FOX KELLER, EVELYN, and SHUTTLEWORTH, SALLY (eds.) (1990). *Body/Politics: Women and the Discourses of Science* (New York: Routledge).

JAGOE, CATHERINE (1992). 'Krausism and the Pygmalion Motif in Galdós's *La familia de León Roch*', *Romance Quarterly*, 39: 41–52.

—— (1993a). 'Disinheriting the Feminine: Galdós and the Rise of the Realist Novel in Spain', *Revista de Estudios Hispánicos*, 27: 225–48.

—— (1993b). 'Noncanonical Novels and the Question of Quality', *Revista de Estudios Hispánicos*, 27: 427–36.

—— (1994). *Ambiguous Angels: Gender in the Novels of Galdós* (Berkeley and Los Angeles: University of California Press).

—— Blanco, Alda, and Enríquez de Salamanca, Cristina (1998). *La mujer en los discursos de género del siglo XIX: textos y contextos* (Barcelona: Icaria).
James, Paul (1996). *Nation Formation: Towards a Theory of Abstract Community* (London: Sage).
Janovitz, Anne (1990). *England's Ruins: Poetic Purpose and the National Landscape* (Oxford: Blackwell).
Jiménez Fraud, Alberto (1973). *Juan Valera y la generación de 1868* (Madrid: Taurus).
Johnson, Paul (1991). *The Birth of the Modern: World Society 1815–1830* (London: Weidenfeld & Nicolson).
Jones, Colin, and Porter, Roy (eds.) (1998). *Reassessing Foucault: Power, Medicine and the Body* (London: Routledge).
Jongh-Rossel, Elena de (1985). *El krausismo y La generación de 1898* (Valencia: Albatros Hispanófila).
—— (1986). 'El paisaje castellano y sus descubridores: anticipando al 98', *Hispanic Journal*, 7: 73–80.
Jordanova, Ludmilla (ed.) (1986). *Languages of Nature: Critical Essays on Science and Nature* (London: Free Association Books).
—— (1989). *Sexual Visions: Images of Gender in Science and Medicine between the Eighteenth Century and Nineteenth Century* (New York: Harvester Wheatsheaf).
Jutglar, Antoni (1971). *Ideologías y clases en la España contemporánea: aproximación a la historia social de las ideas*, ii: *1875–1931* (Madrid: edicusa).
Kahane, Claire (1995). *Passions of the Voice: Hysteria, Narrative, and the Figure of the Speaking Woman* (Baltimore: Johns Hopkins University Press).
Kennedy, Ellen, and Mendus, Susan (eds.) (1987). *Women in Western Political Philosophy* (Brighton: Harvester Wheatsheaf).
Kenny, Michael, and Miguel, Jesús María de (1980). *La antropología médica en España* (Barcelona: Anagrama).
Kern, Robert W. (1974). *Liberals, Reformers and Caciques in Restoration Spain 1875–1909* (Albuquerque: University of North Mexico Press).
Kern, Stephen (1983). *The Culture of Time and Space 1880–1918* (Cambridge, Mass.: Harvard University Press).
Kirkpatrick, Susan (1978). 'The Ideology of Costumbrismo', *Ideologies and Literature*, 2: 28–44.
—— (1989). *Las Románticas: escritoras y subjetividad en España, 1835–1850* (Madrid: Cátedra).
Kolodny, Annette (1975). *The Lay of the Land* (Chapel Hill: North Carolina University Press).
Kronik, John W. (1977). '*El amigo Manso* and the Game of Fictive Autonomy', *Anales Galdosianos*, 12: 71–94.

KRONIK, JOHN W. (1981). '*Misericordia* as Metafiction', in *Homenaje a Antonio Sánchez Barbudo*, ed. Benito Brancaforte, Edward R. Mulvihill, and Roberto G. Sánchez (Madison: University of Wisconsin), 37–49.

—— (1982). 'Galdosian Reflections: Feijoo and the Fabrication of Fortunata', *Modern Language Notes*, 97: 272–310; repr. in Peter B. Goldman (ed.), *Conflicting Realities: Four Readings of a Chapter by Pérez Galdós ('Fortunata y Jacinta', Part III, Chapter IV)* (London: Támesis, 1984).

—— and TURNER, HARRIET S. (1994). *Textos y contextos de Galdós* (Madrid: Castalia).

KUKLICK, HENRIKA (1991). *The Savage Within: The Social History of British Anthropology, 1885–1945* (Cambridge: Cambridge University Press).

LABANYI, JO (1986). 'City, Country and Adultery in *La Regenta*', *Bulletin of Hispanic Studies*, 63: 53–65.

—— (1988). 'The Raw, the Cooked and the Indigestible in *Fortunata y Jacinta*', *Romance Studies*, 13: 55–66.

—— (1990). 'The Problem of Framing in *La de Bringas*', *Anales Galdosianos*, 25: 25–34.

—— (1991). 'Mysticism and Hysteria in *La Regenta*: The Problem of Female Identity', in Lisa Condé and Stephen Hart (eds.), *Feminist Readings on Spanish and Latin-American Literature* (Lampeter: Edwin Mellen), 37–46.

—— (ed.) (1993*a*). *Galdós* (Harlow: Longman).

—— (1993*b*). 'Representing the Unrepresentable: Monsters, Mystics and Feminine Men in Galdós's *Nazarín*', *Journal of Hispanic Research*, 1: 227–37.

—— (1999). 'Galateas in Revolt: Women and Self-Making in the Late Nineteenth-Century Spanish Novel', *Women: A Cultural Review*, 10: 87–96.

LAERMANS, RUDI (1993). 'Learning to Consume: Early Department Stores and the Shaping of Modern Consumer Culture (1860–1914)', *Theory, Culture and Society*, 10.4: 79–102.

LANDES, JOAN (1988). *Women and the Public Sphere* (Ithaca, NY: Cornell University Press).

LANGFORD TAYLOR, TERESIA (1997). *The Representation of Women in the Novels of Juan Valera* (New York: Peter Lang).

LANNON, FRANCES (1987). *Privilege, Persecution and Prophecy: The Catholic Church in Spain 1875–1975* (Oxford: Oxford University Press).

LAQUEUR, THOMAS (1990). *Making Sex: Body and Gender from the Greeks to Freud* (Cambridge, Mass.: Harvard University Press).

—— (1992). 'Sexual Desire and the Market Economy during the Industrial Revolution', in Domna C. Stanton (ed.), *Discourses of Sexuality: From Aristotle to AIDS* (Ann Arbor: University of Michigan Press), 185–215.

LARRA, MARIANO JOSÉ DE (1951). *Artículos completos* (Madrid: Aguilar).

LARSEN, KEVIN S. (1998). 'Dr Pulido y Fernández's "Brave New" Pharmacy', *Romance Quarterly*, 45: 45–54.
LASLETT, PETER, and WALL, RICHARD (eds.) (1972). *Household and Family in Past Time* (Cambridge: Cambridge University Press).
LEDGER, SALLY (1995). 'Gissing, the Shopgirl and the New Woman', *Women: A Cultural Review*, 6: 263–74.
LEE SIX, ABIGAIL (1994–5). 'Beyond Words: Valera's Use of Gaze in *Pepita Jiménez*', *Journal of Hispanic Research*, 3: 251–8.
LEPS, MARIE-CHRISTINE (1992). *Apprehending the Criminal: The Production of Deviance in Nineteenth-Century Discourse* (Durham, NC: Duke University Press).
LIDA, CLARA E., and ZAVALA, IRIS M. (eds.) (1970). *La Revolución de 1868: historia, pensamiento, literatura* (New York: Las Américas).
LIDA, DENAH (1967). 'Sobre el "krausismo" de Galdós', *Anales Galdosianos*, 2: 1–27.
LISSORGUES, YVAN (ed.) (1980–1). *Clarín político*, 2 vols. (Toulouse: Université de Toulouse-Le Mirail).
—— (1983). *La Pensée philosophique et religieuse de Leopoldo Alas (Clarín) 1875–1901* (Paris: CNRS).
—— (ed.) (1988). *Realismo y naturalismo en España en la segunda mitad del siglo XIX* (Barcelona: Anthropos).
LITVAK, LILY (1974). 'La sociología criminal y su influencia en los escritores españoles de fin de siglo', *Revue de littérature comparée*, 48: 12–32.
—— (1991). *El tiempo de los trenes: el paisaje español en el arte y la literatura del realismo (1849–1918)* (Barcelona: Ediciones del Serbal).
LLOYD, GENEVIÈVE (1984). *The Man of Reason: 'Male' and 'Female' in Western Philosophy* (London: Methuen).
LÓPEZ, IGNACIO-JAVIER (1988). 'Representación y escritura diferente en *La desheredada* de Galdós', *Hispanic Review*, 56: 455–80.
LÓPEZ-CORDÓN, MARÍA VICTORIA (1976). *La revolución de 1868 y la I República* (Madrid: Siglo XXI).
LÓPEZ DE LA VEGA, DR (1878). *La higiene del hogar* (Madrid: Administración de La Guirnalda y Episodios Nacionales).
LÓPEZ GARRIDO, DIEGO (1982). *La Guardia Civil y los orígenes del Estado centralista* (Barcelona: Crítica).
LÓPEZ JIMÉNEZ, LUIS (1977). *El naturalismo en España: Valera frente a Zola* (Madrid: Alhambra).
LÓPEZ-LANDY, RICARDO (1979). *El espacio novelesco en la obra de Galdós* (Madrid: Cultural Hispánica).
LÓPEZ MORILLAS, JUAN (1956). *El krausismo español: perfil de una aventura* (Mexico City: Fondo de Cultura Económia).
—— (1968). 'Galdós y el krausismo: *La familia de León Roch*', *Revista de Occidente*, 2nd series, 60: 331–57.
—— (1977). *Krausismo: estética y literatura* (Barcelona: Labor).

LÓPEZ PIÑERO, JOSÉ MARÍA (1964). *Medicina y sociedad en la España del siglo XIX* (Madrid: Sociedad de Estudios y Publicaciones).
—— (1985). *Orígenes históricos del concepto de neurosis* (Madrid: Alianza).
—— GARCÍA BALLESTER, LUIS, and FAUS SEVILLA, PILAR (1964). *Medicina y sociedad en la España del siglo XIX* (Madrid: Sociedad de Estudios y Publicaciones).
LOTT, ROBERT E. (1970). *Language and Psychology in 'Pepita Jiménez'* (Urbana: University of Illinois Press).
MACCORMACK, CAROL P., and STRATHERN, MARILYN (eds.) (1980). *Nature, Culture and Gender* (Cambridge: Cambridge University Press).
MACCURDY, G. GRANT (1983). 'Mysticism, Love and Illumination in *Pepita Jiménez*', *Revista de Estudios Hispánicos*, 17.3: 323–34.
MACPHERSON, C. B. (1990). *The Political Theory of Possessive Individualism*, 13th edn. (Oxford: Oxford University Press).
MADARIAGA DE LA CAMPA, BENITO (1986). *Crónica del regionalismo en Cantabria* (Santander: Ediciones Tantín).
—— (ed.) (1989). *Antología del regionalismo en Cantabria* (Santander: no publisher).
—— (1991). *José María de Pereda: biografía de un novelista* (Santander: Ediciones de Librería Estudios).
MAINER, JOSÉ CARLOS (1988). *La doma de la quimera (ensayos sobre nacionalismo y cultura en España)* (Barcelona: Servei de Publicacions de la Universitat Autònoma).
MANDRELL, JAMES (1992). *Don Juan and the Point of Honor: Seduction, Patriarchal Society, and Literary Tradition* (University Park: Pennsylvania State University Press).
MAQUIEIRA D'ANGELO, VIRGINIA (ed.) (1989). *Mujeres y hombres en la formación del pensamiento occidental*, vol. ii (Madrid: Universidad Autónoma de Madrid).
MARISTANY, LUIS (1973). *El gabinete del doctor Lombroso (Delicuencia y fin de siglo en España)* (Barcelona: Anagrama).
—— (1983). 'Lombroso y España', *Anales de Literatura Española*, 2: 361–81.
MAR-MOLINERO, CLARE, and SMITH, ÁNGEL (eds.) (1996). *Nationalism and the Nation in the Iberian Peninsula: Competing and Conflicting Identities* (Oxford: Berg).
MARTÍNEZ CACHERO, JOSÉ MARÍA (ed.) (1978). *Leopoldo Alas 'Clarín'* (Madrid: Taurus).
MARTÍNEZ CUADRADO, MIGUEL (1973). *La burguesía conservadora (1874–1931)* (Madrid: Alianza).
MARX, KARL (1990). *Selected Writings*, ed. David McLellan (Oxford: Oxford University Press).
—— and ENGELS, FRIEDRICH (1974). *The Communist Manifesto*, introd. A. J. P. Taylor (Harmondsworth: Penguin).

MASIELLO, FRANCINE (1992). *Between Civilization and Barbarism: Women, Nation, and Literary Culture in Modern Argentina* (Lincoln: University of Nebraska Press).

MASON, JOHN HOPE (ed.) (1979). *The Indispensable Rousseau* (London: Quartet Books).

MASON, MICHAEL (1995a). *The Making of Victorian Sexual Attitudes* (Oxford: Oxford University Press).

—— (1995b). *The Making of Victorian Sexuality* (Oxford: Oxford University Press).

MASSON, JEFFRY MOUSSAIEFF (1986). *A Dark Science: Women, Sexuality and Psychiatry in the Nineteenth Century* (New York: Farrar, Strauss & Giroux).

MATA, PEDRO (1868). *Criterio médico-psicológico para el diagnóstico diferencial de la pasión y la locura*, 2 vols. (Madrid: Imprenta a cargo de R. Berenguillo Torres).

MATLOCK, JANN (1994). *Scenes of Seduction: Prostitution, Hysteria, and Reading Difference in Nineteenth-Century France* (New York: Columbia University Press).

MAURICE, JACQUES, and SERRANO, CARLOS (1977). *Joaquín Costa: crisis de la Restauración y populismo (1875–1911)* (Madrid: Siglo XXI).

MAYORAL, MARINA (ed.) (1989). *Estudios sobre 'Los Pazos de Ulloa'* (Madrid: Cátedra-Ministerio de Cultura).

MEDINA, JEREMY T. (1979). *Spanish Realism: The Theory and Practice of a Concept in the Nineteenth Century* (Potomac, Md.: José Porrúa Turanzas).

MENDUS, SUSAN, and RENDALL, JANE (eds.) (1989). *Sexuality and Subordination: Interdisciplinary Studies of Gender in the Nineteenth Century* (London: Routledge).

MICALE, MARK S. (1995). *Approaching Hysteria: Disease and its Interpretations* (Princeton: Princeton University Press).

MICHAELS, WALTER B. (1987). *The Gold Standard and the Logic of Naturalism* (Berkeley and Los Angeles: University of California Press).

MILL, JOHN STUART (1988). *The Subjection of Women*, ed. Susan Moller Okin (Indianapolis: Hackett Publishing Company).

MILLER, ANDREW H. (1995). *Novels behind Glass: Commodity Culture and Victorian Narrative* (Cambridge: Cambridge University Press).

MILLINGTON, MARK I., and SMITH, PAUL JULIAN (eds.) (1994). *New Hispanisms: Literature, Culture, Theory* (Ottawa: Dovehouse).

MINSON, JEFFREY (1986). *Genealogies of Morals: Nietzsche, Foucault, Donzelot and the Eccentricity of Ethics* (London: Macmillan).

MITCHELL, JULIET (1975). *Psychoanalysis and Feminism* (Harmondsworth: Penguin).

MONLAU, PEDRO FELIPE (1860). *Nociones de higiene doméstica y gobierno de la casa para uso de las escuelas de primera enseñanza de niñas y colegios de señoritas* (Madrid: Imprenta de M. Rivadeneyra).
—— (1865). *Higiene del matrimonio o libro de los casados*, 3rd rev. edn. (Madrid: Imprenta de M. Rivadeneyra).
—— (1868). *Estudios superiores de higiene pública y epidemiología (curso de 1868 á 1869: lección inaugural)* (Madrid: Imprenta y Estereotipia de M. Rivadeneyra).
—— (1875). *Elementos de higiene privada*, 5th rev. edn. (Madrid: Moya y Plaza).
—— and SALARICH, JOAQUIM (1984). *Condiciones de vida y trabajo obrero en España a mediados del siglo XIX*, ed. Antoni Jutglar (Barcelona: Anthropos).
MONTESINOS, JOSÉ F. (1957). *Valera o la ficción libre: ensayo de interpretación de una anomalía literaria* (Madrid: Gredos).
—— (1966). *Introducción a una historia de la novela en España en el siglo XIX*, 2nd edn. (Madrid: Castalia).
—— (1968–73). *Galdós*, 3 vols. (Madrid: Castalia).
—— (1969). *Pereda o la novela idilio* (Madrid: Castalia).
—— (1980). *Costumbrismo y novela*, 4th edn. (Madrid: Castalia).
MOOERS, COLIN (1991). *The Making of Bourgeois Europe: Absolutism, Revolution, and the Rise of Capitalism in England, France and Germany* (London: Verso).
MORETTI, FRANCO (1987). *The Way of the World: The 'Bildungsroman' in European Culture* (London: Verso).
—— (1998). *An Atlas of the European Novel 1800–1900* (London: Verso).
MOSCUCCI, ORNELLA (1990). *The Science of Women: Gynaecology and Gender in England, 1800–1929* (Cambridge: Cambridge University Press).
MOSSE, GEORGE L. (1985). *Nationalism and Sexuality: Middle-Class Morality and Sexual Norms in Modern Europe* (Madison: University of Wisconsin Press).
—— (1996). *The Image of Man: The Creation of Modern Masculinity* (New York: Oxford University Press).
MOSSMAN, CAROL A. (1993). *Politics and Narratives of Birth: Gynocolonization from Rousseau to Zola* (Cambridge: Cambridge University Press).
MOYA, MIGUEL (1879). *Conflictos entre los poderes del Estado*, prol. Gumersindo de Azcárate (Madrid: Casa Editorial de Medina).
MUÑOZ ROJAS, JOSÉ ANTONIO (1956). 'Notas sobre la Andalucía de don Juan Valera', *Papeles de Son Armadans*, 3.7: 9–22.
NADAL, JORDI (1994). *El fracaso de la revolución industrial en España, 1814–1913* (Barcelona: Ariel).
NASH, MARY (1983). *Mujer, familia y trabajo en España, 1875–1936* (Barcelona: Anthropos).

NASSAUER, DR MAX (n.d.), *El cuerpo y la vida de la mujer en estado de salud y enfermedad* (Madrid: Librería Médica R. Chena y Compañía).
NEAD, LYNDA (1988). *Myths of Sexuality: Representations of Women in Victorian Britain* (Oxford: Blackwell).
NICHOLSON, LINDA J. (1986). *Gender and History: The Limits of Social Theory in the Age of the Family* (New York: Columbia University Press).
NIETO, ALEJANDRO (1968). 'La administración y el derecho administrativo durante el gobierno provisional de 1868–69', *Revista de Occidente*, 2nd series, 67: 64–93.
NIMETZ, MICHAEL (1971). 'Eros and Ecclesia in Clarín's Vetusta', *Modern Language Notes*, 86: 242–53.
NOCHLIN, LINDA (1991). *The Politics of Vision: Essays on Nineteenth-Century Art and Society* (London: Thames & Hudson).
NUEZ, SEBASTIÁN DE LA (ed.) (1990). *Biblioteca y archivo de la Casa Museo Pérez Galdós* (Las Palmas de Gran Canaria: Cabildo Insular de Gran Canaria).
NÚÑEZ ROLDÁN, FRANCISCO (1995). *Mújeres públicas: historia de la prostitución en España* (Madrid: Temas de Hoy).
NYE, ROBERT A. (1982). 'Degeneration and the Medical Model of Cultural Crisis in the French Belle Époque', in Seymour Drescher, David Sabean, and Allan Sharlin (eds.), *Political Symbolism in Modern Europe: Essays in Honor of George L. Mosse* (New Brunswick: Transaction Books), 19–41.
OKIN, SUSAN MOLLER (1979). *Women in Western Political Thought* (Princeton: Princeton University Press).
ONG, WALTER (1982). *Orality and Literacy: The Technologizing of the Word* (London: Methuen).
ORDÓÑEZ, ELIZABETH J. (1986). 'Paradise Regained, Paradise Lost: Desire and Prohibition in *La madre naturaleza*', *Hispanic Journal*, 8: 7–18.
ORTEGA, JOSÉ, and CARENAS, FRANCISCO (1975). *La figura del sacerdote en la moderna narrativa española* (Madrid: Casuz).
ORTÍ Y BRULL, VICENTE (1893). *La cuestión monetaria* (Madrid: Imprenta y Litografía de los Huérfanos).
ORTIZ ARMENGOL, PEDRO (1996). *Vida de Galdós* (Barcelona: Crítica).
ORTNER, SHERRY B., and WHITEHEAD, HARRIET (eds.) (1989). *Sexual Meanings: The Cultural Construction of Gender and Sexuality* (Cambridge: Cambridge University Press).
OSBORNE, ROBERT E. (1964). *Emilia Pardo Bazán: su vida y sus obras* (Mexico City: Ediciones de Andrea).
OTERO CARVAJAL, LUIS E., and BAHAMONDE, ÁNGEL (eds.) (1986). *Madrid en la sociedad del siglo XIX*, 2 vols. (Madrid: Comunidad de Madrid).

OTIS, LAURA (1995). 'Science and Signification in the Early Writings of Emilia Pardo Bazán', *Revista de Estudios Hispánicos*, 29: 72–106.

OVERTON, BILL (1996). *The Novel of Female Adultery: Love and Gender in Continental European Fiction, 1830–1900* (London: Macmillan).

PALACIO VALDÉS, ARMANDO (1991). *La aldea perdida*, ed. Álvaro Ruiz de la Peña, 12th edn. (Madrid: Espasa Calpe).

PARDO BAZÁN, EMILIA (1966). *La cuestión palpitante*, ed. Carmen Bravo Villasante (Salamanca: Anaya).

—— (1972). *La vida contemporánea*, ed. Carmen Bravo-Villasante (Madrid: Editorial Magisterio Español).

—— (1975). *Cartas a Benito Pérez Galdós (1889–1890)*, ed. Carmen Bravo Villasante (Madrid: Turner).

—— (1981). *'La mujer española' y otros artículos feministas*, ed. Leda Schiavo (Madrid: Editora Nacional).

—— (1985). *La madre naturaleza* (Madrid: Alianza).

—— (1986). *Los Pazos de Ulloa* (Madrid: Castalia).

—— (1994). *Crónicas en 'La Nación' de Buenos Aires (1909–1921)*, ed. Cyrus DeCoster (Madrid: Pliegos).

PARKER, ANDREW, RUSSO, MARY, SOMMER, DORIS, and YAEGER, PATRICIA (eds.) (1992). *Nationalisms and Sexualities* (New York: Routledge).

PATEMAN, CAROLE (1983). 'Feminist Critiques of the Public/Private Dichotomy', in S. I. Benn and G. F. Gaus (eds.), *Public and Private in Social Life* (London: Croom Helm).

—— (1989). *The Sexual Contract* (Cambridge: Polity).

—— (1990). *The Disorder of Women* (Cambridge: Polity).

—— and GROSS, ELIZABETH (eds.) (1986). *Feminist Challenges: Social and Political Theory* (London: Allen & Unwin).

PATTISON, WALTER T. (1965). *El naturalismo español: historia externa de un movimiento literario* (Madrid: Gredos).

—— (1971). *Emilia Pardo Bazán* (New York: Twayne).

PAYNE, STANLEY G. (ed.) (1996). *Identidad y nacionalismo en la España contemporánea: el Carlismo, 1933–1975* (Madrid: Actas).

PENA LÓPEZ, MARÍA DEL CARMEN (1982). 'El paisaje español del siglo XIX: del naturalismo al impresionismo', doctoral thesis (Madrid: Universidad Complutense).

—— (1990). 'El concepto de lo femenino y lo masculino en la teoría del paisaje español', in *La imagen de la mujer en el arte español* (Madrid: Universidad Autónoma de Madrid), 141–8.

—— (ed.) (1993–4). *Centro y periferia en la modernización de la pintura española 1880–1918* (Madrid: Ministerio de Cultura).

PENNY, RALPH (1980). 'El dialectismo de *Peñas arriba*', *Boletín de la Biblioteca de Menéndez Pelayo*, 56: 377–86.

PERAZA DE AYALA, TRINO (1947). *La psiquiatría española en el siglo XIX* (Madrid: CSIC).

PEREDA, JOSÉ MARÍA DE (1897). *Discursos leídos ante la Real Academia Española en la recepción pública del Señor Don José María de Pereda* (Madrid: Est. Tip. de la viuda e hijos de Tello).
—— (1959). *Obras completas*, 2 vols. (Madrid: Aguilar).
—— (1988). *Peñas arriba*, ed. Antonio Rey (Madrid: Cátedra).
PÉREZ, JANET (1995). 'Subversion of Victorian Values and Ideal Types: Pardo Bazán and the Ángel del hogar', *Hispania*, 113: 31–44.
PÉREZ GALDÓS, BENITO (1895). *Nazarín* (Madrid: Casa Editorial 'La Guirnalda').
—— (1923). *Obras inéditas de Benito Pérez Galdós*, ed. Alberto Ghiraldo, vol. iii. (Madrid: Renacimiento).
—— (1966). *Obras completas*, 6th edn., vol. iv, ed. Federico Carlos Sainz de Robles (Madrid: Aguilar).
—— (1970). *Obras completas*, 7th edn., vol. v, ed. Federico Carlos Sainz de Robles (Madrid: Aguilar).
—— (1972). *Ensayos de crítica literaria*, ed. Laureano Bonet (Barcelona: Península).
—— (1981). *Galdós, periodista* (Madrid: Banco de Crédito Industrial).
—— (1982). *Los artículos políticos en la 'Revista de España' 1871–1872*, ed. Brian J. Dendle and Joseph Schraibman (Lexington, Ky.: Dendle & Schraibman).
—— (1985). *La de Bringas*, ed. Alda Blanco and Carlos Blanco Aguinaga (Madrid: Cátedra).
—— (1992). *Fortunata y Jacinta*, ed. Francisco Caudet, 2 vols. (Madrid: Cátedra).
PÉREZ GUTIÉRREZ, FRANCISCO (1975). *El problema religioso y la generación de 1868* (Madrid: Taurus).
PERINAT, ADOLFO, and MARRADES, MARÍA ISABEL (1980). *Mujer, prensa y sociedad en España 1800–1939* (Madrid: Centro de Investigaciones Sociológicas).
PERROT, MICHELLE (ed.) (1990). *A History of Private Life*, iv: *From the Fires of Revolution to the Great War* (Cambridge, Mass.: Belknap Press of Harvard University Press).
PESET, JOSÉ LUIS (1983). *Ciencia y marginación: sobre negros, locos y criminales* (Barcelona: Crítica).
—— and PESET, MARIANO (1975). *Lombroso y la escuela positivista italiana* (Madrid: CSIC).
PICK, DANIEL (1989). *Faces of Degeneration: A European Disorder, c.1848–c.1918* (Cambridge: Cambridge University Press).
PI Y MARGALL, FRANCISCO (1973). *Las nacionalidades*, ed. Antoni Jutglar (Madrid: EDICUSA).
PLA, CARLOS, BENITO, PILAR, CASADO, MERCEDES, and POYÁN, JUAN CARLOS (1987). *El Madrid de Galdós* (Madrid: Avapiés).

Pointon, Marcia (1990). *Naked Authority: The Body in Western Painting 1830–1908* (Cambridge: Cambridge University Press).

Polanco, Victoriano, and Pérez de Camino, Fernando (1889). *La Montaña: paisajes, costumbres y marinas de la provincia de Santander, con una carta autógrafa de don José María de Pereda* (Madrid: Establecimiento Tipográfico Sucesores de Rivadeneyra).

Ponce, J. C. (1996). *Literatura y ferrocarril en España: aspectos socioliterarios del ferrocarril en España* (Madrid: Fundación de los Ferrocarriles Españoles).

Porter, Roy, and Hall, Lesley (1995). *The Facts of Life: The Creation of Sexual Knowledge in Britain, 1650–1950* (New Haven: Yale University Press).

Portero, José Antonio (1978). *Púlpito e ideología en la España del siglo XIX* (Zaragoza: Libros Pórtico).

Pratt, Mary Louise (1992). *Imperial Eyes: Travel Writing and Transculturation* (London: Routledge).

Preston, Paul (1993). *Franco* (London: Harper Collins).

Pugh, Simon (1988). *Garden-Nature-Language* (Manchester: Manchester University Press).

Pulido Fernández, Ángel (1876). *Bosquejos médico-sociales para la mujer* (Madrid: Imprenta a cargo de Víctor Saiz).

Quispe-Agnoli, Rocío (1998). 'De la mujer caída al ángel subvertido en *Fortunata y Jacinta*: las funciones ambivalentes de Mauricia la Dura', *Bulletin of Hispanic Studies* (Glasgow), 75: 337–54.

Rabinow, Paul (ed.) (1984). *The Foucault Reader* (Harmondsworth: Penguin).

Raphael, D. D. (1985). *Adam Smith* (Oxford: Oxford University Press).

Reher, David S. (1997). *Perspectives on the Family in Spain, Past and Present* (Oxford: Clarendon Press).

Répide, Pedro de (1989). *Las calles de Madrid* (Madrid: Kaydeda Ediciones).

Resina, Joan Ramon (1994–5). 'The Sublimation of Wealth and the Consciousness of Modernism in Narcís Oller's *La febre d'or*', *Journal of Hispanic Research*, 3: 259–76.

—— (1995). '*Pepita Jiménez*: del idilio a la Restauración', *Bulletin of Hispanic Studies*, 72: 175–93.

Reuben Holo, Selma (1997). 'The Art Museum as a Means of Refiguring Regional Identity in Democratic Spain', in Marsha Kinder (ed.), *Refiguring Spain: Cinema/Media/Representation* (Durham, NC: Duke University Press), 301–26.

Reyero, Carlos (1987). *Imagen histórica de España (1850–1900)* (Madrid: Espasa Calpe).

—— (1989). *La pintura de historia en España: esplendor de un género en el siglo XIX* (Madrid: Cátedra).

REY GONZÁLEZ, ANTONIO (1990). *Estudios médico-sociales sobre marginados en la España del siglo XIX* (Madrid: Ministerio de Sanidad y Consumo).

RIBBANS, GEOFFREY (1977). *Pérez Galdós, 'Fortunata y Jacinta'* (London: Grant & Cutler).

—— (1980). '*Historia novelada* and *Novela histórica*: The Use of Historical Incidents from the Reign of Isabella II in Galdós's *Episodios* and *Novelas contemporáneas*', in John England (ed.), *Hispanic Studies in Honour of Frank Pierce* (Sheffield: University of Sheffield), 133–47.

—— (1982). ' "La historia como debiera ser": Galdós's Speculations on Nineteenth-Century Spanish History', *Bulletin of Hispanic Studies*, 59: 267–74.

—— (1986). 'Galdós's Literary Presentations of the Interregnum, Reign of Amadeo and the First Republic (1868–1874)', *Bulletin of Hispanic Studies*, 63: 1–17.

—— (1992). 'The Making of a Minor Character: Galdós's Plácido Estupiñá', *Symposium*, 46: 147–57.

—— (1993). *History and Fiction in Galdós's Narratives* (Oxford: Oxford University Press).

—— (1997). *Conflicts and Conciliations: The Evolution of Galdós's 'Fortunata y Jacinta'* (West Lafayette, Ind.: Purdue University Press).

RICHARDS, THOMAS (1990). *The Commodity Culture of Victorian England: Advertising and Spectacle, 1851–1914* (London: Verso).

—— (1993). *The Imperial Archive: Knowledge and the Fantasy of Empire* (London: Verso).

RILEY, DENISE (1988). *'Am I that Name?': Feminism and the Category of 'Women' in History* (London: Macmillan).

RISLEY, WILLIAM R. (1978). 'Setting in the Galdós Novel, 1881–1885', *Hispanic Review*, 46: 23–40.

RIVIÈRE GÓMEZ, AURORA (1994). *La educación de la mujer en el Madrid de Isabel II* (Madrid: Dirección General de la Mujer).

—— (1994). *'Caídas, miserables, degeneradas': estudio sobre la prostitución en el siglo XIX* (Madrid: Dirección General de la Mujer).

RODRÍGUEZ, ADNA ROSA (1991). *La cuestión feminista en los ensayos de Emilia Pardo Bazán* (La Coruña: Ediciós do Castro).

RODRÍGUEZ ESTEBAN, JOSÉ ANTONIO (1994). 'La Institución Libre de Enseñanza y la Sociedad Geográfica de Madrid: la geografía decimonónica en la regeneración interior y exterior', *Boletín Institución Libre de Enseñanza*, 2nd series, 19 (Apr.): 33–44.

RODRÍGUEZ OCAÑA, ESTEBAN (1987). *La constitución de la medicina social como disciplina en España (1882–1923)* (Madrid: Ministerio de Sanidad y Consumo).

RODRÍGUEZ PUÉRTOLAS, JULIO (1975). *Galdós, burguesía y revolución* (Madrid: Turner).

RODRÍGUEZ PUÉRTOLAS, JULIO (ed.) (1988). *Madrid en Galdós, Galdós en Madrid* (catalogue of the exhibition held in the Palacio de Cristal del Retiro, May 1988) (Madrid: Comunidad de Madrid).

—— (ed.) (1989). *Galdós en el centenario de 'Fortunata y Jacinta'* (Palma de Mallorca: Prensa Universitaria).

RODRÍGUEZ SÁNCHEZ, MARÍA DE LOS ÁNGELES (1994). '*La del tercero*: aproximación a la histeria en un cuento escrito por una mujer', *Asclepio*, 46.1: 261–90.

ROGIN, MICHAEL (1996). *Blackface, White Noise: Jewish Immigrants in the Hollywood Melting Pot* (Berkeley and Los Angeles: University of California Press).

ROMERO, LEONARDO (ed.) (1992). *Una anatomía electoral: correspondencia familiar de Juan Valera (1855–1864)* (Barcelona: Sirmio).

ROMERO TOBAR (ed.) (1998). *El camino hacia el 98 (Los escritores de la Restauración y la crisis del fin de siglo)* (Madrid: Fundación Duques de Soria-Visor Libros).

ROUND, NICHOLAS G. (1971). 'Rosalía Bringas' Children', *Anales Galdosianos*, 6: 43–50.

RUANO DE LA HAZA, JOSÉ M. (1984). 'La identidad del narrador de los *Paralipómenos* de *Pepita Jiménez*', *Revista Canadiense de Estudios Hispánicos*, 8: 335–50.

RUBIO CREMADES, ENRIQUE (ed.) (1990). *Juan Valera* (Madrid: Taurus).

RUEDA, GERMÁN (1986). *La desamortización de Mendizábal y Espartero en España* (Madrid: Cátedra).

RUIZ, DAVID (1975). *Asturias contemporánea (1808–1936)* (Madrid: Siglo XXI).

RUIZ SALVADOR, ANTONIO (1966). 'La función del trasfondo histórico en *La desheredada*', *Anales Galdosianos*, 1: 53–61.

—— (1971). *El Ateneo Científico, Literario y Artístico de Madrid (1835–1885)* (London: Támesis).

RUSSELL, BERTRAND (1980). *History of Western Philosophy*, 2nd edn. (London: Unwin).

RUSSETT, CYNTHIA EAGLE (1989). *Sexual Science: The Victorian Construction of Womanhood* (Cambridge, Mass.: Harvard University Press).

RUTHERFORD, JOHN (1974). *Leopoldo Alas, 'La Regenta'* (London: Grant & Cutler).

—— (1988). *'La Regenta' y el lector cómplice* (Murcia: Universidad de Murcia).

RYAN, JENNY (1994). 'Women, Modernity and the City', *Theory, Society and Culture*, 11: 35–63.

SAAVEDRA, LUIS (1987). *Clarín, una interpretación* (Madrid: Taurus).

SAID, EDWARD W. (1993). *Culture and Imperialism* (London: Chatto & Windus).

SALAÜN, SERGE, and SERRANO, CARLOS (1991). *1900 en España* (Madrid: Espasa Calpe).

SÁNCHEZ AGESTA, LUIS (1985). *La constitución de 1876 y el Estado de la Restauración* (Madrid: Fundación Santa María).
SÁNCHEZ ALBORNOZ, NICOLÁS (1968). *España hace un siglo: una economía dual* (Barcelona: Península).
—— (ed.) (1985). *La modernización económica de España 1830–1930* (Madrid: Alianza).
SANTERO, FRANCISCO JAVIER (1885). *Elementos de higiene privada y pública*, 2 vols. (Madrid: El Cosmos Editorial).
SANZ DEL RÍO, JULIÁN (1860). *Ideal de la humanidad para la vida* (Madrid: Imprenta de Manuel Galiano).
SARASÚA, CARMEN (1994). *Criados, nodrizas y amos: el servicio doméstico en la formación del mercado de trabajo madrileño, 1758–1868* (Madrid: Siglo XXI).
SARDÁ, JUAN (1948). *La política monetaria y las fluctuaciones de la economía española en el siglo XIX* (Madrid: CSIC).
SCANLON, GERALDINE M. (1984). 'Heroism in an Unheroic Society: Galdós's *Lo prohibido*', *Modern Language Review*, 79: 831–45.
—— (1986). *La polémica feminista en la España contemporánea 1868– 1975*, 2nd edn. (Madrid: Akal).
—— (1990). 'Class and Gender in Pardo Bazán's *La tribuna*', *Bulletin of Hispanic Studies*, 67: 137–50.
SCHIEBINGER, LONDA (1991). *The Mind Has No Sex? Women in the Origins of Modern Science* (Cambridge, Mass.: Harvard University Press).
—— (1993). *Nature's Body: Sexual Politics and the Making of Modern Science* (London: Pandora).
SCHMIDT, RUTH (1969). *Cartas entre dos amigos del teatro: Manuel Tolosa Latour y Benito Pérez Galdós* (Las Palmas de Gran Canaria: Cabildo Insular de Gran Canaria).
SCHWARTZ, JOEL (1984). *The Sexual Politics of Jean-Jacques Rousseau* (Chicago: Chicago University Press).
SCHWARTZ GIRÓN, PEDRO (ed.) (1970). *Ensayos sobre la economía española a mediados del siglo XIX* (Madrid: Banco de España).
Seminario de historia de la acción social (1988). *De la beneficencia al bienestar social: cuatro siglos de acción social* (Madrid: Siglo XXI).
SENNETT, RICHARD (1991). *The Conscience of the Eye: The Design and Social Life of Cities* (New York: Alfred A. Knopf).
—— (1994). *Flesh and Stone: The Body and the City in Western Civilization* (London: Faber & Faber).
SHANLEY, MARY LYNDON, and PATEMAN, CAROLE (eds.) (1991). *Feminist Interpretations and Political Theory* (Cambridge: Polity).
SHELL, MARC (1978). *The Economy of Literature* (Baltimore: Johns Hopkins University Press).
—— (1994). *Money, Language and Thought* (Baltimore: Johns Hopkins University Press).
—— (1995). *Art and Money* (Chicago: Chicago University Press).

SHERIDAN, ALAN (1980). *Michel Foucault: The Will to Truth* (London: Tavistock Publications).
SHIRES, LINDA M. (ed.) (1992). *Rewriting the Victorians: Theory, History, and the Politics of Gender* (London: Routledge).
SHOEMAKER, WILLIAM H. (ed.) (1972). *Los artículos de Galdós en 'La Nación'* (Madrid: Insula).
—— (ed.) (1973). *Las cartas desconocidas de Galdós en 'La Prensa' de Buenos Aires* (Madrid: Cultural Hispánica).
—— (1980). *The Novelistic Art of Galdós*, 2 vols. (Valencia: Albatros/ Hispanófila).
SHOWALTER, ELAINE (1987). *The Female Malady: Women, Madness and English Culture, 1830–1980* (London: Virago Press).
—— (1991). *Sexual Anarchy: Gender and Culture at the Fin de Siècle* (London: Bloomsbury).
SHUBERT, ADRIAN (1990). *A Social History of Spain* (London: Unwin Hyman).
SIEBURTH, STEPHANIE (1990). *Reading 'La Regenta': Duplicitous Discourse and the Entropy of Structure* (Amsterdam: John Benjamins).
—— (1994). *Inventing High and Low: Literature, Mass Culture and Uneven Modernity in Spain* (Durham, NC: Duke University Press).
SIMMEL, GEORG (1984). *On Women, Sexuality and Love*, ed. Guy Oakes (New Haven: Yale University Press).
—— (1990). *The Philosophy of Money*, 2nd edn. (London: Routledge).
—— (1997). *Simmel on Culture*, ed. David Frisby and Mike Featherstone (London: Sage).
SIMÓN PALMER, MARÍA DEL CARMEN (1982). *La mujer madrileña del siglo XIX* (Madrid: Ayuntamiento de Madrid).
—— (1984). 'La higiene y la medicina de la mujer española a través de los libros (siglos XVI a XIX)', in *La mujer en la historia de España (siglos XVI–XX)* (Madrid: Universidad Autónoma de Madrid), 71–84.
—— (1985). 'Escritoras españolas del siglo XIX o el miedo a la marginación', *Anales de Literatura Española*, 2: 477–90.
—— (1991). *El Retiro: parque de Madrid* (Madrid: Ediciones La Librería).
SINCLAIR, ALISON (1992). 'The Consuming Passion: Appetite and Hunger in *La Regenta*', *Bulletin of Hispanic Studies*, 69: 246–61.
—— (1993). *The Deceived Husband: A Kleinian Discussion of the Literature of Infidelity* (Oxford: Clarendon Press).
—— (1994–5). 'Masculine Envy and Desire in *La Regenta*: The Skull and the Foot', *Journal of Iberian and Latin American Studies: Tesserae*, 1: 171–90.
—— (1997). 'Liminal Anxieties: Nausea and Mud in *La Regenta*', *Bulletin of Hispanic Studies* (Glasgow), 74: 155–76.
—— (1998). *Dislocations of Desire: Gender, Identity, and Strategy in 'La Regenta'* (Chapel Hill: University of North Carolina Press).

SINNIGEN, JOHN H. (1974). 'Individual, Class and Society in *Fortunata y Jacinta*', in Robert J. Weber (ed.), *Galdós Studies*, vol. ii, (London: Támesis), 49–68.
—— (1996). *Sexo y política: lecturas galdosianas* (Madrid: Ediciones de la Torre).
SMITH, ADAM (1993). *An Inquiry into the Nature and Causes of the Wealth of Nations*, ed. Kathryn Sutherland (Oxford: Oxford University Press).
SMITH, ANTHONY (1998). *Nationalism and Modernism* (London: Routledge).
SMITH, PAUL JULIAN (1989). 'Galdós, Valera, Lacan', in *The Body Hispanic: Gender and Sexuality in Spanish and Spanish American Literature* (Oxford: Oxford University Press), 69–104.
SOLÉ TURA, JORDI, and AJA, ELISEO (1978). *Constituciones y períodos constituyentes en España (1808–1936)*, 2nd edn. (Madrid: Siglo XXI).
SOMMER, DORIS (1991). *Foundational Fictions: The National Romances of Latin America* (Berkeley and Los Angeles: University of California Press).
SONTAG, SUSAN (ed.) (1982). *The Barthes Reader* (London: Cape).
SPACKMAN, BARBARA (1989). *Decadent Genealogies: The Rhetoric of Sickness from Baudelaire to D'Annunzio* (Ithaca, NY: Cornell University Press).
SPENCER, HERBERT (n.d.*a*). *Estudios políticos y sociales* (Valencia: F. Sempere y Compañia).
—— (n.d.*b*). *Creación y evolución* (Valencia: F. Sempere y Compañía).
—— (1981). *The Man versus the State, with Six Essays on Government, Society and Freedom* (Indianapolis: Liberty Classics).
STEWART, SUSAN (1993). *On Longing: Narratives of the Miniature, the Gigantic, the Souvenir, the Collection* (Baltimore: Johns Hopkins University Press).
STILL, JUDITH (1997). *Feminine Economies: Thinking against the Market in the Enlightenment and the Late Twentieth Century* (Manchester: Manchester University Press).
STOCKING, GEORGE W. (1987). *Victorian Anthropology* (New York: Free Press).
SULEIMAN, SUSAN (ed.) (1985). *The Female Body in Western Culture: Contemporary Perspectives* (Cambridge, Mass.: Harvard University Press).
SYDIE, ROZALIND A. (1987). *Natural Women, Cultured Men: A Feminist Perspective on Sociological Theory* (Milton Keynes: Open University Press).
TAMBLING, JEREMY (1990). *Confession: Sexuality, Sin, the Subject* (Manchester: Manchester University Press).
TANNER, TONY (1979). *Adultery in the Novel: Contract and Transgression* (Baltimore: Johns Hopkins University Press).
—— (1987). *Scenes of Nature, Signs of Men* (Cambridge: Cambridge University Press).

TEICH, MIKULAS, and PORTER, ROY (eds.) (1993). *The National Question in Europe in Historical Perspective* (Cambridge: Cambridge University Press).
THIERS, A. (1848). *De la propriété* (Paris: Paulin, Lhereux et Cie).
THOMPSON, JAMES (1996). *Models of Value: Eighteenth-Century Political Economy and the Novel* (Durham, NC: Duke University Press).
TIERNO GALVÁN, ENRIQUE (1977). 'Don Juan Valera o el buen sentido', in *Idealismo y pragmatismo en el siglo XIX* (Madrid: Tecnos), 95–129.
TIMOTEO ÁLVAREZ, JESÚS (1981). *Restauración y prensa de masas: los engranajes de un sistema (1875–1883)* (Pamplona: EUNSA).
TINTORÉ, MARÍA JOSÉ (1987). *'La Regenta' de Clarín y la crítica de su tiempo* (Barcelona: Lumen).
TOLOSA LATOUR, MANUEL (1889). *Niñerías*, prol. Benito Pérez Galdós (Madrid: Tip. de Manuel Ginés Hernández).
TOMSICH, MARIA GIOVANNA (1986–7). 'Histeria y narración en *La Regenta*', *Anales de Literatura Española*, 5: 495–517.
TORO MÉRIDA, JOAQUÍN, and PRIETO ALBERCA, ASCENSIÓN (1986). *Pedro Mata y Fontanet: vida, obra y pensamiento (1811–1877)* (Madrid: Editorial Técnica Prial).
TORTELLA CASARES, GABRIEL (1970). 'El Estado, la Banca y el desarrollo económico de España en el siglo XIX', in *Teoría y sociedad: homenaje al profesor Aranguren* (Barcelona: Ariel), 349–60.
—— (1973). *Los orígenes del capitalismo en España: banca, industria y ferrocarriles en el siglo XIX* (Madrid: Tecnos).
—— (1974). *La banca española en la Restauración*, 2 vols. (Madrid: Banco de España).
—— (1994). *El desarrollo de la España contemporánea: historia económica de los siglos XIX y XX* (Madrid: Alianza).
TOSCANO, TERESA (1993). *Retórica e ideología de la Generación de 1868 en la obra de Galdós* (Madrid: Pliegos).
TSUCHIYA, AKIKO (1988). 'Maxi and the Signs of Madness: Reading as Creation in *Fortunata y Jacinta*', *Hispanic Review*, 56: 53–7.
—— (1990). *Images of the Sign: Semiotic Consciousness in the Novels of Benito Pérez Galdós* (Columbia: University of Missouri Press).
—— (1993). 'The Construction of the Female Body in Galdós's *La de Bringas*', *Romance Quarterly*, 40: 35–47.
—— (1997). 'On the Margins of Subjectivity: Sex, Gender and the Body in Galdós's *Lo prohibido*', *Revista Hispánica Moderna*, 50: 280–9.
—— (1998). 'The Female Body Under Surveillance: Galdós's *La desheredada*', in Jeanne P. Brownlow and John W. Kronik (eds.), *Intertextual Pursuits: Literary Mediations in Modern Spanish Narrative* (Lewisburg, Pa.: Bucknell University Press), 201–21.

TUBERT, SILVIA (1997). 'Rosalía de Bringas: el erotismo de los trapos', *Bulletin of Hispanic Studies* (Glasgow), 74: 371-87.
TUÑÓN DE LARA, MANUEL (ed.) (1976). *Estudios sobre el siglo XIX español*, 5th edn. (Madrid: Siglo XXI).
—— (ed.) (1993). *Historia de España*, viii: *Revolución burguesa, oligarquía, y constitucionalismo (1834-1923)*, 2nd edn. (Madrid: Labor).
—— ELORZA, ANTONIO, and PÉREZ LEDESMA, M. (eds.) (1975). *Prensa y sociedad en España (1820-1936)* (Madrid: EDICUSA).
TURNER, BRYAN (1982). 'The Discourse of Diet', *Theory, Society and Culture*, 1.1: 23-32.
TURNER, HARRIET (1983). 'Family Ties and Tyrannies: A Reassessment of Jacinta', *Hispanic Review*, 51: 1-22.
—— (1992). *Galdós, 'Fortunata y Jacinta'* (Cambridge: Cambridge University Press).
TWITCHELL, JAMES B. (1987). *Forbidden Partners: The Incest Taboo in Modern Culture* (New York: Columbia University Press).
UGARTE, MICHAEL (1990). 'New Historicism and the Story of Madrid: *Fortunata y Jacinta* and *Tiempo de silencio*', *Anales Galdosianos*, 25: 45-52.
ULLMAN, JOAN CONELLY, and ALLISON, GEORGE H. (1974). 'Galdós as Psychiatrist in *Fortunata y Jacinta*', *Anales Galdosianos*, 9: 7-36.
UREY, DIANE F. (1982). *Galdós and the Irony of Language* (Cambridge: Cambridge University Press).
—— (1987a). 'Incest and Interpretation in *Los Pazos de Ulloa* and *La madre naturaleza*', *Anales Galdosianos*, 22: 117-31.
—— (1987b). ' "Rumores estridentes": Ana's Resonance in Clarín's *La Regenta*', *Modern Language Review*, 82: 356-75.
—— (1989). *The Novel Histories of Galdós* (Princeton: Princeton University Press).
UTT, ROGER L. (1974). ' "El pájaro voló": observaciones sobre un leitmotif en *Fortunata y Jacinta*', *Anales Galdosianos*, 9: 37-50.
VALERA, JUAN (1882). *Disertaciones y juicios literarios*, 2 vols. (Seville: Francisco Álvarez y Compañía).
—— (1884). *Estudios críticos sobre literatura, política y costumbres de nuestros días*, 3 vols., 2nd edn. (Madrid: Francisco Álvarez).
—— (1927). *Pepita Jiménez*, prol. Manuel Azaña (Madrid: Ediciones de La Lectura).
—— (1929). *Obras completas*, I: *Discursos políticos 1861-1876 (Congreso y Senado)* (Madrid: Carmen Valera).
—— (1942). *Obras completas*, vol. ii (Madrid: Aguilar).
—— (1958). *Obras completas*, vol. iii (Madrid: Aguilar).
—— (1966). *Artículos de 'El Contemporáneo'*, ed. Cyrus DeCoster (Madrid: Castalia).
—— (1968). 'Cartas inéditas a su mujer', *Revista de Occidente*, 2nd series, 67: 1-18.

VALERA, JUAN (1970). *Doña Luz*, ed. Benito Varela Jácome (Madrid: Iter Ediciones).
—— (1985). *Juanita la Larga*, ed. Enrique Rubio Cremades (Madrid: Castalia).
—— (1989). *Pepita Jiménez*, ed. Leonardo Romero (Madrid: Cátedra).
—— and MENÉNDEZ PELAYO, MARCELINO (1946). *Epistolario de Juan Valera y Menéndez Pelayo, 1877–1905*, ed. Miguel Artigas and Pedro Sainz Rodríguez (Madrid: Espasa Calpe).
VALIS, NOËL M. (1979). 'Pereda's *Peñas arriba*: A Re-examination', *Romanistisches Jahrbuch*, 30: 298–308.
—— (1981). *The Decadent Vision in Leopoldo Alas: A Study of 'La Regenta' and 'Su único hijo'* (Baton Rouge: Louisiana State University Press).
—— (1983). 'Order and Meaning in Clarín's *La Regenta*', *Novel*, 16: 246–58.
—— (ed.) (1990). *'Malevolent Insemination' and Other Essays on Clarín* (Ann Arbor: University of Michigan Press).
—— (1992*a*). 'On Monstrous Birth: Leopoldo Alas's *La Regenta*', in Brian Nelson (ed.), *Naturalism in the European Novel: New Critical Perspectives* (New York: Berg), 191–209.
—— (1992*b*). 'Fabricating Culture in *Cánovas*', *Modern Language Notes*, 107: 250–73.
VARELA, JULIA, and ÁLVAREZ-URÍA, FERNANDO (1979). *El cura Galeote, asesino del obispo de Madrid-Alcalá* (Madrid: Ediciones La Piqueta).
—— (1991). *Arqueología de la escuela* (Madrid: Ediciones de la Piqueta).
VARELA JÁCOME, BENITO (1973). *Estructura novelística de Emilia Pardo Bazán* (Madrid: CSIC).
VARELA ORTEGA, JOSÉ (1977). *Los amigos políticos: partidos, elecciones y caciquismo en la Restauración (1875–1900)* (Madrid: Alianza).
VAREY, JOHN E. (ed.) (1966). 'Francisco Bringas: nuestro buen Thiers', *Anales Galdosianos*, 1: 63–9.
—— (1970). *Galdós Studies* (London: Támesis).
VÁZQUEZ-ROMERO, JOSÉ (1991). 'La ensayística de Valera y la filosofía krausista', *Letras Peninsulares*, 4: 35–59.
VEITH, ILZA (1965). *Hysteria: The History of a Disease* (Chicago: Chicago University Press).
VELASCO SOUTO, CARLOS F. (1987). *A sociedade galega da Restauración na obra literaria de Pardo Bazán (1875–1900)* (Pontevedra: Artes Gráficas Portega).
VERA Y CASADO, BARTOLOMÉ DE (1893). *La administración local* (Madrid: Imprenta y litografía de los Huérfanos).
VICENS VIVES, JAIME (1969). *An Economic History of Spain* (Princeton: Princeton University Press).
VIDAL, HERNÁN (ed.) (1988). *Cultural and Historical Grounding for Hispanic and Luso-Brazilian Feminist Literary Criticism* (Minneapolis: Institute for the Study of Ideologies and Literature).

VIDAL GALACHE, FLORENTINA and BENICIA (1995). *Bordes y bastardos: una historia de la Inclusa de Madrid* (Madrid: Compañía Literaria).
VILANOVA, ANTONIO (1985). *Clarín y su obra: en el centenario de 'La Regenta'* (Barcelona: Universidad de Barcelona).
VILANOVA RIBAS, MERCEDES, and MORENO JULIÀ, XAVIER (1992). *Atlas de la evolución del analfabetismo en España de 1887 a 1981* (Madrid: Ministerio de Educación y Ciencia).
VILAR, PIERRE (1977). *Spain: A Brief History*, 2nd edn. (London: Pergamon).
—— (1991). *A History of Gold and Money 1450–1920* (London: Verso).
VILARÓS, TERESA M. (1993). 'Duelo y suicidio de Isidora de Aransis (*La desheredada*)', *Insula*, 561: 13–15.
—— (1995). *Galdós: invención de la mujer y poética de la sexualidad* (Madrid: Siglo XXI).
VILLACORTA BAÑOS, FRANCISCO (1980). *Burguesía y cultura: los intelectuales españoles en sociedad liberal 1808–1931* (Madrid: Siglo XXI).
VILLANUEVA, DARÍO (1992). *Teorías del realismo literario* (Madrid: Instituto de España-Espasa Calpe).
VRETTOS, ATHENA (1995). *Somatic Fictions: Imagining Illness in Victorian Culture* (Stanford, Calif.: Stanford University Press).
WALBY, SYLVIA (1990). *Theorizing Patriarchy* (Oxford: Blackwell).
WALKOWITZ, JUDITH (1992). *Cities of Dreadful Delight: Narratives of Sexual Danger in Late Victorian London* (London: Virago).
WEBER, EUGEN (1979). *Peasants into Frenchmen: The Modernisation of Rural France* (London: Chatto & Windus).
WEBER, FRANCES W. (1966*a*). 'The Dynamics of Motif in Leopoldo Alas's *La Regenta*', *Romanic Review*, 57: 188–99.
—— (1966*b*). 'Ideology and Religious Parody in the Novels of Leopoldo Alas', *Bulletin of Hispanic Studies*, 43: 197–208.
WEEKS, JEFFREY (1981). *Sex, Politics and Society: The Regulation of Sexuality since 1800* (London: Longman).
WHISTON, JAMES (1977). *Juan Valera, 'Pepita Jiménez'* (London: Grant & Cutler).
WHITE, NICHOLAS, and SEGAL, NAOMI (eds.) (1997). *Scarlet Letters: Fictions of Adultery from Antiquity to the 1990s* (London: Macmillan).
WILLEM, LINDA M. (ed.) (1993). *A Sesquicentennial Tribute to Galdós 1843–1993* (Newark, Del.: Juan de la Cuesta).
—— (1998). *Galdós's 'Segunda manera': Rhetorical Strategies and Affective Response* (Chapel Hill: North Carolina University Press).
WILLIAMS, RAYMOND (1975). *The Country and the City* (London: Paladin).
WILLIAMS, ROSALIND H. (1982). *Dream Worlds: Mass Consumption in Late Nineteenth-Century France* (Berkeley and Los Angeles: University of California Press).

WILSON, ELIZABETH (1991). *The Sphinx in the City: Urban Life, the Control of Disorder, and Women* (Berkeley and Los Angeles: University of California Press).
WOOLF, JANET (1985). 'The Invisible Flâneuse: Women and the Literature of Modernity', *Theory, Culture and Society*, 2–3: 37–46.
WRIGHT, CHAD C. (1982). '*Lo prohibido*: "las cuatro paredes de la Restauración"', *Modern Language Notes*, 97: 391–400.
YEAZELL, RUTH BERNARD (ed.) (1986). *Sex, Politics, and Science in the Nineteenth-Century Novel* (Baltimore: Johns Hopkins University Press).
YOUNG, RICHARD (1993). 'Money, Time and Space in Galdós's *Misericordia*', in Anthony Purdy (ed.), *Literature and Money* (Amsterdam: Rodopi), 181–203.
YOUNG, ROBERT M. (1985). *Darwin's Metaphor: Nature's Place in Victorian Culture* (Cambridge: Cambridge University Press).
YUVAL-DAVIS, NIRA (1997). *Gender and Nation* (London: Sage).
ZAHAREAS, ANTHONY (1968). 'El sentido de la tragedia en *Fortunata y Jacinta*', *Anales Galdosianos*, 3: 25–34.
ZARETSKY, ELI (1976). *Capitalism, the Family and Personal Life* (London: Pluto Press).
ZAVALA, IRIS M. (ed.) (1971). *Ideología y política en la novela española del siglo XIX* (Salamanca: Anaya).
—— (1996). *Breve historia feminista de la literatura española (en lengua castellana)*, iii: *La mujer en la literatura española (del S. XVIII a la actualidad)* (Barcelona: Anthropos).
—— (1998). *Breve historia feminista de la literatura española (en lengua castelana)*, v: *La literatura escrita por la mujer (del S. XIX a la actualidad)* (Barcelona: Anthropos).
ZULUETA, CARMEN DE (1984). *Feministas, misioneras y educadoras* (Madrid: Castalia).
—— (1998). ' "El nuevo renacer de España": la Institución Libre de Enseñanza', *Revista Hispánica Moderna*, 51: 161–77.

Index

Alas, Leopoldo 8, 13, 15, 21, 32, 33, 53 n. 1, 58, 209–62, 303, 404; *La Regenta* 2 n. 1, 5, 11 n. 11, 28, 66, 209–62, 289, 386, 391–2, 406, 407, 411–12, 413, 414, 416
Alfonso XII 57, 73, 108, 126 n. 31, 179, 342 n. 4, 347 n. 12
Allsop, Mariana 69
Altamira, Rafael 304
Amadeo I 265–6, 404
Amador de los Ríos, José 11 n. 9
Anderson, Benedict 1, 5, 6–7, 8, 16, 18, 77, 168 n. 2, 209, 392
anthropology 45, 76–7, 79–80, 81, 192, 308
Arana, Sabino 302
Arenal, Concepción 84, 86 n. 24
Arnold, Matthew 10
Asís Méndez, Francisco de 69
Ateneo Científico, Literario y Artístico de Madrid 11, 12, 16, 20, 62, 76, 80, 123 n. 28, 350
Augustine, St 238–9
Azcárate, Gumersindo de 42 n. 10, 57 n. 3, 60, 62, 63, 93 n. 1, 182 n. 13, 224, 303, 304, 315 n. 17, 405–6
Azorín (José Martínez Ruiz) 299, 398

Baroja, Pío 299, 398
Bastiat, Claude-Frédéric 63, 151 n. 7, 173, 240
Bebel, August 184–5
Benjamin, Walter 46, 111, 112 n. 17, 113, 114, 115, 120, 146–7, 149, 153, 166, 388, 390, 391, 414–15
Bentham, Jeremy 16, 25, 123, 124 n. 29
Bernard, Claude 66, 67
Bismarck, Prince Otto von 228 n. 16, 295
Blanco García, Padre 14
Brañas, Alfredo 302
Butler, Judith 413, 415
Buylla, Adolfo 62

Caballero, Fernán (Cecilia Böhl de Faber) 17–18
caciquismo 268–70, 298, 299, 300, 302, 306, 401, 466–9; in *Fortunata y Jacinta* 166–7, 176; in *La Regenta* 228–31, 241; in *Los Pazos de Ulloa* 346, 348–9, 351–2, 353; in *Peñas arriba* 308, 314, 333; in *Pepita Jiménez* 268, 270–4, 282–3, 284–5, 286, 291, 293–5, 297, 298; *see also* Krausism (critique of State control)
Canalejas, Francisco de Paula 59 n. 5
Cánovas del Castillo, Antonio 3, 5, 11, 15, 20, 23, 24, 25, 44, 49, 56, 57, 62, 114, 177, 212, 222, 228, 229, 230, 231 n. 21, 270, 271, 309, 347 n. 12, 404, 405, 407, 408
Carlism 19, 177, 212, 235, 271, 308, 309, 310, 347, 351, 352, 367, 404
Castelar, Emilio 3, 115
Castro, Carlos María de 50, 72
Catholic Church 39, 44, 212, 226; and social control 66, 67–9, 97, 100–2, 191, 194, 219, 234–7, 240, 241–4, 337, 338, 362–6; and State 23, 26, 37, 172, 177, 230, 307; Catholicism 58, 82, 239, 278, 308; *see also* disentailments
centralization 2, 3, 4, 5, 19–22, 23, 24–7, 78, 209–10, 265, 267–8, 301–2, 306–7, 309–10, 343, 345, 349, 353, 393, 403, 409; and Pereda 300, 305–8, 312–13, 317, 321, 325, 333; and Valera 276, 295, 298; in *La Regenta* 230–1; in *Los Pazos de Ulloa* 343, 345, 349, 353; see also *caciquismo*, Carlism, customary law, federalism, Krausism (critique of State control), regionalism, State administration
Cerdá, Ildefonso 50, 247

Index

Cervantes, Miguel de 13, 14 n. 15, 162, 296, 329, 389; *Don Quixote* 296 n. 36, 332, 364 n. 30, 389, 390
Charcot, Jean Martin 203, 246, 413
Claret, Padre Antonio María 276 n. 19
collecting 147–51, 152–3, 330; *see also* commodity fetishism, consumerism, museums, world exhibitions
Comisión de Reformas Sociales 62–5, 77, 199 n. 31, 214 n. 7, 242 n. 30
commodity fetishism 146–51, 156, 161, 164, 174, 290, 394–6; *see also* consumerism
confession 232, 235, 240, 245, 247, 277, 372, 380, 411
consumerism 49, 212; and circulation 100, 109–15, 127, 130–3, 155–8, 168–73, 180–2, 184–6; and commodification 101–2, 290; and excess 98–9, 141; and exhaustion of resources 175, 187–91, 250–1; and representation 206, 208, 232–4, 287–8, 297, 298, 354–5, 385, 386, 387, 395–6, 414, 415; and women 47–8, 86, 106, 135, 136–8, 323–4, 325, 330; *see also* commodity fetishism, fashion, waste
contract: economic 37–8, 44, 95, 116, 142, 173, 182–3, 242, 313–14, 343; marriage 39–44, 46, 82; social 38–44, 305, 332, 371, 375, 402; *see also* Krausism (critique of contract theory), market, Rousseau
Costa, Joaquín 28, 217, 299, 303–5, 316, 317, 348, 369, 398, 407–8
costumbrismo 15, 17–18, 283, 313
Cuesta, Francisco de la 305, 307, 318 n. 22
customary law (*fueros*): abolition of 24–5; concessions to 19; defence of 300–5, 309, 349; in *Los Pazos de Ulloa* 343–4, 345; in *Peñas arriba* 313–14, 318, 328, 332

Darwin, Charles 63, 132, 134, 216, 223, 224, 226 n. 15, 251, 252, 355–6, 359, 379
degeneration 28, 125–6, 132–4, 136–8, 158, 189, 200–6, 254 n. 37, 315 n. 17, 337, 398; degeneracy theory 78–80, 86, 125, 132–4, 214, 232, 239, 256, 338, 379, 380
Derrida, Jacques 331
Desmaisières, Micaela (Vizcondesa de Jorbalán) 68, 194, 195 n. 27
disentailments 23–4, 38, 106, 150, 169, 272–3, 343–4

Echegaray, José 27
economic discourse, figurative use of: in religion 234, 240–2; in social reform 73, 120–1, 125, 198, 204–5; re. the body 102, 117, 173, 183–4, 204–5, 225–8; *see also* sewage, waste
education 277; and Pardo Bazán 349, 362; and Pereda 307–8, 311, 332; and Valera 281, 286; medical 67, 69–70, 71; role in nation formation 18–19, 26–7, 178, 275 n. 17; *see also* Krausism
Engels, Friedrich 45, 94, 154, 185
Escuder, J. M. 75–6
Esquerdo, José María 75, 202
Estébanez Calderón, Serafín 15, 17, 283

fashion: and excess 98–9, 141, 146–7; and feminization 9, 155–6, 169, 170, 171–2, 204, 232–4, 254; and foreign influence 109, 114, 122, 148, 170; and representation 206, 291; and spectacle 110–11, 244; and standardization 113, 156, 160, 179–80, 198–9; *see also* commodity fetishism, consumerism
federalism 19–20, 52, 267, 308, 317 n. 21, 347 n. 11, 350 n. 15
Fernández y González, Manuel 44 n. 12
Ferry, Jules 68
Figuerola, Laureano 154
Filmer, Sir Robert 38, 45
finance: banks 21, 22, 48–9, 129, 310–11; credit 48, 109, 154, 165, 290–1, 390, 399; stock exchange 21, 49, 120, 128–9, 130, 131, 325, 395, 399; *see also* money, national debt
Flaubert, Gustave 207 n. 38; *Bouvard et Pécuchet* 258; *Madame Bovary* 47, 136, 218 n. 10

Foucault, Michel 26 n. 29, 54–5, 65, 72, 80, 86, 235 n. 24, 253, 389–90, 396, 409–10, 411
free trade 22, 44, 49, 128, 139–40, 142, 158, 169, 170 n. 3, 172, 173; *see also* contract, market
Freud, Sigmund 38, 43 n. 11, 45, 134, 189, 203, 213, 215, 217, 246, 256, 285, 379, 413

García Arenal, Fernando 214 n. 7, 242 n. 30
gardens 97, 124–5, 159, 249–51, 259, 288–90, 314
Giddens, Anthony 20, 22–3, 25 n. 28, 37, 49, 55–6, 57, 250–1, 390, 393, 402
Gide, André 163
Giner de los Ríos, Francisco 13 n. 14, 27, 42 n. 10, 57 n. 3, 58, 60, 83, 93 n. 1, 152, 182 n. 13, 220–3, 232, 248, 257 n. 41, 261, 303, 319, 323, 355 n. 24, 372 n. 36
Giné y Partagás, Juan 71, 76, 81
Goncourt brothers 381–2
González de Linares, Augusto 355 n. 24
González de Linares, Gervasio 305–7, 320
González Serrano, Urbano 63, 214, 363 n. 28

Habermas, Jürgen 5, 32–5, 86, 94, 177, 402–3
Haes, Carlos de 27, 319
Hauser, Philiph 73, 134, 195
Hegel, Georg Wilhelm Friedrich 42–3, 83, 220, 406
hellenism 82–3, 239, 277–8, 317, 377–8
Hobsbawm, Eric J. 1, 2, 8, 18, 20, 22, 77, 106–7, 174 n. 9, 316, 401
hysteria 133, 202–3, 238, 246, 257, 356–7, 365, 413

Institución Libre de Enseñanza 62, 64, 83, 303; *see also* Krausism (and education)
Isabel II 144–5, 159, 276 n. 19, 292

John of the Cross, St 239

Kant, Immanuel 36
Kempis, Thomas à 199, 210, 245

Krausism 11–12, 69, 108, 143, 200, 355 n. 24, 367–8; and education 51, 54, 64, 83–4, 185, 191–2, 214, 215, 371–2; and freedom of expression 14, 275; and psychology 58, 214; critique of contract theory 41–4, 54–5, 221, 222–3; critique of particularism (*armonismo*) 99, 102, 107, 220–2, 229, 231, 244–5, 279; critique of State control 26, 33, 57–65, 93, 95, 213, 220, 223, 228 n. 16, 303; defence of representative government 61, 403–6; natural law 42, 58, 59–61, 221–4, 252–3, 284; organicism 66–7, 92–3, 219–20, 274, 299, 312, 370, 376; respect for the body 27, 82–3, 97, 239, 277–8, 281; *see also* Azcárate, Giner de los Ríos, González Serrano, hellenism, Moret, Sanz del Río

Labra, Rafael María de 43–4
Lafuente, Modesto 3
Larra, Mariano de 407 n. 11
law: and abstraction 207, 222, 348, 408; and *caciquismo* 228–9, 231, 285–6, 295, 347; and illegitimacy 183, 353; and marriage 38–9, 40 n. 7, 41, 44, 374; and prostitution 116; legal medicine 75–6; national codification of 3, 5, 10, 21–6, 309, 344; women's unsuitability for 83; *see also* customary law, Krausism (natural law)
León, Fray Luis de 281, 362, 363, 381
Le Play, Frédéric 65, 86
literacy 6, 9, 18–19, 25 n. 28, 355, 380, 384
Locke, John 36, 37, 38, 45, 61, 152, 220, 222
Lombroso, Cesare 79, 210 n. 1
Luys, Jules 246

Machado, Antonio 27
Macías Picavea, Ricardo 408
Macpherson, C. B. 35–7, 46
Madoz, Pascual 23, 27, 103, 143, 169
Mallada, Lucas 299 n. 1, 398
Mallarmé, Stéphane 388
Malthus, Thomas 186–7

market: as basis of liberal individual freedom 35–8, 154–5, 157, 182–3; creation of a national 19, 22, 48; Mercado de San Miguel 181–2; Mercado de Santa Cruz 171–2; separation from household 33–5, 169, 172, 326–7; 351; *see also* consumerism, contract, free trade, money
Marx, Karl 94, 116, 154, 162, 390, 391, 392, 394, 395, 396, 398, 411
Mata, Pedro 70, 75, 81, 126 n. 31, 173
Maudsley, Henry 246
Mendizábal, Juan Álvarez 23
medicine: and sexual difference 81–2, 187, 202, 226–7, 361–2; and social control 65–76, 78, 80–1, 86, 180 n. 12, 188 n. 22, 196, 214–19, 245–7, 253, 315, 355–7, 359–61, 365, 373, 380, 413; medical discourse 97–8, 102, 117–19, 122, 133, 181–2, 183–4, 190, 192, 234, 236, 237–8, 240, 248, 299, 323; *see also* Mata, Monlau, prostitution, Pulido, Santero, Tolosa Latour
Menéndez Pelayo, Marcelino 14, 18, 19, 266 n. 3 and 4, 287 n. 31, 290, 316
Mesonero Romanos, Ramón 15–17
Mill, John Stuart 39, 63, 97, 137, 217, 376 n. 40, 379–80, 403, 405, 411
Mon, Alejandro 25, 400 n. 7
money: abandonment of convertibility into gold 129, 163, 298, 387, 399–401; and abstraction 162–4, 165–6, 292, 294, 296, 298, 345–6, 387–401; circulation of 94–6, 127, 130, 131, 150, 156–7, 158, 160, 161, 165, 171, 173, 291, 345–7; fiduciary 129, 162–3, 165, 170, 292–6, 299, 334, 389, 390, 395–6, 399–400; issue of 21, 48–9, 169, 292, 334, 399; *see also* consumerism, finance, free trade, market, national debt
Monlau, Pedro 69, 71, 73, 81, 133–4, 136 n. 40, 184, 186 n. 18, 202, 216, 218, 227, 238, 248, 254, 356, 357, 362, 366 n. 32
Morel, Bénédict 78, 125, 126 n. 31, 202
Moret, Segismundo 61 n. 6, 62–3, 143–4, 301, 312, 405

Moya, Miguel 57 n. 3, 405
museums 11, 16, 98, 100, 149, 157, 161, 241, 251, 298; *see also* collecting, world exhibitions

national debt 23, 96, 104, 129, 160, 399; debt conversion 129, 397, 399–400
naturalism 8, 12, 13, 67, 201, 224, 245, 337, 338, 361
Neoplatonism 297–8, 330–1, 336, 381, 384, 387–8, 390, 396, 397
neurasthenia 133–4, 322–3, 369, 377, 378
Nocedal, Cándido 271

Oller, Narcís 49

painting: historical 2, 3–4, 77, 174, 192, 249, 317; landscape 27–8, 248, 318–19, 381 n. 43
Pardo Bazán, Emilia 8, 12, 13, 21, 32, 39, 45, 113, 184, 228 n. 16, 290, 337–84, 387, 394, 411, 413–14; *La madre naturaleza* 6, 83, 281, 337–84, 387, 412, 413; *La tribuna* 347 n. 11; *Los Pazos de Ulloa* 45, 337–84, 407, 412
parks, *see* gardens
Pateman, Carole 38–40, 43 n. 11, 45, 46, 376
Pereda, José María de 4, 11 n. 11, 13, 15, 19, 21, 28, 299–336, 387, 388, 411, 416; *Don Gonzalo de la Gonzalera* 308, 333; *El sabor de la tierruca* 310; *Escenas montañesas* 313; *La Montálvez* 310 n. 13; *Los hombres de pro* 333; *Pedro Sánchez* 310 n. 13; *Peñas arriba* 5–6, 299–336, 370, 396; *Sotileza* 331
Pérez de Camino, Fernando 319
Pérez Galdós, Benito 3, 4, 7–8, 9, 11, 13–14, 15, 20–1, 22, 28, 32, 45, 57 n. 3, 71, 75, 76, 91–208, 214, 230 n. 19, 276, 289, 303, 331, 336, 363, 387, 389, 395, 396, 399, 404–5, 407, 411, 414; *Ángel Guerra* 68, 254 n. 37, 255 n. 39; *Doña Perfecta* 412; *El amigo Manso* 188 n. 22, 412; *Episodios nacionales* 2, 11 n. 11; *Fortunata y Jacinta* 6, 7, 8, 16, 21, 28, 31, 34–5, 40, 45, 63, 68, 69, 70, 77, 91–2, 126, 135, 144, 165–208, 218 n. 10,

221 n. 12, 241, 258, 362, 377, 378, 386, 407, 412, 413, 416; *Gloria* 46, 412; *La de Bringas* 47, 56, 91, 92, 109, 113, 128, 139–64, 167, 171, 206, 218 n. 10, 245, 295 n. 35, 390, 394, 396, 407, 414, 416; *La desheredada* 70, 75, 91, 92, 103–26, 131, 133, 134, 136, 139, 156, 162, 182, 201, 395–6, 412, 416; *La familia de León Roch* 56, 61, 91–103, 135, 136, 139, 237, 412; *Lo prohibido* 91, 92, 126–37, 180, 201, 322, 407, 412; *Miau* 25, 92, 269; *Misericordia* 21, 111; *Nazarín* 54, 71, 186, 396–7; *Tormento* 91, 92, 139–60; *Torquemada* series 397; *Tristana* 409, 412
philanthropy 64, 93, 95, 124, 140, 234, 311, 314–15, 371, 411; and women 68–9, 84–7, 131–2, 174, 193–201, 243–4, 245, 253; *see also* social control
picaresque novel 14 n. 15, 162, 389
Pidal y Mon, Alejandro 230
Pi y Margall, Francisco 20, 115, 151 n. 8, 305
Polanco, Victoriano 319
political economy: Alas as Chair of 222–3; Mesía as expert in 227; Valera as expert in 266; *see also* contract, market, property ownership
Pontejos, Marqués de 16, 170
Posada, Adolfo 210 n. 1
Prat de la Riba, Enric 302
press 5, 6, 12, 32, 75, 93, 177, 209, 266, 285, 349–50, 405, 407
property ownership 236; as basis of liberal individual freedom 23, 35–8, 44, 152; and marriage 99–100; and women 38–9; *see also* disentailments, market (as basis of liberal individual freedom)
prostitution 51, 91–2, 107, 117–19, 126, 138, 139, 160, 184, 190, 201, 233, 236, 244, 245, 248, 386; and entry to the market 46–7, 105–6, 155, 157, 182, 189, 197; regulation of 70, 74–5, 106, 112, 116, 131, 194–5
Proudhon, Pierre Joseph 63, 115, 151 n. 8

Pulido, Ángel 79–81, 192, 203, 216, 238, 247, 356, 357
Pygmalion myth 192, 193, 195, 196, 282, 377, 411–12

ragpickers 98, 120, 153, 196, 197, 414–15
Real Academia de Ciencias Morales y Políticas 11, 52, 63, 406
Real Academia Española de la Lengua 12, 19, 81 n. 21, 106, 316 n. 19
regeneration 137–8, 315, 323, 324, 327; regenerationism 28, 299–300, 303, 306, 308, 311, 369, 398; *see also* degeneration, Costa
regionalism 5, 19, 283, 302–3, 310, 312–13, 318, 332, 334, 349
Renan, Ernest 20
representation 161–6, 206–8, 233–4, 245, 256–62, 288, 294, 296, 297–8, 306, 330–6, 369, 381–4, 385–416
republicanism 57, 105, 107 n. 10, 108, 115, 212, 347 n. 12, 349
Riancho, Agustín 319
Ríos, Ángel de los 313, 316–17
Romero Robledo, Francisco 177, 230, 270, 271, 309
Rousseau, Jean-Jacques 40–2, 43, 45, 83, 123 n. 28, 220, 222, 223, 249, 359, 367, 371–2, 374–6, 380, 381
rubbish, *see* ragpickers, sewage, waste

Sagasta, Mateo Práxedes 5, 24, 56, 57, 62, 82, 229, 230, 231 n. 21, 309, 347 n. 12, 403, 405, 408
Sand, Georges 247
Santero, Francisco Javier 66, 70 n. 12, 71, 192, 216, 218, 227, 238, 248, 356, 357
Sanz del Río, Julián 12 n. 12, 42, 60, 61, 92–3, 102, 106, 220, 239, 281, 392
Sereñana y Partagás, Prudencio 74
Serrano, General Francisco 265, 268
sewage 50, 74, 121, 160, 211, 236–8, 239–40, 244, 415; *see also* waste
Silvela, Francisco 309
Simmel, Georg 111, 113, 130 n. 35, 147 n. 2, 150–1, 165–6, 221 n. 12, 368, 387, 391, 392, 393, 394, 397, 410, 414
slavery 37 n. 5, 55, 365, 371

Smith, Adam 34, 42, 134, 187, 216, 241, 390
social control: and representation 386, 409–14, 415; in *Fortunata y Jacinta* 178, 191–201, 205; in *La desheredada* 104, 122–6; in *La madre naturaleza* 367–76, 377, 379–80; in *La Regenta* 213–20, 232, 234–6; through law 25, 393; through reform 52–87; *see also* Catholic Church, education, Krausism, law (national codification of), medicine, philanthropy, Pygmalion myth
socialism 5, 105 n. 8, 106, 107, 111, 114, 116, 151–2, 212, 350 n. 15; 'socialismo de Estado' 56–7, 78, 120, 142
Sociedad Española de Higiene 11, 71, 73, 75, 123 n. 28, 190 n. 25; *see also* medicine
Soria, Arturo 50–1, 72–3, 237, 248
Spencer, Herbert 59, 63, 119, 123 n. 28, 128, 132, 134, 137, 204–5, 216, 219, 224, 258 n. 44, 299, 405 n. 10
State administration 18–19, 20, 24, 25, 78, 84, 94, 95, 104, 120, 140, 141–5, 175–8, 179; *see also caciquismo*, centralization
suffrage 10, 20, 23, 24, 35–6, 108, 172, 229, 309, 342, 402, 403

Tarde, Gabriel 113–14, 132, 199, 210, 257 n. 42, 391
Teresa, St 245, 332, 413
Thiers, Adolphe 151–2, 158
Tolosa Latour, Manuel 75, 81, 122–3, 125, 136 n. 40
Tolstoy, Count Leo 305 n. 7; *Anna Karenina* 255 n. 38, 328

town planning 15–16, 49–50, 72–3, 104, 124–5, 127–8, 153–4, 162, 172, 210–12, 247–8

Unamuno, Miguel de 299, 303, 304, 319–20, 348, 398

vagrancy 23, 36–7, 39, 53, 75, 93, 105–6, 107, 120, 122, 125–6, 131, 176, 197–8
Valera, Juan 3, 11, 14–15, 18, 21, 32, 228–9, 231, 265–98, 387, 393; *Doña Luz* 293–4, 295, 393; *Juanita la Larga* 293, 294–6, 321; *Pepita Jiménez* 5, 265–98, 299, 311, 314, 321, 322, 323, 324, 329, 330, 370, 377, 412
Vázquez de Mella, Juan 310
Velasco, Pedro 79–80
Velázquez, Diego 13, 390
Vera y Casado, Bartolomé de 406–7
Viguera, Baltasar de 67
Villena, Ernestina Manuel de 84, 123 n. 28, 197 n. 28
Vives, Juan Luis 362

waste 101–2, 117–22, 136, 140–3, 189, 205, 241, 242, 415; recycling of 98, 124–5, 152–3, 191–2, 193, 194, 195, 198, 200; *see also* consumerism, ragpickers, sewage
wet-nurses 75, 172, 188, 286, 356, 358–9
Williams, Raymond 24
world exhibitions 49 n. 14, 97, 98–9, 112, 128, 131–2, 146, 147–8, 157, 161, 289; *see also* consumerism, museums

Zola, Émile 67, 80, 134, 171 n. 5, 207 n. 38, 224, 245, 338, 381